2016 EDITION

Payroll Accounting

Bernard J. Bieg
Bucks County Community College

Judith A. Toland
Bucks County Community College

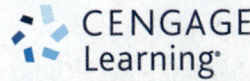

CENGAGE
Learning®

Australia • Brazil • Mexico • Singapore • United Kingdom • United States

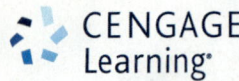

Payroll Accounting, 2016 Edition
Bernard J. Bieg and Judith A. Toland

Vice President, General Manager, Math & Quantitative Business: Balraj Kalsi

Product Director: Mike Schenk

Product Manager: Javan Kline

Associate Content Developer: Andrea Meyer

Product Assistant: Trisha Makley

Associate Marketing Manager: Charisse Darin

Sr. Content Project Manager: Tim Bailey

Content Digitization Project Manager: Thomas Burns

Manufacturing Planner: Doug Wilke

Production Service: Cenveo Publisher Services

Sr. Art Director: Linda May

Cover & Internal Designer: Lou Ann Thesing

Cover and title page image: © haveseen/ Shutterstock.com

Money image used on openers and end-of-chapter: © Stockbyte/Getty Images

Computer monitor image used with front and end matter section titles: © robuart/ Shutterstock.com

Icon used in "Similar to Example" callout: VoodooDot/Shutterstock.com

Intellectual Property:

Analyst: Brittani Morgan

Project Manager: Betsy Hathaway

For product information and technology assistance, contact us at
Cengage Learning Customer & Sales Support, 1-800-354-9706

For permission to use material from this text or product, submit all requests online at **www.cengage.com/permissions**
Further permissions questions can be emailed to **permissionrequest@cengage.com**

Microsoft Excel® is a registered trademark of Microsoft Corporation. © 2015 Microsoft.

Library of Congress Control Number: 2015948940

Student Edition ISBN: 978-1-305-66590-3
Student Edition with Access Card ISBN: 978-1-305-66591-0

Cengage Learning
20 Channel Center Street
Boston, MA 02210
USA

Cengage Learning is a leading provider of customized learning solutions with employees residing in nearly 40 different countries and sales in more than 125 countries around the world. Find your local representative at **www.cengage.com**.

Cengage Learning products are represented in Canada by Nelson Education, Ltd.

To learn more about Cengage Learning Solutions, visit **www.cengage.com**

Purchase any of our products at your local college store or at our preferred online store **www.cengagebrain.com**

Printed in Canada
Print Number: 01   Print Year: 2015

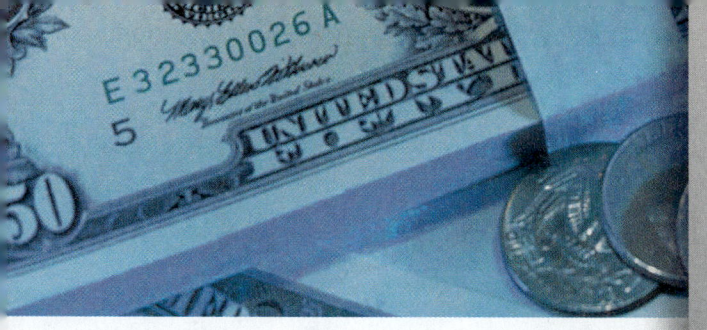

Chapter 2

Affordable Care Act

Forms 1094-C (Transmittal of Employer-Provided Health Insurance Offer and Coverage Information Returns) and 1095-C (Employer-Provided Health Insurance Offer and Coverage) are required to be filed in early 2016. A separate Form 1065-C is filed with each employee along with a copy for the IRS. Form 1094-C is a single transmittal form for all of the returns filed for a given calendar year. Substitute forms can be used that include all of the information required to be reported on Forms 1094-C and 1095-C.

White Collar Employee Exemption Increase

The Department of Labor has proposed increasing the minimum salary for employees meeting white collar exemption to $50,440 annually or $970 a week.

Chapter 3

FICA–OASDI Taxable Wage Base

In this edition of the textbook, we have used the 2015 wage base of $118,500 and current projections have the projected 2016 wage base to remain at $118,500.

Penalties

Penalties for incorrect information returns now range from $50 a return if corrected within 30 days of filing to $500 per return for intentional errors. These fines also apply to health care information returns.

Chapter 4

IRAs

Some states want firms without retirement plans to offer payroll deduction IRAs to employees who do not opt out. Illinois's program is to take effect in 2017 and requires employers in business for at least two years and with 25 or more employees to offer automatic IRAs. The IRAs would be funded with payroll deductions of 3 percent of salary with an employee's option to change the pay in percentage. No employer matching is required.

Chapter 7

Effective July 1, 2015, until June 30, 2016, the Philadelphia Wage Tax is 3.9102 percent (resident) and 3.4828 percent (non-resident).

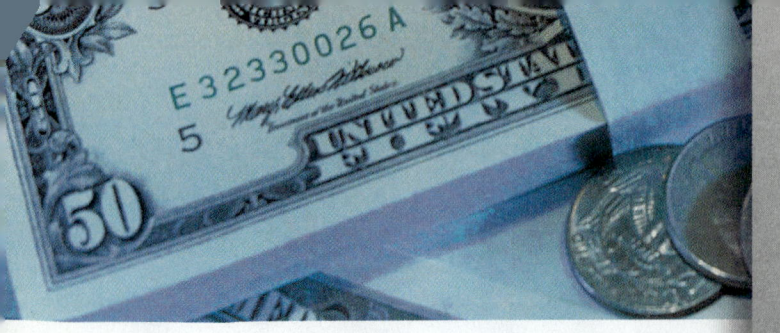

PAYROLL ACCOUNTING AND TODAY'S BUSINESS ENVIRONMENT

Today's payroll accountant is a major player on a company's management team. Management's need for timely and accurate payroll cost data as a part of the total planning step has moved payroll from a disbursement and recording function to an integral part of the management process.

With constant changes in the legal environment, technology advancements in the administration of payroll functions and with tax withholding responsibilities, the payroll accounting occupation has become proactive. During this time when the need for accurate information is so critical, *Payroll Accounting* has established a record of being the most thorough book on the market for over 20 years. Each edition has been updated with the most current data available.

The 2016 edition of *Payroll Accounting* continues to provide the most user-friendly payroll accounting coverage, in addition to significant resources that will aid instructors and students alike in their mastery of payroll accounting.

CengageNOWv2

Payroll Accounting 2016 is fully integrated with CengageNOWv2, a powerful course management and online homework tool that provides robust instructor control and customization to optimize the student learning experience and meet desired outcomes.

CengageNOWv2 Includes

- Integrated eBook
- End-of-chapter homework with static and algorithmic versions
- New Continuing Problems in CLGL
- Adaptive Study Plan and multimedia study tools
- Test bank
- Course management tools and flexible assignment options
- Reporting and gradebook options
- Blueprint Problems
- Animated Activities for Chapters 1 through 4
- Robust feedback

"To students, it's quick feedback, and they can improve the grades by working on the questions multiple times; to instructors, it's less grading time, and easy to evaluate students' performance."

-Jack Wu,
Chemeketa Community College

NEW! Continuing Problems in CLGL

- Problems allow students to apply the techniques learned in each chapter continuously building as they move from chapter to chapter.
- Students gain experience in computing wages and salaries and preparing a payroll register.
- Students become familiar with CLGL prior to the Payroll Project in Appendix A.

Unique to Payroll Accounting

- Detailed **Check My Work** and **Post-Submission feedback** with explanations and tips for completing the problem

"I love CengageNOW and so do most of my students because of the immediate and helpful feedback."

-Penny Hahn,
Henderson Community College

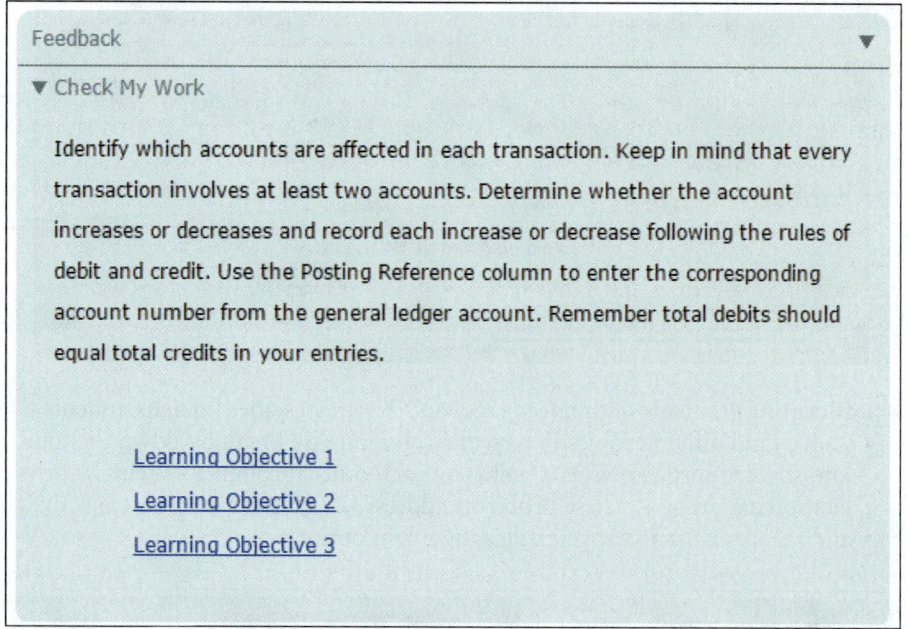

Feedback ▼

▼ Check My Work

Identify which accounts are affected in each transaction. Keep in mind that every transaction involves at least two accounts. Determine whether the account increases or decreases and record each increase or decrease following the rules of debit and credit. Use the Posting Reference column to enter the corresponding account number from the general ledger account. Remember total debits should equal total credits in your entries.

Learning Objective 1

Learning Objective 2

Learning Objective 3

▼ Post Submission Feedback

(a) $750 / 1 − 0.25 (supplemental federal rate) − 0.062 (OASDI) − 0.0145 (HI) − 0.05 (Utah tax)

(b) $750/(1 − 0.3765) = $750/0.6235 = $1,202.89

(c)		
Gross bonus amount	$1,202.88*	
Federal income tax withheld	(300.72)	
OASDI tax withheld	(74.58)	
HI tax withheld	(17.44)	
Utah income tax withheld	(60.14)	
Take-home bonus check	$750.00	

*Need to subtract $0.01 in order to arrive at net of $750.00 (due to rounding).

"Animated Activities help present the topics in another way to students who may learn differently than reading or practicing problems. They are fun and students do not mind watching them."

-Cammy Wayne,
William Rainey Harper College

- **Animated Activities** are video assignments, for Chapters 1 through 4, that visually guide students through selected core topics using a realistic company example. The illustrative videos explain how payroll concepts relate to the everyday activities of a business.

"Blueprint Problems allow students to reinforce the concept presented by me and the textbook. They are also presented in a different learning style to help engage all students."

-Nancy Cowett,
Northern Maine Community College

- **Blueprint Problems** within CengageNOWv2 are designed to help students understand difficult topics in payroll accounting by breaking down the topic into smaller parts. Each part builds on each other through a systematic problem solving process. These problems address key chapter learning objectives and are algorithmic for versatile assignment options.

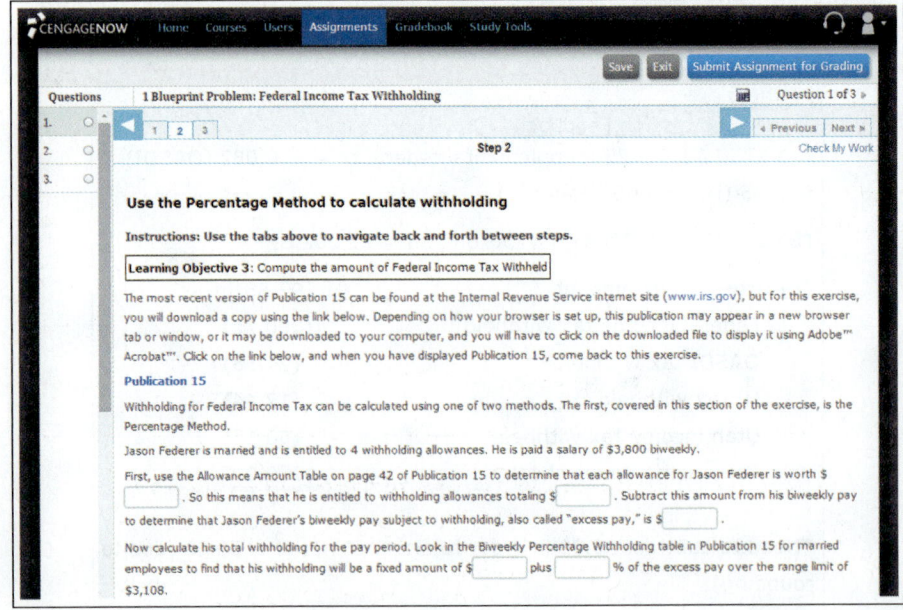

- CengageNOWv2 contains numerous algorithmic problems that allow instructors to have more flexibility and assurance that students are completing the projects on their own.
- Randomized Test Bank answers within CengageNOWv2 allow instructors to assign the same multiple choice test problems, but CNOW will randomize the selection choices. The selection order for each student changes, combating student cheating. See the example below.

The entry to deposit FICA taxes and federal income taxes withheld involves all of the following accounts *except*: **a. Payroll Taxes.** b. FICA Taxes Payable –OASDI. c. Cash. d. FICA Taxes Payable—HI e. Employees FIT	The entry to deposit FICA taxes and federal income taxes withheld involves all of the following accounts *except*: a. Cash b. Employees FIT **c. Payroll Taxes.** d. FICA Taxes Payable—HI e. FICA Taxes Payable –OASDI.

KEY FEATURES

- **Mastery, Application, Motivation**—*Payroll Accounting 2016* and Cengage-NOWv2 help you elevate student thinking with unique content that addresses each stage of the learning process, prepares students to learn, provides practice opportunities that better prepare students for the exam, and helps students achieve mastery with tolls that help them make connections and see the big picture.
- **The Washington Update**—The Washington Update, which appears within Chapters 2, 3, 4, and 5, advises the student of the tax code and tax laws that were used in the current edition. However, because tax code, tables, and laws may be changed by Congress after the text has been printed, the student is advised on how, in practice, they can find the most current tax code, tables, and laws.
- **Enhanced Excel Templates**—The Excel Templates include a feedback section giving instructors the option for adding a comment/grade and an area for students to show their work.
- **Superior Examples**—Examples are identified and numbered within the text. Various end-of-chapter problems are identified as a problem similar to an example within the text. See the examples below.

MASTERY
APPLICATION
MOTIVATION

EXAMPLE 3-7

Yeld Company failed to pay its employment taxes of $5,000 for March (due April 15) until May 20. The failure to pay penalty assessed against Yeld Company is:

Failure to Pay Tax ($5,000 × 0.5% × 2)	=	$50.00
Interest on Taxes Due ($5,000 × 0.03 × 35/365)	=	14.38
Total Penalty		$64.38

Note: In addition, a penalty for failure to make a timely deposit will also be assessed.

3-16A • LO 5 Similar to Example 3-5 on page 3-19, Example 3-6 on page 3-28, Example 3-7 on page 3-29

Vulcan Company is a monthly depositor whose tax liability for March 2016 is $2,505.

1. What is the due date for the deposit of these taxes? _____

2. Assume that no deposit was made until May 2. Compute the following penalties:

   a. Penalty for failure to make timely deposit. $ _____
   b. Penalty for failure to fully pay tax. $ _____
   c. Interest on taxes due and unpaid. $ _____
   d. Total penalty imposed. $ _____

> "Excellent! In the past it was often difficult to point students to a particular example when there was more than one on a page."
>
> -Karen Spray,
> *Northeast Community College*

> "I like this connection; students can easily test themselves on a specific example."
>
> -Jennifer Morton,
> *Ivy Tech Community College*

COMPUTERIZED PAYROLL PROJECT

Chapter 7—The Payroll Project

Chapter 7 consists of a practice set or simulation. The student applies the knowledge acquired in the first six chapters to a practical payroll simulation as the payroll accountant for the Glo-Brite Paint Company. The Payroll Project can be completed manually using fold-out Payroll Registers located at the back of the text or by completing the Excel templates located on the *Payroll Accounting* Web site: **www.cengagebrain.com.**

Appendix A—Payroll Project Using Online General Ledger

The computerized payroll project, located in Appendix A, is identical to the manual payroll project in Chapter 7, although students will now be using Cengage Learning's Online General Ledger in CengageNOWv2. Appendix A provides step-by-step instructions for completing payroll periods within a 3-month time period. See an example of CLGL below.

Shortened Payroll Project

The Shortened Payroll Project takes students through payroll periods for one month only. This is an option for instructors who want to assign a Payroll Project but do not have the time to assign the full version. The Shortened Payroll Project can be completed using the Excel templates provided or by using Cengage Learning's Online General Ledger in CengageNOWv2. See an example on the next page.

Start of Short Version of Payroll Project (Continuation of Payroll Project)

December 3

No. 18 Deposit with the state of Pennsylvania the amount of state income taxes withheld from the November 20 payroll and complete the information worksheet.

December 4

No. 19 Prepare the payroll for the first pay period of December from Time Clerk's Report Nos. 46 and 47, and record the paychecks issued all employees. Record this payroll at the top of the third payroll register sheet.

Note: Thursday, November 26, is a paid holiday for all workers.

Also, record the employer's payroll taxes.

Time Clerk's Report No. 46 For the Week Ending November 21, 20--									
Employee	**Time Record**							**Time Worked**	**Time Lost**
	S	M	T	W	T	F	S		
Bonno, A. V. ...		8	8	8	8	8		40 hrs.	...
Ford, C. L.		8	8	8	8	8		40 hrs.	...
Russell, V. A. ...		8	8	8	8	8		40 hrs.	...
Ryan, N. A.		8	8	8	4	8		36 hrs.	4 hrs.*
Student........		8	8	8	4	8		36 hrs.	...
Woods, B. A. ...		...	8	8	8	8		32 hrs.	...

*Time lost on account of personal business; deduct 4 hours' pay.

OUTSTANDING PEDAGOGY

Learning Objectives

Learning Objectives are enumerated at the beginning of each chapter, and the numbers are repeated next to the start of the applicable text coverage for easy navigation.

Credits Against FUTA Tax

The actual FUTA tax paid is usually only *0.6 percent*, since employers are entitled to a credit against their FUTA tax liability for contributions made under approved state unemployment compensation laws. The maximum credit permitted is 5.4 percent (90% of 6%). Thus, in the preceding example where the **gross** FUTA tax rate is 6.0 percent, the **net** FUTA rate would be 0.6 percent if the full 5.4 percent credit applied. Even if employers pay a SUTA rate of less than 5.4 percent, they still get the full credit against the FUTA tax.

LO 3

Compute the federal unemployment tax, the credit against the tax, and any credit reductions that might apply.

Self-Study Quizzes

Self-Study Quizzes appear throughout each chapter and test the understanding of major concepts. Answers to the quizzes are available within each chapter.

SELF-STUDY QUIZ 3-1

Which of the following are covered by FICA (indicate Yes or No)?

_____ 1. Andrian Mitchell, a full-time life insurance salesperson.
_____ 2. John Sain, a federal government employee, hired in 1990.
_____ 3. Bonnie Stone, a real estate agent.
_____ 4. Stuart Schuck, who offers lawn care service to homeowners in the neighborhood.

Note: Answers are on page 3-30.

Over the Line Real World Ethics Cases

The Over the Line feature illustrates cases of companies either intentionally or unintentionally crossing the boundaries of fairness in their interpretation of payroll laws.

> ### Over the Line
>
> After nearly a year on the job in New York, an employee moved to Florida and telecommuted for another two years. She was laid off and received benefits from New York. The employer appealed, and a state appeals court ruled that she was ineligible because she had not worked in New York during the base period. Her out-of-state work must be incidental to the in-state work. That was not the case since actual work was performed in Florida.

Check Figures Included at the End of This Text

Check figures provide help and assist users in staying on track as they learn the intricacies of payroll accounting.

Key Points Summary

This summary at the end of the chapter ties the key points in the chapter to the Learning Objectives.

Use of Marginal Icons

Use of marginal icons ("On the Net," "News Alert," "IRS Connection," and "On the Job") helps integrate the real world applications of this facts-intensive area of study. "On the Net" icons allow optional integration of Internet research sites for learners.

The icons in each chapter highlight the most current forms, instructions, and wage and tax laws available.

ON THE JOB

If you need to determine if a certain type of payment or individual is subject to income tax withholding, check **Circular E, Employer's Tax Guide**. Special classes of employment and payments are listed, along with their treatment under employment tax laws.

NEWS ALERT

When an employer provides a cell phone to an employee "primarily for noncompensatory business reasons," the IRS will treat the employee's business use of the cell phone as a working condition fringe benefit, the value of which is excludable from the employee's income. Also, personal use of the employer-provided cell phone will be treated as a de minimis fringe benefit.[1]

THOROUGH END-OF-CHAPTER MATERIALS

End-of-chapter assignable materials include matching quizzes, review questions, discussion questions, practical problems, case problems, and continuing payroll problems, which can also be completed using Excel or CLGL.

CONTINUING PAYROLL PROBLEM · A

Refer to the partially completed payroll register that you worked on at the end of Chapter 4. You will now compute the employer's liability for unemployment taxes (FUTA and SUTA) for the pay of January 14. These computations will be used at the end of Chapter 6 in recording the payroll tax entries.

To compute the employer's liability for unemployment taxes, proceed as follows:

1. Enter each employee's gross earnings in the Taxable Earnings—FUTA and SUTA columns.
2. Total the Taxable Earnings—FUTA and SUTA columns.
3. At the bottom of your payroll register, compute the following:

a. Net FUTA tax. Since this is the first pay period of the year, none of the employees are near the $7,000 ceiling; therefore, each employee's gross earnings is subject to the FUTA tax.
b. SUTA tax. Since Kipley Company is a new employer, Pennsylvania has assigned the company a contribution rate of 3.6785% on the first $9,000 of each employee's earnings. Employees pay 0.07% on total gross pay.

Note: Retain your partially completed payroll register for use at the end of Chapter 6.

Up-to-the-Minute Tax Law Changes

Up-to-date knowledge is especially important for today's payroll specialists. This edition has been completely updated to reflect the tax law changes that affect payroll accounting. Users can find these changes listed on the "As We Go To Press" page in the text and on **www.cengagebrain.com**.

INSTRUCTOR RESOURCES

Solutions Manual/Test Bank (Exams)/Achievement Tests (ISBN: 9781305665958)

This robust printed manual contains the Learning Objectives, Chapter Outline, and solutions to all end-of-chapter exercises and problems including the Continuing Payroll Problems, Case Problems, and the Payroll Project. The Test Bank questions and solutions are included to assist with choosing True/False, Multiple-Choice questions, and problems for examinations. Achievement Tests and keys are provided for additional testing and can also be reproduced.

Test Bank Available with Cengage Learning Testing Powered by Cognero

What is Cognero?

- Full-featured, online-assessment system allows instructors to manage test bank content from multiple Cengage Learning solutions.
- Create multiple test versions in an instant.
- Deliver tests from your LMS, your classroom, or wherever you want.
- Works on any operating system or browser.
- No special installs or downloads needed.
- Create tests from school, home, the coffee shop—anywhere with Internet access.

How to access?

- Log into your Cengage Learning SSO account at **login.cengage.com.**
- Add *Payroll Accounting 2016* to your bookshelf (ISBN: 9781305665910).
- Once the book is added to your bookshelf, a link to access Cognero for *Payroll Accounting 2016* will appear, along with the link to the instructor and student companion sites.

"I am very satisfied with the ability to create a different version of a test at any given time."

-Vernon Bogan,
Brown Mackie College

How do I start?
- Online resources, user guides, and instructional videos are available on the instructor companion Web site at **login.cengage.com.**
- Please address any other technical questions to Cengage Learning Technical Support at **support.cengage.com.**

Instructor Web Site (login.cengage.com)

In addition to the material available to students online, the instructor site contains password-protected instructor resources. Instructors can find the following resources:

- Solutions Manual in Microsoft Word
- Comprehensive PowerPoint slides
- Achievement Tests and Keys
- Excel solutions for all end-of-chapter problems
- Excel solutions for Payroll Project (Chapter 7)

STUDENT RESOURCES

Student Companion Web Site (www.cengagebrain.com)

Accessible through **www.cengagebrain.com,** the student Web site contains Interactive Quizzes, Check Figures, Quizzes, Puzzles, Web Links, PowerPoint slides, and the student guide for CLGL. The Excel templates are posted for the full version of the Glo-Brite Payroll Project (short-version templates are available from the instructor), Continuing Payroll Problems A and B, and selected end-of-chapter problems designated by the Excel icon. In addition, the student has access to Appendix B, Excel Template Instructions for the Glo-Brite Payroll Project, as well as important information contained in Appendix C: Social Security Benefits and Appendix D: Unemployment Benefits.

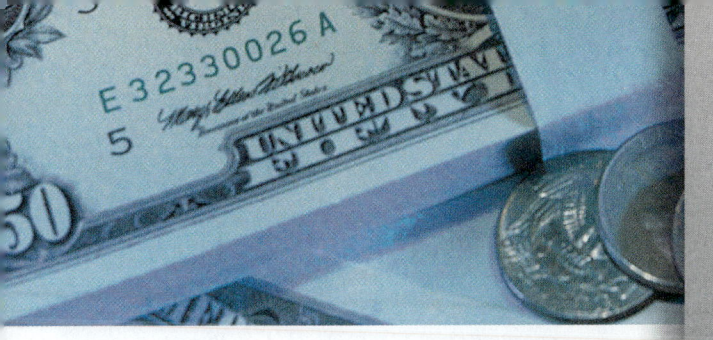

ACKNOWLEDGMENTS

Our sincere appreciation is extended to the many instructors and students who have contributed suggestions to make the textbook more interesting, understandable, and practical to those who pursue the study of payroll accounting. As a result of their very helpful recommendations, the textbook will better satisfy the learning needs of students and the teaching needs of instructors. We would like to thank the following instructors for their valuable comments and suggestions:

Steven Barela
Santa Fe Community College

Gretta Biggs
Nunez Community College

Melissa D. Boback
Cambria-Rowe Business College

Robert Bolmer
Everest Institute

Sharon Brown
Kaplan University

Tracy Carmichael
Fletcher Technical Community College

John Chappell
Northland Community and Technical College

Amy Chataginer
Mississippi Gulf Coast Community College

Diane Clugston
Cambria-Rowe Business College

Nancy Cowett
Northern Maine Community College

Bruce Creech
Sampson Community College

Margaret Lynn Crossman
Laney College

Amy Crouch
International Business College

Cher Cuppari
Everest University

William H. Dams
Lenoir Community College

Judy Daulton
Piedmont Technical College

Stephanie Desormeaux
Delta Tech

Shelly Dhir
Unitek

Barbara Dickson
MTI College

Kerry Dolan
Great Falls College Montana State University

Marianne Edmunds
Daymar College

Annette Edwards
Tennessee College of Applied Technology

Dustin Emhart
North Georgia Technical College

Brian Fink
Danville Area Community College

David Forester
Haywood Community College

Paul Franklin
Kaplan University

Connie Robin Gibson
TriCounty Community College

Marina Grau
Houston Community College

Susan Greene
Cloud County Community College

Steve Groves
Ivy Tech Community College

Bruce Gunning
Kent State University at East Liverpool

Penny Hahn
Henderson Community College

Diann Hammon
JF Drake State Community College

Toni R. Hartley
Laurel Business Institute

Lyle Hicks
Danville Area Community College

JoLynn Hightower
Texas State Technical College West Texas

Kim Hurt
Central Community College

Connie Jones
Wake Tech

Lynn Krausse
Bakersfield College

Jessica Lancaster
McCann School of Business and Technology

Greg Lauer
North Iowa Area Community College

Gil Logan
Bryant & Stratton College

Angel Luper
Tri-County Technical College

Jason Marconi
McCann School of Business and Technology

Dan Marlow
American Business and Technology University

Sharon Martinez
Brown Mackie College

Michelle Masingill
North Idaho College

Carole Maske
Southwestern Community College

Drew McCabe
Brown Mackie College

Linda McCarley
Bevill State Community College

Dawn McKinley
Harper College

Lori Meseke
Vandalia Community Schools

Joseph Malino Nicassio
Westmoreland County Community College

Michelle Parker
Coastal Pines Technical College

Jamie Payton
Gadsden State Community College

Ann Price
Blue Ridge Community and Technical College

Barbara Rice
Gateway Community and Technical College

Patricia Scales
Brookstone College

Tracy Schmeltzer
Wayne Community College

Karen Spray
Northeast Community College

Marie Stewart
Laurel Technical Institute

Juanita Sweet
Cape Cod Community College

Shunda Ware
Atlanta Technical College

Cammy Wayne
William Rainey Harper College

Lynn Whiddon
Central Georgia Technical College

Michele Wilkens
Minnesota State University

Tomeika Williams
Rasmussen College

Jack Wu
Chemeketa Community College

Jessica York
National College

In addition, the authors would like to thank the following content providers and verifiers for the 2016 edition:

Bernie Hill, *Spokane Falls Community College*, retired instructor, for preparing the Excel templates and the Instructor and Student PowerPoint slides and for verifying the text and all the elements on the Web site

Sergey Dyadyura, Project Manager Competentum, for creation and verification of Payroll Project using Cengage Learning General Ledger.

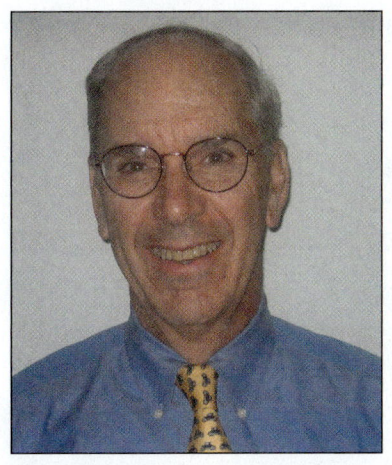

Bernard J. Bieg

After receiving his Master's in Business Administration from the University of Notre Dame and passing the Certified Public Accountants' exam in the early 1970s, Bernard Bieg turned his attention toward a career in teaching. He has been a professor at Bucks County Community College for more than 30 years. During that time, he has taught the whole spectrum of accounting offerings, including payroll accounting. He has maintained strong connections with today's business world by serving as an internal auditor for a local nonprofit organization. His association with this textbook began in 1977 as a co-author with one of the originators of the book, Bill Keeling.

Judith A. Toland

Judith Toland received her Master's Degree in Education from Temple University in 2002, her Bachelor's Degree in Business Administration—Accounting from Bloomsburg University in 1981, and her Associate's Degree from Bucks County Community College in Business Administration in 1979. Judy has taught Accounting courses at BCCC since 1989 and is currently a professor in the Business Studies Department. Judy earned the prestigious Certified Payroll Professional (CPP) designation in 2011.

CONTENTS

AS WE GO TO PRESS iii

PREFACE iv

ACKNOWLEDGMENTS xiii

ABOUT THE AUTHORS xv

1 The Need for Payroll and Personnel Records 1-1

The Payroll Profession 1-2

Fair Labor Standards Act 1-3

Federal Insurance Contributions Act 1-3

Income Tax Withholding Laws 1-4

Unemployment Tax Acts 1-4

Recordkeeping Requirements 1-4

Fair Employment Laws 1-4

Other Federal Laws Affecting the Need for Payroll
and Personnel Records 1-7

Other State Laws Affecting the Need for Payroll and
Personnel Records 1-11

Human Resources and Payroll Accounting Systems 1-12

Human Resources System 1-13

Recordkeeping System 1-20

Payroll Accounting System 1-20

Questions and Problems 1-25

2 Computing Wages and Salaries 2-1

The Fair Labor Standards Act 2-1

Determining Employee's Work Time 2-13

Records Used for Timekeeping 2-17

Methods of Computing Wages and Salaries 2-20

Questions and Problems 2-31

3 Social Security Taxes 3-1

Coverage Under FICA 3-1

A Self-Employed Person 3-12

Employer Identification Number 3-14
Employee's Application for Social Security Card (Form SS-5)............ 3-14
Returns Required for Social Security Purposes 3-16
Preparing Form 941 (Employer's Quarterly Federal Tax Return) 3-21
Failure-to-Comply Penalties.. 3-27
Questions and Problems 3-32

4   Income Tax Withholding 4-1
Coverage Under Federal Income Tax Withholding Laws 4-1
Tax-Deferred Retirement Accounts 4-8
Withholding Allowances.. 4-9
Federal Income Tax Withholding 4-15
Other Methods of Withholding... 4-17
Supplemental Wage Payments 4-18
Wage and Tax Statements 4-21
Returns Employers Must Complete 4-27
Information Returns 4-28
Independent Contractor Payments... 4-28
Backup Withholding.. 4-29
Electronic Filing Form W-2 and Information Returns 4-30
Withholding State Income Tax 4-30
Questions and Problems 4-36

5   Unemployment Compensation Taxes 5-1
Coverage Under FUTA and SUTA... 5-2
Unemployment Compensation Taxes and Credits............................... 5-8
Unemployment Compensation Reports Required
of the Employer 5-18
Questions and Problems 5-30

6   Analyzing and Journalizing Payroll... 6-1
The Payroll Register 6-1
The Employee's Earnings Record 6-4
Recording the Gross Payroll and Withholdings................................... 6-6
Methods of Paying Wages and Salaries 6-12
Recording Payroll Taxes... 6-16
Recording Workers' Compensation Insurance Expense 6-20
Recording the Deposit or Payment of Payroll Taxes 6-21
Recording End-of-Period Adjustments.. 6-22
Summary of Accounts Used in Recording Payroll Transactions 6-23
Illustrative Case 6-24
Questions and Problems 6-33

7   Payroll Project **7-1**
Books of Account and Payroll Records 7-2
General Information 7-3
Start of Payroll Project.. 7-6
**Start of Short Version of Payroll Project
(Continuation of Payroll Project)**......................... 7-16
Questions on the Payroll Project................................. 7-22

**APPENDIX A: Payroll Project Using Online
              General Ledger (CLGL)** **A-1**
              Payroll Project A-1
              Payroll Project (Short Version) A-20
              Optional Activities............................... A-32
              Student Project Audit Tests....................... A-35

TAX TABLE A: TABLES FOR PERCENTAGE METHOD
OF INCOME TAX WITHHOLDING T-1

TAX TABLE B: WAGE BRACKET METHOD
TABLES FOR INCOME TAX WITHHOLDING............................ T-5

CHECK FIGURES CF-1

GLOSSARY G-1

INDEX I-1

Online Web Appendices (cengagebrain.com)

Controlling Costs: Payroll, Benefits, and Taxes....................... **CC-1**

**APPENDIX B: Excel Template Instructions for the
              Glo-Brite Payroll Project
              (Using Excel 2010 or 2013)**.................... **B-1**
              Getting to Know Excel B-1

APPENDIX C: Social Security Benefits............................ **C-1**
              What Factors Are Used to Determine Social
              Security Benefits? C-1
              What Benefits Are Provided by Social Security? ... C-2
              What Are Reduced Benefits?....................... C-4
              How Does Working After Retirement Affect Social
              Security Benefits? C-5
              How Do You Apply for Social Security Benefits? ... C-6
              What Is Medicare?............................... C-7

APPENDIX D: Unemployment Benefits **D-1**
              Unemployment Compensation Benefits D-1

CHAPTER 1

The Need for Payroll and Personnel Records

The Horner Company in our Animated Activities for this chapter is not a lone ranger. Each year close to 100,000 claims involving workplace discrimination are filed with the Equal Employment Opportunity Commission with resulting judgments around $300 million.

On employment applications and in job interviews be careful of "hot button" topics concerning: mental status, living arrangements, age, children, home ownership, church affiliation, political affiliation, credit history, and insurance coverage. Questions relating to these topics will give the appearance of discrimination and could put us on the "slippery slope" to the courthouse.

LEARNING OBJECTIVES

After studying this chapter, you should be able to:

1 Identify the various laws that affect employers in their payroll operations.
2 Examine the recordkeeping requirements of these laws.
3 Describe the employment procedures generally followed in a Human Resources Department.
4 Recognize the various personnel records used by businesses and know the type of information shown on each form.
5 Identify the *payroll register* and the *employee's earnings record.*

No matter the size of the company, the profitability, the product or service being sold, or the type of organization, employees have to be paid. This task has become more difficult as numerous regulations have been enacted. Recent legislation has only added to the administrative burden, and future legislation will continue this trend. The payroll person is no longer the employee stuck in the corner who only appears on payday to distribute paychecks. The job responsibilities have multiplied and now require persons with advanced knowledge in the area of payroll to handle the position. In many cases, the payroll specialist has been on the leading edge of change and automation.

Payroll professionals are responsible for processing over 4 billion pay statements each year to over 100 million people in the workforce of the United States. The processing of payrolls allows no margin for error. Employees, employers, and government agencies monitor the work performed by payroll professionals. A payroll accounting system is the only operation in a business that is almost completely governed by various federal, state, and local laws and regulations. Rules establish who is an employee, what is time worked, when overtime is to be paid, what deductions are made, when to pay an employee, what benefits have to be provided, and when taxes are paid. Lack of compliance with these laws and regulations can result in both fines and back-pay awards.

The payroll professional has risen in the ranks of the accounting profession and now demands salaries commensurate with his or her peers. The confidentiality of the payroll information from each employee's pay rate to the garnishments imposed on some employees has tightened the link to the upper management teams. The confidence and trust that must be placed in payroll professionals have made them an integral part of the "inner circle." This chapter briefly examines the various laws that affect employers in their payroll operations and the payroll and personnel records that they use to meet the requirements of the laws. First, however, let's take a brief look at payroll accounting as a profession.

The Payroll Profession

A 2015 payroll survey of large employers conducted by Robert Half Associates revealed a range of salaries for payroll managers of $58,000–$91,500 and for payroll administrators of $42,500–$57,750.

Typically, an entry-level payroll clerk collects, reviews, approves, and records time records. The clerk also updates attendance records, including vacation, sick, and personal days. Once a payroll is processed, the clerk reviews the information to ensure the accuracy of each employee's pay statement. Job responsibilities will include entering the following information into the payroll system:

1. Time-worked data.
2. Pay rate changes.
3. Tax rate changes.
4. Employee-authorized payroll deductions.
5. New employee information.
6. Marital and employee allowance changes.

Providing information to the Finance Department concerning the amounts to be paid for taxes, health insurance premiums, retirement plans, etc., may also be part of the evolving duties of the advancing payroll professional. One of the final stages involves the completion of payroll tax returns, employee information returns, federal and state census surveys, and fringe benefit and welfare plan returns.

Payroll professionals must keep abreast of the changes in their field so that they can remain technically proficient. This need has been met by an association of payroll practitioners—the American Payroll Association (APA). Membership in the association is open to anyone interested in or engaged in the support of payroll accounting. The APA offers professional training seminars and various publications to its members. Each year, the APA administers examinations for the payroll accountant and awards certificates to those who pass the exams, Fundamental Payroll Certification (to demonstrate a baseline of payroll competency) and Payroll Professional Certification (for the experienced professional to demonstrate the full-range of payroll competency). This testing and certification process has helped the payroll profession to gain recognition in the business community. The APA has also established guidelines for the conduct of the payroll professional. This "Code of Ethics," shown in Figure 1.1, sets the direction for the profession.[1]

One of a number of publications designed to provide current information to the practitioner is published by the Research Institute of America, Inc. This biweekly publication is entitled *Payroll Guide*, and it is a comprehensive review of changes in regulations affecting payroll reporting.[2]

---

1 For more information on the organization, write to American Payroll Association, 660 North Main Avenue, Suite 100, San Antonio, TX 78205-1217; Tel: 210-224-6406; APA@americanpayroll.org.

2 *Payroll Guide* is published by the Research Institute of America, Inc., 195 Broadway, New York, NY 10007; Tel: 1-800-323-8724.

FIGURE 1.1
APA Code of Ethics

1. To be mindful of the personal aspect of the payroll relationship between employer and employee, and to ensure that harmony is maintained through constant concern for the Payroll Professional's fellow employees.
2. To strive for perfect compliance, accuracy, and timeliness of all payroll activities.
3. To keep abreast of the state of the payroll art with regard to developments in payroll technologies.
4. To be current with legislative developments and actions on the part of regulatory bodies, insofar as they affect payroll.
5. To maintain the absolute confidentiality, of the payroll within the procedures of the employer.
6. To refrain from using Association activities for one's personal self-interest or financial gain.
7. To take as one's commitment the enhancement of one's professional abilities through the resources of the American Payroll Association.
8. To support one's fellow Payroll Professionals, both within and outside one's organization.

Source: For more information on the organization, write to American Payroll Association, 660 North Main Avenue, Suite 100, San Antonio, TX 78205-1217; Tel: 210-224-6406; APA@americanpayroll.org.

Fair Labor Standards Act

The Fair Labor Standards Act (FLSA), referred to as the Federal Wage and Hour Law, is covered in Chapter 2. The outline of the law deals with:

- Minimum wage ($7.25 per hour) and overtime pay requirements. In addition, equal pay for equal work, employment of child labor, public service contracts, and wage garnishment.
- Coverage of employers engaged in interstate commerce or in production of goods and services for interstate commerce.
- Maintaining records that explain the basis of wage differentials paid to employees of opposite sex for equal work.
- Displaying a poster (from the regional office of the Wage and Hour division) informing employees of the provisions of the law.
- States' Minimum Wage and Maximum Hour Laws that also establish minimum wage rates for covered employees. Where both federal and state laws cover the same employee, the higher of two rates prevails (e.g., Washington—$9.47 per hour).
- The State's wage orders that also can affect pay periods, pay for call-in and waiting times, rest and meal periods, absences, meals and lodging, uniforms, etc.

LO 1
Identify the various laws that affect employers in their payroll operations.

ON THE JOB

Up until July 24, 2009, the minimum wage was $6.55 per hour.

ON THE NET

http://www.dol.gov/whd/minwage/america.htm This Web site contains the minimum wage laws by state in map and text form.

Federal Insurance Contributions Act

Chapter 3 covers FICA (social security) in detail; however, the basic provisions of the act deal with:

- Tax on employees (set percent of their gross wages) and employers for the Federal Old-Age and Survivors' Trust Fund and the Federal Disability Insurance Trust Fund.
- Separate tax on employees and employers to finance the Health Insurance Plan—Medicare.
- Tax on net earnings of the self-employed individual (Self-Employment Contributions Act—SECA).
- Making payments to persons who are entitled to benefits under these social security taxes.

Income Tax Withholding Laws

ON THE NET

http://www.payroll-taxes.com/
Premiere Payroll Tax Research
Library. This site contains
addresses, phone numbers,
form numbers (with
explanations), and filing dates
for federal and state taxing
authorities.

Chapter 4 covers income tax withholding, but basically:

- Income tax is levied on the earnings of most employees and is deducted from their gross pay.
- Income taxes can be imposed by federal, state, and local governments.
- Federal Income Tax (FIT) employs a percentage formula used by each employer to withhold a specified amount from each wage payment.
- State tax rates vary from state to state.

Unemployment Tax Acts

Chapter 5 covers unemployment taxes with a detailed discussion of:

- Tax levied on employers (Federal Unemployment Tax Act—FUTA) that is used to pay state and federal administrative expenses of the unemployment program.
- A credit granted against most of the FUTA tax if the employer pays a state unemployment tax. A smaller credit is granted to states that have not paid back borrowings from the federal government which were used to pay the cost of benefits to their eligible unemployed workers.
- State unemployment taxes (SUTA) on employers imposed by all states. These taxes are used to pay unemployment benefits.
- Standards set by the Social Security Act that result in a high degree of uniformity in the requirements of state unemployment laws.
- Employers' need to be aware of the SUTA laws in the states where they operate.

Recordkeeping Requirements

LO 2
Examine the recordkeeping
requirements of these laws.

Although the laws do impose recordkeeping requirements on employers, no specific form of record is mandated. Figure 1.2 lists the specific information needed and the retention time periods required.

Fair Employment Laws

Federal and state legislations have been enacted to enforce fair employment practices. Many of these laws deal with discrimination on the basis of age, race, color, religion, gender, or national origin.

ON THE NET

http://www.eeoc.gov/ This
EEOC homepage overviews
guidelines and services of the
Equal Employment
Opportunity Commission
(EEOC).

Civil Rights Act of 1964

Title VII of the Civil Rights Act of 1964, entitled "Equal Employment Opportunity," provides for several fair employment practices. The act, as amended, forbids employers to discriminate in hiring, firing, promoting, compensating, or in any other condition of employment on the basis of race, color, religion, gender, or national origin. Guidelines, established by the Equal Employment Opportunity Commission (EEOC), also include physical characteristics in the definition of national origin discrimination. For example, unnecessary height or weight requirements could exclude some individuals on the basis of their national origin. The EEOC has also declared that sexual harassment violates the Civil Rights Act. Unwelcome sexual advances, requests for sexual favors, and other verbal or physical conduct of a sexual nature can constitute sexual harassment.

FIGURE 1.2

Summary of Information Required by Major Federal Payroll Laws

	Item	Fair Labor Standards Act	Social Security	Income Tax Withholding	Unemployment Tax
EMPLOYEE DATA	Name	Yes	Yes	Yes	Yes
	Address	Yes	Yes	Yes	Yes
	Gender	Yes	. . . .	. . . .	. . . .
	Date of birth	Yes	. . . .	. . . .	. . . .
	Social Security Number	Yes	Yes	Yes	Yes
	Withholding allowances claimed	. . . .	. . . .	Yes	. . . .
	Occupation	Yes	Yes	Yes	Yes
	Period employed	. . . .	Yes	Yes	Yes
	State where services rendered	. . . .	Yes	. . . .	Yes
EMPLOYMENT DATA	Beginning and ending dates of employee's employment	. . . .	Yes	Yes	. . . .
	Day and time of day when workweek begins	Yes	. . . .	. . . .	. . . .
	Regular hourly rate of pay	Yes	. . . .	. . . .	. . . .
	Basis of wage payments; e.g., $9.25 per hour; $74.00 per day	Yes	. . . .	. . . .	. . . .
	Hours worked each day	Yes	. . . .	. . . .	. . . .
	Hours worked each week	Yes	. . . .	. . . .	. . . .
	Daily or weekly straight-time pay, exclusive of overtime pay	Yes	. . . .	. . . .	. . . .
	Amount and nature of exempt pay	Yes	. . . .	. . . .	. . . .
	Weekly overtime pay	Yes	. . . .	. . . .	. . . .
	Total additions to or deductions from wages	Yes	. . . .	. . . .	. . . .
	Total remuneration for payroll period	Yes	Yes	Yes	. . . .
	Total remuneration for calendar year	. . . .	Yes	. . . .	Yes
	Date of payment	Yes	Yes	Yes	Yes
	Payroll period	Yes	Yes	Yes	Yes
TAX DATA	Employee's wages subject to tax for payroll period	. . . .	Yes	Yes	. . . .
	Employee's wages subject to tax for calendar year	. . . .	Yes	. . . .	Yes
	Taxable remuneration—if different from total remuneration, reason for difference	. . . .	Yes	Yes	Yes
	Tax deductions from employee's wages	. . . .	Yes	Yes	Yes
	Date tax collected if other than date of payment	. . . .	Yes	Yes	. . . .
	Tax paid by employer but not deducted from employee's wages	. . . .	Yes	Yes	Yes
GEN'L	Specific form of records	No	No	No	No
	Number of years records must be kept	2–3	4*	4*	4*

*Four years after the due date of the payment of the tax to which the records relate.

The EEOC prohibits unions from excluding or segregating their members on these bases, and employment agencies may not refer or refuse to refer applicants for employment on the basis of race, color, religion, gender, or national origin.

This act covers all employers who engage in an industry "affecting commerce" and who employ 15 or more workers for each working day in each of 20 or more weeks in the current or preceding calendar year. Employers specifically excluded from coverage of the fair employment practices include the U.S. government (state and local governments are covered), a corporation wholly owned by the United States, Indian tribes, private membership clubs (other than labor unions) exempt from federal income tax, and religious societies in the employment of members of a particular religion to work on the societies' religious activities. Although the U.S. government is classified as an exempt employer, the act states that the policy of the U.S. government provides equal employment opportunities without discrimination and that the president should use his existing authority to implement this policy.

Title VII does not protect an employee from arbitrary treatment or dismissal. As long as the employer applies these policies in a nondiscriminatory manner, Title VII requirements have not been violated.

Over the Line

Yellow Transportation has a policy that new employees can be fired if they are late for work during their first 30 days of employment. A non-white employee who was late twice during this period was fired. He then sued the company for racial bias, stating that long-term white employees were not held to the same standard. The court rejected his claim and stated that in order to prove bias the comparison had to be made with newly hired white employees. This ruling confirms the right of a company to set stricter rules during an initial training period.[3]

To accomplish the purpose of eliminating discrimination, the EEOC tries to obtain voluntary compliance with the law before filing a court action for an injunction. It can institute court proceedings for an injunction if it believes that any person or group of persons is not complying with the law. Where a state or local law forbids discriminatory practices, relief must first be sought under the state or local law before a complaint is filed with the Commission. In most states, a special commission or the state Department of Labor administers the laws and may authorize cease-and-desist orders that are enforceable in the courts.

The Civil Rights Act of 1991 grants compensatory and punitive damages in cases where the discrimination is intentional. It also provides for the repayment of attorney fees and the possibility of a jury trial.

Executive Orders

Employers not subject to the Title VII coverage discussed above may come within the scope of the Civil Rights Act by reason of a contract or a subcontract involving federal funds. In a series of **executive orders**, the federal government has banned, in employment on government contracts, discrimination based on race, color, religion, gender, or national origin.

---

3 *HR Specialist*, March 2012, p. 3.

Age Discrimination in Employment Act

The Age Discrimination in Employment Act of 1967 (ADEA) prohibits employers, employment agencies, and labor unions from discriminating on the basis of age in their employment practices. The act covers employers engaged in an industry affecting interstate commerce (who employ 20 or more workers), employment agencies, and labor unions. The act also covers federal, state, and local government employees, other than elected officials and certain aides not covered by civil service. The ADEA provides protection for virtually all workers over 40. A key exception is executives who are 65 or older and who have held high policy-making positions during the two-year period prior to retirement. If such an employee is entitled to an annual retirement benefit from the employer of at least $44,000, the employee can be forcibly retired.

In order to prove compliance with the various fair employment laws, employers must keep accurate personnel and payroll records. All employment applications, along with notations as to their disposition and the reasons for the disposition, should be retained. All records pertaining to promotions, discharges, seniority plans, merit programs, incentive payment plans, etc., should also be retained.

> **ON THE JOB**
>
> Court rulings have updated the regulations to state that favoring an older individual over a younger individual because of age is not unlawful discrimination under the ADEA.

Americans with Disabilities Act

The Americans with Disabilities Act of 1990 (ADA) prohibits employers with 15 or more employees, employment agencies, labor organizations, or joint labor-management committees from discriminating against qualified persons with disabilities because of their disability.

The prohibition of disability-based discrimination applies to job application procedures, hiring, advancement, termination, compensation, job training, and other conditions of employment. In addition, reasonable accommodations, such as wheelchair-accessible restrooms and ramps for qualified disabled job applicants and workers, must be provided.

Under the ADA, a person is considered "qualified" if he or she can perform the essential functions of the job with or without reasonable accommodation.

Other Federal Laws Affecting the Need for Payroll and Personnel Records

Generally, the payroll and personnel records and reports that a business prepares and retains to meet the requirements of the laws already discussed provide sufficient information needed under the laws outlined in Figure 1.3, on page 1-8, and discussed below.

Federal Personal Responsibility and Work Opportunity Reconciliation Act of 1996

The Federal Personal Responsibility and Work Opportunity Reconciliation Act of 1996 (PRWORA) mandates that all states must establish new-hire reporting programs. Every employer is required to report the name, address, and social security number on each new employee and the employer's name, address, and federal employer identification number *within 20 days of hire* to the appropriate state agency. In many states, submission of a copy of the employee's W-4 form (Employee's Withholding Allowance Certificate) will satisfy the reporting requirement. This information must then be forwarded by the state to the federal Office of Child Support Enforcement (OCSE) for entry into the National Directory of New Hires.

Employers with operations in more than one state may file one report with the state of their choice. That state is then to share the information with the other states.

FIGURE 1.3

Federal Laws Affecting the Need for Payroll and Personnel Records

Law	Coverage	Contract Dollar Minimum	Major Provisions
Davis-Bacon Act (1931)	Laborers for contractors or subcontractors on federal government contracts for construction, alteration, or repair of public buildings or works.	$ 2,000	Minimum wage set by secretary of labor (weight is given to union wage scale prevailing in the project area).
Walsh-Healey Public Contracts Act (1936)	Laborers for contractors who furnish materials, supplies, articles, and equipment to any agency of the United States.	$10,000	Single minimum wage determined by secretary of labor for all covered employees in a given industry.
McNamara-O'Hara Service Contract Act (1965)	Service employees on contracts with the United States or the District of Columbia for the furnishing of services.	$ 2,500	Minimum wage set by secretary of labor based on minimum wage found to be prevailing in that locality.
Occupational Safety and Health Act (OSHA) (1970)	Any business involved in interstate commerce.	$ 0	Sets specific occupational and health standards for employers; requires that records be kept of work-related injuries, illnesses, and deaths.
Vocational Rehabilitation Act (1973)	Companies with federal agency contracts.	$ 2,500	Must include in the contract an affirmative action clause requiring that the handicapped applicant or employee will be given appropriate consideration.
Vietnam Era Veterans' Readjustment Act (1974)	Government contractors with federal contracts or subcontracts.	$10,000	Requires contractors to take affirmative action to employ and advance in employment qualified veterans of the Vietnam era and disabled veterans.

The main reason for this requirement is to help in the enforcement of child support obligations. In addition, it will reduce fraud in the unemployment, workers' compensation, and public assistance programs. Failure to report this information can result in fines of up to $25.00 per new hire. Even though under federal law employers do not have to report this same information on independent contractors, some states do require such reporting.

Immigration Reform and Control Act of 1986

The Immigration Reform and Control Act of 1986 (IRCA) bars employers from hiring and retaining aliens unauthorized to work in the United States. It also requires all employers to verify employment eligibility for all individuals by examining the employee's verification documents and having the employee complete Form I-9, Employment Eligibility Verification. Form I-9 lists the documents that an employee can choose from to furnish to the employer. These documents identify the employee and, if an alien, verify authorization to work in the United States. The employer must examine the documents to verify their authenticity and then record the appropriate information on the employee's Form I-9. Employers must also follow up on documents (with an expiration date) that limit the employee's authorization to work. The employer cannot ask an applicant about his or her immigration status before a conditional job offer.

Photocopying new employees' I-9 documents is permitted but not required. If done, photocopying should apply to *all* new employees.

Section 1 of the form must be signed by the employee no later than the first day of employment, but not before accepting a job offer. Section 2 must be signed by the employer or authorized representative within three business days of the employee's first day of employment. The person signing Section 2 must be the same person who examined the employee's documents.

Failure to produce the required documents can result in termination as long as the employer applies this rule uniformly to all employees. If it is confirmed that an employee is not legally authorized to work in this country, the employee must be fired immediately. Failure to do so can result in fines to the employer of

NEWS ALERT

The U.S. Immigration and Customs Enforcement Agency audited more than 3,100 organizations in 2013 and has levied fines of $91 million since 2009.

$3,000 in criminal penalties (civil penalties range from $350–$16,000 depending on occurrence) for each unauthorized alien and/or six months in jail.

The process of collecting, filing, and retaining I-9 forms should be a centralized function so that inconsistencies are eliminated. The forms (I-9) should be filed separately from other personnel records so that the information contained in the forms is kept private. The form must be retained for three years after the date of hiring or for one year after the date the employment is terminated, whichever is later. Terminated employees who are rehired within three years of the date of the initially filed Form I-9 need only reverify the information to the employer.

The U.S. Citizenship and Immigration Services (USCIS) can levy fines if an audit uncovers recordkeeping violations. Civil penalties can be $1,100 for each violation. Any person or entity found to have knowingly employed an unauthorized alien is subject to civil fines of up to $16,000 for each worker. Criminal penalties are assessed where a pattern of discriminatory practice is found.

E-Verify

This is a government-run Internet-based system that allows employers to check the employment eligibility of new hires by comparing the information on an employee's Form I-9 with databases of the Social Security Administration and the Department of Homeland Security. E-Verify requires a Social Security Number (SSN) for the employee, so even though a newly hired employee is not required to have applied for a SSN before completing Form I-9, the employee must apply for it as soon as possible.

For most employers, this is a voluntary program; however, if the employer has a federal contract or subcontract that contains an E-verify clause, the new hires of that organization and the employees performing work on the federal contract must be verified. All new federal employees must have their employment eligibility confirmed through E-verify. State laws can also require employers to E-verify (mandatory in 20 states for some or all employees).

If there is a record mismatch, a tentative nonconfirmation is issued to the employer who must then notify the affected employee. If the employee had voluntarily provided his or her email address on Form I-9, E-verify will inform the employee at the same time as the employer. In case of a mismatch, the employee has eight working days to correct the discrepancy or be fired.

Family and Medical Leave Act of 1993

The Family and Medical Leave Act of 1993 (FMLA) requires employers that have 50 or more employees within a 75-mile radius, for at least 20 weeks in the current or preceding calendar year, to grant workers *unpaid leave* for a family or medical emergency. In cases of childbirth, adoption, or serious illness of the employee or the employee's child, spouse, or parent, the employer must offer the worker as many as 12 weeks of unpaid leave. The leave may be used all at once, or in separate weeks, days, or hours. However, the leave must be taken within 12 months of the qualifying event.

During the leave, employers must continue health-care coverage, and they must also guarantee that the employee will return to the same job or to a comparable position. The employer can substitute an employee's earned paid leave for any part of the 12-week family leave as long as notification is given to the employee within two business days of receiving the request for the leave and it does not violate an existing employment contract.

An expansion of FMLA allowed employees to take leave (up to 12 weeks) when a family member is on active duty or when the employee cares for a family member with a serious injury or illness incurred in the line of duty (up to 26 weeks).

Employers can exempt the following:

1. The highest-paid 10 percent of their workforce.
2. Those who have not worked at least one year and at least 1,250 hours in the previous 12 months for the company.

ON THE JOB

FMLA absenteeism is highest among Health Care employees with 39 percent of their workforce with open FMLA leave (average length of 28 days).

A few states have implemented *paid* family leave plans. For example, New Jersey now allows workers six weeks' paid leave (at two-thirds of their salary up to $604/week) to care for family members with a serious health condition, or to be with a child during the first 12 months after his or her birth or adoption. The program is funded through payroll deductions that are estimated to cost employees a maximum of $38.40 a year.

Current regulations allow employers to contact employees' doctors for clarification on the information on the employees' certification forms. This contact cannot be made by the employees' direct supervisors, but must be done by human resources professionals, leave administrators, or management officials.[4]

Uniformed Services Employment and Reemployment Rights Act of 1994

The Uniformed Services Employment and Reemployment Rights Act (USERRA) gives military personnel the right to take leaves of absences from their civilian jobs for active military service and to return to their jobs with accrued seniority. The reinstatement must be to the employee's original position or its equivalent, except for the dishonorably discharged. In addition, the return must be granted within two weeks of the job request, and health benefits must be started without any waiting period.

Employee Retirement Income Security Act of 1974

The Employee Retirement Income Security Act of 1974 (ERISA) covers employee pension and welfare plans established or maintained by any employer or employee organization representing employees engaged in commerce or in any industry or activity affecting commerce. The legislation safeguards pension funds by regulating how the funds are to be raised and disbursed, who controls them, and what is to be done when funds are insufficient to pay promised benefits. The law *does not* require every employer to establish a pension plan; however, if there is an employer's pension plan, every employee is eligible *after reaching age 21 or completing one year of service,* whichever is later.

ERISA was designed primarily to ensure that workers covered by private pension plans receive benefits from those plans in accordance with their credited years of service with their employers. Vesting conveys to employees the right to share in a retirement fund if they are terminated before the normal retirement age. The vesting process is linked to the number of years needed for workers to earn an equity in their retirement plans and to become entitled to full or partial benefits at some future date if they leave the company before retirement. Once vested, a worker has the right to receive a pension at retirement age, based on years of covered service, even though the worker may not be working for the firm at that time. Currently, the law provides for full vesting of the employer's contributions *in three years or gradually over six years* (20 percent after two years and 20 percent a year for the next four years). The plan administrator must file an annual report (Form 5500) with the federal government by the end of the seventh month following the close of the plan year.

To protect against potential benefit losses because of a plan's termination, ERISA set up a government insurance program, the Pension Benefit Guaranty Corporation, to pay any benefits that could not be met with funds from the plan.

Disclosure Requirements

Informational reports must be filed with the U.S. Department of Labor, the IRS, and the government insurance program. In general, the reports consist of descriptions of the plans and the annual financial data. The plan descriptions include the eligibility requirements for participation and for benefits; provisions for

---

4 "Compensation and Benefits," *HR Specialist,* March 2012, p. 2.

nonforfeitable pension benefits; circumstances that may result in disqualification, loss, or denial of benefits; and procedures for presenting claims. The annual reports include financial statements and schedules showing the current value of plan assets and liabilities, receipts and disbursements, and employer contributions; the assets held for investment purposes; insurance data; and an opinion by an independent qualified public accountant. Upon written request from the participants, the administrator must also furnish a statement, not more than once in a 12-month period, of the total benefits accrued, accrued benefits that are vested, if any, or the earliest date on which accrued benefits will become vested.

Affordable Care Act of 2010 (ACA)

The Affordable Care Act (Obamacare) consists of two pieces of legislation: Patient Protection and Affordable Care Act and Health Care and Education Reconciliation Act. The act was designed to expand health insurance coverage to more Americans while increasing benefits and lowering costs for consumers. Insurance coverage for individuals and their dependents is required for most citizens and legal residents. A small penalty will apply if coverage is not obtained. Employers with 50 or more full-time employees during the previous year (applicable large employers—ALEs) are required to provide coverage for all full-time employees (beginning in 2016, also for their dependents). If an employer does not offer coverage, the employer will owe a penalty for each full-time employee who, under the health law, is eligible for and receives federally subsidized health care coverage.

State-based health insurance exchanges are established for those who do not have access to employer-provided coverage or do not qualify for public programs like Medicaid. These will be marketplaces where individuals can comparison shop. Individuals and families with incomes between 100 percent and 400 percent of the federal poverty level will receive subsidies to buy coverage. Exchanges are also set up for small businesses who will receive tax credits to help pay for coverage for their employees.

A sliding scale income tax credit is established for small employers (fewer than 25 full-time equivalent employees with average annual wages of less than $50,000) who offer health insurance coverage to their employees. If the employer pays at least 50 percent of the cost (the premium rate for an employee with single coverage), there is a 50 percent maximum credit of the employer's premium cost (35 percent for tax-exempt employers) against the employer's income tax liability. It also provides for a Medicare tax increase on wages over $200,000 for single filers and $250,000 for joint filers. This tax must be withheld by the employer of any worker whose wages exceed $200,000 (see page 3-9).

There are two information reporting obligations for applicable large employers:

- A return to be filed with the IRS for each employee with information about the health coverage offered, or not offered, to that employee during the previous year. This return is due to the IRS by February 28 on paper or March 31 if filed electronically.
- An information statement to each full-time employee containing certain health coverage facts. This statement is due by January 31.

Other State Laws Affecting the Need for Payroll and Personnel Records

States have enacted other laws that have a direct bearing on the payroll and personnel records that an employer must maintain and on the rights that must be extended to employees.

Workers' Compensation Laws

Workers' compensation insurance protects employees and their dependents against losses due to work-related injury, illness, or death. Most states have passed laws that require employers to provide workers' compensation insurance through one of the following plans:

1. Contribution to a state compensation insurance fund administered by an insurance department of the state.
2. Purchase of workers' compensation insurance from a private insurance company authorized by the state to issue this type of policy.
3. Establishment of a self-insurance plan, approved by the state, under which the company bears all risk itself.

Benefits are paid to cover medical bills and also to provide a percentage of the worker's regular wages during the time that the employee is unable to work. The employer bears the cost of the workers' compensation insurance premiums, except in Montana, New Mexico, Oregon, and Washington, where both the employer and the employee contribute to the workers' compensation fund.

The insurance premiums are often based upon the total gross payroll of the business and may be stated in terms of an amount for each $100 of weekly wages paid to employees. The premium rates vary among types of jobs.

EXAMPLE 1-1

The rate for office workers of Volpe Parts Company is $0.30 per $100 of payroll, while the rate for machine-shop workers is $1.90 per $100 of payroll.

State Disability Benefit Laws

California, Hawaii, New Jersey, New York, Rhode Island, and Puerto Rico have passed laws to provide **disability benefits** to employees absent from their jobs because of illness, accident, or disease *not arising out of their employment*. Chapter 5 presents further discussion of state disability benefit laws.

Human Resources and Payroll Accounting Systems

Up to this point, we have seen that a business must keep human resources and payroll records to meet the requirements of the various laws under which it operates. In developing its human resources and payroll accounting systems, a business should design basic forms and records that satisfy the requirements of all the laws applicable to that organization. Properly designed forms and records, as described later in this chapter, not only supply the information required by the various laws but also provide management with information needed in its decision-making process. They also result in savings in both time and work because the necessary information is recorded, stored, retrieved, and distributed economically, efficiently, and quickly.

Before studying the employment process, it is important to examine the close relationship between the Payroll Department and the Human Resources Department. Some businesses consider payroll to be strictly an accounting function and, as such, place it under the direct control of the chief financial officer. However, because of the need for frequent interchange of information between the Payroll and Human Resources departments, the trend has been to place payroll under the control of the director of human resources. This movement toward centralization eliminates the duplication of many tasks. With the required information in one department, the process of completing these forms is shortened. Further, questions from employees concerning sick pay, vacation pay, and other benefits can be answered from one source.

Individual computer programs have been developed for the combined needs of payroll and human resources. Information concerning such diverse activities as attendance, retirement benefits, health insurance coverages, and bonus pay is now available to designated employees in the Human Resources Department through a computer terminal.

Human Resources System

In many medium-size and large companies, the **human resources system** embodies all those procedures and methods related to recruiting, selecting, orienting, training, and terminating personnel. Extensive recordkeeping procedures are required in order to:

LO 3
Describe the employment procedures generally followed in a Human Resources Department.

1. Provide data for considering promotions and changes in the status and earnings of workers.
2. Provide the information required by various federal, state, and local laws.
3. Justify company actions if investigated by national or state labor relations boards.
4. Justify company actions in discussions with local unions or plant committees.

Before the Payroll Department can pay newly hired employees, the Human Resources Department must process those employees. Figure 1.4 charts the procedure that the Human Resources Department follows in this hiring process.

A number of companies that manufacture business forms have available standard personnel forms and records that may be successfully used if a business does not care to design its own special forms. In small companies, an application form or an employee history record may be the only document needed. Throughout the remainder of this chapter, several illustrations augment the discussion of the various human resources and payroll records. In these examples, we shall follow Cheryl Crowson from her initial application for employment with Palmero Maintenance Company to her entry onto the company's payroll records.

FIGURE 1.4

Human Resources Department Procedure in the Hiring Process

Job Descriptions

One way to protect companies from discrimination charges in hiring practices is to have true and clear job descriptions for every position in the organization. This is one of the items that courts examine in determining the validity of a discrimination charge. The descriptions must be accurate and must have been prepared before the job was advertised or the interviewing began.

The descriptions should highlight:

- The job's essential functions, including any physical requirements.
- Secondary duties.
- Attendance requirements.
- Education requirements and special skills needed.
- Job holder's supervisor.
- Positions that the applicant will be responsible for overseeing.[5]

In today's world, many of the paper forms presented in this chapter have been replaced with electronic substitutes. They are illustrated here to show the type of information that should be included on these forms no matter what format is used.

Requisition for Personnel

The **requisition for personnel** form notifies the Human Resources Department of the need for additional or replacement employees. The requisition for new employees can be initiated in a number of ways. Some companies utilize a memo that is forwarded to the Human Resources Department stating the title of the position to be filled, a brief description of the duties of the job, and the salary range. Other companies may use preprinted forms. A preprinted form should indicate the type and number of persons needed, the position to be filled, the rate of pay for the job, the salary range, the date the employee is needed, a summary of any special qualifications, and whether the position is permanent or temporary. This process can also be completed electronically, through the use of a company's e-mail system.

Application for Employment

LO 4

Recognize the various personnel records used by businesses and know the type of information shown on each form.

Every business, regardless of size, should have an application form (similar to that in Figure 1.5, on pages 1-15 and 1-16) to be filled out by a person seeking employment. The **application form** gives the applicant an opportunity to provide complete information as to:

1. Personal information including the name, address, telephone number, and social security number of the applicant.
2. Educational background including a summary of the schools attended, whether the applicant graduated, and degrees conferred.
3. Employment and experience record.
4. Type of employment desired.
5. References.

The application form also provides information for the checking of references, serves as a guide to effective interviewing, and provides information for correlation with data obtained from employment tests. It serves as a permanent record for the business. This form can also be set up to be completed electronically by the applicant.

---

5 "Employment Law," *HR Specialist*, December 2011, p. 2.

FIGURE 1.5
Application for Employment

APPLICATION FOR EMPLOYMENT
An Affirmative Action/Equal Opportunity Employer

POSITION APPLIED FOR *Payroll Specialist*

This job application is valid only for the position you have listed above. If you wish to be considered for other positions, you will need to complete and/or submit a separate application for each position.

PERSONAL

Name *Cheryl Crowson*

Address *1630 West End Ave.   Huntington, WV 25703*
STREET   CITY   STATE   ZIP

Telephone *(304) 555-2192*   *(304) 555-1618*
WORK   HOME   OTHER

Social Security Number *000-00-6357*

Have you worked for Palmero Maintenance Company before? YES ☐ NO ☑
If Yes, when? _____

If hired, can you provide proof of identity and eligibility to work in the U.S.? YES ☑ NO ☐

NAMES	ADDRESS	ACADEMIC MAJOR	NO. OF YEARS ATTENDED	DEGREE
HIGH SCHOOL *Centennial Senior*	*Stanford Road Huntington, WV*	*Business*	*4*	*Yes*
COLLEGE, JUNIOR COLLEGE, OR UNIVERSITY *Huntington Community College*	*Swamp Road Huntington, WV*	*Business— Occupational*	*2*	*Associate*
TECHNICAL OR VOCATIONAL				

Other details of training: (Courses)   (Cert.)

FIGURE 1.5 (concluded)
Application for Employment

EMPLOYMENT HISTORY

List in sequence all employers, beginning with present/most recent employer, including military experience and apprenticeship. Explain any gaps in employment in comments section below. If additional space is needed, please attach sheet(s).

EMPLOYER	TELEPHONE	DATES EMPLOYED		Summarize the nature of the work performed and job responsibilities
		FROM Month Year	TO Month Year	
Brennan Shipping Co.	*(304) 555-1119*			
ADDRESS *193 Mountain Blvd., Huntington, WV*		*5/10*	*Present*	*Input time worked*
JOB TITLE *Payroll Assistant*		Hourly Rate/Salary		*information, checked*
IMMEDIATE SUPERVISOR AND TITLE *Helen Young—Payroll Manager*		*$ 3,850*	Per *Month*	*payroll, distributed*
REASON FOR LEAVING *Want to have more responsibility*		Full-time ✔	Part-time	*checks*
MAY WE CONTACT FOR REFERENCE? ☑ YES ☐ NO ☐ LATER				

EMPLOYER	TELEPHONE	DATES EMPLOYED		Summarize the nature of the work performed and job responsibilities
		FROM Month Year	TO Month Year	
AVS Drug	*(304) 555-0101*			
ADDRESS *Broad & Cherry Sts., Huntington, WV*		*9/08*	*5/10*	*Served as head cashier*
JOB TITLE *Clerk/Cashier*		Hourly Rate/Salary		*and maintained inventory*
IMMEDIATE SUPERVISOR AND TITLE *John Stumley—Manager*		*$ 10.15*	Per *Hour*	
REASON FOR LEAVING *Graduated college—Full-time position*		Full-time	Part-time ✔	
MAY WE CONTACT FOR REFERENCE? ☑ YES ☐ NO ☐ LATER				

REFERENCES

Give names of persons we may contact to verify your qualifications for the position:

Edna White	*Instructor*	*Teacher*	*Huntington Community College*
Name	(Title)	(Occupation)	(Organization)

Swamp Road, Huntington, WV Bus. No.: *(304) 555-8000* Home No.: *(304) 555-2111*
(Address)

Henry Stone	*Controller*	*Finance*	*Brennan Shipping Co.*
Name	(Title)	(Occupation)	(Organization)

193 Mountain Blvd., Huntington, WV Bus. No.: *(304) 555-1119* Home No.: *(304) 555-8710*
(Address)

I hereby certify that all statements made in this application (and accompanying résumé, if any) are true and complete. I understand that any false or misleading statement on this application constitutes sufficient grounds for dismissal, if hired. I further certify that I may lawfully be employed in this country and, if employed, will provide required documentation to verify identity and employment eligibility. In addition, in making this application for employment, I understand that the Company may investigate my employment and educational records. I hereby authorize my current and/or former employer(s) and school(s) to furnish the information requested by the Palmero Maintenance Company.

Signature of Applicant *Cheryl Crowson*   Date *June 10, 20--*

Employers subject to fair employment laws must make certain that all aspects of the pre-hire inquiries are free of discrimination on the basis of race, color, religion, gender, national origin, or age. A number of states have instituted a "lifestyle discrimination law" that deals with discrimination based on employees' use of legal products on their own time, e.g., tobacco use. Pre-hire inquiries include questions asked in the employment interview and on application forms, résumés of experience or education required of an applicant, and any kind of written testing. None of the federal civil rights laws specifically outlaws questions concerning the race, color, religion, gender, national origin, or age of an applicant. However, if the employer can offer no logical explanation for asking such questions, the EEOC and the Wage and Hour Administrator view such questions as discriminatory. Of course, pre-hire questions pertaining to religion, gender, national origin, or age are allowed when these factors are bona fide occupational qualifications for a job. Many states have banned the use of a check box relating to an applicant's criminal past; however, employers can still ask about arrest records during the job interview. The EEOC has stated that criminal background checks can only be used if there is a solid business reason for them. Asking for arrest records is illegal.

Testing applicants can also be an area fraught with legal ramifications. Aptitude and psychological testings are unlawful unless results can be related to job performance. The use of online personality tests has surged in the past decade. These tests are used to assess the personality, skills, cognitive abilities, and other traits of 60 to 70 percent of prospective workers in the United States. These types of tests must be approved by the EEOC. Lie detector tests are strictly illegal.

With regard to drug testing, employers must consult their state's laws. Close to one-half of the states have laws covering this type of testing. It can be used in a limited number of situations or in a narrow range of job categories.

Asking an applicant's age or date of birth may tend to deter the older worker. Thus, if an application form calls for such information, a statement should appear on that form notifying the applicant that the ADEA prohibits discrimination on the basis of age with respect to individuals who are at least 40. Questions on the application and during the interview process should be used only to determine the applicant's ability to do the job.

The final part of the application form should be a statement affirming the employer's right to:

- Verify the information on the application.
- Terminate the employee for providing false information on the application or during the interview process.
- Obtain authorization for any planned credit or background checks.

The application should then be signed by the applicant.

Federal anti-discrimination laws require employers to keep all applications for at least one year from the date of hiring decision, even those from unqualified candidates.

Reference Inquiry

Before employing an applicant, a company may check some of the references given on the application. Many businesses use a standard reference inquiry form, which can be mailed or e-mailed to the person or company given as a reference. Other companies prefer a telephone reference check because they feel that a more frank opinion of the candidate is received over the telephone. Some companies prefer not to check on personal references given by the job applicant, since these tend to be less objective than business references (e.g., prior employers).

ON THE **JOB**

The EEOC civil rights groups and unions employ "testers." These are persons who are sent out as applicants to check whether employers are hiring legally.

Today, any type of reference checking has taken on new meaning—expensive litigation. In most cases, respondents to these inquiries will verify dates of employment only, with no information on former employees' work habits. To reduce the increasing number of "failure-to-warn" lawsuits, a number of states have passed laws providing protection from liability to employers who want to provide references. Recent court decisions have held the reference process to be priviledged.[6] Some companies have also made an "Employment Reference Release" part of the employment application.

The Fair Credit Reporting Act of 1968 subjects employers to certain disclosure obligations when they seek an **investigative consumer report** from a consumer reporting agency on a job applicant or in certain instances on present employees. An investigative consumer report usually contains information about the individual's character, general reputation, and mode of living. Generally, the employer must notify the applicant or the employee in writing that such a report is being sought. In the event employment is denied because of the consumer report information, the employer must inform the individual that this was the reason or part of the reason for denying employment. Also, the employer must furnish the applicant with the name and address of the consumer reporting agency that made the report.

Hiring Notice

After the successful applicant is notified of employment and the starting date, time, and to whom to report, a **hiring notice** is sent to the Payroll Department so that the new employee can be added properly to the payroll. A hiring notice, such as

FIGURE 1.6
Hiring Notice

HIRING NOTICE		
		NO. 220
SOCIAL SECURITY NO. 000 - 00 - 6357		
	DATE ___ June 28, 20--	
NAME Cheryl Crowson	**CLOCK NO.** 418	
ADDRESS 1630 West End Ave., Huntington, WV **ZIP** 25703	**PHONE NO.** 555-1618	
OCCUPATION Payroll Specialist	**DEPT.** Accounting	**GROUP NO.** – –
STARTING DATE July 1, 20-- **TIME** 8:00	**A.M. P.M.**	**RATE** $48,000 yr.
MARRIED **SINGLE** X	**BIRTH DATE** 8/1/--	
LAST EMPLOYMENT Brennan Shipping Co.	**LOCATION** Huntington, WV	
DATE LEFT June 30, 20--	**REASON** Advancement	
NO. OF WITHHOLDING ALLOWANCES 1		
IN EMERGENCY NOTIFY Robert Crowson	**PHONE NO.** 555-5136	
EMPLOYEE'S SIGNATURE IN FULL *Cheryl Crowson*		
SUPERVISOR'S SIGNATURE *Margaret T. Johnson*		
EMPLOYMENT DEPARTMENT		
ORIGINAL TO PAYROLL DEPT. **DUPLICATE RETAINED BY HUMAN RESOURCES DEPT.**		

6 "HIRE AT WILL," *HR Specialist*, 2010, p. 28.

that shown in Figure 1.6, usually gives the name, address, and telephone number of the new employee, the department in which employed, the starting date, the rate of pay, the number of withholding allowances claimed, and any other information pertaining to deductions that are to be made from the employee's wages.

Employee History Record

Although many businesses keep no personnel records other than the application, a more detailed record is needed to provide a continuous record of the relationship between the employer and the employee. The employee history record is such a record and, in addition to providing personal and other information usually found on an application, provides space to record the employee's progress, attendance, promotions, performance appraisals, and salary increases. As with most records, the individual employee must have access to his or her human resource files.

Change in Payroll Rate

The change in payroll rate form notifies the proper departments of a change in the employee's rate of remuneration. The change in rate may originate in the Human Resources Department or with the head of the department in which the employee works. In either event, the Payroll Department must be informed of the change for the employee so that the rate change is put into effect at the proper time and so that the records reflect the new rate. Figure 1.7 shows a form that may be used for this purpose.

Terminating an Employee

If an employee has an employee contract or if promises were made to the employee, termination can only be done with "good cause." This means the firing must be based on reasons related to business needs and goals. An "at-will" employee can

> **IRS CONNECTION**
>
> In 2015, April 24 was the day on which the average American worker's income, since the beginning of the year, equaled the tax obligations to federal, state, and local governments.

FIGURE 1.7
Change in Status Form

CHANGE OF STATUS

Please enter the following change(s) as of _____ January 1, 20 -- _____

Name _____ Cheryl Crowson _____ Clock or Payroll No. __418__ Soc. Sec. Number __000-00-6357__

FROM

Job	Dept.	Shift	Rate
Payroll Specialist	Acct.	—	$48,000

TO

Job	Dept.	Shift	Rate
Accounting Analyst	Acct.	—	$51,500

REASON FOR CHANGE:

☐ Hired   ☐ Length of Serv. Increase
☐ Re-hired   ☐ Re-eval. of Existing Job
☒ Promotion   ☐ Resignation
☐ Demotion   ☐ Retirement
☐ Transfer   ☐ Layoff
☐ Merit Increase   ☐ Discharge
☐ Leave of Absence to _____
                        Date

Other reason or explanation: _____
_____
_____

AUTHORIZED BY ___ *Margaret T. Johnson* ___ APPROVED BY ___ *E. J. Dunn* ___

Prepare in triplicate: (1) Human Resources (2) Payroll (3) Employee's Department be discharged for any reason as long as it is not a discriminatory reason, even if the employee just does not work well together with the staff. In cases where the company has made past mistakes in the handling of the employee, it would be wise to consult a lawyer before making the final decision. The lawyer can check all the angles in order to protect the company from lawsuit liability.

Recordkeeping System

Whether the system is paper-based or computer-based or records in the cloud, it is advantageous to have four separate sets of records for each employee:

- Personnel file—basic information (e.g., name, address, etc.)
- Payroll file—salary and benefits
- Medical file—insurance and private medical data
- I-9 file—copies of the forms and the appropriate documents[7]

Employee Access—Personnel Files

Even though personnel files are the property of the employer, employees may have the right to view and receive a copy of their own files. Even though no federal law guarantees it, more than half of the states allow current employees access to their records.

Even with this right, some documents are considered confidential, and employers should not allow employees to view anything that would be considered an invasion of privacy (e.g., reference letters, investigative notes, etc.). Before granting access to personnel files, the payroll professional should check all applicable state laws and their own company's written policy.

Payroll Accounting System

LO 5

Identify the *payroll register* and the *employee's earnings record*.

A payroll accounting system embodies all those procedures and methods related to the disbursement of pay to employees. A typical payroll accounting system includes the procedures shown in Figure 1.8. The nature of the payroll records depends to a great extent on the size of the workforce and the degree to which the recordkeeping is automated. This course describes and illustrates manual payroll accounting systems. Appendix A describes computerized payroll accounting systems, along with operating instructions for using the software available with this text. In most payroll systems—manual or automated—the payroll register and the employee's earnings record are the two basic records that are utilized.

Payroll Register

The payroll register is a multicolumn form used to assemble and summarize the data needed at the end of each payroll period. It provides a detailed listing of a company's complete payroll for that particular pay period. Thus, the payroll register lists all the employees who earned remuneration, the amount of remuneration, the deductions, and the net amount paid. The information provided in the payroll register is used primarily to meet the requirements of the Fair Labor Standards Act. However, the register also provides information for recording the payroll entries and for preparing reports required by other federal, state, and local laws. Figure 1.9 shows one form of payroll register. Another form, used in the Continuing Payroll Problem at the end of Chapters 2 through 6, is shown in the fold-out at the back of this book.

---

7 "Nuts & Bolts," HR Specialist: Employment Law, December 2012, p. 7.

FIGURE 1.8
Procedures in a Payroll Accounting System

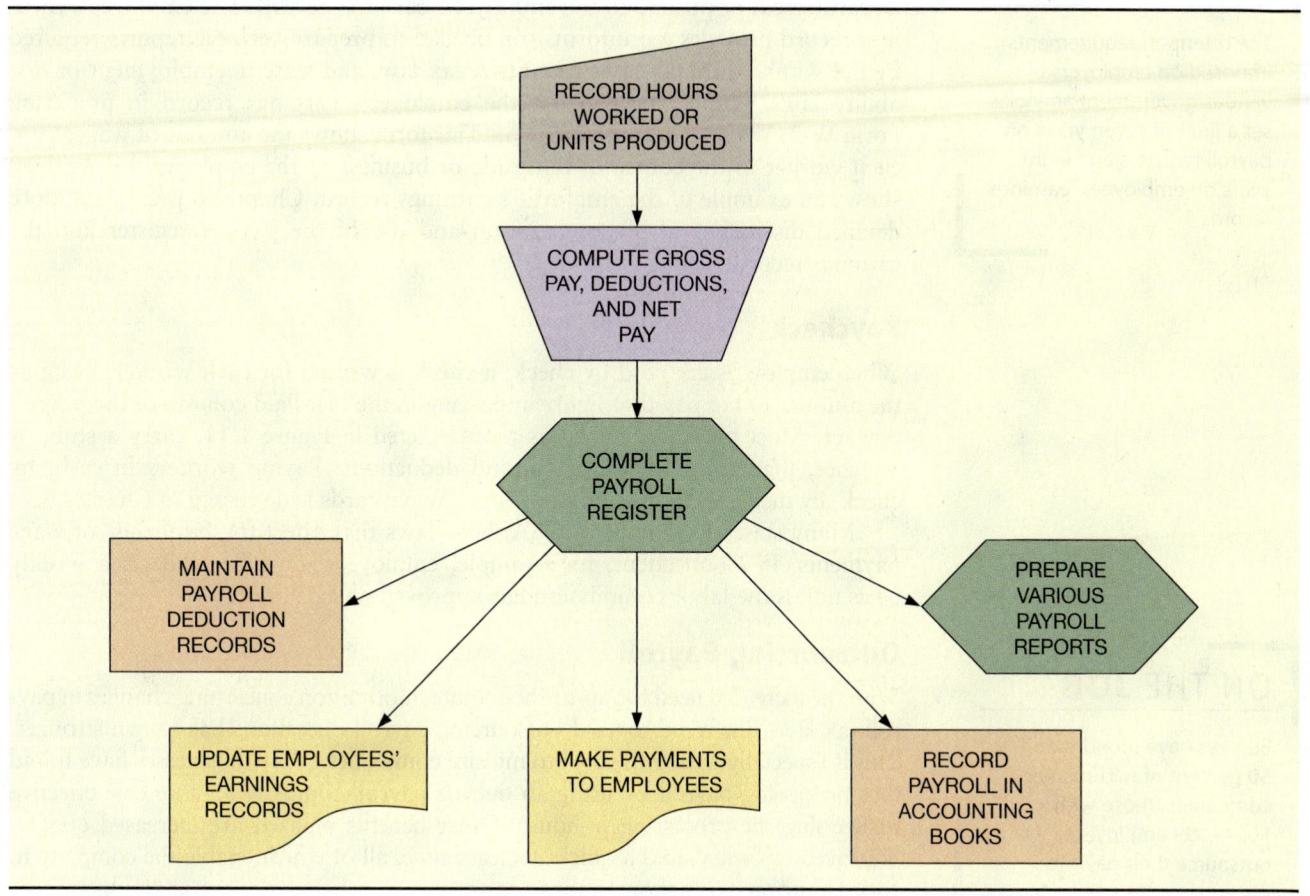

FIGURE 1.9
Payroll Register

PAYROLL REGISTER

FOR WEEK ENDING   *January 19*   20 - -

No.	Name	Total Hours Worked	Regular Earnings Hrs.	Regular Earnings Rate	Regular Earnings Amount	Overtime Earnings Hrs.	Overtime Earnings Rate	Overtime Earnings Amount	Total Earnings	OASDI Tax	HI Tax	Fed. Income Tax	State Income Tax	Check No.	Net Paid Amount
1 403	*Springs, Carl A.*	*40*	*40*	*10.75*	*430.00*				*430.00*	*26.66*	*6.24*	*38.00*	*15.00*	*504*	*344.10*
2 409	*Wiegand, Sue T.*	*42*	*40*	*10.50*	*420.00*	*2*	*15.75*	*31.50*	*451.50*	*27.99*	*6.55*	*6.00*	*13.00*	*505*	*397.96*
3 412	*O'Neill, John B.*	*38*	*38*	*11.10*	*421.80*				*421.80*	*26.15*	*6.12*	*11.00*	*13.00*	*506*	*365.53*
4 413	*Bass, Marie S.*	*44*	*40*	*10.80*	*432.00*	*4*	*16.20*	*64.80*	*496.80*	*30.80*	*7.20*	*59.00*	*20.00*	*507*	*379.80*
5 418	*Crowson, Cheryl*	*40*	*40*	*S*	*990.38*				*990.38*	*61.40*	*14.36*	*138.00*	*46.00*	*508*	*730.62*
47	*Totals*				*9,895.75*			*917.20*	*10,812.95*	*670.40*	*156.79*	*2,008.00*	*542.00*		*7,435.76*

Employee's Earnings Record

In addition to the information contained in the payroll register, businesses must provide more complete information about the accumulated earnings of each employee. For that reason, it is necessary to keep a separate payroll record on each employee—the **employee's earnings record**. Each payday, after the information has been recorded in the payroll register, the information for each employee is transferred, or posted, to the employee's earnings record. The employee's earnings record provides the information needed to prepare periodic reports required by the withholding tax laws, the FICA tax law, and state unemployment or disability laws. Employers also use the employee's earnings record in preparing **Form W-2, Wage and Tax Statement**. This form shows the amount of wages paid each worker in the course of the trade or business of the employer. Figure 1.10 shows an example of the employee's earnings record. Chapter 6 presents a more detailed discussion of the preparation and use of the payroll register and the earnings record.

Paycheck

When employees are paid by check, a check is written for each worker, using as the amount of net pay that figure appearing in the Net Paid column of the payroll register. Most paychecks, such as that depicted in Figure 1.11, carry a stub, or voucher, that shows the earnings and deductions. Paying workers in cash, by check, by means of electronic transfer or by paycards is discussed in Chapter 6.

Many states (but not the FLSA) have laws that affect the frequency of wage payments. In Connecticut, for example, employees must be paid on a weekly basis unless the labor commission has approved an exception.

Outsourcing Payroll

With the increased need for up-to-the-minute information concerning changes in payroll tax laws, the trend toward outsourcing payroll operations has grown stronger. This is especially true with small to midsize companies. Many businesses have found that processing payroll by using an outside payroll company is more cost effective than doing the processing in-house. Other benefits realized are increased quality, improved efficiency, and a quicker release time, all of which enable the company to concentrate on its other operations.

Basically, the payroll operations at the company's site need only deal with the entry of new employee information and the number of hours worked by each employee. This information is sent to the payroll processing company electronically. The input is then processed by the outside firm. Once the processing is completed, the output package (paychecks, payroll, and management reports) is returned to the company.

FIGURE 1.10
Employee's Earnings Record

EMPLOYEE'S EARNINGS RECORD

Week	Week Ending	Total Hours Worked	Regular Earnings Hrs.	Regular Earnings Rate	Regular Earnings Amount	Overtime Earnings Hrs.	Overtime Earnings Rate	Overtime Earnings Amount	Total Earnings	OASDI Tax	HI Tax	Fed. Income Tax	State Income Tax	Check No.	Net Paid Amount	Cumulative Earnings
1	1/5	40	40	S	990.38				990.38	61.40	14.36	138.00	46.00	419	730.62	990.38
2	1/12	42	40	S	990.38	2	37.14	74.28	1,064.66	66.01	15.44	155.00	53.00	463	775.21	2,055.04
3	1/19	40	40	S	990.38				990.38	61.40	14.36	138.00	46.00	508	730.62	3,045.42

Sex	Department	Occupation	State Employed	S.S.No.	Name—Last First Middle	No.W/HAllow.
F M √	Accounting	Accounting Analyst (A)	West Virginia	000-00-6357	Crowson, Cheryl	1
						Marital Status **S**

FIGURE 1.11
Paycheck with Stub Showing Current and Year-to-Date Earnings and Deductions

REGULAR HOURS	O.T.B. HOURS	REGULAR EARNINGS	O.T.B. EARNINGS	GROSS EARNINGS	OASDI	HI	FIT	SIT	CODE	DEDUCTIONS
40		990.38		990.38	61.40	14.36	138.00	46.00		

DEDUCTIONS			
1. MISC.	5. SPECIAL INSURANCE	9. TOOLS	
2. BONDS	6. WELFARE FUND	10. RELIEF ASSOC.	
3. CREDIT UNION	7. ADVANCES	11. SHOES	
4. GROUP INSURANCE	8. UNIFORMS	12.	

CLOCK NO.	RATE	PERIOD ENDING	GROSS EARNINGS	OASDI	HI	FIT	SIT		
418	S	1 19	3,045.42	188.81	44.16	431.00	145.00		
			YEAR TO DATE						730.62

RETAIN THIS STUB
IT IS A STATEMENT OF YOUR
EARNINGS AND DEDUCTIONS

NET PAY ↑

Palmero Maintenance

CLOCK NO.

418   *Palmero Maintenance*

Huntington, WV

DATE January 19, 20 – –

69-21
513

No. 508

PAYROLL ACCOUNT

PAY TO THE ORDER OF   Cheryl Crowson

	DOLLARS	CENTS
730.62	730	62

the 1st national bank
Huntington, WV

BY   *S. Hollis Stevenson*

⑈051300212⑈ 6139 ⁣‴

Leading companies in the industry, such as ADP,[8] will custom-make a comprehensive and integrated program that will meet the needs of each individual business at a cost that many businesses find affordable.

When outsourcing payroll, in order to reduce the risk of unpaid payroll taxes, the following steps should be followed:

• Hire only bonded service bureaus
• Do not allow the service bureau to sign tax returns
• Do not allow tax correspondence to be sent to the service bureau.
• Request regular IRS transcripts of the company accounts[9]

KEY TERMS

application form (p. 1-14)

change in payroll rate form (p. 1-19)

disability benefits (p. 1-12)

employee history record (p. 1-19)

employee's earnings record (p. 1-22)

executive orders (p. 1-6)

fair employment practices (p. 1-4)

Form I-9, Employment Eligibility Verification (p. 1-8)

Form W-2, Wage and Tax Statement (p. 1-22)

hiring notice (p. 1-18)

human resources system (p. 1-13)

income tax (p. 1-4)

8 The ADP Logo is a registered trademark of ADP (Automatic Data Processing) of North America, Inc.

9 "Outsourcing Your Payroll May Not Be a Good Idea, After All" *Payroll Legal Alert*, June 2012, p. 1.

investigative consumer report (p. 1-18)

payroll accounting system (p. 1-20)

payroll register (p. 1-20)

pre-hire inquiries (p. 1-17)

reference inquiry form (p. 1-17)

requisition for personnel (p. 1-14)

vesting (p. 1-10)

workers' compensation insurance (p. 1-12)

KEY POINTS SUMMARY

	Learning Objectives	Key Points	Practical Problems A & B
L01	Identify the various laws that affect employers in their payroll operations.	• Fair Labor Standards Act—minimum wage and overtime. • Federal Insurance Contributions Act—social security taxes on employers and employees. • Income Tax Withholding Laws—deductions from employees' pays for federal and state income taxes. • Unemployment Tax Acts—federal tax on employers to pay administrative costs and state tax on employers to cover benefits.	N/A
L02	Examine the record-keeping requirements of these laws.	• No specific forms are mandated, but information to be collected and retention periods are. • Fair employment laws on the federal and state levels deal with discrimination on the basis of age, race, color, religion, gender, or national origin. • Laws requiring verification of employment eligibility of new hires.	N/A
L03	Describe the employment procedures generally followed in a Human Resources Department.	• From the request for a new employee to applications and interviews, to administering tests, to checking references, to notifying payroll.	N/A
L04	Recognize the various personnel records used by businesses and know the type of information shown on each form.	• Application form is used by most companies to get personal information, educational background, experience records, and references on each applicant. • Order forms that may be used—hiring notice, history record, change in payroll note.	N/A
L05	Identify the *payroll register* and the *employee's earnings record*.	• Payroll register is a list of all employees for each pay period showing their gross pay, deductions, and net pay. • Employee's earnings record is a separate record for each employee showing the same information as the payroll register; used to prepare W-2s.	N/A

MATCHING QUIZ

_____ 1. Employee's earnings record
_____ 2. Payroll register
_____ 3. Executive orders
_____ 4. Fair Labor Standards Act
_____ 5. Immigration Reform and Control Act
_____ 6. Unemployment insurance taxes
_____ 7. Vesting
_____ 8. Workers' compensation insurance
_____ 9. Family and Medical Leave Act
_____ 10. Civil Rights Act

A. Also known as the Federal Wage and Hour Law.
B. Record used in preparing employee's W-2.
C. Protection against losses due to work-related injuries.
D. Multicolumn form used to summarize data needed each pay date.
E. Highest-paid 10 percent of workforce can be exempted.
F. Antidiscrimination orders for employers with contracts involving federal funds.
G. A fair employment law.
H. Form I-9 to be completed by all new employees.
I. Levied by both federal and state governments.
J. Conveys to employees the right to share in a retirement fund.

QUESTIONS FOR REVIEW

1. Which act sets the minimum wage, and what is the current wage rate?
2. Under the FLSA, what information concerning employees' wages earned must be maintained by the employer?
3. Who pays the social security taxes that are levied by the Federal Insurance Contributions Act?
4. How are the funds used which are provided by FUTA and SUTA?
5. What types of unfair employment practices are prohibited by the Civil Rights Act of 1964 as amended?
6. What is the purpose of the Age Discrimination in Employment Act (ADEA)?
7. Are there any exceptions to the protection afforded older workers by the Age Discrimination in Employment Act?
8. Who is covered by the Walsh-Healey Public Contracts Act?
9. What are the major provisions of the Occupational Safety and Health Act (OSHA)?
10. Under the Family and Medical Leave Act, what is the maximum number of weeks of unpaid leave that a covered employer is required to offer an employee whose spouse is seriously ill?
11. What is the primary purpose of the Employee Retirement Income Security Act (ERISA)?
12. Explain the concept of vesting.
13. Under ERISA, if requested in writing, what information must the administrator of the pension fund supply to the participants?
14. Summarize the procedure that may be followed by the Human Resources Department in hiring new employees.
15. What information is commonly provided by a job-seeker on the application for employment form?
16. What is the significance of the Civil Rights Act of 1964 and the Age Discrimination in Employment Act in the employer's use of pre-hire inquiries?
17. What obligations are imposed upon the employer by the Fair Credit Reporting Act of 1968?
18. What procedures are usually included in a typical payroll accounting system?
19. What two basic records are generated in most payroll accounting systems?
20. What uses are made of the information shown in the employee's earnings record?

QUESTIONS FOR DISCUSSION

1. What personnel records would you suggest for a small retailer with three employees?
2. What kind of problem can be encountered when requesting references from previous employers of job applicants?
3. In staffing their offices, some firms encourage in-house referrals (recommendations of their present employees). What are some possible objections to this practice as a means of obtaining job applicants? What advantages may be realized by the firm that uses in-house referrals?
4. The main office of a large bank has an annual turnover of 500 office workers. As an employment officer of this bank, discuss the sources you would use in obtaining replacement employees.

5. Among the questions asked on the application for employment form of Horner Company are the following:
   a. What is the name of your church and what religious holidays do you observe?
   b. What is the name of your birthplace?
   c. Are you a citizen of the United States?
   d. What foreign languages can you read, write, or speak fluently?

   In view of federal and state civil rights laws, do you believe that Horner Company is acting legally or illegally in asking each of the questions listed above?

CASE PROBLEM

C1. Paychecks Kept Coming. LO 3.

Ken, a salaried employee, was terminated from his company in April of this year. Business had been slow since the beginning of the year, and each of the operating plants had laid off workers.

Ken's dismissal was processed through the Human Resources Department, but the information was not relayed to the corporate payroll office.

As had been the policy, checks for workers at remote sites were mailed to the employees. The mailing of Ken's checks continued for the next four weekly paydays. It wasn't until the monthly payroll reports were sent to Ken's supervisor that the error was detected.

Ken refused to return the four extra checks. What actions should the company take?[10]

---

10 Reprinted with permission from *Payroll Guide Newsletter*. Volume 60, No. 21, Copyright © 2001 by Research Institute of America, 395 Hudson Street, New York, NY 10014. All rights reserved.

CHAPTER 2

Computing Wages and Salaries

A s our Animated Feature points out, the Federal Labor Standards Act has many tentacles. It's not just about minimum wage and overtime. The Durmont Company found out the hard way that it also deals with equal pay/equal work. In the Durmont case, there must have been other extenuating circumstances to have the equal pay provision apply to the employee, Denise Harris. Did the company have similar instances with male employees where payment was made right away?

LEARNING OBJECTIVES

After studying this chapter, you should be able to:

1 Explain the major provisions of the Fair Labor Standards Act.
2 Define *hours worked*.
3 Describe the main types of records used to collect payroll data.
4 Calculate regular and overtime pay.
5 Identify distinctive compensation plans.

This chapter examines the major provisions of the Fair Labor Standards Act, how to determine hours worked by employees, commonly used methods to record time worked, and the major methods of computing salaries and wages. Tracing its origin back to the 1930s, the Fair Labor Standards Act is the most encompassing of all the labor laws. However, it is also the one most violated.

WASHINGTON UPDATE

AS MORE STATES INCREASE THEIR MINIMUM WAGE RATES, THERE HAS BEEN MUCH DISCUSSION OF CHANGING THE FEDERAL MINIMUM WAGE. THE MOST DISCUSSED OPTION INVOLVES A SERIES OF STEP INCREASES THAT WILL EVENTUALLY PUSH THE MINIMUM WAGE TO $10.25 PER HOUR. DUE TO THE UNCERTAINTY AND THE FACT THAT NO CHANGES HAVE BEEN SET, THE MINIMUM WAGE USED THROUGHOUT THIS TEXTBOOK WAS THE RATE IN EFFECT AT THE CURRENT TIME—$7.25 PER HOUR. DEPENDING ON THE TIMING, ANY CHANGE THAT TAKES PLACE WILL BE ENUMERATED IN THE "AS WE GO TO PRESS" SECTION AT THE BEGINNING OF THE BOOK AND OUR ONLINE VEHICLE—CENGAGE.NOW.COM

The Fair Labor Standards Act

The Fair Labor Standards Act (FLSA), commonly known as the Federal Wage and Hour Law, contains provisions and standards concerning minimum wages, equal pay for equal work regardless of sex, overtime pay, recordkeeping, and child labor. The Wage and Hour Division of the U.S. Department of Labor (DOL) administers the act.

LO 1
Explain the major provisions of the Fair Labor Standards Act.

ON THE **JOB**

A National Call Center has been established by the Department of Labor to answer employees' and employers' questions on a range of employment issues. The toll-free number is 1-866-4-USA-DOL.

ON THE **NET**

http://www.dol.gov/
U.S. Department of Labor Employment Standards Administration homepage. This site contains various sections of code, such as affirmative action and workers' compensation. To find the most useful information, choose the ESA program that interests you.

IRS CONNECTION

If you want the IRS to determine whether a worker is an employee, file **Form SS-8, Determination of Employee Work Status** for purposes of Federal Employment Taxes and Income Tax Withholding. Over 90 percent of these filed forms were determined to be for employees.

Coverage

The FLSA provides for two bases of coverage—enterprise coverage and individual employee coverage.

Enterprise Coverage

Enterprise coverage includes all employees of an enterprise if:

1. At least two employees engage in interstate commerce or produce goods for interstate commerce. Interstate commerce refers to the trade, transportation, or communication among several states or between a state and any place outside that state. The law also covers employees if they handle, sell, or otherwise work on goods or materials that have been moved in or produced for interstate commerce, and
2. The business has annual gross sales of at least $500,000.

Coverage extends, *without regard to annual sales volume,* to those who operate:

1. A hospital.
2. A nursing home.
3. An institution for the mentally ill.
4. A school for mentally or physically handicapped or gifted children.
5. A preschool, elementary, or secondary school.
6. An institution of higher education.
7. A public agency.

The enterprise coverage under the FLSA does not apply to family establishments, often referred to as "mom and pop stores." Thus, if the only regular employees of an establishment include the owner, parent, spouse, child, or other immediate family members, the establishment is exempt from FLSA coverage.

Individual Employee Coverage

Under individual employee coverage, the FLSA covers a worker if the employee either engages in interstate commerce or produces goods for such commerce. Coverage also includes employment in a fringe occupation closely related and directly essential to the production of goods for interstate commerce. Coverage depends on the activities of the individual employee and not on the work of fellow employees, the nature of the employer's business, or the character of the industry as a whole. Thus, even though a business does not meet the enterprise coverage test, it must pay FLSA wages to those workers eligible for individual coverage.

Glenn Morris works for a small manufacturing firm that has an annual sales volume of $370,000. Although the firm does not meet the $500,000 volume-of-sales requirement for enterprise coverage, Morris is *individually* covered since he operates machinery used to produce goods for interstate commerce.

Employer

The FLSA defines an employer as "any person acting directly or indirectly in the interest of an employer" in relation to an employee. In order to protect employees, courts have defined "employers" in the broadest sense. Co-owners who control the day-to-day operations of the business are employers who are individually liable for violations of the law.

Employee

An individual is an employee if he or she performs services in a covered employment. As long as the common-law relationship of employer and employee exists and the employment is not exempt from the provisions of the law, both are covered and must observe its provisions. No differentiation is made between regular, temporary, substitute, or part-time workers.

A **common-law relationship** of employer and employee exists when the employer has the right to control both what work will be done and how it will be done. How the relationship is labeled is immaterial; it is the substance of the relationship that governs the worker's status.

To determine if a worker may be classified as an employee and if the employer has the right to control, the Internal Revenue Service uses a test based on behavioral control, financial control, and the relationship between the worker and the employer.

A shortened "ABC test" defines an independent contractor (nonemployee) as one who:

1. is free of direction and control in the performance of the work.
2. performs services outside the usual course of business of the company that has hired the contractor.
3. customarily engages in an independent occupation.

Several other factors to consider would be the amount of instruction or training given to the worker, the amount of the worker's investment in the business, the ability to hire and supervise others, and the worker's offering of services to the public.

Employees of a Corporation

Managers, superintendents, supervisors, department heads, and other executives of a corporation are considered employees under the FICA tax law. All officers, such as the president, vice president, secretary, and treasurer, are also employees of the corporation. Their salaries are taxable the same as the wages paid to other employees. A *director of a corporation* who performs no services other than attending and participating in meetings of the board of directors is not an employee.

Partnerships

Partners generally are not employees of the partnership. In some cases, however, a partnership may operate as an association that may be classified as a corporation. In such situations, any partner who renders services similar to those of corporate officers would be an employee.

Domestics

Domestic workers also must be paid the minimum wage if:

1. They perform services in one or more homes for a total of eight hours or more in any workweek, *or if*
2. They earn wages of at least $1,900 from an employer in a calendar year.

Domestic service consists of services of a household nature performed in or about a private home of the person who employs the domestic. Some typical domestics include cooks, butlers, maids, caretakers, gardeners, and chauffeurs. The term also includes a baby sitter employed on other than a casual basis, such as a person who sits for a child five days a week. If the domestics do not live in the household, they must be paid overtime compensation as well as the minimum wage. However, live-in domestics do not have to be paid overtime. A casual baby sitter (one employed on an irregular or intermittent basis) or a companion for the aged or infirmed is not covered.

Direct care workers provide essential home care assistance to the elderly and people with injuries, illnesses, or disabilities. These workers if employed directly by a family or individual are not covered unless they are performing medically-related duties or are providing more than a limited amount of care in addition to fellowship and protection. Direct care workers, employed by third-party employers, were scheduled to receive minimum wage and overtime coverage starting in 2015. A U.S. District Court has voided this requirement and that decision is currently being appealed by the Department of Labor in the U.S. Court of Appeals for the District of Columbia.

Statutory Employees

Workers who qualify as independent contractors under common law, but are taxed as employees for social security, are statutory employees. This status

ON THE JOB

Today, nearly 25 percent of the workforce is made up of temporary workers, consultants, and independent contractors.

applies to agent or commission drivers, industrial home workers, full-time insurance agents, and full-time traveling or city salespeople.

Statutory Nonemployees

There are two categories of statutory nonemployees—direct sellers and licensed real estate agents. For federal tax purposes, they are considered to be self-employed as long as their earnings are based on the amount of sales and their services are performed under a written contract stating that they will not be treated as employees for federal tax purposes.

Interns

In the public and nonprofit sectors, volunteer interns who do not expect compensation are generally exempt from FLSA requirements. Interns in the for-profit sector may be exempt from the minimum wage and overtime requirements of the FLSA when they receive training for their own educational benefit.

Wages

Wages include the remuneration or compensation of paid employees. The terms wages and salaries are commonly used interchangeably. However, wage usually refers to remuneration paid on an hourly or a piecework basis. Salary usually refers to the remuneration paid on a weekly, biweekly (every two weeks), semimonthly (twice a month), monthly, or yearly basis.

The Minimum Wage

The FLSA of 1938 established a minimum wage of 25 cents per hour for a straight-time workweek of 44 hours. With the objective of improving the purchasing power of covered workers, succeeding amendments to the FLSA increased the minimum hourly rate and reduced the workweek. The Fair Minimum Wage Act of 2007 increased the minimum wage to $7.25 beginning on July 24, 2009.

Included in the regular rate of pay is all remuneration for employment paid to or on behalf of the employee. Some examples are:

1. Commission payments.
2. Earned bonuses (nondiscretionary bonus—which is a bonus normally based on hours worked, units produced, production efficiency, or work quality).
3. Severance pay.
4. On-call pay.
5. Shift or weekend differentials.

A discretionary bonus, which is a bonus not agreed upon, announced, or promised before payment, is not included in an employee's regular rate of pay. The employer retains discretion both to the granting and to the amount of the bonus until close to the end of the period for which the bonus is paid (discussion of nondiscretionary bonus, page 2-28).

The law also allows employers to credit the reasonable cost of housing, meals, and transportation to work that they provide towards payment of the minimum wage. To qualify, these facility credits must be furnished for the employee's benefit and must be accepted voluntarily by the employee.

Some other payments are not included in the regular rate of pay. Examples are:

1. Gifts made as a reward for service.
2. Payments for a bona fide profit-sharing or savings plan.
3. Payments for periods when no work is performed—vacations, holidays, sick days, or jury duty days.
4. Payments reported as part of a guaranteed minimum number of hours paid that are more than the actual hours worked.
5. Allowances for vehicles, tools, and uniforms that are considered an offset of employee expenses.

Paying Less than the Minimum Wage

Under certain conditions, wages lower than the minimum wage may be paid to some employees.

1. A training wage allows employers to pay $4.25 per hour to newly hired employees under 20 years of age (opportunity wage). This only applies to the first 90 consecutive calendar days of employment.
2. Retail or service establishments and farms may employ full-time students at 85 percent of the minimum wage ($6.1625 per hour, government rounds to $6.17 in favor of the employee).
3. Institutions of higher education may employ their own full-time students at 85 percent of the minimum wage.
4. Student-learners may be employed at 75 percent of the minimum wage if they are participating in a bona fide vocational training program conducted by an accredited school ($5.44 per hour).
5. Firms whose principal business is the delivery of letters and messages may employ messengers at not less than 95 percent of the minimum wage.
6. Persons whose earning capacity is impaired by age, physical or mental deficiency, or injury may be employed at special minimum wage rates. However, a certificate authorizing employment at such rates must first be obtained.

Paying More than the Minimum Wage

In some cases, wages higher than the minimum must be paid to some employees.

1. Employees of federal contractors must be paid at least $10.10 per hour, and beginning in 2016, the rate will be increased every year by the Secretary of Labor based on increases in the Consumer Price Index.
2. Employees in states that have a higher minimum wage rate than the federal rate must be paid the higher rate.

SELF-STUDY QUIZ 2-1

Indicate which of the following statements regarding the Fair Labor Standards Act are false.

_____ 1. Under the FLSA, wages include sales commissions and bonuses paid for employee performance.
_____ 2. Direct care workers must always be paid overtime compensation in addition to the minimum wage.
_____ 3. A son working for his parents in a family-owned business is not covered under the FLSA.
_____ 4. Individual employee coverage under the FLSA applies only if fellow employees are engaged in similar activities.
_____ 5. A college may pay its own full-time students less than the minimum wage.

Note: Answers are on page 2-30.

State Laws

All states except for Alabama, Louisiana, Mississippi, South Carolina, and Tennessee have minimum wage and overtime rules that apply both to employees covered by the FLSA and to those not covered. The FLSA requires payment of the higher wage standard if it is more than the federal $7.25 per hour.

Paying a "Living Wage"

Over 100 cities have enacted local ordinances to require employers who do business with the government to pay a "living wage" to their low-wage workers. The movement, started by local advocates, grew out of the failure to keep the national minimum wage on pace with the needs of the working poor. Recently, some living wage

---

NEWS ALERT

The Department of Labor has ruled that illegal aliens must also be paid at least the minimum wage and overtime as stipulated in the FLSA.

ON THE JOB

In 2015, the minimum wage was raised in 21 states, and now, in over half of the states the minimum wage rate is more than the federal standard.

NEWS ALERT

In 2007, Maryland became the first state to have a living wage law (covers contractors and subcontractors with a state contract for services at $100,000 or more).
Depending on the area of the state, in 2015 the wage rates ranged from $10.06 to $13.39 per hour.

laws have been passed that also include private industry doing business within the cities' jurisdiction. In Miami, all city workers and workers for companies that have contracts (over $100,000) with the city must be paid $12.46 per hour with health insurance coverage or $14.27 per hour without coverage. In Santa Fe, New Mexico, the living wage rate is set at $10.84 per hour with the value of any employer-provided health benefits credited against this minimum.

Tips

A tip (to ensure promptness) is a gift or gratuity given by a customer in recognition of some service performed for him or her. A tipped employee is one who engages in an occupation in which tips of more than $30 a month are customarily and regularly received. An employer may consider, within prescribed limits, the tips received by a tipped employee as part of the employee's wages. In 1996, the Small Business Job Protection Act froze the minimum cash wage required for tipped employees at *2.13* per hour. Tips received by the employee are credited toward the remainder ($5.12) of the total minimum wage ($7.25 − $2.13). The employee is required to report tips to the employer each month (if more than $20.00). If tips received do not amount to at least $5.12 per hour, the employer must increase the hourly rate of pay so that the hourly wage plus the equivalent hourly rate of tips received equal, at a minimum, $7.25 per hour. In 2015, the minimum wage for tipped employees of federal contractors was set at $4.90 and was to be increased each year by 95 cents an hour until it equals 70 percent of the standard minimum wage. Through a combination of tips and wages, these tipped employees must earn at least $10.00 per hour.

In order to take the tip credit, employers must notify the affected employees of the minimum wage requirements and of their intention to take the tip credit. This information can be provided orally to the employees.

EXAMPLE 2–1

James Rudolph, a waiter, earns a weekly wage of $100.00 for a 40-hour workweek and receives tips of $100.00 each week. Even though the hourly rate paid to Rudolph ($100.00 ÷ 40 hours = $2.50) exceeds the minimum wage rate of $2.13, the employer must pay Rudolph an extra $90.00 so that the tips received plus the wages paid equal the minimum wage of $7.25 per hour.

$7.25 × 40 = ...	$290.00
Weekly wage	(100.00)*
Tips received	(100.00)
Extra weekly pay	$ 90.00

*$100.00 + $90.00 = $190.00; $190.00 ÷ 40 hours = $4.75/hour

ON THE JOB

Companies that accept credit cards can deduct the amount of the credit card company's administrative fee that relates to the tip from the tip amount before giving it to the employee. These tips must be paid to the employee by the next regular payday.

All of the tips are the property of the employee and must be retained by the tipped employee unless there is a pooling of tips among the tipped employees. If employees are required to share the tips with employees not automatically tipped such as janitors, dishwashers, chefs, etc., the tip credit will be lost. To be included for the credit, the tip must be voluntarily paid by a customer. If any portion of the tips is turned over to the employer, no credit is allowed.

Service charges imposed on patrons by the employer do not count toward the tip credit. The IRS has begun to classify automatic gratuities (e.g. event fees, room service charges, and bottle service charges) as service charges which are treated as wages subject to tax withholdings. This will entail more paperwork and extra cost to the employer.

An alternative tip-reporting system can be used in which the employer and the IRS determine a predetermined tip rate for the employer's various occupations. At least 75 percent of the employees must sign agreements to report tips at or above the predetermined rate. The employer is then required to report any employee violations to the IRS.

In cases of two jobs performed by one worker, the tip credit can only be applied to the job that qualifies as tipped employment.

Karl Marx worked for the Hilton Hotel in Las Vegas as a waiter. In addition, on his days off, he worked on Hilton's maintenance crew. Hilton can only claim the tip credit against Marx's wages on his waiter job.

Over the Line

A waitress for Frisch's Dixie was assigned duties over an extended period of time where no tips were possible, while the employer continued to pay the waitress at the sub-minimum wage allowed under the tip credit rule for those hours. The courts found Frisch's Dixie guilty of a willful violation of the FLSA and ordered the company to pay three years backpay.[1]

Under state laws, the states' tip credit percentage (different in each state) is applied to the federal minimum wage to calculate the actual tip credit and the resulting minimum wage required under state law. In states where the tip credit differs from the federal, employers must determine the credit and the resulting minimum wage under both federal and state law and pay their employees the higher cash wage.

SELF-STUDY QUIZ 2-2

Genna Harrison, a waitress, earns $85.20 a week for a 40-hour workweek. During one week, Harrison received tips of $90.

1. What hourly rate is being paid to Harrison?
   $_____
2. How much must the employer pay Harrison in addition to her $85.20 weekly wage?
   $_____

Workweek

The FLSA defines a **workweek** as a fixed and regularly recurring period of 168 hours—seven consecutive 24-hour periods. The individual employee's workweek is the statutory or contract number of hours to be worked regularly during that period. The workweek may begin on any day of the week and need not coincide with the calendar week. An employer may establish the same workweek for the business operations as a whole or assign different workweeks to individual workers or groups of workers.

An employer may change the day a workweek begins if intended to be a permanent change and not just to evade the overtime pay requirements of the FLSA. If, however, a union contract fixes the workweek, the employer's right to change the workweek depends upon the wording in the contract. Each workweek stands alone, and the overtime hours worked in one week may not be shifted to another workweek. Thus, each workweek is a separate unit for the purpose of computing overtime pay.

Overtime Hours and Overtime Pay

The FLSA requires overtime pay for all hours worked in excess of 40 in a workweek. The FLSA requires no overtime pay for daily hours worked in excess of any given number or for work on Saturdays, Sundays, holidays, or other special days. The law requires overtime pay to be *one and one-half times* the employee's regular hourly rate of pay, which must not be less than the statutory minimum. If the state's overtime rule is more generous than the FLSA's, the state law is followed. The payment for the overtime worked must generally be made on the regular payday for the time period in which the overtime work took place.

---

1 *PAYROLL GUIDE*, Jul 5, 2013, p.18, 237, paragraph 18260.

EXAMPLE 2-2

If an employee's regular rate of pay is $18.40 an hour, the overtime rate must be at least $18.40 × 1.5, or $27.60 an hour.

ON THE **JOB**

California defines overtime as any hours worked over eight in one day, and 40 in a workweek, and also provides for double-time pay for hours over 12 in one day and over 8 on the seventh consecutive day worked.

With some restrictions, employees covered under the FLSA can be required by their employers to work overtime. If they refuse, they can be fired under the law. There is also no limit on the overtime that can be required. However, in these cases, the state laws may be the governing force. On the other side, employees should only work overtime if authorized in advance by a supervisor and this should be a written policy. The consequences of unauthorized overtime must be communicated to all employees. Discipline for violating this policy must be administered equally, but payment must still be made for these non-approved hours. If reprimands do not work, suspension and even termination can legally result.

If an hourly-rate employee works in pay periods of two weeks or longer, the employer can elect to give the employee 1.5 hours off for every overtime hour. However, the time off must be in the same pay period as the overtime hours worked, e.g., an employee works *44* hours the first week of a biweekly pay period; he works 34 hours in the second week and is paid for a total of 80 hours [40 + (4 O.T. × 1.5) + 34].

In the case of *tipped employees,* the same tip credit also applies to overtime hours. The regular rate of pay for a tipped employee is the current minimum wage—$2.13 plus $5.12 tip credit = $7.25/hour. Time and one-half of $7.25 is $10.88. Since the employer can use the same tip credit for overtime hours, the employee's overtime cash wages are *$5.76/hour ($10.88 – $5.12).*

EXAMPLE 2-3

Alfred Sims is a tipped employee who normally works a 40-hour week and averages over $300 in tips each week. If his employer takes the maximum tip credit against the minimum wage ($5.12 per hour), in a week in which Alfred worked 44 hours, the restaurant would pay him:

40 hours × $2.13	=	$ 85.20
4 hours × $5.76	=	23.04
Gross pay		$108.24

Exceptions to Overtime Hours and Overtime Pay Provisions

An exception to overtime hours and overtime pay applies to *hospital employees.* Hospitals may enter into an agreement with their employees under which a 14-day period, rather than a workweek, becomes the basis for computing overtime pay. Employees entering such an agreement must receive overtime pay at not less than one and one-half times their regular hourly rate for hours worked in excess of eight hours in any workday or in excess of 80 hours in a 14-day period, whichever is the greater number of overtime hours. Although employers have the option of using the normal workweek or the 14-day period, they cannot change from one method to the other arbitrarily.

Donna Maloney, a lab technician, agreed that a 14-day period would be used to figure her overtime pay. Maloney works 12 hours in one day during the period and 8 hours in each of the 9 other days worked during the period, a total of 84 hours.

Maloney is entitled to 80 hours of straight-time pay and 4 hours of overtime pay for the 14-day period.

If Maloney worked only 7 hours in each of the 9 other days during the period, or a total of 75 hours, she would be entitled to 71 hours of straight-time pay and 4 hours of overtime pay for the 14-day period.

Employees in retail or service industries are exempt from the overtime provisions as long as their regular weekly rate of pay, including commissions, is at least one and one-half times the federal minimum wage rate ($10.88) and more than half of their pay over a monthly period comes from commissions. The overtime exemption is lost for any week in which the pay drops below $10.88 per hour.

Minimum wage legislation also provides an exception for *employees receiving remedial education.* Under this law, employees who receive remedial education offered by their employers are permitted to work up to 10 hours overtime each week without receiving overtime compensation. The remedial training, which does not include training for a specific job, must be designed to provide reading and other basic skills at an eighth-grade level or below.

Compensatory Time Off

A state, a political subdivision of a state, or an interstate governmental agency may grant employees (not covered by a collective bargaining agreement) compensatory time off in lieu of overtime compensation. Employees working in public safety, emergency response, or seasonal activities may accumulate compensatory time off up to 480 hours. (The 480-hour limit represents 320 hours of overtime actually worked at the one and one-half overtime rate.) Employees may "bank" their hours and use them later as time off at time and one-half during the course of their employment.

Employees whose work does not include the preceding activities may bank 240 hours for compensatory time off. Upon reaching the 480- or 240-hour limit, an employee must receive either cash for additional hours of overtime worked or use some compensatory time before receiving further overtime compensation in the form of compensatory time off. Note that not all 480 or 240 hours have to be accrued before compensatory time off may be used. The FLSA also provides for the payment of cash for unused comp time when the employee terminates employment.

Exemptions from FLSA Requirements

Exempt employees (see Figure 2.1 on page 2-10) are those workers exempt from some, or all, of the FLSA requirements, such as minimum wages, equal pay, and overtime pay.

White-Collar Workers

The FLSA exempts some workers, such as executives, administrators, professional employees, highly compensated employees, computer professionals, and outside salespersons, from the minimum wage and overtime pay provisions if they satisfy certain tests.

Test of Exemption

To be eligible for this exemption, the employee must be paid on a *salary basis*, must be paid at least $455 per week, $23,660 annually, and must meet the "primary duty" requirements as listed in Figure 2.2 on page 2-10. This salary must be a predetermined amount that cannot be reduced because of fluctuations in the quantity or quality of the work performed.

The exemption is not lost if the wages are computed on an hourly, daily, or shift basis as long as the arrangement includes a guarantee of at least the minimum weekly required amount, paid on a salary basis. The guaranteed amount must be equivalent to the employee's usual earnings at the hourly, daily, or shift rate for the normal scheduled workweek. This would also apply to exempt employees paid on a fee basis for a single job.

Salary Basis

These white-collar employees must be paid their full salary in any week in which any work is performed without regard to the number of hours worked. However, deductions can be made from the salary if an exempt employee misses one or more full days of work for personal reasons, other than sickness or accident. If the employee does not qualify for the employer's sick pay plan or has used up all available sick time, deductions can also be made for these full-day absences. However, if there is not a bona fide sick leave plan, an employer cannot make deductions from the salaries of exempt employees for absences due to sickness.

FIGURE 2.1
Exemption Status of Workers Under FLSA

Employee Job Description	Minimum Wage Exemption	Equal Pay Exemption	Full Overtime Exemption
Agricultural employees.			X
Agricultural workers who are members of the employer's immediate family.	X	X	X
Air carrier employees if the carrier is subject to Title II of the Railway Labor Act.			X
Amusement or recreational establishment employees, provided the business has seasonal peaks.	X	X	X
Announcers, news editors, and chief engineers of radio or television stations in small communities.			X
Baby sitters (casual) and companions to ill or aged persons unable to care for themselves.	X	X	X
Drivers and drivers' helpers who make local deliveries and are paid on a trip-rate or similar basis following a plan approved by the government.			X
Executive, administrative, and professional employees, including teachers and academic administrative personnel in schools.	X		X
Fruit and vegetable employees who are engaged in the local transportation of these items or of workers employed or to be employed in the harvesting of fruits or vegetables.			X
Household domestic service employees who reside in the household.			X
Motion picture theater employees.			X
Motor carrier employees if the carrier is subject to regulation by the secretary of transportation.			X
Newspaper employees if the newspaper is published on a weekly, semiweekly, or daily basis and if the circulation is less than 4,000 copies, with the major circulation in the county of publication or contiguous counties.	X	X	X
Railroad, express company, and water carrier employees if the companies are subject to Part I of the Interstate Commerce Act.			X
Salespersons for automobile, truck, or farm implement dealers; parts stock clerks or mechanics; salespersons for boat, trailer, or aircraft dealers.			X
Taxicab drivers.			X

FIGURE 2.2
Indications of Exempt Status

Executive	Administrative	Professional	Business Owner
1. Primary duty—managing 2. Supervises two or more employees 3. Authority to hire, fire, promote	1. Primary duty—performs office work 2. Regularly uses discretion and independent judgment	1. Work requires advanced knowledge (science or learning) 2. Knowledge acquired by prolonged course of instruction	1. Owns at least 20 percent of equity 2. Actively manages business operations
Highly Compensated	**Computer Professionals**	**Creative Professional**	**Outside Salespeople**
1. Earns $100,000 or more 2. Performs nonmanual work 3. Regularly performs one of the exempt duties of an executive, professional, or administrative employee	1. Salary of at least $455/week or $27.63/hour 2. Duties consist of system analysis techniques, design of computer systems or programs	1. Requires invention, imagination, originality, or talent in an artistic or a creative endeavor	1. Primary duty—makes sales or obtains orders for services or use of facilities 2. Regularly away from the employer's place of business 3. No salary test

A proportionate share of an exempt employee's salary for the time actually worked is allowed only for the employee's first or last week of employment.

Partial-day absences cannot be deducted from the exempt employee's salary. However, the Wage and Hour Division has stated that the employer can require the employee to use any accumulated leave time to offset the time absent. Employers should keep records that describe the workweek and the wages paid for that work time and can require exempt employees to record and track hours worked, to work a specified schedule, and to work as many hours as the employer desires as long as their salaries are paid.

Exempt status can be lost when employers make improper deductions from the pays of exempt employees. This loss of status only applies to the pay periods when the deductions were made.

An exception to the FLSA salary pay requirement is the use of FMLA leave. If an employee works half a day, the other half a day taken for FMLA can be unpaid (if personal time is not used to cover the FMLA part of the day).

Over the Line

A store manager at a Family Dollar store in Florida was paid a weekly salary of $700 and, even though she spent 60 to 70 percent of her time doing nonexempt work, she did handle many exempt managerial duties—scheduling, directing employees' work, etc. When the employee sued for overtime, the court determined that time alone is not the sole test of an employee's primary duty, and recognized the concept of multi-tasking: concurrent performance of exempt and nonexempt duties. The court ruled against the employee stating that her managerial duties were more important that the other duties performed.[2]

Blue-Collar Workers

The exemption from overtime pay based on the duties and salary tests does not apply to blue-collar workers (manual workers). No matter how highly paid, these workers are still entitled to overtime pay. This also applies to police officers, firefighters, paramedics, emergency medical technicians, and licensed practical nurses.

Equal Pay Act

The Equal Pay Act amended the FLSA to require that men and women performing equal work must receive equal pay. The Equal Pay Act applies to any employer having workers subject to the minimum pay provisions of the Wage and Hour Law. The equal-pay requirements also apply to white-collar workers and outside salespersons, even though they are exempt from the minimum wage standards.

The Equal Pay Law prohibits an employer from discriminating by paying wages to employees of one sex at a lower rate than those paid the opposite sex for equal work on jobs that require equal skill, effort, and responsibility and that are performed under similar working conditions. However, wage differentials between sexes are allowable if based on a seniority system, a merit system, a payment plan that measures earnings by quantity or quality of production, or any factor other than sex. If an unlawful pay differential between men and women exists, the employer must raise the lower rate to equal the higher rate.

Child-Labor Restrictions

The FLSA prohibits a business from the interstate shipment of its goods or services if it employs child labor unlawfully. Under the FLSA, the secretary of labor issues regulations that restrict the employment of individuals under the age of 18.

ON THE **JOB**

The Department of Labor prohibits occupational driving for minors except on an occasional or incidental basis. Permitted driving can only be done during daylight hours and in vehicles not exceeding 6,000 pounds. In New York state, 16- and 17-year-olds are prohibited from driving in Manhattan.

The restrictions divide child employment into nonfarm occupations and agricultural occupations.

Nonfarm Occupations

The basic minimum age for most jobs is 16 years. This is the minimum age for work in manufacturing and processing jobs or in any other occupations except those declared by the secretary of labor as hazardous for minors under 18. The FLSA lists 17 occupations that are considered too dangerous. These include mining, forestry, excavation, roofing work, operation of certain power-driven tools, and most on-the-job driving. However, employees ages 16 and 17 may work an unlimited number of hours each week in nonhazardous jobs.

Within certain limits, 14- and 15-year-olds may be employed in retail, food service, and gasoline service establishments. For example, this age group may be employed in office and clerical work, including the operation of office machines; cashiering; selling; price marking and tagging by hand or by machine; errand and delivery work; kitchen work and other work involved in preparing and serving food and beverages; dispensing gasoline and oil; and car cleaning.

The employment of minors between the ages of 14 and 16 cannot interfere with their schooling, health, and well-being. In addition, the following conditions must be met:

1. All work must be performed outside school hours.
2. There is a maximum three-hour day and 18-hour week when school is in session (eight hours and 40 hours when not in session).
3. All work must be performed between 7 A.M. and 7 P.M. (9 P.M. during the summer).

Agricultural Occupations

The employment of children under age 12 is generally prohibited in agricultural occupations, as described below.

1. During hours when school is in session.
2. Outside school hours on farms, including conglomerates, that used more than 500 man-days of labor in any quarter of the preceding calendar year.
3. Outside school hours on noncovered farms without parental consent.

However, children may work on farms owned or operated by their parents or guardians. Children 10 and 11 years old can work as hand harvest laborers outside school hours for up to eight weeks between June 1 and October 15, with a number of strict conditions on the employer. Children aged 12 and 13 may be employed only during hours when school is not in session provided there is parental consent or the employment is on a farm where the parents are employed. Children aged 14 and 15 may be employed, but only during hours when school is not in session. No child under the age of 16 may be employed in a hazardous farm occupation, such as operating large tractors, corn pickers, cotton pickers, grain combines, and feed grinders.

Certificate of Age

Employers cannot be charged with having violated the child-labor restrictions of the law if they have on file an officially executed *certificate of age* which shows that the minor has reached the stipulated minimum age. In most states, a state employment or age certificate, issued by the Federal Wage and Hour Division or by a state agency, serves as proof of age. In some states, a state or federal certificate of age, a state employment certificate, or a work permit may not be available. In such cases, the employer may rely on any one of the following documents as evidence of age for minor employees:

1. Birth certificate (or attested transcript thereof) or a signed statement of the recorded date and place of birth issued by a registrar of vital statistics or other officer charged with the duty of recording births.

2. Record of baptism (or attested transcript thereof) showing the date of birth of the minor.
3. Statement on the census records of the Bureau of Indian Affairs and signed by an administrative representative thereof showing the name, date, and place of the minor's birth.

The employer should maintain a copy of the document or indicate in the payroll records which document verified the minor's age.

Penalties

The U.S. government may bring civil or criminal actions against employers who violate the FLSA. In cases of misclassified workers, the assessments are:

- unintentional with a filed Form 1099 (showing nonemployee compensation)— 1.5 percent of wages paid + 20 percent of the employee's social security tax.
- unintentional without a filed Form 1099—above penalties are doubled.
- intentional—100 percent of the worker's federal income tax and social security taxes.

In addition to the above, the employer remains liable for any penalties for failure to withhold, to file returns, and to pay taxes.

Employers who willfully violate the wage and hour provisions of the law or the wage orders fixed by the Administrator of the Wage and Hour Division of the Department of Labor will be prosecuted and will be subject to a fine of not more than $10,000, or imprisonment for up to six months, or both. However, no person may be imprisoned for a first offense violation. If an imposed fine goes unpaid, however, the courts have the power to order imprisonment as an incident to the nonpayment. Violators of the child-labor provisions of the act are subject to fines of $11,000 for each violation. If the violation results in death or serious injury to an employee under age 18, the maximum penalty is $50,000 for each violation. Willful or repeated violations will cause a maximum penalty of $100,000.

It is unlawful to discharge or discriminate against an employee because he or she has filed a wage-hour complaint. This could result in a lawsuit in which lost wages, liquidated damages, and even punitive damages are awarded.

Areas Not Covered by the FLSA

The FLSA does not require employers to:

1. Pay extra wages for work on Saturdays, Sundays, or holidays.
2. Pay for holidays, vacations, or severance.
3. Limit the number of hours or work for persons 16 years of age or over.
4. Give holidays off.
5. Grant vacation time.
6. Grant sick leave.

Determining Employee's Work Time

To avoid paying for time not actually spent on the job and to eliminate payment for unnecessary overtime work, employers must know what types of employee activities count as working time under the law. Generally, the hours counted as working time include all the time that employees actually work or must be on duty. A distinction must be made between an employee's principal activities and the preliminary and postliminary activities.

Principal Activities

The **principal activities** of employees include those tasks employees must perform and include any work of consequence performed for the employer. Principal activities include those indispensable to the performance of productive work and those that are an integral part of a principal activity.

IRS CONNECTION

Employees have two years to sue for pay mistakes involving unpaid minimum wage and unpaid overtime, and three years to sue for willful mistakes. Last year, in settlements of over 8,000 lawsuits, the U.S. Department of Labor collected more than $250 million from employers.

LO 2
Define *hours worked*.

The test of compensability with respect to principal activities requires that there be physical or mental exertion, controlled or required by the employer and performed for the employer's benefit.

Chad Quinn is a lathe operator who oils and cleans his machines at the beginning of each workday and installs new cutting tools. These activities performed by Quinn are part of his principal activity.

Clothes-Changing Time and Wash-Up

Because of the nature of their work, some employees change clothes or wash on the employer's premises. Statutes or ordinances may require clothes changing or washing. Employees who spend time changing clothes or washing on the employer's premises regard this time as part of their principal activities. However, even where the nature of the job or the law requires clothes changing or wash-up, it may be excluded from time worked either expressly or by custom and practice under a collective bargaining contract. The U.S. Supreme Court has ruled that time spent donning and doffing protective gear qualified as "clothes changing" under a collective bargaining agreement between the employer and the unionized workforce, and was non-compensable. This ruling affects all employers of a unionized workforce that have uniform or other dress requirements.

Over the Line

A District of Columbia federal court ruled that time spent donning and doffing protective gear and firearms by police officers was compensable time unless the time was too short to monitor. However, changing into uniforms was not considered to be an integral nor indispensable part of their policing duties. Since the officers could change clothes at home, this time is not considered "time worked."[3]

Travel Time

The time spent by employees in traveling to and from work needs to be counted as time worked only if contract, custom, or practice so requires. In some situations, however, travel time between home and work counts as time worked. If an employee who regularly works at a fixed location is given a special one-day work assignment in another city, time worked includes the travel time.

Dana MacAvoy receives an emergency call outside regular working hours and must travel a substantial distance to perform a job away from MacAvoy's usual work site for one of the employer's customers. The travel time counts as time worked.

When performed during the workday as part of an employee's principal activities, the travel time counts as time worked.

Rena Thorpe travels throughout the city to various job sites during regular working hours, 9 A.M. to 5 P.M., Mondays through Fridays. Such travel time counts as work time.

When Thorpe travels between workdays from one city to another, the travel time counts as working time when the hours correspond to regular working hours, even though the hours may occur on Saturday and Sunday.

For example, if Thorpe is sent on a trip requiring travel on Saturday and Sunday to be at a job the first thing Monday morning, the travel time on Saturday and Sunday between the hours of 9 A.M. and 5 P.M. counts as time worked, but travel time before 9 A.M. and after 5 P.M. does not count.

---

3 *Payroll Manager's Letter,* March 7, 2012, Volume 28, Issue 5, p. 8.

Idle Time

Readiness to serve can also be considered employment. If the time spent while idle was primarily for the benefit of the employer, this time must be compensated. However, if workers are required to carry a beeper, pager, or cell phone, this on-call time is not compensable, provided they can use this time for their own purposes. Also, travel limitations during this on-call time does not make it work time.

Waiting Time

If an employee is "engaged to wait," this is work time. For example, workers required to be at a car wash at a scheduled time while waiting for car wash service volume are considered to be working. On the other hand, if an employee is "waiting to be engaged," this is not work time. An employee completely relieved from duty until a certain hour is not working during the time spent waiting for that hour.

Rest Periods and Coffee Breaks

The FLSA does not require that an employer give employees a rest period or a coffee break. However, the employer may grant such rest periods voluntarily; or the union contract or municipal or state legislation may require them. In these cases, the time spent on a rest period of 20 minutes or less counts as part of the hours worked. If longer than 20 minutes, the compensability for the time depends upon the employee's freedom during that time or upon the provisions of the union contract.

Meal Periods

Bona fide meal periods (not including coffee breaks or snack times) during which the employee is completely relieved from duty are not considered working time. Lunch periods during which the employee must perform some duties while eating are not bona fide meal periods. The general rule sets a bona fide meal period at 30 minutes or longer.

In cases where the employer and employee agree that it is sufficient, a 15-minute lunch period can be considered a bona fide meal period. However, the lunchroom facilities must be readily accessible.

Virginia Sherr, an office worker, must eat at her desk and operate the switchboard at lunch time. Sherr must be paid for the lunch period.

ON THE **JOB**

Over 40 states have laws covering meals and rest periods. California requires a 30-minute break (unpaid) after five hours and a 10-minute rest period per four hours of work. If nonexempt employees do not get this break, they must be given an additional hour of pay.

Taking Work Home

With more and more employees taking work home with them, it is important to understand that this is compensable time. Nonexempt employees must be paid for *all hours worked,* even those outside the regular workplace. This holds true whether the work was assigned or the employees took on the extra workload themselves. Even if told not to take work home, the employer must pay for the time worked. The only recourse for the employer would be future warnings and if the practice continues, dismissal of the employee.

Another area of concern for employers would be employees sending work-related e-mails, even when they are technically off the clock. This time spent is considered work time and could trigger overtime pay. A clear statement on e-mail usage for hourly staff should be part of an employee policy manual.

Sleep Time

If required to be on duty for less than 24 hours, the employee is considered to be working even though the employee is sleeping or engaging in other personal activities. If over 24 hours, an agreement to exclude a sleeping period of not more than eight hours from time worked is binding. Adequate sleeping facilities must be provided, and the employee must be permitted at least five hours of uninterrupted sleep.

Over the Line

Self Pride, a Maryland-based residential facilities operator, altered employees' records to reduce hours worked during the 48-hour weekend shift. Based on testimony from the employees, they were not able to sleep during these 48-hour shifts, breaks were routinely interrupted, calls had to be made each hour to the main office or pay was docked, and leaving the facility during breaks was not practical. After receiving all the testimony, the Fourth Circuit Court ruled that the entire 48 hours of the shift constituted work time as defined by the FLSA—break time was interrupted by duties carried out for Self Pride's benefit.[4]

Training Sessions

Generally, working time includes the time spent by employees in attending lectures and meetings for training purposes.

The working time spent by postal clerks in learning mail distribution practices and the operation of letter-sorting machines counts as compensable time because it is (a) controlled and required by the employer, (b) for the primary benefit of the employer, and (c) an integral and indispensable part of the employees' principal work activities.

However, time spent in training sessions need not be counted as working time if ALL the following conditions are met:

1. Attendance by the employee is voluntary.
2. The employee does not produce any goods or perform any other productive work during the meeting or lecture.
3. The meeting or lecture takes place outside regular working hours.
4. The meeting or lecture is not directly related to the employee's work.

Doctor's Appointments

Time spent waiting for and receiving medical assistance on the employer's premises or at the employer's direction during the employee's normal working hours during the workweek is considered time worked. As such, it cannot be deducted from the employee's accrued leave.

Preliminary and Postliminary Activities

Activities regarded as *preliminary* and *postliminary* need not be counted as time worked unless required by contract or custom. Under the *Portal-to-Portal Act*, these activities are not compensated unless they are an "integral and indispensable part of the employee's principal activities and not specifically excluded by the Act." Some examples of activities regarded as preliminary and postliminary include: walking, riding, or traveling to or from the actual place where employees engage in their principal activities; checking in and out at the plant

ON THE JOB

Most states require time off to vote if voting cannot be done before or after the workday even though there is no such federal law. A few states require employees to be paid for this time.

or office and waiting in line to do so; changing clothes for the convenience of the employee, washing up and showering unless directly related to the specific type of work the employee is hired to perform; and waiting in line to receive paychecks.

Activities that qualify as "work time" but the time spent on them is so short that they are considered *de minimis* (insignificant) need not be compensated.

Fractional Parts of an Hour

The FLSA requires that employees be paid for *all* time worked, including fractional parts of an hour. An employer cannot use an arbitrary formula or an estimate as a substitute for determining precisely the compensable working time which is part of an employee's fixed or regular hours.

Uncertain and indefinite working periods beyond the scheduled working hours cannot be practically determined. Therefore, a few seconds or minutes may be disregarded. Some courts have allowed from 10 to 20 minutes to be ignored, while other courts have refused to apply the law to periods as small as 10 minutes. Generally, a few minutes of time spent by employees on the company premises for their own convenience before or after their workdays are not included in the hours worked.

Employers using time clocks may round starting and stopping times of their employees to the nearest five minutes, or to the nearest six minutes (tenth of an hour), or 15 minutes (quarter of an hour). However, consistently rounding time *down* to the nearest five minutes or one-tenth or one-quarter of an hour would be a violation in that employees would not be properly compensated for all time worked. These rules must be administered fairly and consistently.

In the case of union or other employment contracts, the method of computing regular and overtime rates may be prescribed in the contracts.

Absences

The FLSA does not require an employer to pay an employee for hours not worked because of illness. For employees on an hourly wage basis, the time card shows the exact hours worked. In addition, the time off for absences does not count toward the 40 hours for overtime pay purposes even if the employee is paid for the absences. In practice, most U.S. employers provide vacation days, sick days, and/or paid time off (PTO) days for full-time employees. Only one-third of employers offer paid leave to part-time employees.

Tardiness

Employers may handle tardiness in many ways. Frequently, when an employee is late or leaves early, the supervisor must O.K. the time card. Some companies require the employee to sign a special slip indicating the reason for being late or leaving early. Some companies keep time according to the decimal system, whereby each hour is divided into units of tens (six minutes times 10 periods in each hour). An employee who is late one through six minutes is penalized or "docked" one-tenth of an hour. One who is seven through 12 minutes late is "docked" one-fifth of an hour, etc.

> ## ON THE **JOB**
>
> In the case of bad weather that prevents exempt employees from getting to work, a full day's pay can be deducted from their pay. However, the employees could be required to use their leave time to cover the missed day. If the business closes, the employer could require the use of leave time, but cannot deduct a day's pay.

Records Used for Timekeeping

The FLSA requires employers subject to the law to keep certain time and pay records. For example, employers must keep records that indicate the hours each employee worked each workday and each workweek.

How the employer chooses the methods of keeping time records depends on the size of the company and whether employees are paid on an hourly, weekly,

> **LO 3**
> Describe the main types of records used to collect payroll data.

biweekly, semimonthly, or monthly basis. Employees on a salary basis usually work a given number of hours each day and can be required to record and track their hours and to work a specified schedule. Employees on an hourly wage basis may work a varying number of hours with some "down time" and layoffs and some overtime work. All of this time must be recorded in some way.

Time Sheets

A time sheet provides the information required by law and the data used to compute the payroll. Many small businesses that must keep a record of time worked by each employee require each person to submit and sign a time sheet, indicating the times of arrival and departure from work. These time reports are approved by the appropriate supervisor or department head at the end of the pay period. They are then forwarded to the Payroll Department for entry into the payroll system. Time sheets offer a simple method of accumulating employees' working times.

Time Cards

Under this timekeeping system, each employee receives a time card on which the time worked is recorded manually by the employee or automatically by a time clock. The time card is designed to fit various lengths of pay periods. Figure 2.3 shows one type of time card frequently used for a weekly pay period. The card provides space to record the hours worked, the rate of pay, deductions, and net pay. The Payroll Department inserts the handwritten figures to be used in computing total earnings, deductions, and net pay for the payroll period.

Some time clocks use the continental system of recording time, where each day consists of one 24-hour period, instead of two 12-hour periods. The time runs from 12 midnight to 12 midnight. Eight o'clock in the morning is recorded as 800; eight o'clock in the evening, as 2000.

Computerized Time and Attendance Recording Systems

The main kinds of computerized time and attendance recording systems include:

1. *Card-generated systems*—employees use time cards similar to the traditional time cards illustrated earlier. Daily and weekly totals are calculated and printed on the time cards for data entry into the firm's computer system.
2. *Badge systems*—employees are issued plastic laminated badges containing punched holes or having magnetic strips or bar codes. The badges are used with electronic time clocks that collect and store data, which later become input to the computer system.
3. *Cardless and badgeless systems*—employees enter only their personal identification numbers (PIN) on a numerical or alphanumerical key pad. This system, like the badge system, uses time clocks to collect and store data for transmission to, and processing by, the firm's computer system.
4. *Personal computer-based systems*—employees swipe their identification cards across bar code readers connected to personal computers for easy recording of time worked.

For example, the Timekeeper, a self-contained, wall-mounted time clock, contains a computer system.[5] This time clock accepts time and attendance data from time cards and computes complex payroll and on-the-job information. Time-clock systems, such as the Timekeeper, eliminate most manual payroll processing operations. Employees receive their own time cards that show their daily attendance record, thus complying with federal, state, and union regulations. The Timekeeper also totals employee hours and rounds out employee time to fractions of an hour in accordance with the payroll practice of the firm.

---

5 Information supplied by Kronos, Incorporated.

The Timekeeper card, shown in Figure 2.4, is similar to the time card illustrated in Figure 2.3. The mark-sense field at the bottom of the card identifies each employee or supervisor and authorizes access to and use of the Timekeeper.

When an employee places the card in the time clock, the computer scans the card, optically verifies the employee's number, and locates the last print line on the card. The time of entry is then printed on the next line. Simultaneously, the computer stores the punch-in time in the system's memory. When an employee punches out, the Timekeeper again verifies the employee's identification number and computes and rounds off the daily and cumulative payroll hours. Next, the actual punch-out time and the computed cumulative hours are printed on the card and stored within the Timekeeper for transmission to a computer for payroll processing.

Next Generation

With more and more employees working outside the traditional office environment, the time clock has not been able to keep up with most companies' needs for time and attendance information. Many companies have been forced to acquire more automated systems. These systems allow for:

1. quicker and more accurate data assembly.
2. elimination of calculation errors.
3. easier tracking of labor cost to projects.
4. faster and more reliable scheduling.

FIGURE 2.3
Time Card

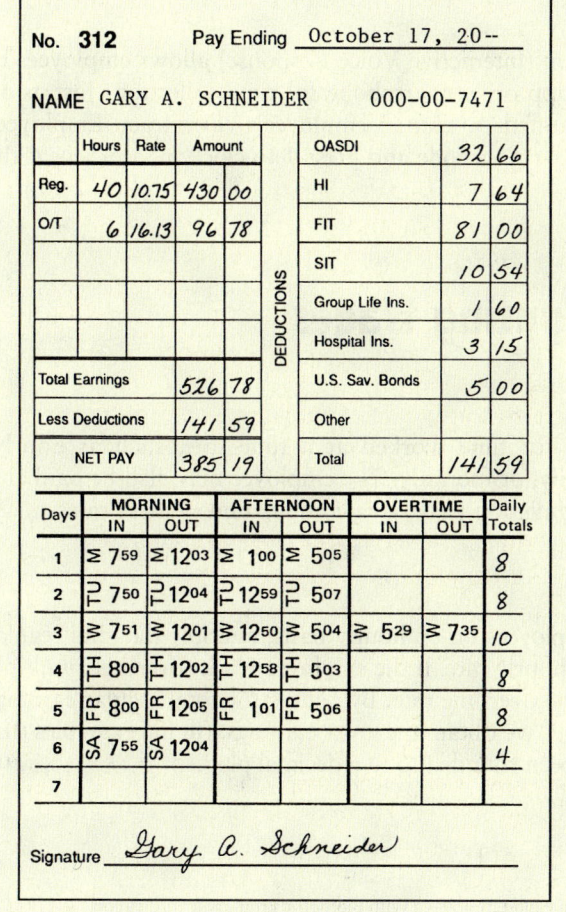

FIGURE 2.4
Mark-Sense Time Card Used in the Timekeeper Computerized System

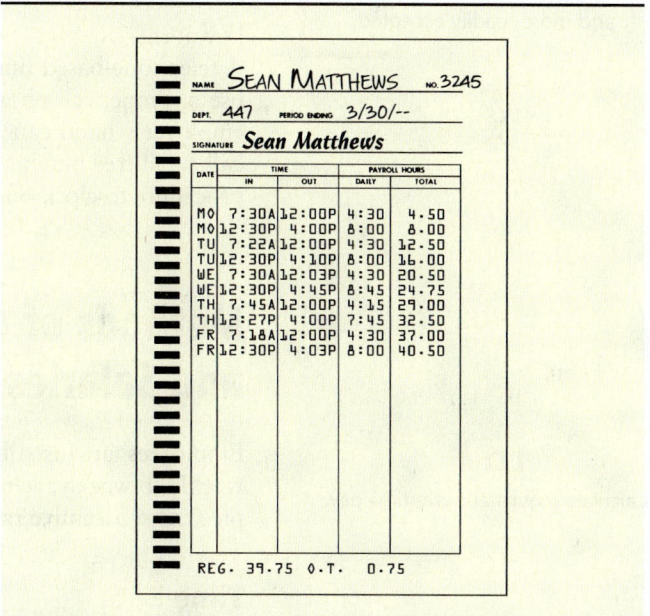

Touch-Screen Technology

In this system, data can be collected and processed instantaneously. The system requires employees to punch in and out on touch-screen personal computers (PCs), which are connected to the company's main computer server. These touch-screen kiosks are also used to provide information back to the employee regarding the organization.

Internet

Some Web-based time accounting systems now allow employees to "clock" in and out via the Internet. Employees use passwords to log on to a secured Web site. This site can also be used by the employees to check their hours worked, vacation time accrued, and messages from the Human Resources Department. This can also be accomplished through the use of mobile and wireless data collection devices (cell phones, personal digital assistants, and Global Positioning Satellite—GPS—enabled smartphones). Without ever visiting their office, employees can enter time and labor information.

Biometrics

The need for greater security and precision has recently produced a more affordable alternative to companies that are searching for time and attendance systems. A biometric time system uses a time clock that reads an employee's unique fingerprint or hand geometry (size and shape) to validate the employee. This technology is also available in other forms—voice recognition, iris scan, and even whole-face recognition.

IVR

A telephone-based time system (Interactive Voice Response) allows employees to use a phone, cell phone, or app on a smartphone for time collection. Just as an employee's hand can be identified, so can an employee's voice tract. Employees call a toll-free number, say their pass code and press 1 to clock in, and repeat the procedure to clock out.[6]

Methods of Computing Wages and Salaries

LO 4
Calculate regular and overtime pay.

Employees are usually paid for time worked at a time rate, such as hourly, weekly, biweekly, semimonthly, or monthly. The employee may also be paid at a piece rate, incentive rate, commission basis, or a combination of these rates.

Time Rate

To compute the wages of employees on an hourly basis, multiply the total regular hours worked by the regular hourly rate. If the employee works overtime, multiply the total overtime hours by the overtime rate. By adding the total regular earnings and the total overtime earnings, we obtain the **gross earnings**. (In the examples that follow, if needed, rates have been rounded to two decimal places.)

6 "Time Collection for Remote, Mobile Field Employees With Biometric Employee Verification," *PAYTECH*, October 2009, p. 44.

Joanne French works a 40-hour week at $12.40 an hour with overtime hours paid at $1^{1}/_{2}$ times the regular rate.

EXAMPLE 2-4

Regular weekly earnings are	$496.00 (40 × $12.40)
The overtime rate is..	$18.60 ($12.40 × 1.5)
If French works 4 hours overtime, additional earnings for the	
4 hours are	$74.40 (4 × $18.60)
French's weekly gross earnings are..	$570.40 ($496.00 + $74.40)
If paid only for time actually worked and she works only 36 hours during a week,	
French earns	$446.40 (36 × $12.40)

The employee's regular rate of pay includes ***all payments*** given for working a particular job. This does not include discretionary bonuses, gifts on special occasions, and contributions to certain welfare plans (see page 2-4).

In the case of factory workers, many factories compute the actual time spent on a certain job so that amount can be charged to that job.

Sonja Patel spent 100 minutes on a certain job. The wages chargeable to that job at the regular hourly rate of $11.58 would be computed as follows:

EXAMPLE 2-5

$$\$11.58 \times \frac{100}{60} = \$19.30$$

Calculating Overtime Pay

In calculating the gross pay of an employee who worked overtime, one of two methods can be used, both of which will result in the same total gross pay.

The most common method is to calculate the gross pay for the 40 hours and then calculate the overtime pay by multiplying the number of hours over 40 by a pay rate of one and one-half times the employee's regular rate of pay.

John Dilcher is paid an hourly rate of $18.50 per hour, and he worked 49 hours this week. His gross pay is:

EXAMPLE 2-6

$$
\begin{aligned}
40 \text{ hours} \times \$18.50 &= \quad \$740.00 \\
9 \text{ hours} \times \$27.75 \ (\$18.50 \times 1.5) &= \quad \underline{249.75} \\
\text{Total gross pay} &= \quad \underline{\underline{\$989.75}}
\end{aligned}
$$

The other method is the **overtime premium** approach. In this case, the total hours worked (including overtime hours) are multiplied by the regular rate of pay. Then the overtime premium pay is calculated by multiplying the overtime hours by an overtime premium rate of one-half the regular hourly rate.

John Dilcher's (the prior example) pay would be calculated as follows:

EXAMPLE 2-7

$$
\begin{aligned}
49 \text{ hours} \times \$18.50 &= \quad \$906.50 \\
9 \text{ hours} \times \$9.25 \ (\$18.50 \times 0.5) &= \quad \underline{83.25} \\
\text{Total gross pay} &= \quad \underline{\underline{\$989.75}}
\end{aligned}
$$

By using the overtime premium approach, an employer could save on the calculation of workers' compensation insurance. Most states do not include the overtime premium in the determination of the workers' compensation insurance costs to employers.

Plans in which overtime is *paid in advance* do not violate the pay requirements of the FLSA. In these plans, in weeks in which an employee works less than the applicable statutory workweek (e.g., 40 hours), the employer will advance the difference in pay to raise it to the standard for the statutory workweek. When overtime is worked, the advances (computed at the time and one-half rate) will offset the overtime pay. A running account must be maintained for each employee, and if the prepayment credits are not sufficient to cover the overtime compensation, the difference must be paid on the following payday.

In cases where an employee works at *different rates for different jobs* during the same workweek, the employers can, at their option, calculate the overtime in one of three ways. (1) One could pay at the higher rate for the overtime hours. (2) One could calculate it by taking the total earnings for both jobs, dividing by the total hours worked, then taking one-half of this rate, and multiplying by the overtime hours. (3) One could use an overtime rate based on the rate for the job performed after the 40th hour (the employee must have agreed to this in advance).

EXAMPLE 2-8

Steve Timko worked at two different pay rates during the past week. His main job paid $17.30/hour, while the extra job rate was $20.50. He worked the first 36 hours at Job "A" and 8 hours at Job "B."

Method (1)

Regular earnings	$ 622.80 (36 × $17.30)
Job B	$ 164.00 (8 × $20.50)
Overtime rate (higher rate)	$ 10.25 (0.5 × $20.50)
Overtime pay	$ 41.00 (4 × $10.25)
Total pay	$ 827.80 ($622.80 + $164.00 + $41.00)

Method (2)

Job A	$ 622.80 (36 × $17.30)
Job B	$ 164.00 (8 × $20.50)
Overtime rate (1/2)	$ 8.94 ($786.80 ÷ 44 × 0.5)
Extra overtime pay	$ 35.76 (4 × $8.94)
Total pay	$ 822.56 ($622.80 + $164.00 + $35.76)

Method (3)

Job A	$ 622.80 (36 × $17.30)
Job B	$ 164.00 (8 × $20.50)
Overtime pay (Job B)	$ 41.00 (4 × $10.25)
Total pay	$ 827.80 ($622.80 + $164.00 + $41.00)

Converting Weekly Wage Rates to Hourly Rates

When paying on a weekly basis, sometimes employers must convert the weekly wage rate to an hourly rate, especially to figure overtime earnings. To do this, divide the weekly wage rate by the number of hours in the regular workweek.

EXAMPLE 2-9

John Hazelton earns $412 a week for a workweek consisting of 40 hours. If Hazelton worked 43 hours in a particular week, compute gross pay as follows:

$$\$412.00 \div 40 \text{ hours} = \$10.30 \text{ hourly wage rate}$$
$$\$10.30 \text{ hourly wage rate} \times 1.5 = \$15.45 \text{ overtime wage rate}$$
$$\text{Gross pay} = \$412.00 + (3 \text{ hours} \times \$15.45) = \$458.35$$

Converting Biweekly Wage Rates to Hourly Rates

If paying employees biweekly, divide the biweekly earnings by 2 to arrive at the weekly rate, and divide the weekly rate by the standard number of hours.

Glenda Rome earns $980 biweekly and works a standard 40-hour workweek. Compute Rome's hourly and overtime rates as follows:

EXAMPLE 2-10

$$\$980.00 \div 2 = \$490.00 \text{ regular weekly earnings}$$
$$\$490.00 \div 40 = \$12.25 \text{ regular hourly rate}$$
$$\$12.25 \times 1.5 = \$18.38 \text{ overtime hourly rate}$$

Converting Monthly Salary Rates to Hourly Rates

If workers paid on a monthly basis earn overtime pay for work beyond a 40-hour week, compute the hourly overtime rate by converting the monthly salary rate to an hourly rate. To do this correctly, you must extend the monthly salary to an annual figure, divide by 52, and then divide by the regular number of hours worked each week.

Al Carmen earns $5,200 per month and works a standard 40-hour week. During one week, Carmen earned 6 hours of overtime.

EXAMPLE 2-11

Step 1
Convert the monthly salary rate to a weekly rate by first annualizing the monthly salary. Then divide the annual salary by 52 weeks.

$5,200 monthly salary × 12 months = $62,400 annual salary
$62,400 annual salary ÷ 52 weeks = $1,200 weekly salary

Step 2
Divide the weekly rate by the standard number of hours in the workweek.

$1,200 weekly salary ÷ 40 hours = $30.00 hourly rate

Step 3
Compute the overtime rate by multiplying the hourly rate by 1.5.

$30.00 hourly rate × 1.5 = $45.00 overtime rate

Step 4
Compute the *gross pay* for the week by adding the overtime earnings to the regular weekly earnings.

Regular weekly earnings	$1,200.00
Overtime earnings (6 × $45.00)	270.00
Gross pay	$1,470.00

Converting Semimonthly Salary Rates to Hourly Rates

Semimonthly salary rates are converted the same as monthly rates except semimonthly earnings are multiplied by 24 instead of by 12 to compute the annual earnings.

Margaret Johnson earns $1,175 semimonthly.

EXAMPLE 2-12

Step 1
Annualize the salary.

$1,175 × 24 = $28,200 annual rate

Step 2
Compute the weekly salary.

$28,200 ÷ 52 = $542.31 weekly rate

Step 3
Compute the hourly rate.

$542.31 ÷ 40 = $13.56 hourly rate

Step 4
Compute the overtime rate.

$13.56 × 1.5 = $20.34 overtime rate

Numerous tables of decimal equivalents, such as the one shown in Figure 2.5, help in converting wages to an hourly rate.

FIGURE 2.5

Table of Decimal Equivalents to Convert into Weekly, Hourly, and Hourly Overtime Salary Rates

To convert into:	Weekly Salary Rate	Hourly Salary Rate	Hourly Overtime Salary Rate
Multiply the:			
Weekly salary rate by	. . .	0.025	0.0375
Semimonthly salary rate by	0.4615	0.01154	0.0173
Monthly salary rate by	0.2308	0.00577	0.00866
Yearly salary rate by	0.01923	0.00048	0.000721

EXAMPLE 2-13

Weekly salary $550: $550 × 0.025 = $13.75 hourly rate; $550 × 0.0375 = $20.63 hourly overtime rate
Monthly salary $1,800: $1,800 × 0.00577 = $10.39 hourly rate; $1,800 × 0.00866 = $15.59 hourly overtime rate

Salaried Nonexempt Employees

LO 5

Identify distinctive compensation plans.

In order to cut administrative costs, salaries can be paid to nonexempt employees; however, these employees are still subject to the FLSA's overtime rules. The employee's *regular rate* of pay is found by dividing the number of *hours expected to be worked* each week into the weekly salary. The employee is then entitled to be paid at the regular rate of pay for the first 40 hours and at one and one-half times the regular rate of pay for the hours over 40.

If an employee's normal workweek is less than 40 hours, as long as an agreement exists between the employee and the employer that the salary covers all hours worked up to and including 40 hours, the employer does not have to pay for the "overtime hours" up to the 40 hours.

EXAMPLE 2-14

Rob Hau, a nonexempt employee, works a standard 35-hour week and is paid a salary of $1,080.00. Last week, Hau worked 39 hours and was paid his normal salary of $1,080.00 since he has an agreement with his employer that the salary covers all hours worked with the exception of the work hours over 40.

If he had worked 43 hours, his pay would have been:

Regular (up to 40 hours) = $1,080.00
Overtime pay:
$1,080.00 ÷ 35 = $30.86 per hour
$30.86 × 1.5 = $46.29
$46.29 × 3 = $138.87
$1,080.00 + $138.87 = $1,218.87 gross pay

Salaried with Fluctuating Workweek

Employers may pay employees who work fluctuating schedules a fixed salary, regardless of the number of hours worked.

Both parties must agree, prior to the workweek, that this pay calculation method will be used, and the salary must cover at least the minimum wage rate for the total hours worked each workweek. In such cases, overtime pay is found by dividing the normal salary by the total hours worked. An *extra half rate* is then paid for all hours worked over 40. Some states prohibit or limit the use of this method of payment.

Matt Leonard earns $739.20 a week with fluctuating workweek hours. If he worked 48 hours in one week, his gross pay would be calculated as follows:

EXAMPLE 2-15

$$739.20 \div 48 \text{ hours} = \$15.40 \text{ regular rate}$$
$$\$15.40 \times 0.5 = \$7.70 \text{ extra half pay rate}$$
$$8 \text{ hours O.T.} \times \$7.70 = \$61.60 \text{ extra pay}$$
$$\$739.20 + \$61.60 = \$800.80 \text{ weekly gross pay}$$

This calculation also applies to employees who receive a day rate compensation. The total pay for the week would be divided by the hours worked. The extra half rate would then be applied to the hours worked over 40 to determine the overtime pay.

An alternative method of calculating the overtime is to use the fixed salary divided by 40 hours to determine the regular rate of pay. This way, the overtime premium will be the same no matter how many hours are worked. This method eliminates the need to recalculate the regular rate of pay each week as the number of hours worked changes.[7]

Same as the example above.

EXAMPLE 2-16

$$739.20 \div 40 \text{ hours} = \$18.48 \text{ regular rate}$$
$$\$18.48 \times 0.5 = \$9.24 \text{ extra half pay rate}$$
$$8 \text{ hours O.T.} \times \$9.24 = \$73.92 \text{ extra pay}$$
$$\$739.20 + \$73.92 = \$813.12 \text{ weekly gross pay}$$

As a true "fixed salary arrangement," employers cannot make deductions from the salary for absences occasioned by the employee. The exception would apply to disciplinary deductions.

BELO Plan An alternative salary method to compensate employees working fluctuating schedules is the BELO plan. It is more restrictive than the fluctuating workweek method, and the following conditions must be met:

- Irregular work hours are the nature of the job.
- There are large variations in weekly hours above and below 40 hours.
- Rate of pay cannot include additional forms of compensation—bonuses, commissions, etc.
- Guaranteed compensation cannot be for more than 60 hours—beyond 60 hours requires one and one-half times the regular rate.
- Agreement must exist between the employer and the employee.

Basically, the salary is figured by calculating the wages for the maximum number of hours at straight time and then adding 50 percent (one-half) of the regular rate for the overtime hours.

The agreement between John Kalas and his employer provides for a pay rate of $14 per hour with a maximum of 48 hours per week.

EXAMPLE 2-17

$$48 \text{ hours} \times \$14 = \$672.00$$
$$8 \text{ hours} \times 0.5 \times \$14 = \underline{56.00}$$
$$\text{John's weekly salary} = \underline{\$728.00}$$

No matter how many hours John works each week (above and below 40), his gross pay would be $728.00. However, if John works beyond the agreed-upon maximum of 48 hours, he must be paid at one and one-half times his regular rate of pay (1.5 × $14 = $21) for the hours over 48.

---

7 Robert Ditmer, "Using a Fluctuating Worksheet May Save You Money," *PAYTECH,* April 2003, pp. 42–44.

SELF-STUDY QUIZ 2-3

Compute the hourly and overtime rates for a standard 40-hour workweek for the following amounts:

	Hourly Rate	Overtime Rate
1. $525.00 weekly	_____	_____
2. $892.00 biweekly	_____	_____
3. $1,450.00 semimonthly	_____	_____
4. $2,600.00 monthly	_____	_____

Piece Rate

Under the piece-rate system, the employer pays workers according to their output, such as an amount for each unit or piece produced. Thus, the wages increase as production increases. The employer keeps production records for each employee so that these records will be available when computing the wages earned by each employee. The Fair Labor Standards Act specifies that under a piece-rate system, the regular hourly rate of pay is computed as shown in the following example.

EXAMPLE 2-18

Sally Ray produced 13,000 items during a 40-hour workweek. Ray is paid 4 cents per unit and receives a bonus of 2 cents for each unit over 12,000 in a week. Ray's weekly earnings are:

Step 1
Add the total weekly earnings from piece rates and all other sources, such as incentive bonuses.

Regular earnings	$13,000 \times \$0.04 =$	$520.00
Incentive earnings	$1,000 \times \$0.02 =$	20.00
Total weekly earnings		$540.00

Step 2
Divide the weekly earnings by total number of hours worked in the week for which such compensation was paid.

$$\text{Total weekly earnings} \over \text{Total hours worked} \quad = \frac{\$540.00}{40} = \$13.50 \text{ per hour}$$

The piece rate must at least equal the statutory minimum wage rate. In some instances, an employer may pay a worker an hourly rate for some hours and a piece rate for other hours during the week. In such cases, both the hourly rate and the piece-rate earnings must be at least the minimum rate.

Overtime Earnings for Pieceworkers—Method A

For overtime work, the pieceworker is entitled to be paid, in addition to piecework earnings for the entire period, a sum equal to one-half the regular hourly rate of pay multiplied by the number of hours worked in excess of 40 in the week.

EXAMPLE 2-19

Paul Fritz produced 3,073 pieces in a 44-hour workweek and is paid $18\frac{3}{4}$ cents for every unit produced.

Step 1
Compute the total regular weekly earnings.

$3,073 \times \$0.1875 = \$576.19$ regular weekly earnings

Step 2
Compute the regular hourly rate of pay.

$\$576.19 \div 44 \text{ hours} = \$13.10$ regular hourly rate of pay

Step 3

Compute the overtime rate of pay and compute the overtime earnings. The regular earnings include the pay for the overtime hours at the regular rate. This is for the extra one-half time.

$$0.5 \times \$13.10 = \$6.55 \text{ overtime rate of pay}$$
$$4 \text{ hours} \times \$6.55 = \$26.20 \text{ overtime earnings}$$

Step 4

Compute the total regular and overtime earnings for the week.

$$\$576.19 + \$26.20 = \$602.39 \text{ piecework}$$
$$\text{and overtime earnings}$$

Overtime Earnings for Pieceworkers—Method B

Another method of computing overtime payment for pieceworkers complies with the requirements of the FLSA. Before doing the work, piece-rate employees may agree with their employer, in advance of the work being done, to be paid at a rate not less than one and one-half times the piece rate for each piece produced during the overtime hours. No additional overtime pay will be due to the employees.

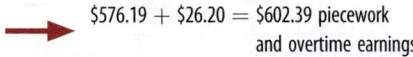

Assume that in the preceding example, Fritz earned overtime at a piece rate of one and one-half times the regular rate for all pieces produced during overtime hours. Of the total 3,073 pieces produced, 272 were produced in the 4 overtime hours. Fritz's total piecework and overtime earnings are as follows:

$$2,801 \times \$0.1875 = \$525.19 \text{ piecework earnings}$$
$$272 \text{ pieces} \times 0.2813 \ (\$0.1875 \times 1.5) = \$76.51 \text{ overtime earnings}$$
$$\$525.19 + \$76.51 = \$601.70 \text{ piecework and overtime earnings}$$

SELF-STUDY QUIZ 2-4

Bruce Eaton is paid 10 cents per unit under the piece-rate system. During one week, Eaton worked 46 hours and produced 5,520 units. Compute the following:

1. The piecework earnings $ _____
2. The regular hourly rate $ _____
3. The overtime hourly rate $ _____
4. The overtime earnings $ _____
5. The total earnings $ _____

Special Incentive Plans

Most wage systems involving special incentives are modifications of the piece-rate system described previously. Under many incentive plans, the company determines a standard for the quantity that an average worker can produce in a certain period of time. Workers failing to reach the standard earn a lower piece rate, while those who produce more than the standard receive a higher rate. With incentive plans, the computation of the payroll is usually more complicated than under the time-rate or piece-rate systems. Records of time worked as well as the production of each employee must be available in computing wages under most incentive plans.

ON THE NET

http://www.incentivelogic.com
There are companies that specialize in setting up different forms of employee incentive plans.

Chu Wang, Inc., pays its blade polishers according to the following piece-rate incentive plan:

No. of Blades Polished per 8-Hour Workday	Earnings per Blade Polished
less than 1,850	0.0150
1,850 to 1,999	0.0165
2,000 (Daily Standard)	0.0180
2,001 to 2,100	0.0198
2,101 to 2,250	0.0217
over 2,250	0.0240

Commissions

The entire remuneration, or at least part of the remuneration, of certain employees may be on a commission basis. A **commission** is a stated percentage of revenue paid to an employee who transacts a piece of business or performs a service. Thus, a salesperson working in a certain territory may have a fixed salary each year plus a bonus for sales in excess of a certain amount.

EXAMPLE 2-21

Kate Kline receives an annual $35,000 base salary for working a certain territory. A sales quota of $800,000 has been set for that territory for the current year. Kline will receive a 6 percent commission on all sales in excess of $800,000. For the current year, the sales in the territory are $1,030,000. The bonus paid Kline would be:

$13,800 (6% of $230,000)

Kline's total earnings for the year would be:

$48,800 ($35,000 + $13,800)

There are numerous variations of the commission method of remuneration. Some businesses offer special premiums or bonuses for selling certain merchandise. For example, to help move merchandise in a ready-to-wear department, a department store will frequently pay a premium or a bonus to the salesperson who sells specific items of merchandise. Commissions are considered to be payments for hours worked and must be included in determining the regular hourly rate. This applies regardless of whether the commission is the sole source of the employee's compensation or is paid in addition to a salary or hourly rate. It does not matter whether the commission earnings are computed daily, weekly, monthly, or at some other interval. However, in the case of outside salespeople who are exempt from the FLSA, commissions paid to them do not have to meet the minimum wage criteria.

Commissions are treated as straight-time pay. To calculate overtime, the weekly commission is divided by the *total hours* worked. This is the employee's regular rate of pay. The overtime pay would be one-half the regular rate of pay for all hours worked over 40 in the workweek.

Nondiscretionary Bonuses

A bonus that is part of employees' wage rates must be allocated to the wages for the period covered by the bonus. Bonuses that are known in advance, or that are set up as inducements to achieve goals, would fit into this category. The employer has only to add the bonus to the wages for the week and divide the sum by the total hours worked to determine the regular rate of pay. One-half of the regular rate would be the premium needed to apply to the overtime hours.

Garrison Heard earns $12.00 per hour and has earned a production bonus this week of $27.60. Since Heard worked 46 hours this week, his gross pay would be:

EXAMPLE 2-22

$$46 \text{ hours} \times \$12.00 = \$552.00 + \$27.60 = \$579.60$$
$$\$579.60 \div 46 \text{ hours} = \$12.60 \text{ regular rate of pay}$$
$$\$12.60 \times 0.5 = \$6.30 \times 6 \text{ hours} = \$37.80$$
$$\$579.60 + \$37.80 = \$617.40 \text{ gross pay}$$

Els Company instituted a perfect attendance program. The bonus ($2,184) is paid in January for the previous year. John Garcia worked 42 hours each week during the year and earned the bonus. The extra overtime pay due Garcia is:

EXAMPLE 2-23

$$\$2,184 \div 52 = \$42/\text{week}$$
$$\$42 \div 42 \text{ hours} = \$1.00 \text{ bonus for each hour}$$
$$\$1.00 \times 0.5 = \$0.50 \text{ extra overtime rate}$$
$$\$0.50 \times 2 \text{ overtime hours/week} \times 52 \text{ weeks} = \$52 \text{ extra earnings}$$

Profit-Sharing Plans

Many businesses have developed **profit-sharing plans** whereby the employer shares with the employees a portion of the profits of the business. Generally, profit-sharing plans include the following three types:

1. Cash payments based upon the earnings of a specified period.
2. Profits placed in a special fund or account to be drawn upon by employees at some future time. This plan may be in the form of a savings account, a pension fund, or an annuity.
3. Profits distributed to employees in the form of capital stock.

   The payments made pursuant to a bona fide profit-sharing plan that meets the standards fixed by the secretary of labor's regulations are not deemed wages in determining the employee's regular rate of pay for overtime purposes.

KEY TERMS

biweekly (p. 2-4)

commission (p. 2-28)

common-law relationship (p. 2-3)

continental system (p. 2-18)

discretionary bonus (p. 2-4)

domestic service (p. 2-3)

employee (p. 2-2)

enterprise coverage (p. 2-2)

exempt employees (p. 2-9)

gross earnings (p. 2-20)

individual employee coverage (p. 2-2)

nondiscretionary bonus (p. 2-4)

overtime premium (p. 2-21)

piece-rate system (p. 2-26)

principal activities (p. 2-13)

profit-sharing plans (p. 2-29)

salary (p. 2-4)

semimonthly (p. 2-4)

time card (p. 2-18)

time sheet (p. 2-18)

tip (p. 2-6)

tipped employee (p. 2-6)

wage (p. 2-4)

wages (p. 2-4)

workweek (p. 2-7)

ANSWERS TO SELF-STUDY QUIZZES

Self-Study Quiz 2-1
1. True.
2. False. Direct care workers employed by a family or individual are not covered if only performing fellowship and protection services.
3. True.
4. False. Individual employee coverage is not affected by the work of fellow employees.
5. True.

Self-Study Quiz 2-2
1. $ 2.13
2. $114.80 $ 290.00 ($7.25 × 40 hours)
             −85.20 weekly wage
             −90.00 tip credit claimed by employer
             $ 114.80

Self-Study Quiz 2-3

	Hourly Rate	Overtime Rate
1.	$13.13	$19.70
2.	$11.15	$16.73
3.	$16.73	$25.10
4.	$15.00	$22.50

Self-Study Quiz 2-4
1. $552.00
2. $12.00 ($552.00 ÷ 46)
3. $6.00 ($12.00 × 0.50)
4. $36.00 ($6.00 × 6)
5. $588.00

KEY POINTS SUMMARY

	Learning Objectives	Key Points	Problem Sets A & B
L01	Explain the major provisions of the Fair Labor Standards Act.	• Minimum wage ($7.25/hour) but tipped employees ($2.13/hour).	2-1, 2-2
		• Overtime pay at time and one-half for hours over 40.	
		• Exemption for white-collar workers (paid at least $455/week and meet "primary duty" requirements).	
		• Equal pay for equal work.	
		• Child labor laws (basic minimum is 16 years).	
L02	Define *hours worked*.	• Principal activities are indispensable to performance of productive work.	2-7
		• "Gray areas"—clothes-changing, travel, rest periods, meal periods, training.	
		• Preliminary/postliminary activities not counted unless by contract or custom.	
L03	Describe the main types of records used to collect payroll data.	• From time sheets to time cards to computerized record systems.	2-9, 2-10, 2-11
		• Next generation—biometrics.	

Learning Objectives	Key Points	Problem Sets A & B
L04 Calculate regular and over-time pay.	• Regular pay (hours worked × hourly rate of pay), overtime pay (hours over 40 × time and one-half the hourly rate).	2-3, 2-4, 2-5, 2-6, 2-8, 2-9, 2-11, 2-12, 2-13, 2-14, 2-15, 2-16
	• Converting weekly $\dfrac{\text{salary}}{\text{regular hours worked}}$ biweekly $\dfrac{\text{salary}}{2}$ = weekly semimonthly $\dfrac{\text{salary} \times 24}{52}$ = weekly monthly $\dfrac{\text{salary} \times 12}{52}$ = weekly	
L05 Identify distinctive compensation plans.	• Salaried nonexempt (salary ÷ hours expected to be worked = regular rate of pay, then one and one-half that rate for hours over 40).	2-17, 2-18, 2-19, 2-20, 2-21, 2-22
	• Fluctuating workweek (salary ÷ total hours worked with an extra half for hours over 40).	
	• Piece-rate $\dfrac{\text{piece-rate total}}{\text{hours worked}}$ = hourly rate of pay, then one-half rate for hours over 40.	
	• Commissions—treated as straight-time pay.	
	• Nondiscretionary bonuses—add to wages and divide total by hours worked to get regular rate of pay.	

MATCHING QUIZ

_____ 1. Biweekly
_____ 2. Commission
_____ 3. Tipped employee
_____ 4. Common-law relationship
_____ 5. Gross earnings
_____ 6. Individual employee coverage
_____ 7. Overtime premium
_____ 8. Exempt employees
_____ 9. Piece-rate system
_____ 10. Semimonthly

A. Remuneration paid twice a month
B. Exempt from some or all of the FLSA requirements
C. Employee engages in interstate commerce or produces goods for such commerce
D. Remuneration paid every two weeks
E. Employer has the right to control both what work will be done and how it will be done
F. Engaged in a job in which tips of more than $30 a month are regularly received
G. Payment to employee based on a stated percentage of revenue
H. Regular earnings plus overtime earnings
I. Pay system based on an amount paid to the employee per units produced
J. One-half the regular hourly rate

QUESTIONS FOR REVIEW

1. Explain the two bases of coverage provided by the FLSA.
2. In determining the existence of an employer/employee relationship, the IRS groups the items of evidence into which general categories?
3. What kinds of establishments may employ full-time students at 85 percent of the minimum wage?
4. What is Miami's living wage rate?
5. To what extent are tips considered wages under the FLSA?

6. Explain how a state employee working in the area of public safety may use compensatory time off in lieu of overtime compensation.

7. Under what conditions would an employee of a state receive cash for his or her compensatory time off?

8. The following employees are exempt from various requirements of the FLSA. Indicate from which requirement or requirements each of the following employees is exempt:
   a. Amusement park employee
   b. Taxicab driver
   c. Casual baby sitter
   d. Elementary school teacher
   e. Outside salesperson

9. What are the types of exempt white-collar employees?

10. What requirements need be met in order to be classified as a "highly compensated" employee?

11. In order not to interfere with the schooling and well-being of minors between the ages of 14 and 16, employers of these minors must satisfy what three conditions?

12. In determining the working time of employees, how are the principal activities of employees defined?

13. Under what conditions is travel time counted as time worked?

14. What is the difference between "engaged to wait" and "waiting to be engaged" as far as working time?

15. In order to get caught up, an employee takes work home. Must the employee be paid for this extra time?

16. When is time spent by employees in attending lectures and meetings for training purposes not counted as working time?

17. Under what conditions would preliminary and postliminary activities be counted as time worked?

18. How does a biometric time system identify an employee?

19. What is the Wage and Hour Division's position on the rounding off of fractional parts of an hour in determining an employee's time worked?

20. If the overtime premium approach is used, how is the overtime premium pay calculated?

21. Explain how to calculate the overtime hourly rate for employees who are paid biweekly.

22. In the case of a salaried nonexempt employee, how is the regular rate of pay determined?

23. How is overtime pay calculated for a nonexempt employee who works on fluctuating schedules and is paid a fixed salary?

24. Are commissions included in determining an employee's regular rate of pay?

25. What is a nondiscretionary bonus?

QUESTIONS FOR DISCUSSION

1. Abreu Company allows employees the option of carrying over unused vacation days or "cashing" them out. If they cash out, does the employer count the time or earnings when calculating overtime for these nonexempt employees?[8]

2. Along with many other companies, Sanchez Printers observes the Friday after Thanksgiving as a paid holiday. The company requires each employee to make up Friday's lost hours in the following workweek by working extra hours without pay. Is Sanchez Printers proceeding legally by requiring its employees to work extra hours without compensation to make up for the hours lost on the Friday holiday? Explain.

3. Lidle Company needs time to calculate employees' overtime payments by the end of the pay period in which the overtime is worked. Can it pay the overtime payments with the following period's paycheck?

4. The Payroll Department of DuMont has a policy of waiting one full week before correcting any paycheck errors of $30 or less. However, any pay shortages that exceed $30 are made up the same day. Also, any amounts less than $30 are made up the same day when the particular circumstances of the employees indicate that it would place an undue hardship on them to wait until the next pay one week later.

   Denise Harris, an order checker in DuMont's Shipping Department, discovered an error of $28.34 in her weekly check. When Harris reported the error, a payroll clerk informed her that she would have to wait until the next week's paycheck to recover the amount, since the underpayment was less than $30.

   What is your reaction to DuMont's policy of providing for paycheck corrections? Assume that Harris protests the delay and in court argues that her earned wages should be paid on the date due. As the judge hearing the case, how would you decide?

5. Mack Banta, a nonexempt account representative, worked extra hours this week as a call operator. A number of operators were out for the week and Banta was asked to pick up some of their hours. Can the company pay Banta at a lower pay rate for the hours he worked as an operator? These extra hours also pushed Banta's work time over 40 hours. How should the company calculate Banta's overtime pay?

PROBLEM SET · A

Special forms required to solve the problems are provided along with the problems in each chapter.

Note: In this chapter and in all succeeding work throughout the course, *unless instructed otherwise,* calculate hourly rates and overtime rates as follows:

1. Carry the hourly rate and the overtime rate to 3 decimal places and then round off to 2 decimal places (round the hourly rate to 2 decimal places before multiplying by one and one-half to determine the overtime rate).
2. If the third decimal place is 5 or more, round to the next higher cent.
3. If the third decimal place is less than 5, simply drop the third decimal place.
   Examples: Monthly rate $1,827
   Weekly rate ($1,827 × 12)/52 = $421.615 rounded to $421.62
   Hourly rate $421.62/40 = $10.540 rounded to $10.54
   O.T. rate $10.54 × 1.5 = $15.81

Also, use the minimum hourly wage of $7.25 in solving these problems and all that follow.

2-1A · LO 1 Similar to Example 2-4 on page 2-21

Carson Beck works at the local Worst Buy Shop. As a full-time student at the local university, he is being paid an hourly rate of $4.20 an hour. One week, Beck worked 37 hours.

a. Beck's earnings for the week are .... $ _____

b. Is the hourly rate in violation of the FLSA? Explain.

_____

_____

c. If the hourly rate is in violation of the FLSA, the amount the shop should pay Beck is .. $ _____

2-2A · LO 1 Similar to Example 2-1 on page 2-6

Ben Lieber is a waiter at Harbor House, where he receives a weekly wage of $80 plus tips for a 40-hour workweek. Lieber's weekly tips usually range from $280 to $400.

a. Under the Fair Labor Standards Act, the minimum amount of wages that Lieber must receive for a 40-hour workweek is .... $ _____

b. Since Harbor House is in violation of the FLSA, the additional amount it should pay Lieber each week to meet the minimum wage requirement for a tipped employee is ...... $ _____

2-3A · LO 4 Similar to Example 2-4 on page 2-21

The hours worked and the hourly wage rates for five employees of Kagan Company for the week ended September 9 follow.

a. For each employee, compute the gross earnings.
b. Compute the total gross earnings for all employees.

2-3A (concluded)

Employee	Hours Worked	Regular Hourly Wage Rate	(a) Gross Earnings
Darley, R.	38	$11.70	$
Waxman, B.	40	12.35	
Isaac, J.	37	13.00	
Bruner, H.	40	10.75	
Kellogg, P.	32½	12.40	
		(b) Total gross earnings	$

2-4A • LO 4   Similar to Example 2-6 on page 2-21

The wages and hours information for five employees of McNeese Enterprises for the week ended July 8 is given below. Employees work a standard 40-hour workweek and are paid time and one-half for all hours over 40 in each workweek.

a. For each employee, compute the regular earnings, overtime rate, overtime earnings, and total gross earnings.

b. Compute the total gross earnings for all employees.

Employee	Hours Worked	Regular Hourly Wage Rate	Regular Earnings	Overtime Rate	Overtime Earnings	Total Gross Earnings
Carman, T.	47	$ 12.45	$	$	$	$
Galasso, A.	42	11.90				
Jones, B.	48	10.85				
Rodna, G.	44	11.25				
Wilmon, W.	45½	13.40				
				(b) Total gross earnings		$

2-5A • LO 4   Similar to Example 2-3 on page 2-8

Gabrielle Hunter, a waitress at the Hole-in-the-Wall restaurant, worked 42 hours this week and collected over $500 in tips. The restaurant uses the full tip credit against the minimum wage and pays Hunter the minimum required for tipped employees. Determine her gross pay from the restaurant.

a. Pay for the 40 hours.. $ _____

b. Pay for the overtime hours .... $ _____

2-6A • LO 4   Similar to Example 2-13 on page 2-24

Connie Duffy started working for Dexter Company on Thursday of this week. She worked 9 hours on Thursday and 8 hours on Friday. Her annual salary is $80,000, and she is an exempt white-collar employee. Determine her gross pay for her first partial week of work.

Gross pay.............................. $ _____

2-7A • LO 2   Similar to Example 2-6 on page 2-21

John Porter is an hourly employee of Motter Company located in New York City. This week, Porter had to travel to the company's regional office in Albany. He left Sunday at noon and arrived in Albany at 3:00 P.M. During the week, he worked his normal 40 hours in the Albany office (Monday through Friday—9 A.M. to 5 P.M.). In addition, he attended the company's 4-hour work training session on Wednesday evening. Porter's hourly rate of pay is $14.80 per hour.

a. Porter's overtime earnings for the week are .... $ _____

b. Porter's total earnings for the week are... $ _____

2-8A • LO 4   Similar to Example 2-7 on page 2-21

Joseph Cavato is paid $12.96 per hour. During the past week, he worked 46 hours, and he is a covered employee who must be paid for overtime. Calculate his gross pay using the overtime premium approach.

a. Regular pay (46 hours) .... $ _____

b. Overtime premium pay .... _____

c. Gross pay .... $ _____

2-9A • LO 3, 4   Similar to Example 2-6 on page 2-21

The following time card shows the time worked one week by Ken Pace. The employer disregards any time before 8:00 A.M. or between 12:00 and 1:00 P.M. and after 5:00 P.M. Employees do not begin work until 8:00 A.M. or 1:00 P.M., and do not work beyond 5:00 P.M., unless they are asked to work overtime.

Hours worked beyond the regular 8-hour day and on Saturday are paid at one and one-half times the regular rate. Hours worked on Sunday are paid double the regular rate. Fractions of the hour for time worked are based on full quarter-hour increments.

No. 72 Name Ken Pace						(a)
Day	Morning		Afternoon		Overtime		Hours Worked
	In	Out	In	Out	In	Out	
M	7:50	12:00	12:50	5:01			
T	7:56	12:01	12:49	5:02	5:30	7:31	
W	7:59	12:02	12:58	5:03			
T	7:45	12:00	12:55	5:00	5:29	8:02	
F	8:01	12:01	1:00	5:01	6:00	7:30	
S	7:48	12:02					
S			2:00	6:03			
Total Hours Worked							
Remarks							

Pace's regular wage rate is $13.50 per hour, and the regular workweek is 40 hours with five 8-hour days. Compute:

a. The hours worked each day. (Ignore the one-minute tardiness on Friday.) .... _____

b. The total hours worked... _____

c. The regular earnings... $ _____

d. The overtime earnings... _____

e. The total earnings .... $ _____

2-10A • LO 3   **Similar to Example 2-4 on page 2-21**

Under the decimal system of computing time worked at Timmerman Company, production workers who are tardy are "docked" according to the schedule shown below.

Minutes Late in Ringing in	Fractional Hour Deducted
1 through 6	1/10
7 through 12	2/10
13 through 18	3/10
19 through 24, etc.	4/10

The regular hours of work, Monday through Friday, are from 7:30 to 11:30 A.M. and from 12:30 to 4:30 P.M. During one week, Henry Vanderhoff, who earns $12.15 an hour, reports in and checks out as shown below. Employees are not paid for ringing in a few minutes before 7:30 and 12:30 nor for ringing out a few minutes after 11:30 and 4:30.

(a)

DAY	AM		PM		HRS WORKED
	In	Out	In	Out	
M	7:28	11:31	12:29	4:31	
T	7:35	11:30	12:30	4:30	
W	7:50	11:33	12:27	4:32	
Th	7:27	11:31	12:50	4:33	
F	7:28	11:32	12:40	4:30	

Refer to the partial time card and compute:

a. The hours worked each day .... _____

b. The total hours worked .... _____

c. The gross earnings for the week .... $ _____

2-11A • LO 3, 4   **Similar to Example 2-4 on page 2-21**

Potts, Inc., recently converted from a 5-day, 40-hour workweek to a 4-day, 40-hour workweek, with overtime continuing to be paid at one and one-half times the regular hourly rate for all hours worked beyond 40 in the week. In this company, time is recorded under the continental system, as shown on the time card at the right.

Sue Ellen Boggs is part of the Group B employees whose regular workweek is Tuesday through Friday. The working hours each day are 800 to 1200; 1230 to 1630; and 1800 to 2000. The company disregards any time before 800, between 1200 and 1230, and between 1630 and 1800, and permits employees to ring in up to 10 minutes late before any deduction is made for tardiness. Deductions are made to the nearest 1/4 of an hour for workers who are more than 10 minutes late in ringing in.

Refer to the time card and compute:

a. The daily total hours .... _____

b. The total hours for the week .... _____

c. The regular weekly earnings .... $ _____

d. The overtime earnings (company rounds O.T. rate to 3 decimal places) .... _____

e. The total weekly earnings .... $ _____

2-11A (concluded)

Time		Mon	Tues	Wed	Thurs	Fri	Sat	
No. 160						Hr. Rate $10.45		
Name Sue Ellen Boggs						O.T. Rate $15.675		
Evening	Out		2002	2001	2005	2000		
Evening	In		1801	1809	1802	1800		
Afternoon	Out		1630	1631	1630	1635		
Afternoon	In		1230	1231	1230	1238		
Morning	Out		1200	1202	1200	1203	1201	
Morning	In		755	750	813	759	800	Total for Week
Daily Totals		(a)						(b)

Remarks *13 minutes late Thursday - deduct ¼ hr.*

2-12A • LO 4 Similar to Example 2-8 on page 2-22

Kyle Forman worked 47 hours during the week for Erickson Company at two different jobs. His pay rate was $14.00 for the first 40 hours, and his pay rate was $11.80 for the other 7 hours. Determine his gross pay for that week if the company uses the one-half average rate method.

a. Gross pay .... $ _____

b. If prior agreement existed that overtime would be paid at the rate for the job performed after the 40th hour, the gross pay would be .... $ _____

2-13A • LO 4 Similar to Example 2-9 on page 2-22

Barbara Ripa, a nonexempt employee, receives $695 for a regular 40-hour week and time and one-half for overtime. For a workweek of 45 hours, compute:

a. The regular earnings... $ _____

b. The overtime earnings .... _____

c. The total earnings .... $ _____

2-14A • LO 4 Similar to Example 2-11 on page 2-23

Cal DiMangino earns $2,875 each month and works 40 hours each week. Compute:

a. The hourly rate .... $ _____

b. The overtime rate at time and one-half .... $ _____

2-15A • LO 4   Similar to Example 2-14 on page 2-24

Sheila Williams, a medical secretary, earns $2,575 monthly for a 35-hour week. For overtime work, she receives extra pay at the regular hourly rate up to 40 hours and time and one-half beyond 40 hours in any week. During one semimonthly pay period, Williams worked 10 hours overtime. Only 2 hours of this overtime were beyond 40 hours in any one week. Compute:

a. The regular semimonthly earnings .... $ _____

b. The overtime earnings .... _____

c. The total earnings .... $ _____

2-16A • LO 4   Similar to Example 2-17 on page 2-25

Kenneth Caplan is a salaried employee who normally works a 37½-hour week and is paid a weekly salary of $675.00. The agreement that he has with his employer states that his salary is to cover all hours worked up to and including 40. This week, Caplan worked 42 hours. Calculate his gross pay.

Gross pay.. $ _____

2-17A • LO 5   Similar to Example 2-15 on page 2-25

Carrie Overwood works fluctuating work schedules. Besides her fixed salary of $1,050 per week, her employment agreement provides for overtime pay at an extra half-rate for hours worked over 40. This week she worked 48 hours. Compute:

a. The overtime earnings .... $ _____

b. The total earnings .... $ _____

c. If this was a BELO plan with a pay rate of $22.00 per hour and a maximum of 53 hours, how much would Overwood be paid for 48 hours? .... $ _____

2-18A • LO 5   Similar to Example 2-19 on page 2-26

During the first week in November, Erin Mills worked 45½ hours and produced 1,275 units under a piece-rate system. The regular piece rate is $0.45 a unit. Mills is paid overtime according to the FLSA ruling for overtime work under a piece-rate system. Compute:

a. The piecework earnings .... $ _____

b. The regular hourly rate .... $ _____

   The overtime hourly rate... $ _____

c. The overtime earnings .... $ _____

d. The total earnings .... $ _____

2-19A • LO 5   Similar to Example 2-20 on page 2-27

Refer to Problem 2-18A. Assume that Mills had agreed with her employer prior to the performance of the work that she would be paid one and one-half times the regular piece rate for all pieces produced during the overtime hours. Assume that her production totals for the week were 1,075 pieces during regular hours and 200 pieces during overtime hours. Compute:

a. The piecework earnings .... $ _____

b. The overtime earnings .... _____

c. The total earnings .... $ _____

2-20A • LO 5   Similar to Example 2-22 on page 2-29

Wendy Epstein, a sales representative, earns an annual salary of $29,500 and receives a commission on that portion of her annual sales that exceeds $150,000. The commission is 8.5% on all sales up to $50,000 above the quota. Beyond that amount, she receives a commission of 10%. Her total sales for the past year were $295,000. Compute:

a. The regular annual salary................ $ _____

b. The commission ....   _____

c. The total annual earnings............... $ _____

2-21A • LO 5   Similar to Example 2-22 on page 2-29

Jill Connor is employed as a salesperson in the men's department of Fashion Line. In addition to her weekly base salary of $440, Connor is paid a commission of 2% on her total net sales for the week (total gross sales less any customer returns). During the past week, to promote the sale of its fine cashmere sweaters, Fashion Line agreed to pay Connor an additional PM (push money) of 2% of the total net sales of cashmere sweaters. Connor's weekly sales tally is given below.

Item	Gross Sales	Customer Returns
Regular sweaters.........	$400	$48
Cashmere sweaters	995	75
Ties.............................	190	0
Dress shirts	445	39
Sports shirts	185	25

Compute Connor's total weekly earnings, showing her (a) weekly base salary, (b) commission, (c) PM, and (d) total weekly earnings.

a. Weekly base salary.. $ 440.00

   Weekly gross sales.. $ _____

     Less customer returns ....   _____

   Weekly net sales .... $ _____

b. Commission: $ _____ × 2%...   _____

   Weekly gross sales of cashmere sweaters .... $ _____

     Less customer returns ....   _____

   Weekly net sales of cashmere sweaters.. $ _____

c. PM: $ _____ × 2% ....   _____

d. Total weekly earnings .... $ ____

2-22A • LO 5   Similar to Example 2-23 on page 2-29

Casey Collins' average workweek during the first quarter of the year (13 weeks) was 43 hours. As part of his company's perfect attendance program, he earned a bonus of $975. Determine the extra overtime pay due Collins for the first quarter.

   Extra overtime pay .... $ _____

PROBLEM SET · B

Special forms required to solve the problems are provided along with the problems in each chapter.

Note: In this chapter and in all succeeding work throughout the course, **unless instructed otherwise,** calculate hourly rates and overtime rates as follows:

1. Carry the hourly rate and the overtime rate to 3 decimal places and then round of to 2 decimal places (round the hourly rate to 2 decimal places before multiplying by one and one-half to determine the overtime rate).
2. If the third decimal place is 5 or more, round to the next higher cent.
3. If the third decimal place is less than 5, simply drop the third decimal place.
   Examples: Monthly rate $1,827
                  Weekly rate ($1,827 × 12)/52 = $421.615 rounded to $421.62
                  Hourly rate $421.62/40 = $10.540 rounded to $10.54
                  O.T. rate $10.54 × 1.5 = $15.81

Also, use the minimum hourly wage of $7.25 in solving these problems and all that follow.

2-1B · LO 1   Similar to Example 2-4 on page 2-21

Genna Cross, a full-time student at Kirby University, is employed by The Boot Shop as a salesperson. Her hourly rate is $5.25. One week, Cross worked 33¼ hours.

    a. Cross's earnings for the week are .... $ _____

    b. Is the hourly rate in violation of the FLSA? Explain.

    _____

    _____

    c. If the hourly rate is in violation of the FLSA, the amount The Boot Shop should pay Cross is... $ _____

2-2B · LO 1   Similar to Example 2-1 on page 2-6

Bert Garro is a waiter at La Bron House, where he receives a weekly wage of $75 plus tips for a 40-hour workweek. Garro's weekly tips usually range from $300 to $350.

    a. Under the Fair Labor Standards Act, the minimum amount of wages that Garro must receive for a 40-hour workweek is .... $ _____

    b. Since La Bron House is in violation of the FLSA, the additional amount it should pay Garro each week to meet the minimum wage requirement for a tipped employee is....... $ _____

2-3B · LO 4   Similar to Example 2-4 on page 2-21

The hours worked and the hourly wage rates for five employees of Koogel Company for the week ended June 10 follow.

    a. For each employee, compute the gross earnings.

    b. Compute the total gross earnings for all employees.

2-3B (concluded)

Employee	Hours Worked	Regular Hourly Wage Rate	(a) Gross Earnings
Duffy, M.	35	$11.90	$ _____
Hazelton, G.	28	14.15	_____
Inman, T.	39½	10.90	_____
Palmer, C.	24½	16.40	_____
Diaz, O.	31	12.90	_____
		(b) Total gross earnings	$ _____

2-4B • LO 4   Similar to Example 2-6 on page 2-21

The wages and hours information for five employees of Somja Enterprises for the week ended April 1 is given below. Employees work a standard 40-hour workweek and are paid time and one-half for all hours over 40 in each workweek.

a. For each employee, compute the regular earnings, overtime rate, overtime earnings, and total gross earnings.

b. Compute the total gross earnings for all employees.

Employee	Hours Worked	Regular Hourly Wage Rate	Regular Earnings	Overtime Rate	Overtime Earnings	Total Gross Earnings
Wilson, H.	43	$ 11.90	$ _____	$ _____	$ _____	$ _____
Aha, C.	42	14.20	_____	_____	_____	_____
Shoup, K.	47	13.90	_____	_____	_____	_____
Carlyn, D.	41½	10.70	_____	_____	_____	_____
McMurray, J.	45	17.10	_____	_____	_____	_____
				(b) Total gross earnings		$ _____

2-5B • LO 4   Similar to Example 2-3 on page 2-8

Hunter Sobitson, a waiter at the Twentieth Hole restaurant, worked 43½ hours this week and collected over $650 in tips. The restaurant uses the full tip credit against the minimum wage and pays Sobitson the minimum required for tipped employees. Determine his gross pay from the restaurant.

a. Pay for the 40 hours......................... $ _____

b. Pay for overtime hours.................... $ _____

2-6B • LO 4   Similar to Example 2-13 on page 2-24

Cam Fitzer, a white-collar exempt employee, started working for Villan Company on Thursday of this week. He worked 9 hours on both Thursday and Friday. His annual salary is $77,000, and he is paid weekly for a 5-day week. Determine his gross pay for his first partial week of work.

Gross pay... $ _____

2-7B • LO 2   Similar to Example 2-6 on page 2-21

Jamie Kerr is an hourly employee of Noonan Company located in Los Angeles. This week, Kerr had to travel to the company's regional office in Santa Fe. He left Sunday at noon and arrived in Santa Fe at 3:30 P.M. During the week, he worked his normal 40 hours in the Santa Fe office (Monday through Friday—9 A.M. to 5 P.M.). In addition, he

2-7B (concluded)

attended the company's 3$\frac{1}{2}$-hour work training session on Wednesday evening. Kerr's hourly rate of pay is $16.90 per hour.

a. Kerr's overtime earnings for the week are .... $ _____

b. Kerr's total earnings for the week are .... $ _____

2-8B • LO 4   Similar to Example 2-7 on page 2-21

Peter Case is paid $13.76 per hour. During the past week, he worked 44 hours, and he is a covered employee who must be paid for overtime. Calculate his gross pay using the overtime premium approach.

a. Regular pay (44 hours) .... $ _____

b. Overtime premium pay .... _____

c. Gross pay .... $ _____

2-9B • LO 3, 4   Similar to Example 2-6 on page 2-21

The following time card shows the time worked one week by Hal Carsom. The employer disregards any time before 8:00 A.M. or between 12:00 and 1:00 P.M. and after 5:00 P.M. Employees do not begin work until 8:00 A.M. or 1:00 P.M., and do not work beyond 5:00 P.M., unless they are asked to work overtime.

Hours worked beyond the regular 8-hour day and on Saturday are paid at one and one-half times the regular rate. Hours worked on Sunday are paid double the regular rate. Fractions of the hour for time worked are based on full quarter-hour increments.

No.	72						(a)
Name	Hal Carsom						
Day	Morning		Afternoon		Overtime		Hours Worked
	In	Out	In	Out	In	Out	
M	7:47	12:00	12:50	5:01			
T	7:50	12:01	12:49	5:02	5:30	8:31	
W	8:05	12:02	12:58	5:03			
T	7:45	12:00	12:55	5:00	5:29	7:35	
F	8:01	12:01	1:00	5:01	6:00	8:01	
S	7:48	12:02					
S			2:00	6:03			
	Total Hours Worked						
Remarks_____							

Carsom's regular wage rate is $14.10 per hour, and the regular workweek is 40 hours with five 8-hour days. Compute:

a. The hours worked each day. (Ignore the one-minute tardiness on Friday.)............... _____

b. The total hours worked... _____

c. The regular earnings... $ _____

d. The overtime earnings .... _____

e. The total earnings .... $ _____

2-10B • LO 3   Similar to Example 2-4 on page 2-21

Under the decimal system of computing time worked at Carman's Company, production workers who are tardy are "docked" according to the schedule shown below.

Minutes Late in Ringing in	Fractional Hour Deducted
1 through 6	1/10
7 through 12	2/10
13 through 18	3/10
19 through 24, etc.	4/10

The regular hours of work, Monday through Friday, are from 7:30 to 11:30 A.M. and from 12:30 to 4:30 P.M. During one week, Bernard Hoskins, who earns $12.95 an hour, reports in and checks out as shown below. Employees are not paid for ringing in a few minutes before 7:30 and 12:30 nor for ringing out a few minutes after 11:30 and 4:30.

(a)

DAY	AM		PM		HRS WORKED
	In	Out	In	Out	
M	7:28	11:31	12:50	4:31	
T	7:35	11:30	12:30	4:30	
W	7:44	11:33	12:27	4:32	
Th	7:27	11:31	12:32	4:33	
F	7:34	11:32	12:40	4:30	

Refer to the partial time card and compute:

a. The hours worked each day .... _____

b. The total hours worked.. _____

c. The gross earnings for the week .... $_____

2-11B • LO 3, 4   Similar to Example 2-4 on page 2-21

Costa, Inc., recently converted from a 5-day, 40-hour workweek to a 4-day, 40-hour workweek, with overtime continuing to be paid at one and one-half times the regular hourly rate for all hours worked beyond 40 in the week. In this company, time is recorded under the continental system, as shown on the time card at the right.

Barbara Bansta is part of the Group B employees whose regular workweek is Tuesday through Friday. The working hours each day are 800 to 1200; 1230 to 1630; and 1800 to 2000. The company disregards any time before 800, between 1200 and 1230, and between 1630 and 1800, and permits employees to ring in up to 10 minutes late before any deduction is made for tardiness. Deductions are made to the nearest 1/4 of an hour for workers who are more than 10 minutes late in ringing in.

Refer to the time card and compute:

a. The daily total hours... _____

b. The total hours for the week .... _____

c. The regular weekly earnings.. $_____

d. The overtime earnings (company rounds O.T. rate to 3 decimal places)................... _____

e. The total weekly earnings .... $_____

2-11B (concluded)

No.	160			Hr. Rate	$13.85	
Name	Barbara Bansta			O.T. Rate	$20.775	

Time		Mon	Tues	Wed	Thurs	Fri	Sat	
Evening	Out		2002	2001	2005	2000		
	In		1801	1809	1802	1800		
Afternoon	Out		1630	1631	1630	1635		
	In		1230	1231	1230	1238		
Morning	Out		1200	1202	1200	1203	1201	
	In		755	750	825	759	800	Total for Week
Daily Totals	(a)							(b)

Remarks _25 minutes late Thursday – deduct ½ hr._

2-12B • LO 4 Similar to Example 2-8 on page 2-22

Kenneth Johanson worked 49 hours during the week for Luben Company at two different jobs. His pay rate was $15.00 for the first 40 hours, and his pay rate was $13.10 for the other 9 hours. Determine his gross pay for that week if the company uses the one-half average rate method.

a. Gross pay .... $ _____

b. If prior agreement existed that overtime would be paid at the rate for the job performed after the 40th hour, the gross pay would be .... $ _____

2-13B • LO 4 Similar to Example 2-9 on page 2-22

Pat Kunz, a nonexempt employee, receives $725 for a regular 40-hour week and time and one-half for overtime. For a workweek of 44 hours, compute:

a. The regular earnings.. $ _____

b. The overtime earnings.. _____

c. The total earnings .... $ _____

2-14B • LO 4 Similar to Example 2-11 on page 2-23

Carl La Duca earns $3,875 each month and works 40 hours each week. Compute:

a. The hourly rate .... $ _____

b. The overtime rate at time and one-half .... $ _____

2-15B • LO 4   Similar to Example 2-14 on page 2-24

Stefani Wilson, a medical secretary, earns $2,650 monthly for a 37½-hour week. For overtime work, she receives extra pay at the regular hourly rate up to 40 hours and time and one-half beyond 40 hours in any week. During one semimonthly pay period, Wilson worked 6 hours overtime. Only 2 hours of this overtime were beyond 40 hours in any one week. Compute:

  a. The regular semimonthly earnings .... $_____

  b. The overtime earnings.. _____

  c. The total earnings .... $_____

2-16B • LO 4   Similar to Example 2-17 on page 2-25

Jody Baush is a salaried employee who normally works a 35-hour week and is paid a weekly salary of $735.00. The agreement that he has with his employer states that his salary is to cover all hours worked up to and including 40. This week, Baush worked 42 hours. Calculate his gross pay.

  Gross pay... $_____

2-17B • LO 5   Similar to Example 2-15 on page 2-25

Colleen Prescott is a salaried employee who works fluctuating work schedules. She is paid a fixed salary of $920 each week, with an agreement with her employer that overtime (over 40 hours) will be paid at an extra half-rate, based on the actual hours worked. This week she worked 42 hours. Compute:

  a. The overtime earnings.. $_____

  b. The total earnings .... $_____

  c. If this was a BELO plan with a pay rate of $21 per hour and a maximum of
      45 hours, how much would Prescott be paid for 42 hours? .... $_____

2-18B • LO 5   Similar to Example 2-19 on page 2-26

During the first week in April, Courtney Nelson worked 46 hours and produced 1,450 units under a piece-rate system. The regular piece rate is $0.38 a unit. Nelson is paid overtime according to the FLSA ruling for overtime work under a piece-rate system. Compute:

  a. The piecework earnings .... $_____

  b. The regular hourly rate .... $_____

      The overtime hourly rate... $_____

  c. The overtime earnings.. _____

  d. The total earnings .... $_____

2-19B • LO 5   Similar to Example 2-20 on page 2-27

Refer to Problem 2-18B. Assume that Nelson had agreed with her employer prior to the performance of the work that she would be paid one and one-half times the regular piece rate for all pieces produced during the overtime hours. Assume that her production totals for the week were 1,120 pieces during regular hours and 330 pieces during overtime hours. Compute:

  a. The piecework earnings .... $_____

  b. The overtime earnings.. _____

  c. The total earnings .... $_____

2-20B • LO 5 Similar to Example 2-22 on page 2-29

Warrenda Spuhn, a sales representative, earns an annual salary of $34,500 and receives a commission on that portion of her annual sales that exceeds $150,000. The commission is 9.5% on all sales up to $50,000 above the quota. Beyond that amount, she receives a commission of 12%. Her total sales for the past year were $315,000. Compute:

a. The regular annual salary.. $_____

b. The commission .... _____

c. The total annual earnings... $_____

2-21B • LO 5 Similar to Example 2-22 on page 2-29

Maria Cohen is employed as a salesperson in the men's department of Lee's Fashions. In addition to her weekly base salary of $400 (35-hour week), Cohen is paid a commission of 1% on her total net sales for the week (total gross sales less any customer returns). During the past week, to promote the sale of its fine cashmere sweaters, Lee's agreed to pay Cohen an additional PM (push money) of 3% of the total net sales of cashmere sweaters. Cohen's weekly sales tally is given below.

Item	Gross Sales	Customer Returns
Regular sweaters................................	$600	$58
Cashmere sweaters	895	75
Ties..	190	0
Dress shirts	445	39
Sports shirts	585	45

Compute Cohen's total weekly earnings, showing her (a) weekly base salary, (b) commission, (c) PM, and (d) total weekly earnings.

a. Weekly base salary .... $ 400.00

    Weekly gross sales .... $_____

      Less customer returns .... _____

    Weekly net sales.. $_____

b. Commission: $_____ × 1% .... _____

    Weekly gross sales of cashmere sweaters................................ $_____

      Less customer returns .... _____

    Weekly net sales of cashmere sweaters .... $_____

c. PM: $_____ × 3% .... _____

d. Total weekly earnings .... $_____

2-22B • LO 5 Similar to Example 2-23 on page 2-29

Connie Gibbs collected a $2,000 bonus for her department's safety record for the year (52 weeks). During that year, Gibbs worked an average of 44 hours each week. Calculate the extra overtime pay due Gibbs for that year.

    Extra overtime pay .... $_____

CONTINUING PAYROLL PROBLEM • A   CLGL

In the Continuing Payroll Problem A, presented at the end of succeeding chapters, you will gain experience in computing wages and salaries and preparing a payroll register for Kipley Company, Inc., a newly formed corporation. At the end of subsequent chapters, information will be presented so that the payroll register can be completed step by step as you proceed through the discussion material relating to that particular section of the payroll register.

Kipley Company is a small manufacturing firm located in Pittsburgh, Pennsylvania. The company has a workforce of both hourly and salaried employees. Each employee is paid for hours actually worked during each week, with the time worked being recorded in quarter-hour increments. The standard workweek consists of 40 hours, with all employees being paid time and one-half for any hours worked beyond the 40 regular hours.

Wages are paid every Friday, with one week's pay being held back by the company. Thus, the first payday for Kipley Company is January 14 for the workweek ending January 8 (Saturday).

The information below will be used in preparing the payroll for the pay period ending January 8.

Time Card No.	Employee Name	Hourly Wage or Salary
11	Fran M. Carson	$ 17.50 per hour
12	William A. Wilson	17.25 per hour
13	Harry T. Utley	18.10 per hour
21	Lawrence R. Fife	17.90 per hour
22	Lucy K. Smith	19.75 per hour
31	Gretchen R. Fay	515 per week
32	Glenda B. Robey	2,700 per month
33	Thomas K. Schork	3,350 per month
51	Barbara T. Hardy	2,510 per month
99	Carson C. Kipley	52,000 per year

Ms. Glenda B. Robey prepares the time clerk's report for each pay period. Her report for the first week of operations is given below.

	TIME CLERK'S REPORT NO. 1								
	For Period Ending January 8, 20--								
	Employee	**Time Record**						**Time Worked***	**Time Lost**
		M	**T**	**W**	**T**	**F**	**S**		
11	Fran M. Carson	8	8	8	8	8	—	40	
12	William A. Wilson	8	8	8	8	8	8	48	
13	Harry T. Utley	8	5½	8	8	8	—	37½	2½ hrs. tardy
21	Lawrence R. Fife	10	10	8	8	10	—	46	
22	Lucy K. Smith	8	8	8	8	8	—	40	
31	Gretchen R. Fay	9	8	8	8	8	1¼	41¼	
32	Glenda B. Robey	8	8	8	8	8	—	40	
33	Thomas K. Schork	8	8	8	8	8	—	40	
51	Barbara T. Hardy	8	8	8	8	8	4	44	
99	Carson C. Kipley	8	8	8	8	8	—	40	

*All employees, except for Carson Kipley, are paid for hours worked beyond 40 at one and one-half times their regular hourly rate of pay.

Using the payroll register for Kipley Company, which is reproduced on a fold-out at the back of the book (PR-1), proceed as follows:

1. Enter each employee's time card number and name in the appropriate columns.
2. Record the regular hours and the overtime hours worked for each employee, using the time clerk's report as your reference.
3. Complete the Regular Earnings columns (Rate per Hour and Amount) and the Overtime Earnings columns (Rate per Hour and Amount) for each hourly employee. For salaried workers, complete the Regular Earnings column and show the hourly overtime rate and earnings only if overtime was worked.
4. Record the Total Earnings for each employee by adding the Regular Earnings and the Overtime Earnings.

Note: Retain your partially completed payroll register for use at the end of Chapter 3.

CONTINUING PAYROLL PROBLEM • B

In the Continuing Payroll Problem B, presented at the end of succeeding chapters, you will gain experience in computing wages and salaries and preparing a payroll register for Olney Company, Inc., a newly formed corporation. At the end of subsequent chapters, information will be presented so that the payroll register can be completed step by step as you proceed through the discussion material relating to that particular section of the payroll register.

Olney Company is a small manufacturing firm located in Allentown, Pennsylvania. The company has a workforce of both hourly and salaried employees. Each employee is paid for hours actually worked during each week, with the time worked being recorded in quarter-hour increments. The standard workweek consists of 40 hours, with all employees being paid time and one-half for any hours worked beyond the 40 regular hours.

Wages are paid every Friday, with one week's pay being held back by the company. Thus, the first payday for Olney Company is January 14 for the workweek ending January 8 (Saturday).

The information below will be used in preparing the payroll for the pay period ending January 8.

Time Card No.	Employee Name	Hourly Wage or Salary
11	Rob A. Mangino	$ 18.50 per hour
12	Inga C. Flores	19.25 per hour
13	Carson S. Palmetto	17.80 per hour
21	Randy F. Waters	20.70 per hour
22	Cathy T. Kroll	23.80 per hour
31	Carmen V. Ruppert	800 per week
32	William M. Scott	780 per week
33	Sarah A. Wickman	3,500 per month
51	Lucas T. Foley	4,500 per month
99	Marshal W. Olney	78,000 per year

Ms. Carmen V. Ruppert prepares the time clerk's report for each pay period. Her report for the first week of operations is given on the following page.

Using the payroll register for Olney Company, which is reproduced on a fold-out at the back of the book (PR-1), proceed as follows:

1. Enter each employee's time card number and name in the appropriate columns.
2. Record the regular hours and the overtime hours worked for each employee, using the time clerk's report as your reference.
3. Complete the Regular Earnings columns (Rate per Hour and Amount) and the Overtime Earnings columns (Rate per Hour and Amount) for each hourly employee. For salaried workers, complete the Regular Earnings column and show the hourly overtime rate and earnings only if overtime was worked.
4. Record the Total Earnings for each employee by adding the Regular Earnings and the Overtime Earnings.

Note: Retain your partially completed payroll register for use at the end of Chapter 3.

		Time Record						Time	Time
	Employee	M	T	W	T	F	S	Worked*	Lost
11	ROB A.MANGINO	8	8	8	8	8	—	40	
12	INGA C.FLORES	8	8	8	8	10	8	50	
13	CARSON S.PALMETTO	8	5½	8	8	9	—	38½	1 ½ hrs. tardy
21	RANDY F.WATERS	10	10	8	8	11	—	47	
22	CATHY T.KROLL	8	8	8	8	8	—	40	
31	CARMEN V.RUPPERT	8	8	8	8	8	1¼	41¼	
32	WILLIAM M.SCOTT	8	8	8	8	8	—	40	
33	SARAH A.WICKMAN	8	8	8	8	8	—	40	
51	LUCAS T.FOLEY	8	8	8	8	9	4	45	
99	MARSHAL W.OLNEY	8	8	8	8	8	—	40	

TIME CLERK'S REPORT NO. 1
For Period Ending January 8, 20--

*All employees, except for Marshal Olney, are paid for hours worked beyond 40 at one and one-half times their regular hourly rate of pay.

CASE PROBLEMS

C1. Reducing the Cost of Compensated Leave Time. LO 1.

For the past several weeks, Adele Delgado, payroll manager for Petrillo Packing Company, has been studying the mounting costs of accrued vacations and sick leave. Most of her firm's employees are entitled to two weeks' vacation each year and the privilege of accruing their vacation time for future use. Also, the workers have a generous sick-leave plan that reimburses them while they are ill at home or in the hospital.

Scanning the employees' accrued vacation times on the computer printout, Delgado notes the line entry for John Mannick. Mannick recently retired and cashed in

14 weeks of accrued vacation—all paid at his current wage, which was much more than when he originally earned the vacations. And, of course, the firm's payroll taxes for the accrued vacation payout were significantly increased.

Delgado also knows that some workers feel short-changed if they do not use their sick leave each year. They realize that if the leave is not used, they lose it for that year. Probably, she thinks, this accounts for those who regularly become ill on Mondays or Fridays.

What solutions can you offer to limit the cost of and more effectively manage the firm's policies for compensated leave time?

C2. Payment of Personal Time Off at Year-End. LO 5.

Huche Company allows its employees to carry over unused personal time off (PTO) days (vacation, sick days, etc.) from year to year. In addition, employees have the option to "cash out" their unused days at the end of the year.

John Keevens was just paid $685 for his unused PTO days. Since he is a nonexempt employee, John has questioned the amount of his last paycheck (which includes the $685). The PTO days push the paid hours over 40, and he wants to be paid for his overtime hours.

What would you tell John?

Social Security Taxes

I n this chapter's animated activities we see Emerald and Sons Company. What risks does Emerald and Sons Company take when they do not timely remit payroll taxes including social security taxes? Employers act as middlemen—collection agents for the federal government. Employers are required to do the following: file employment tax returns, fully pay taxes when due, make timely deposits, furnish wage and tax statements, file or provide information tax returns, and supply identification numbers.

Let's see how an employer acts as collection agent of payroll taxes, such as social security. We'll also learn the civil and criminal penalties that are awaiting unethical companies like Emerald and Sons.

LEARNING OBJECTIVES

After studying this chapter, you should be able to:

1 Identify, for social security purposes, those persons covered under the law and those services that make up employment.

2 Identify the types of compensation that are defined as wages.

3 Apply the current tax rates and wage base for FICA and SECA purposes.

4 Describe the different requirements and procedures for depositing FICA taxes and income taxes withheld from employees' wages.

5 Complete Form 941, Employer's Quarterly Federal Tax Return.

This chapter covers the government's old-age, survivors, and disability insurance benefits program (OASDI) and the retirees' health insurance program (HI). These programs are funded by social security and Medicare taxes imposed on employees and their employers. The taxes are calculated at a standard flat rate for every employee and employer. The statutes that provide the taxes include:

1. **Federal Insurance Contributions Act (FICA)**, which imposes two taxes on employees and two taxes on employers. One of the taxes finances the federal old-age, survivors, and disability insurance program (OASDI). The other finances the hospital insurance (HI), or Medicare, program.
2. **Self-Employment Contributions Act (SECA)**, which levies a tax upon the net earnings of the self-employed.

Coverage Under FICA

The retirement and disability parts of the social security program cover most workers in the United States. However, before an individual is considered to be "covered" for social security purposes, the following must be determined:

1. If the individual is an "employee," as defined by the common-law relationship of employer and employee.
2. If the service the individual renders is "employment," as defined by FICA tax law.
3. If the compensation the individual receives is "taxable wages," as defined by FICA tax law.

LO 1

Identify, for social security purposes, those persons covered under the law and those services that make up employment.

By identifying a "covered" employee and "covered" employment, it can then be determined who pays the tax and who will be entitled to benefits. An employee who is receiving social security benefits must pay the tax on his or her current earned wages. Part-time employees and seasonal employees are taxed in the same way as full-time employees.

Employer

Every **person** is an **employer** if the person employs one or more individuals for the performances of services in the United States, unless such services or employment are specifically exempted by the law. The term "person," as defined in the law, means an individual, a trust or estate, a partnership, or a corporation.

The term **employment** applies to any service performed by employees for their employer, regardless of the citizenship or residence of either. FICA covers most types of employment, but there are specific exclusions. Some types of employment are wholly exempt from coverage, and others are exempt only if the cash wages received are less than a stipulated dollar amount, as shown in Figure 3.1.

If an employee's services performed during one-half or more of any period constitute covered employment, then all the employee's services for that pay period must be counted as covered employment, and vice versa. In these cases, a pay period cannot exceed 31 consecutive days.

Employee

As explained in Chapter 2, the test used by the IRS to determine a worker's classification is the common-law test. Basically, if a business tells, or has a right to tell, a worker how, when, and where to work, then the worker is an employee.

Occupations Specifically Covered by FICA

In addition to the common-law test, FICA law also provides specific coverage for the following list of four occupations. Even though these workers are independent contractors under common law, they are treated by statute as employees.

FIGURE 3.1
Exempt Employment

Employment Type	Conditions of Exclusion
Agricultural services	Compensation of all farm workers is less than $2,500 in any calendar year, or compensation is less than $150 for each worker in a calendar year. Remuneration other than cash is not taxed.
Domestic service	Service performed in a local college club or a chapter of a college fraternity or sorority by a student who is *enrolled* and *regularly attending classes* at the school, college, or university.
Services performed by civilians for the U.S. government	Of any of its agencies if such agencies are specifically exempt from the employer portion of the FICA tax, or if such services are covered by a retirement system established by law.
Services performed by railroad workers	For employers covered by the Railroad Retirement Tax Act.
Services performed in the employment of foreign governments	Ambassadors, ministers, and other diplomatic officers and employees.
Services performed by an individual under the age of 18, as a newspaper distributor	Delivery or distribution of newspapers or shopping news, excluding delivery or distribution to a point for subsequent delivery or distribution.
Services performed by student nurses	In the employ of a hospital or a nurses' training school chartered or approved under state law, and the nurses are *enrolled* and *regularly attending classes* in that school. FICA exempts only the pay received by student nurses if the pay is nominal and their work is part time and an integral part of the curriculum.
Services performed by students for their public or private school, college, or university	Working as "noncareer" employees while enrolled academically at least half time (for undergraduates, at least six credit hours). This student FICA exception does not apply to an employee who regularly works 40 or more hours a week.

However, such persons are not covered by FICA if they have a substantial interest in the facilities used in connection with their jobs or if the services consist of a single transaction. The list includes:

1. *Agent-drivers* and *commission-drivers* who distribute food and beverage products or handle laundry or dry cleaning.
2. Full-time *life insurance salespersons.*
3. Full-time *traveling or city salespersons* for one firm or person.
4. An individual who works *at home* on materials or goods that you supply and that must be returned to you or to a person you name if you also furnish specifications for the work to be done.

Government Employees

Different rules apply.

- Federal   Hired after 1983—full coverage.
                      Hired prior to 1984—only Medicare (HI) applies.
- State and local   Work done after July 1, 1991, and not in public retirement plan—full coverage.
                      Hired after March 31, 1986, and covered by a public retirement plan—Medicare (HI) only.
- Military   Basic pay—full FICA taxes.
                      Excess of basic pay—not subject to FICA tax.
                      Temporary service with National Guard—difference in pay covered by civilian employer—subject to FICA tax.

International Agreements

Totalization agreements with over 20 foreign countries have eliminated dual taxation and dual coverage. Inpatriates (employees transferred from a foreign country to company's home country) who are working in the United States from one of these countries will not have social security taxes withheld on U.S.-sourced income. If the worker is from a country that has no such agreement, social security tax must be withheld.

Expatriates (employees transferred from company's home country to foreign country) will be subject to U.S. social security tax and could also be subject to foreign social security taxes.

Family Employment

Work performed for a parent by a child under the age of 18 is exempt from FICA. If the work is not in the course of the parent's business and the child is under 21, the exemption also applies. However, if the child's services are done for a corporation, a partnership (unless each partner is a parent of the child), or an estate, the exemption does not apply.

Household Employee

If a worker performs household services in or around your home subject to your will and control, as to both what must be done and how it will be done, that worker is your household employee. It does not matter whether you exercise this control as long as you have the legal right to control the method and result of the work.

However, in order for the household employee and the employer to be liable for the FICA taxes, the household employee must receive *$1,900 or more in cash wages* from any one employer in the year.[1] Household employees do not include people (a) who work for you in your business; (b) who follow an independent trade, business, or profession in which they offer services to the general public; and (c) who are under the age of 18 unless their principal occupation is household employment.

ON THE JOB

Some examples of workers who may be household employees include:

- Babysitters   • Gardeners
- Caretakers   • Nannies
- Cooks   • Housekeepers
- Drivers   • Maids

---

1 For election workers, it is $1,600 or more.

Exempt Employees

Employees of not-for-profit organizations are subject to FICA taxes. Some services, such as those performed by duly ordained ministers of churches, remain exempt from FICA taxes, but the individuals are then subject to self-employment tax on their net earnings. Ministers, certain members of religious orders, and Christian Science practitioners previously electing exemption from social security coverage may now be covered by filing a waiver form with the IRS. Once an election to be covered by social security is made, it is irrevocable.

The following are also exempt from both the OASDI and HI portions of the tax:

- Medical interns.
- Student nurses.
- Inmates of U.S. penal institutions.
- Those serving temporarily in case of emergency (storm, flood, etc.).

Voluntary Coverage

Coverage under FICA can be extended to certain classes of services that otherwise would be excluded. For example, service in the employ of a state or local government that began prior to April 1, 1986, is still exempt for the OASDI portion of the FICA tax. However, coverage can be extended to these employees by means of a voluntary agreement entered into by the state and secretary of health and human services. When a state elects voluntary coverage, it becomes responsible for the collection and payment of the FICA tax as if it were covered employment.

SELF-STUDY QUIZ 3-1

Which of the following are covered by FICA (indicate Yes or No)?

_____ 1. Andrian Mitchell, a full-time life insurance salesperson.
_____ 2. John Sain, a federal government employee, hired in 1990.
_____ 3. Bonnie Stone, a real estate agent.
_____ 4. Stuart Schuck, who offers lawn care service to homeowners in the neighborhood.

Note: Answers are on page 3-30.

Independent Contractor

The FICA tax law identifies **independent contractors** as persons who follow an independent trade, business, or profession where they offer their services to the public. The Small Business Administration estimates that nearly 5 million workers are independent contractors. The test in Figure 3.2 determines independent contractor status.

Employers do not pay or withhold payroll taxes on payments made to independent contractors. However, the individual contractors are liable for social security taxes (self-employment taxes) on the net earnings of their businesses.

Misclassifying employees carries a penalty for the employer. Generally, the penalty will be the employer's share of FICA taxes plus the income and FICA taxes that were not withheld from the employee's earnings. If the employee did report the earnings on his or her federal tax return, the penalty is voided. If not reported, the employer may qualify for a reduced rate of 1.5 percent of the employee's wage if a Form 1099 (see page 4-29) was filed (3.0 percent if not filed). A reduced rate might also apply to the employee's share of FICA taxes—20 percent of the full FICA tax if Form 1099 was filed (40 percent if not filed).

FIGURE 3.2

Test for Independent Contractor Status

Workers *may* be classified as independent contractors if they:
1. Hire, supervise, and pay assistants.
2. Determine the sequence of their work.
3. Set their own hours of work.
4. Work for as many employers as they wish.
5. Are paid by the job.
6. Make their services available to the public.
7. Have an opportunity for profit or loss.
8. Furnish their own tools.
9. Have a substantial investment in their trade.
10. May be dismissed only under terms of contract.

Taxable Wages

The amount of wages paid by employers to their employees during the calendar year determines the amount of OASDI/HI taxes. The basis of payment may be hourly, daily, weekly, biweekly, semimonthly, monthly, annually, piece rate, or a percentage of profits. Wages include the following:

1. Actual money received by employees, whether called wages or salaries.
2. Cash value of meals and lodging provided for the convenience of the *employees*.
3. Bonuses and commissions paid by the employer with respect to employment.

Other common types of payments that are considered wages under FICA are listed in Figure 3.3 (on page 3-6).

Tips

FICA considers cash tips of $20 or more in a calendar month to be taxable wages. Employees must report their tips in writing to their employers by the 10th of the month following the month in which the tips were received. Employers can require more frequent reporting. Rules for reporting tips by employees and employers are summarized as follows:

1. Employees can report tips on *Form 4070, Employee's Report of Tips to Employer*, shown in Figure 3.4 (on page 3-7).
2. Employees failing to report tips to their employers may be penalized 50 percent of the FICA tax due on the tips. The tax court may rule that the non-reporting of tip income constitutes fraud.
3. Employers must collect the employee's FICA tax on the tips that each employee reports. The employer deducts the employee's FICA tax from the wages due the employee or from other funds the employee makes available. The employer should deduct the FICA taxes (on the reported tips plus the wage payment) from the first pay after the reporting of the previous month's tips.
4. Employers are also liable for their share of the FICA tax on any tips subject to the employee's FICA tax. Employers are allowed a business tax credit (Form 8846) on their income tax return for FICA taxes paid on their employees' tip income.
5. Large food and beverage establishments (11 or more employees where tipping is customary) are required to allocate to their tipped employees the excess of 8 percent of the establishment's gross receipts over the tips actually reported by their employees. However, employers withhold FICA taxes only on the tips reported by employees, not from tips that are allocated. The amount of allocated tip income is shown separately on the employee's *Wage and Tax Statement (Form W-2)*, explained in Chapter 4.

LO 2

Identify the types of compensation that are defined as wages.

ON THE JOB

Many restaurants now use software to help in tracking tips. Some programs add a "prompt" that freezes the computer screen as employees try to clock out if they have not entered their tips for the day.

6. Every large food or beverage establishment must report the amount of its receipts from food and beverage operations annually to the IRS and the amount of tips reported by its employees. [*Form 8027, Employer's Annual Information Return of Tip Income and Allocated Tips* (not illustrated)]

7. Employers can claim a credit for social security and Medicare taxes paid on certain employees' tips on *Form 8846, Credit for Employer Social Security and Medicare Taxes Paid on Certain Employee Tips.* The tips on which the credit is claimed is the amount of tips in excess of those treated as wages for purposes of satisfying the minimum wage.

FIGURE 3.3

Other Types of Taxable Wages

Type of Wage	Conditions
Advance payments	For future work to be done by the individual receiving the advance where the employer considers the work satisfaction for the advance.
Back-pay awards	Pay received in one period for employment in an earlier period, unless it is a settlement for failure to employ workers.
Bonuses	For services rendered by employees for an employer.
Cash and noncash prizes and awards	For outstanding work, exceeding sales quotas, contributing suggestions that increase productivity or efficiency.
Christmas gifts	Except noncash gifts of nominal value (such as a turkey or a ham).
Commissions	On sales or insurance premiums paid as compensation for services performed.
Death benefits	Wage payments (not gratuity) to an employee's beneficiaries or estate after the employee's death. Payments made after the calendar year in which the employee died and employer-provided death-benefit plans are not taxed.
Employees' federal income and social security taxes paid for by the employer	Payment of the employee portion of the FICA tax by the employer for domestics working in the employer's home and for agricultural laborers is an exception to this rule.
Fringe benefits—noncash	Personal use of company car, employer-provided vehicles for commuting, flights on employer-provided airplanes, and free or discounted flights on commercial airlines.
Guaranteed annual wage payments	Union contract agreements whereby an employer guarantees certain employees will either work during or be paid for each normal workweek in a calendar year.
Idle time or standby payments	Amounts paid workers who are at the beck and call of an employer but who are performing no work.
Insurance premiums paid by the employer for an employee's group-term life insurance coverage	Exceeding $50,000 of coverage. For retired workers, their group-term life insurance that exceeds $50,000 is also subject to FICA.
Jury duty pay	The difference between the employee's regular wages and the amount received for jury duty, paid by employers.
Moving expense reimbursements	Unless the employee will be entitled to deduct these moving expenses in determining taxable income for federal income tax purposes.
Retroactive wage increases	Treated as wages in the period paid.
Severance pay	Severance payments are taxable wages for FICA.
Sick pay—first six months	For sickness or accident disability. Payments under a state temporary disability law are also subject to FICA taxes.
Stock payments	The fair market value of stock transferred by employers to employees as remuneration for services.
Vacation pay	Whether the leave is taken or not.

FIGURE 3.4

Form 4070, Employee's Report of Tips to Employer

Form **4070** (Rev. August 2005) Department of the Treasury Internal Revenue Service	**Employee's Report of Tips to Employer**	OMB No. 1545-0074	

Employee's name and address Carmen T. Perez 1704 Elm St., San Diego, CA 92121-8837a	Social security number 000 : 00 : 7220	
Employer's name and address (include establishment name, if different) Holland House Inn 9 Fairway, San Diego, CA 92123-1369	**1** Cash tips received $389.10	
	2 Credit and debit card tips received —	
	3 Tips paid out —	
Month or shorter period in which tips were received from July 1, 20-- , to July 31, 20--	**4** Net tips (lines **1 + 2 - 3**) $389.10	
Signature *Carmen T. Perez*	Date August 10, 20--	

For Paperwork Reduction Act Notice, see the instructions on the back of this form.   Cat. No. 41320P   Form **4070** (Rev. 8-2005)

Source: Internal Revenue Service.

An alternative tip reporting method (*The Attributed Tip Income Program—ATIP*) can be used. Under ATIP, a formula based on the employer's credit card sales determines the amount of tips that must be reported to the IRS. The employer then assigns the required amount of tips among all tipped employees. To be eligible to use ATIP, the employer must have at least 20 percent of its gross receipts from charged receipts that show charged tips and at least 75 percent of its tipped employees must sign a participation agreement.

Exempt Payments

FICA tax only applies to types of compensation considered taxable under the law. Examples of compensation that the law excludes from the tax follow.

Meals and Lodging FICA exempts the value of meals or lodging furnished to employees for the *convenience of the employer*. The value of meals or lodging not meeting this test will be subject to FICA tax. The IRS places no specific value on meals or lodging furnished by employers to employees. Instead, the IRS relies on state valuations. Where a state has no law or regulation on the subject, fair value is defined as the reasonable prevailing value of the meals or lodging.

Sick Pay The *first six months of sick pay* an employee receives is considered wages and is subject to FICA tax. Payments made *after* the expiration of the six consecutive calendar months following the last month in which the employee worked for the employer are not taxed. The period off the job must be continuous for six months. Any return to work starts a new six-month period. FICA defines sick pay as any payment made to individuals due to personal injury or sickness that does not constitute wages. Sick pay payments must be part of a plan to which the employer is a party. Sick pay must not include amounts paid to individuals who are permanently disabled.

Sick pay payments may also be made by a third party, including insurance companies, trusts providing sick and accident benefits, and employers' associations funded to pay sickness and accident benefits. The third party is treated as a separate employer and must withhold and deposit the employees' FICA taxes.

ON THE NET

http://www.ssa.gov/ **Social Security Online**. Maintained by the Social Security Administration, it contains general FICA information. http://www.socialsecurity.gov /employer/ "Employer W-2 Filing Instructions & Information."

However, the third party may be relieved of the liability for the employer's share of the FICA taxes if the third party fulfills each of these requirements:

1. Withholds and deposits the employee portion of the FICA tax.
2. Notifies the employer of the amount of wages or compensation involved.

The liability for that share of the taxes then reverts back to the employer. For convenience, an employer may contract to have the third party deposit the employer portion of the tax as well as the employee portion.

Generally, payments made to employees or their dependents for medical or hospital expenses in connection with sickness or accident disability are not considered wages. However, these payments must be part of a plan established by the employer for all employees or for a particular class of employees. However, employer payments made directly to employees and their dependents in lieu of health insurance coverage are taxable wages.

Makeup Pay for Military Duty Wage supplements paid by employers to cover the difference between employees' salary and their military pay or payment of their full salary are exempt from FICA and Medicare taxes (though subject to income tax withholding). This applies to active-duty soldiers and reservists activated for *more than 30 days.*

Contributions to Deferred Compensation Plans

Employee pretax (federal income tax) contributions under a qualified cash or deferred compensation arrangement (*Tax-Deferred Retirement Plans*, as discussed in Chapter 4) are subject to FICA tax. However, the employers' matching contributions are tax-free.

Over the Line

The University of Pittsburgh made early retirement payouts to tenured faculty, which were treated as FICA nontaxable since the payments were for the surrender of tenure rights (a property transaction not subject to FICA taxes). The IRS contended that the rights relinquished were gained through the employees' past services and, therefore, were a form of compensation for services rendered. The U.S. Court of Appeals ruled that tenure is a form of compensation for past services and the purpose was to provide for employees' early retirement (paid like severance payments), and, as such, the payments were taxable.[2]

Payments for Educational Assistance

Educational assistance refers to the expenses that an employer pays for an employee's education, such as tuition, fees, and payments for books, supplies, and equipment. Also, educational assistance includes the cost of employer-provided courses of instruction (books, supplies, and equipment). Educational assistance excludes payment for tools or supplies that employees keep after they complete a course of instruction. Payments for job-related educational expenses are not subject to FICA taxes if the education maintains or improves skills required by the individual's employment. Payments for non–job-related educational expenses up to $5,250 are also exempt from FICA taxes.

---

2 *Payroll Manager's Letter,* Aspen Publishers, March 7, 2008, Volume 24, No. 5, p. 4.

SELF-STUDY QUIZ 3-2

Which of the following are subject to FICA tax (indicate Yes or No)?

_____ 1. A $15 gift certificate for a local grocery store given to employees as a Christmas gift.

_____ 2. Sales representatives using their company cars for personal use on weeknights and weekends.

_____ 3. Employer's contributions to a Simplified Employee Pension Plan (SEP) for its employees.

_____ 4. A tuition reimbursement plan that pays tuition for employees successfully completing job-related courses.

_____ 5. Severance pay made to an employee discharged for theft.

Tax Rates

> **LO 3**
>
> Apply the current tax rates and wage base for FICA and SECA purposes.

The Social Security Act, as amended, imposes a separate tax on employees and employers for old-age, survivors, and disability insurance (OASDI) benefits and for hospital insurance (HI) benefits. The 2015 tax rates for both the employee and the employer portions of the tax follow:

	Rate	Wage Base	Maximum Tax
Employee and Employer OASDI:	6.20%	$118,500	$7,347
Employee* and Employer HI:	1.45%	No limit	No maximum

*Employee HI: Plus an additional 0.9% on wages over $200,000.

Taxable Wage Base

The employer must consider the **taxable wage base** when computing the OASDI portion of the FICA tax. The law exempts wages that exceed this base during the calendar year ($118,500 for 2015, *please see "AS WE GO TO PRESS" for estimated 2016 OASDI*). Once the OASDI taxable wage base has been reached, all payments made to the employee during the remainder of the year are not taxable. The wage base applies to amounts *paid* employees in a calendar year and not to the time when the services were performed by the employees. The HI portion of the FICA tax is 1.45 percent withheld on total earnings plus an additional 0.9 percent on wages over $200,000. The employer does not "match" the Employee's Supplemental HI rate of 0.9 percent on wages in excess of $200,000. The employer HI rate is 1.45 percent on all wages. Just as social security benefits increase each year based on changes in the Consumer Price Index, the taxable wage base is increased also.

This means that an employee who makes $34,000 would pay the FICA tax (6.2% + 1.45%) on his or her total earnings, while an employee who makes $1 million would pay the HI portion (1.45%) on his or her total earnings plus additional HI tax (0.9%) on wages in excess of $200,000, but only $118,500 of the $1 million would be taxed at 6.2 percent.

WASHINGTON UPDATE

RECENT LEGISLATION INCLUDED A SPECIAL 3.8 PERCENT MEDICARE SURTAX ON NET INVESTMENT INCOME OF SINGLE FILERS WITH MODIFIED ADJUSTED GROSS INCOME OVER $200,000 AND OVER $250,000 FOR JOINT FILERS. PLEASE SEE "AS WE GO TO PRESS" FOR THE MOST CURRENT UPDATES.

Determining OASDI Tax:

If:

Cumulative Wages	+	Current Wage Payment	<	OASDI Wage Base, then
$52,400	+	$6,000	=	$58,400

compute the OASDI tax on the entire wage payment. ($6,000 × 0.062 = $372.00)

If:

Cumulative Wages	+	Current Wage Payment	>	OASDI Wage Base, then
$108,800	+	$16,000	=	$124,800

compute the OASDI tax on the part of the current wage payment that brings the cumulative wages up to the OASDI taxable wage limit. ($108,800 + $9,700 = $118,500)

$$\$9,700 \times 0.062 = \$601.40$$

Employees' FICA (OASDI/HI) Taxes and Withholdings

FICA requires employers to collect the OASDI/HI taxes from their employees and pay the taxes to the IRS at the same time they pay their own tax. The employer deducts the tax from the wages at the time of payment. The amount of each tax to be withheld is computed by applying to the employee's taxable wages the tax rate in effect at the time that the wages are received. In calculating the amounts of FICA taxes to withhold from employees' pays, the employer may disregard any fractional part of a cent, unless it is one-half cent or more, which must be rounded up one cent.

Ruth Engle receives pay on January 1, 2016, for work done during the last week of December 2015. The wages would be taxed as income in the calendar year 2016, using 2016 tax rates.

The liability for the tax extends to both the employee and the employer, but after the employer has collected the tax, the employee's liability ceases. The following examples illustrate the computation of the FICA taxes to be withheld.

EXAMPLE 3-1

1. Casey Berra, employed by Gobel Company, earned $460 during the week ended January 29, 2016. Prior to January 29, Berra's cumulative gross earnings for the year were $2,765.70. FICA taxes to be withheld on $460 are computed as follows:

OASDI		HI	
Taxable Wages..................................	$ 460	Taxable Wages............................	$ 460
Tax Rate	× 6.2%	Tax Rate	× 1.45%
OASDI Tax to Be Withheld..............	$ 28.52	HI Tax to Be Withheld	$ 6.67

2. Francis Aha, a salaried employee of Wilson Advertising Agency, is paid every Friday. She earned $1,925 for this pay. Prior to the pay of November 4, 2016, she had earned $118,050. The FICA taxes to be withheld from Aha's pay on November 4 are computed as follows:

OASDI		HI	
Taxable Wage Limit........................	$118,500	Taxable Wage Limit...................	NONE
Wages Paid to Date........................	118,050	Wages Paid to Date...................	$118,050
Taxable Wages This Pay.................	$ 450	Taxable Wages This Pay.............	$ 1,925
Tax Rate	× 6.2%	Tax Rate	× 1.45%
OASDI Tax to Be Withheld..............	$ 27.90	HI Tax to Be Withheld	$ 27.91

(continued)

3. Marc Todd, president of Uni-Sight, Inc., is paid $5,200 semimonthly. Prior to his last pay on December 23, 2016, Todd had earned $119,600. The FICA taxes to be withheld from Todd's pay on December 23 are computed as follows:

OASDI		HI	
Taxable Wage Limit..........................	$118,500	Taxable Wage Limit....................	NONE
Wages Paid to Date..........................	119,600	Wages Paid to Date....................	$119,600
Taxable Wages This Pay..................	$ -0-	Taxable Wage This Pay..............	$ 5,200
OASDI Tax to Be Withheld...............	$ -0-	Tax Rate	×1.45%
		HI Tax to Be Withheld	$ 75.40

4. Jennifer Matthews employed by Quality Company is paid $5,000 weekly. Prior to the pay of September 30, she had earned $200,000. The FICA taxes to be withheld from Jennifer's pay on September 30 are computed as follows:

OASDI		HI	
Taxable Wage Limit..........................	$118,500	Taxable Wage Limit (applicable	
Wages Paid to Date..........................	200,000	on Wages at 1.45%)...........	NONE
Taxable Wages this Pay	-0-	Wages paid to date....................	$200,000
OASDI to be Withheld......................	$ -0-	Taxable Wage this Pay..............	$ 5,000
		Tax Rate	1.45%
		HI Tax to Be Withheld	$ 72.50
		Additional .9% HI Tax on wages in	
		excess of $200,000 = $5,000	
		× 0.9% =	45.00
		Total HI Tax to be Withheld......	$ 117.50

Sometimes an employee has paid FICA taxes on wages in excess of the taxable base because of having worked for more than one employer. If so, the employee is entitled to a refund for the overpayment. The amount of the overpayment is credited against the employee's federal income taxes for that year. Instructions are given on the ***Individual Income Tax Return (Form 1040)*** that explain how the overpayment should be treated.

Employer's FICA (OASDI) Taxes

In addition to withholding the correct amount of FICA tax from the employees' taxable earnings, the employer must make contributions to the program. The employer's portion of the tax is based on the wages paid to the employees. The employer's taxes, however, are not computed on the wages paid each employee, but on the total taxable wages paid all employees. As with employee withholdings, once the OASDI taxable wage base is reached, the employer no longer contributes for that particular employee. The employer's OASDI tax is 6.2 percent of total employees' wages paid, and the HI tax is 1.45 percent of total employees' wages paid.

Wallington Company has 100 employees, each earning $525.25 a week.   **EXAMPLE 3-2**

OASDI

Amount of OASDI tax withheld from each employee's paycheck		
each week:	$32.57	(6.2% × $525.25)
Total tax withheld from the 100 employees' wages:	$3,257.00	($32.57 × 100)
Tax on employer:	$3,256.55	[6.2% × ($525.25 × 100)]

HI

Amount of HI tax withheld from each employee's paycheck		
each week:	$7.62	(1.45% × $525.25)
Total tax withheld from the 100 employees' wages is:	$762.00	($7.62 × 100)
Tax on employer:	$761.61	[1.45% × ($525.25 × 100)]

Successor Employer

Wages paid by the prior employer can be counted towards the annual OASDI wage base by a successor employer if all the following criteria are met:

1. The successor has acquired all the property used in the prior employer's business.
2. The affected employees were employed immediately before and continued working right after the transfer of the business.
3. Wages were paid by the prior employer during the calendar year of acquisition.

SELF-STUDY QUIZ 3-3

Patrick's Fine Foods employs five people. For each person, compute the amount of OASDI and HI tax for the first week in January.

Employee	Weekly Wage	OASDI	HI
Tammy Wolf	$225.00		
Bill Young	300.00		

Employee	Weekly Wage	OASDI	HI
Howard Feldman	$ 175.00		
Carin Clever	1,000.00		
Bud McAvoy	2,350.00		

Compute the employer's portion of the FICA taxes, based on the payroll data above.

Will any of the employees exceed the taxable wage base during the year? If yes, on which payday will it occur?

A Self-Employed Person

The Self-Employment Contributions Act (SECA) extended coverage under the social security system to the self-employed in 1951. Over the years, most self-employed persons have become covered by the law.

Self-Employment Income

SECA uses an individual's self-employment income as the basis for levying taxes and for determining the amount of income to credit toward OASDI insurance benefits or HI coverage. Self-employment income generally consists of the net earnings derived by individuals from a business or profession carried on as a sole proprietorship or as a partnership. Self-employed persons determine their net earnings by finding the sum of the following:

1. The *gross income* derived by an individual from any business or profession carried on, less allowable deductions attributable to such a business or profession, and
2. The *individual's distributive share* (whether or not distributed) of the ordinary net income or loss from any business or profession carried on by a partnership of which the individual is a member.

ON THE NET

http://www.irs.gov/pub/irs-pdf/p1779.pdf Lists IRS criteria for determining employee versus independent contractor status.

Self-Employment OASDI/HI Taxes

The projected self-employed tax rate for 2016 on the net earnings is 15.3 percent— 12.4 percent for OASDI and 2.9 percent for HI (double the employee rate). Self-employment income is subject to 0.9 percent additional HI tax on earned income in excess of $200,000.

Svetlana Priosky's net self-employment earnings for the year were $63,210. Her self-employment tax would be:

$$\$63,210 \times 0.153 = \$9,671.13$$

EXAMPLE 3-3

Usually, the net business income of individuals, as shown in their income tax returns, makes up their net earnings from self-employment for the purpose of the Social Security Act.

Earnings of less than $400 from self-employment are ignored. For computing the OASDI taxes, the maximum self-employment taxable income of any individual is $118,500 (2015). For the HI taxes, however, the total self-employment income is taxable. If the individual is also an employee of another company, the wages received can reduce the amount of self-employment income that is taxed for OASDI (wages + self-employment income > $118,500).

Roberta Wurst receives wages of $120,000 from her job. She also earned $15,000 in net self-employment income during the year. In computing her OASDI taxes, none of her self-employment income is considered, since her wages exceed the taxable wage base of $118,500. However, in computing her HI taxes, all of her earnings from self-employment are taxed.

If the wages received amount to less than $118,500, any net self-employment earnings amounting to $400 or more must be counted as self-employment income up to an aggregate amount of $118,500 for OASDI taxes.

George Talbot receives wages amounting to $93,500. His net earnings from self-employment amount to $28,600. Talbot must count $25,000 of his earnings in determining taxable self-employment income for OASDI taxes.

EXAMPLE 3-4

FICA Taxable Wage Base	—	Wages Received	=	Taxable Self — Employment Income
$118,500	—	$93,500	=	$25,000

Taxable Year

In computing the taxes on self-employment income, sole proprietors use the same taxable year as that used for income tax purposes. In the case of a partnership, the taxable year of the partners may not correspond with that of the partnership. In such instances, the partners are required to include in computing net earnings from self-employment their distributive share of the income or loss from the partnership for any taxable year ending with or within their taxable year.

Reporting Self-Employment Income

Sole proprietors report their self-employment income by transferring certain data from *Schedule C (Form 1040), Profit or Loss from Business to Schedule SE (Form 1040), Self-Employment Tax*. SECA requires self-employed persons to include SECA taxes in their quarterly payment of estimated income taxes. The taxpayer's estimated tax is the sum of the estimated income taxes and SECA taxes less any credits against the tax.

Lori Kinmark works as a jeweler for a local company. She earns $1,000 per week, plus a year-end bonus of $2,000. Kinmark also earns an additional net self-employment income of $28,000 per year.

$_____ 1. Compute Kinmark's annual earnings from employment.

$_____ 2. Compute Kinmark's total earnings from her job and from self-employment income.

$_____ 3. How much self-employment income should Kinmark include in computing taxable self-employment income for OASDI taxes?

$_____ 4. What are the total FICA taxes on her self-employment earnings?

Employer Identification Number

Every employer of one or more persons must file an application for an identification number (employer identification number—EIN). EINs can be obtained directly from the Internet (http://www.irs.gov). No preregistration is required, and the number that is issued is immediately recognized by IRS systems. The Internal Revenue Service also offers employers a toll-free number (800-829-4933) where they can request an employer identification number. Businesses can still obtain EINs by mailing or faxing Form SS-4. This form must be sent to the IRS service center where the employer's federal tax returns are filed. Figure 3.5 shows a filled-in copy of Form SS-4.

The employer must enter this EIN on all returns, forms, and correspondence sent to the District Director of Internal Revenue that relate to the taxes imposed under FICA. The employer uses the EIN in any correspondence with the Social Security Administration (SSA) and enters the number on forms issued by the SSA. Regardless of how many different business locations are operated, the employer receives only one EIN. The penalty for failing to supply the identification number is discussed later in this chapter. If the owner sells or otherwise transfers a business, the new owner must file an application for a new identification number.

Employee's Application for Social Security Card (Form SS-5)

ON THE JOB

The employer must obtain each employee's SSN to enter on Form W-2 (discussed in Chapter 4). If the employer does not provide the correct name and SSN, he or she may owe a penalty.

Under the Social Security Act, every employee and every self-employed person must have a social security number (SSN). The application for a SSN is available at any social security or IRS office. The *Application for a Social Security Card (Form SS-5)* can be filed with any field office of the SSA.

The Social Security Act requires applicants for a social security card to furnish evidence of their age, identity, and U.S. citizenship or lawful alien status. Applicants may either apply by mailing the required documents and forms to their nearest social security office or apply in person. If they are age 18 or older and have never had a social security card, or are aliens whose immigration documents should not be sent through the mail, they must apply in person.

Upon receipt of their SSN, employees should inform their employers of the number assigned them. If employees change positions, they must notify the new employer of their SSN when they begin employment. If an employee changes his or her name by court order or by marriage, the individual should request a new social security card by completing a new Form SS-5. Employees may have their SSN changed at any time by applying to the SSA and showing good reasons for a change. Otherwise, only one number is assigned to an employee, and the employee will continue to use that number regardless of the changes in positions or employers.

FIGURE 3.5

Form SS-4, Application for Employer Identification Number

Form **SS-4** (Rev. January 2010) Department of the Treasury Internal Revenue Service	**Application for Employer Identification Number** (For use by employers, corporations, partnerships, trusts, estates, churches, government agencies, Indian tribal entities, certain individuals, and others.) ▶ See separate instructions for each line. ▶ Keep a copy for your records.	OMB No. 1545-0003 **EIN**

Type or print clearly.

1 Legal name of entity (or individual) for whom the EIN is being requested
Myers Payroll Services, Inc.

2 Trade name of business (if different from name on line 1)

3 Executor, administrator, trustee, "care of" name
Care of Martin Myers

4a Mailing address (room, apt., suite no. and street, or P.O. box)
P.O. Box 212

5a Street address (if different) (Do not enter a P.O. box.)
3401 Atrium Way

4b City, state, and ZIP code (if foreign, see instructions)
Sacramento, CA 95814-1212

5b City, state, and ZIP code (if foreign, see instructions)
Sacramento, CA 95814-0340

6 County and state where principal business is located
Orange County, CA

7a Name of responsible party
Catherine Myers

7b SSN, ITIN, or EIN
000-00-6119

8a Is this application for a limited liability company (LLC) (or a foreign equivalent)? ☐ Yes ☒ No

8b If 8a is "Yes," enter the number of LLC members ▶

8c If 8a is "Yes," was the LLC organized in the United States? ☐ Yes ☐ No

9a **Type of entity** (check only one box). **Caution.** If 8a is "Yes," see the instructions for the correct box to check.

☐ Sole proprietor (SSN) _____
☐ Partnership
☑ Corporation (enter form number to be filed) ▶ _1120_
☐ Personal service corporation
☐ Church or church-controlled organization
☐ Other nonprofit organization (specify) ▶ _____
☐ Other (specify) ▶

☐ Estate (SSN of decedent) _____
☐ Plan administrator (TIN) _____
☐ Trust (TIN of grantor) _____
☐ National Guard ☐ State/local government
☐ Farmers' cooperative ☐ Federal government/military
☐ REMIC ☐ Indian tribal governments/enterprises
Group Exemption Number (GEN) if any ▶

9b If a corporation, name the state or foreign country (if applicable) where incorporated

State: California

Foreign country:

10 **Reason for applying** (check only one box)

☑ Started new business (specify type) ▶ _____
Payroll Processing
☐ Hired employees (Check the box and see line 13.)
☐ Compliance with IRS withholding regulations
☐ Other (specify) ▶

☐ Banking purpose (specify purpose) ▶ _____
☐ Changed type of organization (specify new type) ▶ _____
☐ Purchased going business
☐ Created a trust (specify type) ▶ _____
☐ Created a pension plan (specify type) ▶ _____

11 Date business started or acquired (month, day, year). See instructions.
July 3, 20--

12 Closing month of accounting year December

13 Highest number of employees expected in the next 12 months (enter -0- if none).

If no employees expected, skip line 14.

Agricultural	Household	Other
		1

14 If you expect your employment tax liability to be $1,000 or less in a full calendar year **and** want to file Form 944 annually instead of Forms 941 quarterly, check here. (Your employment tax liability generally will be $1,000 or less if you expect to pay $4,000 or less in total wages.) If you do not check this box, you must file Form 941 for every quarter. ☒

15 First date wages or annuities were paid (month, day, year). **Note.** If applicant is a withholding agent, enter date income will first be paid to nonresident alien (month, day, year) . . . . ▶ July 15, 20--

16 Check **one** box that best describes the principal activity of your business.

☐ Construction ☐ Rental & leasing ☐ Transportation & warehousing ☐ Health care & social assistance ☐ Wholesale-agent/broker
☐ Real estate ☐ Manufacturing ☐ Finance & insurance ☐ Accommodation & food service ☐ Wholesale-other ☐ Retail
☒ Other (specify) Payroll Services

17 Indicate principal line of merchandise sold, specific construction work done, products produced, or services provided.
Payroll Processing

18 Has the applicant entity shown on line 1 ever applied for and received an EIN? ☐ Yes ☑ No
If "Yes," write previous EIN here ▶

Third Party Designee

Complete this section **only** if you want to authorize the named individual to receive the entity's EIN and answer questions about the completion of this form.

Designee's name

Designee's telephone number (include area code)
( )

Address and ZIP code

Designee's fax number (include area code)
( )

Under penalties of perjury, I declare that I have examined this application, and to the best of my knowledge and belief, it is true, correct, and complete.

Name and title (type or print clearly) ▶ Catherine Myers, President

Applicant's telephone number (include area code)
(919) 555-2111

Signature ▶ *Catherine Myers* Date ▶ 6/4/--

Applicant's fax number (include area code)
(919) 555-2119

For Privacy Act and Paperwork Reduction Act Notice, see separate instructions. Cat. No. 16055N Form **SS-4** (Rev. 1-2010)

Source: Internal Revenue Service.

For aliens who must file U.S. tax returns but are not eligible to receive a social security number, the IRS has instituted *Form W-7, Application for IRS Individual Taxpayer Identification Number (ITIN).* An ITIN (begins with the number 9) is intended for tax purposes only.

The secretary of health and human services is authorized to ensure that SSNs are issued to or on behalf of children who are below school age at the request of their parents or guardians and to children of school age when they first enroll in school. Further, SSNs must be obtained for children age one or over who are claimed as dependents on federal income tax returns.

Criminal penalties (of up to $5,000 or imprisonment of up to five years, or both) exist for persons involved in the following situations:

1. Knowingly and willfully using a SSN obtained with false information.
2. Using someone else's SSN.
3. Altering a social security card.
4. Buying or selling a card claimed to be issued by the secretary.
5. Possessing a card or counterfeit card with the intent to sell or alter it.

Verifying Social Security Numbers

The Social Security Administration offers employers an online system to check current and former employees' names and social security numbers. Employers can verify up to 10 names and SSNs per screen or upload files of up to 250,000 names and SSNs with verification results the next day (http://www.ssa.gov/employer/ssnv.htm).

Returns Required for Social Security Purposes

Employers covered under FICA are liable for their own FICA taxes and their employees' FICA and income taxes withheld from wages. Withholding of income taxes is discussed in Chapter 4. Every employer (except those employing agricultural workers) who is required to withhold income taxes from wages or who is liable for social security taxes must file:

1. A *quarterly* or an *annual* tax and information return (Form 941 or 944). This return shows the total FICA wage paid and the total FICA taxes (employer and employee contributions) and federal income taxes withheld.
2. An *annual* return of withheld federal income taxes (Form 945). This return covers *nonpayroll* items such as backup withholding, withholding on gambling winnings, pensions, annuities, IRAs, and military retirement.

Generally, an employer must electronically transfer to the IRS the income taxes and social security taxes withheld and the employer's matching social security taxes.

Any employer who fails to pay the withheld income taxes and FICA taxes, fails to make deposits and payments, or does not file the tax returns as required by law may be required to deposit such taxes in a special trust account for the U.S. government and file monthly tax returns. Figure 3.6 lists and briefly describes the major forms used to prepare FICA tax returns and deposits.

Deposit Requirements (Nonagricultural Workers)

LO 4

Describe the different requirements and procedures for depositing FICA taxes and income taxes withheld from employees' wages.

The requirements for depositing *FICA taxes and income taxes withheld* from employees' wages vary according to the amount of such taxes reported during a **lookback period**. Depending on the total amount of taxes involved (federal income tax and FICA tax withheld from employees' earnings plus the employer's portion of the FICA tax), employers may have to pay their taxes several

FIGURE 3.6
Major Forms for Preparing FICA Tax Returns and Deposits

Form 941, Employer's Quarterly Federal Tax Return	Required of all covered employers, except employers of household and agricultural employees, who withhold income tax and social security taxes (see Figure 3.8 on pages 3-22 and 3-23).
Form 941-PR, Employer's Quarterly Federal Tax Return	Required of employers to report social security taxes for workers in Puerto Rico.
Form 941-SS, Employer's Quarterly Federal Tax Return	Required of employers to report social security taxes for workers in American Samoa, Guam, the Northern Mariana Islands, and the Virgin Islands.
Form 941-V, Form 941 Payment Voucher	Filled in by employers with a total tax liability of less than $2,500 for the quarter who are making payment with Form 941.
Form 941-X, Adjusted Employer's Quarterly Federal Tax Return or Claim for Refund	Use to correct previously filed Forms 941, 941-SS, 943, 944, and 945.
Form 943, Employer's Annual Tax Return for Agricultural Employees	Used by employers of agricultural workers for reporting FICA and income taxes on wages paid.
Form 944, Employer's Annual Federal Tax Return	Can be used by employers who owe $1,000 or less in employment taxes each year (in place of Form 941).
Form 945, Annual Return of Withheld Federal Income Tax	Required of employers to report income tax withheld from nonpayroll payments.

times a month or monthly. Some employers may not have to make any deposits but, instead, may pay their taxes at the time of filing their quarterly return, Form 941, discussed later in this chapter.

The amount of employment taxes that the employer reported on the quarterly returns for the *four quarters in the lookback period* determines if the employer is a monthly or a semiweekly depositor. A lookback period consists of four quarters beginning July 1 of the second preceding year and ending June 30 of the prior year. These four quarters are the employer's lookback period even if no taxes were reported for any of the quarters. Figure 3.7 shows the lookback period for 2016.

Each November, the IRS notifies employers whether they will be a monthly or a semiweekly depositor for the next calendar year.

FIGURE 3.7
Lookback Period for Calendar Year 2016

2014		2015	
July–Sept.	Oct.–Dec.	Jan.–Mar.	Apr.–June

Monthly Depositor	Reported—$50,000 or less in lookback period. Required deposits—By the 15th of the following month (if not a banking day, next banking day).
Semiweekly Depositor	Reported—More than $50,000 in lookback period. Required deposits (Within three business days of the semiweekly period. If any of the three weekdays is a nonbusiness day, add one additional business day to the due date.) • Payday on Wednesday, Thursday, or Friday—due following Wednesday. • Payday on Saturday, Sunday, Monday, or Tuesday—due following Friday. Separate liabilities and deposits—When deposit period spans two separate quarters.

IRS CONNECTION

At the end of the year, the IRS sends a notice to employers whose deposit schedules will change for the upcoming year.

(Continued)

One-Day Rule	Reported—$100,000 or more in undeposited taxes on any day during a deposit period.
	Required deposit—Close of the next banking day.
	Semiweekly status—If an employer falls under the one-day rule at any time during this year or last year.
No Deposits	Reported—Accumulated employment taxes of less than $2,500 for the whole calendar quarter.
	Required deposit—Pay with the filing of quarterly Form 941 or deposit by the end of month following the calendar quarter.
	Unsure of $2,500 total—Use the appropriate rules above.

Monthly

1. Robart Company's deposit status for 2016 was determined by using the lookback period shown in Figure 3.7 on page 3-17. During the two quarters of 2014, Robart reported employment taxes (FICA & employees' income tax) of $16,000. For each of the two quarters in 2015, the company reported taxes of $10,000. Since the taxes reported by Robart during the lookback period do not exceed $50,000, the company is classed as a monthly depositor and follows the monthly rule for the current year, 2016.

2. Vu-Tu, Inc., is a monthly depositor. For July taxes of $11,000, Vu-Tu must deposit the $11,000 on or before August 15, 2016.

Semiweekly

1. Meyer Company's deposit status for 2016 was determined by using the lookback period shown in Figure 3.7 on page 3-17. In the two quarters of 2014, Meyer reported taxes of $35,000. The taxes reported in the two quarters of 2015 totaled $30,000. Since the total taxes reported during the four quarters of the lookback period exceeded $50,000, Meyer is subject to the semiweekly rule for the current year, 2016.

2. The employees of Franchild, a semiweekly depositor, are paid every Monday. On September 19, 2016, Franchild has accumulated taxes totaling $24,000. Franchild is required to deposit the $24,000 on or before the following Friday, September 23.

One-Day

1. On Wednesday, January 6, 2016, Wycheck Company accumulated $105,000 in employment taxes for wages paid on that day. Regardless of Wycheck's deposit status, the firm is required to deposit the $105,000 by the next banking day, Thursday, January 7. Note that if Wycheck was not subject to the semiweekly rule on January 7, 2016, the company would become subject to that rule as of January 8, 2016.

2. Blastein Company is subject to the semiweekly rule. On Monday, February 1, 2016, Blastein accumulated $120,000 in employment taxes. The firm is required to deposit the $120,000 by the next banking day, Tuesday, February 2.

    On Tuesday, February 2, Blastein accumulates $30,000 more in employment taxes. Even though Blastein had a previous $120,000 deposit obligation that occurred earlier in the semiweekly period, Blastein now has an additional and separate deposit obligation that must be met by the following Friday, February 5.

A *new employer* becomes a **monthly depositor** until a lookback period that can be used to determine deposit frequency is established. However, if an unsatisfied deposit of $100,000 or more triggers the $100,000 one-day rule (see Figure 3.7) at any time during the year, the new employer becomes a **semiweekly depositor** for the remainder of the current calendar year and the subsequent calendar year.

The Safe Harbor Rule (98 Percent Rule)

The amount deposited by an employer may be affected by the safe harbor rule. Under this rule, an employer satisfies the deposit obligations provided:

1. The amount of any shortfall (under deposit) does not exceed the greater of $100 or 2 percent of the amount of employment taxes required to be deposited.
2. The employer deposits the shortfall on or before the shortfall makeup date.

A shortfall is the excess of the amount of employment taxes required to be deposited over the amount deposited on or before the last date prescribed for the deposit. The shortfall makeup rules follow:

1. *Monthly depositors:* The shortfall must be deposited or remitted by the quarterly return due date, in accordance with the applicable form and instruction.
2. *Semiweekly depositors and those subject to the $100,000 one-day rule:* The shortfall must be deposited on or before the first Wednesday or Friday, whichever is earlier, falling on or after the 15th day of the month following the month in which the deposit was required to be made.
3. *Shortfall over $100,000:* If the shortfall is more than $100,000, the one-day rule overrides the safe harbor rule.

EXAMPLE 3-5

1. On Friday, May 27, 2016, Rogers, Ltd., a semiweekly depositor, pays wages and accumulates employment taxes. Rogers makes a deposit on Wednesday, June 1, in the amount of $4,000. Later it was determined that Rogers was actually required to deposit $4,080 by Wednesday.

   Rogers has a shortfall of $80. The shortfall is less than the greater of $100 or 2 percent of the amount required to be deposited. Therefore, Rogers satisfies the safe harbor rule so long as the $80 shortfall is deposited by Wednesday, July 13.

2. On Friday, October 7, 2016, Vargan Company, a semiweekly depositor, pays wages and accumulates employment taxes. Vargan makes a deposit of $30,000 but later finds that the amount of the deposit should have been $32,000.

   The $2,000 shortfall ($32,000 − $30,000) exceeds the greater of $100 or 2 percent of the amount required to be deposited (2% × $32,000 = $640). Thus, the safe harbor rule was not met. As a result, Vargan is subject to a failure-to-deposit penalty, as described later in this chapter.

Deposit Requirements for Employers of Agricultural Workers

The deposit-making rules that apply to employers of agricultural laborers resemble those for employers of nonagricultural workers. However, there are exceptions, explained in the instructions accompanying *Form 943, Employer's Annual Tax Return for Agricultural Employees.*

Deposit Requirements for Employers of Household Employees

Household or domestic employees are usually not subject to federal income tax withholding, but they may voluntarily request that federal income taxes be withheld from their wages. Even though federal income taxes are not withheld from their wages, they are subject to FICA taxes if each worker has been paid cash wages of $1,900 or more in a calendar year. Noncash items given to household employees are not subject to FICA tax.

Employers who withhold and pay FICA taxes and federal income taxes for household services must report these taxes on *Form W-2, Wage and Tax Statement*, for each household employee.

Deposit Requirements for State and Local Government Employers

Each state and local government employer must file its return on Form 941 with the IRS and deposit its FICA taxes through the federal deposit system. State and local government employers must make their tax deposits according to the same deposit schedule used by private employers.

Procedures for Making Deposits

The original paper-based system has been replaced by an electronic depositing system.

Electronic Deposits Most employers must now make their deposits via the Electronic Federal Tax Payment System (EFTPS). The major exception will be for businesses with $2,500 or less in quarterly tax liabilities that pay when they file their returns (see Form 941). A deposit using this system must be initiated at least one business day before it is due in order to be considered timely.

This system is a communications network that facilitates the direct transfer of funds from the employer's bank to the Treasury Department. Generally, these transfers are transacted by touch-tone phone, personal computer, or online.

To use the online option, the employer must have Internet access. Enrollment in EFTPS Online can be done at http://www.eftps.gov.

Over the Line

Fallu Productions, a Joe Pesci film company, deposited its payroll taxes in full and on time at an approved bank for parts of 2001 and 2002. Penalties were charged by the IRS since the deposits were not made electronically. The penalties were challenged in federal court on grounds that there was no underpayment; the court ruled that the deposits must meet the requirements of the Internal Revenue Code. Since a regulatory requirement (electronic deposits) was violated, the penalties apply.[3]

Once enrolled in the EFTPS program, an employer can switch between computer software or online methods anytime. The linkage on all the methods is provided by the company's employer identification number.

There are two electronic methods of deposit:

1. EFTPS (direct)—the employer can instruct the Treasury Financial Agent for the area to withdraw funds from the employer's bank account and route them to the Treasury's account at the Federal Reserve Bank (ACH debit method).
2. EFTPS (through a financial institution)—the employer could also instruct the bank to send each payment directly to the Treasury's account at the Federal Reserve Bank (ACH credit method).

To enroll, an employer must complete *Form 9779, EFTPS Business Enrollment Form*. Enrollment takes from three to six weeks, and a confirmation package will be sent by the IRS to the employer with a personal identification number (PIN) and payment instructions.

ON THE JOB

If a deposit is required and the employer has not yet received the Employer Identification Number, the deposit must be mailed directly to the Internal Revenue Service with an explanation attached.

SELF-STUDY QUIZ 3-5

_____ 1. Johnson Industries, a semiweekly depositor, pays its employees every Friday. When should the company deposit the employment taxes for each weekly payday?

_____ 2. What rule should Bartlett Repair, a new company, follow in making its deposits for accumulated employment taxes?

_____ 3. Quail Hollow Motors (a semiweekly depositor) accumulates taxes of $105,000 on Monday and must deposit this amount on Tuesday, the next banking day. On Tuesday, the company accumulates additional taxes of $20,000. What deposit rule should Quail Hollow Motors follow for depositing the additional $20,000?

Preparing Form 941 (Employer's Quarterly Federal Tax Return)

Generally, the employer must make a quarterly return of FICA taxes and withheld income taxes for the three months of each calendar quarter, using *Form 941, Employer's Quarterly Federal Tax Return*. Figure 3.8 on page 3-22 shows a completed copy of Form 941. Form 941 may be submitted electronically using the Form 941 e-file program.

All nonpayroll items (backup withholding and withholding from pensions, annuities, IRAs, military retirement, and gambling winnings) are reported on *Form 945, Annual Return of Withheld Federal Income Tax* (Chapter 4).

Completing the Return

In making entries on the form:

a. Dollar signs and decimal points—not used.
b. Zero value line item—leave blank.
c. Negative amounts—use "minus" sign.
d. No rounding to nearest dollar.

Part 1

Most of the entries required on this part are self-explanatory. Other sources of information are shown in Figure 3.9 on page 3-24. The tax adjustments relate to:

5f. Employer's share of FICA taxes on tips reported on *Form 4137, Social Security and Medicare Tax on Unreported Tip Income.*
7. Fractions of cents—employees' share (one-half) of amounts on lines 5(a)–5(d) may differ slightly from amounts actually withheld (due to rounding).
8. Sick pay—adjustment for employees' share of FICA taxes that were withheld by third-party sick pay payer.
9. Tips and group-term life insurance—uncollected FICA taxes on tips and group-term life insurance premiums.

Part 2

14. Check the appropriate box. If the monthly schedule applies, enter a summary of your *tax liability* by month.

In addition, semiweekly and next-day depositors must complete Schedule B of *Form 941, Report of Tax Liability for Semiweekly Schedule Depositors*, instead of Form 941, line 14 (if the tax liability for the quarter was $2,500 or more). The employer's tax liability is listed by each payday (see Figure 3.10 on page 3-25).

Part 3

15. and 16. Complete if either situation applies.

Part 4

Complete if the employer wants to allow an employee, a paid tax preparer, or another person to discuss Form 941 with the IRS.

Part 5

The form must be signed by the employer or other person who is required to withhold and pay the tax. If the employer is:

1. An *individual*, the return should be signed by that person.
2. A *corporation*, the return should be signed by its president, vice president, or other principal officer authorized to sign the return. Corporate officers or duly authorized agents may use facsimile signatures under certain conditions.

LO 5
Complete Form 941, Employer's Quarterly Federal Tax Return.

ON THE JOB

The balance due on Form 941 can be paid by credit card. This does not apply to making federal tax deposits.

IRS CONNECTION

Internal Revenue Service forms and publications are available by calling 1-800-829-3676 or by accessing its Internet Web site at http://www.irs.gov/formspubs/

ON THE JOB

For most entities, the "responsible party" is the person who can control, manage, or direct the entity and the disposition of the entity's funds and assets.

FIGURE 3.8

Form 941, Employer's Quarterly Federal Tax Return

Form **941 for 20--:** **Employer's QUARTERLY Federal Tax Return**
(Rev. January 2015)

Department of the Treasury — Internal Revenue Service

OMB No. 1545-0029

Employer identification number (EIN) `0 0 — 0 0 0 7 7 7 9`

Name *(not your trade name)* JOHN GRANATELLI

Trade name *(if any)* GRANATELLI MOTORS

Address 3709 FIFTH

Number / Street / Suite or room number

CHICAGO / IL / 60605

City / State / ZIP code

Foreign country name / Foreign province/county / Foreign postal code

Report for this Quarter of 20--
(Check one.)

☑ **1:** January, February, March

☐ **2:** April, May, June

☐ **3:** July, August, September

☐ **4:** October, November, December

Instructions and prior year forms are available at *www.irs.gov/form941*.

Read the separate instructions before you complete Form 941. Type or print within the boxes.

Part 1:   Answer these questions for this quarter.

1   Number of employees who received wages, tips, or other compensation for the pay period including: *Mar. 12* (Quarter 1), *June 12* (Quarter 2), *Sept. 12* (Quarter 3), or *Dec. 12* (Quarter 4)   **1**   26

2   Wages, tips, and other compensation **2**   74895.92

3   Federal income tax withheld from wages, tips, and other compensation **3**   12372.13

4   If no wages, tips, and other compensation are subject to social security or Medicare tax   ☐ Check and go to line 6.

	Column 1		Column 2
5a Taxable social security wages . .	74895.92	× .124 =	9287.09
5b Taxable social security tips . . .	.	× .124 =	.
5c Taxable Medicare wages & tips. .	74895.92	× .029 =	2171.98
5d Taxable wages & tips subject to Additional Medicare Tax withholding	.	× .009 =	.

5e   Add Column 2 from lines 5a, 5b, 5c, and 5d **5e**   11459.07

5f   Section 3121(q) Notice and Demand—Tax due on unreported tips (see instructions)   .   .   **5f**   .

6   Total taxes before adjustments. Add lines 3, 5e, and 5f **6**   23831.20

7   Current quarter's adjustment for fractions of cents   .   .   .   .   .   .   **7**   — .15

8   Current quarter's adjustment for sick pay **8**

9   Current quarter's adjustments for tips and group-term life insurance   .   .   .   .   .   **9**   .

10   Total taxes after adjustments. Combine lines 6 through 9   .   .   .   .   .   **10**   23831.05

11   Total deposits for this quarter, including overpayment applied from a prior quarter and overpayments applied from Form 941-X, 941-X (PR), 944-X, 944-X (PR), or 944-X (SP) filed in the current quarter **11**   23831.05

12   Balance due. If line 10 is more than line 11, enter the difference and see instructions   .   .   **12**   .

13   Overpayment. If line 11 is more than line 10, enter the difference   [.]   Check one: ☐ Apply to next return. ☐ Send a refund.

▶ You MUST complete both pages of Form 941 and SIGN it.

Next ▶

For Privacy Act and Paperwork Reduction Act Notice, see the back of the Payment Voucher.   Cat. No. 17001Z   Form **941** (Rev. 1-2015)

FIGURE 3.8 (concluded)

Form 941, Employer's Quarterly Federal Tax Return

Name *(not your trade name)*	Employer identification number (EIN)
JOHN GRANATELLI	00-0007779

Part 2:	**Tell us about your deposit schedule and tax liability for this quarter.**

If you are unsure about whether you are a monthly schedule depositor or a semiweekly schedule depositor, see Pub. 15 (Circular E), section 11.

14 Check one: ☐ **Line 10 on this return is less than $2,500 or line 10 on the return for the prior quarter was less than $2,500, and you did not incur a $100,000 next-day deposit obligation during the current quarter.** If line 10 for the prior quarter was less than $2,500 but line 10 on this return is $100,000 or more, you must provide a record of your federal tax liability. If you are a monthly schedule depositor, complete the deposit schedule below; if you are a semiweekly schedule depositor, attach Schedule B (Form 941). Go to Part 3.

☐ **You were a monthly schedule depositor for the entire quarter.** Enter your tax liability for each month and total liability for the quarter, then go to Part 3.

Tax liability: Month 1   [.   ]

Month 2   [.   ]

Month 3   [.   ]

Total liability for quarter   [.   ]   Total must equal line 10.

☑ **You were a semiweekly schedule depositor for any part of this quarter.** Complete Schedule B (Form 941), Report of Tax Liability for Semiweekly Schedule Depositors, and attach it to Form 941.

Part 3:	**Tell us about your business. If a question does NOT apply to your business, leave it blank.**

15 If your business has closed or you stopped paying wages . . . .   ☐ Check here, and

enter the final date you paid wages   [/   /   ] .

16 If you are a seasonal employer and you do not have to file a return for every quarter of the year . .   ☐ Check here.

Part 4:	**May we speak with your third-party designee?**

Do you want to allow an employee, a paid tax preparer, or another person to discuss this return with the IRS? See the instructions for details.

☐ Yes. Designee's name and phone number   [   ]   [   ]

Select a 5-digit Personal Identification Number (PIN) to use when talking to the IRS.   [ ] [ ] [ ] [ ] [ ]

☑ No.

Part 5:	**Sign here. You MUST complete both pages of Form 941 and SIGN it.**

Under penalties of perjury, I declare that I have examined this return, including accompanying schedules and statements, and to the best of my knowledge and belief, it is true, correct, and complete. Declaration of preparer (other than taxpayer) is based on all information of which preparer has any knowledge.

X Sign your name here   *John Granatelli*

Print your name here   JOHN GRANATELLI

Print your title here   OWNER

Date   05 /02 /16

Best daytime phone   (773)555-2119

Paid Preparer Use Only   Check if you are self-employed . . . ☐

Preparer's name		PTIN	
Preparer's signature		Date	/ /
Firm's name (or yours if self-employed)		EIN	
Address		Phone	
City		State	ZIP code

Source: Internal Revenue Service.

FIGURE 3.9

Sources of Information for Completing Form 941

Line Number	Source of Information
1	Payroll register.
2	General ledger accounts for wages and salaries; Forms 4070, or employees' written statements reporting cash tips.
3	General ledger accounts.
4	General ledger balances.
5a	Payroll register; include any social security taxes (OASDI) paid for employees, sick pay, and taxable fringe benefits subject to OASDI. Do not include any tips. Do not report any employees' wages that exceed $118,500, the taxable wage base for 2015.
5b	Forms 4070, or employees' written statements to report cash tips. Enter all tips reported until tips and wages for each employee reach $118,500. Report this information even if you are unable to withhold the employee OASDI tax. Do not include allocated tips, which should be reported on Form 8027.
5c	Payroll register; Forms 4070, or employees' written statements to report cash tips. Report amounts paid to certain federal, state, and local government employees who are subject only to the HI portion of the FICA tax.
5d	Payroll register; enter all wages, tips, sick pay, and taxable fringe benefits that are subject to additional Medicare tax withholding. You are required to begin withholding additional Medicare tax in the pay period in which you pay wages in excess of $200,000 to an employee and continue to withhold it each pay period until the end of the calendar year. Additional Medicare tax is only imposed on the employee. There is no employer share of additional Medicare tax. All wages that are subject to Medicare tax are subject to additional Medicare tax withholding if paid in excess of the $200,000 withholding threshold.
5e	Add lines 5a, 5b, 5c and 5d.
5f	Enter the tax due from Notice and Demand on line 5f. The IRS issues a Notice and Demand to advise an employer of the amount of tips received by employees who failed to report or underreported tips to the employer.
7	To adjust for fractions of cents: If there is a difference between the total tax on line 6 and the total deducted from your employees' wages or tips plus the employer's tax on those wages or tips (general ledger accounts) because of fractions of cents added or dropped in collecting the tax, report the difference. Enter this difference in the space for "Fractions of Cents." If a negative number is to be used, use a minus sign −.
8	To adjust for the tax on third-party sick pay: Deduct the social security tax on third-party sick pay for which you are not responsible. Enter the amount of the adjustment in the space for "Sick Pay."
9	To adjust for the tax on tips and group-term life insurance: Include the total uncollected employee social security tax for lines 5b and 5d.
10	Total of lines 6 through 9.
11	General ledger accounts, previous Form 941; record the total deposits for the quarter, including any overpayment applied from previous quarter.
12	Compute balance due by subtracting line 11 from line 10. Pay the balance due IRS.
13	Compute overpayment by subtracting line 11 from line 10 and indicate if amount is to be applied to the next return or refunded.

Source: Internal Revenue Service.

3. A *partnership or other unincorporated organization*, a responsible and duly authorized partner or officer having knowledge of the firm's affairs should sign the return.

4. A *trust* or *estate*, the return should be signed by the fiduciary of the trust or estate.

5. A *political body*, such as a state or territory, the return should be signed by the officer or employee having control of the wage payments or officer properly designated for that purpose.

6. An *agent*, who pays the wages for the employer, may be authorized by the employer to sign the appropriate tax returns.

Employment tax forms can be signed by a facsimile-rubber stamp, mechanical device, or computer software program.

Employers can use credit cards to pay the balance due as shown on Form 941—this does not apply to tax deposits.

FIGURE 3.10
Report of Tax Liability for Semiweekly Schedule Depositors

Schedule B (Form 941):

Report of Tax Liability for Semiweekly Schedule Depositors

(Rev. January 2014)   Department of the Treasury — Internal Revenue Service

OMB No. 1545-0029

Employer identification number (EIN): 0 0 – 0 0 0 7 7 7 9

Name (not your trade name): JOHN GRANATELLI

Calendar year: 2 0 1 6   (Also check quarter)

Report for this Quarter...
(Check one.)

- ✔ 1: January, February, March
- ☐ 2: April, May, June
- ☐ 3: July, August, September
- ☐ 4: October, November, December

Use this schedule to show your TAX LIABILITY for the quarter; DO NOT use it to show your deposits. When you file this form with Form 941 or Form 941-SS, DO NOT change your tax liability by adjustments reported on any Forms 941-X or 944-X. You must fill out this form and attach it to Form 941 or Form 941-SS if you are a semiweekly schedule depositor or became one because your accumulated tax liability on any day was $100,000 or more. Write your daily tax liability on the numbered space that corresponds to the date wages were paid. See Section 11 in Pub. 15 (Circular E), Employer's Tax Guide, for details.

Month 1

Day	Amount	Day	Amount	Day	Amount	Day	Amount
1	3389.11	9	.	17	.	25	.
2	.	10	.	18	.	26	.
3	.	11	.	19	.	27	.
4	.	12	.	20	.	28	.
5	.	13	.	21	.	29	3396.81
6	.	14	.	22	.	30	.
7	.	15	3189.34	23	.	31	.
8	.	16	.	24	.		

Tax liability for Month 1: 9975.26

Month 2

Day	Amount	Day	Amount	Day	Amount	Day	Amount
1	.	9	.	17	.	25	.
2	.	10	.	18	.	26	3477.18
3	.	11	.	19	.	27	.
4	.	12	3283.95	20	.	28	.
5	.	13	.	21	.	29	.
6	.	14	.	22	.	30	.
7	.	15	.	23	.	31	.
8	.	16	.	24	.		

Tax liability for Month 2: 6761.13

Month 3

Day	Amount	Day	Amount	Day	Amount	Day	Amount
1	.	9	.	17	.	25	3780.06
2	.	10	.	18	.	26	.
3	.	11	3314.60	19	.	27	.
4	.	12	.	20	.	28	.
5	.	13	.	21	.	29	.
6	.	14	.	22	.	30	.
7	.	15	.	23	.	31	.
8	.	16	.	24	.		

Tax liability for Month 3: 7094.66

Fill in your total liability for the quarter (Month 1 + Month 2 + Month 3) ▶
Total must equal line 10 on Form 941 or Form 941-SS.

Total liability for the quarter: 23831.05

For Paperwork Reduction Act Notice, see separate instructions.   IRS.gov/form941   Cat. No. 11967Q   **Schedule B (Form 941)** (Rev. 1-2014)

Source: Internal Revenue Service.

Filing Form 941

The law requires employers to file Form 941 on or before the last day of the month following the close of the calendar quarter for which the return applies. If an employer makes timely tax deposits for the quarter, the employer may file Form 941 on or before the 10th day of the second month following the close of the calendar quarter.

Payments can be made with Form 941 only if either the net taxes for the quarter (line 10) are less than $2,500 or the payment serves as a deposit for a monthly depositor in accordance with the accuracy of deposits rule (can be more than $2,500). In both cases, a Form 941-V (Payment Voucher) must be filed with Form 941.

If the last day for filing a quarterly return falls on Saturday, Sunday, or a legal holiday, the employer may file the return on the next business day. If the return is filed by mailing, the employer should mail the return in sufficient time for it to reach the IRS Center no later than the next business day under ordinary handling of the mail.

---

1. An employer files a return by May 2 for the calendar quarter ending March 31 (April 30 is a Saturday).
2. An employer makes timely deposits for the quarter ending March 31. The form can be filed on or before May 10.
3. Pruit Company was not required to make any deposits for FICA taxes during the quarter ending March 31. The company makes its deposit for the first quarter taxes on April 22 for taxes due. Pruit can still file Form 941 on or before May 10 for the first quarter return.

Individual employers file quarterly returns with the IRS Center of the region in which the employer's principal place of business, office, or agency is located. The return may still be filed at the local office of the district director of the IRS if the taxpayer hand delivers the return.

After filing their first Form 941, employers must file returns for each quarter even if there were no taxes to report (unless they had checked box 15—business closed—in their last filing). The exception to this is for *seasonal employers* who do not have to file for quarters when they have no tax liability (they must check line 16 for every quarter that they do file).

Electronic Filing of Form 941

Several programs allow for the electronic filing of Form 941 information:

- 941 e-file programs: Business taxpayers, reporting agents, software developers, and transmitters can transmit the return electronically via an IRS-provided and certified secure Internet transport. The program sends electronic acknowledgements and builds records to be processed by IRS computer systems. An e-file application must be completed in order to participate in the program.
- 941 online filing programs: Taxpayers can file electronically through an authorized third-party transmitter using this Web-based system. To participate, businesses must apply for a PIN (Personal Identification Number) by completing the PIN registration online at the IRS Web site.
- Electronic 941 filing for reporting agents: Reporting agents may directly file their clients' Forms 941 electronically under the 941 e-file program.

Non-Filers

Certain employers are not required to file this form.

- Seasonal employers—for quarters when they have no payroll tax liability because no wages were paid.
- Small employers—whose estimated annual tax liability is $1,000 or less.
- Employers of farmworkers—file an annual tax return, Form 943.
- Household employers—report and pay FICA taxes on their personal income tax return, Form 1040.

Form 941-X

Adjusted Employer's Quarterly Federal Tax Return or Claim for Refund is used to correct errors on previously filed Form 941s. It is a stand-alone form that is not attached to Form 941.

Form 944

Employer's Annual Federal Tax Return can be used by employers who owe $1,000 or less in employment taxes per year and have not been late with any deposits for two years. These employers have to file the form and pay their employment taxes only once a year. Employers who believe they are eligible can contact the IRS and express their wish to file Form 944. The IRS will then send a notification letter to qualified Form 944 employers. Eligible employers who exceed the $1,000 threshold during the year can still file Form 944 for that year. However, they must start filing Form 941 at the beginning of the next year.

This return can also be used by new employers who expect to pay wages of $4,000 or less this year. Employers that are required to file Form 944 can notify the IRS if they want to file Form 941 quarterly instead.

The form (which is not illustrated) is basically the same as Form 941.

> **NEWS** ALER T
>
> Approximately 17 percent of tax filers are eligible to file Form 944.

Failure-to-Comply Penalties

Employers act as collection agents for the government by collecting employment taxes and paying them to the appropriate government agency. Employers who fail to carry out their duties as collection agents are subject to civil and criminal penalties. The penalties may be additions to the tax, interest charges, and fines and imprisonment. Penalties also apply to federal income taxes (Chapter 4) and federal unemployment taxes (Chapter 5) and are imposed on employers who fail to do the following:

1. File employment tax returns.
2. Fully pay taxes when due.
3. Make timely deposits.
4. Furnish wage and tax statements.
5. File or provide information returns.
6. Supply identification numbers.

> **NEWS** ALER T
>
> Over $58 billion in unpaid payroll taxes is owed by nearly 2 million businesses. Over 100,000 businesses owe more than two years of payroll taxes. Many of these businesses are insolvent or defunct.

The penalty depends on the degree of willfulness present in the employer's conduct. Persons other than the employer who have the duty or responsibility for collecting, accounting for, and paying any taxes may also be assessed penalties. Passing bad checks in payment of any employment tax also carries a penalty.

Once Form 941 is received, it usually takes the IRS about five weeks to notify an employer of any tax delinquencies.

Failure to File Employment Tax Returns

IRS CONNECTION

The IRS reports that over 6.6 million employers file more than 23 million 941s every year.

If an employer fails to file an employment tax return on the date prescribed for filing, a certain percentage of the amount of tax required to be reported will be added to the tax. Employers may avoid this addition if they show to the satisfaction of the IRS that failure to file was due to reasonable cause and not willful conduct.

Additions to the Tax	5 percent combined penalty of the net amount of tax that should have been reported less any amounts timely paid; an additional 5 percent for each additional month or fraction of a month during which failure continues, not to exceed 25 percent.
	15 percent per month, not to exceed 75 percent, for fraudulent failure to file.
	Minimum penalty for failing to file within 60 days of its due date is the lesser of $135, or 100 percent of the amount required to be shown on the return.
Criminal Penalties	Not more than $25,000 ($100,000 for corporations), imprisonment of not more than one year, or both.
	Not more than $100,000, imprisonment of no more than three years, or both for willfully signing a return not true and correct as to every material statement.

EXAMPLE 3-6

Ned Fromton, an employer, files his employment tax return 20 days after the due date of the return. The amount of tax that was unpaid is $6,000. Fromton's penalty is:
    Failure to file (5% × $6,000) = $300 *Note:* Any fraction of a month counts as a whole month.

Failure to Fully Pay Employment Taxes

IRS CONNECTION

Nearly one-third of small firms are hit with penalties for payroll mistakes, with the average fine being $848.

Employers who fail to pay the amount as shown on a return by the due date are faced with the following civil and criminal penalties:

Additions to the Tax	0.5 percent of the amount shown as tax on a return per month or fraction of a month, not to exceed 25 percent. The amount on which the penalty is calculated can be reduced by payments made on or before the beginning of the month. If both penalties for filing a late return and for not fully paying the tax apply in the same month, the failure to file penalty is reduced by the amount of the failure to pay full penalty. There is also a separate 0.5 percent per month penalty for failing to pay a tax amount due that was not shown on the return within 21 days of the notice (10 days if the amount is $100,000 or greater) and demand from the IRS. The penalty is based on the amount in the IRS notice. In addition, any taxes due will bear *interest at the rate of 3 percent* per year. Large corporate underpayments ($100,000) will carry the rate of 5 percent.[4]
Additions to the Tax	20 percent of the underpayment for negligence (failure to make a reasonable attempt to comply) or intentional disregard (careless, reckless, or intentional disregard of the law) of the payment rules.
	75 percent of the underpayment if underpayment is due to fraud with the intent to evade the tax.
The 100% Penalty	100 percent of the tax due for willfully failing to collect, account for, or pay employment taxes or willfully attempting to evade or defeat the taxes.
Tax Levies	Levy on and seize any property and property rights held by the employer at the time of levy for failure of the employer to pay any taxes, 10 days after notice and demand for payment.
Criminal Penalties	Not more than $10,000, imprisonment of no more than five years, or both, for willful failure to pay the tax. These penalties are in addition to the 75 percent fraud penalty.

---

4 The IRS sets the interest rate each calendar quarter, based on the short-term Treasury bill rate for the first month in each calendar quarter, plus three percentage points, and applies it for the following calendar quarter. The rate stated is for the first quarter of 2015.

Yeld Company failed to pay its employment taxes of $5,000 for March (due April 15) until May 20. The failure to pay penalty assessed against Yeld Company is:

EXAMPLE 3-7

Failure to Pay Tax ($5,000 × 0.5% × 2)	=	$50.00
Interest on Taxes Due ($5,000 × 0.03 × 35/365)	=	14.38
Total Penalty		$64.38

Note: In addition, a penalty for failure to make a timely deposit will also be assessed.

Failure to Make Timely Deposits

Penalties may apply if employers do not make required deposits on time in an authorized government depository.

Deposits made 1 to 5 calendar days late	2 percent of the undeposited taxes
Deposits made 6 to 15 days late	5 percent of the undeposited taxes
Deposits made 16 or more days late	10 percent of the undeposited taxes
Deposits made at unauthorized financial institutions or directly to IRS	10 percent of the undeposited taxes
Deposits subject to electronic deposit requirements but not deposited by EFTPS	10 percent of the tax deposit required
Amounts unpaid more than 10 days after IRS notice	15 percent of the undeposited taxes

ON THE JOB

Deposits are applied to the most recent tax liabilities within the quarter; however, a depositor can designate to the IRS the period to which a deposit is to be applied. The employer has 90 days from the date of a penalty notice to make the designation.

Greerson Inc. must make a deposit of $1,800 on June 15. The deposit was made 11 days late. The penalty assessed against Greerson is:

EXAMPLE 3-8

Failure to make timely deposit ($1,800 × 5%) = $90

Failure to Furnish Payee Statements

If employers willfully fail to furnish their employees with properly executed wage and tax statements or willfully furnish false or fraudulent statements (employee's copy of W-2 or recipient's Form 1099—discussed in Chapter 4), the civil penalty is $100 for each statement.

Maximum Penalty	$1,500,000 in any calendar year ($500,000 for small businesses).
Intentional Disregard	$260 per statement with no limit on the maximum penalty for the calendar year.
Criminal Penalties	$5,000 or more, plus may be subject to criminal sanctions.

Failure to Furnish Information Returns

Employers who fail to timely file their information returns *with the government* (any 1099 series or Forms W-2) are subject to fines for each failure. These penalties also apply to failures to include all required information on the forms, to supply only correct information, to file magnetically if required, and to report correct taxpayer identification numbers. The penalty is based on when the correct information is filed.

Correction within 30 days	$30 per failure, maximum fine of $250,000 ($75,000 for small businesses).[5]
Correction after 30 days, before August 1	$60 per failure, maximum fine $500,000 ($200,000 for small businesses).
Not filed correctly by August 1	$100 per return, maximum fine $1,500,000 ($500,000 for small businesses).
Intentional disregard	$260 per statement with no limit on the maximum penalty for the calendar year.

Bad Checks

Checks or money orders not tendered in good faith	2 percent of the amount. If the check or electronic payment is less than $1,250, penalty is $25 or the amount of the check, whichever is less.

KEY TERMS

educational assistance (p. 3-8)

employer (p. 3-2)

employment (p. 3-2)

independent contractors (p. 3-4)

lookback period (p. 3-16)

monthly depositor (p. 3-18)

person (p. 3-2)

safe harbor rule (p. 3-19)

self-employment income (p. 3-12)

semiweekly depositor (p. 3-18)

shortfall (p. 3-19)

sick pay (p. 3-7)

taxable wage base (p. 3-9)

ANSWERS TO SELF-STUDY QUIZZES

Self-Study Quiz 3-1

1. Yes. Full-time life insurance salespersons are covered as statutory employees for social security, Medicare, and FUTA tax purposes.
2. Yes. Federal government employees hired after 1983 are subject to full FICA coverage.
3. No. Real estate agents are considered independent contractors.
4. No. Schuck offers his services to the general public and is considered an independent contractor.

Self-Study Quiz 3-2

1. Yes. The gift certificates are considered cash equivalents.
2. Yes. Personal use of a company vehicle for non–business-related activities constitutes a taxable fringe benefit.
3. No. An employer may contribute to an SEP set up by or on behalf of its employees. The employer's contributions are exempt from FICA taxes if reason to believe exists that employees will be entitled to deduct the employer contributions for federal income tax purposes.

4. No. Generally, employers do not have to include in wages or withhold on the value of payment made for job-related training for their employees.
5. Yes. Payments by employers for involuntary separation of an employee from the employer's service are taxable under FICA.

Self-Study Quiz 3-3

Employee	OASDI	HI
Tammy Wolf	$ 13.95	$ 3.26
Bill Young	18.60	4.35
Howard Feldman	10.85	2.54
Carin Clever	62.00	14.50
Bud McAvoy	145.70	34.08
Totals	$251.10	$58.73
Employer's taxes (based on $4,050 gross wages)	$251.10	$58.73

Bud McAvoy will earn an annual salary of $122,200, which exceeds the wage base for OASDI taxes ($118,500).

---

5 Small business is a concern whose average annual gross receipts for the three years before the year in question were $5 million or less. If less than three years, the entire period in existence is used.

Through the 50th weekly payday, McAvoy will have cumulative wages of $117,500.

When the payment is made on the 51st payday, McAvoy will exceed the wage base for OASDI taxes:

Cumulative wages taxes	$117,500
Current wage payment	2,350
	$119,850

Therefore, only $1,000 is taxable.

Self-Study Quiz 3-4
1. $54,000 [($1,000 per week × 52) + $2,000 bonus]
2. $82,000 ($54,000 + $28,000)
3. $28,000 (Taxable wage base $118,500)
4. $4,284 [($28,000 × 0.124) + ($28,000 × 0.029)]

Self-Study Quiz 3-5
1. Johnson should pay its taxes by the following Wednesday.
2. During the first calendar year for a new business, the company is a monthly depositor. However, if during the year it has an undeposited tax liability of $100,000 (which triggers the one-banking-day rule), the company becomes a semiweekly depositor for the remainder of the year.
3. The additional taxes are not accumulated with the previous liability of $105,000. The company should follow the semiweekly deposit rules and pay the $20,000 by Friday.

KEY POINTS SUMMARY

	Learning Objectives	Key Points	Practical Problems A & B
L01	Identify, for social security purposes, those persons covered under the law and those services that make up employment.	• Employer/employee relationship, service is employment and compensation is taxable wages. • Specific coverage—agent-drivers, life insurance salespersons, traveling salespersons, and home workers. • Independent contractors are not employees but are taxed for FICA on earnings of their business.	
L02	Identify the types of compensation that are defined as wages.	• Wages, bonuses, and commissions are taxed. • Tips of $20 or more a month are taxable—employer collects tax from the wage payments to the tipped employee.	3-3, 3-4, 3-17
L03	Apply the current tax rates and wage base for FICA and SECA purposes.	• Employee's OASDI—6.2 percent on first $118,500; HI—1.45 percent on total wages plus additional 0.9 percent on wages in excess of $200,000. • Employer's OASDI—6.2 percent on first $118,500. HI—1.45 percent on total wages. • Employer collects tax from the employees' wages and calculates the employer's share. • Rate for all self-employed is 12.4 percent and 2.9 percent, respectively. Self-employed also subject to supplemental 0.9 percent HI tax on earned income in excess of $200,000. • Employer ID number—Form SS-4. • Employee social security number—Form SS-5. • Form 941—employers' quarterly information return.	3-1, 3-2, 3-3, 3-4, 3-5, 3-6, 3-7, 3-8, 3-9, 3-10, 3-17

Learning Objectives	Key Points	Practical Problems A & B
LO4 Describe the different requirements and procedures for depositing FICA taxes and income taxes withheld from employees' wages.	• Amount of taxes reported in the "lookback" period determines status. • Deposits—Employees' Withheld FICA Taxes + Employer's FICA Taxes + Employees' FIT Taxes. • Monthly depositors—15th of following month. • Semiweekly depositors—Wednesday, Thursday, or Friday payday (following Wednesday); Saturday, Sunday, Monday, or Tuesday payday (following Friday). • One-day rule—$100,000 or more in undeposited taxes on any day during a deposit period. • Deposits made electronically.	3-15
LO5 Complete Form 941, Employer's Quarterly Federal Tax Return.	• Form 941 due one month after the end of each quarter. • Semiweekly and one-day depositors must also complete Schedule B—Report of Tax Liability. • Penalties for failure to file returns and to pay employment taxes.	3-11, 3-12, 3-13, 3-14, 3-15, 3-16

MATCHING QUIZ

_____ 1. Employee's FICA tax rates
_____ 2. Form SS-4
_____ 3. Semiweekly depositor
_____ 4. Taxable for FICA
_____ 5. Nontaxable for FICA
_____ 6. Self-employed's FICA tax rates
_____ 7. Form 941
_____ 8. Monthly depositor
_____ 9. Taxable wage base
_____ 10. Form SS-5

A. Cash value of meals provided for employees' convenience
B. By the 15th day of the following month
C. Employer's Quarterly Federal Tax Return
D. Application for Employer Identification Number
E. 6.2 percent and 1.45 percent
F. Employee's application for social security card
G. Applies only to the OASDI portion of the FICA tax
H. More than $50,000 in employment taxes in the lookback period
I. 12.4 percent and 2.9 percent
J. Employer's matching contributions into employees' deferred compensation arrangements

QUESTIONS FOR REVIEW

1. For social security purposes, what conditions must an individual meet to be classified as a "covered" employer?
2. For social security purposes, what conditions must an individual meet to be classified as a "covered" employee?
3. Under what conditions does a common-law relationship exist between an employee and an employer?
4. Summarize the test conditions under which a worker is classified as an independent contractor.

5. What are an employer's responsibilities for FICA taxes on:
   a. Tips reported by employees?
   b. Wages paid tipped employees?
6. What conditions exclude sick pay from the definition of wages for FICA tax purposes?
7. What is the FICA tax liability status of pretax contributions to a qualified deferred compensation arrangement?
8. John Luis receives wages from three employers during 2016. Is he entitled to a refund on the OASDI

taxes paid on wages in excess of the $118,500 limit? If so, how can he receive a refund?

9. What are the self-employment tax rates for 2015? Explain how the tax is computed.

10. How does an employer file an application for an employer identification number?

11. Summarize the deposit rules for nonagricultural employers.

12. Which employers must deposit their employment taxes electronically?

13. How are the electronic tax deposits transferred from the employer's account to the IRS?

14. How often must an employer file Form 941?

15. List the penalties imposed on the employer for the following:
    a. Filing Form 941 late.
    b. Seven days late making a deposit.
    c. Issuing a bad check to the IRS.

QUESTIONS FOR DISCUSSION

1. In order to improve the cash flow of the company, Neal Emerald decided to postpone depositing all employment taxes a few months ago. He told his sales manager, "I'll pay up before the IRS catches up with me." What risks does Emerald face by not upholding his responsibility for the collection and payment of employment taxes?

2. During the year employee Sean Matthews earned wages in the amount of $250,000. Discuss how the employee's HI tax will differ from the employer's HI tax for this employee.

3. During a recent strike at the Ultima Hotel, union members were paid strike benefits by their union. Don Volmer, a union representative, participates in negotiations with the hotel. Are the payments Volmer receives for his services as a union negotiator subject to FICA taxes?

4. When employees of County Bank are summoned to serve on jury duty, the firm pays its workers the difference between their regular wages and the amount received for jury duty. One such employee has been receiving $365 per week. She just completed a five-day week of jury duty, for which she was paid $65 ($9 per day plus 20 cents per mile from her house to the courthouse, a 20-mile round trip). How much of the employee's earnings are subject to FICA tax?

PROBLEM SET · A

Note: In this chapter and in all succeeding work throughout the course, **unless instructed otherwise,** use the following rates, ceiling, and maximum taxes.

Employee and Employer OASDI:	.6.20%	$118,500	$7,347
Employee* and Employer HI:	1.45%	No limit	No maximum
Self-employed OASDI:	12.4%	$118,500	$14,694
Self-employed HI:	2.9%	No limit	No maximum

For rounding rules refer to page 2-33.

*Employee HI: Plus an additional 0.9% on wages over $200,000. Also applicable to self-employed.

3-1A · LO 3   Similar to Example 3-1 on pages 3-10 and 3-11

The biweekly taxable wages for the employees of Rite-Shop follow. Compute the FICA taxes for each employee and the employer's FICA taxes.

		Biweekly Taxable	FICA Taxes	
Employee No.	Employee Name	Wages	OASDI	HI
711	Castro, Manny	$1,000.00	$	$
512	Corrales, Pat	968.00		
624	Guitar, Joseph	1,004.00		
325	Moore, Connie	1,046.40		
422	Morrison, Harry	1,200.00		
210	Robertson, Catherine	1,044.80		
111	Swarez, Joseph	1,122.00		
		Totals	$	$

Employer's OASDI	$_____	$_____	
	Total Taxable Wages	Employer's OASDI Tax	
Employer's HI Tax	$_____	$_____	
	Total Taxable Wages	Employer's HI Tax	

3-2A · LO 3   Similar to Example 3-1 on pages 3-10 and 3-11

During 2016, Rachael Parkins, president of Mathieson Company, was paid a semimonthly salary of $7,000. Compute the amount of FICA taxes that should be withheld from her:

	OASDI	HI
a. 9th paycheck	$_____	$_____
b. 17th paycheck	$_____	$_____
c. 24th paycheck	$_____	$_____

d. If Rachael Parkin's year-to-date earnings as of her 24th paycheck are $168,000, and her year-end bonus is $100,000, how much is the additional 0.9% HI tax withheld?

$_____

3-3A • LO 2, 3   Similar to Example 3-1 on pages 3-10 and 3-11

Ernie Gilmore began working as a part-time waiter on June 1, 2016, at Sporthouse Restaurant. The cash tips of $390 that he received during June were reported on Form 4070, which he submitted to his employer on July 1. During July, he was paid wages of $525 by the restaurant. Compute OASDI and HI:

		OASDI	HI
a.	The amount of FICA taxes that the employer should withhold from Gilmore's wages during July.	$_____	$_____
b.	The amount of the employer's FICA taxes on Gilmore's wages and tips during July.	$_____	$_____

3-4A • LO 2, 3   Similar to Example 3-1 on pages 3-10 and 3-11

Ken Gorman is a maitre d' at Carmel Dinner Club. On February 5, his gross pay was $800 (three days working, one paid vacation day, and one paid sick day). He also reported to his employer tips of $900 for the previous month (applicable taxes to be deducted out of this pay). Gorman belongs to the company's 401(k) plan and has 5 percent of his gross pay ($800) deducted each week (salary reduction). Carmel Dinner Club also provides a matching contribution ($40) into the plan for Gorman. This week's pay would have a:

a. Deduction for OASDI tax $_____

b. Deduction for HI tax $_____

3-5A • LO 3   Similar to Example 3-1 on pages 3-10 and 3-11

In 20-- the annual salaries paid each of the officers of Abrew, Inc., follow. The officers are paid semimonthly on the 15th and the last day of the month. Compute the FICA taxes to be withheld from each officer's pay on (a) November 15 and (b) December 31.

a.

		November 15			
Name and Title	Annual Salary	OASDI Taxable Earnings	OASDI Tax	HI Taxable Earnings	HI Tax
Hanks, Timothy, President	$141,600	_____	_____	_____	_____
Grath, John, VP Finance	119,000	_____	_____	_____	_____
James, Sally, VP Sales	69,600	_____	_____	_____	_____
Kimmel, Joan, VP Mfg.	54,000	_____	_____	_____	_____
Wie, Pam, VP Personnel	51,600	_____	_____	_____	_____
Grant, Mary, VP Secretary	49,200	_____	_____	_____	_____

b.

		December 31			
Name and Title	Annual Salary	OASDI Taxable Earnings	OASDI Tax	HI Taxable Earnings	HI Tax
Hanks, Timothy, President	$141,600	_____	_____	_____	_____
Grath, John, VP Finance	119,000	_____	_____	_____	_____
James, Sally, VP Sales	69,600	_____	_____	_____	_____
Kimmel, Joan, VP Mfg.	54,000	_____	_____	_____	_____
Wie, Pam, VP Personnel	51,600	_____	_____	_____	_____
Grant, Mary, VP Secretary	49,200	_____	_____	_____	_____

3-6A • LO 3 Similar to Example 3-1 on pages 3-10 and 3-11, Example 3-2 on page 3-11

Audrey Martin and Beth James are partners in the Country Gift Shop, which employs the individuals listed below. Paychecks are distributed every Friday to all employees. Based on the information given, compute the amounts listed below for a weekly payroll period.

Name and Position	Salary	OASDI Taxable Earnings	OASDI Tax	HI Taxable Earnings	HI Tax
Zena Vertin, Office	$ 700 per week				
Nicole Norge, Sales	2,980 per month				
Bob Mert, Delivery	485 per week				
Audrey Martin, Partner	950 per week				
Beth James, Partner	950 per week				
Totals		$	$	$	$

Employer's OASDI Tax $_____
Employer's HI Tax $_____

3-7A • LO 3 Similar to Example 3-1 on pages 3-10 and 3-11, Example 3-2 on page 3-11

Volpe Corporation has only five employees who are all paid $850 per week. Compute the total FICA taxes that the employer would withhold from the five employees each week and the amount the company would pay as its own liability for the employer's share of the FICA taxes on the weekly wages of the five employees:

Employees' total OASDI................ $_____

Employees' total HI .... $_____

Employer's total OASDI............... $_____

Employer's total HI .... $_____

3-8A • LO 3 Similar to Example 3-4 on page 3-13

Ralph Henwood was paid a salary of $64,600 during 20-- by Odesto Company. In addition, during the year Henwood started his own business as a public accountant and reported a net business income of $60,000 on his income tax return for 20--. Compute the following:

a. The amount of FICA taxes that was withheld from his earnings during 20-- by Odesto Company. OASDI $_____ HI $_____

b. Henwood's self-employment taxes on the income derived from the public accounting business for 20--. OASDI $_____ HI $_____

3-9A • LO 3 **Similar to Example 3-1 on pages 3-10 and 3-11, Example 3-2 on page 3-11**

Empty Fields Company pays its salaried employees monthly on the last day of each month. The annual salary payroll for 20-- follows. Compute the following for the payroll of December 31:

Employee	Annual Salary	OASDI Taxable Wages	OASDI Tax	HI Taxable Wages	HI Tax
Utley, Genna	$ 37,040				
Werth, Norm	48,900				
Bass, John	40,000				
Ruiz, Sam	120,000				
Compton, Sue	36,900				
Williams, Mary	48,500				
Patel, Raymond	106,080				
Carson, Abe	56,900				
Livinsky, Sarah	37,850				
Harper, Mark	51,200				
Totals		$	$	$	$

Employer's OASDI Tax $ _____
Employer's HI Tax $ _____

3-10A • LO 3 **Similar to Example 3-1 on pages 3-10 and 3-11**

The monthly and hourly wage schedule for the employees of Quirk, Inc., follows. No employees are due overtime pay. Compute the following for the last monthly pay of the year:

- **a.** The total wages of each part-time employee for December 2016.
- **b.** The OASDI and HI taxable wages for each employee.
- **c.** The FICA taxes withheld from each employee's wages for December.
- **d.** Totals of columns.
- **e.** The employer's FICA taxes for the month.

Employees	Total Monthly Payroll	OASDI Taxable Wages	OASDI Tax	HI Taxable Wages	HI Tax
Full-Time Office:					
Adaiar, Gene	$2,450.00				
Crup, Jason	2,300.00				
Essex, Joan	2,975.00				
Garza, Irma	2,985.00				
Leason, Mel	2,900.00				
Pruit, Marne	7,000.00				
Rubble, Deanne	2,400.00				
Simpson, Dick	3,985.00				
Truap, Ann	5,000.00				
Wilson, Trudy	2,440.00				

3-10A (concluded)

	Hours Worked	Hourly Rate	Total Monthly	OASDI Taxable Wages	OASDI Tax	HI Taxable Wages	HI Tax
Part-Time Office:							
Kyle, Judy	170	$12.50					
Laird, Sharon	170	12.60					
Maxwell, Sara	140	14.00					
Nelson, Donna	145	14.20					
Scott, Kim	162	15.65					
Totals for all employees			$	$	$	$	$
Employer's FICA taxes				OASDI $		HI $	

3-11A • LO 5   See page 3-22

Cruz Company has gathered the information needed to complete its Form 941 for the quarter ended September 30, 2016. Using the information presented below, complete Part 1 of Form 941, reproduced on the next page.

    # of employees for pay period that included September 12—14 employees
    Wages paid third quarter—$79,750.17
    Federal income tax withheld in the third quarter—$9,570.00
    Taxable social security and Medicare wages—$79,750.17
    Total tax deposits for the quarter—$21,771.83

3-12A • LO 5   See page 3-23

Refer to Problem 3-11A. Complete Parts 2, 4, and 5 of Form 941 (on page 3-41) for Cruz Company for the third quarter of 2016. Cruz Company is a monthly depositor with the following monthly tax liabilities for this quarter:

July	$7,193.10
August	7,000.95
September	7,577.78

State unemployment taxes are only paid to California. The company does not use a third-party designee and the tax returns are signed by the president, Carlos Cruz (Phone: 916-555-9739).

Form **941 for 20--:** **Employer's QUARTERLY Federal Tax Return**
(Rev. January 2015) Department of the Treasury — Internal Revenue Service

OMB No. 1545-0029

Employer identification number (EIN) 0 0 – 0 0 0 6 5 0 9

Name *(not your trade name)* CARLOS CRUZ

Trade name *(if any)* CRUZ COMPANY

Address 901 KEYSTONE
Number   Street   Suite or room number

SACRAMENTO   CA   95916
City   State   ZIP code

Foreign country name   Foreign province/county   Foreign postal code

Report for this Quarter of 20--
(Check one.)

☐ **1:** January, February, March

☐ **2:** April, May, June

☐ **3:** July, August, September

☐ **4:** October, November, December

Instructions and prior year forms are available at *www.irs.gov/form941*.

Read the separate instructions before you complete Form 941. Type or print within the boxes.

Part 1: **Answer these questions for this quarter.**

1 Number of employees who received wages, tips, or other compensation for the pay period including: *Mar. 12* (Quarter 1), *June 12* (Quarter 2), *Sept. 12* (Quarter 3), or *Dec. 12* (Quarter 4) **1** _____

2 Wages, tips, and other compensation . . . . **2** _____ .__

3 Federal income tax withheld from wages, tips, and other compensation . . . . . . **3** _____ .__

4 If no wages, tips, and other compensation are subject to social security or Medicare tax ☐ Check and go to line 6.

		Column 1			Column 2	
5a	Taxable social security wages . .	_____ .__	× .124 =	_____ .__		
5b	Taxable social security tips . . .	_____ .__	× .124 =	_____ .__		
5c	Taxable Medicare wages & tips. .	_____ .__	× .029 =	_____ .__		
5d	Taxable wages & tips subject to Additional Medicare Tax withholding	_____ .__	× .009 =	_____ .__		

5e Add Column 2 from lines 5a, 5b, 5c, and 5d . . . . **5e** _____ .__

5f Section 3121(q) Notice and Demand—Tax due on unreported tips (see instructions) . . **5f** _____ .__

6 Total taxes before adjustments. Add lines 3, 5e, and 5f . . . . **6** _____ .__

7 Current quarter's adjustment for fractions of cents . . . . **7** _____ .__

8 Current quarter's adjustment for sick pay . . . . **8** _____ .__

9 Current quarter's adjustments for tips and group-term life insurance . . . . . . **9** _____ .__

10 Total taxes after adjustments. Combine lines 6 through 9 . . . . . . **10** _____ .__

11 Total deposits for this quarter, including overpayment applied from a prior quarter and overpayments applied from Form 941-X, 941-X (PR), 944-X, 944-X (PR), or 944-X (SP) filed in the current quarter . . . . **11** _____ .__

12 Balance due. If line 10 is more than line 11, enter the difference and see instructions . . . **12** _____ .__

13 Overpayment. If line 11 is more than line 10, enter the difference _____ .__ Check one: ☐ Apply to next return. ☐ Send a refund.

▶ **You MUST complete both pages of Form 941 and SIGN it.** Next ▶

For Privacy Act and Paperwork Reduction Act Notice, see the back of the Payment Voucher. Cat. No. 17001Z Form **941** (Rev. 1-2015)

Name *(not your trade name)*	Employer identification number (EIN)
CARLOS CRUZ	00-0006509

Part 2: Tell us about your deposit schedule and tax liability for this quarter.

If you are unsure about whether you are a monthly schedule depositor or a semiweekly schedule depositor, see Pub. 15 (Circular E), section 11.

14 Check one: ☐ Line 10 on this return is less than $2,500 or line 10 on the return for the prior quarter was less than $2,500, and you did not incur a $100,000 next-day deposit obligation during the current quarter. If line 10 for the prior quarter was less than $2,500 but line 10 on this return is $100,000 or more, you must provide a record of your federal tax liability. If you are a monthly schedule depositor, complete the deposit schedule below; if you are a semiweekly schedule depositor, attach Schedule B (Form 941). Go to Part 3.

☐ **You were a monthly schedule depositor for the entire quarter.** Enter your tax liability for each month and total liability for the quarter, then go to Part 3.

Tax liability: Month 1 [.   ]

Month 2 [.   ]

Month 3 [.   ]

Total liability for quarter [.   ] Total must equal line 10.

☐ **You were a semiweekly schedule depositor for any part of this quarter.** Complete Schedule B (Form 941), Report of Tax Liability for Semiweekly Schedule Depositors, and attach it to Form 941.

Part 3: Tell us about your business. If a question does NOT apply to your business, leave it blank.

15 If your business has closed or you stopped paying wages . . . . ☐ Check here, and

enter the final date you paid wages [/   /   ] .

16 If you are a seasonal employer and you do not have to file a return for every quarter of the year . . ☐ Check here.

Part 4: May we speak with your third-party designee?

Do you want to allow an employee, a paid tax preparer, or another person to discuss this return with the IRS? See the instructions for details.

☐ Yes. Designee's name and phone number [   ] [   ]

Select a 5-digit Personal Identification Number (PIN) to use when talking to the IRS. ☐ ☐ ☐ ☐ ☐

☐ No.

Part 5: Sign here. You MUST complete both pages of Form 941 and SIGN it.

Under penalties of perjury, I declare that I have examined this return, including accompanying schedules and statements, and to the best of my knowledge and belief, it is true, correct, and complete. Declaration of preparer (other than taxpayer) is based on all information of which preparer has any knowledge.

X Sign your name here [   ]

Print your name here [   ]

Print your title here [   ]

Date [   ]

Best daytime phone [   ]

Paid Preparer Use Only

Check if you are self-employed . . . ☐

Preparer's name	[ ]	PTIN	[ ]
Preparer's signature	[ ]	Date	[/ /]
Firm's name (or yours if self-employed)	[ ]	EIN	[ ]
Address	[ ]	Phone	[ ]
City	[ ]	State [ ]	ZIP code	[ ]

Page **2**

Form **941** (Rev. 1-2015)

Source: Internal Revenue Service.

3-13A • LO 5 See pages 3-22 and 3-23

Karen Kluster opened Lube and Wash on January 1, 2016. The business is subject to FICA taxes. At the end of the first quarter of 2016, Kluster, as president of the company, must file Form 941, Employer's Quarterly Federal Tax Return. Using Form 941(Parts 1 through 5), reproduced on pages 3-43 and 3-44, prepare, sign, and date the return on the basis of the information shown below.

Employer's address:	234 Oak, Austin, TX 78711-0234
Employer's ID number:	00-0005874
Phone number:	(512) 555–1111

Each employee is paid semimonthly on the 15th and last day of each month. Shown below is the payroll information for the first quarter of 2016. All pay periods were the same.

PAYROLL INFORMATION FOR JANUARY–MARCH

Employee	SSN	Quarterly Wage	OASDI Tax	HI Tax	Federal Income Tax	Total Deductions	Net Pay
Paul Purson	000-00-7233	$12,000.00	$ 744.00	$174.00	$1,260.00	$2,178.00	$ 9,822.00
Matt Dirkson	000-00-8451	12,600.00	781.20	182.70	1,200.00	2,163.90	10,436.10
Joan Howard	000-00-3668	12,500.00	775.02	181.26	1,080.00	2,036.28	10,463.72
Dorrie Smith	000-00-6527	10,800.00	669.60	156.60	1,140.00	1,966.20	8,833.80
Totals		$47,900.00	$2,969.82	$694.56	$4,680.00	$8,344.38	$39,555.62

Employer's FICA taxes	$2969.80	$694.55
for the quarter	OASDI	HI

The total taxes per payday are:

Employees' FICA Tax—OASDI	$ 494.97
Employer's FICA Tax—OASDI	494.97
Employees' FICA Tax—HI	115.76
Employer's FICA Tax—HI	115.76
Employees' FIT	780.00
Total	$2,001.46 × 6 deposits = $12,008.76 for the quarter

None of the employees reported tips during the quarter.

Note: Lines 5a and 5c of Form 941, tax on total taxable wages, are computed by multiplying by the combined tax rate for both employer and employee. Small differences due to rounding may occur between this total and the total taxes withheld from employees each pay period and the amount of the employer's taxes calculated each pay period. This difference is reported on line 7 as a deduction or an addition as "Fractions of Cents."

Form **941 for 20--:** **Employer's QUARTERLY Federal Tax Return**

(Rev. January 2015)   Department of the Treasury — Internal Revenue Service

OMB No. 1545-0029

Employer identification number (EIN) 0 0 – 0 0 0 5 8 7 4

Name (not your trade name)   KAREN KLUSTER

Trade name (if any)   LUBE AND WASH

Address   234 OAK

Number   Street   Suite or room number

AUSTIN   TX   78711-0234

City   State   ZIP code

Foreign country name   Foreign province/county   Foreign postal code

Report for this Quarter of 20--
(Check one.)

☐ **1:** January, February, March

☐ **2:** April, May, June

☐ **3:** July, August, September

☐ **4:** October, November, December

Instructions and prior year forms are available at *www.irs.gov/form941.*

Read the separate instructions before you complete Form 941. Type or print within the boxes.

Part 1:   **Answer these questions for this quarter.**

1   Number of employees who received wages, tips, or other compensation for the pay period including: *Mar. 12* (Quarter 1), *June 12* (Quarter 2), *Sept. 12* (Quarter 3), or *Dec. 12* (Quarter 4)   **1** [＿＿＿＿]

2   Wages, tips, and other compensation   .   .   .   .   **2** [＿＿＿＿]

3   Federal income tax withheld from wages, tips, and other compensation   .   .   .   .   .   .   **3** [＿＿＿＿]

4   If no wages, tips, and other compensation are subject to social security or Medicare tax   ☐ Check and go to line 6.

	Column 1	Column 2
5a Taxable social security wages . .	[＿＿＿]	× .124 =	[＿＿＿]
5b Taxable social security tips . . .	[＿＿＿]	× .124 =	[＿＿＿]
5c Taxable Medicare wages & tips. .	[＿＿＿]	× .029 =	[＿＿＿]
5d Taxable wages & tips subject to Additional Medicare Tax withholding	[＿＿＿]	× .009 =	[＿＿＿]

5e   Add Column 2 from lines 5a, 5b, 5c, and 5d   .   .   .   .   **5e** [＿＿＿＿]

5f   Section 3121(q) Notice and Demand—Tax due on unreported tips (see instructions)   .   .   **5f** [＿＿＿＿]

6   Total taxes before adjustments. Add lines 3, 5e, and 5f   .   .   .   .   **6** [＿＿＿＿]

7   Current quarter's adjustment for fractions of cents   .   .   .   .   **7** [＿＿＿＿]

8   Current quarter's adjustment for sick pay   .   .   .   .   **8** [＿＿＿＿]

9   Current quarter's adjustments for tips and group-term life insurance   .   .   .   .   .   **9** [＿＿＿＿]

10   Total taxes after adjustments. Combine lines 6 through 9   .   .   .   .   .   .   **10** [＿＿＿＿]

11   Total deposits for this quarter, including overpayment applied from a prior quarter and overpayments applied from Form 941-X, 941-X (PR), 944-X, 944-X (PR), or 944-X (SP) filed in the current quarter   .   .   .   .   **11** [＿＿＿＿]

12   Balance due. If line 10 is more than line 11, enter the difference and see instructions   .   .   .   **12** [＿＿＿＿]

13   Overpayment. If line 11 is more than line 10, enter the difference   [＿＿＿]   Check one: ☐ Apply to next return.   ☐ Send a refund.

▶ **You MUST complete both pages of Form 941 and SIGN it.**   Next ▶

For Privacy Act and Paperwork Reduction Act Notice, see the back of the Payment Voucher.   Cat. No. 17001Z   Form **941** (Rev. 1-2015)

3-13A (concluded)

Name *(not your trade name)*	Employer identification number (EIN)
KAREN KLUSTER	00 - 0005874

Part 2:   Tell us about your deposit schedule and tax liability for this quarter.

If you are unsure about whether you are a monthly schedule depositor or a semiweekly schedule depositor, see Pub. 15 (Circular E), section 11.

14   Check one: ☐   Line 10 on this return is less than $2,500 or line 10 on the return for the prior quarter was less than $2,500, and you did not incur a $100,000 next-day deposit obligation during the current quarter. If line 10 for the prior quarter was less than $2,500 but line 10 on this return is $100,000 or more, you must provide a record of your federal tax liability. If you are a monthly schedule depositor, complete the deposit schedule below; if you are a semiweekly schedule depositor, attach Schedule B (Form 941). Go to Part 3.

☐   **You were a monthly schedule depositor for the entire quarter.** Enter your tax liability for each month and total liability for the quarter, then go to Part 3.

Tax liability: Month 1   [.   ]

Month 2   [.   ]

Month 3   [.   ]

Total liability for quarter   [.   ]   Total must equal line 10.

☐   **You were a semiweekly schedule depositor for any part of this quarter.** Complete Schedule B (Form 941), Report of Tax Liability for Semiweekly Schedule Depositors, and attach it to Form 941.

Part 3:   Tell us about your business. If a question does NOT apply to your business, leave it blank.

15   If your business has closed or you stopped paying wages . . . .   ☐ Check here, and

enter the final date you paid wages   [/   /   ] .

16   If you are a seasonal employer and you do not have to file a return for every quarter of the year   .   .   ☐ Check here.

Part 4:   May we speak with your third-party designee?

Do you want to allow an employee, a paid tax preparer, or another person to discuss this return with the IRS? See the instructions for details.

☐   Yes.   Designee's name and phone number   [   ]   [   ]

Select a 5-digit Personal Identification Number (PIN) to use when talking to the IRS.   ☐ ☐ ☐ ☐ ☐

☐   No.

Part 5:   Sign here. You MUST complete both pages of Form 941 and SIGN it.

Under penalties of perjury, I declare that I have examined this return, including accompanying schedules and statements, and to the best of my knowledge and belief, it is true, correct, and complete. Declaration of preparer (other than taxpayer) is based on all information of which preparer has any knowledge.

X   **Sign your name here**   [   ]

Print your name here   [   ]

Print your title here   [   ]

Date   [   ]   Best daytime phone   [   ]

Paid Preparer Use Only   Check if you are self-employed . . . ☐

Preparer's name	[ ]	PTIN	[ ]
Preparer's signature	[ ]	Date	[/ /]
Firm's name (or yours if self-employed)	[ ]	EIN	[ ]
Address	[ ]	Phone	[ ]
City	[ ] State [ ]	ZIP code	[ ]

Form **941** (Rev. 1-2015)

Source: Internal Revenue Service.

3-14A • LO 5   **See pages 3-22 and 3-23**

During the third calendar quarter of 20--, Bayview Inn, owned by Diane R. Peters, employed the persons listed below. Also given are the employees' salaries or wages and the amount of tips reported to the owner. The tips were reported by the 10th of each month. The federal income tax and FICA tax to be withheld from the tips were estimated by the owner and withheld equally over the 13 weekly pay periods. The employer's portion of FICA tax on the tips was estimated as the same amount.

Employee	Salary or Wage	Quarter's Wages	Quarter's Tips	Quarter's OASDI	Quarter's HI	Quarter's FIT
Grant Frazier	$78,000/year	$ 19,500.00		$1,209.00	$ 282.75	$1,500.00
Joseph LaVange	52,000/year	13,000.00		806.00	188.50	1,100.00
Susanne Ayers	800/week	10,400.00	$ 2,240.90	783.77	183.30	750.00
Howard Cohen	650/week	8,450.00	2,493.10	678.47	158.73	740.00
Lee Soong	675/week	8,775.00	2,640.30	707.72	165.49	660.00
Mary Yee	750/week	9,750.00	2,704.00	772.20	180.70	900.00
Helen Woods	750/week	9,750.00		604.50	141.44	800.00
Koo Shin	600/week	7,800.00		483.60	113.10	1,100.00
Aaron Abalis	750/week	9,750.00		604.50	141.44	800.00
David Harad	600/week	7,800.00		483.60	113.10	750.00
		$104,975.00	$10,078.30	$7,133.36	$1,668.55	$9,100.00

Employees are paid weekly on Friday. The following paydays occurred during this quarter:

July	August	September
5 weekly paydays	4 weekly paydays	4 weekly paydays

Taxes withheld for the 13 paydays in the third quarter follow:

Employees' Federal Income Tax	Weekly FICA Taxes Withheld on Wages		Weekly FICA Taxes on Tips	
	OASDI	HI	OASDI	HI
$700 per week	Employees' $500.65	$117.11	Employees' $48.07	$11.24
	Employer's 500.65	117.09	Employer's 48.07	11.24

Based on the information given, complete Form 941 on the following pages for Diane R. Peters.
Phone number: (901) 555-7959

3-14A (continued)

Form **941 for 20--:** **Employer's QUARTERLY Federal Tax Return**
(Rev. January 2015) Department of the Treasury — Internal Revenue Service
OMB No. 1545-0029

Employer identification number (EIN) 0 0 – 0 0 0 3 6 0 7

Name *(not your trade name)* DIANE R. PETERS

Trade name *(if any)* BAYVIEW INN

Address 404 UNION AVE.
Number   Street   Suite or room number

MEMPHIS   TN   38112
City   State   ZIP code

Foreign country name   Foreign province/county   Foreign postal code

Report for this Quarter of 20--
(Check one.)

☐ **1:** January, February, March

☐ **2:** April, May, June

☐ **3:** July, August, September

☐ **4:** October, November, December

Instructions and prior year forms are available at *www.irs.gov/form941*.

Read the separate instructions before you complete Form 941. Type or print within the boxes.

Part 1: **Answer these questions for this quarter.**

1 Number of employees who received wages, tips, or other compensation for the pay period including: *Mar. 12* (Quarter 1), *June 12* (Quarter 2), *Sept. 12* (Quarter 3), or *Dec. 12* (Quarter 4) **1**

2 Wages, tips, and other compensation **2**

3 Federal income tax withheld from wages, tips, and other compensation **3**

4 If no wages, tips, and other compensation are subject to social security or Medicare tax   ☐ Check and go to line 6.

	Column 1		Column 2
5a Taxable social security wages . .		× .124 =	
5b Taxable social security tips . . .		× .124 =	
5c Taxable Medicare wages & tips. .		× .029 =	
5d Taxable wages & tips subject to Additional Medicare Tax withholding		× .009 =	

5e Add Column 2 from lines 5a, 5b, 5c, and 5d **5e**

5f Section 3121(q) Notice and Demand—Tax due on unreported tips (see instructions) . . **5f**

6 Total taxes before adjustments. Add lines 3, 5e, and 5f **6**

7 Current quarter's adjustment for fractions of cents **7**

8 Current quarter's adjustment for sick pay **8**

9 Current quarter's adjustments for tips and group-term life insurance **9**

10 Total taxes after adjustments. Combine lines 6 through 9 . . . . **10**

11 Total deposits for this quarter, including overpayment applied from a prior quarter and overpayments applied from Form 941-X, 941-X (PR), 944-X, 944-X (PR), or 944-X (SP) filed in the current quarter **11**

12 Balance due. If line 10 is more than line 11, enter the difference and see instructions . . . **12**

13 Overpayment. If line 11 is more than line 10, enter the difference   Check one: ☐ Apply to next return. ☐ Send a refund.

▶ You MUST complete both pages of Form 941 and SIGN it.   Next ▶

For Privacy Act and Paperwork Reduction Act Notice, see the back of the Payment Voucher.   Cat. No. 17001Z   Form **941** (Rev. 1-2015)

3-14A (concluded)

Name (not your trade name)	Employer identification number (EIN)
DIANE R. PETERS	00-0003607

Part 2: **Tell us about your deposit schedule and tax liability for this quarter.**

If you are unsure about whether you are a monthly schedule depositor or a semiweekly schedule depositor, see Pub. 15 (Circular E), section 11.

14 **Check one:** ☐ Line 10 on this return is less than $2,500 or line 10 on the return for the prior quarter was less than $2,500, and you did not incur a $100,000 next-day deposit obligation during the current quarter. If line 10 for the prior quarter was less than $2,500 but line 10 on this return is $100,000 or more, you must provide a record of your federal tax liability. If you are a monthly schedule depositor, complete the deposit schedule below; if you are a semiweekly schedule depositor, attach Schedule B (Form 941). Go to Part 3.

☐ **You were a monthly schedule depositor for the entire quarter.** Enter your tax liability for each month and total liability for the quarter, then go to Part 3.

Tax liability: **Month 1** [_____ .]

Month 2 [_____ .]

Month 3 [_____ .]

Total liability for quarter [_____ .]   **Total must equal line 10.**

☐ **You were a semiweekly schedule depositor for any part of this quarter.** Complete Schedule B (Form 941), Report of Tax Liability for Semiweekly Schedule Depositors, and attach it to Form 941.

Part 3: **Tell us about your business. If a question does NOT apply to your business, leave it blank.**

15 **If your business has closed or you stopped paying wages** . . . . ☐ Check here, and

enter the final date you paid wages [/ /] .

16 **If you are a seasonal employer and you do not have to file a return for every quarter of the year** . . ☐ Check here.

Part 4: **May we speak with your third-party designee?**

Do you want to allow an employee, a paid tax preparer, or another person to discuss this return with the IRS? See the instructions for details.

☐ **Yes.** Designee's name and phone number [_____] [_____]

Select a 5-digit Personal Identification Number (PIN) to use when talking to the IRS. ☐ ☐ ☐ ☐ ☐

☐ **No.**

Part 5: **Sign here. You MUST complete both pages of Form 941 and SIGN it.**

Under penalties of perjury, I declare that I have examined this return, including accompanying schedules and statements, and to the best of my knowledge and belief, it is true, correct, and complete. Declaration of preparer (other than taxpayer) is based on all information of which preparer has any knowledge.

X **Sign your name here** [_____]

Print your name here [_____]

Print your title here [_____]

Date [/ /]

Best daytime phone [_____]

Paid Preparer Use Only

Check if you are self-employed . . . ☐

Preparer's name	[_____]	PTIN	[_____]
Preparer's signature	[_____]	Date	[/ /]
Firm's name (or yours if self-employed)	[_____]	EIN	[_____]
Address	[_____]	Phone	[_____]
City	[_____] State [_____]	ZIP code	[_____]

Page **2**   Form **941** (Rev. 1-2015)

3-15A • LO 4, 5   Similar to Example 3-5 on page 3-19 and see page 3-25

The taxable wages and withheld taxes for Stafford Company (EIN 00-0001462), semiweekly depositor, for the first quarter of 2016 follow.

Semimonthly Paydays	Gross and Taxable Wages	FICA Withheld OASDI	FICA Withheld HI	Federal Income Tax Withheld
1/15	$ 24,500	$1,519.00	$ 355.25	$ 3,185.00
1/29	23,985	1,487.07	347.78	3,090.00
2/15	25,190	1,561.78	365.26	3,410.00
2/29	25,530	1,582.86	370.19	3,497.00
3/15	24,950	1,546.90	361.78	3,385.00
3/31	25,100	1,556.20	363.95	3,400.00
	$149,255	$9,253.81	$2,164.21	$19,967.00

a. Complete Schedule B of Form 941 on page 3-49 for the first quarter for Steve Hazelton, the owner of Stafford Company.

b. Below list the due dates of each deposit in the first quarter.

Paydays	Deposit Due Dates
January 15	1. _____
January 29	2. _____
February 15	3. _____
February 29	4. _____
March 15	5. _____
March 31	6. _____

3-16A • LO 5   Similar to Example 3-5 on page 3-19, Example 3-6 on page 3-28, Example 3-7 on page 3-29

Vulcan Company is a monthly depositor whose tax liability for March 2016 is $2,505.

1. What is the due date for the deposit of these taxes?   _____

2. Assume that no deposit was made until May 2. Compute the following penalties:

   a. Penalty for failure to make timely deposit. $ _____

   b. Penalty for failure to fully pay tax. $ _____

   c. Interest on taxes due and unpaid. $ _____

   d. Total penalty imposed. $ _____

3-15A (concluded)

Schedule B (Form 941):

Report of Tax Liability for Semiweekly Schedule Depositors

(Rev. January 2014)   Department of the Treasury — Internal Revenue Service

OMB No. 1545-0029

Employer identification number (EIN)

Name *(not your trade name)*

Calendar year   (Also check quarter)

Report for this Quarter...
(Check one.)

☐ **1:** January, February, March

☐ **2:** April, May, June

☐ **3:** July, August, September

☐ **4:** October, November, December

Use this schedule to show your **TAX LIABILITY** for the quarter; DO NOT use it to show your deposits. When you file this form with Form 941 or Form 941-SS, DO NOT change your tax liability by adjustments reported on any Forms 941-X or 944-X. You must fill out this form and attach it to Form 941 or Form 941-SS if you are a semiweekly schedule depositor or became one because your accumulated tax liability on any day was $100,000 or more. Write your daily tax liability on the numbered space that corresponds to the date wages were paid. See Section 11 in Pub. 15 (Circular E), Employer's Tax Guide, for details.

Month 1

1	9	17	25	**Tax liability for Month 1**
2	10	18	26	
3	11	19	27	
4	12	20	28	
5	13	21	29	
6	14	22	30	
7	15	23	31	
8	16	24		

Month 2

1	9	17	25	**Tax liability for Month 2**
2	10	18	26	
3	11	19	27	
4	12	20	28	
5	13	21	29	
6	14	22	30	
7	15	23	31	
8	16	24		

Month 3

1	9	17	25	**Tax liability for Month 3**
2	10	18	26	
3	11	19	27	
4	12	20	28	
5	13	21	29	
6	14	22	30	
7	15	23	31	
8	16	24		

Fill in your total liability for the quarter (Month 1 + Month 2 + Month 3) ▶

Total must equal line 10 on Form 941 or Form 941-SS.

Total liability for the quarter

For Paperwork Reduction Act Notice, see separate instructions.   IRS.gov/form941   Cat. No. 11967Q   Schedule B (Form 941) (Rev. 1-2014)

Source: Internal Revenue Service.

3-17A • LO 2, 3 📄 **Similar to Example 3-1 on pages 3-10 and 3-11**

At Vision Club Company, office workers are employed for a 40-hour workweek on either an annual or a monthly salary basis.

Given on the form below are the current annual and monthly salary rates for five office workers for the week ended December 9, 2016 (50th payday of the year). In addition, with this pay, these employees are paid their sliding-scale annual bonuses. The bonuses are listed on the register.

For each worker, compute:

1. Regular earnings for the weekly payroll ended December 9, 2016.
2. Overtime earnings (if applicable).
3. Total regular, overtime earnings, and bonus.
4. FICA taxable wages for this pay period.
5. FICA taxes to be withheld for this pay period.

VISION CLUB COMPANY

Employee	Salary	Hours Worked	Annual Bonus	Regular Earnings	Overtime Earnings	Total Earnings
Marx, A.	$97,240/yr.	40	$30,000	_____	_____	_____
Boxer, C.	91,000/yr.	40	25,000	_____	_____	_____
Lundy, R.	6,240/mo.	40	20,000	_____	_____	_____
Ruth, B.	4,680/mo.	40	15,000	_____	_____	_____
Gehrig, L.	4,900/mo.	48	8,000	_____	_____	_____
Totals				_____	_____	_____

(left side)

VISION CLUB COMPANY

Cumulative Earnings as of Last Pay Period	FICA Taxable Wages This Pay Period		FICA Taxes to Be Withheld		Employee
	OASDI	HI	OASDI	HI	
$91,630.00	_____	_____	_____	_____	Marx, A.
85,750.00	_____	_____	_____	_____	Boxer, C.
70,560.00	_____	_____	_____	_____	Lundy, R.
− 52,920.00	_____	_____	_____	_____	Ruth, B.
34,890.00	_____	_____	_____	_____	Gehrig, L.
					Totals

(right side)

Employer's FICA taxes for week ended December 9, 2016: $ _____ $ _____

OASDI   HI

PROBLEM SET • B

Note: In this chapter and in all succeeding work throughout the course, ***unless instructed otherwise***, use the following rates, ceiling, and maximum taxes.

Employee and Employer OASDI:	6.20%	$118,500	$7,347
Employee* and Employer HI:	1.45%	No limit	No maximum
Self-employed OASDI:	12.4%	$118,500	$14,694
Self-employed HI:	2.9%	No limit	No maximum

For rounding rules refer to page 2-33.

*Employee HI: Plus an additional 0.9% on wages over $200,000. Also applicable to self-employed.

3-1B • LO 3 Similar to Example 3-1 on pages 3-10 and 3-11

The biweekly taxable wages for the employees of Wee-Ones Foods follow. Compute the FICA taxes for each employee and the employer's FICA taxes.

		Biweekly Taxable	FICA Taxes	
Employee No.	Employee Name	Wages	OASDI	HI
711	Adams, Jane	$1,100.00	$_____	$_____
512	Candy, James	1,000.00	_____	_____
624	Guiterrez, Roberta	1,050.00	_____	_____
325	Harrison, Ken	1,250.00	_____	_____
422	Lowland, Harriet	1,600.00	_____	_____
210	Ranger, Ralph	1,310.50	_____	_____
111	Sweat, Rudy	1,419.45	_____	_____
		Totals	$_____	$_____

Employer's OASDI $_____ $_____

        Total Taxable Wages   Employer's OASDI Tax

Employer's HI Tax $_____ $_____

        Total Taxable Wages   Employer's HI Tax

3-2B • LO 3 Similar to Example 3-1 on pages 3-10 and 3-11

During 2016, Matti Conners, president of Maggert Company, was paid a semimonthly salary of $5,500. Compute the amount of FICA taxes that should be withheld from her:

	OASDI	HI
a. 9th paycheck	$_____	$_____
b. 22nd paycheck	$_____	$_____
c. 24th paycheck	$_____	$_____
d. If Matti Conner's year-to-date earnings as of her 24th paycheck are $132,000 and her year-end bonus is $100,000, how much is the additional 0.9% HI tax withheld?		$_____

3-3B • LO 2, 3   Similar to Example 3-1 on pages 3-10 and 3-11

Eric Sherm began working as a part-time waiter on April 1, 2016, at Yardville Restaurant. The cash tips of $475 that he received during April were reported on Form 4070, which he submitted to his employer on May 2. During May, he was paid wages of $630 by the restaurant. Compute OASDI and HI:

	OASDI	HI
a. The amount of FICA taxes that the employer should withhold from Sherm's wages during May.	$	$
b. The amount of the employer's FICA taxes on Sherm's wages and tips during May.	$	$

3-4B • LO 2, 3   Similar to Example 3-1 on pages 3-10 and 3-11

Moisa Evans is a maitre d' at Red Rock Club. On September 2, his gross pay was $900 (three days working, one paid vacation day, and one paid sick day). He also reported to his employer tips of $860 for the previous month (applicable taxes to be deducted out of this pay). Evans belongs to the company's 401(k) plan and has 5 percent of his gross pay ($900) deducted each week (salary reduction). Red Rock Club also provides a matching contribution ($45) into the plan for Evans. This week's pay would have a:

a. Deduction for OASDI tax $ _____

b. Deduction for HI tax $ _____

3-5B • LO 3   Similar to Example 3-1 on pages 3-10 and 3-11

In 20-- the annual salaries paid each of the officers of Perez, Inc., follow. The officers are paid semimonthly on the 15th and the last day of the month. Compute the FICA taxes to be withheld from each officer's pay on (a) November 15 and (b) December 31.

a.

		November 15			
Name and Title	Annual Salary	OASDI Taxable Earnings	OASDI Tax	HI Taxable Earnings	HI Tax
Perez, Paul, President	$136,800				
Donald, Donna, VP Finance	120,000				
Funke, Jack, VP Sales	76,800				
Weis, Al, VP Mfg.	92,400				
Lang, Hope, VP Personnel	78,000				
Lee, Amy, VP Secretary	52,800				

b.

		December 31			
Name and Title	Annual Salary	OASDI Taxable Earnings	OASDI Tax	HI Taxable Earnings	HI Tax
Perez, Paul, President	$136,800				
Donald, Donna, VP Finance	120,000				
Funke, Jack, VP Sales	76,800				
Weis, Al, VP Mfg.	92,400				
Lang, Hope, VP Personnel	78,000				
Lee, Amy, VP Secretary	52,800				

3-6B • LO 3 Similar to Example 3-1 on pages 3-10 and 3-11, Example 3-2 on page 3-11

Amanda Autry and Carley Wilson are partners in A & W Gift Shop, which employs the individuals listed below. Paychecks are distributed every Friday to all employees. Based on the information given, compute the amounts listed below for a weekly payroll period.

Name and Position	Salary	OASDI Taxable Earnings	OASDI Tax	HI Taxable Earnings	HI Tax
Kelly Simon, Office	$ 750 per week	_____	_____	_____	_____
Jim Tress, Sales	3,450 per month	_____	_____	_____	_____
May Aha, Delivery	520 per week	_____	_____	_____	_____
Amanda Autry, Partner	1,900 per week	_____	_____	_____	_____
Carley Wilson, Partner	1,900 per week	_____	_____	_____	_____
Totals		$ _____	$ _____	$ _____	$ _____

Employer's OASDI Tax $ _____
Employer's HI Tax $ _____

3-7B • LO 3 Similar to Example 3-1 on pages 3-10 and 3-11, Example 3-2 on page 3-11

Funke Corporation has only five employees who are all paid $1,050 per week. Compute the total FICA taxes that the employer would withhold from the five employees each week and the amount the company would pay as its own liability for the employer's share of the FICA taxes on the weekly wages of the five employees:

Employees' total OASDI................ $ _____
Employees' total HI .... $ _____
Employer's total OASDI............... $ _____
Employer's total HI .... $ _____

3-8B • LO 3 Similar to Example 3-4 on page 3-13

George Parker was paid a salary of $74,700 during 20-- by Umberger Company. In addition, during the year, Parker started his own business as a public accountant and reported a net business income of $50,000 on his income tax return for 20--. Compute the following:

a. The amount of FICA taxes that was withheld from his earnings during 20-- by Umberger Company.
  OASDI $ _____
  HI $ _____

b. Parker's self-employment taxes on the income derived from the public accounting business for 20--.
  OASDI $ _____
  HI $ _____

3-9B • LO 3 Similar to Example 3-1 on pages 3-10 and 3-11, Example 3-2 on page 3-11

Haggerty Company pays its salaried employees monthly on the last day of each month. The annual salary payroll for 20-- follows. Compute the following for the payroll of December 31:

Employee	Annual Salary	OASDI Taxable Wages	OASDI Tax	HI Taxable Wages	HI Tax
Stern, Myra	$ 42,150				
Lundy, Hal	39,500				
Franks, Rob	46,000				
Haggerty, Alan	161,280				
Ward, Randy	40,800				
Hoskin, Al	39,600				
Wee, Pam	106,800				
Prince, Harry	76,800				
Maven, Mary	52,000				
Harley, David	68,960				
Totals		$	$	$	$

Employer's OASDI Tax $ _____
Employer's HI Tax $ _____

3-10B • LO 3 Similar to Example 3-1 on pages 3-10 and 3-11

The monthly and hourly wage schedule for the employees of Quincy, Inc., follows. No employees are due overtime pay. Compute the following for the last monthly pay of the year:

a. The total wages of each part-time employee for December 2016.

b. The OASDI and HI taxable wages for each employee.

c. The FICA taxes withheld from each employee's wages for December.

d. Totals of columns.

e. The employer's FICA taxes for the month.

Employees	Total Monthly Payroll	OASDI Taxable Wages	OASDI Tax	HI Taxable Wages	HI Tax
Full-Time Office:					
Hutchings, Jean	$3,250.00				
Florio, Anne	4,000.00				
Trabert, Judy	3,500.00				
Williams, Justin	3,100.00				
Galzano, Jared	4,250.00				
Sussex, Jude	8,000.00				
Robinson, Dave	6,300.00				
Prender, Hank	4,985.00				
Sorenson, Deb	5,600.00				
Hutchinson, Wendy	5,200.00				

3-10B (concluded)

	Hours Worked	Hourly Rate	Total Monthly	OASDI Taxable Wages	OASDI Tax	HI Taxable Wages	HI Tax
Part-Time Office:							
Fox, Mandy	180	$12.50					
Billings, Clara	160	13.00					
Nau, Kevin	170	19.75					
Millis, Toby	142	15.00					
Cummings, Cheryl	162	14.50					
Totals for all employees			$	$	$	$	$
Employer's FICA taxes				OASDI $		HI $	

3-11B • LO 5 See page 3-22

Gallagher Company has gathered the information needed to complete its Form 941 for the quarter ended September 30, 2016. Using the information presented below, complete Part 1 of Form 941, reproduced on the next page.

# of employees for pay period that included September 12 —15 employees
Wages paid third quarter—$89,352.18
Federal income tax withheld in the third quarter—$10,195.00
Taxable social security and Medicare wages—$89,352.18
Total tax deposits for the quarter—$23,865.92

3-12B • LO 5 See page 3-23

Refer to Problem 3-11B. Complete Parts 2, 4, and 5 of Form 941 (on page 3-57) for Gallagher Company for the third quarter of 2016. Gallagher Company is a monthly depositor with the following monthly tax liabilities for this quarter:

July	$7,891.75
August	7,984.90
September	7,989.27

State unemployment taxes are only paid to California. The company does not use a third-party designee, and the tax returns are signed by the president, James Gallagher (Phone: 916-555-9739).

3-11B

Form **941 for 20--:** **Employer's QUARTERLY Federal Tax Return**
(Rev. January 2015)
Department of the Treasury — Internal Revenue Service

OMB No. 1545-0029

Employer identification number (EIN) 0 0 — 0 0 0 6 5 0 9

Name *(not your trade name)* JAMES GALLAGHER

Trade name *(if any)* GALLAGHER COMPANY

Address 901 KEYSTONE
Number   Street   Suite or room number

SACRAMENTO   CA   95916
City   State   ZIP code

Foreign country name   Foreign province/county   Foreign postal code

Report for this Quarter of 20--
(Check one.)

☐ **1:** January, February, March

☐ **2:** April, May, June

☐ **3:** July, August, September

☐ **4:** October, November, December

Instructions and prior year forms are available at *www.irs.gov/form941.*

Read the separate instructions before you complete Form 941. Type or print within the boxes.

Part 1:   Answer these questions for this quarter.

1   Number of employees who received wages, tips, or other compensation for the pay period including: *Mar. 12* (Quarter 1), *June 12* (Quarter 2), *Sept. 12* (Quarter 3), or *Dec. 12* (Quarter 4)   **1** ☐

2   Wages, tips, and other compensation . . . .   **2** ☐ .

3   Federal income tax withheld from wages, tips, and other compensation . . . .   **3** ☐ .

4   If no wages, tips, and other compensation are subject to social security or Medicare tax   ☐ Check and go to line 6.

		Column 1		Column 2
5a	Taxable social security wages . .	☐ .	× .124 =	☐ .
5b	Taxable social security tips . . .	☐ .	× .124 =	☐ .
5c	Taxable Medicare wages & tips. .	☐ .	× .029 =	☐ .
5d	Taxable wages & tips subject to Additional Medicare Tax withholding	☐ .	× .009 =	☐ .

5e   Add Column 2 from lines 5a, 5b, 5c, and 5d . . . .   **5e** ☐ .

5f   Section 3121(q) Notice and Demand—Tax due on unreported tips (see instructions) . .   **5f** ☐ .

6   Total taxes before adjustments. Add lines 3, 5e, and 5f . . . .   **6** ☐ .

7   Current quarter's adjustment for fractions of cents . . . .   **7** ☐ .

8   Current quarter's adjustment for sick pay . . . .   **8** ☐ .

9   Current quarter's adjustments for tips and group-term life insurance . . . .   **9** ☐ .

10   Total taxes after adjustments. Combine lines 6 through 9 . . . .   **10** ☐ .

11   Total deposits for this quarter, including overpayment applied from a prior quarter and overpayments applied from Form 941-X, 941-X (PR), 944-X, 944-X (PR), or 944-X (SP) filed in the current quarter . . . .   **11** ☐ .

12   Balance due. If line 10 is more than line 11, enter the difference and see instructions . . .   **12** ☐ .

13   Overpayment. If line 11 is more than line 10, enter the difference ☐ . Check one: ☐ Apply to next return. ☐ Send a refund.

▶ **You MUST complete both pages of Form 941 and SIGN it.**

For Privacy Act and Paperwork Reduction Act Notice, see the back of the Payment Voucher.

Cat. No. 17001Z

Next ▶

Form **941** (Rev. 1-2015)

Name (not your trade name)

JAMES GALLAGHER

Employer identification number (EIN)

00-0006509

Part 2:   **Tell us about your deposit schedule and tax liability for this quarter.**

If you are unsure about whether you are a monthly schedule depositor or a semiweekly schedule depositor, see Pub. 15 (Circular E), section 11.

14   **Check one:** ☐   Line 10 on this return is less than $2,500 or line 10 on the return for the prior quarter was less than $2,500, and you did not incur a $100,000 next-day deposit obligation during the current quarter. If line 10 for the prior quarter was less than $2,500 but line 10 on this return is $100,000 or more, you must provide a record of your federal tax liability. If you are a monthly schedule depositor, complete the deposit schedule below; if you are a semiweekly schedule depositor, attach Schedule B (Form 941). Go to Part 3.

☐   **You were a monthly schedule depositor for the entire quarter.** Enter your tax liability for each month and total liability for the quarter, then go to Part 3.

       Tax liability: **Month 1**   [_____ .]

                     Month 2   [_____ .]

                     Month 3   [_____ .]

       Total liability for quarter   [_____ .]   **Total must equal line 10.**

☐   **You were a semiweekly schedule depositor for any part of this quarter.** Complete Schedule B (Form 941), Report of Tax Liability for Semiweekly Schedule Depositors, and attach it to Form 941.

Part 3:   **Tell us about your business. If a question does NOT apply to your business, leave it blank.**

15   **If your business has closed or you stopped paying wages** . . . . ☐ Check here, and

    enter the final date you paid wages   [/   /   ] .

16   **If you are a seasonal employer and you do not have to file a return for every quarter of the year** . . ☐ Check here.

Part 4:   **May we speak with your third-party designee?**

Do you want to allow an employee, a paid tax preparer, or another person to discuss this return with the IRS? See the instructions for details.

☐ **Yes.** Designee's name and phone number   [_____]   [_____]

          Select a 5-digit Personal Identification Number (PIN) to use when talking to the IRS.   [☐ ☐ ☐ ☐ ☐]

☐ **No.**

Part 5:   **Sign here. You MUST complete both pages of Form 941 and SIGN it.**

Under penalties of perjury, I declare that I have examined this return, including accompanying schedules and statements, and to the best of my knowledge and belief, it is true, correct, and complete. Declaration of preparer (other than taxpayer) is based on all information of which preparer has any knowledge.

X   **Sign your name here**   [_____]

    Print your name here   [_____]

    Print your title here   [_____]

    Date   [/   /   ]   Best daytime phone   [_____]

Paid Preparer Use Only   Check if you are self-employed . . . ☐

Preparer's name   [_____]   PTIN   [_____]

Preparer's signature   [_____]   Date   [/   /   ]

Firm's name (or yours if self-employed)   [_____]   EIN   [_____]

Address   [_____]   Phone   [_____]

City   [_____]   State [_____]   ZIP code   [_____]

Page **2**   Form **941** (Rev. 1-2015)

Source: Internal Revenue Service.

3-13B • LO 5   See pages 3-22 and 3-23

Stan Barker opened Quik-Stop Market on January 1, 2016. The business is subject to FICA taxes. At the end of the first quarter of 2016, Barker, as president of the company, must file Form 941, Employer's Quarterly Federal Tax Return. Using Form 941 (Parts 1 through 5), reproduced on pages 3-59 and 3-60, prepare, sign, and date the return on the basis of the information shown below.

Employer's address:	234 Oak, Austin, TX 78711-0234
Employer's ID number:	00-0005874
Phone number:	(512) 555–1111

Each employee is paid semimonthly on the 15th and last day of each month. Shown below is the payroll information for the first quarter of 2016. All pay periods were the same.

PAYROLL INFORMATION FOR JANUARY–MARCH

Employee	SSN	Quarterly Wage	OASDI Tax	HI Tax	Federal Income Tax	Total Deductions	Net Pay
Albert Greer	000-00-7233	$10,440	$ 647.28	$151.38	$1,260.00	$2,058.66	$ 8,381.34
Patty Dilts	000-00-8451	10,530	652.86	152.70	1,200.00	2,005.56	8,524.44
Jerod Hughs	000-00-3668	23,220	1,439.64	336.72	1,080.00	2,856.36	20,363.64
Denise Eaton	000-00-6527	11,700	725.40	169.68	1,140.00	2,035.08	9,664.92
Totals		$55,890	$3,465.18	$810.48	$4,680.00	$8,955.66	$46,934.34

Employer's FICA taxes $3,465.18 $810.41

For the Quarter OASDI HI

The total taxes per payday are:

Employees' FICA Tax—OASDI	$ 577.53
Employer's FICA Tax—OASDI	577.53
Employees' FICA Tax—HI	135.08
Employer's FICA Tax—HI	135.07
Employees' FIT Tax	780.00

Total $2,205.21 × 6 deposits = $13,231.26 for the quarter

None of the employees reported tips during the quarter.

Note: Lines 5a and 5c of Form 941, tax on total taxable wages, are computed by multiplying by the combined tax rate for both employer and employee. Small differences due to rounding may occur between this total and the total taxes withheld from employees each pay period and the amount of the employer's taxes calculated each pay period. This difference is reported on line 7 as a deduction or an addition as "Fractions of Cents."

3-13B (continued)

Form **941 for 20--:** **Employer's QUARTERLY Federal Tax Return**
(Rev. January 2015) Department of the Treasury — Internal Revenue Service

OMB No. 1545-0029

Employer identification number (EIN) `0` `0` – `0` `0` `0` `5` `8` `7` `4`

Name *(not your trade name)* STAN BARKER

Trade name *(if any)* QUIK-STOP MARKET

Address 234 OAK
Number Street Suite or room number

AUSTIN TX 78711-0234
City State ZIP code

Foreign country name Foreign province/county Foreign postal code

Report for this Quarter of 20--
(Check one.)

☐ 1: January, February, March

☐ 2: April, May, June

☐ 3: July, August, September

☐ 4: October, November, December

Instructions and prior year forms are available at *www.irs.gov/form941.*

Read the separate instructions before you complete Form 941. Type or print within the boxes.

Part 1:	Answer these questions for this quarter.

1 Number of employees who received wages, tips, or other compensation for the pay period including: *Mar. 12* (Quarter 1), *June 12* (Quarter 2), *Sept. 12* (Quarter 3), or *Dec. 12* (Quarter 4) **1** ☐

2 Wages, tips, and other compensation . . . . **2** ☐ .

3 Federal income tax withheld from wages, tips, and other compensation . . . . . . **3** ☐ .

4 If no wages, tips, and other compensation are subject to social security or Medicare tax ☐ Check and go to line 6.

		Column 1		Column 2
5a	Taxable social security wages . .	☐ .	× .124 =	☐ .
5b	Taxable social security tips . . .	☐ .	× .124 =	☐ .
5c	Taxable Medicare wages & tips. .	☐ .	× .029 =	☐ .
5d	Taxable wages & tips subject to Additional Medicare Tax withholding	☐ .	× .009 =	☐ .

5e Add Column 2 from lines 5a, 5b, 5c, and 5d . . . . **5e** ☐ .

5f Section 3121(q) Notice and Demand—Tax due on unreported tips (see instructions) . . **5f** ☐ .

6 Total taxes before adjustments. Add lines 3, 5e, and 5f . . . . **6** ☐ .

7 Current quarter's adjustment for fractions of cents . . . . **7** ☐ .

8 Current quarter's adjustment for sick pay . . . . **8** ☐ .

9 Current quarter's adjustments for tips and group-term life insurance . . . . . . **9** ☐ .

10 Total taxes after adjustments. Combine lines 6 through 9 . . . . . . **10** ☐ .

11 Total deposits for this quarter, including overpayment applied from a prior quarter and overpayments applied from Form 941-X, 941-X (PR), 944-X, 944-X (PR), or 944-X (SP) filed in the current quarter . . . . **11** ☐ .

12 Balance due. If line 10 is more than line 11, enter the difference and see instructions . . . **12** ☐ .

13 Overpayment. If line 11 is more than line 10, enter the difference ☐ . Check one: ☐ Apply to next return. ☐ Send a refund.

▶ **You MUST complete both pages of Form 941 and SIGN it.**

For Privacy Act and Paperwork Reduction Act Notice, see the back of the Payment Voucher. Cat. No. 17001Z Next ▶ Form **941** (Rev. 1-2015)

3-13B (concluded)

Name *(not your trade name)*	Employer identification number (EIN)
STAN BARKER	00-0005874

Part 2: Tell us about your deposit schedule and tax liability for this quarter.

If you are unsure about whether you are a monthly schedule depositor or a semiweekly schedule depositor, see Pub. 15 (Circular E), section 11.

14 Check one: ☐ Line 10 on this return is less than $2,500 or line 10 on the return for the prior quarter was less than $2,500, and you did not incur a $100,000 next-day deposit obligation during the current quarter. If line 10 for the prior quarter was less than $2,500 but line 10 on this return is $100,000 or more, you must provide a record of your federal tax liability. If you are a monthly schedule depositor, complete the deposit schedule below; if you are a semiweekly schedule depositor, attach Schedule B (Form 941). Go to Part 3.

☐ **You were a monthly schedule depositor for the entire quarter.** Enter your tax liability for each month and total liability for the quarter, then go to Part 3.

Tax liability: Month 1 [.   ]

Month 2 [.   ]

Month 3 [.   ]

Total liability for quarter [.   ] Total must equal line 10.

☐ **You were a semiweekly schedule depositor for any part of this quarter.** Complete Schedule B (Form 941), Report of Tax Liability for Semiweekly Schedule Depositors, and attach it to Form 941.

Part 3: Tell us about your business. If a question does NOT apply to your business, leave it blank.

15 If your business has closed or you stopped paying wages . . . . ☐ Check here, and

enter the final date you paid wages [/   /   ] .

16 If you are a seasonal employer and you do not have to file a return for every quarter of the year . . ☐ Check here.

Part 4: May we speak with your third-party designee?

Do you want to allow an employee, a paid tax preparer, or another person to discuss this return with the IRS? See the instructions for details.

☐ Yes. Designee's name and phone number [   ] [   ]

Select a 5-digit Personal Identification Number (PIN) to use when talking to the IRS. [ ][ ][ ][ ][ ]

☐ No.

Part 5: Sign here. You MUST complete both pages of Form 941 and SIGN it.

Under penalties of perjury, I declare that I have examined this return, including accompanying schedules and statements, and to the best of my knowledge and belief, it is true, correct, and complete. Declaration of preparer (other than taxpayer) is based on all information of which preparer has any knowledge.

✗ Sign your name here [   ] Print your name here [   ]

Print your title here [   ]

Date [/   /   ] Best daytime phone [   ]

Paid Preparer Use Only Check if you are self-employed . . . ☐

Preparer's name [ ]	PTIN	[ ]
Preparer's signature [ ]	Date	[/ /]
Firm's name (or yours if self-employed) [ ]	EIN	[ ]
Address [ ]	Phone	[ ]
City [ ] State [ ]	ZIP code	[ ]

Page **2** Form **941** (Rev. 1-2015)

Source: Internal Revenue Service.

3-14B • LO 5   See pages 3-22 and 3-23

During the third calendar quarter of 20--, the Beechtree Inn, owned by Dawn Smedley, employed the persons listed below. Also given are the employees' salaries or wages and the amount of tips reported to the owner. The tips were reported by the 10th of each month. The federal income tax and FICA tax to be withheld from the tips were estimated by the owner and withheld equally over the 13 weekly pay periods. The employer's portion of FICA tax on the tips was estimated as the same amount.

Employee	Salary or Wage	Quarter's Wages	Quarter's Tips	Quarter's OASDI	Quarter's HI	Quarter's FIT
Jennifer Pasco	$104,000/year	$ 26,000.00		$1,612.00	$ 337.00	$1,980.00
Shelby Toland	78,000/year	19,500.00		1,209.00	282.75	1,290.00
Casey Riordan	800/week	10,400.00	$ 3,240.90	845.78	197.73	600.00
Howard Cohen	650/week	8,450.00	3,493.10	740.48	173.29	630.00
Rebecca Somerville	675/week	8,775.00	3,640.30	769.73	180.05	690.00
Matthew Chalfont	750/week	9,750.00	3,704.00	834.21	195.13	540.00
Sean Matthews	750/week	9,750.00		604.50	141.44	910.00
Holly Perry	600/week	7,800.00		483.60	113.10	653.00
Margaret Levine	750/week	9,750.00		604.50	141.44	364.00
Mary Bullen	600/week	7,800.00		483.60	113.10	559.00
		$117,975.00	$14,078.30	$8,187.40	$1,915.03	$8,216.00

Employees are paid weekly on Friday. The following paydays occurred during this quarter:

July	August	September
5 weekly paydays	4 weekly paydays	4 weekly paydays

Taxes withheld for the 13 paydays in the third quarter follow:

Employees' Federal Income Tax	Weekly FICA Taxes Withheld on Wages		Weekly FICA Taxes on Tips	
	OASDI	HI	OASDI	HI
$632 per week	Employees' $562.65	$131.61	Employees' $67.15	$15.70
	Employer's 562.65	131.59	Employer's 67.14	15.70

Based on the information given, complete Form 941 on the following pages for Dawn Smedley.
Phone number: (901) 555-7959

3-14B (continued)

Form **941 for 20--:** **Employer's QUARTERLY Federal Tax Return**
(Rev. January 2015)

Department of the Treasury — Internal Revenue Service

OMB No. 1545-0029

Employer identification number (EIN) 0 0 — 0 0 0 3 6 0 7

Name *(not your trade name)* DAWN SMEDLEY

Trade name *(if any)* BEECHTREE INN

Address 404 UNION AVE.

Number   Street   Suite or room number

MEMPHIS   TN   38112

City   State   ZIP code

Foreign country name   Foreign province/county   Foreign postal code

Report for this Quarter of 20--
(Check one.)

☐ **1:** January, February, March

☐ **2:** April, May, June

☐ **3:** July, August, September

☐ **4:** October, November, December

Instructions and prior year forms are available at *www.irs.gov/form941.*

Read the separate instructions before you complete Form 941. Type or print within the boxes.

Part 1: **Answer these questions for this quarter.**

1   Number of employees who received wages, tips, or other compensation for the pay period including: *Mar. 12* (Quarter 1), *June 12* (Quarter 2), *Sept. 12* (Quarter 3), or *Dec. 12* (Quarter 4)   **1**

2   Wages, tips, and other compensation **2**

3   Federal income tax withheld from wages, tips, and other compensation **3**

4   If no wages, tips, and other compensation are subject to social security or Medicare tax   ☐ Check and go to line 6.

	Column 1		Column 2
5a Taxable social security wages . .		× .124 =	
5b Taxable social security tips . . .		× .124 =	
5c Taxable Medicare wages & tips. .		× .029 =	
5d Taxable wages & tips subject to Additional Medicare Tax withholding		× .009 =	

5e   Add Column 2 from lines 5a, 5b, 5c, and 5d **5e**

5f   Section 3121(q) Notice and Demand—Tax due on unreported tips (see instructions)   . .   **5f**

6   Total taxes before adjustments. Add lines 3, 5e, and 5f **6**

7   Current quarter's adjustment for fractions of cents **7**

8   Current quarter's adjustment for sick pay **8**

9   Current quarter's adjustments for tips and group-term life insurance **9**

10   Total taxes after adjustments. Combine lines 6 through 9   . . . .   **10**

11   Total deposits for this quarter, including overpayment applied from a prior quarter and overpayments applied from Form 941-X, 941-X (PR), 944-X, 944-X (PR), or 944-X (SP) filed in the current quarter **11**

12   Balance due. If line 10 is more than line 11, enter the difference and see instructions   . . .   **12**

13   Overpayment. If line 11 is more than line 10, enter the difference   Check one: ☐ Apply to next return. ☐ Send a refund.

▶ You MUST complete both pages of Form 941 and SIGN it.

For Privacy Act and Paperwork Reduction Act Notice, see the back of the Payment Voucher.

Cat. No. 17001Z

Next ▶

Form **941** (Rev. 1-2015)

Name *(not your trade name)*	Employer identification number (EIN)
DAWN SMEDLEY	00-0003607

Part 2: Tell us about your deposit schedule and tax liability for this quarter.

If you are unsure about whether you are a monthly schedule depositor or a semiweekly schedule depositor, see Pub. 15 (Circular E), section 11.

14 Check one: ☐ Line 10 on this return is less than $2,500 or line 10 on the return for the prior quarter was less than $2,500, and you did not incur a $100,000 next-day deposit obligation during the current quarter. If line 10 for the prior quarter was less than $2,500 but line 10 on this return is $100,000 or more, you must provide a record of your federal tax liability. If you are a monthly schedule depositor, complete the deposit schedule below; if you are a semiweekly schedule depositor, attach Schedule B (Form 941). Go to Part 3.

☐ **You were a monthly schedule depositor for the entire quarter.** Enter your tax liability for each month and total liability for the quarter, then go to Part 3.

Tax liability: Month 1 [_____ . ___]

Month 2 [_____ . ___]

Month 3 [_____ . ___]

Total liability for quarter [_____ . ___] **Total must equal line 10.**

☐ **You were a semiweekly schedule depositor for any part of this quarter.** Complete Schedule B (Form 941), Report of Tax Liability for Semiweekly Schedule Depositors, and attach it to Form 941.

Part 3: Tell us about your business. If a question does NOT apply to your business, leave it blank.

15 If your business has closed or you stopped paying wages . . . . ☐ Check here, and

enter the final date you paid wages [/ /] .

16 If you are a seasonal employer and you do not have to file a return for every quarter of the year . . ☐ Check here.

Part 4: May we speak with your third-party designee?

Do you want to allow an employee, a paid tax preparer, or another person to discuss this return with the IRS? See the instructions for details.

☐ Yes. Designee's name and phone number [_____] [_____]

Select a 5-digit Personal Identification Number (PIN) to use when talking to the IRS. ☐ ☐ ☐ ☐ ☐

☐ No.

Part 5: Sign here. You MUST complete both pages of Form 941 and SIGN it.

Under penalties of perjury, I declare that I have examined this return, including accompanying schedules and statements, and to the best of my knowledge and belief, it is true, correct, and complete. Declaration of preparer (other than taxpayer) is based on all information of which preparer has any knowledge.

X **Sign your name here** [_____]   Print your name here [_____]

Print your title here [_____]

Date [/ /]   Best daytime phone [_____]

Paid Preparer Use Only   Check if you are self-employed . . . ☐

Preparer's name	[_____]	PTIN	[_____]
Preparer's signature	[_____]	Date	[/ /]
Firm's name (or yours if self-employed)	[_____]	EIN	[_____]
Address	[_____]	Phone	[_____]
City	[_____] State [____]	ZIP code	[_____]

Source: Internal Revenue Service.

3-15B • LO 4, 5 **Similar to Example 3-5 on page 3-19 and see page 3-25**

The taxable wages and withheld taxes for Hamilton Company (EIN 00-0001462), semiweekly depositor, for the first quarter of 2016 follow.

Semimonthly Paydays	Gross and Taxable Wages	FICA Withheld OASDI	FICA Withheld HI	Federal Income Tax Withheld
1/15	$ 34,200	$ 2,120.40	$ 495.90	$ 4,180.00
1/29	32,900	2,039.80	477.05	4,090.00
2/15	31,750	1,968.50	460.38	3,996.00
2/29	28,970	1,796.14	420.07	3,797.00
3/15	28,800	1,785.60	417.60	3,790.00
3/31	29,400	1,822.80	426.30	3,999.00
	$186,020	$11,533.24	$2,697.30	$23,852.00

a. Complete Schedule B of Form 941 on page 3-65 for the first quarter for Harry Conway, the owner of Hamilton Company.

b. Below list the due dates of each deposit in the first quarter.

Paydays	Deposit Due Dates
January 15	1. _____
January 29	2. _____
February 15	3. _____
February 29	4. _____
March 15	5. _____
March 31	6. _____

3-15B (concluded)

Schedule B (Form 941):
Report of Tax Liability for Semiweekly Schedule Depositors

OMB No. 1545-0029

(Rev. January 2014)   Department of the Treasury — Internal Revenue Service

Employer identification number (EIN) ☐☐ – ☐☐☐☐☐☐☐

Name *(not your trade name)*

Calendar year ☐☐☐☐   (Also check quarter)

Report for this Quarter...
(Check one.)

☐ **1:** January, February, March
☐ **2:** April, May, June
☐ **3:** July, August, September
☐ **4:** October, November, December

Use this schedule to show your TAX LIABILITY for the quarter; DO NOT use it to show your deposits. When you file this form with Form 941 or Form 941-SS, DO NOT change your tax liability by adjustments reported on any Forms 941-X or 944-X. You must fill out this form and attach it to Form 941 or Form 941-SS if you are a semiweekly schedule depositor or became one because your accumulated tax liability on any day was $100,000 or more. Write your daily tax liability on the numbered space that corresponds to the date wages were paid. See Section 11 in Pub. 15 (Circular E), Employer's Tax Guide, for details.

Month 1

								Tax liability for Month 1
1	.	9	.	17	.	25	.	
2	.	10	.	18	.	26	.	
3	.	11	.	19	.	27	.	
4	.	12	.	20	.	28	.	.
5	.	13	.	21	.	29	.	
6	.	14	.	22	.	30	.	
7	.	15	.	23	.	31	.	
8	.	16	.	24	.			

Month 2

								Tax liability for Month 2
1	.	9	.	17	.	25	.	
2	.	10	.	18	.	26	.	
3	.	11	.	19	.	27	.	.
4	.	12	.	20	.	28	.	
5	.	13	.	21	.	29	.	
6	.	14	.	22	.	30	.	
7	.	15	.	23	.	31	.	
8	.	16	.	24	.			

Month 3

								Tax liability for Month 3
1	.	9	.	17	.	25	.	
2	.	10	.	18	.	26	.	.
3	.	11	.	19	.	27	.	
4	.	12	.	20	.	28	.	
5	.	13	.	21	.	29	.	
6	.	14	.	22	.	30	.	
7	.	15	.	23	.	31	.	
8	.	16	.	24	.			

Total liability for the quarter

Fill in your total liability for the quarter (Month 1 + Month 2 + Month 3) ▶

Total must equal line 10 on Form 941 or Form 941-SS.   .

For Paperwork Reduction Act Notice, see separate instructions.   IRS.gov/form941   Cat. No. 11967Q   Schedule B (Form 941) (Rev. 1-2014)

Source: Internal Revenue Service.

3-16B • LO 5 **Similar to Example 3-5 on page 3-19, Example 3-6 on page 3-28, Example 3-7 on page 3-29**

Yelman Company is a monthly depositor whose tax liability for June 2016 is $3,930.

1. What is the due date for the deposit of these taxes?   _____

2. Assume that no deposit was made until August 5. Compute the following penalties:

    a. Penalty for failure to make timely deposit. $ _____

    b. Penalty for failure to fully pay tax. $ _____

    c. Interest on taxes due and unpaid. $ _____

    d. Total penalty imposed. $ _____

3-17B • LO 2, 3 **Similar to Example 3-1 on pages 3-10 and 3-11**

At Gleeson Brewing Company, office workers are employed for a 40-hour workweek on either an annual or a monthly salary basis.

Given on the form below are the current annual and monthly salary rates for five office workers for the week ended December 9, 2016 (50th payday of the year). In addition, with this pay, these employees are paid their sliding-scale annual bonuses. The bonuses are listed on the register.

For each worker, compute:
1. Regular earnings for the weekly payroll ended December 9, 2016.
2. Overtime earnings (if applicable).
3. Total regular, overtime earnings, and bonus.
4. FICA taxable wages for this pay period.
5. FICA taxes to be withheld for this pay period.

GLEESON BREWING COMPANY

Employee	Salary	Hours Worked	Annual Bonus	Regular Earnings	Overtime Earnings	Total Earnings
Won, H.	$99,840/yr.	40	$30,000			
Park, B.	96,200/yr.	40	25,000			
James, R.	7,280/mo.	40	20,000			
Oho, J.	5,265/mo.	40	15,000			
Mack, K.	3,400/mo.	46	8,000			
Totals						

(left side)

GLEESON BREWING COMPANY

Cumulative Earnings as of Last Pay Period	FICA Taxable Wages This Pay Period		FICA Taxes to Be Withheld		Employee
	OASDI	HI	OASDI	HI	
$94,080.00					Won, H.
90,650.00					Park, B.
82,320.00					James, R.
59,535.00					Oho, J.
38,446.38					Mack, K.
					Totals

(right side)

Employer's FICA taxes for week ended December 9, 2016: $ _____ $ _____

                                             OASDI   HI

CONTINUING PAYROLL PROBLEM • A

Refer to the partially completed payroll register you started at the end of Chapter 2. You will now determine the amount of FICA taxes to be withheld from each employee's pay for the pay period ending January 8, 20--.

1. In the Taxable Earnings columns, record the amount of each employee's weekly earnings that is subject to FICA taxes.

2. Using the amount recorded in step 1, compute the taxes for each employee and record in the appropriate column.

Note: Keep your partially completed payroll register for use at the end of Chapter 4.

CONTINUING PAYROLL PROBLEM • B

Refer to the partially completed payroll register you started at the end of Chapter 2. You will now determine the amount of FICA taxes to be withheld from each employee's pay for the pay period ending January 8, 20--.

1. In the Taxable Earnings columns, record the amount of each employee's weekly earnings that is subject to FICA taxes.

2. Using the amount recorded in step 1, compute the taxes for each employee and record in the appropriate column.

Note: Keep your partially completed payroll register for use at the end of Chapter 4.

CASE PROBLEMS

C1. Auditing Form 941. LO 4, 5.

Your assistant has just completed a rough draft of Form 941, shown on pages 3-70 and 3-71, for the quarter ending March 31, 20--. As the supervisor and authorized signer, you are auditing the form before it is mailed to ensure its accuracy.

Four of the company's general ledger accounts are shown on the following two pages. Employees are paid on the 15th and last day of each month. The company is a semiweekly depositor. Indicate any changes that should be made on the form before it is signed, dated, and mailed.

C1 (continued)

FICA TAXES PAYABLE—OASDI   Account No. 214

Date		Debit	Credit	Balance Debit	Balance Credit
20--					
Jan.	15		773.94		773.94
	15		773.96		1,547.90
	19	1,547.90			—
	31		843.78		843.78
	31		843.78		1,687.56
Feb.	2	1,687.56			—
	15		833.74		833.74
	15		833.72		1,667.46
	22	1,667.46			—
	28		803.79		803.79
	28		803.79		1,607.58
Mar.	3	1,607.58			—
	15		786.73		786.73
	15		786.72		1,573.45
	20	1,573.45			—
	31		787.87		787.87
	31		787.88		1,575.75
Apr.	5	1,575.75			—

FICA TAXES PAYABLE—HI   Account No. 215

Date		Debit	Credit	Balance Debit	Balance Credit
20--					
Jan.	15		181.01		181.01
	15		181.01		362.02
	19	362.02			—
	31		197.32		197.32
	31		197.34		394.66
Feb.	2	394.66			—
	15		194.98		194.98
	15		194.98		389.96
	22	389.96			—
	28		187.98		187.98
	28		187.98		375.96
Mar.	3	375.96			—
	15		183.99		183.99
	15		184.01		368.00
	20	368.00			—
	31		184.24		184.24
	31		184.26		368.50
Apr.	5	368.50			—

C1 (continued)

EMPLOYEES FEDERAL INCOME TAX PAYABLE Account No. 216

Date		Debit	Credit	Balance Debit	Balance Credit
20--					
Jan.	15		1,980.00		1,980.00
	19	1,980.00			—
	31		2,217.00		2,217.00
Feb.	2	2,217.00			—
	15		2,016.00		2,016.00
	22	2,016.00			—
	28		2,007.00		2,007.00
Mar.	3	2,007.00			—
	15		1,970.00		1,970.00
	20	1,970.00			—
	31		1,887.00		1,887.00
Apr.	5	1,887.00			—

WAGES AND SALARIES Account No. 511

Date		Debit	Credit	Balance Debit	Balance Credit
20--					
Jan.	15	12,483.16		12,483.16	
	31	13,609.40		26,092.56	
Feb.	15	13,447.13		39,539.69	
	28	12,964.43		52,504.12	
Mar.	15	12,689.02		65,193.14	
	31	12,707.69		77,900.83	

C1 (continued)

Form **941 for 20--:** **Employer's QUARTERLY Federal Tax Return**
(Rev. January 2015) Department of the Treasury — Internal Revenue Service

OMB No. 1545-0029

Employer identification number (EIN) 0 0 – 0 0 0 7 1 4 2

Name *(not your trade name)*

Trade name *(if any)* COASTAL COMPANY

Address 77 CASTRO
Number   Street   Suite or room number

SAN FRANCISCO   CA   94117
City   State   ZIP code

Foreign country name   Foreign province/county   Foreign postal code

Report for this Quarter of 20--
(Check one.)

☐ **1:** January, February, March

☐ **2:** April, May, June

☐ **3:** July, August, September

☐ **4:** October, November, December

Instructions and prior year forms are available at *www.irs.gov/form941.*

Read the separate instructions before you complete Form 941. Type or print within the boxes.

Part 1: **Answer these questions for this quarter.**

1	Number of employees who received wages, tips, or other compensation for the pay period including: *Mar. 12* (Quarter 1), *June 12* (Quarter 2), *Sept. 12* (Quarter 3), or *Dec. 12* (Quarter 4)	1	17
2	Wages, tips, and other compensation	2	77900.38
3	Federal income tax withheld from wages, tips, and other compensation	3	12077.00
4	If no wages, tips, and other compensation are subject to social security or Medicare tax	☐ Check and go to line 6.	

		Column 1		Column 2
5a	Taxable social security wages	77900.38	× .124 =	9659.65
5b	Taxable social security tips	.	× .124 =	.
5c	Taxable Medicare wages & tips	77900.38	× .029 =	2259.11
5d	Taxable wages & tips subject to Additional Medicare Tax withholding	.	× .009 =	.

5e	Add Column 2 from lines 5a, 5b, 5c, and 5d	5e	11918.76
5f	Section 3121(q) Notice and Demand—Tax due on unreported tips (see instructions)	5f	.
6	Total taxes before adjustments. Add lines 3, 5e, and 5f	6	23995.76
7	Current quarter's adjustment for fractions of cents	7	.04
8	Current quarter's adjustment for sick pay	8	.
9	Current quarter's adjustments for tips and group-term life insurance	9	.
10	Total taxes after adjustments. Combine lines 6 through 9	10	23995.80
11	Total deposits for this quarter, including overpayment applied from a prior quarter and overpayments applied from Form 941-X, 941-X (PR), 944-X, 944-X (PR), or 944-X (SP) filed in the current quarter	11	23995.80
12	Balance due. If line 10 is more than line 11, enter the difference and see instructions	12	18.00
13	Overpayment. If line 11 is more than line 10, enter the difference	.	Check one: ☐ Apply to next return. ☐ Send a refund.

▶ You MUST complete both pages of Form 941 and SIGN it.

Next ▶

For Privacy Act and Paperwork Reduction Act Notice, see the back of the Payment Voucher.   Cat. No. 17001Z   Form **941** (Rev. 1-2015)

C1 (concluded)

Name (not your trade name)	Employer identification number (EIN)
COASTAL COMPANY	00-0007142

Part 2:	**Tell us about your deposit schedule and tax liability for this quarter.**

If you are unsure about whether you are a monthly schedule depositor or a semiweekly schedule depositor, see Pub. 15 (Circular E), section 11.

14 Check one: ☐ Line 10 on this return is less than $2,500 or line 10 on the return for the prior quarter was less than $2,500, and you did not incur a $100,000 next-day deposit obligation during the current quarter. If line 10 for the prior quarter was less than $2,500 but line 10 on this return is $100,000 or more, you must provide a record of your federal tax liability. If you are a monthly schedule depositor, complete the deposit schedule below; if you are a semiweekly schedule depositor, attach Schedule B (Form 941). Go to Part 3.

☐ **You were a monthly schedule depositor for the entire quarter.** Enter your tax liability for each month and total liability for the quarter, then go to Part 3.

Tax liability:	Month 1	8189.14
	Month 2	8063.96
	Month 3	7742.70
Total liability for quarter		23995.80	**Total must equal line 10.**

☐ **You were a semiweekly schedule depositor for any part of this quarter.** Complete Schedule B (Form 941), Report of Tax Liability for Semiweekly Schedule Depositors, and attach it to Form 941.

Part 3:	**Tell us about your business. If a question does NOT apply to your business, leave it blank.**

15 If your business has closed or you stopped paying wages . . . . ☐ Check here, and

enter the final date you paid wages [/ /] .

16 If you are a seasonal employer and you do not have to file a return for every quarter of the year . . ☐ Check here.

Part 4:	**May we speak with your third-party designee?**

Do you want to allow an employee, a paid tax preparer, or another person to discuss this return with the IRS? See the instructions for details.

☐ Yes. Designee's name and phone number [_____] [_____]

Select a 5-digit Personal Identification Number (PIN) to use when talking to the IRS. ☐ ☐ ☐ ☐ ☐

☐ No.

Part 5:	**Sign here. You MUST complete both pages of Form 941 and SIGN it.**

Under penalties of perjury, I declare that I have examined this return, including accompanying schedules and statements, and to the best of my knowledge and belief, it is true, correct, and complete. Declaration of preparer (other than taxpayer) is based on all information of which preparer has any knowledge.

X **Sign your name here** [_____]

Print your name here [_____]

Print your title here [_____]

Date [/ /]

Best daytime phone [_____]

Paid Preparer Use Only   Check if you are self-employed . . . ☐

Preparer's name	[_____]	PTIN	[_____]
Preparer's signature	[_____]	Date	[/ /]
Firm's name (or yours if self-employed)	[_____]	EIN	[_____]
Address	[_____]	Phone	[_____]
City	[_____]	State	☐ ZIP code	[_____]

Source: Internal Revenue Service.

C2. Household Employee? LO 1.

Nelson operates a placement service for companion-sitting for the elderly. He placed Martha Jackson with Mrs. Mock, an elderly woman who needed a person to assist with her personal needs, household care, and companionship. Jackson is paid directly from Mrs. Mock. Jackson had to pay a placement fee of $50 to Nelson. Is Jackson an employee of Nelson or a household employee of Mrs. Mock? Explain.

Income Tax Withholding

In this chapter's animated activities, we look at Barbri Company. Barbri Company pays its employees weekly. One of Barbri's employees takes a three-week vacation. Should Barbri Company pay their employee based on the gross earnings for the three-week period or should Barbri pay the employee on three separate wage payments? Vacation pay is considered supplemental wages. Other types of supplemental wages include bonuses, commissions, exercised nonqualified stock options, and dismissal pay.

Let's take a look at supplemental wages and other topics including Federal Income Tax Withholding Law, completing Form 941 and Form W-2 (Wage and Tax Statement).

LEARNING OBJECTIVES

After studying this chapter, you should be able to:

1. Explain coverage under the Federal Income Tax Withholding Law by determining: (a) the employer-employee relationship, (b) the kinds of payments defined as wages, and (c) the kinds of pretax salary reductions.

2. Explain: (a) the types of withholding allowances that may be claimed by employees for income tax withholding and (b) the purpose and use of Form W-4.

3. Compute the amount of federal income tax to be withheld using: (a) the percentage method; (b) the wage-bracket method; (c) alternative methods such as quarterly averaging, annualizing of wages, and part-year employment; and (d) withholding of federal income taxes on supplementary wage payments.

4. Explain: (a) Form W-2, (b) the completion of **Form 941, Employer's Quarterly Federal Tax Return,** (c) major types of information returns, and (d) the impact of state and local income taxes on the payroll accounting process.

Due to printing schedules, the tax tables at the end of the book are the tables that were in effect until December 31, 2015.

At the beginning of World War II, the income tax became the principal source of revenue to finance government operations. The Ruml plan put the collection of this tax on a pay-as-you-go basis. This chapter describes the employer's responsibility for withholding income taxes from employees' wages and paying these taxes to the federal government. In addition, many employers must also comply with state, city, and county income tax withholding laws. Employers must be aware of these laws to avoid possible penalties.

Coverage Under Federal Income Tax Withholding Laws

Before an individual withholds any tax under the tax law, the following conditions must exist:

1. There must be, or have been, an employer-employee relationship.
2. The payments received by the employee must be defined as wages under the law.
3. The employment must not be exempted by the law.

LO 1

Explain coverage under the Federal Income Tax Withholding Law by determining: (a) the employer-employee relationship, (b) the kinds of payments defined as wages, and (c) the kinds of pretax salary reductions.

Employer-Employee Relationship

As discussed in Chapter 3, establishing the correct relationship between the employer and employee is a very important factor in complying with the Social Security Tax Law. This also applies to the Federal Income Tax Withholding Law.

If a business has the right to control and direct the worker, it meets the definition of an employer under the common-law criteria.

Employers can be sole proprietorships, partners, corporations, not-for-profit corporations, and federal and state governments. No distinctions are made between classes or grades of employees—from executives to entry-level personnel. Directors of a corporation are not considered employees unless they perform services other than participation in board meetings. Partners are also eliminated from the definition of an employee.

If the employer-employee relationship exists, the pay is subject to federal income tax withholding.

Statutory Employees/Nonemployees

If a worker does not qualify as an employee under the common-law test, federal income taxes are not withheld. However, by statute, under certain conditions he or she may be considered *an employee* for FICA and FUTA taxes. As discussed in Chapter 3, this applies to agent drivers, full-time life insurance salespersons, homeworkers, and traveling or city salespersons.

Direct sellers and qualified real estate agents are considered *nonemployees* by statute. They are treated as self-employed for *all* federal tax purposes.

Taxable Wages

For withholding purposes, the term **wages** includes the total compensation paid to employees for services. Employers withhold federal income taxes on the *gross amount* of wages before deductions such as state and local taxes, insurance premiums, savings bonds, profit-sharing contributions, and union dues. Examples of employee compensation subject to withholding include:

- Wages and salaries
- Vacation allowances
- Supplemental payments
- Bonuses and commissions
- Taxable fringe benefits
- Tips
- Cash awards

Employees may receive compensation in ways other than their regular wage payments. Figure 4.1 shows some special types of payments that are also subject to federal income tax withholding.

Payments to employees in a medium other than cash are also taxed. Payments in the form of goods, lodging, food, clothing, or services are taxed at their fair market value at the time that they are given.

If wages received in the same payroll period are in part subject to withholding and in part exempt, all wages received are treated alike. If one-half or more of the wages is subject to withholding, then withholding is required on all wages. If more than one-half of the pay is exempt from withholding, then no withholding is required for the total pay.

FIGURE **4.1**
Taxable Payments to Employees

Disabled Worker's Wages	Withhold for wages paid after the year in which the worker became entitled to disability insurance under the Social Security Act.
Drawing Account Advances	Advance payments to salespersons against their commissions or unearned salaries for which they are to perform services, but for which they are not legally obligated to repay.
Gift Certificates (cards)	Considered cash equivalent, and therefore taxable.
Meals and Lodging	Unless furnished for the employer's convenience and on the employer's premises, as a condition of employment. Cash allowances for meals and lodging are taxable. If more than half of the meals provided to employees on the employer's premises are for the convenience of the employer, then these meals are treated as for the employer's convenience.
Moving Expenses	Nonqualified reimbursed and employer-paid expenses are subject to withholding. Nonqualified expenses include cost of sale of old residence, purchase of new residence, house hunting, temporary living expenses, and meals.
Partially Exempt Employment	If the employee spends half or more time in a pay period performing services subject to employment taxes, all pay in that pay period is taxable.
Payments to Nonresident Aliens	Subject to withholding (unless excepted by regulations).
Scholarship	Cash or reduced tuition is taxable if paid for teaching, research, or other services as a condition of receiving the scholarship.
Sick Pay	Subject to withholding whether paid by the employer or third party (to the extent of the employer's contribution into the plan).
Supplemental Unemployment Compensation	To the extent it is includible in an employee's gross income. It does not include separation due to disciplinary problems or age.
Travel and Business Expenses (nonaccountable plans)	If (1) the employee is not required to or does not substantiate expenses with receipts or (2) the employee receives travel advances and does not or is not required to return any unused amount of the advance.

Fringe Benefits

Unless the law says otherwise, fringe benefits are subject to federal income tax withholding. In general, the taxable portion is the amount by which the fair market value of the benefits exceeds what the employee paid, plus any amount the law excludes. Fringe benefits include employer-provided items such as those listed here.

- Cars
- Free or discounted flights
- Discounts on property or services
- Vacations
- Memberships in social or country clubs
- Tickets for entertainment and sporting events

Withholding on Fringe Benefits

Determination of the value of the fringe benefit must be made by January 31 of the following year. For withholding and depositing purposes, reasonable estimates may be used before that date. The employer may add the value of fringe benefits to regular wages for a payroll period and figure withholding taxes on the total or may withhold the tax on the value of the benefits at the *flat 25* percent supplemental wage rate.

The employer may choose not to withhold income tax on the value of an employee's personal use of a vehicle. The employer must, however, withhold social security, Medicare, or railroad retirement taxes on the use of the vehicle.

Flexible Reporting

With noncash fringe benefits, the employer has the option of treating the benefits as being paid on any basis (paying monthly, at year-end, etc.). As long as the benefits are treated as paid by December 31, the employer can choose any option.

Due to a *special period rule,* employers can even use October 31 as the cutoff date for valuing the noncash fringe benefit. This rule allows employers to treat noncash fringe benefits of November and December as being provided in the following year and therefore taxed in the next year.

If this special rule is applied to a particular benefit, it must apply to all employees who receive this benefit. Also, if applied, the employer must notify the employees of this special rule treatment prior to giving them their W-2 forms.

Employers may treat the value of a single fringe benefit as paid on one or more dates in the same calendar year even if the employee receives the entire benefit at one time.

A one-time receipt of a $1,000 fringe benefit in 2016 can be treated as four payments of $250, each in a different pay period of 2016.

ON THE **JOB**

If you need to determine if a certain type of payment or individual is subject to income tax withholding, check **Circular E, Employer's Tax Guide**. Special classes of employment and payments are listed, along with their treatment under employment tax laws.

NEWS ALERT

When an employer provides a cell phone to an employee "primarily for noncompensatory business reasons," the IRS will treat the employee's business use of the cell phone as a working condition fringe benefit, the value of which is excludable from the employee's income. Also, personal use of the employer-provided cell phone will be treated as a de minimis fringe benefit.[1]

Nontaxable Fringe Benefits

Fringe benefits that are nontaxable include:

- Services provided at no additional cost
- Qualified employee discounts
- Working condition fringes
- Qualified transportation fringes
- Use of on-premises athletic facilities
- Reduced tuition for education
- Job-placement assistance

Services the employer provides at no additional cost, qualified employee discounts, meals at employer-run eating establishments, and reduced tuition are excluded from their income only if the benefits are given to employees on a nondiscriminatory basis.

De Minimis Fringe Benefit

Any property or service the value of which is so small that accounting for it would be unreasonable or impractical is labeled a de minimis fringe benefit (i.e., coffee, doughnuts, local telephone calls). There is no dollar cap on this type of nontaxable fringe benefit.

Taxable Tips

As reported in Chapter 3, employees must report cash tips to the employer by the 10th of the month following the month they receive the tips. This report includes tips paid by the employer for charge customers and tips the employee receives directly from the customers. Tips of *less than $20* in a month and noncash tips need not be reported.

---

1 *Payroll Currently,* October 7, 2011, Issue 10, p. 3.

Withholding from Tips

The employer collects income tax, as well as social security taxes, on reported tips. The following procedures apply to withholding income tax on reported tips:

1. The employer collects the tax from the employee's wages or from other funds the employee makes available.
2. When tips are reported in connection with employment where the employee also receives a regular wage, compute the withholding tax on the aggregate—treat tips as a supplemental wage payment.
3. If the withholding tax exceeds the amount of wages paid to the employee, the employee must pay the uncollected portion of the taxes directly to the IRS when filing the annual income tax return (Form 1040).
4. The employer is not required to audit or verify the accuracy of the tip income reported.

Allocated Tips

Large food and beverage establishments that have customary tipping and normally had more than 10 employees on a typical business day in the preceding year may be required to allocate tips among employees if:

The total tips reported by the employees during any payroll period are less than 8 percent of the establishment's gross receipts for that period.

The amount of allocated tips to employees equals:

The difference between tips reported and 8 percent of gross receipts, other than carryout sales and sales with at least a 10 percent service charge added.

The tip allocation may be made using one of three methods: hours worked, gross receipts, good faith agreement. Federal income taxes are to be withheld only on the tips reported to the employer; no taxes are withheld on the tips that are merely allocated.

Traveling Expenses

Accountable Plan

Employee expense reimbursement amounts paid under an accountable plan are not subject to income tax withholding. An accountable plan requires the employer's reimbursement or allowance arrangement to meet all three of the following rules:

1. Business connected.
2. Adequate accounting within a reasonable time period (generally, 60 days).
3. Employee return of excess of substantiated amounts (generally, 120 days).

Nonaccountable Plan

A nonaccountable plan is an arrangement that does not meet all of the previous requirements. All amounts paid under this plan are considered wages and are subject to income tax withholding.

Payments Exempt from Withholding

The law excludes certain payments and payments to certain individuals from federal income tax withholding, as shown in Figure 4.2 on page 4-6.

Pretax Salary Reductions

An employee can authorize an employer to deduct certain withholdings from his or her pay on a pretax basis. These withholdings are taken from the gross pay and therefore reduce the amount of pay that is subject to federal income tax.

Cafeteria Plans

Some employers offer their employees a choice between cash (pay) or qualified (nontaxable) benefits. Employees can select various levels of health, accident, and life insurance coverage or choose to contribute to cash or deferred plans. The salary reductions are used to pay for the desired benefit, and these pretax contributions are not included in taxable wages for FIT. These salary reductions, which are allowed under a cafeteria plan, are also exempt from FICA and FUTA taxes and from most states' taxes.

FIGURE 4.2
Exempt Payments

Type of Payment or Individual	Conditions
Advances	For travel and other business expenses reasonably expected to be incurred.
Accident and Health Insurance Payments	Exempt except 2 percent shareholder-employees of S corporations.
Deceased Person's Wages	Paid to the person's beneficiary or estate.
Dependent Care Assistance	To the extent it is reasonable to believe the amounts will be excludable from gross income. Up to $5,000 can be excluded from an employee's gross income without being subject to social security, Medicare, or income tax withholding.
Domestic Service	Private home, local college club, or local chapter of college fraternity or sorority.
Educational Assistance	If education maintains or improves employee's skills required by the job. For the non–job-related educational assistance, up to $5,250 per year of employer-provided assistance for undergraduate and graduate education is tax-free. Also applies to "downsized" employees and can be used after voluntary or involuntary termination.
Employee Business Expense Reimbursements	Accountable plans for amounts not exceeding specified government rates for mileage, lodging, meals, and incidental expenses.
Employee-Safety and Length-of-Service Awards	If merchandise costs $400 or less. Rises to $1,600 for a written nondiscriminatory plan.
Employer-Provided Parking	Up to $250 per month.
Foreign Service by U.S. Citizens	As employees for affiliates of American employers if entitled to exclusion under section 911 or required by law of foreign country to withhold income tax on such payment.
Group-Term Life Insurance Costs	The employer's cost of group-term life insurance less than $50,000.
Health Reimbursement Arrangements (HRA)	As long as no person has the right to receive cash or any other taxable or nontaxable benefit other than medical care reimbursement.
Individuals Under 18	For delivery or distribution of newspapers, shopping news, and vendors of newspapers and magazines where payment is the difference between the purchase and sales price.
Long-Term Care Insurance Premiums	Employer-paid premiums for long-term care insurance up to a limit. For example, for an employee age 40 or under, the first $380 of premiums are nontaxable.
Ministers of Churches, Members of Religious Orders	Performing services for the order agency of the supervising church or associated institution.
Moving Expense Reimbursements	For qualified expenses, if the employee is entitled to a deduction for these expenses on the individual's federal income tax return.
Public Officials	For fees only, not salaries.
Retirement and Pension Plans	• Employer contributions to a qualified plan. • Employer contributions to IRA accounts under an SEP [see section 402(g) for salary reduction limitation]. • Employer contributions to section 403(b) annuity contract [see section 402(g) for limitation]. • Elective contributions and deferrals to plans containing a qualified cash or deferred compensation arrangement, such as 401(k).
Sickness or Injury Payments	Payments made under worker's compensation law or contract of insurance.
Transportation in a Commuter Highway Vehicle and Transit Pass	Up to $130 per month.

SELF-STUDY QUIZ 4-1

Check any item of employee compensation not subject to withholding:

_____ 1. Company-provided lunches at the plant to reduce tardiness by keeping employees on the premises.

_____ 2. Year-end bonuses to managers and supervisors.

_____ 3. Work-out room for employee use during lunch hours.

_____ 4. Travel advances to salespersons for overnight sales calls out of town.

_____ 5. Employer-paid sick pay.

_____ 6. Memberships in the local country club for department managers.

_____ 7. Meals provided by a local restaurant for its employees.

Note: Answers are on page 4-34.

The following benefits may be included in the plan:

- Accident and health insurance
- Self-insured medical reimbursement plan
- Group-term life insurance (first $50,000 of coverage)
- Dependent care assistance (first $5,000)
- Health savings accounts (discussed below)

These benefits cannot be included in a cafeteria plan:

- Transportation fringe benefits
- Educational assistance
- Scholarships and fellowship grants
- Meals and lodging for the convenience of employer
- Dependent group-term life insurance
- Deferred compensation except for 401(k) contributions

Flexible-Spending Accounts

These accounts allow employees to have money deducted from their paychecks to cover their out-of-pocket medical expenses. The deductions from the employees' pays are made with pretax dollars. Regulations now allow employers the option to extend the time period to spend the unused money in these accounts from the end of the year until March 15 of the following year. Reimbursements are made to employees from an employer-controlled account, and unused monies in these accounts are forfeited by the participants. In 2015, a limit on flexible spending arrangements in the amount of $2,550 per year was implemented.

Health Savings Accounts

These accounts are used by employees who have high-deductible health insurance (for 2016, $1,300 for self-only coverage and $2,600 for family coverage and with maximum out-of-pocket expenses of $6,550 and $13,100, respectively) to pay for medical expenses for themselves and their dependents. Contributions made into the plan by the employer are excluded from the employees' taxable income. For a single person in 2016, the maximum contribution is $3,350 or the amount of the annual deductible, if less (for family coverage—$6,750). Employees who are 55 or older by the end of the year can contribute an additional $1,000 to their HSA. If married and both are age 55 or older, both can contribute an additional $1,000. Employee contributions into the account (through payroll deductions) must be included in wages and are subject to withholding taxes. However, if these contributions are part of a salary reduction arrangement in a qualified cafeteria plan, they are not subject to withholding taxes.

Archer Medical Savings Accounts

These accounts are for employees of small businesses (50 or fewer employees) and are set up in conjunction with high-deductible insurance plans. Employees'

ON THE **JOB**

Children who have not reached age 27 as of the end of the tax year will qualify for health insurance, including cafeteria plans.

payroll deductions are subject to federal income tax withholding (FICA also). However, employees can deduct the contributions on their tax returns, and they have full control over the account. Employer contributions are not subject to tax withholding. Unused monies in this type of account carry over from year to year.

Deferred Arrangements

Many deferred arrangements are usually set up as retirement plans. The most common of these is the **defined contribution plan** that provides future benefits based solely on the amount paid by each employee and employer into the account, plus investment gains. These plans are tax-deferred savings or stock accounts held in trust for employees. The most popular types of retirement accounts are the 401(k) and IRAs.

EXAMPLE 4-1   Carl Jamison, an employee for the Scharman School, belongs to a tax-deferred retirement plan to which he contributes 3 percent of his pay which is matched by the school. His biweekly pay is $2,500. Because of the deferral (3% × $2,500 = $75), $2,425 is subject to federal income tax withholding.

Tax-Deferred Retirement Accounts

These types of accounts allow employees to contribute amounts from their wages into retirement accounts. These contributions reduce the amount of the employees' wages that are subject to federal income tax. These tax-deferred plans set limits on the amounts that employees can contribute tax-free and also provide for additional contributions to be made into the accounts by the employers. Upon retirement, the employees will receive their contributions back in the form of regular payments from their retirement plans. These payments are then subject to federal income tax. The advantage to tax-deferred retirement accounts is that the taxpayer may be in a lower tax bracket when the income is taxed.

- *401(k) Plan.* A standard tax-deferred retirement plan. A set percentage of an employee's wages is contributed on a pretax basis. Employers can limit the percentage of an employee's pay that can be contributed. This limit can be lower than the maximum set by law. Employees can add after-tax contributions to this total, and the employer can contribute to the employees' plan.
- *Simple Plans.* A small company plan for a company with up to 100 employees. The employer can offer a SIMPLE plan as part of a 401(k) plan. This plan allows employees to contribute a percentage of their pay toward retirement.
- *Section 403(b) Plan.* A plan for employees of tax-exempt organizations.
- *Section 457(b) Plan.* A plan for employees of state and local governments and of tax-exempt organizations other than churches.

The following information applies to 2015:

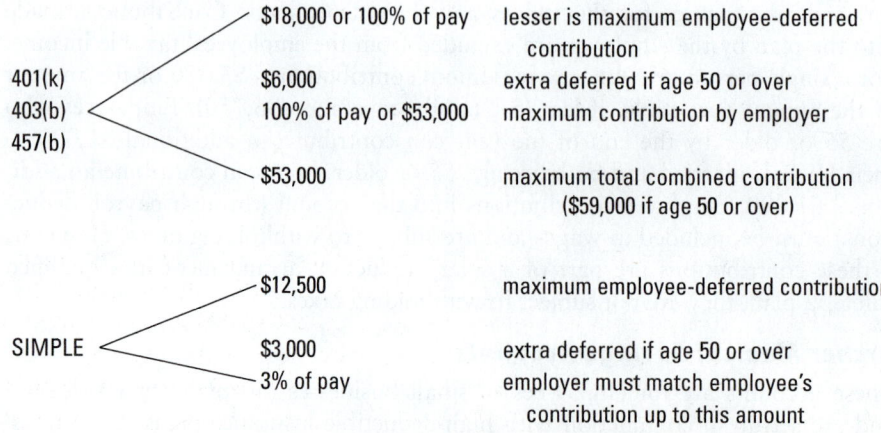

	$18,000 or 100% of pay	lesser is maximum employee-deferred contribution
401(k)	$6,000	extra deferred if age 50 or over
403(b)	100% of pay or $53,000	maximum contribution by employer
457(b)	$53,000	maximum total combined contribution ($59,000 if age 50 or over)
	$12,500	maximum employee-deferred contribution
SIMPLE	$3,000	extra deferred if age 50 or over
	3% of pay	employer must match employee's contribution up to this amount

Individual Retirement Accounts

Beyond the various payroll-related tax-deferred accounts, individuals can set up their own retirement accounts. In 2015, under certain conditions, an employee may put aside each year the lesser of $5,500 or 100 percent of their compensation without paying federal income taxes on their contributions. If an employee is age 50 or older before 2016, the most that can be contributed to a traditional IRA is the lesser of $6,500 or 100 percent of their compensation. Eligible employees may make an additional $5,500 contribution on behalf of a nonworking or low-earning spouse provided the combined compensation is at least equal to the total combined IRA contribution. To be eligible for such deductible (tax-free) contributions, either of the following two conditions must be met (for 2015):

1. The individual does not belong to a company-funded retirement plan.
2. The individual has modified adjusted gross income less than $61,000. (In the case of a married employee, the combined adjusted gross income must be less than $98,000.)

If the employee belongs to another qualified plan, full and partial tax-free deductions are allowed if:

1. The employee is single or head of household and has modified adjusted gross income less than $61,000 with phaseout at $71,000.
2. The employee is married, filing a joint return, and has modified adjusted gross income less than $98,000 with phaseout at $118,000.
3. The employee is married, filing separately, and has zero adjusted gross income with phaseout at $10,000.

If an employee's spouse belongs to a company-funded retirement plan, the employee is not considered an active participant in the plan. However, the nonactive spouse's tax-free IRA deduction ($5,500) will begin to phase out between $183,000 to $193,000 of their total adjusted gross income.

Even though these contributions can be made through payroll deductions, the employer is not considered a pension plan sponsor and is not subject to ERISA as long as the following guidelines are met:

1. The employer makes no matching contributions.
2. Participation is not mandatory.
3. The employer does not endorse any IRA sponsors.

Roth IRA

Another type of IRA that allows taxpayers and their spouses to make annual *nondeductible* contributions of up to $5,500 ($6,500 if age 50 or older) is the Roth IRA. The amount that may be contributed is reduced by the amount contributed into other IRAs. Allowable contributions are phased out for those with adjusted gross income of between $116,000 to $131,000 for single taxpayers, $183,000 to $193,000 for joint taxpayers, and $0 to $10,000 for married taxpayers filing separately.

The advantage of this type of IRA is that distributions made out of the fund at retirement are tax-free.

Withholding Allowances

The law entitles employees to exempt a portion of their earnings from withholding by claiming a personal allowance and allowances for their dependents if they furnish their employers with a claim for the allowances. Employees may also claim special allowances and allowances for itemized deductions and tax credits. However, employees cannot claim the same withholding allowances with more than one employer at the same time.

LO 2

Explain: (a) the types of withholding allowances that may be claimed by employees for income tax withholding and (b) the purpose and use of Form W-4.

Personal Allowances

Employees can claim a **personal allowance** for themselves and each qualified dependent, provided they are not claimed on another person's tax return. In 2015, the amount of the personal allowance was $4,000, and this was treated as a deduction in computing taxable income. A married employee may also claim one personal allowance for his or her spouse if the spouse is not claimed as a dependent on another person's tax return.

If the employee has a second job or if the spouse also works, the personal allowances that the employee is entitled to should not also be claimed on the other job.

Allowances for Dependents

Employees may claim one allowance for each dependent (other than a spouse) who will be claimed on their federal income tax returns. To qualify as a dependent, the person must meet specific requirements that are listed in the instructions accompanying the individual's federal income tax return (six tests are involved—relationship, support, domicile, age, joint return, and citizenship).

Additional Withholding Allowance

Employees can also reduce the amount of withholding by claiming a **special withholding allowance**, whether or not they plan to itemize deductions on their tax returns. An additional withholding allowance can be claimed by a person under any one of the following situations:

1. Single person who has only one job.
2. Married person who has only one job with nonworking spouse.
3. Person's wages from a second job or the spouse's wages (or both) equal $1,500 or less.

This allowance is only used to compute the employee's income tax withholding. The employee *cannot claim* this allowance on his or her income tax return.

Other Withholding Allowances

Withholding allowances reduce the overwithholding of income taxes on employees' wages. In addition to the allowances already discussed, employees may be entitled to withholding allowances based on estimated tax credits, such as child care, and itemized deductions for medical expenses, mortgage interest, and charitable contributions. Employees take these credits when filing their federal income tax returns. The number of withholding allowances is determined on the worksheet that accompanies *Form W-4, Employee's Withholding Allowance Certificate,* and is then reported on that form.

Form W-4 (Employee's Withholding Allowance Certificate)

The employer uses the information from *Form W-4, Employee's Withholding Allowance Certificate,* to compute the amount of income tax to withhold from employees' wages. The employer must have Form W-4 on file for each employee. This form contains the withholding allowance certificate (shown in Figure 4.3), detailed instructions, and worksheets for employees to use in completing the certificate.

Completing Form W-4

The employee completes Form W-4 when he or she begins work for an employer. Employers must retain the withholding certificate as a supporting record of the withholding allowances used in deducting income taxes from the employees'

FIGURE 4.3

Form W-4, Employee's Withholding Allowance Certificate

---------------------------- Separate here and give Form W-4 to your employer. Keep the top part for your records. ----------------------------

Form **W-4** Department of the Treasury Internal Revenue Service	**Employee's Withholding Allowance Certificate** ▶ Whether you are entitled to claim a certain number of allowances or exemption from withholding is subject to review by the IRS. Your employer may be required to send a copy of this form to the IRS.	OMB No. 1545-0074 **20--**

1 Your first name and middle initial	Last name	2 Your social security number
Harry M.	Weir	000 00 6921

Home address (number and street or rural route)	3 ☒ Single ☐ Married ☐ Married, but withhold at higher Single rate.
421 Eastmont	**Note.** If married, but legally separated, or spouse is a nonresident alien, check the "Single" box.

City or town, state, and ZIP code	4 If your last name differs from that shown on your social security card,
Richland, WA 99352	check here. You must call 1-800-772-1213 for a replacement card. ▶ ☐

5	Total number of allowances you are claiming (from line **H** above **or** from the applicable worksheet on page 2)	**5**	4
6	Additional amount, if any, you want withheld from each paycheck	**6** $	0

7   I claim exemption from withholding for 2015, and I certify that I meet **both** of the following conditions for exemption.
  • Last year I had a right to a refund of **all** federal income tax withheld because I had **no** tax liability, **and**
  • This year I expect a refund of **all** federal income tax withheld because I expect to have **no** tax liability.
  If you meet both conditions, write "Exempt" here . . . . ▶ | **7** |

Under penalties of perjury, I declare that I have examined this certificate and, to the best of my knowledge and belief, it is true, correct, and complete.

Employee's signature
(This form is not valid unless you sign it.) ▶ *Harry M. Weir*   **Date** ▶ *January 1, 20- -*

8 Employer's name and address (Employer: Complete lines 8 and 10 only if sending to the IRS.)	**9** Office code (optional)	**10** Employer identification number (EIN)

For Privacy Act and Paperwork Reduction Act Notice, see page 2.	Cat. No. 10220Q	Form **W-4** (2015)

Source: Internal Revenue Service.

salaries and wages. Once filed, the certificate remains in effect until an amended certificate takes effect. Withholding certificates should be retained as long as they are in effect and for four years thereafter. If the employee does not complete the W-4, the employer withholds taxes as if the employee is *single, with no withholding allowances.*

Since the employers are required to get each employee's social security number on Form W-4, they can request to see the employee's social security card, and they can photocopy the card for their files.

Withholding Allowances

The number of withholding allowances claimed on Form W-4 may differ from the number of exemptions claimed on the employee's tax return. The process of determining the correct number of withholding allowances begins with the number of personal exemptions the employee expects to claim on his or her tax return. The employee then increases or decreases this number based on the employee's eligibility and desire for a higher paycheck or a higher tax refund. The worksheets provided with Form W-4 enable the employee to determine the exact number of allowances to enter on the certificate.

Changing Form W-4

If the status of an employee changes with respect to the number of withholding allowances or marital status, the employee files an amended W-4. If there is a decrease in the number of allowances, the employee must furnish the employer with a new certificate within 10 days. If there is an increase in the number of allowances, the employee can either file a new certificate or allow the current certificate to remain in effect.

The employer makes the certificate effective no later than the start of the first payroll period ending on or after the 30th day from the date the replacement Form W-4 is received. The employer may not repay or reimburse the employee

ON THE **NET**

The IRS has created a page on its Web site (**www.irs.gov/w4**) for updates to **Form W-4, Employee's Withholding Allowance Certificate**.

for income taxes overwithheld before the effective date of the new certificate but may reimburse the employee after that date if the employer failed to implement the new certificate.

Exemption from Income Tax Withholding

Employees may claim exemption from income tax withholding if they had no income tax liability last year and expect none in the current year. The exemption is valid for one year and must be claimed on a new Form W-4 filed by February 15 of each succeeding year. If a new certificate is not filed, taxes are withheld at the single rate with zero withholding allowances.

Single persons who made less than $10,300 in 2015 owed no federal income tax. Married couples filing jointly with combined wages up to $20,600 incurred no tax liability.

Employees may not claim exemption from withholding if (1) another person claims the employee as a dependent on his or her tax return, *and* (2) income exceeds $1,050 annually and includes more than $350 of unearned income (interest or dividends); or if unearned income is less than $350, but the total income exceeds $6,300.

Additional and Voluntary Withholding Agreements

In some instances, employees want additional federal income taxes withheld from their wages, such as a person with two or more jobs, or a married couple where both work. The simplest way to increase the amount of tax withheld is to reduce the number of withholding allowances claimed. Another method is to request that the employer withhold an additional amount from the employee's pay. These requests must be done on Forms W-4 by filling in the additional amounts to be withheld on line 6. There is a worksheet on the back of Form W-4 that can be used to calculate the additional amount to be withheld.

If an employee receives payments not classified as wages, or an employer-employee relationship does not exist, individuals can voluntarily request that the employer or the one making the payments withhold federal income taxes from their payments. These individuals need only furnish a Form W-4. Requests for additional and voluntary withholding become effective when the employer accepts them and begins to withhold tax. The agreements remain in effect until the specified termination date or until the termination is mutually agreed upon. Either party may terminate an agreement prior to a specified date or mutual agreement by furnishing the other party with a signed, written notice of termination.

Individuals who may wish to request additional withholding or a voluntary agreement to withhold include:
- Clergy
- Two wage-earner married couples
- Domestic workers in a private home
- Individuals receiving significant amounts of interest or dividends
- Individuals receiving self-employment income

Electronic Filing of Form W-4

Employers may establish a system that requires employees to file and make changes to their W-4s by using a computer network or interactive voice response technology. However, the employer must make available the paper W-4 option to any employee who objects to using the system or whose access to the system is limited.

Invalid Forms W-4

Employers are not required to verify the authenticity of the information on employees' W-4s. However, if the form is altered in any way or if the employee acknowledges that the information is false, the employer cannot accept the invalid W-4. The employer can ask for a new W-4. If the employee refuses to submit a new one, the employer can use the employee's most recent correct W-4 on file or, if a new hire, withhold as if the employee were single with no allowances.

Requested Forms W-4

Regulations require employers to only submit copies of employees' Forms W-4 that are requested in a written notice from the IRS.

Figure 4.4 outlines the procedures to follow in submitting Forms W-4 to the IRS.

Employee Penalties

Employees who willfully file false information statements (Form W-4) are, in addition to any other penalty, subject to fines of up to $1,000 or imprisonment for up to one year or both.

Employees claiming excess deductions are subject to a $500 civil penalty for each offense.

Withholding on Nonresident Aliens

Resident aliens (those with green cards) are lawful citizens and are taxed similar to U.S. citizens. To avoid underwithholding, nonresident aliens (who cannot claim the standard exemption and are limited to one allowance when filing their personal U.S. income tax returns) should (1) not claim exemption from income tax withholding; (2) request withholding as single, regardless of actual status; (3) claim only one allowance (residents of Canada, Mexico, Japan, or Korea may claim more than one allowance); (4) add an extra amount to wages, then determine withholding based on the total amount (e.g., $51.00 for a weekly payroll period); and (5) write "Nonresident Alien" on dotted line on line 6 on Form W-4.

Other Withholdings

Federal income taxes are also withheld from other kinds of payments made to current and former employees, as described below.

Withholding for Pension or Annuity Payments

Generally, the withholding of federal income taxes applies to payments made from pension, profit-sharing, stock bonus, annuity, and certain deferred compensation plans and individual retirement arrangements. You treat the payments

FIGURE 4.4
Procedures for Submitting Forms W-4

- Send copies of Forms W-4 only after the IRS requests them in writing.
- The IRS can also issue "lock-in" letters to employers specifying the maximum number of withholding exemptions permitted for an employee without obtaining a copy of the employee's W-4.
- An "employee notice" is sent along with the lock-in letter. This notice must be given to the employee within 10 business days of the receipt. If no longer employed, the employer must notify the IRS in writing.
- Withhold federal income tax based on lock-in letter starting with the first pay period 60 days after the date of the letter, unless the IRS contacts the employer.
- Challenges to the lock-in letter must be sent in writing along with a new Form W-4 by the employee directly to the IRS.
- Employer should disregard any new W-4 (unless claiming fewer exemptions than the IRS notice) submitted by the employee until notified to do so by the IRS.

from any of these sources as wages for the purpose of withholding. Unless the recipients of pension or annuity payments elect *not* to have federal income taxes withheld from such payments, the taxes will be withheld. Payers must withhold on monthly pension and annuity payments exceeding $20,640 a year, unless the payees elect otherwise. If the recipients do not instruct the payers to the contrary, the payers are required to withhold income taxes as if the recipients were *married and claiming three withholding allowances.*

By completing Form W-4P or a substitute form furnished by the payer, an employee can elect to have no income tax withheld from the payments received. The form may also be used to change the amount of tax that would ordinarily be withheld by the payers. Once completed, Form W-4P remains in effect until the recipient changes or revokes the certificate. The payer must notify the recipients each year of their right to elect to have no taxes withheld or to revoke their election.

Withholding from Sick Pay

Form W-4S, Request for Federal Income Tax Withholding from Sick Pay, must be filed with the payer of sick pay if the employee wants federal income taxes to be withheld from the payments. Form W-4S is filed only if the payer is a third party, such as an insurance company. The form should not be filed with the worker's employer, who makes such payments, since employers already must withhold income taxes from sick pay.

Withholding on Government Payments

Form W-4V can be used to request federal income tax withholding on government payments (such as social security benefits or unemployment compensation). This request is voluntary.

Over the Line

The former owner of an employee leasing business, Excell Personnel, Inc., has been sentenced to 36 months in prison and ordered to pay $4,234,670.16 in restitution to the IRS. The company which "leased" employees made deductions for withholding of income taxes and FICA taxes; however, the owner admitted that he was aware of his legal obligations but deliberately chose not to remit the withheld taxes to the IRS.[2]

SELF-STUDY QUIZ 4-2

1. Grace Kyle submitted a new Form W-4 claiming one additional withholding allowance. Kyle also requested to be reimbursed for the overwithholding prior to the change. How should the payroll manager respond to Kyle?

2. Bob Bradley is upset because his paycheck on February 12, 2016, has federal income tax withheld, even though he filed a W-4 in 2015 claiming exemption from withholding. What should the payroll manager say to Bradley?

3. Greg Volmer, married with a nonemployed spouse, has three dependent children. How many allowances can Volmer claim on his W-4?

---

2 Anne S. Lewis, "Employee Leasing Company Owner Sentenced to Prison, Ordered to Pay over $4 Million in Payroll Taxes," *PAYTECH*, June 2008, p. 57.

WASHINGTON UPDATE

THE 2016 FEDERAL INCOME TAX RATES WERE NOT AVAILABLE DURING THE
PRODUCTION OF THIS TEXTBOOK. WE HAVE USED THE 2015 FEDERAL INCOME
TAX RATES, 2015 FICA TAX RATES, AND 2015 OASDI TAX BASE IN THIS TEXTBOOK.
PRESIDENT OBAMA'S FISCAL YEAR 2016 BUDGET ENTAILED SEVERAL
EMPLOYMENT TAX PROPOSALS INCLUDING A PROPOSAL TO REDUCE ELECTRONIC
W-2/W-3 REPORTING THRESHOLD FROM 250 TO 5 EMPLOYEES. PLEASE SEE "AS WE
GO TO PRESS" FOR THE MOST CURRENT UPDATES.

Federal Income Tax Withholding

After the employer learns from Form W-4 the number of withholding allowances
for an employee, the employer selects a withholding method. Employers usually
choose either the **percentage method** or the **wage-bracket method**. Both distin-
guish between married and unmarried persons, and both methods provide the full
benefit of the allowances claimed by the employee on Form W-4.

The choice of methods is usually based on the number of employees and the payroll accounting system used. The employer can change from one method to another
at any time, and different methods may be used for different groups of employees.

Both methods take into account a **standard deduction**, an amount of money
used to reduce an individual's adjusted gross income in arriving at the taxable
income. For 2015, the following standard deductions apply:

Joint return filers and surviving spouses	$12,600
Married persons filing separately	6,300
Head of household filers	9,250
Single filers	6,300

> **LO 3**
>
> Compute the amount of federal
> income tax to be withheld using:
> (a) the percentage method; (b) the
> wage-bracket method; (c) alterna-
> tive methods such as quarterly
> averaging, annualizing of wages,
> and part-year employment; and
> (d) withholding of federal income
> taxes on supplementary wage
> payments.

These amounts are increased for single and married individuals or surviving
spouses age 65 or older or blind. Each year, the standard deductions are adjusted
for inflation. The adjustment also applies to the additional standard deductions
available to elderly or blind persons.

Percentage Method

To compute the tax using the percentage method, follow these steps:

Step 1
Determine the amount of gross wages earned. If the
wage ends in a fractional dollar amount, you may
round the gross pay to the nearest dollar.

> Wilson Goodman, single, claims two allowances and
> earns $915.60 semimonthly.
>
> Round Gross Wages to $916.00

Step 2
Multiply the number of allowances claimed by the
amount of one allowance for the appropriate payroll
period, as shown in the Table of Allowance Values in
Figure 4.5 on page 4-16.

> Table of Allowance Values for semimonthly payroll
> period shows $166.70.
>
> Multiply $166.70 × 2 = $333.40

> **ON THE JOB**
>
> The basic income tax rates for
> 2015 are 10%, 15%, 25%, 28%,
> 33%, 35% and 39.6%.

Step 3
Subtract the amount for the number of allowances
claimed from the employee's gross pay to find the
excess of wages over allowances claimed.

> | | |
> |---|---:|
> | Gross pay | $916.00 |
> | Less: Allowances | 333.40 |
> | Excess wages | $582.60 |

Step 4
Determine the withholding tax on the excess of wages
over allowances claimed by referring to the
appropriate Percentage Method Withholding Table.

> Compute tax from Tax Table 3(a), page T-3.
>
> $53.79 = [15%($582.60 − $480.00) + $38.40]

FIGURE 4.5

Table of Allowance Values for 2015

Weekly	76.90	Biweekly	153.80	Semimonthly	166.70	Monthly	333.30
Quarterly	1,000.00	Semiannual	2,000.00	Annual	4,000.00	Daily/Misc.	15.40

SELF-STUDY QUIZ 4-3

Tiffany Moulder, married and claiming three allowances, receives a salary of $1,100.25 each week. Compute the amount to withhold for federal income tax using the percentage method and Figure 4.5 above. Show the results of each step, as described for figuring withholding using the percentage method.

Step 1 Result _____   Step 2 Result _____

Step 3 Result _____   Step 4 Result _____

NEWS ALERT

The top 1 percent of taxpayers by income paid 40.4 percent of federal taxes collected, while the bottom half of taxpayers paid 2.9 percent.

Wage-Bracket Method

The IRS provides statutory wage-bracket tables for weekly, biweekly, semimonthly, monthly, and daily or miscellaneous pay periods. Copies may be obtained from the District Director of Internal Revenue. Tax Table B at the end of the textbook provides tables for weekly, biweekly, semimonthly, monthly, and daily pay periods for single and married persons.

To use the wage-bracket method, follow these steps:

Step 1
Select the withholding table that applies to the employee's marital status and pay period.

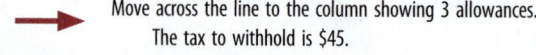

Adrienne Huff is married and claims 3 allowances. She is paid weekly at a rate of $810.

Step 2
Locate the wage bracket (the first two columns of the table) in which the employee's gross wages fall.

Locate the appropriate wage bracket (see Figure 4.6):
   At least $810 but less than $820

Step 3
Follow the line for the wage bracket across to the right to the column showing the appropriate number of allowances. Withhold this amount of tax.

Move across the line to the column showing 3 allowances. The tax to withhold is $45.

If the employee's wages are higher than the last amount listed on the appropriate wage-bracket table, the percentage method must be used for that employee.

In cases where an employee claims more than 10 allowances, the employer has two methods for determining the amount to withhold when using the wage-bracket tables.

1. Withhold as if the employee claimed only 10 allowances, or
2. Multiply the value of one allowance for the applicable payroll period by the number of withholding allowances exceeding 10; subtract this amount from the employee's gross wage that is subject to federal income tax withholding. Use the resulting amount and column 10 for allowances in the wage-bracket table to determine the tax to withhold.

FIGURE 4.6
Married Persons—Weekly Payroll Period

Wage Bracket Method Tables for Income Tax Withholding

MARRIED Persons—WEEKLY Payroll Period

(For Wages Paid through December 31, 2015)

| And the wages are— | | And the number of withholding allowances claimed is— | | | | | | | | | | |
At least	But less than	0	1	2	3	4	5	6	7	8	9	10
		The amount of income tax to be withheld is—										
$750	$760	$71	$59	$48	$36	$28	$21	$13	$5	$0	$0	$0
760	770	72	61	49	38	29	22	14	6	0	0	0
770	780	74	62	51	39	30	23	15	7	0	0	0
780	790	75	64	52	41	31	24	16	8	0	0	0
790	800	77	65	54	42	32	25	17	9	1	0	0
800	810	78	67	55	44	33	26	18	10	2	0	0
810	820	80	68	57	45	34	27	19	11	3	0	0
820	830	81	70	58	47	35	28	20	12	4	0	0
830	840	83	71	60	48	37	29	21	13	5	0	0
840	850	84	73	61	50	38	30	22	14	6	0	0

Source: Internal Revenue Service.

WITHHOLDING WITH OVER 10 ALLOWANCES. Genevieve Minster is married and claims 12 allowances. She is paid $2,600 semimonthly. To determine her federal tax withholding using the wage-bracket tables, do the following:

> **EXAMPLE 4-2**

Step 1—Multiply the amount of a withholding allowance for a semimonthly payroll period by 2.

$$\$166.70 \times 2 = \$333.40$$

Step 2—Subtract that number from the gross wages.

$$\$2,600.00 - \$333.40 = \$2,266.60$$

Step 3—Go to the wage-bracket table for a semimonthly pay period for a married person under the column for 10 allowances. (Page T-10)

$$\$25$$

SELF-STUDY QUIZ 4-4

Quirk Motors uses the wage-bracket method to withhold from the semimonthly earnings of its employees. For each employee, compute the amount to be withheld from their earnings for the payroll period ending April 15.

Employee	Marital Status	No. of Allowances	Salary	Federal Income Tax Withheld
Kyle Lamb	S	1	$1,100	_____
Zed Nurin	S	0	850	_____
Carol Hogan	M	4	975	_____
Marla Vick	M	2	2,600	_____
Al Marks	S	3	1,200	_____

Other Methods of Withholding

In addition to the two principal methods of withholding previously described, employers may use other methods such as **quarterly averaging**, **annualizing wages**, and **part-year employment**.

EXAMPLE 4-3

QUARTERLY AVERAGING. Jackson, Inc., estimates that Cal Hudson will be paid $6,690 during the second quarter of the year. Hudson is married, claims two withholding allowances, and is paid semimonthly.

Step 1—Divide the estimated quarterly wages by 6 (the number of semimonthly pay periods in the quarter).

$$\$6,690 \div 6 = \$1,115$$

Step 2—Find the amount of federal income tax to withhold from each semimonthly payment.

MARRIED Persons—SEMIMONTHLY Payroll Period

Wages at least $1,100 but not more than $1,120 for 2 allowances = $42

The withholding is based on the average payment instead of the actual payment.

EXAMPLE 4-4

ANNUALIZING WAGES. Marc Field, married with three allowances, receives $1,350 semimonthly. Under the annualizing method, do the following:

Step 1—Multiply the semimonthly wage by 24 pay periods to compute his annual wage.

$$\$1,350 \times 24 = \$32,400$$

Step 2—Subtract withholding allowances of $12,000 (3 × $4,000).

$$\$32,400 - \$12,000 = \$20,400$$

Step 3—Use Tax Table 7(b) and apply the percentage method to the taxable wages.

10% of the excess over $11,800 ($20,400 − $8,600) × 0.10 = $1,180.

$1,180 ÷ 24 semimonthly payrolls = $49.17 per paycheck

EXAMPLE 4-5

PART-YEAR EMPLOYMENT METHOD. Jack Matthews, previously unemployed for the calendar year, has agreed to begin temporary employment on September 6. He has made a written request for the part-year employment method of withholding. He claims single with zero allowances on his W-4. For the biweekly period from September 6 to September 17, he earns a total of $7,600.

Step 1—Wages for the current payroll period are added to the wages paid previously.

$$\$7,600 + 0 = \$7,600$$

Step 2—The number of payroll periods worked in step 1 is added to the number of payroll periods between the employee's past and current employment.

$$1 + 19 = 20$$

Step 3—Divide the step 1 amount by the total number of payroll periods.

$$\$7,600 \div 20 = \$380$$

Step 4—Tax on the step 3 amount (from wage-bracket table for single/biweekly, zero allowances).

$30

Step 5—Total number of payroll periods from step 2 multiplied by step 4 equals the withholding for the pay period.

$$20 \times \$30 = \$600$$

ON THE JOB

In order to reduce federal income tax withholding, a part-time employee who figures the federal income tax on a calendar-year basis can request in writing that the employer withhold tax by the part-year employment method.

Supplemental Wage Payments

Supplemental wage payments include items such as vacation pay, bonuses, commissions, exercised nonqualified stock options, and dismissal pay. Since these types of payments may be paid at a different time from the regular payroll and not related to a particular payroll, the employer must decide whether to lump the regular wages and supplemental wages together or withhold from the supplemental wages separately. The first distinction is the treatment of vacation pays versus other types of supplemental pays.

Vacation Pay

Vacation pay is subject to withholding as though it were a regular payment made for the payroll period or periods occurring during the vacation. If the vacation pay is for a time longer than your usual payroll period, spread it over the pay period(s) for which you pay it. If an employee is paid weekly and is paid for two weeks of vacation, treat each vacation week separately and calculate the tax on each vacation week using the weekly tax tables or wage brackets.

However, if vacation pay is in lieu of taking vacation time, treat it as a regular supplemental wage payment and calculate the tax on the total as a single payment. A lump-sum vacation payment on termination of employment is also treated as a supplemental wage payment.

Supplemental Wages Paid with Regular Wages

If the employer pays supplemental wages with regular wages but does not specify the amount of each type of wage, the employer withholds as if the total were a single payment for a regular payroll period.

Mandi Robinson, married with three allowances, earns a monthly salary of $2,400. She also receives a bonus on sales that exceed her quota for the year. For this year, her bonus amounts to $4,600. Robinson's employer pays her the regular monthly salary and the bonus together on her December paycheck. The withholding for the December pay is computed on the total amount of $7,000 ($2,400 + $4,600). After deducting the allowances, using the percentage Tax Table 4(b), the amount to withhold is $715.62 [$7,000 − 3($333.30) = $6,000.10 − $2,254.00 = $3,746.10 × 15% = $561.92 + $153.70].

EXAMPLE 4-6

However, if the employer indicates specifically the amount of each payment, the employer may withhold at *a flat 25 percent rate* on the supplemental wages if the tax is withheld on the employee's regular wages at the appropriate rate.

If you indicate separately on Robinson's paycheck stub the amount of each payment, the amount of federal income tax to be withheld is computed as follows:

EXAMPLE 4-7

		Taxes Withheld	
Regular monthly earnings	$2,400	$ 70.00	(from wage-bracket tax tables*)
Annual bonus	4,600	1,150.00	($4,600 × 25%)
Totals	$7,000	$1,220.00	

*The percentage table could also be used.

If the employee has already received supplemental wages for the year in excess of $1 million, a **39.6 percent** withholding rate must be used for the amount above $1 million (the aggregate method cannot be used).

States that have income taxes usually set up their own flat rate for withholding on these supplemental pays. Some require that the supplemental pay be added to a regular pay and the total taxed.

Supplemental Wages Paid Separately from Regular Wages

If the supplemental wages are paid separately, the income tax withholding method depends on whether or not you withheld income tax from the employee's last regular wage payment. If you withheld income tax from the employee's regular wages, you can use either of the following methods for supplemental wages.

Method A

Add the supplemental wages and regular wages for the most recent payroll period. Then, figure the income tax as if the total were a single payment. Subtract the tax already withheld from the regular wage. Withhold the remaining tax from the supplemental wage.

EXAMPLE 4-8

Louis Ernst, married with two allowances, is paid $985 semimonthly. The tax to be withheld under the wage-bracket method on each semimonthly pay is $30. Ernst is paid his regular wage on June 11. On June 14, he receives a bonus of $500. The tax on the bonus is computed as follows:

Regular wage payment..	$ 985
Bonus...	500
Total..	$1,485
Tax on total from the wage-bracket table in Tax Table B...	$ 81
Less: Tax already withheld on $985...	30
Tax to be withheld from $500 bonus...	$ 51

If you did not withhold income tax from the employee's regular wage payment, use Method A.

Method B

Withhold a flat 25 percent (39.6 percent if over $1 million) on the supplemental pay.

EXAMPLE 4-9

The tax withheld on Louis Ernst's June 15 bonus of $500 is computed as follows:

Bonus...	$ 500
Tax rate	× 25%
Tax withheld on bonus	$ 125

SELF-STUDY QUIZ 4-5

Fred Burdette, married with two allowances, received his regular semimonthly wage of $1,450 on June 10. On June 17, he received a semiannual bonus of $500. Compute the amount of federal income tax to be withheld on the bonus using each method for computing supplemental wage payments. The employer uses the wage-bracket tables.

Method A _____

Method B _____

If a supplemental payment is paid in a year where no regular wages are paid, the payment is treated as a regular wage payment, and withholding is determined by the rules that apply to a miscellaneous payroll period.

Gross-Up Supplementals

In order to give an employee the intended amount of a supplemental payment, the employer will need to gross up the payment so that after the appropriate payroll taxes are withheld, the net amount left is equal to the original intended payment.

A special "**gross-up**" formula can be applied in this situation:

$$\text{Grossed-Up Amount} = \frac{\text{Intended Payment}}{1 - \text{Applicable Tax Rates (FICA, 25\% federal income tax rate, and state tax rate)}}$$

EXAMPLE 4-10

GROSSING-UP. Cotter Company wants to award a $4,000 bonus to Donna D'Amico. In addition, it wants the net bonus payment to equal $4,000. Assuming D'Amico is still under the OASDI/FICA limit, the calculation would be:

A. 　$\dfrac{\$4,000}{1 - 0.25 \text{ (supplemental W/H rate)} - 0.062 \text{ (OASDI)} - 0.0145 \text{ (HI)}}$

B. 　$\dfrac{\$4,000}{0.6735} = \$5,939.12$ grossed-up bonus

If state or local taxes apply, they must also be included in the formula.

Wage and Tax Statements

Employers must furnish **wage and tax statements** to employees informing them of the wages paid during the calendar year and the amount of taxes withheld from those wages. The employer sends copies of these statements to the federal government and, in many cases, to state, city, and local governments.

Form W-2

Form W-2, Wage and Tax Statement (2015 version), shown in Figure 4.7, on page 4-22, is prepared if any of the following items apply to an employee during the calendar year:

1. Income tax or social security taxes were withheld.
2. Income tax would have been withheld if the employee had not claimed more than one withholding allowance or had not claimed exemption from withholding on Form W-4.
3. Any amount was paid for services if the employer is in a trade or business. The cash value of any noncash payments made should be included.

Figure 4.8, on pages 4-23 and 4-24, summarizes the instructions for completing each of the boxes on Form W-2. Employees' names should appear exactly as shown on the employee's social security card (do not include titles or suffixes). If an entry does not apply to the firm or employee, leave the box blank. Employers must give employees Form W-2 on or before January 31 following the close of the calendar year.

The Affordable Care Act requires the reporting of the cost of employer-sponsored health coverage on Form W-2 in Box 12, coded as DD (see page 4-23, Figure 4.8). This includes coverage provided for domestic partners. The value of the employer's excludable contribution to health coverage continues to be excludable from an employee's income, and it is not taxable. This reporting is for informational purposes only. Employers that provide "applicable employer-sponsored coverage" under a group health plan are subject to the reporting requirement.

When employees leave the service of the employer, you may give them Form W-2 any time after employment ends. If employees ask for Form W-2, the employer should give it to them within 30 days of their request or the final wage payment, whichever is later. In instances where terminated workers may be rehired at some time before the year ends, the employer may delay furnishing the form until January 31 following the close of the calendar year. Employers distribute Form W-2 copies as follows:

Copy A—To the Social Security Administration *by the end of February* following the year for which Form W-2 is applicable. If filed *electronically, March 31* is the due date.

LO 4

Explain: (a) Form W-2, (b) the completion of *Form 941, Employer's Quarterly Federal Tax Return,* (c) major types of information returns, and (d) the impact of state and local income taxes on the payroll accounting process.

ON THE JOB

Employers can create "fill-in" versions of Forms W-2 and W-3 for filing with the Social Security Administration and print out copies for employees at **http://www .socialsecurity.gov/employer/**

FIGURE **4.7**

Form W-2, Wage and Tax Statement

a Employee's social security number 000-00-7478	For Official Use Only ▶ OMB No. 1545-0008		

22222 | Void ☐

b Employer identification number (EIN) 00-0007221	1 Wages, tips, other compensation 29360.18	2 Federal income tax withheld 4610.00
c Employer's name, address, and ZIP code	3 Social security wages 29360.18	4 Social security tax withheld 1820.33
Keevey Motors	5 Medicare wages and tips 29360.18	6 Medicare tax withheld 425.72
600 Third Avenue Philadelphia, PA 19103-5600	7 Social security tips	8 Allocated tips
d Control number	9	10 Dependent care benefits
e Employee's first name and initial Richard M. Last name Cabor Suff.	11 Nonqualified plans	12a See instructions for box 12 C 78.00
	13 Statutory employee ☐ Retirement plan ☒ Third-party sick pay ☐	12b
483 Monroe Street Philadelphia, PA 19119-4821	14 Other BC/BS Premium w/h 296.00	12c
		12d
f Employee's address and ZIP code		

15 State Employer's state ID number	16 State wages, tips, etc.	17 State income tax	18 Local wages, tips, etc.	19 Local income tax	20 Locality name
PA 00-0-0013	29282.18	898.96	29282.18	1150.20	Phila

Form **W-2** Wage and Tax Statement **20- -** Department of the Treasury—Internal Revenue Service

Copy A For Social Security Administration — Send this entire page with Form W-3 to the Social Security Administration; photocopies are **not** acceptable.

For Privacy Act and Paperwork Reduction Act Notice, see the separate instructions.

Cat. No. 10134D

Do Not Cut, Fold, or Staple Forms on This Page — Do Not Cut, Fold, or Staple Forms on This Page

Source: Internal Revenue Service.

Copy 1—To the state, city, or local tax department.
Copy B—To employees for filing with their federal income tax return.
Copy C—To employees for their personal records.
Copy 2—To employees for filing with their state, city, or local income tax returns.
Copy D—Retained by the employer.

If 250 or more Forms W-2 are being filed, reporting must be done electronically. An extended deadline of March 31 applies to any W-2s filed electronically.

Employers that are going out of business must send W-2 forms to the employees by the date the final Form 941 is due. One month later, the W-2 forms are due at the Social Security Administration.

If Form W-2 has been lost or destroyed, employers are authorized to furnish substitute copies to the employee. The substitute form should be clearly marked **REISSUED STATEMENT**. Do not send Copy A of the substitute statement to the Social Security Administration. If, after a reasonable effort, the employer cannot deliver a Form W-2, the employer retains the employee's copies of the form for a four-year period. A "reasonable effort" means the forms were mailed to the last known address of the employee.

The IRS allows employers to put W-2s on a secure Web site and provide employees with passwords to access their individual W-2s. As long as an employee has affirmatively consented, his or her W-2 can be sent electronically. The consent by the employee must also be made electronically in a manner that indicates that the employee will be able to access the W-2. The W-2 must be posted on or before January 31 (kept until October 15), and the employee must be notified of its availability and must be given instructions on how to access and print the W-2.

Form W-2c

To correct errors in previously filed Forms W-2, employers file *Form W-2c, Corrected Wage and Tax Statement* shown in Figure 4.9 on page 4-25. File Copy A with the Social Security Administration and the remaining copies as noted on the bottom of each form.

IRS CONNECTION

Time extensions for filing W-2s can be requested by sending Form 8809 (Request for Extension of Time to File Information Returns) to the IRS by February 28. An additional 30-day extension can be requested by submitting another Form 8809 before the end of the initial extension period. An online request for an extension of time for Forms W-2 is available via the FIRE (Filing Information Returns Electronically) system at https://fire.irs.gov

FIGURE 4.8
How to Complete Form W-2

Box A—Employee's social security number: Filers may use truncated taxpayer identification numbers (TTINs) on electronically furnished payee statements. An employee who does not have an SSN should apply for one by completing Form SS-5.

Void: Put an X in this box when an error has been made. Amounts shown on void forms should not be included in your subtotal Form W-2.

Box B—Employer identification number (EIN): Enter the number assigned to you by the IRS. Do not use a prior owner's EIN. If you do not have an EIN when filing Forms W-2, enter "Applied For." You can get an EIN by filing Form SS-4.

Box C—Employer's name, address, and ZIP code: This entry should be the same as shown on your Form 941 or 943.

Box D—Control number: For the employer to identify the individual Forms W-2. Up to 7 digits may be used to assign the number, which the employer uses when writing the Social Security Administration about the form. The employer does not have to use this box.

Box E—Employee's name: The name should be entered exactly as shown on the employee's social security card.

Box F—Employee's address and ZIP code: This box is combined with Box E on all copies except Copy A, to allow you to mail employee's copies in a window envelope or as a self-mailer.

Box 1—Wages, tips, other compensation: Record, before any payroll deductions, the total of (1) wages, prizes, and awards paid; (2) noncash payments (including certain fringe benefits); (3) tips reported by employee to employer (not allocated tips); (4) certain employee business expense reimbursements; (5) cost of accident and health insurance premiums paid on behalf of 2% or more shareholder employees by an S corporation; (6) taxable benefits made from a Section 125 (cafeteria plan); and (7) all other compensation including certain scholarships and fellowship grants and payments for moving expenses. Other compensation is an amount you pay your employee from which federal income tax is not withheld. You may show other compensation on a separate Form W-2. Do not include elective deferrals [i.e., 401(k)].

Box 2—Federal income tax withheld: Record the amount of federal income tax withheld from the employee's wages for the year.

Box 3—Social security wages: Enter the total wages paid (before payroll deductions) subject to employee social security (OASDI) tax. Do not include social security tips and allocated tips. Generally, noncash payments are considered wages. Include employee business expenses reported in Box 1. Include employer contributions to qualified cash or deferred compensation plans and to retirement arrangements described in Box 12 (Codes D, E, F, and G), even though the deferrals are not includible in Box 1 as wages, tips, and other compensation. Include any employee OASDI and HI taxes and employee state unemployment compensation taxes you paid for your employee rather than deducting it from wages. Report in this box the cost of group-term life insurance coverage over $50,000 that is taxable to former employees. Report the cost of accident and health insurance premiums paid on behalf of 2% or more shareholder-employees by an S corporation only if the exclusion under Section 312(a)(2)(B) is not satisfied. Do not enter more than the maximum OASDI taxable wage base for the year.

Box 4—Social security tax withheld: Record the total social security (OASDI) tax (not the employer's share) withheld or paid by the employer for the employee. Include only taxes withheld for the year's wages.

Box 5—Medicare wages and tips: Enter the Medicare (HI) wages and tips. Be sure to enter tips the employee reported even if you did not have enough employee funds to collect the HI tax for those tips. Report in this box the cost of group-term life insurance coverage over $50,000 that is taxable to former employees.

Box 6—Medicare tax withheld: Enter the total employee Medicare (HI) tax (not the employer's share) including the Additional Medicare Tax withheld or paid by the employer for the employee. Include only taxes withheld for the year's wages.

Box 7—Social security tips: Record the amount the employee reported even if you did not have enough employee funds to collect the social security (OASDI) tax for the tips. The total of Boxes 3 and 7 should not be more than the maximum OASDI wage base for the year. But report all tips in Box 1 along with wages and other compensation.

Box 8—Allocated tips: If you are a large food or beverage establishment, record the amount of tips allocated to the employee. Do not include this amount in Boxes 1, 3, 5, or 7.

Box 9—BLANK

Box 10—Dependent care benefits: Record the total amount of dependent care benefits paid or incurred by you for your employee. This total should include any amount in excess of the exclusion ($5,000).

Box 11—Nonqualified plans: Enter the amount from a nonqualified deferred compensation plan or Section 457 plan that was distributed or became taxable because the substantial risk of forfeiture lapsed. Include this amount in Box 11 only if it is also includible in Boxes 1, 3, and 5. Report distributions to beneficiaries of deceased employees on Form 1099-R.

Box 12—Complete and code this box for all applicable items listed in the Reference Guide. Additional information about any coded item may be found in the IRS's Instructions for Form W-2. Do not enter more than four codes in this box. If you are reporting more than four items, use a separate Form W-2 or a substitute Form W-2 to report the additional items. Use a capital letter when entering each code and enter the dollar amount on the same line. Use decimal points.

FIGURE 4.8 (concluded)

How to Complete Form W-2

Box 13—Mark the boxes that apply.

Statutory employee: Mark this box for statutory employees whose earnings are subject to social security (OASDI) and Medicare (HI) taxes but not subject to federal income tax withholding.

Retirement plan: Mark this box if the employee was an active participant (for any part of the year) in a retirement plan such as 401(k) and SEP.

Third-party sick plan: Mark this box only if you are a third-party, sick-pay payer filing a Form W-2 for an insured's employee.

Box 14—Other: Use this box for any other information you want to give your employee. Label each item. Examples are union dues, health insurance premiums deducted, moving expenses paid, nontaxable income, or educational assistance payments.

Boxes 15 through 20—State or local income tax information: You do not have to complete these boxes, but you may want to if you use copies of this form for your state and local returns. The ID number is assigned by each individual state. The state and local information boxes can be used to report wages and taxes on two states and two localities. Keep each state's and locality's information separated by the dotted line.

Reference Guide for Box 12 Codes

A—Uncollected social security (OASDI) tax on tips

B—Uncollected Medicare (HI) tax on tips

C—Group-term life insurance over $50,000

D—Elective deferrals to a Section 401(k) cash or deferred arrangement

E—Elective deferrals to a Section 403(b) salary reduction agreement

F—Elective deferrals to a Section 408(k)(6) salary reduction SEP

G—Elective and nonelective deferrals to a Section 457(b) deferred compensation plan (state and local government and tax-exempt employers)

H—Elective deferrals to a Section 501(c)(18)(D) tax-exempt organization plan

J—Nontaxable sick pay

K—20% excise tax on excess golden parachute payments

L—Substantiated employee business expense (federal rate)

M—Uncollected social security (OASDI) tax on group-term life insurance coverage

N—Uncollected Medicare (HI) tax on group-term life insurance coverage

P—Excludable reimbursed moving expenses

Q—Military employee basic housing, subsistence, and combat zone pay

R—Employer contributions to medical savings account

S—Employee salary reduction contributions to a 408(p) SIMPLE retirement plan

T—Employer-provided qualified adoption benefits

V—Exercise of nonstatutory stock options

W—Employer contributions to an employee's health savings account (HSA)

Y—Deferrals under a Section 409A nonqualified deferred compensation plan

Z—Income under a Section 409A nonqualified deferred compensation plan

AA—Designated Roth contributions to a 401(k) plan

BB—Designated Roth contributions under a 403(b) salary reduction agreement

DD—Cost of employer-sponsored health coverage. The amount reported with code DD is not taxable. This reporting requirement is for information purposes only.

EE—Designated Roth contributions under a governmental Section 457(b) plan. This amount does not apply to elective deferrals under Code G.

Source: Internal Revenue Service.

Form W-3c should accompany all corrected wage and tax statements unless the correction is for only one employee or to correct employees' names, addresses, or social security numbers. In the case of an incorrect address, the employer can mail the "incorrect" W-2 in an envelope bearing the corrected address.

Form W-3

Form W-3, Transmittal of Wage and Tax Statements, must be filed with the Social Security Administration by employers and other payers as a transmittal for Forms W-2. On Form W-3, the employer indicates the number of documents being transmitted. Form W-3 and the accompanying documents enable the Social Security Administration and the IRS to compare the totals to the amounts for the income tax withholdings, social security wages, social security tips, and Medicare wages and tips, as reported on the employer's 941s for the year.

ON THE NET

For access to all federal tax forms, see the **Forms and Publications** download page:
http://www.irs.gov/formspubs/

FIGURE **4.9**

Form W-2c, Corrected Wage and Tax Statement

DO NOT CUT, FOLD, OR STAPLE THIS FORM

44444	For Official Use Only ▶ OMB No. 1545-0008

a Employer's name, address, and ZIP code

Comcart Company
1600 Fourth Avenue
Princeton, NJ 09109

b Employer's Federal EIN
00-0007221

Note. Only complete money fields that are being corrected (exception: for corrections involving MQGE, see the General Instructions for Forms W-2 and W-3, under Specific Instructions for Form W-2c, boxes 5 and 6).

c Tax year/Form corrected   20-- / **W-2**

d Employee's correct SSN   000-00-6399

e Corrected SSN and/or name (Check this box and complete boxes f and/or g if incorrect on form previously filed.) ☐

Complete boxes f and/or g only if incorrect on form **previously filed** ▶

f Employee's **previously reported** SSN

g Employee's **previously reported** name

h Employee's first name and initial   Last name   Suff.
Marge A.   Mangano

8911 State Street
Trenton, NJ 08033

i Employee's address and ZIP code

Previously reported	Correct information	Previously reported	Correct information
1 Wages, tips, other compensation	1 Wages, tips, other compensation	2 Federal income tax withheld 3,293.00	2 Federal income tax withheld 3,923.00
3 Social security wages	3 Social security wages	4 Social security tax withheld	4 Social security tax withheld
5 Medicare wages and tips	5 Medicare wages and tips	6 Medicare tax withheld	6 Medicare tax withheld
7 Social security tips	7 Social security tips	8 Allocated tips	8 Allocated tips
9	9	10 Dependent care benefits	10 Dependent care benefits
11 Nonqualified plans	11 Nonqualified plans	12a See instructions for box 12	12a See instructions for box 12
13 Statutory employee Retirement plan Third-party sick pay ☐ ☐ ☐	13 Statutory employee Retirement plan Third-party sick pay ☐ ☐ ☐	12b	12b
14 Other (see instructions)	14 Other (see instructions)	12c	12c
		12d	12d

State Correction Information

Previously reported	Correct information	Previously reported	Correct information
15 State Employer's state ID number	15 State Employer's state ID number	15 State Employer's state ID number	15 State Employer's state ID number
16 State wages, tips, etc.	16 State wages, tips, etc.	16 State wages, tips, etc.	16 State wages, tips, etc.
17 State income tax	17 State income tax	17 State income tax	17 State income tax

Locality Correction Information

Previously reported	Correct information	Previously reported	Correct information
18 Local wages, tips, etc.	18 Local wages, tips, etc.	18 Local wages, tips, etc.	18 Local wages, tips, etc.
19 Local income tax	19 Local income tax	19 Local income tax	19 Local income tax
20 Locality name	20 Locality name	20 Locality name	20 Locality name

For Privacy Act and Paperwork Reduction Act Notice, see separate instructions.

Copy A—For Social Security Administration

Form **W-2c** (Rev. 8-2014)   **Corrected Wage and Tax Statement**   Cat. No. 61437D   Department of the Treasury Internal Revenue Service

Source: Internal Revenue Service.

FIGURE 4.10

Form W-3, Transmittal of Wage and Tax Statements

DO NOT STAPLE

a Control number: 33333	For Official Use Only ▶ OMB No. 1545-0008	

b Kind of Payer (Check one): 941 [X], CT-1 [ ], Military [ ], Hshld. emp. [ ], 943 [ ], Medicare govt. emp. [ ], 944 [ ]

Kind of Employer (Check one): None apply [ ], State/local non-501c [X], 501c non-govt. [ ], State/local 501c [ ], Federal govt. [ ]

Third-party sick pay (Check if applicable) [ ]

c Total number of Forms W-2: 132	d Establishment number	1 Wages, tips, other compensation: 2620736.40	2 Federal income tax withheld: 330317.19
e Employer identification number (EIN): 00-0006281		3 Social security wages: 2485210.05	4 Social security tax withheld: 154083.02
f Employer's name: Grove Electronics 33 Vista Road Vallejo, CA 94590-0033		5 Medicare wages and tips: 2620736.40	6 Medicare tax withheld: 38000.68
		7 Social security tips	8 Allocated tips
		9	10 Dependent care benefits
		11 Nonqualified plans	12a Deferred compensation
g Employer's address and ZIP code			
h Other EIN used this year		13 For third-party sick pay use only	12b
15 State: CA	Employer's state ID number: 00-004132	14 Income tax withheld by payer of third-party sick pay	
16 State wages, tips, etc.: 2620736.40	17 State income tax: 111381.29	18 Local wages, tips, etc.	19 Local income tax
Employer's contact person: Roger Damron		Employer's telephone number: (415) 555-3200	For Official Use Only
Employer's fax number: (415) 555-2229		Employer's email address: RDamron@grove.com	

Under penalties of perjury, I declare that I have examined this return and accompanying documents and, to the best of my knowledge and belief, they are true, correct, and complete.

Signature ▶ *Carl W. Tolan*   Title ▶ President   Date ▶ 2/28/20- -

Form **W-3** Transmittal of Wage and Tax Statements   20- -

Department of the Treasury
Internal Revenue Service

Source: Internal Revenue Service.

The IRS will require explanations of any differences and corrections to any errors. Figure 4.10 above shows a completed Form W-3. The employer files all Forms W-2 with one W-3. Forms W-3 and the related documents are filed with the Social Security Administration by the end of February each year. Form W-3 is mailed to employers during the fourth quarter.

The information shown on Form W-3 is matched against the employer's Forms 941 for the year. If the totals do not match, the IRS notifies the employer of the discrepancy, and the employer is required to provide additional information.

Penalties

The following penalties are imposed for late or incorrect filing of W-2s:

1. If filed correctly within 30 days after the due date, $30 per return ($250,000 maximum penalty/$75,000 for small businesses).
2. If filed between 30 days after the due date and August 1, $60 per return ($500,000 maximum penalty/$200,000 for small businesses).
3. After August 1, $100 per return ($1,500,000 maximum penalty/$500,000 for small businesses).
4. Penalties of $250 per return, or if greater, 10 percent of the amount to be reported correctly for intentional disregard of the requirements for filing, providing payee statements, and reporting incorrect information (no maximum penalty).
5. Filing W-2s with mismatched names and social security numbers, $100 per form.
6. Penalties of $100 per statement ($1,500,000 maximum) for failure to furnish the statements to *employees* on time, or furnishing incorrect information on the statements.

Form W-3c

The *Transmittal of Corrected Income and Tax Statements, Form W-3c,* is used to accompany copies of Form W-2c, sent to the Social Security Administration. This form can also be used to correct a previously filed Form W-3.

Privately Printed Forms

Employers may use their own forms by obtaining specifications for the private printing of Forms W-2 from any IRS center or district office. To the extent that the privately printed forms meet the specifications, the employer may use them without prior approval of the IRS.

SELF-STUDY QUIZ 4-6

1. Marquat Company deducts union dues from its employees' paychecks each month during the year and sends them to the local union office. How should the company report this deduction on the employees' Forms W-2?
2. Gringle's terminated 10 of its employees on July 8. The company informed each employee that it may rehire them again during its peak season in September. When should the company furnish each employee with a W-2 statement?
3. While preparing her 2015 personal income tax return, Connie Becker, an employee of Trident Mills, discovered that she had lost her Form W-2. What procedures should the company follow to prepare a new Form W-2 for Becker?

Returns Employers Must Complete

Employers must file returns reporting the amount of wages paid and the amount of taxes withheld at designated times, beginning with the first quarter in which taxable wages are paid. Rules that require different returns for different types of employees further complicate the accounting tasks and payroll procedures. Figure 4.11 briefly summarizes the major returns completed by employers.

The most recent information with regard to withholding, deposit, and payment and reporting of federal income taxes, FICA taxes, and FUTA taxes is available in *Circular E, Employer's Tax Guide.* This circular is sent to employers prior to the start of the new year and is also available at district offices of the IRS.

FIGURE 4.11

Major Returns Filed by Employers

Form 941, Employer's Quarterly Federal Tax Return	For reporting federal income taxes withheld during the calendar quarter and the employer and employee portions of the FICA taxes. Form 941 is illustrated in Chapter 3.
Form 943, Employer's Annual Tax Return for Agricultural Employees	For reporting the withholding of federal income taxes and FICA taxes on wages paid to agricultural workers. Form 943 is used for agricultural employees even though the employer may employ nonagricultural workers.
Form 944, Employer's Annual Federal Tax Return	Replaces Form 941 for employers who owe $1,000 or less in employment taxes for the year.
Form 945, Annual Return of Withheld Federal Income Tax	Used to report tax liability for nonpayroll items such as backup withholding and withholding on gambling winnings, pensions, and annuities, and deposits made for the year. **Backup withholding** occurs when an individual receives taxable interest, dividends, and certain other payments and fails to furnish the payer with the correct taxpayer identification numbers. Payers are then required to withhold 28 percent of those payments. Backup withholding does not apply to wages, pensions, annuities, or IRAs.

Information Returns

The IRS requires employers to file **information returns** to report compensation paid to certain individuals who are not employees. These returns allow the IRS to determine if taxpayers are reporting their true income. Figure 4.12, briefly summarizes the major information returns required by the IRS. The employer sends copies of the returns to the payee by the end of January. These forms can be sent to the contractors electronically as long as they agree in advance to this method of delivery. The payer's name, address, and phone number are included on the recipient's copy of Form 1099.

To transmit each type of Form 1099 to the IRS, the employer uses *Form 1096, Annual Summary and Transmittal of U.S. Information Returns.* Employers use a separate Form 1096 to transmit each type of information return. For example, one Form 1096 is used to transmit all Forms 1099-MISC (see Figure 4.13) and another Form 1096 is used to transmit all Forms 1099-INT. The employer files Form 1096 and all accompanying forms to the IRS on or before the last day of February of the year following the payment. For returns filed electronically, the due date is March 31. Penalties previously listed for late submission of Forms W-2 also apply to the Form 1099 series (see page 4-26).

IRS CONNECTION

The IRS estimates that self-employed taxpayers are underpaying their taxes by at least $81 billion. These nonwage workers are not caught because payers do not always report these payments to the IRS.

Independent Contractor Payments

Payments made to independent contractors (individuals or partnerships) of at least $600 must be reported on Form 1099-Miscellaneous Income. This does not apply to contractors who are incorporated unless the payments are medical or health-care related. Since payments to these independent contractors are not generated by payroll departments, the accounts payable departments usually complete the appropriate 1099 forms.

Form 1099-MISC can also be provided electronically to any recipient who has consented to receive the form in this manner.

FIGURE 4.12
Major Information Returns

Form 1099-DIV, Dividends and Distributions	For reporting dividends totaling $10 or more to any person; foreign tax withheld and paid on dividends and other distributions on stock for a person; distributions made by corporations and regulated investment companies (including money market funds) as part of liquidation.
Form 1099-G, Certain Government Payments	For reporting unemployment compensation payments, state and local income tax refunds of $10 or more, taxable grants, income tax refunds, and agricultural subsidy payments.
Form 1099-INT, Interest Income	For reporting payments of (a) interest of $10 or more paid or credited on earnings from savings and loans, credit unions, bank deposits, corporate bonds, etc.; (b) interest of $600 or more from other sources; (c) forfeited interest due on premature withdrawals of time deposits; (d) foreign tax eligible for the recipient's foreign tax credit withheld and paid on interest; (e) payments of any interest on bearer certificates of deposit.
Form 1099-MISC, Miscellaneous Income (See Figure 4.13)	For reporting miscellaneous income, such as rents, royalties, commissions, fees, prizes, and awards of at least $600 paid to nonemployees, and any backup withholding. Gross royalty payments of $10 or more must also be reported on this form. Life insurance companies may use either 1099-MISC or Form W-2 to report payments to full-time life insurance sales agents.
Form 1099-PATR, Taxable Distributions Received from Cooperatives	For cooperatives to report patronage dividends paid and other distributions made that total $10 or more during the year.
Form 1099-R, Distributions from Pensions, Annuities, Retirement or Profit-Sharing Plans, IRAs, Insurance Contracts, etc.	For reporting all distributions that total $10 or more from pensions, annuities, profit-sharing and retirement plans, and individual retirement arrangements made by employees' trusts or funds; federal, state, or local government retirement system; life insurance companies.
Form 5498, IRA Contribution Information	For reporting contributions received from each person to an IRA or simplified employee pension plan (SEP) and qualified deductible voluntary employee contributions to a plan maintained by the employer.
Form 8027, Employer's Annual Information Return of Tip Income and Allocated Tips	For large food or beverage establishments to report to the IRS the receipts from food and beverage operations and tips reported by employees.

FIGURE 4.13

Form 1099-MISC, Miscellaneous Income

9595	□ VOID	□ CORRECTED		
PAYER'S name, street address, city or town, state or province, country, ZIP or foreign postal code, and telephone no. Worldwide Publishing Co. 40 Fifth Avenue New York, NY 10011-4000 (212) 555-2000	**1 Rents** $ **2 Royalties** $ 34,970.65	OMB No. 1545-0115 20-- Form **1099-MISC**	**Miscellaneous Income**	
	3 Other income $	**4 Federal income tax withheld** $	**Copy A**	
PAYER'S federal identification number	RECIPIENT'S identification number	**5 Fishing boat proceeds**	**6 Medical and health care payments**	**For Internal Revenue Service Center**
00-0003736	000-00-4821	$	$	**File with Form 1096.**
RECIPIENT'S name Laurie T. Musberger		**7 Nonemployee compensation**	**8 Substitute payments in lieu of dividends or interest**	For Privacy Act and Paperwork Reduction Act Notice, see the
Street address (including apt. no.) 1043 Maple Drive		$	$	**20-- General Instructions for Certain Information Returns.**
		9 Payer made direct sales of $5,000 or more of consumer products to a buyer (recipient) for resale ▶ □	**10 Crop insurance proceeds** $	
City or town, state or province, country, and ZIP or foreign postal code Chicago, IL 60615-3443		**11**	**12**	
Account number (see instructions)	FATCA filing requirement □	2nd TIN not. □	**13 Excess golden parachute payments** $	**14 Gross proceeds paid to an attorney** $	
15a Section 409A deferrals $	**15b** Section 409A income $	**16 State tax withheld** $ $	**17 State/Payer's state no.** 00-03378	**18 State income** $ $

Form **1099-MISC**   Cat. No. 14425J   www.irs.gov/form1099misc   Department of the Treasury - Internal Revenue Service

Do Not Cut or Separate Forms on This Page — Do Not Cut or Separate Forms on This Page

Source: Internal Revenue Service.

Backup Withholding

Independent contractors must provide taxpayer identification numbers (TIN) to their employers (orally, in writing, or on Form W-9). If this is not done and the company anticipates paying the contractor $600 or more, the company must withhold federal income taxes of *28 percent* of the payments made. This backup withholding must continue until the number is reported. Failure to withhold will result in the payer being held liable by the IRS for the 28 percent withholding.

NEWS ALERT

Recipient's identification number is truncated on employee's copy of Form 1099-MISC.

Nonpayroll Reporting

Payroll income tax withholdings are reported on Form 941, while nonpayroll items are reported on *Form 945, Annual Return of Withheld Federal Income Tax*. Nonpayroll items include backup withholdings and withholdings on pensions, IRAs, gambling winnings, and military retirement pay. Generally, all income tax witholdings that are reported on Form 1099 or Form W-2G belong on Form 945.

Over the Line

The IRS assessed employment taxes, penalties, and interest to Bruecher Foundation Services, Inc., in reference to workers that were misclassified as independent contractors. Section 530 of the Internal Revenue Code gives "safe harbor" for the misclassification of employees if the employer can show that it filed all federal tax and information returns. However, the IRS said Bruecher would not qualify for safe harbor because it did not file information returns (Forms 1099) on a timely basis.[3]

Electronic Filing Form W-2 and Information Returns

ON THE NET

For electronic filing of tax return and payment options, go to: **Electronic Filing for Businesses: https://www.eftps.gov/eftps/**

If employers file 250 or more Forms W-2 or other information returns (for each type of information return), they must use electronic filing instead of paper forms. Filing Forms W-2 does not require approval of the medium by the Social Security Administration. The employer must complete *Form 4419, Application for Filing Information Returns Electronically (FIRE)*, and file it with the IRS.

Withholding State Income Tax

In addition to federal income taxes, many states also have income tax withholding requirements. The situation is further complicated if an employer has employees in several states. This requires employers to know how much tax to withhold, what types of employees and payments are exempt, and how to pay the tax.

In general, state income taxes should be withheld based on where the services are performed unless there is a **reciprocal agreement** between the states. If there is no such agreement and the employee works in one state and lives in another, the laws of both states must be considered.

The three different methods of withholding are:

ON THE JOB

Only nine states do not have a state income tax on wages—Alaska, Florida, Nevada, New Hampshire, South Dakota, Tennessee, Texas, Washington, and Wyoming.

1. Full taxation—both resident's state and work state calculate the taxes without any credits.
2. Leftover taxation—pay the full tax to the work state, and then pay the rest to the resident state.
3. Reciprocity—withhold only for the work state or resident state depending on the reciprocal agreement between the states.[4]

Employers must also be informed about each state's regulations regarding:

1. The required frequency of making wage payments.
2. The acceptable media of payment.
3. The maximum interval between the end of a pay period and the payday for that period.
4. The time limits for making final wage payments to employees who are discharged, are laid off, quit, or go on strike.
5. How often to inform employees of the deductions made from their wages.
6. The maximum amount of unpaid wages to pay the surviving spouse or family of a deceased worker.

---

3 Anne S. Lewis, "Employer That Failed to File Timely Information Returns for Misclassified Workers Was Not Entitled to Section 530 Relief," *PAYTECH*, October 2007, p. 73.

4 "State Tax Issues for Travelling and Telecommuting Employees," *Pay State Update,* American Payroll Association, May 30, 2002, Issue 11, p. 2.

Wage-bracket tables and percentage method formulas are used in many states to determine the amount of state income taxes to withhold from their employees' wages. Each state also determines for state income tax purposes the taxability status of the various fringe benefits discussed in this chapter. Even though most states do not tax deductions made for cafeteria plans and 401(k) accounts, some states do not allow for the tax sheltering of these deductions from employees' wages. Once again, it is the employers' responsibility to know the laws of the states in which they conduct business.

Most states having income tax laws require employers to withhold tax from both nonresidents and residents, unless a **reciprocal agreement** exists with one or more states to the contrary. For example, a reciprocal agreement may exist between two states where both states grant an exemption to nonresidents who work in each of those states.

Even though there is no law requiring an employer to withhold income tax from the employee's home state if the employer has no physical presence in that state, most employers do this as a courtesy to their out-of-state employees.

State Income Tax Returns and Reports

Payroll managers should be familiar with four main types of state income tax returns or reports:

1. **Periodic withholding returns** on which you report the wages paid and the state tax withheld during the reporting period. Figure 4.14 shows the *Payroll Tax Deposit Coupon* used by employers in California. Depending on the amount of state income taxes withheld for each quarterly period, employers may be required to pay the taxes semimonthly, monthly, or quarterly. Some states require employers to deposit their withheld income taxes through electronic funds transfer (EFT).

2. **Reconciliation returns** that compare the total amount of state tax paid as shown on the periodic returns with the amounts of state tax declared to have been withheld from employees' wages. Figure 4.15, on page 4-32, shows the *Quarterly Contribution Return and Report of Wages (Continuation)* for use by employers in California. Employers may submit their information on magnetic media.

FIGURE 4.14
Form DE 88ALL, California Payroll Tax Deposit

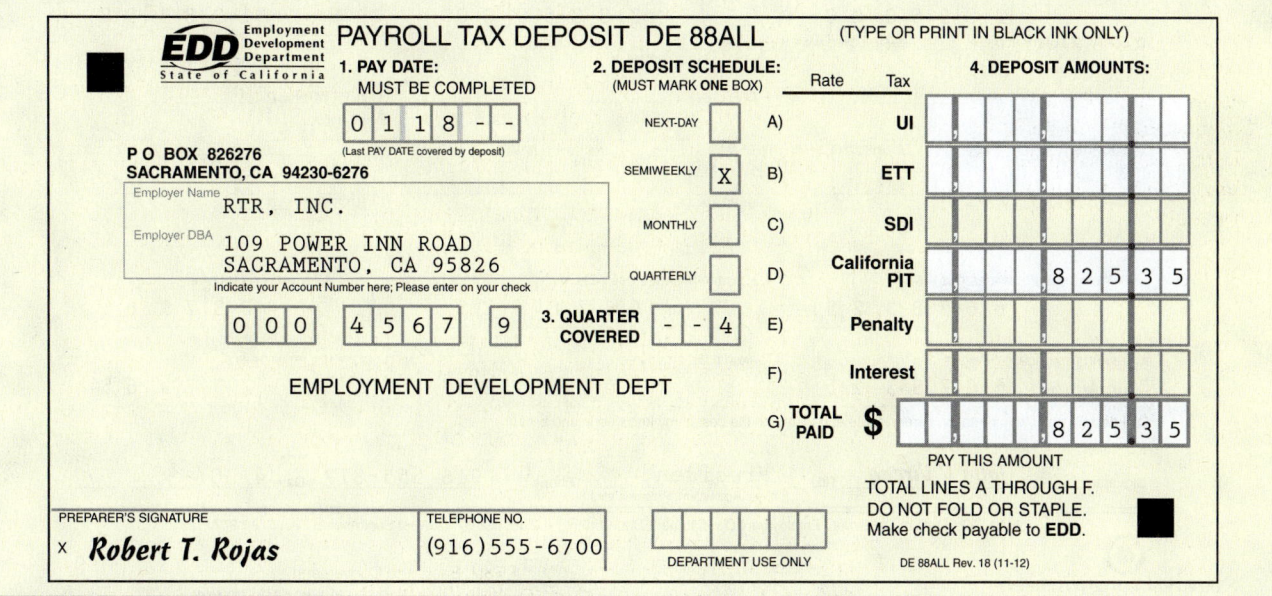

Source: CA Employment Development Department.

FIGURE 4.15

Form DE 9c, California Quarterly Contribution Return and Report of Wages (Continuation)

EDD Employment Development Department
State of California

QUARTERLY CONTRIBUTION RETURN AND REPORT OF WAGES (CONTINUATION)

REMINDER: File your DE 9 and DE 9C together.

009C0111

Page number _____ of _____

You must FILE this report even if you had no payroll. If you had no payroll, complete Items C and O.

	YR	QTR
	- -	1

QUARTER ENDED
331

DUE
4 30 - -

DELINQUENT IF NOT POSTMARKED OR RECEIVED BY
4 30 - -

EMPLOYER ACCOUNT NO.
0 0 0 0 3 2 1 1

Vireng Company
1817 Kresson Road
Sacramento, CA 95826

DO NOT ALTER THIS AREA

P1 ☐   C ☐   T ☐   S ☐   W ☐   A ☐

EFFECTIVE DATE
Mo.   Day   Yr.   WIC

A. EMPLOYEES full-time and part-time who worked during or received pay subject to UI for the payroll period which includes the 12th of the month.

1st Mo.	2nd Mo.	3rd Mo.
5	5	5

B. ☐ Check this box if you are reporting ONLY Voluntary Plan Disability Insurance wages on this page.
☐ Report Personal Income Tax (PIT) Wages and PIT Withheld, if appropriate. (See instructions for Item B.)

C. ☐ NO PAYROLL

D. SOCIAL SECURITY NUMBER	E. EMPLOYEE NAME (FIRST NAME)	(M.I.) (LAST NAME)	
000 00 6399	Maria	L Goshen	
F. TOTAL SUBJECT WAGES	**G. PIT WAGES**	**H. PIT WITHHELD**	
5 0 0 9 2 5	5 0 0 9 2 5	5 5 2 5	

D. SOCIAL SECURITY NUMBER	E. EMPLOYEE NAME (FIRST NAME)	(M.I.) (LAST NAME)	
000 00 7931	Carmen	M Rodgers	
F. TOTAL SUBJECT WAGES	**G. PIT WAGES**	**H. PIT WITHHELD**	
7 1 9 5 0 0	7 1 9 5 0 0	9 5 0 3	

D. SOCIAL SECURITY NUMBER	E. EMPLOYEE NAME (FIRST NAME)	(M.I.) (LAST NAME)	
000 00 8001	Joseph	N Nyugen	
F. TOTAL SUBJECT WAGES	**G. PIT WAGES**	**H. PIT WITHHELD**	
1 0 3 1 9 0 0	1 0 3 1 9 0 0	1 2 0 7 7	

D. SOCIAL SECURITY NUMBER	E. EMPLOYEE NAME (FIRST NAME)	(M.I.) (LAST NAME)	
000 00 9114	Elaine	M Schmidt	
F. TOTAL SUBJECT WAGES	**G. PIT WAGES**	**H. PIT WITHHELD**	
1 5 9 1 0 0 0	1 5 9 1 0 0 0	7 2 4 6 2	

D. SOCIAL SECURITY NUMBER	E. EMPLOYEE NAME (FIRST NAME)	(M.I.) (LAST NAME)	
000 00 4091	John	V Vireng	
F. TOTAL SUBJECT WAGES	**G. PIT WAGES**	**H. PIT WITHHELD**	
2 8 3 5 0 0 0	2 8 3 5 0 0 0	1 3 8 3 9 8	

D. SOCIAL SECURITY NUMBER	E. EMPLOYEE NAME (FIRST NAME)	(M.I.) (LAST NAME)	
F. TOTAL SUBJECT WAGES	**G. PIT WAGES**	**H. PIT WITHHELD**	

D. SOCIAL SECURITY NUMBER	E. EMPLOYEE NAME (FIRST NAME)	(M.I.) (LAST NAME)	
F. TOTAL SUBJECT WAGES	**G. PIT WAGES**	**H. PIT WITHHELD**	

I. TOTAL SUBJECT WAGES THIS PAGE	J. TOTAL PIT WAGES THIS PAGE	K. TOTAL PIT WITHHELD THIS PAGE
6 6 7 8 3 2 5	6 6 7 8 3 2 5	2 3 7 9 6 5

L. GRAND TOTAL SUBJECT WAGES	M. GRAND TOTAL PIT WAGES	N. GRAND TOTAL PIT WITHHELD
6 6 7 8 3 2 5	6 6 7 8 3 2 5	2 3 7 9 6 5

O. I declare that the information herein is true and correct to the best of my knowledge and belief.

Signature _Required_ **John V Vireng**   Title __President__   Phone ( ) 916 555-8121 Date 4/30/--
(Owner, Accountant, Preparer, etc.)

MAIL TO: State of California / Employment Development Department / P.O. Box 989071 / West Sacramento CA 95798-9071

DE 9C Rev. 1 (1-12) **(INTERNET)**

Page 1 of 2

e-Services   Fast, Easy, and Convenient!
Visit EDD's Web site at **www.edd.ca.gov**

CU

Source: CA Employment Development Department.

3. **Annual statements** to employees showing the amount of wages paid during the year and the state tax withheld from those wages.

4. **Information returns** used to report payments to individuals that are not subject to withholding and/or are not reported on the annual employee wage and tax statements. See Figure 4.12, on page 4-28, for a listing of the major information returns.

Since the requirements for transmitting returns and reports vary from state to state, employers should become familiar with the tax regulations of the state in which their business is located and of the state or states in which their employees reside. Because federal regulations require filing of information returns on magnetic media, many states permit employers to submit wage information on magnetic disk or tape. Also, many states take part in the Combined Federal/ State Filing Program, which enables employers to file information returns with the federal government and authorize release of the information to the applicable state. To participate in this program, employers must first obtain permission from the IRS.

Withholding Local Income Taxes

In addition to state income tax laws, many cities and counties have passed local income tax legislation requiring employers to deduct and withhold income taxes or license fees on salaries or wages paid. In Alabama, several cities have license fee ordinances that require the withholding of the fees from employees' wages. Certain employees in Denver, Colorado, are subject to the withholding of the Denver Occupational Privilege Tax from their compensation. In Kentucky, a number of cities and counties impose a license fee (payroll tax).

Figure 4.16 shows the coupon that must be completed by employers in Philadelphia. All must withhold the city income tax from compensation paid their employees. Depending upon the amount of taxes withheld, employers may be required to make deposits weekly, monthly, or quarterly. Employer's with more than 250 W-2s must remit electronically. For any late payments of the tax, the city imposes a penalty on the underpayment. Employers must file annual reconciliation returns by the end of February, reporting the amount of taxes deducted during the preceding calendar year.

FIGURE 4.16
Philadelphia Wage Tax Coupon

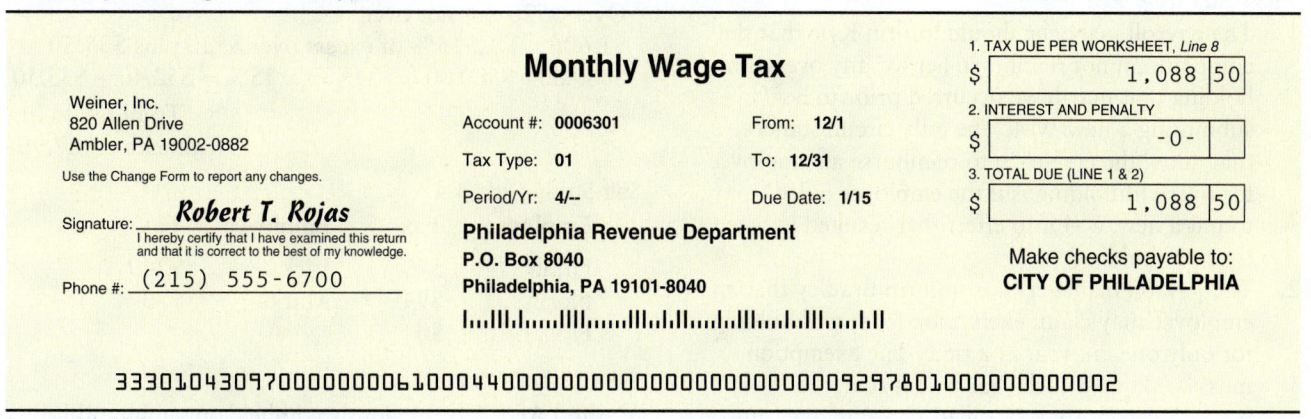

Source: Philadelphia Revenue Department.

KEY TERMS

annualizing wages (p. 4-17)

backup withholding (p. 4-29)

de minimis fringe benefit (p. 4-4)

defined contribution plan (p. 4-8)

gross-up (p. 4-21)

information returns (p. 4-28)

part-year employment (p. 4-17)

percentage method (p. 4-15)

personal allowance (p. 4-10)

quarterly averaging (p. 4-17)

reciprocal agreement (p. 4-31)

special withholding allowance (p. 4-10)

standard deduction (p. 4-15)

supplemental wage payments (p. 4-18)

wage and tax statements (p. 4-21)

wage-bracket method (p. 4-15)

wages (p. 4-2)

ANSWERS TO SELF-STUDY QUIZZES

Self-Study Quiz 4-1

✓   1. Meals provided to employees for the convenience of the employer on the employer's premises.

___   2. Bonuses to managers and supervisors are considered compensation for services rendered as employees and are subject to withholding.

✓   3. The use of on-site athletic facilities by employees is considered a nontaxable fringe benefit.

✓   4. Advances for business expenses reasonably expected to be incurred.

___   5. Sick pay is subject to withholding.

___   6. Memberships in social or country clubs are taxable fringe benefits and are subject to withholding.

✓   7. No-additional-cost meals provided to employees at an employer-operated eating establishment.

Self-Study Quiz 4-2

1. The payroll manager should inform Kyle that the company cannot reimburse her for any overwithholding that may have occurred prior to her submitting a new W-4. The only circumstances that allow the employer to reimburse an employee for overwithholding is if the employer failed to put a new W-4 into effect that resulted in overwithholding.

2. The payroll manager must inform Bradley that an employee may claim exemption from withholding for only one tax year at a time. The exemption must be claimed each year by February 15. If a new certificate is not filed, the employer must withhold at the single rate with zero withholding allowances.

3. Volmer may claim six personal allowances, as identified on the personal allowance worksheet accompanying Form W-4:

a. One allowance for himself.

b. One allowance for his spouse.

c. One allowance for being married, having one job, and his spouse not working.

d. One allowance for each dependent child (total of 3).

Self-Study Quiz 4-3

Step 1—Round gross wages: **$1,100**

Step 2—Multiply the number $3 \times \$76.90 = \$230.70$
of allowances by the weekly
allowance amount:

Step 3—Subtract the value of the $\$1,100 - \$230.70 =$
allowances from the gross pay: **$869.30**

Step 4—Compute the tax from
the percentage tax table for
WEEKLY MARRIED person:

Over $520 But not over
$1,606 .... 15% of excess over $520 plus $35.50

$869.30 - $520.00 = $349.30 × 15% = $52.40 + $35.50

**Total tax to be
withheld = $87.90**

Self-Study Quiz 4-4

Employee	Tax	Employee	Tax
Lamb	$108	Vick	$249
Nurin	$94	Marks	$73
Hogan	$0		

Self-Study Quiz 4-5

Method A: Tax previously withheld on semimonthly
wage of $1,450 = $76

Tax on wage and bonus ($1,950): $150
Less tax previously withheld: 76
Withholding on bonus: $ 74

Method B: 25% × $500 = $125

Self-Study Quiz 4-6

1. The company should report the total amount deducted from each employee in Box 14 of Form W-2. This box is to provide "other" information the company wants to give the employees. The company should label the amount as "union dues" in Box 14.

2. If an employee leaves the service of the employer, the employer may furnish Form W-2 any time after employment ends. If the employee requests Form W-2, the employer should give it to him/her within 30 days of the request or final wage payment, whichever is later. If there is a reasonable expectation that the employees may be rehired before the end of the year, the employer may delay providing Form W-2 until January following the close of the calendar year.

3. If Form W-2 has been destroyed or lost, employers are authorized to furnish substitute copies to the employee. Trident should provide a substitute form to Becker. The form should be clearly marked "Reissued Statement," and the company should not send the substitute statement to the Social Security Administration.

KEY POINTS SUMMARY

	Learning Objectives	Key Points	Practical Problems A & B
L01	Explain coverage under the Federal Income Tax Withholding Law by determining: (a) the employer-employee relationship, (b) the kinds of payments defined as wages, and (c) the kinds of pretax salary reductions.	• Statutory employees/nonemployees. • Fringe benefit is added to regular wages—W/H taxes on total or 25 percent of fringe benefit. • Tips—tax on tips taken from regular wage payments. • Pretax salary reductions—from cafeteria plans to retirement contributions.	4-1, 4-7, 4-11
L02	Explain: (a) the types of withholding allowances that may be claimed by employees for income tax withholding and (b) the purpose and use of Form W-4.	• Allowances claimed on W-4 for personal (themselves and spouse), dependents, special withholding, tax credits, and itemized deductions on personal tax return. • Can claim exemption from W/H if no tax last year and none expected this year.	
L03	Compute the amount of federal income tax to be withheld using: (a) the percentage method; (b) the wage-bracket method; (c) alternative methods such as quarterly averaging, annualizing of wages, and part-year employment; and (d) withholding of federal income taxes on supplementary wage payments.	• Use *Percentage Method W/H* table or *Wage-Bracket* table to determine federal tax withholding. • Supplemental—vacation (tax as separate wage payment) versus nonvacation (added to regular pay and total taxed or 25 percent of supplemental). • Gross-up formula.	4-2, 4-3, 4-4, 4-5, 4-6, 4-8, 4-9, 4-10, 4-13
L04	Explain: (a) Form W-2, (b) the completion of **Form 941, Employer's Quarterly Federal Tax Return,** (c) major types of information returns, and (d) the impact of state and local income taxes on the payroll accounting process.	• *Wage and Tax Statement* (W-2) give to employees with copies to taxing authorities. • Quarterly Form 941 reports federal income taxes and FICA taxes withheld. • Form 1099—payments to consultants.	4-12, 4-13

MATCHING QUIZ

_____ 1. Taxable tips
_____ 2. Personal allowance
_____ 3. Backup withholding
_____ 4. Form 1099-MISC
_____ 5. Roth IRA
_____ 6. Standard deduction
_____ 7. Pretax salary reductions
_____ 8. Form 1096
_____ 9. Nontaxable fringe benefits
_____ 10. Flexible reporting

A. Payments of at least $600 to independent contractors
B. Annual nondeductible contributions of up to $5,500
C. Annual summary and transmittal of U.S. information returns
D. Allows employers to use any basis as the time period for payment of noncash fringe benefits
E. $4,000 deduction in computing taxable income
F. Withholdings from gross pay that reduce the amount of pay subject to federal income tax
G. Qualified employee discounts
H. Amount of money used to reduce an individual's adjusted gross income to taxable income
I. Withhold federal income taxes of 28 percent of payments made
J. $20 or more in a month

QUESTIONS FOR REVIEW

Note: Use Tax Tables A and B at the back of this textbook and the tax regulations presented in this chapter to answer all questions and solve all problems.

1. How is the amount of a fringe benefit that is taxable to an employee determined?
2. To what extent are cash tips treated as remuneration subject to federal income tax withholding?
3. For each of the following kinds of wage payments, indicate whether or not the wages are exempt from the withholding of federal income taxes:
   a. Three weeks' vacation pay.
   b. Weekly advance to a sales representative for traveling expenses to be incurred.
   c. Weekly wages paid the housekeeper in a college fraternity.
   d. Monthly salary received by Rev. Cole Carpenter.
   e. Payments under a worker's compensation law for sickness or injury.
4. What is the maximum contribution that an employer can make to an employee's SIMPLE account?
5. What is the maximum amount that an employee can shelter into a 401(k) plan?
6. What is a personal allowance? What was the amount of a personal allowance for 2015?
7. Orrin D'Amato, single, participates in his firm's pension retirement plan. This year, his modified adjusted gross income will be about $75,000. How much of his compensation may D'Amato contribute to an IRA this year without paying federal income taxes on the contribution?

8. Are employer contributions into employees' health savings accounts taxed as earnings of the employees?
9. Under what conditions may employees be exempt from the withholding of federal income taxes during 2015? How do such employees indicate their no-tax-liability status?
10. How is the *special period rule* for the reporting of fringe benefits applied?
11. Commencing in June, Alan Oldt is eligible to receive monthly payments from a pension fund. What procedure should Oldt follow if he does not wish to have federal income taxes withheld from his periodic pension payments?
12. Rhonda Gramm is single, and her wages are paid weekly. Under the percentage method, what is the amount of Gramm's one weekly withholding allowance? Howard Heinz, married, claims two withholding allowances, and his wages are paid semimonthly. What is the total amount of his semimonthly withholding allowances?
13. What formula is used to "gross-up" supplemental payments in order to cover the taxes on the supplemental payments?
14. Trowbridge Company has just completed the processing of its year-end payroll and distributed all the weekly paychecks. The payroll department is now computing the amount of the annual bonus to be given each worker. What methods may be used by the company in determining the amount of federal income taxes to be withheld from the annual bonus payments?

15. What is Form 944?
16. Why must some employers file Form 1096?
17. What is the penalty for filing W-2s with mismatched names and social security numbers?
18. What are the penalties imposed on employees for filing false information on Form W-4?
19. Under what conditions must employers submit copies of Form W-4 to the IRS?
20. Besides the name and address of the payer, what other information should be listed in the address box of the payer on the recipient's copy of Form 1099-MISC?

QUESTIONS FOR DISCUSSION

1. Alex Oberstar, a cook in the Lagomarsino Company cafeteria, is furnished two meals each day during his eight-hour shift. Oberstar's duties require him to have his meals on the company's premises. Should the cash value of Oberstar's meals be included as part of his taxable wages? Explain.

2. Barbri Company ordinarily pays its employees on a weekly basis. Recently, one of the employees, Bernard Nagle, was sent from the home office on a three-week trip. Nagle has now returned to the office, and you are preparing a single check covering his three-week services. Should you withhold federal income taxes on the total gross earnings for the three-week period, or should you compute the federal income taxes as if Nagle were receiving three separate weekly wage payments?

3. Investigate your state's income tax withholding law (or that of some other state assigned by your instructor), and find the answers to the following questions:
   a. Who must withhold the tax?
   b. How are covered employers and covered employees defined?
   c. Are there any reciprocal agreements into which the state has entered? If so, describe them.
   d. How is the withholding rate determined?
   e. What payments are subject to withholding?
   f. What payments are not subject to withholding?
   g. Are there any employee withholding exemptions?
   h. What methods of withholding are permitted?
   i. Describe each of the returns required by the state.
   j. What kinds of information must be retained by employers in their withholding tax records?
   k. What penalties are imposed for failure to comply with the withholding law?
   l. Are any employers required to deposit their withheld income taxes through electronic funds transfer (EFT)? If so, what requirements does the state impose?

4. Rena Reynolds, one of your firm's workers, has just come into the payroll department and says to you: "I am thinking of amending my Form W-4 so that an additional $10 is withheld each week. That way I will get a fat refund next year. What do you think of my idea?" How would you reply to Reynolds?

5. Anita Leland, a waitress in Atlantis Casino, reported tips of $467 to her employer last year. Two months after she filed her federal income tax return, Leland received a letter from the IRS informing her that she had earned $5,260 in tips rather than the $467 reported and that she owed the government $1,872.94 in back taxes.
   a. How is the IRS able to determine the amount of tips received by a waitress in a casino?
   b. If the IRS is correct in its determination of the tips received, is Atlantis subject to a penalty for not having withheld payroll taxes on all the tips Leland received during the year?

6. Justin Holmes, an ex-employee, is entitled to a taxable fringe benefit during the first part of this year. Because he wasn't paid any wages this year, can his employer report the taxable fringe benefit on Form 1099?

PROBLEM SET • A

As we go to press, the federal income tax rates for 2016 are being determined by budget talks in Washington and not available for publication. For this edition, the 2015 federal income tax tables and 2015 FICA rates have been used.

4-1A • LO 1   See page 4-16

Sean Matthews is a waiter at the Duluxe Lounge. In his first weekly pay in March, he earned $300.00 for the 40 hours he worked. In addition, he reports his tips for February to his employer ($500.00), and the employer withholds the appropriate taxes for the tips from this first pay in March.

   Calculate his net take-home pay assuming the employer withheld federal income tax (*wage-bracket*, married, 2 allowances), social security taxes, and state income tax (2%) .... $ _____

4-2A • LO 3   See page 4-15

Use the *percentage method* to compute the federal income taxes to withhold from the wages or salaries of each employee.

Employee No.	Employee Name	Marital Status	No. of Withholding Allowances	Gross Wage or Salary	Amount to Be Withheld
1	Amoroso, A.	M	4	$1,610 weekly	_____
2	Finley, R.	S	0	825 biweekly	_____
3	Gluck, E.	S	5	9,630 quarterly	_____
4	Quinn, S.	M	8	925 semimonthly	_____
5	Treave, Y.	M	3	2,875 monthly	_____

4-3A • LO 3   See pages 4-15 and 4-16

Use (a) the percentage method and (b) the wage-bracket method to compute the federal income taxes to withhold from the wages or salaries of each employee.

Employee	Marital Status	No. of Withholding Allowances	Gross Wage or Salary	Amount to Be Withheld Percentage Method	Amount to Be Withheld Wage-Bracket Method
Corn, A.	S	2	$ 675 weekly	_____	_____
Fogge, P.	S	1	1,960 weekly	_____	_____
Felps, S.	M	6	1,775 biweekly	_____	_____
Carson, W.	M	4	2,480 semimonthly	_____	_____
Helm, M.	M	9	5,380 monthly	_____	_____

4-4A • LO 3   See page 4-16

Eaton Enterprises uses the *wage-bracket method* to determine federal income tax withholding on its employees. Find the amount to withhold from the wages paid each employee.

Employee	Marital Status	No. of Withholding Allowances	Payroll Period W=Weekly S=Semimonthly M=Monthly D=Daily	Wage	Amount to Be Withheld
Hal Bower	M	1	W	$1,350	_____
Ruth Cramden	S	1	W	590	_____
Gil Jones	S	3	W	675	_____
Teresa Kern	M	6	M	4,090	_____
Ruby Long	M	2	M	2,730	_____
Katie Luis	M	8	S	955	_____
Susan Martin	S	1	D	108	_____
Jim Singer	S	4	S	2,610	_____
Martin Torres	M	4	M	3,215	_____

4-5A • LO 3   See page 4-16

The names of the employees of Hogan Thrift Shop are listed on the following payroll register. Employees are paid weekly. The marital status and the number of allowances claimed are shown on the payroll register, along with each employee's weekly salary, which has remained the same all year. Complete the payroll register for the payroll period ending December 16, the 51st weekly payday. The state income tax rate is 2% of total earnings, the city income tax rate is 1.5% of the total gross earnings, and the *wage-bracket method* is used for federal income taxes.

HOGAN THRIFT SHOP
PAYROLL REGISTER

FOR PERIOD ENDING _____ 20____

EMPLOYEE NAME	MARITAL STATUS	NO. OF W/H ALLOW.	TOTAL EARNINGS	DEDUCTIONS (a) FICA OASDI	HI	(b) FIT	(c) SIT	(d) CIT	(e) NET PAY
John, Matthew	M	3	2 3 5 0 00						
Smith, Jennifer	S	1	2 7 5 00						
Bullen, Catherine	M	0	2 5 0 00						
Matthews, Mary	S	3	3 2 0 25						
Hadt, Bonnie	S	1	4 5 0 00						
Camp, Sean	S	2	5 6 0 50						
Wilson, Helen	S	1	4 7 5 50						
Gleason, Josie	M	3	8 9 0 00						
Totals									

Compute the employer's FICA taxes for the pay period ending December 16.

OASDI Taxes		HI Taxes	
OASDI taxable earnings	$_____	HI taxable earnings	$_____
OASDI taxes	$_____	HI taxes	$_____

4-6A • LO 3   Similar to Example 4-10 on page 4-21

Damerly Company (a California employer) wants to give a holiday bonus check of $250 to each employee. Since it wants the check amount to be $250, it will need to gross-up the amount of the bonus. Calculate the withholding taxes and the gross amount of the bonus to be made to John Rolen if his cumulative earnings for the year are $46,910. Besides being subject to social security taxes and federal income tax (supplemental rate), a 6.6% California income tax must be withheld on supplemental payments... $_____

4-7A • LO 1 Similar to Example 4-8 on page 4-8

Julie Whiteweiler made $930 this week. Only social security (fully taxable) and federal income taxes attach to her pay. Whiteweiler contributes $100 each week to her company's 401(k) plan and has $25 put into her health savings account (nonqualified) each week. Her employer matches this $25 each week. Determine Whiteweiler's take-home pay if she is single and claims 2 allowances (use the wage-bracket method) .... $ _____

4-8A • LO 3 Similar to Example 4-6 on page 4-19

The names of the employees of Cox Security Systems and their regular salaries are shown in the following payroll register. Note that Hall and Short are paid monthly on the last payday, while all others are paid weekly.

In addition to the regular salaries, the company pays an annual bonus based on the amount of earnings for the year. For the current year, the bonus amounts to 8% of the annual salary paid to each employee. The bonus is to be paid along with the regular salaries on December 30, but the amount of the bonus and the amount of the regular salary will be shown separately on each employee's earnings statement. Assume that all employees received their regular salary during the entire year.

Prepare the payroll for the pay period ending December 30, showing the following for each employee:

- Use the *wage-bracket method* to withhold federal income tax from the regular salaries.
- Withhold a flat 25% on the annual bonus.
- Total salaries and bonuses are subject to a 2% state income tax and a 1% city income tax.

FOR PERIOD ENDING _____ 20___

EMPLOYEE NAME	MARITAL STATUS	NO. OF W/H ALLOW.	EARNINGS REGULAR	(a) SUPP'L.	(b) TOTAL	(c) FICA OASDI	(c) FICA HI	(d) FIT	(e) SIT	(f) CIT	(g) NET PAY
Hall, Michael	M	5	5 0 0 0 00*								
Short, Joy T.	M	2	2 7 5 0 00*								
Abbott, Linda	S	1	5 2 0 00								
Smith, Joseph	M	4	4 6 5 00								
Tols, Sean M.	M	2	3 8 0 00								
Gillespie, Michelle	S	1	3 5 0 00								
Smart, Jennifer	M	2	5 7 5 00								
White, Matthew J.	S	0	4 2 5 00								
Totals											

*Monthly

Compute the employer's FICA taxes for the pay period ending December 30.

OASDI Taxes
OASDI taxable earnings $ _____
OASDI taxes $ _____

HI Taxes
HI taxable earnings $ _____
HI taxes $ _____

4-9A • LO 3   See page 4-16

Assume during the quarter ending December 31 of the current year, Cox Security Systems had 13 weekly paydays and three monthly paydays. Using the data given in 4-8A, complete the following form to show:

a. Total earnings paid during the quarter, including both the regular and the supplemental earnings.

b. Total amount of FICA taxes withheld during the quarter.

c. Total amount of federal income taxes withheld during the quarter.

d. Total amount of state income taxes withheld during the quarter.

e. Total amount of city income taxes withheld during the quarter.

f. Total net amount paid each employee during the quarter.

EMPLOYEE NAME	(a) TOTAL EARNINGS	(b) FICA		(c) FIT	(d) SIT	(e) CIT	(f) NET PAY
		OASDI	HI	DEDUCTIONS			
Hall, Michael							
Short, Joy T.							
Abbott, Linda							
Smith, Joseph							
Tols, Sean M.							
Gillespie, Michelle							
Smart, Jennifer							
White, Matthew J.							
Totals							

4-10A • LO 3 Similar to Example 4-10 on page 4-21

Mattola Company is giving each of its employees a holiday bonus of $100 on December 16 (a nonpayday). The company wants each employee's check to be $100. The supplemental tax percent is used.

a. What will be the gross amount of each bonus if each employee pays a state income tax of 2.8% (besides the other payroll taxes)? $ _____

b. What would the net amount of each bonus check be if the company did not gross-up the bonus? $ _____

4-11A • LO 1 Similar to Example 4-1 on page 4-8

George Clausen (age 48) is employed by Kline Company and is paid a salary of $42,640. He has just decided to join the company's Simple Retirement Account (IRA form) and has a few questions. Answer the following for Clausen:

a. What is the maximum that he can contribute into this retirement fund? $ _____

b. What would be the company's contribution? $ _____

c. What would be his weekly take-home pay with the retirement contribution deducted (married, 2 allowances, *wage-bracket method*, and a 2.3% state income tax on total wages)? $ _____

d. What would be his weekly take-home pay without the retirement contribution deduction? $ _____

4-12A • LO 4 See pages 3-16, 3-17, 3-21, and 4-31

During the fourth quarter of 2016, there were seven biweekly paydays on Friday (October 7, 21; November 4, 18; December 2, 16, 30) for Quality Repairs. Using the forms supplied on pages 4-44 to 4-47, complete the following for the fourth quarter:

a. Complete the Federal Deposit Information Worksheets reflecting electronic deposits (monthly depositor). The employer's phone number is (501) 555-7331. Federal deposit liability each pay, $677.68.

b. Employer's Quarterly Federal Tax Return, Form 941. The form is signed by you as president on January 31, 2017.

c. Employer's Report of State Income Tax Withheld for the quarter, due on or before January 31, 2017.

Quarterly Payroll Data

Total Earnings 5 Employees	OASDI	HI	FIT	SIT
$18,750.00	$1,162.50	$271.88	$1,875.00	$1,312.50

Employer's OASDI	$1,162.50
Employer's HI	271.88
Federal deposit liability each pay	677.68

4-12A (continued)

EMPLOYER'S REPORT
OF STATE INCOME TAX WITHHELD

(DO NOT WRITE IN THIS SPACE)

IMPORTANT: PLEASE REFER TO THIS NUMBER IN ANY CORRESPONDENCE→

WITHHOLDING IDENTIFICATION NUMBER	MONTH OF OR QUARTER ENDING
00-0-3301	DEC 20--

IF YOU ARE A SEA-SONAL EMPLOYER AND THIS IS YOUR FINAL REPORT FOR THIS SEASON, CHECK HERE ☐ AND SHOW THE NEXT MONTH IN WHICH YOU WILL PAY WAGES.

QUALITY REPAIRS
10 SUMMIT SQUARE
CITY, STATE 00000-0000

IF NAME OR ADDRESS IS INCORRECT, PLEASE MAKE CORRECTIONS.
THIS REPORT MUST BE RETURNED EVEN IF NO AMOUNT HAS BEEN WITHHELD

1. GROSS PAYROLL THIS PERIOD . . . . $

2. STATE INCOME TAX WITHHELD . . . . $

3. ADJUSTMENT FOR PREVIOUS PERIOD(S). (ATTACH STATEMENT) $

4. TOTAL ADJUSTED TAX (LINE 2 PLUS OR MINUS LINE 3) $

5. PENALTY (35% OF LINE 4) $

6. INTEREST . . . .

7. TOTAL AMOUNT DUE AND PAYABLE . . . . $

Under penalties prescribed by law, I hereby affirm that to the best of my knowledge and belief this return, including any accompanying schedules and statements, is true and complete. If prepared by a person other than taxpayer, his affirmation is based on all information of which he has any knowledge.

MAIL THIS REPORT WITH CHECK OR MONEY ORDER PAYABLE TO THE DEPT. OF REVENUE ON OR BEFORE DUE DATE TO AVOID PENALTY.

SIGNATURE: TITLE: DATE:

FEDERAL DEPOSIT INFORMATION WORKSHEET

Employer Identification Number	00-0004701	Name	QUALITY REPAIRS
Month Tax Year Ends	12	Amount of Deposit	
Type of Tax (Form)		Tax Period	
Address	10 SUMMIT SQUARE	Phone Number	
City, State, Zip	CITY, STATE 00000-0000		

To be deposited on or before _____

4-12A (continued)

FEDERAL DEPOSIT INFORMATION WORKSHEET

Employer Identification Number	00-0004701	Name	QUALITY REPAIRS
Month Tax Year Ends	12	Amount of Deposit	_____
Type of Tax (Form)	_____	Tax Period	_____
Address	10 SUMMIT SQUARE	Phone Number	_____
City, State, Zip	CITY, STATE 00000-0000		

To be deposited on or before _____

FEDERAL DEPOSIT INFORMATION WORKSHEET

Employer Identification Number	00-0004701	Name	QUALITY REPAIRS
Month Tax Year Ends	12	Amount of Deposit	_____
Type of Tax (Form)	_____	Tax Period	_____
Address	10 SUMMIT SQUARE	Phone Number	_____
City, State, Zip	CITY, STATE 00000-0000		

To be deposited on or before _____

4-12A (continued)

Form **941** for 20--: **Employer's QUARTERLY Federal Tax Return**
(Rev. January 2015)   Department of the Treasury — Internal Revenue Service

OMB No. 1545-0029

Employer identification number (EIN) 0 0 – 0 0 0 4 7 0 1

Name (not your trade name) QUALITY REPAIRS

Trade name (if any)

Address 10 SUMMIT SQUARE
Number   Street   Suite or room number

CITY   ST   00000-0000
City   State   ZIP code

Foreign country name   Foreign province/county   Foreign postal code

Report for this Quarter of 20--
(Check one.)

☐ 1: January, February, March
☐ 2: April, May, June
☐ 3: July, August, September
☐ 4: October, November, December

Instructions and prior year forms are available at www.irs.gov/form941.

Read the separate instructions before you complete Form 941. Type or print within the boxes.

Part 1:   Answer these questions for this quarter.

1 Number of employees who received wages, tips, or other compensation for the pay period including: Mar. 12 (Quarter 1), June 12 (Quarter 2), Sept. 12 (Quarter 3), or Dec. 12 (Quarter 4)   1

2 Wages, tips, and other compensation   2

3 Federal income tax withheld from wages, tips, and other compensation   3

4 If no wages, tips, and other compensation are subject to social security or Medicare tax   ☐ Check and go to line 6.

	Column 1		Column 2
5a Taxable social security wages		× .124 =	
5b Taxable social security tips		× .124 =	
5c Taxable Medicare wages & tips		× .029 =	
5d Taxable wages & tips subject to Additional Medicare Tax withholding		× .009 =	

5e Add Column 2 from lines 5a, 5b, 5c, and 5d   5e

5f Section 3121(q) Notice and Demand—Tax due on unreported tips (see instructions)   5f

6 Total taxes before adjustments. Add lines 3, 5e, and 5f   6

7 Current quarter's adjustment for fractions of cents   7

8 Current quarter's adjustment for sick pay   8

9 Current quarter's adjustments for tips and group-term life insurance   9

10 Total taxes after adjustments. Combine lines 6 through 9   10

11 Total deposits for this quarter, including overpayment applied from a prior quarter and overpayments applied from Form 941-X, 941-X (PR), 944-X, 944-X (PR), or 944-X (SP) filed in the current quarter   11

12 Balance due. If line 10 is more than line 11, enter the difference and see instructions   12

13 Overpayment. If line 11 is more than line 10, enter the difference   Check one: ☐ Apply to next return. ☐ Send a refund.

► You MUST complete both pages of Form 941 and SIGN it.   Next ►

For Privacy Act and Paperwork Reduction Act Notice, see the back of the Payment Voucher.   Cat. No. 17001Z   Form **941** (Rev. 1-2015)

4-12A (concluded)

Name (not your trade name)	Employer identification number (EIN)
QUALITY REPAIRS	00-0004701

Part 2: Tell us about your deposit schedule and tax liability for this quarter.

If you are unsure about whether you are a monthly schedule depositor or a semiweekly schedule depositor, see Pub. 15 (Circular E), section 11.

14 Check one: ☐ Line 10 on this return is less than $2,500 or line 10 on the return for the prior quarter was less than $2,500, and you did not incur a **$100,000 next-day deposit obligation during the current quarter.** If line 10 for the prior quarter was less than $2,500 but line 10 on this return is $100,000 or more, you must provide a record of your federal tax liability. If you are a monthly schedule depositor, complete the deposit schedule below; if you are a semiweekly schedule depositor, attach Schedule B (Form 941). Go to Part 3.

☐ **You were a monthly schedule depositor for the entire quarter.** Enter your tax liability for each month and total liability for the quarter, then go to Part 3.

Tax liability: Month 1 [.   ]

Month 2 [.   ]

Month 3 [.   ]

Total liability for quarter [.   ] Total must equal line 10.

☐ **You were a semiweekly schedule depositor for any part of this quarter.** Complete Schedule B (Form 941), Report of Tax Liability for Semiweekly Schedule Depositors, and attach it to Form 941.

Part 3: Tell us about your business. If a question does NOT apply to your business, leave it blank.

15 If your business has closed or you stopped paying wages . . . . ☐ Check here, and

enter the final date you paid wages [/   /   ] .

16 If you are a seasonal employer and you do not have to file a return for every quarter of the year . . ☐ Check here.

Part 4: May we speak with your third-party designee?

Do you want to allow an employee, a paid tax preparer, or another person to discuss this return with the IRS? See the instructions for details.

☐ Yes. Designee's name and phone number [   ] [   ]

Select a 5-digit Personal Identification Number (PIN) to use when talking to the IRS. ☐ ☐ ☐ ☐ ☐

☐ No.

Part 5: Sign here. You MUST complete both pages of Form 941 and SIGN it.

Under penalties of perjury, I declare that I have examined this return, including accompanying schedules and statements, and to the best of my knowledge and belief, it is true, correct, and complete. Declaration of preparer (other than taxpayer) is based on all information of which preparer has any knowledge.

✗ **Sign your name here** [   ] Print your name here [   ]

Print your title here [   ]

Date [/   /   ] Best daytime phone [   ]

Paid Preparer Use Only Check if you are self-employed . . . ☐

Preparer's name	[ ]	PTIN	[ ]
Preparer's signature	[ ]	Date	[/ /]
Firm's name (or yours if self-employed)	[ ]	EIN	[ ]
Address	[ ]	Phone	[ ]
City	[ ] State [ ]	ZIP code	[ ]

Page **2** Form **941** (Rev. 1-2015)

4-13A • LO 3, 4 See pages 4-21, 4-22, 4-23, 4-24, and 4-26

During the first full week of 2017, the Payroll Department of Quigley Corporation is preparing the Forms W-2 for distribution to its employees along with their payroll checks on January 6. In this problem, you will complete six of the forms in order to gain some experience in recording the different kinds of information required.

Assume each employee earned the same weekly salary for each of the 52 paydays in 2016. Using the following information obtained from the personnel and payroll records of the firm, complete Copy A of the six Forms W-2 reproduced on the following pages. Also complete Form W-3. The form is to be signed by the president, Kenneth T. Ford, and is prepared by Ralph I. Volpe.

Company Information:

Address:	4800 River Road		
	Philadelphia, PA 19113-5548	Pennsylvania state identification number:	00-0-1066
Telephone number: (215) 555-0017		Federal identification number:	00-0000972
Fax number: (215) 555-0010		Philadelphia identification number:	0001895

Income Tax Information:

The wage-bracket method is used to determine federal income tax withholding. Calculate the annual federal income tax withheld by using the weekly wage-bracket table and multiply the answer by 52. The other taxes withheld are shown below.

Employee Data	Payroll Data	Annual Taxes Withheld	
Kelly B. Roach	Single, 1 allowance	2,305.16	Social security tax withheld
54 Gradison Place	$715 per week	539.24	Medicare tax withheld
Philadelphia, PA 19113-4054	SS#: 000-00-4310	1,141.40	State income tax withheld
	Deduction for 401(k) plan: $50/week	1,457.56	Local income tax withheld
Ralph I. Volpe	Married, 1 allowance	2,530.84	Social security tax withheld
56 Andrews Court, Apt. 7	$785 per week	591.76	Medicare tax withheld
Philadelphia, PA 19103-3356	SS#: 000-00-8804	1,253.20	State income tax withheld
	Dependent care payment: $950	1,600.04	Local income tax withheld
	$70/week—401(k)		
Randi A. Myer	Single, 0 allowances	2,853.24	Social security tax withheld
770 Camac Street	$885 per week	667.16	Medicare tax withheld
Philadelphia, PA 19101-3770	SS#: 000-00-3316	1,412.84	State income tax withheld
	Union dues withheld: $102	1,803.88	Local income tax withheld
Kenneth T. Ford	Married, 7 allowances	4,368.69	Social security tax withheld
338 North Side Avenue	$1,350 per week	1,021.97	Medicare tax withheld
Philadelphia, PA 19130-6638	SS#: 000-00-6839	2,155.40	State income tax withheld
	Cost of group-term life insurance exceeding $50,000: $262.75	2,751.84	Local income tax withheld
	No income tax withheld on insurance cost, but FICA taxes are withheld.		
	$100/week—401(k)		
Chrissy C. Carman	Married, 3 allowances	2,643.68	Social security tax withheld
4900 Gladwynne Terrace	$820 per week	618.28	Medicare tax withheld
Philadelphia, PA 19127-0049	SS#: 000-00-5771	1,308.84	State income tax withheld
	Union dues withheld: $102	1,671.28	Local income tax withheld
Hal B. Zuber	Single, 1 allowance	2,546.96	Social security tax withheld
480-A Hopkinson Tower	$790 per week	595.92	Medicare tax withheld
Philadelphia, PA 19101-3301	SS#: 000-00-8703	1,261.00	State income tax withheld
	Educational assistance payments (job-required): $675	1,610.44	Local income tax withheld
	$50/week—401(k)		

4-13A (continued)

22222	Void ☐	**a** Employee's social security number	For Official Use Only ► OMB No. 1545-0008	

b Employer identification number (EIN)	**1** Wages, tips, other compensation	**2** Federal income tax withheld
c Employer's name, address, and ZIP code	**3** Social security wages	**4** Social security tax withheld
	5 Medicare wages and tips	**6** Medicare tax withheld
	7 Social security tips	**8** Allocated tips
d Control number	**9**	**10** Dependent care benefits
e Employee's first name and initial Last name Suff.	**11** Nonqualified plans	**12a** See instructions for box 12
	13 Statutory employee ☐ Retirement plan ☐ Third-party sick pay ☐	**12b**
	14 Other	**12c**
		12d
f Employee's address and ZIP code		

15 State Employer's state ID number	**16** State wages, tips, etc.	**17** State income tax	**18** Local wages, tips, etc.	**19** Local income tax	**20** Locality name

Form **W-2** Wage and Tax Statement   **20 - -**   Department of the Treasury—Internal Revenue Service

Copy A For Social Security Administration — Send this entire page with
Form W-3 to the Social Security Administration; photocopies are **not** acceptable.

For Privacy Act and Paperwork Reduction
Act Notice, see the separate instructions.

Cat. No. 10134D

Do Not Cut, Fold, or Staple Forms on This Page — Do Not Cut, Fold, or Staple Forms on This Page

---

22222	Void ☐	**a** Employee's social security number	For Official Use Only ► OMB No. 1545-0008	

b Employer identification number (EIN)	**1** Wages, tips, other compensation	**2** Federal income tax withheld
c Employer's name, address, and ZIP code	**3** Social security wages	**4** Social security tax withheld
	5 Medicare wages and tips	**6** Medicare tax withheld
	7 Social security tips	**8** Allocated tips
d Control number	**9**	**10** Dependent care benefits
e Employee's first name and initial Last name Suff.	**11** Nonqualified plans	**12a** See instructions for box 12
	13 Statutory employee ☐ Retirement plan ☐ Third-party sick pay ☐	**12b**
	14 Other	**12c**
		12d
f Employee's address and ZIP code		

15 State Employer's state ID number	**16** State wages, tips, etc.	**17** State income tax	**18** Local wages, tips, etc.	**19** Local income tax	**20** Locality name

Form **W-2** Wage and Tax Statement   **20 - -**   Department of the Treasury—Internal Revenue Service

Copy A For Social Security Administration — Send this entire page with
Form W-3 to the Social Security Administration; photocopies are **not** acceptable.

For Privacy Act and Paperwork Reduction
Act Notice, see the separate instructions.

Cat. No. 10134D

Do Not Cut, Fold, or Staple Forms on This Page — Do Not Cut, Fold, or Staple Forms on This Page

Source: Internal Revenue Service.

4-13A (continued)

22222	Void ☐	**a** Employee's social security number	For Official Use Only ▶ OMB No. 1545-0008	

b Employer identification number (EIN)		**1** Wages, tips, other compensation	**2** Federal income tax withheld
c Employer's name, address, and ZIP code		**3** Social security wages	**4** Social security tax withheld
		5 Medicare wages and tips	**6** Medicare tax withheld
		7 Social security tips	**8** Allocated tips
d Control number		**9**	**10** Dependent care benefits
e Employee's first name and initial Last name Suff.		**11** Nonqualified plans	**12a** See instructions for box 12
		13 Statutory employee ☐ Retirement plan ☐ Third-party sick pay ☐	**12b**
		14 Other	**12c**
			12d
f Employee's address and ZIP code			

15 State Employer's state ID number	**16** State wages, tips, etc.	**17** State income tax	**18** Local wages, tips, etc.	**19** Local income tax	**20** Locality name

Form **W-2** Wage and Tax Statement   **20 - -**   Department of the Treasury—Internal Revenue Service

Copy A For Social Security Administration — Send this entire page with Form W-3 to the Social Security Administration; photocopies are **not** acceptable.

For Privacy Act and Paperwork Reduction Act Notice, see the separate instructions.

Cat. No. 10134D

Do Not Cut, Fold, or Staple Forms on This Page — Do Not Cut, Fold, or Staple Forms on This Page

22222	Void ☐	**a** Employee's social security number	For Official Use Only ▶ OMB No. 1545-0008	

b Employer identification number (EIN)		**1** Wages, tips, other compensation	**2** Federal income tax withheld
c Employer's name, address, and ZIP code		**3** Social security wages	**4** Social security tax withheld
		5 Medicare wages and tips	**6** Medicare tax withheld
		7 Social security tips	**8** Allocated tips
d Control number		**9**	**10** Dependent care benefits
e Employee's first name and initial Last name Suff.		**11** Nonqualified plans	**12a** See instructions for box 12
		13 Statutory employee ☐ Retirement plan ☐ Third-party sick pay ☐	**12b**
		14 Other	**12c**
			12d
f Employee's address and ZIP code			

15 State Employer's state ID number	**16** State wages, tips, etc.	**17** State income tax	**18** Local wages, tips, etc.	**19** Local income tax	**20** Locality name

Form **W-2** Wage and Tax Statement   **20 - -**   Department of the Treasury—Internal Revenue Service

Copy A For Social Security Administration — Send this entire page with Form W-3 to the Social Security Administration; photocopies are **not** acceptable.

For Privacy Act and Paperwork Reduction Act Notice, see the separate instructions.

Cat. No. 10134D

Do Not Cut, Fold, or Staple Forms on This Page — Do Not Cut, Fold, or Staple Forms on This Page

Source: Internal Revenue Service.

4-13A (continued)

22222	Void ☐	**a** Employee's social security number	For Official Use Only ▶ OMB No. 1545-0008	

b Employer identification number (EIN)	**1** Wages, tips, other compensation	**2** Federal income tax withheld
c Employer's name, address, and ZIP code	**3** Social security wages	**4** Social security tax withheld
	5 Medicare wages and tips	**6** Medicare tax withheld
	7 Social security tips	**8** Allocated tips
d Control number	**9**	**10** Dependent care benefits

e Employee's first name and initial	Last name	Suff.	**11** Nonqualified plans	**12a** See instructions for box 12

13 Statutory employee ☐ Retirement plan ☐ Third-party sick pay ☐ **12b**

14 Other **12c**

12d

f Employee's address and ZIP code

15 State Employer's state ID number	**16** State wages, tips, etc.	**17** State income tax	**18** Local wages, tips, etc.	**19** Local income tax	**20** Locality name

Form **W-2** Wage and Tax Statement **20- -** Department of the Treasury—Internal Revenue Service

Copy A For Social Security Administration — Send this entire page with Form W-3 to the Social Security Administration; photocopies are **not** acceptable.

For Privacy Act and Paperwork Reduction Act Notice, see the separate instructions.

Cat. No. 10134D

Do Not Cut, Fold, or Staple Forms on This Page — Do Not Cut, Fold, or Staple Forms on This Page

---

22222	Void ☐	**a** Employee's social security number	For Official Use Only ▶ OMB No. 1545-0008	

b Employer identification number (EIN)	**1** Wages, tips, other compensation	**2** Federal income tax withheld
c Employer's name, address, and ZIP code	**3** Social security wages	**4** Social security tax withheld
	5 Medicare wages and tips	**6** Medicare tax withheld
	7 Social security tips	**8** Allocated tips
d Control number	**9**	**10** Dependent care benefits

e Employee's first name and initial	Last name	Suff.	**11** Nonqualified plans	**12a** See instructions for box 12

13 Statutory employee ☐ Retirement plan ☐ Third-party sick pay ☐ **12b**

14 Other **12c**

12d

f Employee's address and ZIP code

15 State Employer's state ID number	**16** State wages, tips, etc.	**17** State income tax	**18** Local wages, tips, etc.	**19** Local income tax	**20** Locality name

Form **W-2** Wage and Tax Statement **20- -** Department of the Treasury—Internal Revenue Service

Copy A For Social Security Administration — Send this entire page with Form W-3 to the Social Security Administration; photocopies are **not** acceptable.

For Privacy Act and Paperwork Reduction Act Notice, see the separate instructions.

Cat. No. 10134D

Do Not Cut, Fold, or Staple Forms on This Page — Do Not Cut, Fold, or Staple Forms on This Page

Source: Internal Revenue Service.

4-13A (concluded)

DO NOT STAPLE

| 33333 | a Control number | For Official Use Only ▶ |
| | | OMB No. 1545-0008 |

| b **Kind of Payer** (Check one) | 941 ☐ | Military ☐ | 943 ☐ | 944 ☐ | | **Kind of Employer** (Check one) | None apply ☐ | 501c non-govt. ☐ | | Third-party sick pay (Check if applicable) ☐ |
| | CT-1 ☐ | Hshld. emp. ☐ | Medicare govt. emp. ☐ | | | | State/local non-501c ☐ | State/local 501c ☐ | Federal govt. ☐ | |

c Total number of Forms W-2	d Establishment number	1 Wages, tips, other compensation	2 Federal income tax withheld
e Employer identification number (EIN)		3 Social security wages	4 Social security tax withheld
f Employer's name		5 Medicare wages and tips	6 Medicare tax withheld
		7 Social security tips	8 Allocated tips
		9	10 Dependent care benefits
		11 Nonqualified plans	12a Deferred compensation
g Employer's address and ZIP code			
h Other EIN used this year		13 For third-party sick pay use only	12b
15 State Employer's state ID number		14 Income tax withheld by payer of third-party sick pay	
16 State wages, tips, etc.	17 State income tax	18 Local wages, tips, etc.	19 Local income tax
Employer's contact person		Employer's telephone number	For Official Use Only
Employer's fax number		Employer's email address	

Under penalties of perjury, I declare that I have examined this return and accompanying documents and, to the best of my knowledge and belief, they are true, correct, and complete.

Signature ▶   Title ▶   Date ▶

Form **W-3** **Transmittal of Wage and Tax Statements**   **20 - -**   Department of the Treasury Internal Revenue Service

Source: Internal Revenue Service.

PROBLEM SET · B

As we go to press, the federal income tax rates for 2016 are being determined by budget talks in Washington and not available for publication. For this edition, the 2015 federal income tax tables and 2015 FICA rates have been used.

4-1B · LO 1 See page 4-16

Herman Swayne is a waiter at the Dixie Hotel. In his first weekly pay in March, he earned $360.00 for the 40 hours he worked. In addition, he reports his tips for February to his employer ($700.00), and the employer withholds the appropriate taxes for the tips from this first pay in March.

Calculate his net take-home pay assuming the employer withheld federal income tax (*wage-bracket*, married, 2 allowances), social security taxes, and state income tax (2%) .... $_____

4-2B · LO 3 See page 4-15

Use the *percentage method* to compute the federal income taxes to withhold from the wages or salaries of each employee.

Employee No.	Employee Name	Marital Status	No. of Withholding Allowances	Gross Wage or Salary	Amount to Be Withheld
1	Skymer, A.	M	4	$ 1,575 weekly	_____
2	Wolfe, T.	S	0	1,200 biweekly	_____
3	Klein, G.	S	5	12,600 quarterly	_____
4	Carey, P.	M	8	1,090 semimonthly	_____
5	Wu, M.	M	3	8,120 monthly	_____

4-3B · LO 3 See pages 4-15 and 4-16

Use (a) the percentage method and (b) the wage-bracket method to compute the federal income taxes to withhold from the wages or salaries of each employee.

Employee	Marital Status	No. of Withholding Allowances	Gross Wage or Salary	Amount to Be Withheld Percentage Method	Wage-Bracket Method
Ruiz, S.	S	2	$1,040 weekly	_____	_____
Flume, X.	S	1	2,190 weekly	_____	_____
Farley, H.	M	6	1,890 biweekly	_____	_____
Comey, P.	M	4	2,315 semimonthly	_____	_____
Hanks, R.	M	9	4,200 monthly	_____	_____

4-4B · LO 3 See page 4-16

Ernesto Enterprises uses the *wage-bracket method* to determine federal income tax withholding on its employees. Find the amount to withhold from the wages paid each employee.

Employee	Marital Status	No. of Withholding Allowances	Payroll Period W=Weekly S=Semimonthly M=Monthly D=Daily	Wage	Amount to Be Withheld
Ed Boone	M	1	W	$1,250	_____
Ray Ortega	S	1	W	695	_____
Carl Lopez	S	3	W	915	_____
Terri Kim	M	6	M	5,070	_____
Kathy Horace	M	2	M	3,730	_____
John Gleam	M	8	S	1,200	_____
Rob Abreu	S	1	D	115	_____
Carmen Sanchez	S	4	S	2,040	_____
Howard Nee	M	4	M	4,500	_____

4-5B • LO 3   See page 4-16

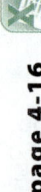

The names of the employees of Hogan Thrift Shop are listed on the following payroll register. Employees are paid weekly. The marital status and the number of allowances claimed are shown on the payroll register, along with each employee's weekly salary, which has remained the same all year. Complete the payroll register for the payroll period ending December 16, the 51st weekly payday. The state income tax rate is 3.1% of total earnings, the city income tax rate is 1% of the total gross earnings, and the *wage-bracket method* is used for federal income taxes.

HOGAN THRIFT SHOP

PAYROLL REGISTER

FOR PERIOD ENDING _____   20 ____

EMPLOYEE NAME	MARITAL STATUS	NO. OF W/H ALLOW.	TOTAL EARNINGS	(a) FICA OASDI	HI	(b) FIT	(c) SIT	(d) CIT	(e) NET PAY
Gold, Ken	M	3	2 0 8 0 00						
Morton, Cam	S	1	6 9 0 00						
Wendal, Hal	M	0	6 7 5 00						
Cox, Debbie	S	3	5 1 0 00						
Hurley, Don	S	1	1 0 1 0 00						
Hand, Cheryl	S	2	8 5 0 00						
Welsh, Ronda	S	1	5 9 0 90						
Ruiz, Stacy	M	3	6 1 1 15						
Totals									

Compute the employer's FICA taxes for the pay period ending December 16.

OASDI Taxes		HI Taxes	
OASDI taxable earnings	$ _____	HI taxable earnings	$ _____
OASDI taxes	$ _____	HI taxes	$ _____

4-6B • LO 3   Similar to Example 4-10 on page 4-21

Youngston Company (a Utah employer) wants to give a holiday bonus check of $750 to each employee. Since it wants the check amount to be $750, it will need to gross-up the amount of the bonus. Calculate the withholding taxes and the gross amount of the bonus to be made to Genna Fredrich if her earnings for the year are $55,920. Besides being subject to social security taxes and federal income tax (supplemental rate), a 5% Utah income tax must be withheld on supplemental payments .... $ _____

4-7B • LO 1 Similar to Example 4-1 on page 4-8

Jen Miller made $1,090 this week. Only social security (fully taxable) and federal income taxes attach to her pay. Miller contributes $125 each week to her company's 401(k) plan and has $40 put into her health savings account (nonqualified) each week. Her employer matches this $40 each week. Determine Miller's take-home pay if she is married and claims 2 allowances (use the wage-bracket method)....................... $ _____

4-8B • LO 3 Similar to Example 4-6 on page 4-19

The names of the employees of Matson Office Systems and their regular salaries are shown in the following payroll register. Note that Wayne and Young are paid monthly on the last payday, while all others are paid weekly.

In addition to the regular salaries, the company pays an annual bonus based on the amount of earnings for the year. For the current year, the bonus amounts to 8% of the annual salary paid to each employee. The bonus is to be paid along with the regular salaries on December 30, but the amount of the bonus and the amount of the regular salary will be shown separately on each employee's earnings statement. Assume that all employees received their regular salary during the entire year.

Prepare the payroll for the pay period ending December 30, showing the following for each employee:

- Use the *wage-bracket method* to withhold federal income tax from the regular salaries.
- Withhold a flat 25% on the annual bonus.
- Total salaries and bonuses are subject to a 2% state income tax and a 1% city income tax.

FOR PERIOD ENDING _____ 20___

EMPLOYEE NAME	MARITAL STATUS	NO. OF W/H ALLOW.	EARNINGS REGULAR	EARNINGS (a) SUPPL.	(b) TOTAL	(c) FICA OASDI	(c) FICA HI	DEDUCTIONS (d) FIT	DEDUCTIONS (e) SIT	DEDUCTIONS (f) CIT	(g) NET PAY
Wayne, Bret	M	5	4 2 0 0 00 *								
Young, Gina	M	2	4 1 5 0 00 *								
Course, Rudy	S	1	8 1 0 00								
Dickson, Emile	M	4	7 1 5 00								
Woodrow, Walt	M	2	6 9 5 00								
Noblet, Jim	S	1	5 2 5 00								
Ono, Joan	M	2	8 0 0 00								
Jones, Carrie	S	0	6 4 5 00								
Totals											

*Monthly

Compute the employer's FICA taxes for the pay period ending December 30.

OASDI Taxes			HI Taxes		
OASDI taxable earnings	$ _____		HI taxable earnings	$ _____	
OASDI taxes	$ _____		HI taxes	$ _____	

4-9B • LO 3   See page 4-16

Assume during the quarter ending December 31 of the current year, Matson Office Systems had 13 weekly paydays and three monthly paydays. Using the data given in 4-8B, complete the following form to show:

a. Total earnings paid during the quarter, including both the regular and the supplemental earnings.

b. Total amount of FICA taxes withheld during the quarter.

c. Total amount of federal income taxes withheld during the quarter.

d. Total amount of state income taxes withheld during the quarter.

e. Total amount of city income taxes withheld during the quarter.

f. Total net amount paid each employee during the quarter.

EMPLOYEE NAME	(a) TOTAL EARNINGS	(b) FICA OASDI	(b) FICA HI	(c) FIT	(d) SIT	(e) CIT	(f) NET PAY
Wayne, Bret							
Young, Gina							
Course, Rudy							
Dickson, Emile							
Woodrow, Walt							
Noblet, Jim							
Ono, Joan							
Jones, Carrie							
Totals							

DEDUCTIONS

4-10B • LO 3   Similar to Example 4-10 on page 4-21

Harrington Company is giving each of its employees a holiday bonus of $250 on December 16 (a nonpayday). The company wants each employee's check to be $250. The supplemental tax percent is used.

a. What will be the gross amount of each bonus if each employee pays a state income tax of 3.01% (besides the other payroll taxes)? $ _____

b. What would the net amount of each bonus check be if the company did not gross-up the bonus? $ _____

4-11B • LO 1   Similar to Example 4-1 on page 4-8

Samantha Montgomery (age 42) is employed by Canon Company and is paid a salary of $62,430. She has just decided to join the company's Simple Retirement Account (IRA form) and has a few questions. Answer the following for Montgomery:

a. What is the maximum that she can contribute into this retirement fund? $ _____

b. What would be the company's contribution? $ _____

c. What would be her weekly take-home pay with the retirement contribution deducted (married, 2 allowances, *wage-bracket method,* and a 2.3% state income tax on total wages)? $ _____

d. What would be her weekly take-home pay without the retirement contribution deduction? $ _____

4-12B • LO 4   See pages 3-16, 3-17, 3-21, and 4-31

During the fourth quarter of 2016, there were seven biweekly paydays on Friday (October 7, 21; November 4, 18; December 2, 16, 30) for Clarke's Roofing. Using the forms supplied on pages 4-58 to 4-61, complete the following for the fourth quarter:

a. Complete the Federal Deposit Information Worksheets, reflecting electronic deposits (monthly depositor). The employer's phone number is (501) 555-1212. Federal deposit liability each pay, $1,304.56.

b. Employer's Quarterly Federal Tax Return, Form 941. The form is signed by you as president on January 31, 2017.

c. Employer's Report of State Income Tax Withheld for the quarter, due on or before January 31, 2017.

Quarterly Payroll Data

Total Earnings 5 Employees	OASDI	HI	FIT	SIT
$37,450.00	$2,321.90	$543.06	$3,402.00	$2,621.50
Employer's OASDI	$2,321.90			
Employer's HI	543.06			
Federal deposit liability each pay	1,304.56			

EMPLOYER'S REPORT
OF STATE INCOME TAX WITHHELD

(DO NOT WRITE IN THIS SPACE)

IMPORTANT : PLEASE REFER TO THIS NUMBER IN ANY CORRESPONDENCE

WITHHOLDING IDENTIFICATION NUMBER	MONTH OF OR QUARTER ENDING
00-0-8787	DEC 20--

IF YOU ARE A SEA-SONAL EMPLOYER AND THIS IS YOUR FINAL REPORT FOR THIS SEASON, CHECK HERE ☐ AND SHOW THE NEXT MONTH IN WHICH YOU WILL PAY WAGES.

CLARKE'S ROOFING
20 SUMMIT SQUARE
CITY, STATE 00000-0000

IF NAME OR ADDRESS IS INCORRECT, PLEASE MAKE CORRECTIONS.
THIS REPORT MUST BE RETURNED EVEN IF NO AMOUNT HAS BEEN WITHHELD

Under penalties prescribed by law, I hereby affirm that to the best of my knowledge and belief this return, including any accompanying schedules and statements, is true and complete. If prepared by a person other than taxpayer, his affirmation is based on all information of which he has any knowledge.

SIGNATURE: TITLE: DATE:

1. GROSS PAYROLL THIS PERIOD	$
2. STATE INCOME TAX WITHHELD	$
3. ADJUSTMENT FOR PREVIOUS PERIOD(S). (ATTACH STATEMENT)	$
4. TOTAL ADJUSTED TAX (LINE 2 PLUS OR MINUS LINE 3)	$
5. PENALTY (35% OF LINE 4)	
6. INTEREST	
7. TOTAL AMOUNT DUE AND PAYABLE	$

MAIL THIS REPORT WITH CHECK OR MONEY ORDER PAYABLE TO THE DEPT. OF REVENUE ON OR BEFORE DUE DATE TO AVOID PENALTY.

FEDERAL DEPOSIT INFORMATION WORKSHEET

Employer
Identification Number   00-0004701   Name   CLARKE'S ROOFING

Month Tax Year Ends   12   Amount of Deposit   _____

Type of Tax (Form)   _____   Tax Period   _____

Address   20 SUMMIT SQUARE   Phone Number   _____

City, State, Zip   CITY, STATE 00000-0000

To be deposited on or before _____

4-12B (continued)

FEDERAL DEPOSIT INFORMATION WORKSHEET

Employer Identification Number	00-0004701	Name	CLARKE'S ROOFING
Month Tax Year Ends	12	Amount of Deposit	_____
Type of Tax (Form)	_____	Tax Period	_____
Address	20 SUMMIT SQUARE	Phone Number	_____
City, State, Zip	CITY, STATE 00000-0000		

To be deposited on or before _____

FEDERAL DEPOSIT INFORMATION WORKSHEET

Employer Identification Number	00-0004701	Name	CLARKE'S ROOFING
Month Tax Year Ends	12	Amount of Deposit	_____
Type of Tax (Form)	_____	Tax Period	_____
Address	20 SUMMIT SQUARE	Phone Number	_____
City, State, Zip	CITY, STATE 00000-0000		

To be deposited on or before _____

Form **941 for 20--:** **Employer's QUARTERLY Federal Tax Return**
(Rev. January 2015)   Department of the Treasury — Internal Revenue Service

OMB No. 1545-0029

Employer identification number (EIN) 0 0 – 0 0 0 4 7 0 1

Name *(not your trade name)* CLARKE'S ROOFING

Trade name *(if any)*

Address 20 SUMMIT SQUARE
Number   Street   Suite or room number

CITY   ST   00000-0000
City   State   ZIP code

Foreign country name   Foreign province/county   Foreign postal code

Report for this Quarter of 20--
(Check one.)

☐ **1:** January, February, March

☐ **2:** April, May, June

☐ **3:** July, August, September

☐ **4:** October, November, December

Instructions and prior year forms are available at *www.irs.gov/form941*.

Read the separate instructions before you complete Form 941. Type or print within the boxes.

Part 1: **Answer these questions for this quarter.**

1 Number of employees who received wages, tips, or other compensation for the pay period including: *Mar. 12* (Quarter 1), *June 12* (Quarter 2), *Sept. 12* (Quarter 3), or *Dec. 12* (Quarter 4)   **1** ⬚

2 Wages, tips, and other compensation . . . .   **2** ⬚ .

3 Federal income tax withheld from wages, tips, and other compensation . . . . . .   **3** ⬚ .

4 If no wages, tips, and other compensation are subject to social security or Medicare tax   ☐ Check and go to line 6.

		Column 1		Column 2
5a	Taxable social security wages . .	⬚ .	× .124 =	⬚ .
5b	Taxable social security tips . . .	⬚ .	× .124 =	⬚ .
5c	Taxable Medicare wages & tips. .	⬚ .	× .029 =	⬚ .
5d	Taxable wages & tips subject to Additional Medicare Tax withholding	⬚ .	× .009 =	⬚ .

5e Add Column 2 from lines 5a, 5b, 5c, and 5d . . . .   **5e** ⬚ .

5f Section 3121(q) Notice and Demand—Tax due on unreported tips (see instructions) . .   **5f** ⬚ .

6 Total taxes before adjustments. Add lines 3, 5e, and 5f . . . .   **6** ⬚ .

7 Current quarter's adjustment for fractions of cents . . . .   **7** ⬚ .

8 Current quarter's adjustment for sick pay . . . .   **8** ⬚ .

9 Current quarter's adjustments for tips and group-term life insurance . . . . . .   **9** ⬚ .

10 Total taxes after adjustments. Combine lines 6 through 9 . . . .   **10** ⬚ .

11 Total deposits for this quarter, including overpayment applied from a prior quarter and overpayments applied from Form 941-X, 941-X (PR), 944-X, 944-X (PR), or 944-X (SP) filed in the current quarter . . . .   **11** ⬚ .

12 Balance due. If line 10 is more than line 11, enter the difference and see instructions . . .   **12** ⬚ .

13 Overpayment. If line 11 is more than line 10, enter the difference ⬚ .   Check one: ☐ Apply to next return.   ☐ Send a refund.

▶ You MUST complete both pages of Form 941 and SIGN it.   Next ▶

For Privacy Act and Paperwork Reduction Act Notice, see the back of the Payment Voucher.   Cat. No. 17001Z   Form **941** (Rev. 1-2015)

4-12B (concluded)

Name *(not your trade name)*	Employer identification number (EIN)
CLARKE'S ROOFING	00-0004701

Part 2:	**Tell us about your deposit schedule and tax liability for this quarter.**

If you are unsure about whether you are a monthly schedule depositor or a semiweekly schedule depositor, see Pub. 15 (Circular E), section 11.

14 Check one: ☐ **Line 10 on this return is less than $2,500 or line 10 on the return for the prior quarter was less than $2,500, and you did not incur a $100,000 next-day deposit obligation during the current quarter.** If line 10 for the prior quarter was less than $2,500 but line 10 on this return is $100,000 or more, you must provide a record of your federal tax liability. If you are a monthly schedule depositor, complete the deposit schedule below; if you are a semiweekly schedule depositor, attach Schedule B (Form 941). Go to Part 3.

☐ **You were a monthly schedule depositor for the entire quarter.** Enter your tax liability for each month and total liability for the quarter, then go to Part 3.

Tax liability:	Month 1	.
	Month 2	.
	Month 3	.
Total liability for quarter		. Total must equal line 10.

☐ **You were a semiweekly schedule depositor for any part of this quarter.** Complete Schedule B (Form 941), Report of Tax Liability for Semiweekly Schedule Depositors, and attach it to Form 941.

Part 3:	**Tell us about your business. If a question does NOT apply to your business, leave it blank.**

15 If your business has closed or you stopped paying wages . . . . ☐ Check here, and

enter the final date you paid wages   [/   /] .

16 If you are a seasonal employer and you do not have to file a return for every quarter of the year . . ☐ Check here.

Part 4:	**May we speak with your third-party designee?**

Do you want to allow an employee, a paid tax preparer, or another person to discuss this return with the IRS? See the instructions for details.

☐ Yes. Designee's name and phone number   [   ] [   ]

Select a 5-digit Personal Identification Number (PIN) to use when talking to the IRS. ☐ ☐ ☐ ☐ ☐

☐ No.

Part 5:	**Sign here. You MUST complete both pages of Form 941 and SIGN it.**

Under penalties of perjury, I declare that I have examined this return, including accompanying schedules and statements, and to the best of my knowledge and belief, it is true, correct, and complete. Declaration of preparer (other than taxpayer) is based on all information of which preparer has any knowledge.

X **Sign your name here**

Print your name here
Print your title here

Date   [/   /]

Best daytime phone

Paid Preparer Use Only

Check if you are self-employed . . . ☐

Preparer's name		PTIN	
Preparer's signature		Date	/ /
Firm's name (or yours if self-employed)		EIN	
Address		Phone	
City	State	ZIP code	

Page **2**

Form **941** (Rev. 1-2015)

4-13B • LO 3, 4   See pages 4-21, 4-22, 4-23, 4-24, and 4-26

During the first full week of 2017, the Payroll Department of Omni Corporation is preparing the Forms W-2 for distribution to its employees along with their payroll checks on January 6. In this problem, you will complete six of the forms in order to gain some experience in recording the different kinds of information required.

Assume each employee earned the same weekly salary for each of the 52 paydays in 2016. Using the following information obtained from the personnel and payroll records of the firm, complete Copy A of the six Forms W-2 reproduced on the following pages. Also complete Form W-3. The form is to be signed by the president, Frank Kent, and is prepared by Vince Roper.

Company Information:

Address: 4800 River Road
            Philadelphia, PA 19113-5548

Telephone number: (215) 555-0017
Fax number: (215) 555-0010

Pennsylvania state identification number: 00-0-1066
Federal identification number: 00-0000972
Philadelphia identification number: 0001895

Income Tax Information:

The wage-bracket method is used to determine federal income tax withholding. Calculate the annual federal income tax withheld by using the weekly wage-bracket table and multiply the answer by 52. The other taxes withheld are shown below.

Employee Data	Payroll Data	Annual Taxes Withheld	
Randy A. Kellison 54 Gradison Place Philadelphia, PA 19113-4054	Single, 2 allowances $715 per week SS#: 000-00-4310 Deduction for 401(k) plan: $50/week	2,305.16 539.24 1,141.40 1,457.56	Social security tax withheld Medicare tax withheld State income tax withheld Local income tax withheld
Vince T. Roper 56 Andrews Court, Apt. 7 Philadelphia, PA 19103-3356	Married, 3 allowances $985 per week SS#: 000-00-8804 Dependent care payment: $950 $70/week—401(k)	3,175.64 742.56 1,572.48 2,007.72	Social security tax withheld Medicare tax withheld State income tax withheld Local income tax withheld
Murray T. Rodson 770 Camac Street Philadelphia, PA 19101-3770	Single, 0 allowances $765 per week SS#: 000-00-3316 Union dues withheld: $102	2,466.36 576.68 1,221.48 1,559.48	Social security tax withheld Medicare tax withheld State income tax withheld Local income tax withheld
Frank A. Kent 338 North Side Avenue Philadelphia, PA 19130-6638	Married, 6 allowances $1,875 per week SS#: 000-00-6839 Cost of group-term life insurance exceeding $50,000: $262.75 No income tax withheld on insurance cost, but FICA taxes are withheld.* $100/week—401(k)	6,061.29 1,417.69 2,993.12 3,822.00	Social security tax withheld Medicare tax withheld State income tax withheld Local income tax withheld
Carlie C. Christian 4900 Gladwynne Terrace Philadelphia, PA 19127-0049	Married, 5 allowances $780 per week SS#: 000-00-5771 Union dues withheld: $102	2,514.72 588.12 1,245.40 1,590.16	Social security tax withheld Medicare tax withheld State income tax withheld Local income tax withheld
Zana W. Amelia 480-A Hopkinson Tower Philadelphia, PA 19101-3301	Single, 1 allowance $790 per week SS#: 000-00-8703 Educational assistance payments (job-required): $675 $50/week—401(k)	2,546.96 595.92 1,261.00 1,610.44	Social security tax withheld Medicare tax withheld State income tax withheld Local income tax withheld

*Must use percentage method to calculate federal income tax.

4-13B (continued)

22222	Void ☐	**a** Employee's social security number

For Official Use Only ▶
OMB No. 1545-0008

b Employer identification number (EIN)	**1** Wages, tips, other compensation	**2** Federal income tax withheld
c Employer's name, address, and ZIP code	**3** Social security wages	**4** Social security tax withheld
	5 Medicare wages and tips	**6** Medicare tax withheld
	7 Social security tips	**8** Allocated tips
d Control number	**9**	**10** Dependent care benefits
e Employee's first name and initial Last name Suff.	**11** Nonqualified plans	**12a** See instructions for box 12
	13 Statutory employee ☐ Retirement plan ☐ Third-party sick pay ☐	**12b**
	14 Other	**12c**
		12d
f Employee's address and ZIP code		

15 State Employer's state ID number	**16** State wages, tips, etc.	**17** State income tax	**18** Local wages, tips, etc.	**19** Local income tax	**20** Locality name

Form **W-2** Wage and Tax Statement   **20 - -**

Department of the Treasury—Internal Revenue Service

Copy A For Social Security Administration — Send this entire page with
Form W-3 to the Social Security Administration; photocopies are **not** acceptable.

**For Privacy Act and Paperwork Reduction
Act Notice, see the separate instructions.**

Cat. No. 10134D

Do Not Cut, Fold, or Staple Forms on This Page — Do Not Cut, Fold, or Staple Forms on This Page

---

22222	Void ☐	**a** Employee's social security number

For Official Use Only ▶
OMB No. 1545-0008

b Employer identification number (EIN)	**1** Wages, tips, other compensation	**2** Federal income tax withheld
c Employer's name, address, and ZIP code	**3** Social security wages	**4** Social security tax withheld
	5 Medicare wages and tips	**6** Medicare tax withheld
	7 Social security tips	**8** Allocated tips
d Control number	**9**	**10** Dependent care benefits
e Employee's first name and initial Last name Suff.	**11** Nonqualified plans	**12a** See instructions for box 12
	13 Statutory employee ☐ Retirement plan ☐ Third-party sick pay ☐	**12b**
	14 Other	**12c**
		12d
f Employee's address and ZIP code		

15 State Employer's state ID number	**16** State wages, tips, etc.	**17** State income tax	**18** Local wages, tips, etc.	**19** Local income tax	**20** Locality name

Form **W-2** Wage and Tax Statement   **20 - -**

Department of the Treasury—Internal Revenue Service

Copy A For Social Security Administration — Send this entire page with
Form W-3 to the Social Security Administration; photocopies are **not** acceptable.

**For Privacy Act and Paperwork Reduction
Act Notice, see the separate instructions.**

Cat. No. 10134D

Do Not Cut, Fold, or Staple Forms on This Page — Do Not Cut, Fold, or Staple Forms on This Page

Source: Internal Revenue Service.

4-13B (continued)

22222	Void ☐	**a** Employee's social security number	**For Official Use Only ▶** OMB No. 1545-0008	

b Employer identification number (EIN)

1 Wages, tips, other compensation | **2** Federal income tax withheld

c Employer's name, address, and ZIP code

3 Social security wages | **4** Social security tax withheld

5 Medicare wages and tips | **6** Medicare tax withheld

7 Social security tips | **8** Allocated tips

d Control number | **9** | **10** Dependent care benefits

e Employee's first name and initial | Last name | Suff. | **11** Nonqualified plans | **12a** See instructions for box 12

13 Statutory employee ☐ Retirement plan ☐ Third-party sick pay ☐ | **12b**

14 Other | **12c**

12d

f Employee's address and ZIP code

15 State | Employer's state ID number | **16** State wages, tips, etc. | **17** State income tax | **18** Local wages, tips, etc. | **19** Local income tax | **20** Locality name

Form **W-2** Wage and Tax Statement   20 - -

Department of the Treasury—Internal Revenue Service
For Privacy Act and Paperwork Reduction Act Notice, see the separate instructions.

Copy A For Social Security Administration — Send this entire page with Form W-3 to the Social Security Administration; photocopies are **not** acceptable.

Cat. No. 10134D

Do Not Cut, Fold, or Staple Forms on This Page — Do Not Cut, Fold, or Staple Forms on This Page

---

22222	Void ☐	**a** Employee's social security number	**For Official Use Only ▶** OMB No. 1545-0008	

b Employer identification number (EIN)

1 Wages, tips, other compensation | **2** Federal income tax withheld

c Employer's name, address, and ZIP code

3 Social security wages | **4** Social security tax withheld

5 Medicare wages and tips | **6** Medicare tax withheld

7 Social security tips | **8** Allocated tips

d Control number | **9** | **10** Dependent care benefits

e Employee's first name and initial | Last name | Suff. | **11** Nonqualified plans | **12a** See instructions for box 12

13 Statutory employee ☐ Retirement plan ☐ Third-party sick pay ☐ | **12b**

14 Other | **12c**

12d

f Employee's address and ZIP code

15 State | Employer's state ID number | **16** State wages, tips, etc. | **17** State income tax | **18** Local wages, tips, etc. | **19** Local income tax | **20** Locality name

Form **W-2** Wage and Tax Statement   20 - -

Department of the Treasury—Internal Revenue Service
For Privacy Act and Paperwork Reduction Act Notice, see the separate instructions.

Copy A For Social Security Administration — Send this entire page with Form W-3 to the Social Security Administration; photocopies are **not** acceptable.

Cat. No. 10134D

Do Not Cut, Fold, or Staple Forms on This Page — Do Not Cut, Fold, or Staple Forms on This Page

Source: Internal Revenue Service.

4-13B (continued)

22222	Void ☐	**a** Employee's social security number	**For Official Use Only ▶** **OMB No. 1545-0008**		
b Employer identification number (EIN)			**1** Wages, tips, other compensation		**2** Federal income tax withheld
c Employer's name, address, and ZIP code			**3** Social security wages		**4** Social security tax withheld
			5 Medicare wages and tips		**6** Medicare tax withheld
			7 Social security tips		**8** Allocated tips
d Control number			**9**		**10** Dependent care benefits
e Employee's first name and initial	Last name	Suff.	**11** Nonqualified plans		**12a** See instructions for box 12 C o d e
			13 Statutory employee ☐ Retirement plan ☐ Third-party sick pay ☐		**12b** C o d e
			14 Other		**12c** C o d e
					12d C o d e
f Employee's address and ZIP code					

15 State	Employer's state ID number	**16** State wages, tips, etc.	**17** State income tax	**18** Local wages, tips, etc.	**19** Local income tax	**20** Locality name

Form **W-2** Wage and Tax Statement 20 - - Department of the Treasury—Internal Revenue Service

Copy A For Social Security Administration — Send this entire page with Form W-3 to the Social Security Administration; photocopies are **not** acceptable.

For Privacy Act and Paperwork Reduction Act Notice, see the separate instructions.

Cat. No. 10134D

Do Not Cut, Fold, or Staple Forms on This Page — Do Not Cut, Fold, or Staple Forms on This Page

22222	Void ☐	**a** Employee's social security number	**For Official Use Only ▶** **OMB No. 1545-0008**		
b Employer identification number (EIN)			**1** Wages, tips, other compensation		**2** Federal income tax withheld
c Employer's name, address, and ZIP code			**3** Social security wages		**4** Social security tax withheld
			5 Medicare wages and tips		**6** Medicare tax withheld
			7 Social security tips		**8** Allocated tips
d Control number			**9**		**10** Dependent care benefits
e Employee's first name and initial	Last name	Suff.	**11** Nonqualified plans		**12a** See instructions for box 12 C o d e
			13 Statutory employee ☐ Retirement plan ☐ Third-party sick pay ☐		**12b** C o d e
			14 Other		**12c** C o d e
					12d C o d e
f Employee's address and ZIP code					

15 State	Employer's state ID number	**16** State wages, tips, etc.	**17** State income tax	**18** Local wages, tips, etc.	**19** Local income tax	**20** Locality name

Form **W-2** Wage and Tax Statement 20 - - Department of the Treasury—Internal Revenue Service

Copy A For Social Security Administration — Send this entire page with Form W-3 to the Social Security Administration; photocopies are **not** acceptable.

For Privacy Act and Paperwork Reduction Act Notice, see the separate instructions.

Cat. No. 10134D

Do Not Cut, Fold, or Staple Forms on This Page — Do Not Cut, Fold, or Staple Forms on This Page

Source: Internal Revenue Service.

4-13B (concluded)

DO NOT STAPLE

33333	**a** Control number

For Official Use Only ▶	
OMB No. 1545-0008	

b
Kind of Payer (Check one) ▶
- 941 ☐
- CT-1 ☐
- Military ☐
- Hshld. emp. ☐
- 943 ☐
- Medicare govt. emp. ☐
- 944 ☐

Kind of Employer (Check one) ▶
- None apply ☐
- State/local non-501c ☐
- 501c non-govt. ☐
- State/local 501c ☐
- Federal govt. ☐

Third-party sick pay (Check if applicable) ☐

c Total number of Forms W-2	**d** Establishment number
1 Wages, tips, other compensation	**2** Federal income tax withheld
e Employer identification number (EIN)	
3 Social security wages	**4** Social security tax withheld
f Employer's name	
5 Medicare wages and tips	**6** Medicare tax withheld
	7 Social security tips	**8** Allocated tips
	9	**10** Dependent care benefits
	11 Nonqualified plans	**12a** Deferred compensation
g Employer's address and ZIP code	
h Other EIN used this year	**13** For third-party sick pay use only	**12b**
15 State Employer's state ID number	**14** Income tax withheld by payer of third-party sick pay
16 State wages, tips, etc.	**17** State income tax	**18** Local wages, tips, etc.	**19** Local income tax
Employer's contact person	Employer's telephone number	For Official Use Only
Employer's fax number	Employer's email address	

Under penalties of perjury, I declare that I have examined this return and accompanying documents and, to the best of my knowledge and belief, they are true, correct, and complete.

Signature ▶   Title ▶   Date ▶

Form **W-3** **Transmittal of Wage and Tax Statements**   **20 - -**   Department of the Treasury
Internal Revenue Service

Source: Internal Revenue Service.

CONTINUING PAYROLL PROBLEM · A

Refer to the partially completed payroll register which you worked on at the end of Chapter 3. You will now determine the amount of income tax to withhold for each employee, proceeding as follows:

1. In the appropriate columns of your payroll register, record the marital status and number of withholding allowances claimed for each employee, using the information provided.
2. Record the payroll deductions for the SIMPLE plan that the employer has established for participating employees. All of the employees are participating, and their weekly contributions are listed below. The tax deferral on these deductions applies only to the federal income tax.
3. Record the amount of federal income taxes using the wage-bracket method.
4. Record the state income taxes on the gross weekly earnings for each employee. The rate is 3.07% for the state of Pennsylvania.
5. Record the city income taxes on the gross weekly earnings of each employee. The rate is 3% for the city of Pittsburgh residents.

Time Card No.	Marital Status	No. of Allowances	SIMPLE Deductions
11	S	1	$20
12	S	0	50
13	M	2	40
21	M	4	50
22	S	2	20
31	M	3	40
32	M	6	50
33	S	1	60
51	M	5	30
99	M	7	80

CONTINUING PAYROLL PROBLEM · B

Refer to the partially completed payroll register which you worked on at the end of Chapter 3. You will now determine the amount of income tax to withhold for each employee, proceeding as follows:

1. In the appropriate columns of your payroll register, record the marital status and number of withholding allowances claimed for each employee, using the information provided.
2. Record the payroll deductions for the SIMPLE plan that the employer has established for participating employees. All of the employees are participating, and their weekly contributions are listed below. The tax deferral on these deductions applies only to the federal income tax.
3. Record the amount of federal income taxes using the wage-bracket method. (Must use percentage method for Olney.)
4. Record the state income taxes on the gross weekly earnings for each employee. The rate is 3.07% for the state of Pennsylvania.
5. Record the city income taxes on the gross weekly earnings of each employee. The rate is 1.33% for the city of Allentown residents.

Time Card No.	Marital Status	No. of Allowances	SIMPLE Deductions
11	S	1	$20
12	S	0	50
13	M	2	40
21	M	3	60
22	S	2	20
31	M	3	40
32	M	4	50
33	S	1	50
51	M	5	30
99	M	7	80

CASE PROBLEMS

C1. Answering Employees' Questions About Wage Reporting. LO 4.

During the past week, one of your newly employed payroll associates dropped into your office to ask several questions regarding wage reporting for federal income and social security tax purposes. If you were the payroll supervisor, how would you answer each of the following questions raised by your associate?

1. I just noticed that the social security number is wrong on three of the employees' W-2 forms. How do I go about correcting the forms? Will the employees be penalized for filing incorrect forms?

2. Eileen Huang informed me today that we had withheld too much Medicare tax from her pay last year. She is right! What forms do I use to make the correction?

3. You asked me last week to locate one of our former employees, Warren Bucks. I can't seem to track him down. What should I do with his Form W-2?

4. Is it okay to use titles like "M.D." and "Esq." when I keyboard data in the W-2 forms?

C2. Classified as an Employee and Independent Contractor. LO 1.

Yeager Company pays John Kerr a salary as an employee and also fees for work he does as an independent contractor. Does this violate IRS rules?

CHAPTER 5

Unemployment Compensation Taxes

L et's look at some more taxes that the employer pays. Did you ever wonder where the money comes from to pay benefits to workers who lost their jobs? How about the funds needed to administer the unemployment program? Did you know that an employer pays both a federal and a state unemployment tax?

In our current business environment, many states are hard pressed to fund their paid-out benefits. This will mean higher tax rates for employers and higher taxable wage limits. It will also mean borrowing from the federal government.

There are new deposit requirements and tax forms to digest. Welcome to the world of unemployment taxes.

LEARNING OBJECTIVES

After studying this chapter, you should be able to:

1 Describe the basic requirements for an individual to be classified as an employer or an employee under the Federal Unemployment Tax Act.

2 Identify generally what is defined as taxable wages by the Federal Unemployment Tax Act.

3 Compute the federal unemployment tax, the credit against the tax, and any credit reductions that might apply.

4 Describe how an experience-rating system is used in determining employers' contributions to state unemployment compensation funds.

5 Complete the reports required by the Federal Unemployment Tax Act.

6 Describe the types of information reports under the various state unemployment compensation laws.

The Social Security Act of 1935 ordered every state to set up an unemployment compensation program in order to provide payments to workers during periods of temporary unemployment. Payroll taxes at both the federal and state levels fund this unemployment insurance program. The Federal Unemployment Tax Act (FUTA) imposes a tax on employers based on wages paid for covered employment. It is *not* collected or deducted from employees' wages. The funds collected by the federal government as a result of this tax pay the cost of administering both the federal and the state unemployment insurance programs. The FUTA tax is *not* used for the payment of weekly benefits to unemployed workers. Such benefits are paid by the states in accordance with each state's unemployment tax law (SUTA). These unemployment benefits are paid out of each state's trust fund, which is financed by state unemployment taxes. Because all states conform to standards specified in FUTA, considerable uniformity exists in the provisions of the state unemployment compensation laws. However, many variations in eligibility requirements, rates of contributions, benefits paid, and duration of benefits exist. All the states, Puerto Rico, the Virgin Islands, and the District of Columbia have enacted unemployment compensation laws that have been approved by the Social Security Administration.

NEWS ALERT

The average length of unemployment in June 2015 was 28.1 weeks.

You can realize the extent of the federal-state unemployment insurance program in terms of the people involved by the fact that in June 2015 the number of unemployed persons was 9.4 million out of a civilian labor force of about 157.0 million. At that time, the jobless rate was 5.3 percent. *Unemployed persons* include young people seeking positions for the first time, seasonal workers unemployed a part of each year, and workers who lost their jobs through various causes and cannot find other suitable employment.

Coverage Under FUTA and SUTA

LO 1

Describe the basic requirements for an individual to be classified as an employer or an employee under the Federal Unemployment Tax Act.

Other than a few significant exceptions as explained in this section, the coverage under FUTA is similar to that under FICA, as described in Chapter 3.

Employers—FUTA

The federal law levies a payroll tax on employers for the purpose of providing more uniform administration of the various state unemployment compensation laws. The federal law considers a person or a business an employer if *either* of the following two tests applies:

1. Pays wages of $1,500 or more during any calendar quarter in the current or preceding calendar year, or
2. Employs one or more persons, on at least some portion of one day, in each of 20 or more calendar weeks during the current or preceding taxable year.

A number of points serve to clarify the meaning of the two alternative tests: (a) a calendar week is defined as seven successive days beginning with Sunday; (b) the 20 weeks need not be consecutive; (c) the employees need not be the same employees; (d) regular, part-time, and temporary workers are considered employees; (e) in determining the employer's status, employees include individuals on vacation or sick leave; and (f) members of a partnership are not considered to be employees. As soon as an employer meets either test, the employer becomes liable for the FUTA tax for the entire calendar year.

For Vemor Company (a new employer), the 20th week of having one or more employees does not occur until November of 2016. The company becomes liable for FUTA tax on all taxable wages paid beginning with January 1, 2016.

Other covered employers are:

1. *Agricultural employers* who in the present or previous year paid $20,000 or more to farm workers in any calendar quarter and/or employed 10 or more farm workers during some part of a day during any 20 different weeks. This includes wages paid to aliens who are in this country on a temporary basis to perform farmwork.
2. A *household employer* who during the present or previous year paid $1,000 or more during any quarter for household services in a private home, college club, or local fraternity or sorority club.

Once attained, the employer status continues until the employer fails to meet the test for coverage during a year. In this case, liability under FUTA would end as of January 1 of the next year.

Generally, the nature of the business organization has no relevance in determining employer status. Thus, the employer may be an individual, corporation, partnership, company, association, trust, or estate. There may be instances where

IRS CONNECTION

Generally, religious, educational, scientific, and charitable organizations exempt from federal income tax are not subject to FUTA tax.

it is difficult to determine which of two entities is the employer for purposes of FUTA. As under FICA, the question is answered by determining which entity has the ultimate right to direct and control the employees' activities. It is not necessary that the employer actually direct or control the manner in which the services are performed; it is sufficient if the employer has the right to do so. Other factors characteristic of an employer include the right to discharge and the furnishing of tools and a place to work.

Employers—SUTA

In general, employers specifically excluded under the federal law are also excluded under the state laws. However, as a result of variations found in state unemployment compensation laws, not all employers covered by the unemployment compensation laws of one or more states are covered by FUTA. For example, the services performed by some charitable organizations may be covered by a state's unemployment compensation act, but these same services may be exempt from FUTA coverage.

Employees—FUTA

Every individual is considered an employee if the relationship between the worker and the person for whom the services are performed is the legal common-law relationship of employer and employee. This individual would then be counted in determining whether the employer is subject to FUTA. Chapters 3 and 4 cover the nature of this common-law relationship.

For the purpose of the FUTA tax, the term "employee" also means any of the following who perform service for remuneration:

1. An *agent-driver* or a *commission-driver* who distributes food or beverages (other than milk) or laundry or dry-cleaning services for the principal.
2. A *traveling* or a city *salesperson* engaged in full-time soliciting and transmitting to the principal orders for merchandise for resale or supplies for use in business operations.

Home workers (unless they meet the definition of employee under the common-law test) and full-time life insurance agents (FICA statutory employees) are exempt under FUTA. If a person in one of these categories has a substantial investment in facilities used to perform the services (not including transportation facilities), the individual is an independent contractor and not a covered employee.

The work performed by the employee for the employer includes any services of whatever nature performed within the United States, regardless of the citizenship or residence of either. FUTA coverage also includes service of any nature performed outside the United States by a citizen of the United States for an American employer. The major exception is that service performed in Canada or in any other adjoining country with which the United States has an agreement relating to unemployment does not constitute covered employment.

An employee may perform both included and excluded employment for the same employer during a pay period. In such a case, the services that predominate in the pay period determine the employee's status with that employer for the period. FUTA wholly exempts some services from coverage. Among those *excluded* from coverage in 2016 are:

1. Casual laborers, unless cash remuneration paid for such service is $50 or more in a calendar quarter and the person to whom it is paid is regularly employed by the one for whom the services were performed during that period.
2. Directors of corporations, unless they perform services for the corporation other than those required by attending and participating in meetings of the board of directors.

ON THE NET

http://www.servicelocator.org /OWSLinks.asp This site provides a variety of interactive maps concerning individual states' status on unemployment-related issues.

3. Foreign students and exchange visitors who are carrying out the purposes for which they are admitted into the United States, such as studying, teaching, or conducting research. If employed for other purposes, they would not be excluded.
4. Government employees of international organizations, such as the United Nations.
5. Independent contractors, such as physicians, lawyers, dentists, veterinarians, contractors, subcontractors, public stenographers, auctioneers, and others who follow an independent trade, business, or profession in which they offer their services to the public.
6. Individuals under 18 years of age who deliver or distribute newspapers or shopping news (other than delivery or distribution to any point for subsequent delivery and distribution) and retail vendors of any age who sell and distribute newspapers and magazines to the ultimate consumer.
7. Insurance agents or solicitors paid solely on a commission basis.
8. Members of partnerships.
9. Service performed by an individual for a son, daughter, or spouse, or by a child under the age of 21 for a parent.
10. Services performed by a student who is enrolled and regularly attending classes at a school, college, or university, if service is performed for that school, college, or university.
11. Services performed by employees or employee representatives for employers covered by either the Railroad Retirement Tax Act or the Railroad Unemployment Insurance Act.
12. Services performed by individuals in fishing and related activities if the vessel is less than ten net tons.
13. Services performed in the employ of a religious, educational, or charitable organization that is exempt from federal income tax. This exemption includes service in church-sponsored elementary and secondary schools.
14. Services performed in the employ of foreign, federal, state, or local governments and certain of their instrumentalities. However, taxes imposed by FUTA apply to these federal instrumentalities: federal reserve banks, federal loan banks, and federal credit unions.
15. Students enrolled full time in a work-study or internship program, for work that is an integral part of the student's academic program.
16. Student nurses and hospital interns.

Employees—SUTA

The definition of "employee" as established by FUTA applies to a majority of the states, although minor variations exist in the state laws. Many states apply a simple "ABC" test to determine exclusion from coverage. All of the following requirements must be met for exclusion:

1. Free from control or direction.
2. Performed outside usual course of business.
3. Customarily engaged in an independent trade or business.

All states extend coverage to U.S. citizens working abroad for American employers (except in Canada).

Coverage of Interstate Employees

An interstate employee is an individual who works in more than one state. To prevent duplicate contributions on the services of interstate employees, all states have adopted a uniform four-part definition of employment to determine which state will cover such employees. This definition covers the entire services of an interstate worker in one state only—that state in which the worker will most likely look for a job if he or she becomes unemployed. Several factors that must be considered in determining coverage of interstate employees, in their order of application, include:

1. Place where the work is *localized*.
2. Location of *base of operations*.
3. Location of place from which operations are *directed or controlled*.
4. Location of *employee's residence*.

Over the Line

After nearly a year on the job in New York, an employee moved to Florida and telecommuted for another two years. She was laid off and received benefits from New York. The employer appealed, and a state appeals court ruled that she was ineligible because she had not worked in New York during the base period. Her out-of-state work must be incidental to the in-state work. That was not the case since actual work was performed in Florida.

Place Where the Work Is Localized

Under this main criterion of coverage adopted by the states, if all the work is performed within one state, it is clearly "localized" in that state and constitutes "employment" under the law of that state. In some cases, however, part of the person's work may be performed outside the state. In such instances, the entire work may be treated as localized within the state if the services performed in other states are temporary or transitory in nature.

Carlin Parker is a sales representative whose regular sales territory lies within Arizona. Parker is covered by the laws of Arizona, with respect to his total employment, even though he makes frequent trips to the firm's showrooms in Los Angeles to attend sales meetings and to look over new lines of goods.

Location of Base of Operations

Often, a worker may perform services continually in two or more states. In such situations, the employment in one state is not incidental to the employment in the other state. Thus, the test of localization does not apply, and the base of operations test must be considered. Under this test, the employee's services may be covered by the laws of a single state even though the services are not localized within that state. The base of operation is the place of a more or less permanent nature from which the employee starts work and to which the employee customarily returns. It could be a particular place where his or her (a) instructions are received, (b) business records are maintained, (c) supplies are sent, or (d) office is maintained (may be in the employee's home).

Mathew Hinges travels through four southern states for Irwin Company, which is headquartered in Georgia. His work is equally divided among the four states. When working in Georgia, he reports to the main office for instructions. The location of his base of operations is clearly Georgia, and his services are subject to the Georgia laws.

Location of Place from Which Operations Are Directed or Controlled

Often, an employee's services are not localized in any state. Or, it may be impossible to determine any base of operations. If the place of control can be fixed in a particular state in which some service is performed, that will be the state in which the individual is covered.

Joyce Mendes is a sales representative whose sales territory is so widespread that she does not retain any fixed business address or office. She receives all orders or instructions by mail or wire wherever she may happen to be. Clearly, the work is not localized in any state, and no fixed base of operations exists. However, the services performed by Mendes may still come under the provisions of a single state law—the law of that state in which is located the place of direction or control, provided that some of Mendes's work is also performed in that state.

Location of Employee's Residence

If an employee's coverage cannot be determined by any of the three tests described, a final test, that of the employee's residence, is used. Thus, the worker's service is covered in its entirety in the state in which the employee lives, provided some of the service is performed in that state.

Randy Mueller is employed by Prang Company of Illinois. He lives in Iowa, and his work territory includes Iowa, Minnesota, and Wisconsin. Since neither the base of operations nor the place from which his work is directed is in a state in which he works, he is covered in his state of residence (Iowa).

Reciprocal Arrangements and Transfers of Employment

If coverage of interstate employees cannot be determined using these factors, states may enter into arrangements under which the employer may elect coverage of the employee in one state.

These agreements, known as **reciprocal arrangements**, provide unemployment insurance coverage and payment of benefits to interstate workers. The most widely accepted type of interstate coverage arrangement is the Interstate Reciprocal Coverage Arrangement. Under this arrangement, an employer can elect to cover all of the services of a worker in any one state in which (a) the employee performs any work, (b) the employee maintains a residence, or (c) the employer maintains the place of business.

ON THE JOB

The only states that have not signed the reciprocal arrangements are Alaska, Kentucky, Mississippi, New Jersey, and New York, plus Puerto Rico.

Morris Davidson is a salesperson for Tannenbaum Company. His sales territory includes parts of Rhode Island and Massachusetts, and his services can be considered localized in both states. Under the Interstate Reciprocal Coverage Arrangement, the company elects to cover Davidson under the law of Massachusetts.

Instead of paying into two or more of the 50 states, an employer can elect a state based on such factors as low wage bases and contribution rates. Once the employer chooses the state in which all the services of the interstate workers are to be covered and the employee consents to the coverage, this state approves the election of coverage. Then, the appropriate agencies of the other states in which services are performed are notified so that they can agree to the coverage in the state of election. Since they are usually done on a case-by-case basis, new arrangements must be agreed upon for each employee.

Another aspect of reciprocal arrangements concerns the transfer of an employee from one state to another during the same calendar year. An employer can include, for purposes of determining the taxable wage base in the second state, wages paid an employee with respect to employment covered by the unemployment compensation law of the previous state.

EXAMPLE 5-1

Parlone Company has paid wages of $4,000 to an employee in State A. During the year, the employee is transferred to State B, which has a $7,000 taxable salary limitation for its state unemployment tax. The company has a credit of $4,000 against this $7,000 limit. Thus, the company has to pay State B's unemployment tax on only the next $3,000 of wages earned by that worker in State B during the remainder of the calendar year.

Coverage of Americans Working Overseas

As mentioned before, coverage extends to U.S. citizens working abroad for American employers. The state of the employer's principal place of business would provide the coverage. If the principal place of business cannot be determined, the state of incorporation or the state of residence of the individual owner would be the state of coverage.

Wages—FUTA

Generally, *wages* means all remuneration for employment, including the cash value of all remuneration paid in any medium other than cash, with certain exceptions.

During 2016, taxable wages include only the first $7,000 of remuneration paid by an employer to an employee with respect to employment during any calendar year. The basis upon which the remuneration is paid is immaterial. It may be paid on a piece-work basis or it may be a percentage of profits; it may be paid hourly, daily, weekly, biweekly, semimonthly, monthly, or annually. Some of the more common types of payments made to employees and the taxability status of these payments include the following:

> **LO 2**
>
> Identify generally what is defined as taxable wages by the Federal Unemployment Tax Act.

Taxable Wages for Unemployment Purposes

1. Advance payment for work to be done in the future.
2. Bonuses as remuneration for services.
3. Cash and noncash prizes and awards for doing outstanding work, for exceeding sales quotas, or for contributing suggestions that increase productivity or efficiency.
4. Christmas gifts, excluding noncash gifts of nominal value.
5. Commissions as compensation for covered employment.
6. Contributions by an employer to a supplemental unemployment individual-account plan to which the employee has a fully vested and nonforfeitable right.
7. Dismissal payments.
8. Employer contributions to cash or deferred arrangements to the extent that the contributions are not included in the employee's gross income.
9. Idle time and standby payments.
10. Payment by the employer of the employee's FICA tax or the employee's share of any state unemployment compensation tax without deduction from the employee's wages.
11. Payments representing compensation for services by an employee paid to the dependents after an employee's death. Payments in the nature of a gratuity rather than compensation for services are nontaxable. Any payments made by an employer to an employee's estate or to the employee's survivors after the calendar year in which the employee died are excluded from the definition of wages and thus may not be taxed.
12. Payments to employees or their dependents on account of sickness or accident disability. These payments are **not** taxable after the expiration of six months following the last calendar month in which the employee worked. Payments for work missed due to pregnancy are not classified as taxable wages during the first six months of absence.
13. Payments under a guaranteed annual wage plan.
14. Retroactive wage increases.
15. Tips, including charged tips, reported by the employee to the employer.
16. Transfer of stock by an employer to the employees as remuneration for services. (The fair market value of the stock at the time of payment is the taxable base.)
17. Vacation pay.

Nontaxable Wages for Unemployment Purposes

1. Advances or reimbursement of ordinary and necessary business expenses incurred in the business of the employer.
2. Allowances made to an individual by a prospective employer for expenses incurred in connection with interviews for possible employment.
3. Bonuses under a supplemental compensation plan paid upon retirement, death, or disability of an employee.
4. Caddy fees.
5. Commissions paid to insurance agents and solicitors who are paid solely by commission. Such persons are classified as independent contractors, not employees.
6. Courtesy discounts to employees and their families.
7. Educational assistance payments to workers.
8. Payments made by an employer under a plan established by the employer for health, accident, or life insurance, or retirement benefits on behalf of the employees or their dependents.
9. Reimbursement of an employee's moving expenses if, at the time of payment, it is reasonable to believe that the employee will be entitled to a deduction for those expenses at the time of filing his or her federal income tax return.
10. Retirement pay.
11. Strike benefits paid by a union to its members.
12. Value of meals and lodging furnished employees for the convenience of the employer.
13. Workers' compensation payments.

Wages—SUTA

The definition of taxable wages is fairly uniform under the various state unemployment compensation laws. However, some variations exist among the states as to the status of particular kinds of payments. For example, about one-sixth of the states have ruled that Christmas bonuses or gifts are "wages" when substantial, contractual, or based on a percentage of the employee's wages or length of service. New Hampshire, however, does not include gifts or gratuities of $25 or less as wages, unless paid under a contract related to past or future employment. A further variation in defining taxable wages among the states arises in the treatment of dismissal payments. Generally, such payments are considered wages whether or not the employer must legally make the payments. However, in some states (e.g., Kentucky), dismissal payments under a plan established for all employees or for a class of employees do not constitute wages. Puerto Rico does not consider any type of dismissal payment to be wages, nor are tips considered taxable wages.

Unemployment Compensation Taxes and Credits

The base of the unemployment compensation tax is *wages paid* rather than *wages payable*. Thus, an employer is liable for the unemployment compensation tax in the year in which wages are paid employees, not necessarily in the year in which the services are rendered. Thus, if an employee performs services in 2015 but is not paid for them until 2016, the employer is liable for the tax in 2016, and the 2016 tax rates apply. Wages are considered paid when actually paid or when constructively paid. Wages are considered constructively paid when credited to the account of, or set apart for, an employee so that they may be drawn upon at any time, even though they are not actually possessed by the employee.

Successor employers can include payments against the FUTA wage base that predecessor employers made to the employees who continue to work for the new employer. The predecessor employer must have been an employer for FUTA tax purposes.

Tax Rate—FUTA

Under FUTA, all employers, as defined earlier, are subject to a tax with respect to having individuals in their employ. For 2016, the employer's tax rate is 6.0 percent of the first $7,000 wages paid each employee during the calendar year. Thus, an employer is liable for the FUTA tax on wages paid each employee until the employee's wages reach the $7,000 level. If an employee has more than one employer during the current year, the taxable wage base *applies separately* to each of those employers, unless one employer has transferred the business to the second.

> **EXAMPLE 5-2**

Assume that in 2016, an employer had charged the wages account for $79,850. Of this amount, $720 will not be paid until the first payday in 2017. Further, the wages actually paid to employees in 2016 in excess of $7,000 each amounted to $29,840. The gross FUTA tax imposed on the employer is computed as follows:

Total amount charged to wages during 2016		$79,850.00
Less:		
Wages not to be paid until 2017	$ 720	
Wages paid in excess of $7,000 limit	29,840	30,560.00
Total taxable wages		$49,290.00
Rate of tax		× 6.0%
Amount of gross FUTA tax		$ 2,957.40

Credits Against FUTA Tax

The actual FUTA tax paid is usually only *0.6 percent*, since employers are entitled to a credit against their FUTA tax liability for contributions made under approved state unemployment compensation laws. The maximum credit permitted is 5.4 percent (90% of 6%). Thus, in the preceding example where the *gross* FUTA tax rate is 6.0 percent, the *net* FUTA rate would be 0.6 percent if the full 5.4 percent credit applied. Even if employers pay a SUTA rate of less than 5.4 percent, they still get the full credit against the FUTA tax.

> **LO 3**
> Compute the federal unemployment tax, the credit against the tax, and any credit reductions that might apply.

> **EXAMPLE 5-3**

Total taxable earnings (above example)	$49,290.00
Net rate of tax (6.0% − 5.4%)	× 0.6%
Amount of net FUTA tax	$ 295.74

To obtain the maximum credit of 5.4 percent against the federal tax, the employer must make the state contributions on or before the due date for filing the annual return under FUTA (see page 5-22)—January 31, 2017. If the employer is late in paying the state contributions, the credit is limited to 90 percent of the amount of the deposit that would have been allowed as a credit if the late contributions had been paid on time.

> **ON THE JOB**
>
> Eighty percent of the FUTA tax paid goes to pay federal (4 percent) and state (76 percent) administrative costs. The other 20 percent goes into an extended unemployment benefits account.

EXAMPLE 5-4

Sutcliffe Company had taxable wages totaling $87,500 in 2016. During the year, the company paid some of its state contributions after the January 31, 2017, cutoff. The penalty for tardiness is shown in the following calculation of the firm's net FUTA tax for 2016:

Amount of gross FUTA tax ($87,500 × 6.0%)		$ 5,250.00
State taxable wages	$87,500	
Sutcliffe's SUTA tax rate	× 5.4%	
Sutcliffe's SUTA tax	$ 4,725	
Breakdown of Sutcliffe's SUTA tax payments:		
Before 1/31/17—$3,000 × 100% credit		(3,000.00)
After 1/31/17—$1,725 × 90% credit		(1,552.50)
Amount of net FUTA tax		$ 697.50

If the company had made timely payments of its state contributions, the amount of its net FUTA tax would have been reduced to $525, for a savings of $172.50, as follows:

Amount of gross FUTA tax ($87,500 × 6.0%)		$5,250.00
Total taxable wages	$87,500	
Credit against tax	× 5.4%	
Total credit		4,725.00
Amount of net FUTA tax ($87,500 × 0.6%)		$ 525.00

$697.50 − $525.00 = $172.50 savings

The credit against the FUTA tax for state contributions does not apply to any SUTA payments deducted from employees' pay and penalties and interest not included in the contribution rate assigned by the state.

WASHINGTON UPDATE

THE WHITE HOUSE BUDGET PROPOSES TO RETURN THE NET FUTA TAX TO 0.08 PERCENT (6.2% − 5.4%). IN ANOTHER RECOMMENDATION, THE TAXABLE WAGE BASE WOULD BE RAISED TO $15,000 WITH A REDUCED FUTA RATE OF 5.77 PERCENT, LEADING TO A NET TAX RATE OF 0.37 PERCENT (5.77% − 5.4%).

Experience Rating

In some cases, employers may pay contributions into their state unemployment fund at a rate lower than 5.4 percent. The method by which the employer contributions may be adjusted because of a favorable employment record is referred to as **experience rating** or **merit rating**. Thus, an employer's favorable experience rate (employment record) qualifies the employer for a SUTA rate lower than 5.4 percent. As noted before, FUTA provides for a credit equal to the employer's SUTA rate plus an additional credit so that the *full 5.4 percent credit* still applies. In this way, employers who have steady employment histories, and therefore lower SUTA tax rates, are not penalized when the FUTA tax is paid.

SELF-STUDY QUIZ 5-1

Garo Company pays taxable wages (FUTA and SUTA) of $188,000 during 2016. Garo Company has a state unemployment tax rate of 4.1% for 2016 because of its past employment record. Compute Garo Company's 2016 FUTA and SUTA taxes.

    $_____FUTA
    $_____SUTA

Note: Answers are on page 5-28.

If an employer receives an additional credit against the FUTA tax because the state experience rate is less than 5.4 percent, the additional credit is not subject to the 90 percent FUTA credit limitation for late SUTA payments. The credit reduction applies only to actual SUTA tax payments made after January 31, 2017.

EXAMPLE 5-5

Yeldon Company has a $70,000 federal and state taxable payroll and has earned a reduced state tax rate of 4 percent. If none of its state tax payments are timely, the FUTA tax calculation is as follows:

Gross FUTA tax ($70,000 × 0.060)..		$4,200
Less 90% credit for state taxes paid late ($70,000 × 0.04 × 90%)...............................	$2,520	
Less additional credit for state tax if rate were 5.4% [$70,000 × (0.054 − 0.04)]....................	980	
Total credit...		3,500
Net FUTA tax...		$ 700

If Yeldon Company had made its SUTA payments before the due date of Form 940, the credit for the payments (4%) and the additional credit (1.4%) would have provided a total credit of $3,780 and a FUTA tax savings of $280.

Where contributions are paid into more than one state unemployment compensation fund, the credit against the federal tax is still limited to 5.4 percent.

The contribution rate of Domski Supply in Kansas is 5.5 percent and in Missouri, 2 percent. The credit against the gross FUTA tax on the wages paid is 5.4 percent in each state.

The unemployment compensation laws of certain states set the taxable wage base at a figure higher than the first $7,000 paid to each employee. For example, in Arkansas, the wage base for 2015 was the first $12,000. In such states, the total contributions that the employer must pay into the state fund may exceed 5.4 percent of the taxable wages as established by FUTA (first $7,000 of each employee's earnings). However, the maximum credit that can be claimed against the gross FUTA tax for the state contributions is 5.4 percent of the first $7,000 of each individual employee's earnings.

Title XII Advances

States that experience financial difficulties and are unable to pay their unemployment compensation benefits may borrow funds from the federal government under Title XII of the Social Security Act. The states use these funds, called Title XII advances, to pay their regular unemployment benefits. Under the repayment provisions established by the federal government, if a state defaults in its payments, the credit against the gross FUTA tax is reduced by 0.3 percent beginning the *second taxable year after the advance.* This penalty increases by an additional 0.3 percent for each succeeding year in which there is a balance due the federal government. Thus, employers in those states have their gross FUTA tax rate increased by 0.3 percent the second year after the advance, then by 0.6 percent. The credit reduction is capped (0.6 percent) if certain solvency requirements are met by the state. The credit reduction can be avoided if the state repays the loan by November 10 of the year in which the reduction is scheduled to take effect. This additional FUTA tax is due with the fourth quarter deposit. In addition, a Benefit Cost Ratio (BCR) of 0.5 percent is added to the credit reduction beginning with the third or fourth consecutive year in which the federal loan has not been repaid and the credit reduction state's unemployment insurance rates do not meet the minimum federal levels.

For the 2014 tax year there were seven credit reduction states and the Virgin Islands. The credit reductions ranged from 1.2 percent to 1.7 percent (Connecticut, which had outstanding federal loans for five consecutive years).

Tax Rates—SUTA

Figure 5.1, on pages 5-12 and 5-13, presents a summary of each state's 2015 unemployment compensation laws, including the tax rates and the wage limitations. The tax rate applied to each employer within a particular state yields the funds used by that state in paying benefits to its unemployed workers. Currently, all states have enacted pooled-fund laws as a basis for their unemployment insurance systems. By means of pooled funds, the cost of unemployment benefits is spread among all the employers in a particular state.

FIGURE 5.1

Summary of State Unemployment Compensation Laws (2015)
Warning: The provisions of the state laws are subject to change at any time.

State	Size of Firm (One employee in specified time and/or size of payroll[1])	Contributions (On first $7,000 unless otherwise indicated)		Benefits (Excluding dependency allowances)			
		Employer Min.–Max.	Employee	Waiting Period (weeks)	Max. per Week	Min. per Week	Max. Duration (weeks)
ALABAMA	20 weeks	0.65%–6.8% on first $8,000		none	$265	$ 45	26
ALASKA	any time	1.0%–5.4% on first $38,700	0.57% on first $38,700	1	370	56	26
ARIZONA	20 weeks	0.03%–7.79%**		1	240	60	26
ARKANSAS	10 days	0.9%–12.8% on first $12,000**		1	451	81	26
CALIFORNIA*	over $100 in any calendar quarter	1.5%–6.2%	0.9% on first $104,738 (disability ins)	1	450	40	25
COLORADO	any time	0.78%–10.2% on first $11,800**		1	532	25	26
CONNECTICUT*	20 weeks	1.9%–6.8% on first $15,000		none	590	15	26
DELAWARE	20 weeks	0.3%–8.2% on first $18,500		none	330	20	26
DISTRICT OF COLUMBIA	any time	1.6%–7.0% on first $9,000		1	359	50	26
FLORIDA	20 weeks	0.24%–5.4%		1	275	32	23
GEORGIA	20 weeks	0.04%–8.10% on first $9,500**		none	330	44	26
HAWAII	any time	0.2%–5.8% on first $40,900	0.5% of maximum weekly wages of $951.23, not to exceed $4.76 per week (disability ins)	1	544	5	26
IDAHO	20 weeks or $300 in any calendar quarter	0.453%–5.4% on first $36,000		1	383	72	26
ILLINOIS	20 weeks	0.55%–8.15% on first $12,960		1	413	51	25
INDIANA*	20 weeks	0.51%–7.548% on first $9,500**		1	390	50	26
IOWA	20 weeks	0.0%–7.5% on first $27,300		none	416	62	26
KANSAS	20 weeks	0.07%–7.4% on first $12,000**		1	469	117	26
KENTUCKY*	20 weeks	1.0%–10.0% on first $9,900**		none	415	39	26
LOUISIANA	20 weeks	0.10%–6.2% on first $7,700**		1	247	10	26
MAINE	20 weeks	0.8%–6.92% on first $12,000**		1	386	67	26
MARYLAND	any time	0.6%–9.0% on first $8,500		none	410	25	26
MASSACHUSETTS	13 weeks	0.73%–11.13% on first $15,000**		1	674	31	30
MICHIGAN	20 weeks or $1,000 in calendar year	0.06%–10.3% on first $9,500**		None	362	81	20
MINNESOTA	20 weeks	0.2%–9.1% on first $30,000**		1	640	38	26
MISSISSIPPI	20 weeks	0.39%–5.4% on first $14,000		1	235	30	26
MISSOURI	20 weeks	0.0%–7.8% on first $13,000**		1	320	48	26
MONTANA	Over $1,000 in current or preceding year	0.02%–6.12% on first $29,500		1	471	134	28

[1]This is $1,500 in any calendar quarter in current or preceding calendar year unless otherwise specified.
*2014 FUTA credit reduction state
**Allow voluntary contributions

(continued)

FIGURE 5.1 (concluded)

Summary of State Unemployment Compensation Laws (2015)
Warning: The provisions of the state laws are subject to change at any time.

State	Size of Firm (One employee in specified time and/or size of payroll¹)	Contributions (On first $7,000 unless otherwise indicated) Employer Min.–Max.	Employee	Waiting Period (weeks)	Max. per Week	Min. per Week	Max. Duration (weeks)
NEBRASKA	20 weeks	0.0%–5.4% on first $9,000**		1	362	30	26
NEVADA	$225 in any quarter	0.25%–5.4% on first $27,800		none	398	16	26
NEW HAMPSHIRE	20 weeks	0.1%–7.0% on first $14,000		none	427	32	20
NEW JERSEY	$1,000 in any year	1.2%–7.0% on first $32,000**	0.765% (0.25% for disability ins; 0.515% for unempl. comp./family leave/workforce development funds) on first $32,000	1	636	73	26
NEW MEXICO	20 weeks or $450 in any quarter	0.33%–5.4% on first $23,400**		1	406	75	26
NEW YORK*	$300 in any quarter	2.1%–9.9% on first $10,500**		1	420	100	26
NORTH CAROLINA*	20 weeks	0.72%–6.91% on first $21,700**		1	535	46	26
NORTH DAKOTA	20 weeks	0.1%–9.7% on first $35,600**		1	442	43	26
OHIO*	20 weeks	0.3%–8.6% on first $9,000**		1	400	111	26
OKLAHOMA		0.1%–5.5% on first $17,000		1	368	16	26
OREGON	20 weeks	1.5%–5.4% on first $35,700		1	538	126	26
PENNSYLVANIA	18 weeks or $225 in any quarter	2.801%–10.8937% on first $9,000**	0.07% on total wages	1	573	35	26
PUERTO RICO	any time	2.4%–5.4%	0.3% on first $9,000 (disability ins)	1	133	7	26
RHODE ISLAND	any time	1.69%–9.79% on first $21,200	1.2% on first $64,200 (disability ins)	1	566	43	26
SOUTH CAROLINA	any time	0.06%–6.03% on first $14,000		1	326	42	26
SOUTH DAKOTA	20 weeks	0.0%–10.03% on first $15,000**		1	345	28	26
TENNESSEE	20 weeks	0.15%–10.0% on first $9,000		1	275	30	26
TEXAS	20 weeks	0.47%–7.49% on first $9,000**		1	454	63	26
UTAH	$140 in calendar quarter in current or preceding calendar year	0.3%–7.3% on first $31,300		1	467	25	26
VERMONT	20 weeks	1.3%–8.4% on first $16,400		1	425	59	26
VIRGIN ISLANDS*	any time	1.5%–6.0% on first $22,900		1	495	33	26
VIRGINIA	20 weeks	0.44%–6.54% on first $8,000		1	378	54	26
WASHINGTON	any time	0.17%–5.84% on first $42,100**		1	637	151	26
WEST VIRGINIA	20 weeks	1.5%–8.5% on first $12,000**		1	424	24	26
WISCONSIN	20 weeks	0.27%–12.0% on first $14,000**		none	370	54	26
WYOMING	$500 in current or preceding calendar year	0.27%–10.0% on first $24,700		1	471	34	26

¹This is $1,500 in any calendar quarter in current or preceding calendar year unless otherwise specified.
*2014 FUTA credit reduction state
**Allow voluntary contributions

Employer Contributions

Every state has its own unemployment compensation law with varying tax rates and taxable wage bases.

EXAMPLE 5-6

The Iqbal Company of Georgia had a FUTA taxable payroll of $215,600 and a SUTA taxable payroll of $255,700 with a 5.6 percent SUTA tax rate. The company would pay unemployment taxes of:

FUTA $215,600 × 0.006 = $ 1,293.60
SUTA $255,700 × 0.056 = $14,319.20
TOTAL TAXES $15,612.80

As with FUTA tax, if an employee has more than one employer during the year, the taxable wage base (same state) or bases (different states) applies separately to each employer.

To minimize the impact of unemployment insurance taxes on newly covered employers, each state sets an initial contribution rate for new employers that will apply for a specific period of time. During this period of time, the new employer's employment record can be developed and an experience rating can later be established. A state may assign a contribution rate of not less than 1 percent to newly covered employers on some "reasonable basis" other than employment experience. Once the new employer has accumulated the experience required under the provisions of the state law, a new rate will be assigned. For example, Nevada applies 2.95 percent to new employers plus a 0.05 percent career enhancement program fee.

Employee Contributions

Some states, as shown in Figure 5.1, impose a contributions requirement on employees in addition to the contributions made by the employer.

EXAMPLE 5-7

1. Fay Nannen earns $320 during the first week of February while working for Dango, Inc. Since the company is located in New Jersey, Nannen would have $2.45 deducted from her pay (0.765% of $320). This 0.765 percent tax would be deducted on the first $32,000 paid to her during the year. (In New Jersey, 0.25 percent of the employees' contributions is for the disability benefit plan and 0.515 percent for the unemployment insurance/family leave funds.)

2. Donald Drury works in Puerto Rico and earns $450 each week. He would contribute $1.35 (0.3% of $450) of each pay to a disability fund. This 0.3 percent deduction would continue until his cumulative pay for the year reached $9,000.

SELF-STUDY QUIZ 5-2

Moss Company paid wages of $6,000 to John Castellano in Arizona. During the year, Castellano transferred to the company's office in Colorado, and he received $26,000 for the rest of the year. The company's unemployment tax rate for Colorado is 2.9 percent. What would Moss Company pay to Colorado for unemployment taxes on Castellano's wages? $_____

LO 4

Describe how an experience-rating system is used in determining employers' contributions to state unemployment compensation funds.

Experience Rating

As indicated earlier, the concept of experience rating is based upon the payment of state unemployment taxes according to the employer's stability of employment. As an employer experiences a lower employee turnover, generally the state unemployment tax rate will lower.

In all states, some type of experience-rating plan provides for a reduction in the employer's tax contributions based on the employer's experience with the risk of unemployment. Of the several formulas used to determine the contribution rates, the most commonly used is the **reserve-ratio formula**:

$$\text{Reserve Ratio} = \frac{\text{Contributions} - \text{Benefits Paid}}{\text{Average Payroll}}$$

The amount of the unemployment compensation contributions (taxes paid), the benefits paid by the state, and the employer's payroll are entered by the state on each employer's record. The benefits paid are subtracted from the contributions, and the balance of the employer's account is divided by the average payroll for a stated period of time to determine the reserve ratio. Under this plan, the balance carried forward each year equals the difference between the employer's total contributions and the total benefits paid to former employees by the state. The contribution rates are then established according to a schedule under which the higher the reserve ratio, the lower the tax rate.

Employers who have built up a balance in their reserve account (contributions paid in less benefits charged) are sometimes referred to as **positive-balance employers**. The larger the positive balance in a company's reserve account, the lower its tax rate will be. Employers whose reserve accounts have been charged for more benefits paid out than contributions paid in are referred to as **negative-balance employers**, and their high tax rates reflect this fact.

Computing the Contribution Rate

In an experience-rating system, the rate of contributions for employers is based on the employment experience of the employer. The rate is determined by computing the total of the reserve built up by employer contributions over a certain period of time and by computing the ratio of the amount in the reserve account to the employer's average annual payroll as determined under the state's formula.

EXAMPLE 5-8

Spencili Company is an employer located in a state with an unemployment compensation law containing merit-rating provisions for employers who meet certain requirements. Below is a summary of the total wages for the years 2012 to 2015, inclusive. For the purpose of the illustration, assume that the total wages and taxable wages are the same amount.

Quarter	2012	2013	2014	2015
1st	$11,000	$10,000	$ 8,500	$10,500
2nd	10,000	9,000	9,500	11,000
3rd	10,000	9,500	10,000	11,000
4th	10,500	9,750	9,500	9,500
Total	$41,500	$38,250	$37,500	$42,000

The State Unemployment Compensation Commission maintains a separate account for each employer. The account is credited with contributions paid into the unemployment compensation fund by the employer and is charged with unemployment benefits paid from the fund.

For 2016, the state law set up the following contribution rate schedule for employers:

Reserve Ratio	Rate
Negative reserve balance	6.7%
0% to less than 8%	5.9%
8% to less than 10%	5.0%
10% to less than 12%	4.1%
12% to less than 15%	3.2%
15% and over	2.5%

The state law under discussion defines: *average annual payroll*—average of last three years, *annual payroll*—wages paid from October 1 to September 30 each year.

The following computations show the state contributions made by Spencili Company for the calendar years 2012 to 2015, inclusive, the federal tax imposed under FUTA, and the method of arriving at the contribution rate for the calendar year 2016:

2012

Taxable wages	$41,500	
Rate (SUTA)	× 2.7%	
State contributions		$1,120.50
Federal tax: 0.6% of $41,500 (used 0.6% for whole year)		249.00
Total unemployment tax		$1,369.50

2013

Taxable wages	$38,250	
Rate (SUTA)	× 2.7%	
State contributions		$1,032.75
Federal tax: 0.6% of $38,250		229.50
Total unemployment tax		$1,262.25

2014

Taxable wages	$37,500	
Rate (SUTA)	× 3.4%	
State contributions		$1,275.00
Federal tax: 0.6% of $37,500		225.00
Total unemployment tax		$1,500.00

2015

Taxable wages	$42,000	
Rate (SUTA)	× 3.7%	
State contributions		$1,554.00
Federal tax: 0.6% of $42,000		252.00
Total unemployment tax		$1,806.00

Remember that the average annual payroll is the average of the last three annual payrolls, with each annual payroll period running from October 1 to September 30.

Assume that Spencili Company paid state contributions of $960 in 2010 and $1,010 in 2011 and that $1,850 was charged to the employer's account for unemployment compensation benefits during 2014 and 2015. The contribution rate for 2016 is computed as follows:

Computation of rate for 2016:

Annual payroll period ending 9/30/13	$ 39,000
Annual payroll period ending 9/30/14	37,750
Annual payroll period ending 9/30/15	42,000
Total of last 3 annual payroll periods	$118,750

Average annual payroll:

$$\$118,750 \div 3 = \$39,583$$

Contributions for 2010	$ 960.00
Contributions for 2011	1,010.00
Contributions for 2012	1,120.50
Contributions for 2013	1,032.75
Contributions for 2014	1,275.00
Contributions for 2015 (first nine months)	1,202.50
Total contributions	$6,600.75
Less amount of benefits paid	1,850.00
Balance in reserve account 9/30/15	$4,750.75

$$\$4,750.75 \div \text{Average annual payroll, } \$39,583 = 12\%$$

Since the reserve is 12 percent of the average annual payroll, the tax rate for 2016 is 3.2 percent (the ratio is between 12% and 15%).

Voluntary Contributions

In some states (see Figure 5.1, on pages 5-12 and 5-13), employers may obtain reduced unemployment compensation rates by making **voluntary contributions** to the state fund. Employers deliberately make these contributions in addition to their regularly required payments of state unemployment taxes. The voluntary contributions increase the balance in the employer's reserve account so that a lower contribution rate may be assigned for the following year. Thus, the new lower tax rate will save the employer more in future state unemployment tax payments than the amount of the voluntary contribution itself.

An employer who desires to make a voluntary contribution usually must determine the amount of the contribution needed in order to obtain a lower contribution rate. In some states, the agencies provide worksheets that aid employers in determining the amount of voluntary contributions required. Ohio computes the voluntary contribution amount needed and includes it in the rate notices sent to all employers. As with the regular contributions, the state must receive the voluntary contributions by a certain date before they can be credited to the employer's account and be used in computing a new tax rate. In some states, the employer may have a certain number of days following the mailing of the tax rate notice to make the voluntary contributions. For instance, in Arizona, the voluntary contributions must be paid by January 31.

NEWS ALERT

If there are unpaid taxes and penalties due, states may apply the voluntary contributions to these amounts first.

EXAMPLE 5-9

To illustrate the tax saving that may be realized as a result of making voluntary contributions, consider the following case of Krane Company, which is subject to the unemployment compensation law of a state that uses the reserve-ratio formula to determine experience ratings. The following contribution rate schedule applies for 2017:

Reserve Ratio	Rate
0% to less than 1%	6.2%
1% to less than 1.4%	5.6%
1.4% to less than 1.8%	5.0%
1.8% to less than 2.2%	4.4%
2.2% to less than 2.6%	3.8%
2.6% to less than 3.0%	3.2%
3.0% and over	2.6%

For the three 12-month periods ending on June 30, 2016, the company had an average annual taxable payroll of $330,000. This is the base that the state uses as the average payroll. As of June 30, 2016, the credits to the employer's account exceeded the benefits paid by $6,800. Thus, the 2016 reserve ratio is 2.06 percent ($6,800 ÷ $330,000), which would result in the assignment of a 4.4 percent tax rate, as shown in the preceding table. If the employer's 2017 total taxable payroll were $390,000, the SUTA contribution would amount to $17,160.

If Krane Company makes a voluntary contribution into the state fund within the time period specified by the state law, the tax for 2017 will be less. For example, if the company contributes $460, the reserve ratio will be 2.2 percent ($7,260 ÷ $330,000). As a result, the tax rate will be reduced to 3.8 percent, with the following savings realized in 2017:

Tax payment with no voluntary contribution (4.4% × $390,000)		$17,160
Tax payment with voluntary contribution	$ 460	
Reserve ratio (3.8% × $390,000)	14,820	15,280
Tax savings		$ 1,880

Since these payments are not required payments, these voluntary contributions do not count as part of the credit against the FUTA tax.

Nonprofits

A federal law allows nonprofits the option to reimburse the state for the actual amount of unemployment benefits paid to their former employees, instead of paying a set percentage for state unemployment taxes. The reimbursement takes place on a dollar-for-dollar basis when the state pays the benefits to the former employees.

Dumping

The *SUTA Dumping Prevention Act* requires states to enact laws that stop businesses from changing their business structure to avoid paying their proper amount of SUTA taxes. This law is designed to stop companies with poor experience ratings from forming new companies with lower new employer tax rates and then transferring the employees to the new company ("dumping" the original company's high tax rates).

Unemployment Compensation Reports Required of the Employer

LO 5

Complete the reports required by the Federal Unemployment Tax Act.

Employers liable for both the FUTA and the SUTA tax must file periodic reports with both the federal and the state governments. For FUTA tax reporting, employers file an annual return (Form 940) and generally make quarterly tax payments. Also, employers covered by state unemployment compensation laws generally submit two major kinds of reports. One is a tax return, on which the employer reports the tax due the state. The other is a wage report, which reflects the amount of taxable wages paid to each of the employer's covered employees.

Annual FUTA Return—Form 940

Form 940, Employer's Annual Federal Unemployment (FUTA) Tax Return, is the prescribed form for making the return required of employers in reporting the tax imposed under FUTA. Figure 5.2, on pages 5-19 and 5-20, shows a filled-in copy of this form. Figure 5.3 on page 5-21 provides sources of information for completing the form. If an employer who is not liable for FUTA tax receives a Form 940, check box c in the top corner of the form and sign and return the form to the IRS.

Electronic Filing

Employers can also electronically file Form 940 through their payroll service provider (if they offer this service). In addition, the government provides a web-based Internet system through which taxpayers enter data directly into IRS approved software. The IRS e-file can be used to file Form 940 and e-pay (electronic funds withdrawal) the balance due in a single step.

Completing the Return

In making entries on the form:

a. Dollar signs and decimal points—not used (commas optional).
b. Zero value line—leave blank.
c. Negative amounts—use "minus" sign.
d. Rounding—is optional and can be done to the nearest dollar for all entries.

Part 1

1a. Employers who pay SUTA tax to only one state enter that state (use the two-letter, U.S. Postal Service abbreviation) in this box. If more than one state, check box 1b.
2. Employers who paid wages in a "credit reduction" state would check this box.

FIGURE 5.2
Form 940, Employer's Annual Federal Unemployment (FUTA) Tax Return (page 1)

Form **940 for 20--:** **Employer's Annual Federal Unemployment (FUTA) Tax Return**
Department of the Treasury — Internal Revenue Service

OMB No. 1545-0028

Employer identification number (EIN) 0 0 – 0 0 0 0 3 2 0

Name (not your trade name) SHANNON HEATING COMPANY

Trade name (if any)

Address P.O. BOX 1803
Number   Street   Suite or room number

LANSDOWNE   PA   19019-3636
City   State   ZIP code

Foreign country name   Foreign province/county   Foreign postal code

Type of Return
(Check all that apply.)

- a. Amended
- b. Successor employer
- c. No payments to employees in 20--
- d. Final: Business closed or stopped paying wages

Instructions and prior-year forms are available at *www.irs.gov/form940*.

Read the separate instructions before you complete this form. Please type or print within the boxes.

Part 1:   Tell us about your return. If any line does NOT apply, leave it blank.

1a If you had to pay state unemployment tax in one state only, enter the state abbreviation . **1a** ☐ ☐

1b If you had to pay state unemployment tax in more than one state, you are a multi-state employer . . . . **1b** ☒ Check here. Complete Schedule A (Form 940).

2 If you paid wages in a state that is subject to CREDIT REDUCTION . . . . **2** ☒ Check here. Complete Schedule A (Form 940).

Part 2:   Determine your FUTA tax before adjustments for 20--. If any line does NOT apply, leave it blank.

3 Total payments to all employees **3** 122534.29

4 Payments exempt from FUTA tax **4** 4300.00

Check all that apply: **4a** ☐ Fringe benefits **4c** ☒ Retirement/Pension **4e** ☐ Other
4b ☐ Group-term life insurance **4d** ☐ Dependent care

5 Total of payments made to each employee in excess of $7,000 . . . . **5** 21017.62

6 Subtotal (line 4 + line 5 = line 6) **6** 25317.62

7 Total taxable FUTA wages (line 3 – line 6 = line 7) (see instructions) **7** 97216.67

8 FUTA tax before adjustments (line 7 x .006 = line 8) **8** 583.30

Part 3:   Determine your adjustments. If any line does NOT apply, leave it blank.

9 If ALL of the taxable FUTA wages you paid were excluded from state unemployment tax, multiply line 7 by .054 (line 7 × .054 = line 9). Go to line 12 . . . . **9** .

10 If SOME of the taxable FUTA wages you paid were excluded from state unemployment tax, OR you paid ANY state unemployment tax late (after the due date for filing Form 940), complete the worksheet in the instructions. Enter the amount from line 7 of the worksheet . . **10** .

11 If credit reduction applies, enter the total from Schedule A (Form 940) **11** 419.02

Part 4:   Determine your FUTA tax and balance due or overpayment for 20--. If any line does NOT apply, leave it blank.

12 Total FUTA tax after adjustments (lines 8 + 9 + 10 + 11 = line 12) **12** 1002.32

13 FUTA tax deposited for the year, including any overpayment applied from a prior year . **13** 562.20

14 Balance due (If line 12 is more than line 13, enter the excess on line 14.)
- If line 14 is more than $500, you must deposit your tax.
- If line 14 is $500 or less, you may pay with this return. (see instructions) **14** 440.12

15 Overpayment (If line 13 is more than line 12, enter the excess on line 15 and check a box below.) . . . . **15** .

▶ You **MUST** complete both pages of this form and **SIGN** it.   Check one: ☐ Apply to next return. ☐ Send a refund.

Next ▶

For Privacy Act and Paperwork Reduction Act Notice, see the back of Form 940-V, Payment Voucher.   Cat. No. 11234O   Form **940** (2014)

FIGURE 5.2 (concluded)

Form 940, Employer's Annual Federal Unemployment (FUTA) Tax Return (page 2)

Name (not your trade name)	Employer identification number (EIN)
SHANNON HEATING COMPANY	00-0000320

Part 5: Report your FUTA tax liability by quarter only if line 12 is more than $500. If not, go to Part 6.

16 Report the amount of your FUTA tax liability for each quarter; do NOT enter the amount you deposited. If you had no liability for a quarter, leave the line blank.

16a 1st quarter (January 1 – March 31)	16a	203.42
16b 2nd quarter (April 1 – June 30)	16b	259.95
16c 3rd quarter (July 1 – September 30)	16c	98.83
16d 4th quarter (October 1 – December 31)	16d	440.12

17 Total tax liability for the year (lines 16a + 16b + 16c + 16d = line 17) **17** | 1002.32 | **Total must equal line 12.**

Part 6: May we speak with your third-party designee?

Do you want to allow an employee, a paid tax preparer, or another person to discuss this return with the IRS? See the instructions for details.

☐ **Yes.** Designee's name and phone number

Select a 5-digit Personal Identification Number (PIN) to use when talking to IRS

☒ **No.**

Part 7: Sign here. You MUST complete both pages of this form and SIGN it.

Under penalties of perjury, I declare that I have examined this return, including accompanying schedules and statements, and to the best of my knowledge and belief, it is true, correct, and complete, and that no part of any payment made to a state unemployment fund claimed as a credit was, or is to be, deducted from the payments made to employees. Declaration of preparer (other than taxpayer) is based on all information of which preparer has any knowledge.

X Sign your name here   *J.D. Shannon*

Print your name here   J.D. SHANNON

Print your title here   PRESIDENT

Date   1/31/17

Best daytime phone   (215) 555 – 1234

Paid Preparer Use Only   Check if you are self-employed . ☐

Preparer's name		PTIN	
Preparer's signature		Date	/ /
Firm's name (or yours if self-employed)		EIN	
Address		Phone	( ) –
City		State	ZIP code

Page **2**   Form **940** (2014)

Source: Internal Revenue Service.

FIGURE 5.3

Sources of Information for Completing Form 940

Line No.	Source of Information
Part 1—About Your Return	
1	State unemployment tax forms
Part 2—Determine Your FUTA Tax	
3	General ledger account(s) for wages and salaries
4	Employee information files
5	Employee earnings records
6	Follow directions for addition.
7	Follow directions for subtraction.
8	Follow directions for multiplication.
Part 3—Determine Your Adjustments	
9 and 10	From the appropriate states' unemployment tax returns
11	From the total on Schedule A
Part 4—Determine Your FUTA Tax	
12	Follow directions for addition.
13	From the debit postings to the FUTA taxes payable account in the general ledger
14, 15	Difference between lines 12 and 13
Part 5—FUTA Tax Liability for Each Quarter	
16	From the quarterly balances in the FUTA taxes payable account in the general ledger
17	Follow directions for addition.
Part 6—Third-Party Designee	
	Check the yes or no box.
Part 7—Sign Here	
	Sign, date, and list phone number.

Part 2

Many of the entries are self-explanatory. The taxable wages adjustments relate to:

4.   Some payments that are not included in the FUTA definition of "wages" or services that are not included in the definition of "employment" are entered here. Some of these payments would include the value of certain meals and lodging, contributions to accident or health plans for employees, employer contributions to employees' qualified retirement plans, and payments to children under the age of 21 for services provided to their parent(s). This also applies to the value of group-term life insurance in excess of $50,000—box 4b (taxable for FICA, federal income tax, but not FUTA). Check the appropriate box(es).

5.   Enter the total of the payments over $7,000 that were paid to each employee after subtracting exempt payments (line 4).

Part 3

Adjustments made to the FUTA tax:

9.   If all the wages paid were excluded from state unemployment tax (e.g., wages were paid to employees in a specific excluded occupation), the employer must pay a 6.0 percent FUTA tax.

10. If this applies, the attached worksheet must be completed and the step-by-step process will determine the credit.
11. If the FUTA taxable wages were also subject to state unemployment taxes, enter the amount from Schedule A.

Part 4

Complete lines 12 through 15 to determine the balance due or the overpayment, whichever applies. If a balance is due, depending on the amount of the liability, the employer either deposits, electronically transfers, or remits the balance due directly to the IRS with Form 940. Employers may now use a major credit card to pay the balance due on the form. This does not apply to the payment of the quarterly deposits made during the year (page 5-24).

Part 5

Complete this part only if line 12 is more than $500. Enter the tax liability for each quarter. If a credit reduction applies (line 11), the amount owed for the reduction must be included with the fourth quarter liability.

Part 6

Check the appropriate box. If YES is checked, complete the designee's information.

Part 7

Form 940 must be signed by:

1. The individual, if a sole proprietorship.
2. The president, vice president, or other principal officer, if a corporation.
3. A responsible and duly authorized member, if a partnership or other unincorporated organization.
4. A fiduciary, if a trust or an estate.

Officers and authorized agents may sign the return by rubber stamp, mechanical device, or computer software. In the case of an electronically-filed form, a ten digit Personal Identification Number (PIN) will be used by the authorized signer to electronically sign the Form 940. This PIN is sent to the business once the authorized signer(s) of the Form 94x series have been approved by the IRS.

Schedule A

This schedule (Figure 5.4) is only completed by employers who were required to pay state unemployment taxes in more than one state or paid wages in a state that is subject to the credit reduction.

Enter an "X" in the box for the appropriate states. If the states are subject to a FUTA credit reduction, calculate the credit reduction (FUTA taxable wages for that state, multiplied by the state's credit reduction rate). At the bottom of the schedule, total the amount of the credit reductions and enter this amount on line 11 of Form 940. This schedule will then be submitted along with Form 940.

Filing the Return

The employer must file the annual return no later than January 31 following the close of the calendar year. If, however, the employer has made timely deposits that pay the FUTA tax liability in full, as discussed later, the company may delay the filing of Form 940 until February 10. The return must be filed on a calendar-year basis even though the company operates on a fiscal-year basis different from the calendar year. If January 31 or February 10 falls on Saturday, Sunday, or a legal holiday, the return may be filed on the following business day. A mailed return bearing a postmark indicating it was mailed on or before the due date will be considered to have been timely filed even though received after the due date.

FIGURE 5.4
Required Form for Multi-State Employers

Schedule A (Form 940) for 20--:

Multi-State Employer and Credit Reduction Information

OMB No. 1545-0028

Department of the Treasury — Internal Revenue Service

See the instructions on page 2. File this schedule with Form 940.

Employer identification number (EIN): 0 0 – 0 0 0 0 0 3 2 0

Name (not your trade name): SHANNON HEATING COMPANY

Place an "X" in the box of EVERY state in which you had to pay state unemployment tax this year. For each state with a credit reduction rate greater than zero, enter the FUTA taxable wages, multiply by the reduction rate, and enter the credit reduction amount. Do not include in the *FUTA Taxable Wages* box wages that were excluded from state unemployment tax (see the instructions for Step 2). If any states do not apply to you, leave them blank.

Postal Abbreviation	FUTA Taxable Wages	Reduction Rate	Credit Reduction	Postal Abbreviation	FUTA Taxable Wages	Reduction Rate	Credit Reduction
☐ AK	.	× .000	.	☐ NC	.	× .012	.
☐ AL	.	× .000	.	☐ ND	.	× .000	.
☐ AR	.	× .000	.	☐ NE	.	× .000	.
☐ AZ	.	× .000	.	☐ NH	.	× .000	.
☐ CA	.	× .012	.	☐ NJ	.	× .000	.
☐ CO	.	× .000	.	☐ NM	.	× .000	.
☐ CT	.	× .017	.	☐ NV	.	× .000	.
☐ DC	.	× .000	.	☐ NY	.	× .012	.
☐ DE	.	× .000	.	☒ OH	34918 • 07	× .012	419 • 02
☐ FL	.	× .000	.	☐ OK	.	× .000	.
☐ GA	.	× .000	.	☐ OR	.	× .000	.
☐ HI	.	× .000	.	☒ PA	.	× .000	.
☐ IA	.	× .000	.	☐ RI	.	× .000	.
☐ ID	.	× .000	.	☐ SC	.	× .000	.
☐ IL	.	× .000	.	☐ SD	.	× .000	.
☐ IN	.	× .015	.	☐ TN	.	× .000	.
☐ KS	.	× .000	.	☐ TX	.	× .000	.
☐ KY	.	× .012	.	☐ UT	.	× .000	.
☐ LA	.	× .000	.	☐ VA	.	× .000	.
☐ MA	.	× .000	.	☐ VT	.	× .000	.
☐ MD	.	× .000	.	☐ WA	.	× .000	.
☐ ME	.	× .000	.	☐ WI	.	× .000	.
☐ MI	.	× .000	.	☐ WV	.	× .000	.
☐ MN	.	× .000	.	☐ WY	.	× .000	.
☐ MO	.	× .000	.	☐ PR	.	× .000	.
☐ MS	.	× .000	.	☐ VI	.	× .012	.
☐ MT	.	× .000	.				

Total Credit Reduction. Add all amounts shown in the *Credit Reduction* boxes. Enter the total here and on Form 940, line 11 . . . .   419 • 02

For Privacy Act and Paperwork Reduction Act Notice, see the Instructions for Form 940.   Cat. No. 16997C   Schedule A (Form 940) 2014

Source: Internal Revenue Service.

Upon application of the employer, the district director or the director of a service center may grant a reasonable extension of time in which to file the return, but not for payment of the tax. However, no extension will be granted for a period of more than 90 days. Generally, the application for an extension must be written on or before the filing due date. The return must be filed with the IRS center for the district in which the employer's principal place of business or office or agency is located. The instructions for Form 940 list the addresses of the IRS centers.

Once an employer has filed Form 940, the IRS will send the employer a pre-addressed Form 940 near the close of each subsequent calendar year.

Amending the Return

When filing a corrected return, the employer must complete a new Form 940 for the year being amended. The "Amended" box on Form 940 should be checked, and the correct figures should be completed on the form. The return must be signed, and an explanation of the reasons for filing an amended return should be attached.

Final Return

If a company has ceased doing business, a final Form 940 must be completed (check box on Form 940 to indicate a final return) and the balance of the tax paid. In addition, a statement giving the name and address of the person(s) in charge of the required payroll records must be included with Form 940. If the business was sold or transferred, the name and address of the acquiring company should be included in the statement.

Quarterly Deposit Form—FUTA

The employer computes the net FUTA tax on a quarterly basis during the month following the end of each calendar quarter by multiplying 0.6 percent by that part of the first $7,000 of each of the employee's annual wages that the employer paid during the quarter. If the employer's tax liability exceeds $500, the employer must pay before the last day of the month following the end of the quarter. Amounts owed due to a credit reduction (Title VII Advances) should be included with the fourth-quarter deposit. The employer is required to deposit all federal depository tax liabilities (including FUTA) electronically. Chapter 3 enumerated the requirements for each employer. In order to make timely payments, the Electronic Federal Tax Payment System (EFTPS) payment transaction must be initiated at least one business day before the due date of the deposit.

A similar computation and payment for each of the first three quarters of the year is made. If the tax liability for the first quarter is $500 or less, a payment is not required; however, the employer must add the amount of the liability to the amount subject to payment for the next quarter in order to compare the total tax due with the $500 threshold for that quarter. Amounts owed due to a credit reduction (Title XII advances) should be included with the fourth quarter deposit.

As stated in Chapter 3, businesses are required to make their federal tax deposits electronically unless they have $2,500 or less in quarterly tax liabilities and pay their liability when they file their returns.

As shown in Figure 5.2, on pages 5-19 and 5-20, the accumulated tax liabilities of Shannon Heating Company for the 1st and 2nd quarters of 2016 were less than $500; no payment was made for the first two quarters. Since the accumulated liability at the end of the 3rd quarter exceeded the $500 limit, a payment of $562.20 was made on October 31, 2016.

At the time of filing the annual return on Form 940, the employer pays the balance of tax owed for the prior year and not yet paid. If the amount of tax reportable on Form 940 exceeds by more than $500 the sum of amounts deposited each quarter, the employer must pay the total amount owed electronically on or before January 31 following the year for which Form 940 is filed. If the amount owed is $500 or less, the employer may remit it with the annual form. A payment voucher form,

Form 940V, is completed and filed along with Form 940 and the check or money order. This form allows the government to process the payment more efficiently.

As already stated, e-pay or a major credit card can be used to pay the balance due on the return but cannot be used for the required quarterly deposits.

Taxes—Household Employers

Household employers both report and pay their federal unemployment taxes for their household employees with their personal income tax return (Form 1040). Schedule H, *Household Employment Taxes*, is attached to their tax returns, and payment of the unemployment taxes for the previous year is due by April 15. If there are other employees involved in addition to household employees, the employers can choose to include the household employees on their Form 940.

SELF-STUDY QUIZ 5-3

The FUTA taxable wages of Davies Company during 2016 follow. List the amount and the due date of each deposit of FUTA taxes for the year—not in a credit reduction state.

	Amount	Due Date
1st Quarter—$66,000	$	
2nd Quarter—$64,000	$	
3rd Quarter—$42,000	$	
4th Quarter—$25,000	$	

Penalties—FUTA

As indicated in Chapter 3, the Internal Revenue Code subjects employers to civil and criminal penalties for failing to file returns, pay the employment taxes when due, and make timely deposits. These penalties apply, generally, without regard to the type of tax or return involved. The employer is responsible even if the duties of depositing taxes and filing the return have been outsourced. If the third party fails to perform any required action, the employer is still accountable. The last section of Chapter 3 presents all of the penalties.

Information Reports—SUTA

A wide variation exists in the official forms that the states provide for filing the reports required under the unemployment compensation laws. Therefore, the employer must become familiar with the law and regulations of each state in which liability might be incurred. In an increasing number of states, electronic filing of the reports and electronic payment of tax liabilities are required.

The reports required of the employers by the individual states determine (1) the employer's liability for the contributions, (2) the amount of the contribution due on a quarterly basis, and (3) the amount of benefits to which employees will be entitled if they become unemployed. The most important of the required reports follow:

1. Status reports
2. Contribution reports
3. Wage information reports
4. Separation reports
5. Partial unemployment notices

Status Reports

Under the unemployment compensation laws of most states, new employers must register or file an initial statement or status report. This report determines the employer's liability for making contributions into the state unemployment compensation fund.

> **LO 6**
>
> Describe the types of information reports under the various state unemployment compensation laws.

Contribution Reports

All employers liable for contributions under the unemployment compensation law of any state must submit a quarterly **contribution report** or tax return. This report provides a summary of the wages paid during the period and shows the computation of the tax or contribution. Usually, the report must be filed on or before the last day of the month following the close of the calendar quarter, and the tax or contribution must be paid at the same time. Figure 5.5 shows an illustration of a quarterly tax calculation report (Part I).

Wage Information Reports

In most states, employers must make **wage information reports** concerning individual employees. Usually, employers file these reports with the quarterly contribution reports. Figure 5.6 shows an example of a quarterly wage information report (Part II). On the report are listed all employee names, SSNs, taxable wages, taxable tips, and the employer's federal account number. In addition, the number of credit weeks earned by each employee during the quarter could be required. (A *credit week* is defined by the state's unemployment compensation law; for example, Pennsylvania defines a credit week as any calendar week in the quarter during which the person earned remuneration of not less than $50.)

Most states permit the use of the same magnetic tape for reporting state wage information that is used for federal social security reporting purposes. The payroll manager should contact the state agency to determine whether federal-state combined magnetic tape reporting is acceptable.

Separation Reports

Whenever a worker becomes separated from employment, a **separation report**, providing a wage and employment record of the separated employee and the reason for leaving, might be required. Usually, a copy of the report is given to the worker in order that the individual may be informed of any entitlement to unemployment insurance benefits.

ON THE JOB

State unemployment insurance records must be preserved by employers for a certain number of years based on each state's requirements. The periods range from a low in Mississippi of three years to a high in Tennessee of seven years.

FIGURE 5.5

Pennsylvania Form, UC-2. Employer's Report for Unemployment Compensation—Part I

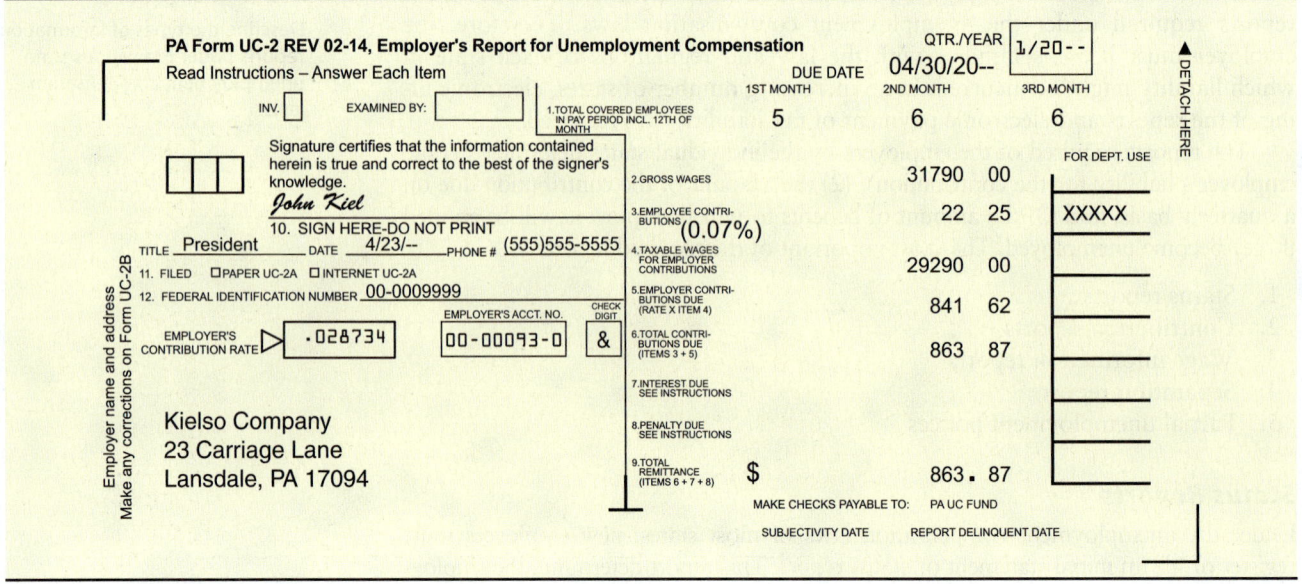

Source: PA Department of Labor & Industry.

FIGURE 5.6

Pennsylvania Form, UC-2A. Employers Report for Unemployment Compensation—Part II

pennsylvania
DEPARTMENT OF LABOR & INDUSTRY

PA Form UC-2A, Employer's Quarterly
Report of Wages Paid to Each Employee

See instructions on separate sheet. Information MUST be typewritten or printed in BLACK ink. Do NOT use commas (,) or dollar signs ($).
If typed, disregard vertical bars and type a consecutive string of characters. If hand printed, print in CAPS and within the boxes as below:

SAMPLE Typed:	1 2 3 4 5 6 . 0 0	SAMPLE Handwritten:	1 2 3 4 5 6 . 0 0	SAMPLE Filled-in: → ●

Employer name (make corrections on Form UC-2B)	Employer PA UC account no.	Check digit	Quarter and year Q / Y Y Y Y	Quarter ending date M M / D D / Y Y Y Y
Kielso Company	00 — 00093-0	&	1/20--	03/31/20--

1. Name and telephone number of preparer	2. Total number of pages in this report	3. Total number of employees listed in item 8 on all pages of Form UC-2A	4. Plant number (if approved)
Nancy Heller (555) 555-5555	1	7	

5. Gross wages, MUST agree with item 2 on UC-2
and the sum of item 11 on all pages of Form UC-2A

▲

	3 1 7 9 0 . 0 0

6. Fill in this circle if you would like the
Department to preprint your employee's
names & SSNs on Form UC-2A next
quarter   →   ◉

7. Employee's Social Security Number	8. Employee's name FI MI LAST	9. Gross wages paid this qtr Example: 123456.00	10. Credit Weeks
0 0 0 0 0 8 2 7 1	J L CARROLL	6 3 0 0 . 0 0	1 3
0 0 0 0 0 1 9 1 8	C H LONG	1 9 0 0 . 0 0	5
0 0 0 0 0 3 7 9 0	H M DORSEY	2 9 9 0 . 0 0	1 3
0 0 0 0 0 6 5 1 0	M F ERNST	2 1 0 0 . 0 0	1 3
0 0 0 0 0 0 0 9 3	J B KIEL	1 0 5 0 0 . 0 0	1 3
0 0 0 0 0 9 0 0 8	A W PINKETT	4 1 0 0 . 0 0	1 3
0 0 0 0 0 1 7 9 2	L B GOLIC	3 9 0 0 . 0 0	1 3
		.	
		.	
		.	
		.	
		.	
		.	
		.	
		.	
		.	
		.	
		.	
		.	
		.	

List any additional employees on continuation sheets in the required format (see instructions).

▲
11. Total gross wages for this page: → | 3 1 7 9 0 . 0 0 |
12. Total number of employees for this page 7

UC-2A REV 07-12   **13. Page** 1 **of** 1

Source: PA Department of Labor & Industry.

Partial Unemployment Notices

Most states require employers to give **partial unemployment notices** to those workers who become "partially unemployed," so that they are informed of their potential eligibility for partial unemployment benefits. **Partial unemployment** refers to employment by the individual's regular employer but on a reduced scale because of lack of work. In most states, the notice must be given to the worker immediately after a week of partial employment has been completed. After that, the employer ordinarily furnishes the worker with some kind of low-earnings report during each week of partial employment so that the worker will be assured of the receipt of supplemental or partial benefits.

Penalties—SUTA

All states have some form of penalty for failure to pay, for the late payment of contributions, and also for failure to file reports. Some states impose a 10 percent penalty if the failure to pay the tax is due to negligence, and in a few states, a 50 percent penalty is imposed if the failure to pay is due to fraud. Many states also deny experience rates to employers who are delinquent in filing reports or paying contributions. In some states, employers who have been delinquent in paying their contributions may be required to pay the contributions monthly rather than quarterly.

KEY TERMS

constructively paid (p. 5-8)	pooled-fund laws (p. 5-11)
contribution report (p. 5-26)	positive-balance employers (p. 5-15)
dismissal payments (p. 5-8)	reciprocal arrangements (p. 5-6)
experience rating (p. 5-10)	reserve-ratio formula (p. 5-15)
interstate employee (p. 5-4)	separation report (p. 5-26)
merit rating (p. 5-10)	status report (p. 5-25)
negative-balance employers (p. 5-15)	Title XII advances (p. 5-11)
partial unemployment (p. 5-28)	voluntary contributions (p. 5-17)
partial unemployment notices (p. 5-28)	wage information reports (p. 5-26)

ANSWERS TO SELF-STUDY QUIZZES

Self-Study Quiz 5-1

4.1% of $188,000 =	$7,708		SUTA tax
6.0% of $188,000 =		$11,280	Gross FUTA tax
4.1% of $188,000 =	$7,708		Credit for SUTA tax paid
1.3% of $188,000 =	2,444	10,152	Additional credit to get to 5.4%
0.6% of $188,000 =		$ 1,128	Net FUTA tax

Self-Study Quiz 5-2

From the Summary of State Unemployment Compensation Laws (Figure 5.1 on page 5-12), the taxable wage in Colorado is $11,800. However, the company receives a credit of $6,000 against this limit because of unemployment taxes paid to Arizona on Castellano's wages in that state. Therefore, the calculation is:

Castellano's wages in Colorado	$26,000
Over taxable limit	14,200
Colorado's SUTA wage limit	$11,800
Credit for wages taxed in Arizona	6,000
Castellano's taxable wages in Colorado	$ 5,800
Moss's SUTA tax rate in Colorado	× 2.9%
Amount of the company's SUTA tax in Colorado	$168.20

Self-Study Quiz 5-3

1st Quarter—$66,000 × 0.006 = $396.00
      no deposit due
2nd Quarter—$64,000 × 0.006 = $384 + $396 = $780
      due on 8/1/2016 (7/31/16 is a Sunday)

3rd Quarter—$42,000 × 0.006 = $252.00
      no deposit due
4th Quarter—($25,000 × 0.006) + $252.00 = $402.00
      due on 1/31/17

KEY POINTS SUMMARY

	Learning Objectives	Key Points	Practical Problems A & B
LO1	Describe the basic requirements for an individual to be classified as an employer or an employee under the Federal Unemployment Tax Act.	• Employer—pays wages or $1,500 or more in a quarter or employs 1 or more in 20 or more weeks. • Employee—legal common-law relationship + agent/commission driver + travelling/city salesperson. • Interstate employees—where localized, base of operations, direction or control, or residence.	5-5, 5-6
LO2	Identify generally what is defined as taxable wages by the Federal Unemployment Tax Act.	• First $7,000 of each employee's earnings is taxed. • Fairly uniform under state laws.	5-14
LO3	Compute the federal unemployment tax, the credit against the tax, and any credit reductions that might apply.	• 6.0 percent of first $7,000 of earnings − 5.4 percent credit (for SUTA taxes paid) = 0.6 percent net FUTA rate. • Experience ratings set SUTA rate for each employer based on past employment record.	5-1, 5-2, 5-3, 5-4, 5-7, 5-9, 5-10, 5-11
LO4	Describe how an experience-rating system is used in determining employers' contributions to state unemployment compensation funds.	• Reserve-ratio formula determines tax rate for each employer (contributions – benefits paid/average payroll). • Some states allow voluntary contributions in order to lower SUTA tax rate.	5-8, 5-12, 5-13, 5-15
LO5	Complete the reports required by the Federal Unemployment Tax Act.	• Annual Form 940 to be completed by January 31st of the following year. • Taxes paid quarterly (if liability each quarter is over $500). • Paid electronically.	5-16, 5-17
LO6	Describe the types of information reports under the various state unemployment compensation laws.	• Information reports, status reports, contribution reports, and wage information reports. • Quarterly contribution reports filed by end of the month following the quarter-end. • Taxes paid with reports.	N/A

MATCHING QUIZ

_____ 1. Reciprocal arrangements
_____ 2. Title XII advances
_____ 3. Negative-balance employers
_____ 4. Dumping
_____ 5. Over $500
_____ 6. Merit rating
_____ 7. Form 940
_____ 8. Household employers
_____ 9. Wage information reports
_____ 10. Voluntary contributions

A. Extra state unemployment contributions made by the employers
B. Favorable employment records result in a lower SUTA tax
C. Annual Federal Unemployment Tax Return
D. Poor experience-rated companies form new companies with lower unemployment tax rates
E. Pay FUTA tax with Schedule H of Form 1040
F. Provide unemployment insurance coverage and payment of benefits to interstate workers
G. Borrowings from federal government to pay unemployment compensation benefits
H. Employers whose reserve account has been charged with more benefits paid out than contributions made
I. Quarterly threshold for mandatory depositing of FUTA taxes
J. Quarterly reports submitted to the state listing employees, SSNs, and taxable wages

QUESTIONS FOR REVIEW

1. What two alternative tests are applied to a business in order to judge whether it is an "employer" and therefore subject to the FUTA tax?
2. What condition would make a household employer a covered employer under FUTA?
3. Charlie Carlson is a full-time student at Wenonah College and works part time in the school's maintenance department. Must the college pay a FUTA tax on Carlson's earnings?
4. Under the Interstate Reciprocal Coverage Arrangement, the services of a worker can be covered in the state of the election of the employer as long as one of three factors exists. What are those three conditions?
5. To what extent does FUTA coverage extend to services that a citizen of the United States performs for an American employer outside the United States?
6. Which of the following types of payments are taxable under FUTA?
   a. Commissions as compensation for covered employment.
   b. Christmas gifts of nominal value.
   c. Courtesy discounts to employees.
   d. Reimbursement of ordinary and necessary business expenses.
   e. Dismissal payments.
7. What is an employer required to do in order to obtain the maximum credit of 5.4 percent against the FUTA tax?
8. An employer, because of a favorable experience rating, is permitted to pay a state contribution at a reduced rate of 1.5 percent. What percentage of taxable wages must be paid in the aggregate to the federal and state governments?
9. What are two situations in which an employer could be liable for a net FUTA tax greater than 0.6 percent?
10. What is the purpose of Title XII advances?
11. In 2015:
    a. Which states had the widest range of SUTA tax rates for employers?
    b. Which state paid the highest weekly maximum benefit (excluding dependency allowances) to qualified unemployed workers?
    c. Which state had the highest taxable wage base for the SUTA tax?
12. How is the SUTA tax rate determined for a new employer?
13. a. For an employer who is subject to FUTA, what is the basic form that must be filed with the federal government?
    b. When must the form be filed?
    c. How are taxable wages computed on the annual return?
14. How are pretax contributions by employees into cafeteria plans presented on Form 940?
15. How does an employer file an amended Form 940?
16. What special steps must be taken when completing Form 940 for a company that has ceased operations during the year?

17. When and how does an employer pay the FUTA taxes?
18. What are the options for paying an amount due (under $500) with the filing of Form 940?
19. How often do employers file wage and contribution reports with their states?
20. What is a separation report?

QUESTIONS FOR DISCUSSION

1. Can the owner of a small business receive unemployment compensation? Explain.
2. What arguments could be made for raising the upper limits of the SUTA tax rates?
3. Check the unemployment compensation law of your state and determine the answers to the following questions:
   a. How do nonprofit organizations, subject to coverage, make payments to the unemployment compensation fund?
   b. Can part-time teachers collect unemployment compensation between school terms?
   c. Can professional athletes receive unemployment compensation?
   d. Are aliens covered by the unemployment compensation law?
   e. How do employers protest or appeal benefit determinations and charges against their accounts?
   f. Briefly describe how a person's weekly benefit rate and maximum benefit amount are determined.
   g. Can an unemployed worker collect additional benefits if he or she has dependents? If so, how much is paid for each dependent?
   h. Does the state provide payment of partial benefits?
   i. Are benefits payable to a female during pregnancy?
   j. Can employers make voluntary contributions to their state unemployment reserve accounts?
   k. For what reasons may an unemployed worker be disqualified from receiving unemployment benefits?
   l. What steps are taken by the state unemployment agency to prevent the improper payment of claims?

4. As a way of curbing the unemployment rate, California has a "shared-work compensation" program. Under this program, a company faced with a layoff of its workers may place its entire workforce on a four-day workweek during the period of hardship. During this period of reduced workweeks, the employees collect partial unemployment benefits. When business rebounds, the firm returns to its normal five-day workweek, and the unemployment compensation benefits cease. Participation in the program must be approved by both the employer and the unions. If, however, the firm is not unionized, management has the discretion of putting the plan into effect.
   a. What are the benefits of such a shared-work compensation program to (1) the employer and (2) the employees?
   b. What disadvantages do you see in the operation of a shared-work compensation program, especially from the viewpoint of organized labor?

PROBLEM SET · A

Since the SUTA rates changes are made at the end of each year and there is much discussion about changes to the FUTA rate, the available 2015 rates were used for FUTA and SUTA.

5-1A · LO 3, 4 Similar to Example 5-3 on page 5-9

During the year, Plum Company has a SUTA tax rate of 4.8%. The taxable payroll for the year for FUTA and SUTA is $123,400. Compute:

   a. Net FUTA tax .... $ _____
   b. Net SUTA tax.. $ _____
   c. Total unemployment taxes .... $ _____

5-2A · LO 3, 4 Similar to Example 5-4 on page 5-10

Peyton Company's payroll for the year is $737,910. Of this amount, $472,120 is for wages paid in excess of $7,000 to each individual employee. The SUTA rate in Peyton Company's state is 2.9% on the first $7,000 of each employee's earnings. Compute:

   a. Net FUTA tax .... $ _____
   b. Net SUTA tax.. $ _____
   c. Total unemployment taxes .... $ _____

5-3A · LO 3, 4 Similar to Example 5-4 on page 5-10

Garrison Shops had a SUTA tax rate of 3.7%. The state's taxable limit was $8,000 of each employee's earnings. For the year, Garrison Shops had FUTA taxable wages of $67,900 and SUTA taxable wages of $83,900. Compute:

   a. Net FUTA tax .... $ _____
   b. Net SUTA tax.. $ _____

5-4A · LO 3, 4 Similar to Example 5-4 on page 5-10

Due to its experience rating, Ianelli, Inc., is required to pay unemployment taxes on its payroll as follows:

   a. Under SUTA for Massachusetts on taxable payroll of $18,000, the contribution rate is 4%.

   b. Under SUTA for New Hampshire on taxable payroll of $24,000, the contribution rate is 2.65%.

   c. Under SUTA for Maine on taxable payroll of $79,000, the contribution rate is 2.9%.

   d. Under FUTA, the taxable payroll is $103,500.

     Compute:

     a. SUTA taxes paid to Massachusetts .... $ _____
     b. SUTA taxes paid to New Hampshire .... $ _____
     c. SUTA taxes paid to Maine... $ _____
     d. FUTA taxes paid .... $ _____

5-5A · LO 1, 3 Similar to Example 5-3 on page 5-9

Donner Company began its operations in September of the current year. During September, the company paid wages of $23,400. For the last quarter of the year, the taxable wages paid amounted to $64,700. None of the employees was paid more than $7,000 this year.

5-5A (concluded)

    a. Is Donner Company liable for FUTA tax this year? Explain.

_____

_____

    b. What is the *net* FUTA tax?... $_____

5-6A • LO 1, 2, 3   Similar to Example 5-2 on page 5-9

In September 2016, Manson Paint Corporation began operations in a state that requires new employers of one or more individuals to pay a state unemployment tax of 3.5% of the first $7,000 of wages paid each employee.

    An analysis of the company's payroll for the year shows total wages paid of $177,610. The salaries of the president and the vice president of the company were $20,000 and $15,000, respectively, for the four-month period, but there were no other employees who received wages in excess of $7,000 for the four months. Included in the total wages were $900 paid to a director who only attended director meetings during the year, $6,300 paid to the factory superintendent, and $2,000 in employee contributions to a cafeteria plan made on a pretax basis—for both federal and state.

    In addition to the total wages of $177,610, a payment of $2,430 was made to Andersen Accounting Company for an audit it performed on the company's books in December 2016. Compute:

    a. Net FUTA tax .... $_____
    b. SUTA tax .... $_____

5-7A • LO 3, 4   Similar to Example 5-1 on page 5-6

In April of the current year, Freeman Steel Company transferred Herb Porter from its factory in Nebraska to its plant in Ohio. The company's SUTA tax rates based on its experience ratings are 3.2% in Nebraska and 3.8% in Ohio. Both states base the tax on the first $9,000 of each employee's earnings. This year, Freeman Steel Company paid Herb Porter wages of $20,900; $2,800 were paid in Nebraska and the remainder in Ohio. Compute:

    a. Amount of SUTA tax the company must pay to Nebraska on Porter's wages .... $_____
    b. Amount of SUTA tax the company must pay to Ohio on Porter's wages .... $_____
    c. Amount of the net FUTA tax on Porter's wages (Ohio is a credit reduction state—
       1.2%.)... $_____

5-8A • LO 4   Similar to Example 5-4 on page 5-10

During 2016, Jeff Smallwood worked for two different employers. Until May, he worked for Rowland Construction Company in Ames, Iowa, and earned $22,000. The state unemployment rate for Rowland is 4.6%. He then changed jobs and worked for Ford Improvement Company in Topeka, Kansas, and earned $29,500 for the rest of the year. The state unemployment rate for Ford is 5.1%. Determine the unemployment taxes (FUTA and SUTA) that would be paid by:

    a. Rowland Construction Company .... $_____
    b. Ford Improvement Company .... $_____

5-9A • LO 3, 4   Similar to Example 5-4 on page 5-10

The partnership of Keenan and Kludlow paid the following wages during this year:

M. Keenan (partner)	$85,000
S. Kludlow (partner)	75,000
N. Perry (supervisor)	53,000
T. Lee (factory worker).............................	34,600
R. Rolf (factory worker)	29,800
D. Broch (factory worker)	6,900
S. Ruiz (bookkeeper)	25,400
C. Rudolph (maintenance).........................	5,100

5-9A (concluded)

In addition, the partnership owed $200 to Rudolph for work he performed during December. However, payment for this work will not be made until January of the following year. The state unemployment tax rate for the company is 2.95% on the first $9,000 of each employee's earnings. Compute:

a. Net FUTA tax for the partnership for this year.................... $ _____

b. SUTA tax for this year .... $ _____

5-10A • LO 3, 4   Similar to Example 5-5 on page 5-11

Peroni Company paid wages of $170,900 this year. Of this amount, $114,000 was taxable for net FUTA and SUTA purposes. The state's contribution tax rate is 3.1% for Peroni Company. Due to cash flow problems, the company did not make any SUTA payments until after the Form 940 filing date. Compute:

a. Amount of credit the company would receive against the FUTA tax for its SUTA contributions.. $ _____

b. Amount that Peroni Company would pay to the federal government for its FUTA tax.. $ _____

c. Amount that the company lost because of its late payments .... $ _____

5-11A • LO 3, 4   Similar to Example 5-7 on page 5-14

During 2016, Jordan Company was subject to the Alaska state unemployment tax of 4.2%. The company's taxable wages for FUTA were $86,700 and for SUTA, $171,000. Compute:

a. SUTA tax that Jordan Company would pay to the state of Alaska............................... $ _____

b. Net FUTA tax for 2016.. $ _____

c. Amount of employees' unemployment tax for 2016 (use the employee's tax rate shown in Figure 5.1 on page 5-12) .... $ _____

5-12A • LO 4   Similar to Example 5-9 on page 5-17

The following unemployment tax rate schedule is in effect for the calendar year 2016 in State A, which uses the reserve-ratio formula in determining employer contributions:

Reserve Ratio	Contribution Rate
0.0% or more, but less than 1.0%	6.7%
1.0% or more, but less than 1.2%	6.4%
1.2% or more, but less than 1.4%	6.1%
1.4% or more, but less than 1.6%	5.8%
1.6% or more, but less than 1.8%	5.5%
1.8% or more, but less than 2.0%	5.2%
2.0% or more, but less than 2.2%	4.9%
2.2% or more, but less than 2.4%	4.6%
2.4% or more, but less than 2.6%	4.3%
2.6% or more, but less than 2.8%	4.0%
2.8% or more, but less than 3.0%	3.7%
3.0% or more, but less than 3.2%	3.4%
3.2% or more	3.1%

Hyram Company, which is located in State A, had an average annual payroll of $850,000 for the three 12-month periods ending on June 30, 2015 (the computation date for the tax year 2016). As of June 30, 2015, the total contributions that had been made to Hyram Company's reserve account, in excess of the benefits charged, amounted to $17,440. Compute:

a. Hyram Company's reserve ratio for 2015.. _____ %

b. 2016 contribution rate for the company .... _____ %

c. Smallest contribution that the company can make in order to reduce its tax rate if State A permits voluntary contributions .... $ _____

d. Tax savings realized by the company, taking into consideration the voluntary contribution made in (c) if the taxable payroll in 2016 is $980,000 .... $ _____

5-13A • LO 4 **Similar to Example 5-9 on page 5-17**

As of June 30, 2015 (the computation date for the 2016 tax rate), Sanchez Company had a negative balance of $1,190 in its unemployment reserve account in State A. The company's average payroll over the last three 12-month periods amounted to $520,000. The unemployment compensation law of State A provides that the tax rate of an employer who has a negative balance on the computation date shall be 7.2% during the following calendar year.

Using the tax rate schedule presented in Problem 5-12A, compute:

a. The smallest voluntary contribution that Sanchez Company should make in order to effect a change in its tax rate .... $ _____

b. The amount of the tax savings as a result of the voluntary contribution if Sanchez Company's taxable payroll for 2016 is $660,000 .... $ _____

5-14A • LO 2, 3, 4 **Similar to Example 5-4 on page 5-10**

Marlene Grady and Pauline Monroe are partners engaged in operating The G&M Doll Shop, which has employed the following persons since the beginning of the year:

V. Hoffman (general office worker)	$1,700 per month
A. Drugan (saleswoman)	$15,000 per year
G. Beiter (stock clerk)	$180 per week
S. Egan (deliveryman)	$220 per week
B. Lin (cleaning and maintenance, part-time) ..	$160 per week

Grady and Monroe are each paid a weekly salary allowance of $950.

The doll shop is located in a state that requires unemployment compensation contributions of employers of one or more individuals. The company is subject to state contributions at a rate of 3.1% for wages not in excess of $8,100. Compute each of the following amounts based upon the 41st weekly payroll period for the week ending October 7, 2016:

a. Amount of FICA taxes (OASDI and HI) to be withheld from the earnings of each person. (Refer to Chapter 3.)

	OASDI	HI
M. Grady	$ _____	$ _____
P. Monroe	_____	_____
V. Hoffman	_____	_____
A. Drugan	_____	_____
G. Beiter	_____	_____
S. Egan	_____	_____
B. Lin	_____	_____

b. Amount of the employer's FICA taxes for the weekly payroll .... _____

c. Amount of state unemployment contributions for the weekly payroll .... $ _____

d. Amount of the net FUTA tax on the payroll .... $ _____

e. Total amount of the employer's payroll taxes for the weekly payroll .... $ _____

5-15A • LO 4 **Similar to Example 5-8 on page 5-15**

Karlson Software Company is located in State H, which enables employers to reduce their contribution rates under the experience-rating system. From 2002 to 2011, inclusive, the company's total contributions to state unemployment compensation amounted to $14,695. For the calendar years 2012 to 2015, inclusive, the contribution rate for Karlson was 2.7%.

The contributions of each employer are credited to an account maintained by the State Unemployment Compensation Commission. This account is credited with contributions paid into the account by the employer and is charged with unemployment benefits that are paid from the account. Starting January 1, 2016, the contributions rate for all employers in State H will be based on the following tax-rate schedule:

5-15A (concluded)

Reserve Ratio	Contribution Rate
Contributions falling below benefits paid...	7.0%
0.0% to 7.9%...	5.5%
8.0% to 9.9%...	4.5%
10.0% to 11.9%..	3.5%
12.0% to 14.9%..	2.5%
15.0% or more	1.5%

The annual payroll for calculation purposes is the total wages payable during a 12-month period ending with the last day of the third quarter of any calendar year. The average annual payroll is the average of the last three annual payrolls. The SUTA tax rate for the year is computed using the information available (benefits received and taxes paid) as of September 30 of the preceding year.

The schedule below shows the total payroll and the taxable payroll for the calendar years 2012 to 2015.

	Calendar Year							
	2012		2013		2014		2015	
	Total Payroll	Taxable Payroll	Total Payroll	Taxable Payroll	Total Payroll	Taxable Payroll	Total Payroll	Taxable Payroll
First Quarter........	$12,000	$12,000	$11,000	$11,000	$13,000	$13,000	$10,000	$10,000
Second Quarter....	11,750	11,750	11,500	11,400	12,750	12,700	9,300	9,300
Third Quarter......	12,500	12,250	12,750	12,400	12,200	12,000	9,350	9,350
Fourth Quarter	13,000	12,500	12,500	12,200	14,000	13,750	—	—

Unemployment benefits became payable to the company's qualified unemployed workers on January 1, 2002. Between that time and September 30, 2015, total benefits amounting to $15,100.90 were charged against the employer's account. Compute:

a. Contribution rate for 2016 .... _____ %

b. Rate for 2016 if $2,000 additional benefits had been charged by mistake to the account of Karlson Software Company by the State Unemployment Compensation Commission .... _____ %

5-16A • LO 5   See pages 5-19, 5-20, and 5-23

As the accountant for Runson Moving Company, you are preparing the company's annual return, Form 940 and Schedule A. Use the following information to complete Form 940 and Schedule A on pages 5-38 to 5-40.

The net FUTA tax liability for each quarter of 2016 was as follows: 1st, $220.10; 2nd, $107.60; 3rd, $101.00; and 4th, $56.10 plus the credit reduction.

Since the net FUTA tax liability did not exceed $500 until the 4th quarter, the company was required to make its first deposit of FUTA taxes on January 31, 2017. Assume that the electronic payment was made on time.

a. One of the employees performs all of his duties in another state—Arizona.

b. Total payments made to employees during calendar year 2016:

California	$102,310
Arizona..	18,490
Total..	$120,800

c. Employer contributions in California into employees' 401(k) retirement plan: $3,500.

d. Payments made to employees in excess of $7,000: $36,500 ($11,490 from Arizona and $25,010 from California).

e. Form is to be signed by Mickey Vixon, Vice President.

f. Phone number—(219) 555-8310.

Form **940 for 20--:** **Employer's Annual Federal Unemployment (FUTA) Tax Return**
Department of the Treasury — Internal Revenue Service

OMB No. 1545-0028

Employer identification number (EIN) 0 0 – 0 0 0 3 7 9 3

Name (not your trade name) RUNSON MOVING COMPANY

Trade name (if any)

Address 423 BRISTOL PIKE

Number   Street   Suite or room number

SACRAMENTO   CA   94203-4523

City   State   ZIP code

Foreign country name   Foreign province/county   Foreign postal code

Type of Return
(Check all that apply.)

☐ **a.** Amended
☐ **b.** Successor employer
☐ **c.** No payments to employees in 20--
☐ **d.** Final: Business closed or stopped paying wages

Instructions and prior-year forms are available at *www.irs.gov/form940.*

Read the separate instructions before you complete this form. Please type or print within the boxes.

Part 1: Tell us about your return. If any line does NOT apply, leave it blank.

1a If you had to pay state unemployment tax in one state only, enter the state abbreviation . **1a** ☐ ☐

1b If you had to pay state unemployment tax in more than one state, you are a multi-state employer . . . . **1b** ☐ Check here. Complete Schedule A (Form 940).

2 If you paid wages in a state that is subject to CREDIT REDUCTION . . . . **2** ☐ Check here. Complete Schedule A (Form 940).

Part 2: Determine your FUTA tax before adjustments for 20--. If any line does NOT apply, leave it blank.

3 Total payments to all employees . . . . **3** | . |

4 Payments exempt from FUTA tax . . . . **4** | . |

Check all that apply: **4a** ☐ Fringe benefits   **4c** ☐ Retirement/Pension   **4e** ☐ Other
                    4b ☐ Group-term life insurance   **4d** ☐ Dependent care

5 Total of payments made to each employee in excess of $7,000 . . . . **5** | . |

6 Subtotal (line 4 + line 5 = line 6) . . . . **6** | . |

7 Total taxable FUTA wages (line 3 – line 6 = line 7) (see instructions) . . . . **7** | . |

8 FUTA tax before adjustments (line 7 x .006 = line 8) . . . . **8** | . |

Part 3: Determine your adjustments. If any line does NOT apply, leave it blank.

9 If ALL of the taxable FUTA wages you paid were excluded from state unemployment tax, multiply line 7 by .054 (line 7 × .054 = line 9). Go to line 12 . . . . **9** | . |

10 If SOME of the taxable FUTA wages you paid were excluded from state unemployment tax, OR you paid ANY state unemployment tax late (after the due date for filing Form 940), complete the worksheet in the instructions. Enter the amount from line 7 of the worksheet . . **10** | . |

11 If credit reduction applies, enter the total from Schedule A (Form 940) . . . . **11** | . |

Part 4: Determine your FUTA tax and balance due or overpayment for 20--. If any line does NOT apply, leave it blank.

12 Total FUTA tax after adjustments (lines 8 + 9 + 10 + 11 = line 12) . . . . **12** | . |

13 FUTA tax deposited for the year, including any overpayment applied from a prior year . **13** | . |

14 Balance due (If line 12 is more than line 13, enter the excess on line 14.)
• If line 14 is more than $500, you must deposit your tax.
• If line 14 is $500 or less, you may pay with this return. (see instructions) . . . . **14** | . |

15 Overpayment (If line 13 is more than line 12, enter the excess on line 15 and check a box below.) . . . . **15** | . |

▶ You **MUST** complete both pages of this form and **SIGN** it.   Check one: ☐ Apply to next return. ☐ Send a refund.

Next ▶

For Privacy Act and Paperwork Reduction Act Notice, see the back of Form 940-V, Payment Voucher.   Cat. No. 11234O   Form **940** (2014)

5-16A (continued)

Name (not your trade name)	Employer identification number (EIN)
RUNSON MOVING COMPANY	00-0003793

Part 5: Report your FUTA tax liability by quarter only if line 12 is more than $500. If not, go to Part 6.

16 Report the amount of your FUTA tax liability for each quarter; do NOT enter the amount you deposited. If you had no liability for a quarter, leave the line blank.

16a **1st quarter** (January 1 – March 31) . . . . 16a [.   ]

16b **2nd quarter** (April 1 – June 30) . . . . 16b [.   ]

16c **3rd quarter** (July 1 – September 30) . . . . 16c [.   ]

16d **4th quarter** (October 1 – December 31) . . . . 16d [.   ]

17 **Total tax liability for the year** (lines 16a + 16b + 16c + 16d = line 17) 17 [.   ] **Total must equal line 12.**

Part 6: May we speak with your third-party designee?

Do you want to allow an employee, a paid tax preparer, or another person to discuss this return with the IRS? See the instructions for details.

☐ **Yes.** Designee's name and phone number [   ] [   ]

Select a 5-digit Personal Identification Number (PIN) to use when talking to IRS [ ][ ][ ][ ][ ]

☐ **No.**

Part 7: Sign here. You MUST complete both pages of this form and SIGN it.

Under penalties of perjury, I declare that I have examined this return, including accompanying schedules and statements, and to the best of my knowledge and belief, it is true, correct, and complete, and that no part of any payment made to a state unemployment fund claimed as a credit was, or is to be, deducted from the payments made to employees. Declaration of preparer (other than taxpayer) is based on all information of which preparer has any knowledge.

✗ **Sign your name here** [   ]   Print your name here [   ]

Print your title here [   ]

Date [/   /   ]   Best daytime phone [   ]

Paid Preparer Use Only   Check if you are self-employed . ☐

Preparer's name	[ ]	PTIN	[ ]
Preparer's signature	[ ]	Date	[/ /]
Firm's name (or yours if self-employed)	[ ]	EIN	[ ]
Address	[ ]	Phone	[ ]
City	[ ] State [ ]	ZIP code	[ ]

Page **2**   Form **940** (2014)

Schedule A (Form 940) for 20--:

Multi-State Employer and Credit Reduction Information
Department of the Treasury — Internal Revenue Service

OMB No. 1545-0028

See the instructions on page 2. File this schedule with Form 940.

Employer identification number (EIN) | 0 | 0 | – | 0 | 0 | 0 | 3 | 7 | 9 | 3 |

Name (not your trade name) RUNSON MOVING COMPANY

Place an "X" in the box of EVERY state in which you had to pay state unemployment tax this year. For each state with a credit reduction rate greater than zero, enter the FUTA taxable wages, multiply by the reduction rate, and enter the credit reduction amount. Do not include in the *FUTA Taxable Wages* box wages that were excluded from state unemployment tax (see the instructions for Step 2). If any states do not apply to you, leave them blank.

Postal Abbreviation	FUTA Taxable Wages	Reduction Rate	Credit Reduction	Postal Abbreviation	FUTA Taxable Wages	Reduction Rate	Credit Reduction
AK	.	× .000	.	NC	.	× .012	.
AL	.	× .000	.	ND	.	× .000	.
AR	.	× .000	.	NE	.	× .000	.
AZ	.	× .000	.	NH	.	× .000	.
CA	.	× .012	.	NJ	.	× .000	.
CO	.	× .000	.	NM	.	× .000	.
CT	.	× .017	.	NV	.	× .000	.
DC	.	× .000	.	NY	.	× .012	.
DE	.	× .000	.	OH	.	× .012	.
FL	.	× .000	.	OK	.	× .000	.
GA	.	× .000	.	OR	.	× .000	.
HI	.	× .000	.	PA	.	× .000	.
IA	.	× .000	.	RI	.	× .000	.
ID	.	× .000	.	SC	.	× .000	.
IL	.	× .000	.	SD	.	× .000	.
IN	.	× .015	.	TN	.	× .000	.
KS	.	× .000	.	TX	.	× .000	.
KY	.	× .012	.	UT	.	× .000	.
LA	.	× .000	.	VA	.	× .000	.
MA	.	× .000	.	VT	.	× .000	.
MD	.	× .000	.	WA	.	× .000	.
ME	.	× .000	.	WI	.	× .000	.
MI	.	× .000	.	WV	.	× .000	.
MN	.	× .000	.	WY	.	× .000	.
MO	.	× .000	.	PR	.	× .000	.
MS	.	× .000	.	VI	.	× .012	.
MT	.	× .000	.				

Total Credit Reduction. Add all amounts shown in the *Credit Reduction* boxes. Enter the total here and on Form 940, line 11 . . . . | . |

For Privacy Act and Paperwork Reduction Act Notice, see the Instructions for Form 940.   Cat. No. 16997C   Schedule A (Form 940) 2014

Source: Internal Revenue Service.

5-17A • LO 5, 6   See pages 5-19, 5-20, 5-26 and 5-27

The information listed below refers to the employees of Lemonica Company for the year ended December 31, 2016. The wages are separated into the quarters in which they were paid to the individual employees.

Name	Social Security #	1st Qtr.	2nd Qtr.	3rd Qtr.	4th Qtr.	Total
Robert G. Cramer......................	000-00-0001	$ 5,800	$ 5,000	$ 5,000	$ 5,200	$ 21,000
Daniel M. English (Foreman)	000-00-0003	13,000	13,400	13,400	13,400	53,200
Ruth A. Small............................	000-00-1998	2,000	2,300	2,300	2,400	9,000
Harry B. Klaus...........................	000-00-7413	11,600	11,700	11,700	11,700	46,700
Kenneth N. George (Manager)..	000-00-6523	13,600	14,000	14,500	15,000	57,100
Mavis R. Jones...........................	000-00-6789	1,600	1,700	1,700	-0-	5,000
Marshall T. McCoy....................	000-00-3334	11,400	11,400	-0-	-0-	22,800
Bertram A. Gompers (President)	000-00-1014	24,500	25,000	25,500	26,300	101,300
Arthur S. Rooks.........................	000-00-7277	-0-	700	1,700	1,700	4,100
Mary R. Bastian	000-00-8111	8,000	8,200	8,200	8,200	32,600
Klaus C. Werner........................	000-00-2623	2,300	2,500	2,500	2,500	9,800
Kathy T. Tyler	000-00-3534	-0-	-0-	11,300	11,700	23,000
Totals		$93,800	$95,900	$97,800	$98,100	$385,600

For 2016, State D's contribution rate for Lemonica Company, based on the experience-rating system of the state, was 2.8% of the first $7,000 of each employee's earnings. The state tax returns are due one month after the end of each calendar quarter. During 2016, the company paid $2,214.80 of contributions to State D's unemployment fund.

Employer's phone number: (613) 555-0029. Employer's State D reporting number: 00596.

Using the forms supplied on pages 5-42 to 5-44, complete the following for 2016:

a. Date and amount of the FUTA tax payment for the fourth quarter of 2016 (State D is not a credit reduction state).

Tax Payment:

Date _____   Amount $_____

b. Employer's Report for Unemployment Compensation, State D—4th quarter only. Item 1 is the number of employees employed in the pay period that includes the 12th of each month in the quarter. For Lemonica Company, the number of employees is eight in October, seven in November, and eight in December. All employees earned 13 credit weeks during the last quarter except for Rooks (8) and Tyler (9).

c. Employer's Annual Federal Unemployment (FUTA) Tax Return—Form 940

Indicate on each form the date that the form should be submitted and the amount of money that must be paid. The president of the company prepares and signs all tax forms.

5-17A (continued)

b.

State D Form UC-2 REV 02-14, Employer's Report for Unemployment Compensation

Read Instructions – Answer Each Item

QTR./YEAR 4/2017

DUE DATE 01/31/2017

1ST MONTH   2ND MONTH   3RD MONTH

DETACH HERE

INV.   EXAMINED BY:

1. TOTAL COVERED EMPLOYEES IN PAY PERIOD INCL. 12TH OF MONTH

Signature certifies that the information contained herein is true and correct to the best of the signer's knowledge.

2. GROSS WAGES

3. EMPLOYEE CONTRIBUTIONS

FOR DEPT. USE

X X X X X X X X X X   XXXXX

10. SIGN HERE-DO NOT PRINT

TITLE _____ DATE _____ PHONE # _____

11. FILED ☐ PAPER UC-2A ☐ INTERNET UC-2A

12. FEDERAL IDENTIFICATION NUMBER _____

4. TAXABLE WAGES FOR EMPLOYER CONTRIBUTIONS

5. EMPLOYER CONTRIBUTIONS DUE (RATE X ITEM 4)

EMPLOYER'S ACCT. NO.   CHECK DIGIT

EMPLOYER'S CONTRIBUTION RATE ▷ 2.8%   00596   1

6. TOTAL CONTRIBUTIONS DUE (ITEMS 3 + 5)

7. INTEREST DUE SEE INSTRUCTIONS

8. PENALTY DUE SEE INSTRUCTIONS

Employer name and address
Make any corrections on Form UC-2B

Lemonica Company
123 Swamp Road
Pikesville, D State 10777-2017

9. TOTAL REMITTANCE (ITEMS 6 + 7 + 8) $.

MAKE CHECKS PAYABLE TO: State D UC FUND

SUBJECTIVITY DATE   REPORT DELINQUENT DATE

State D Form UC-2A, Employer's Quarterly
Report of Wages Paid to Each Employee

See instructions on separate sheet. Information MUST be typewritten or printed in BLACK ink. Do NOT use commas (,) or dollar signs ($).
If typed, disregard vertical bars and type a consecutive string of characters. If hand printed, print in CAPS and within the boxes as below:

SAMPLE Typed: 1 2 3 4 5 6 . 0 0   SAMPLE Handwritten: 1 2 3 4 5 6 . 0 0   SAMPLE Filled-in: → ●

Employer name (make corrections on Form UC-2B)

Employer State D UC account no.

Check digit

Quarter and year Q / YYYY

Quarter ending date MM / DD / YYYY

Lemonica Company   00596   1   4/2017   12/31/2017

1. Name and telephone number of preparer

2. Total number of pages in this report

3. Total number of employees listed in item 8 on all pages of Form UC-2A

4. Plant number (if approved)

5. Gross wages, MUST agree with item 2 on UC-2 and the sum of item 11 on all pages of Form UC-2A ▲

6. Fill in this circle if you would like the Department to preprint your employee's names & SSNs on Form UC-2A next quarter → ◉

7. Employee's Social Security Number	8. Employee's name FI MI LAST	9. Gross wages paid this qtr Example: 123456.00	10. Credit Weeks

List any additional employees on continuation sheets in the required format (see instructions).

11. Total gross wages for this page: →

12. Total number of employees for this page _____

UC-2A REV 07-12

13. Page ____ of ____

5-17A (continued)

c.

Form **940 for 20--:** **Employer's Annual Federal Unemployment (FUTA) Tax Return**

Department of the Treasury — Internal Revenue Service

OMB No. 1545-0028

Employer identification number (EIN)   0 0 — 0 0 0 6 4 2 1

Name *(not your trade name)*   LEMONICA COMPANY

Trade name *(if any)*

Address   123 SWAMP ROAD
Number   Street   Suite or room number

PIKESVILLE   D   10777-2017
City   State   ZIP code

Foreign country name   Foreign province/county   Foreign postal code

Type of Return
(Check all that apply.)

☐ **a.** Amended

☐ **b.** Successor employer

☐ **c.** No payments to employees in 20--

☐ **d.** Final: Business closed or stopped paying wages

Instructions and prior-year forms are available at *www.irs.gov/form940.*

Read the separate instructions before you complete this form. Please type or print within the boxes.

Part 1:   **Tell us about your return. If any line does NOT apply, leave it blank.**

1a   If you had to pay state unemployment tax in one state only, enter the state abbreviation .   **1a** ☐ ☐

1b   If you had to pay state unemployment tax in more than one state, you are a multi-state employer . . . .   **1b** ☐   Check here. Complete Schedule A (Form 940).

2   If you paid wages in a state that is subject to **CREDIT REDUCTION** . . . .   **2** ☐   Check here. Complete Schedule A (Form 940).

Part 2:   **Determine your FUTA tax before adjustments for 20--. If any line does NOT apply, leave it blank.**

3   Total payments to all employees . . . .   **3** [   ] .

4   Payments exempt from FUTA tax . . . .   **4** [   ] .

Check all that apply: **4a** ☐ Fringe benefits   **4c** ☐ Retirement/Pension   **4e** ☐ Other
                        4b ☐ Group-term life insurance   **4d** ☐ Dependent care

5   Total of payments made to each employee in excess of $7,000 . . . .   **5** [   ] .

6   Subtotal (line 4 + line 5 = line 6) . . . .   **6** [   ] .

7   Total taxable FUTA wages (line 3 – line 6 = line 7) (see instructions) . . . .   **7** [   ] .

8   FUTA tax before adjustments (line 7 x .006 = line 8) . . . .   **8** [   ] .

Part 3:   **Determine your adjustments. If any line does NOT apply, leave it blank.**

9   If ALL of the taxable FUTA wages you paid were excluded from state unemployment tax, multiply line 7 by .054 (line 7 × .054 = line 9). Go to line 12 . . . . .   **9** [   ] .

10   If SOME of the taxable FUTA wages you paid were excluded from state unemployment tax, OR you paid ANY state unemployment tax late (after the due date for filing Form 940), complete the worksheet in the instructions. Enter the amount from line 7 of the worksheet . .   **10** [   ] .

11   If credit reduction applies, enter the total from Schedule A (Form 940) . . . .   **11** [   ] .

Part 4:   **Determine your FUTA tax and balance due or overpayment for 20--. If any line does NOT apply, leave it blank.**

12   Total FUTA tax after adjustments (lines 8 + 9 + 10 + 11 = line 12) . . . .   **12** [   ] .

13   FUTA tax deposited for the year, including any overpayment applied from a prior year . . .   **13** [   ] .

14   Balance due (If line 12 is more than line 13, enter the excess on line 14.)
• If line 14 is more than $500, you must deposit your tax.
• If line 14 is $500 or less, you may pay with this return. (see instructions) . . . .   **14** [   ] .

15   Overpayment (If line 13 is more than line 12, enter the excess on line 15 and check a box below.) . . . .   **15** [   ] .

▶ You **MUST** complete both pages of this form and **SIGN** it.

Check one: ☐ Apply to next return.   ☐ Send a refund.

Next ▶

For Privacy Act and Paperwork Reduction Act Notice, see the back of Form 940-V, Payment Voucher.   Cat. No. 11234O   Form **940** (2014)

5-17A (concluded)

c.

Name *(not your trade name)*	Employer identification number (EIN)
LEMONICA COMPANY	00-0006421

Part 5: Report your FUTA tax liability by quarter only if line 12 is more than $500. If not, go to Part 6.

16 Report the amount of your FUTA tax liability for each quarter; do NOT enter the amount you deposited. If you had no liability for a quarter, leave the line blank.

16a **1st quarter** (January 1 – March 31)	**16a**	.
16b **2nd quarter** (April 1 – June 30)	**16b**	.
16c **3rd quarter** (July 1 – September 30)	**16c**	.
16d **4th quarter** (October 1 – December 31)	**16d**	.

17 **Total tax liability for the year** (lines 16a + 16b + 16c + 16d = line 17) **17** .   **Total must equal line 12.**

Part 6: May we speak with your third-party designee?

Do you want to allow an employee, a paid tax preparer, or another person to discuss this return with the IRS? See the instructions for details.

☐ **Yes.**   Designee's name and phone number

        Select a 5-digit Personal Identification Number (PIN) to use when talking to IRS

☐ **No.**

Part 7: Sign here. You MUST complete both pages of this form and SIGN it.

Under penalties of perjury, I declare that I have examined this return, including accompanying schedules and statements, and to the best of my knowledge and belief, it is true, correct, and complete, and that no part of any payment made to a state unemployment fund claimed as a credit was, or is to be, deducted from the payments made to employees. Declaration of preparer (other than taxpayer) is based on all information of which preparer has any knowledge.

✗ Sign your name here

Print your name here

Print your title here

Date   /   /

Best daytime phone

Paid Preparer Use Only   Check if you are self-employed   ☐

Preparer's name	PTIN	
Preparer's signature	Date	/ /
Firm's name (or yours if self-employed)	EIN	
Address	Phone	
City	State	ZIP code

Page **2**   Form **940** (2014)

Source: Internal Revenue Service.

PROBLEM SET · B

Since the SUTA rates changes are made at the end of each year and there is much discussion about changes to the FUTA rate, the available 2015 rates were used for FUTA and SUTA.

5-1B · LO 3, 4 Similar to Example 5-3 on page 5-9

During the year, Zeno Company has a SUTA tax rate of 6.3%. The taxable payroll for the year for FUTA and SUTA is $77,000. Compute:

a. Net FUTA tax .... $ _____
b. Net SUTA tax.. $ _____
c. Total unemployment taxes .... $ _____

5-2B · LO 3, 4 Similar to Example 5-4 on page 5-10

Yengling Company's payroll for the year is $593,150. Of this amount, $211,630 is for wages paid in excess of $7,000 to each individual employee. The SUTA rate in Yengling Company's state is 2.9% on the first $7,000 of each employee's earnings. Compute:

a. Net FUTA tax .... $ _____
b. Net SUTA tax.. $ _____
c. Total unemployment taxes .... $ _____

5-3B · LO 3, 4 Similar to Example 5-4 on page 5-10

Garrison Shops had a SUTA tax rate of 2.7%. The state's taxable limit was $8,000 of each employee's earnings. For the year, Garrison Shops had FUTA taxable wages of $77,900 and SUTA taxable wages of $93,900. Compute:

a. Net FUTA tax .... $ _____
b. Net SUTA tax.. $ _____

5-4B · LO 3, 4 Similar to Example 5-4 on page 5-10

Due to its experience rating, Ianelli, Inc., is required to pay unemployment taxes on its payroll as follows:
1. Under SUTA for New Mexico on taxable payroll of $28,000, the contribution rate is 3.9%.
2. Under SUTA for Colorado on taxable payroll of $23,000, the contribution rate is 2.95%.
3. Under SUTA for Utah on taxable payroll of $65,000, the contribution rate is 4.1%.
4. Under FUTA, the taxable payroll is $94,500.

Compute:

a. SUTA taxes paid to New Mexico................................. $ _____
b. SUTA taxes paid to Colorado .... $ _____
c. SUTA taxes paid to Utah .... $ _____
d. FUTA taxes paid .... $ _____

5-5B · LO 1, 3 Similar to Example 5-3 on page 5-9

Cowen Company began its operations in August of the current year. During August and September, the company paid wages of $2,450. For the last quarter of the year, the taxable wages paid amounted to $3,900. None of the employees were paid more than $7,000 this year.

a. Is Cowen Company liable for FUTA tax this year? Explain.

_____

_____

b. What is the *net* FUTA tax?.. $ _____

5-6B • LO 1, 2, 3   Similar to Example 5-2 on page 5-9

In September 2016, Painter Wax Corporation began operations in a state that requires new employers of one or more individuals to pay a state unemployment tax of 4.1% of the first $7,000 of wages paid each employee.

An analysis of the company's payroll for the year shows total wages paid of $212,640. The salaries of the president and the vice president of the company were $25,000 and $15,000, respectively, for the four-month period, but there were no other employees who received wages in excess of $7,000 for the four months. Included in the total wages were $900 paid to a director who only attended director meetings during the year, $6,300 paid to the factory superintendent, and $2,000 in employee contributions to a cafeteria plan made on a pretax basis—for both federal and state.

In addition to the total wages of $212,640, a payment of $2,000 was made to Andersen Accounting Company for an audit it performed on the company's books in December 2016. Compute:

    a. Net FUTA tax .... $ _____
    b. SUTA tax .... $ _____

5-7B • LO 3, 4   Similar to Example 5-1 on page 5-6

In April of the current year, Steelman Press Company transferred Ken Sherm from its factory in Louisiana to its plant in Florida. The company's SUTA tax rates based on its experience ratings are 3.2% in Louisiana and 3.8% in Florida. The taxable wage limits are $7,700 in Louisiana and $7,000 in Florida. This year, Steelman Press Company paid Ken Sherm wages of $14,190; $4,950 were paid in Louisiana and the remainder in Florida. Compute:

    a. Amount of SUTA tax the company must pay to Louisiana on Sherm's wages... $ _____
    b. Amount of SUTA tax the company must pay to Florida on Sherm's wages....... $ _____
    c. Amount of the net FUTA tax on Sherm's wages .... $ _____

5-8B • LO 4   Similar to Example 5-4 on page 5-10

During 2016, Jake Gore worked for two different employers. Until May, he worked for Wonderman Construction Company in Kansas City, Kansas, and earned $21,500. The state unemployment rate for Wonderman is 4.6%. He then changed jobs and worked for Buxmont Improvement Company in Mobile, Alabama, and earned $33,100 for the rest of the year. The state unemployment rate for Buxmont is 5.1%. Determine the unemployment taxes (FUTA and SUTA) that would be paid by:

    a. Wonderman Construction Company .... $ _____
    b. Buxmont Improvement Company .... $ _____

5-9B • LO 3, 4   Similar to Example 5-4 on page 5-10

The partnership of Cox and Cohen paid the following wages during this year:

M. Cox (partner)	$45,000
S. Cohen (partner)	26,000
N. Tate (supervisor).............................	14,350
T. Gerenski (factory worker)	9,900
R. Sobowski (factory worker)..............	9,450
D. Brunder (factory worker)................	8,910
S. Carsoni (bookkeeper)	11,100
C. Chu (maintenance)...........................	3,900

In addition, the partnership owed $200 to Chu for work he performed during December. However, payment for this work will not be made until January of the following year. The state unemployment tax rate for the company is 2.95% on the first $9,000 of each employee's earnings. Compute:

    a. Net FUTA tax for the partnership for this year............. $ _____
    b. SUTA tax for this year .... $ _____

5-10B • LO 3, 4   Similar to Example 5-5 on page 5-11

Roofling Company paid wages of $319,600 this year. Of this amount, $193,900 was taxable for net FUTA and SUTA purposes. The state's contribution tax rate is 4.3% for Roofling Company. Due to cash flow problems, the company did not make any SUTA payments until after the Form 940 filing date. Compute:

a. Amount of credit the company would receive against the FUTA tax for its SUTA contributions .... $ _____

b. Amount that Roofling Company would pay to the federal government for its FUTA tax .... $ _____

c. Amount that the company lost because of its late payments .... $ _____

5-11B • LO 3, 4   Similar to Example 5-7 on page 5-14

During 2016, Shoupe Company was subject to the New Jersey state unemployment tax of 5.1%. The company's taxable wages for FUTA were $93,400 and for SUTA, $194,300. Compute:

a. SUTA tax that Shoupe Company would pay to the state of New Jersey .... $ _____

b. Net FUTA tax for 2016.. $ _____

c. Amount of employees' unemployment tax for 2016 (use the employee's tax rate shown in Figure 5.1 on page 5-12)... $ _____

5-12B • LO 4   Similar to Example 5-9 on page 5-17

The following unemployment tax rate schedule is in effect for the calendar year 2016 in State A, which uses the reserve-ratio formula in determining employer contributions:

Reserve Ratio	Contribution Rate
0.0% or more, but less than 1.0%...	6.7%
1.0% or more, but less than 1.2%...	6.4%
1.2% or more, but less than 1.4%...	6.1%
1.4% or more, but less than 1.6%...	5.8%
1.6% or more, but less than 1.8%...	5.5%
1.8% or more, but less than 2.0%...	5.2%
2.0% or more, but less than 2.2%...	4.9%
2.2% or more, but less than 2.4%...	4.6%
2.4% or more, but less than 2.6%...	4.3%
2.6% or more, but less than 2.8%...	4.0%
2.8% or more, but less than 3.0%...	3.7%
3.0% or more, but less than 3.2%...	3.4%
3.2% or more	3.1%

Conrad Company, which is located in State A, had an average annual payroll of $1,150,000 for the three 12-month periods ending on June 30, 2015 (the computation date for the tax year 2016). As of June 30, 2015, the total contributions that had been made to Conrad Company's reserve account, in excess of the benefits charged, amounted to $21,560. Compute:

a. Conrad Company's reserve ratio for 2015...................................... _____ %

b. 2016 contribution rate for the company .... _____ %

c. Smallest contribution that the company can make in order to reduce its tax rate if State A permits voluntary contributions .... $ _____

d. Tax savings realized by the company, taking into consideration the voluntary contribution made in (c) if the taxable payroll in 2016 is $1,295,000 .... $ _____

5-13B • LO 4 **Similar to Example 5-9 on page 5-17**

As of June 30, 2015 (the computation date for the 2016 tax rate), Amanda Company had a negative balance of $1,015 in its unemployment reserve account in State A. The company's average payroll over the last three 12-month periods amounted to $525,000. The unemployment compensation law of State A provides that the tax rate of an employer who has a negative balance on the computation date shall be 7.2% during the following calendar year.

Using the tax rate schedule presented in Problem 5-12B, compute:

a. The smallest voluntary contribution that Amanda Company should make in order to effect a change in its tax rate .... $ _____

b. The amount of the tax savings as a result of the voluntary contribution if Amanda Company's taxable payroll for 2016 is $650,000 .... $ _____

5-14B • LO 2, 3, 4 **Similar to Example 5-4 on page 5-10**

Mary Givens and Peggy Moser are partners engaged in operating The G&M Doll Shop, which has employed the following persons since the beginning of the year:

T. Binn (general office worker)	$3,100 per month
W. Ashworth (saleswoman)...	$30,000 per year
K. Bitner (stock clerk)	$280 per week
J. Vern (deliveryman)...	$350 per week
A. Axel (cleaning and maintenance, part-time).....................	$240 per week

Givens and Moser are each paid a weekly salary allowance of $1,000.

The doll shop is located in a state that requires unemployment compensation contributions of employers of one or more individuals. The company is subject to state contributions at a rate of 3.25% for wages not in excess of $10,000.

Compute each of the following amounts based upon the 41st weekly payroll period ending October 7, 2016:

a. Amount of FICA taxes (OASDI and HI) to be withheld from the earnings of each person. (Refer to Chapter 3.)

	OASDI	HI
M. Givens..	$ _____	$ _____
P. Moser	_____	_____
T. Binn..	_____	_____
W. Ashworth	_____	_____
K. Bitner	_____	_____
J. Vern	_____	_____
A. Axel	_____	_____

b. Amount of the employer's FICA taxes for the weekly payroll........... _____
c. Amount of state unemployment contributions for the weekly payroll .... $ _____
d. Amount of the net FUTA tax on the payroll .... $ _____
e. Total amount of the employer's payroll taxes for the weekly payroll .... $ _____

5-15B • LO 4 **Similar to Example 5-8 on page 5-15**

Applebaum Security Company is located in State H, which enables employers to reduce their contribution rates under the experience-rating system. From 2002 to 2011, inclusive, the company's total contributions to state unemployment compensation amounted to $18,135. For the calendar years 2012 to 2015, inclusive, the contribution rate for Applebaum was 3.7%.

5-15B (concluded)

The contributions of each employer are credited to an account maintained by the State Unemployment Compensation Commission. This account is credited with contributions paid into the account by the employer and is charged with unemployment benefits that are paid from the account. Starting January 1, 2016, the contributions rate for all employers in State H will be based on the following tax-rate schedule:

Reserve Ratio	Contribution Rate
Contributions falling below benefits paid......................................	7.0%
0.0% to 7.9%...	5.5%
8.0% to 9.9%...	4.5%
10.0% to 11.9%..	3.5%
12.0% to 14.9%..	2.5%
15.0% or more	1.5%

The annual payroll for calculation purposes is the total wages payable during a 12-month period ending with the last day of the third quarter of any calendar year. The average annual payroll is the average of the last three annual payrolls. The SUTA tax rate for the year is computed using the information available (benefits received and taxes paid) as of September 30 of the preceding year.

The schedule below shows the total payroll and the taxable payroll for the calendar years 2012 to 2015.

	Calendar Year							
	2012		**2013**		**2014**		**2015**	
	Total Payroll	Taxable Payroll	Total Payroll	Taxable Payroll	Total Payroll	Taxable Payroll	Total Payroll	Taxable Payroll
First Quarter.........	$12,000	$12,000	$11,000	$11,000	$13,000	$13,000	$10,000	$10,000
Second Quarter.....	11,750	11,750	11,500	11,400	12,750	12,700	9,300	9,300
Third Quarter.......	12,500	12,250	12,750	12,400	12,200	12,000	9,350	9,350
Fourth Quarter	13,000	12,500	12,500	12,200	14,000	13,750	—	—

Unemployment benefits became payable to the company's qualified unemployed workers on January 1, 2002. Between that time and September 30, 2015, total benefits amounting to $23,194.15 were charged against the employer's account. Compute:

    a. Contribution rate for 2016 .... _____ %

    b. Rate for 2016 if $2,000 additional benefits had been charged by mistake to the account of Applebaum Security Company by the State Unemployment Compensation Commission .... _____ %

5-16B • LO 5   See pages 5-19, 5-20, and 5-23

As the accountant for Monroe Trucking Company, you are preparing the company's annual return, Form 940 and Schedule A. Use the following information to complete Form 940 and Schedule A on pages 5-50 to 5-52.

The net FUTA tax liability for each quarter of 2016 was as follows: 1st, $97.00; 2nd, $87.00; 3rd, $69.70; and 4th, $59.50.

Since the net FUTA tax liability did not exceed $500, the company was not required to make its first deposit of FUTA taxes until January 31, 2017. Assume that the electronic payment was made on time.

    a. One of the employees performs all of his duties in another state—Louisiana.

    b. Total payments made to employees during calendar year 2016:

Texas	$53,450
Louisiana	22,150
Total..........................	$75,600

    c. Employer contributions into employees' 401(k) retirement plan: $1,250.

    d. Payments made to employees in excess of $7,000: $22,150.

    e. Form is to be signed by Vernon Scott, Vice President.

    f. Phone number—(834) 555-5551.

Form **940** for 20--: **Employer's Annual Federal Unemployment (FUTA) Tax Return**

Department of the Treasury — Internal Revenue Service

OMB No. 1545-0028

Employer identification number (EIN) 0 0 – 0 0 0 3 7 9 3

Name (not your trade name) MONROE TRUCKING COMPANY

Trade name (if any)

Address 423 BRISTOL PIKE

Number   Street   Suite or room number

LAREDO   TX   78040-4523

City   State   ZIP code

Foreign country name   Foreign province/county   Foreign postal code

Type of Return
(Check all that apply.)

- ☐ **a.** Amended
- ☐ **b.** Successor employer
- ☐ **c.** No payments to employees in 20--
- ☐ **d.** Final: Business closed or stopped paying wages

Instructions and prior-year forms are available at *www.irs.gov/form940*.

Read the separate instructions before you complete this form. Please type or print within the boxes.

Part 1:   Tell us about your return. If any line does NOT apply, leave it blank.

1a If you had to pay state unemployment tax in one state only, enter the state abbreviation . **1a** ☐ ☐

1b If you had to pay state unemployment tax in more than one state, you are a multi-state employer . . . . **1b** ☐ Check here. Complete Schedule A (Form 940).

2 If you paid wages in a state that is subject to CREDIT REDUCTION . . . . **2** ☐ Check here. Complete Schedule A (Form 940).

Part 2:   Determine your FUTA tax before adjustments for 20--. If any line does NOT apply, leave it blank.

3 Total payments to all employees . . . . **3** ▢ .

4 Payments exempt from FUTA tax . . . . . . **4** ▢ .

Check all that apply: **4a** ☐ Fringe benefits   **4c** ☐ Retirement/Pension   **4e** ☐ Other
4b ☐ Group-term life insurance   **4d** ☐ Dependent care

5 Total of payments made to each employee in excess of $7,000 . . . . **5** ▢ .

6 Subtotal (line 4 + line 5 = line 6) . . . . **6** ▢ .

7 Total taxable FUTA wages (line 3 – line 6 = line 7) (see instructions) . . . . . . **7** ▢ .

8 FUTA tax before adjustments (line 7 x .006 = line 8) . . . . . . **8** ▢ .

Part 3:   Determine your adjustments. If any line does NOT apply, leave it blank.

9 If ALL of the taxable FUTA wages you paid were excluded from state unemployment tax, multiply line 7 by .054 (line 7 × .054 = line 9). Go to line 12 . . . . . . **9** ▢ .

10 If SOME of the taxable FUTA wages you paid were excluded from state unemployment tax, OR you paid ANY state unemployment tax late (after the due date for filing Form 940), complete the worksheet in the instructions. Enter the amount from line 7 of the worksheet . . **10** ▢ .

11 If credit reduction applies, enter the total from Schedule A (Form 940) . . . . . . **11** ▢ .

Part 4:   Determine your FUTA tax and balance due or overpayment for 20--. If any line does NOT apply, leave it blank.

12 Total FUTA tax after adjustments (lines 8 + 9 + 10 + 11 = line 12) . . . . . . **12** ▢ .

13 FUTA tax deposited for the year, including any overpayment applied from a prior year . **13** ▢ .

14 Balance due (If line 12 is more than line 13, enter the excess on line 14.)
- If line 14 is more than $500, you must deposit your tax.
- If line 14 is $500 or less, you may pay with this return. (see instructions) . . . . . . **14** ▢ .

15 Overpayment (If line 13 is more than line 12, enter the excess on line 15 and check a box below.) . . . . **15** ▢ .

► You **MUST** complete both pages of this form and **SIGN** it.

Check one: ☐ Apply to next return.   ☐ Send a refund.

Next ►

For Privacy Act and Paperwork Reduction Act Notice, see the back of Form 940-V, Payment Voucher.   Cat. No. 11234O   Form **940** (2014)

5-16B (continued)

Name *(not your trade name)*	Employer identification number (EIN)
MONROE TRUCKING COMPANY	00-0003793

Part 5: Report your FUTA tax liability by quarter only if line 12 is more than $500. If not, go to Part 6.

16 Report the amount of your FUTA tax liability for each quarter; do NOT enter the amount you deposited. If you had no liability for a quarter, leave the line blank.

    16a 1st quarter (January 1 – March 31) . . . . **16a** [_____ . __]

    16b 2nd quarter (April 1 – June 30) . . . . **16b** [_____ . __]

    16c 3rd quarter (July 1 – September 30) . . . . **16c** [_____ . __]

    16d 4th quarter (October 1 – December 31) . . . . . . **16d** [_____ . __]

17 Total tax liability for the year (lines 16a + 16b + 16c + 16d = line 17) **17** [_____ . __] Total must equal line 12.

Part 6: May we speak with your third-party designee?

Do you want to allow an employee, a paid tax preparer, or another person to discuss this return with the IRS? See the instructions for details.

☐ **Yes.** Designee's name and phone number [_____] [_____]

          Select a 5-digit Personal Identification Number (PIN) to use when talking to IRS [_][_][_][_][_]

☐ **No.**

Part 7: Sign here. You MUST complete both pages of this form and SIGN it.

Under penalties of perjury, I declare that I have examined this return, including accompanying schedules and statements, and to the best of my knowledge and belief, it is true, correct, and complete, and that no part of any payment made to a state unemployment fund claimed as a credit was, or is to be, deducted from the payments made to employees. Declaration of preparer (other than taxpayer) is based on all information of which preparer has any knowledge.

✗ Sign your name here [_____]

  Print your name here [_____]

  Print your title here [_____]

  Date [__ / __ / __]

  Best daytime phone [_____]

Paid Preparer Use Only   Check if you are self-employed . ☐

Preparer's name	[_____]	PTIN	[_____]
Preparer's signature	[_____]	Date	[__ / __]
Firm's name (or yours if self-employed)	[_____]	EIN	[_____]
Address	[_____]	Phone	[_____]
City	[_____] State [_____]	ZIP code	[_____]

Page **2**   Form **940** (2014)

Source: Internal Revenue Service.

Schedule A (Form 940) for 20--:

Multi-State Employer and Credit Reduction Information

Department of the Treasury — Internal Revenue Service

OMB No. 1545-0028

See the instructions on page 2. File this schedule with Form 940.

Employer identification number (EIN) 0 0 – 0 0 0 3 7 9 3

Name *(not your trade name)* MONROE TRUCKING COMPANY

Place an "X" in the box of EVERY state in which you had to pay state unemployment tax this year. For each state with a credit reduction rate greater than zero, enter the FUTA taxable wages, multiply by the reduction rate, and enter the credit reduction amount. Do not include in the *FUTA Taxable Wages* box wages that were excluded from state unemployment tax (see the instructions for Step 2). If any states do not apply to you, leave them blank.

Postal Abbreviation	FUTA Taxable Wages	Reduction Rate	Credit Reduction	Postal Abbreviation	FUTA Taxable Wages	Reduction Rate	Credit Reduction
AK	·	× .000	·	NC	·	× .012	·
AL	·	× .000	·	ND	·	× .000	·
AR	·	× .000	·	NE	·	× .000	·
AZ	·	× .000	·	NH	·	× .000	·
CA	·	× .012	·	NJ	·	× .000	·
CO	·	× .000	·	NM	·	× .000	·
CT	·	× .017	·	NV	·	× .000	·
DC	·	× .000	·	NY	·	× .012	·
DE	·	× .000	·	OH	·	× .012	·
FL	·	× .000	·	OK	·	× .000	·
GA	·	× .000	·	OR	·	× .000	·
HI	·	× .000	·	PA	·	× .000	·
IA	·	× .000	·	RI	·	× .000	·
ID	·	× .000	·	SC	·	× .000	·
IL	·	× .000	·	SD	·	× .000	·
IN	·	× .015	·	TN	·	× .000	·
KS	·	× .000	·	TX	·	× .000	·
KY	·	× .012	·	UT	·	× .000	·
LA	·	× .000	·	VA	·	× .000	·
MA	·	× .000	·	VT	·	× .000	·
MD	·	× .000	·	WA	·	× .000	·
ME	·	× .000	·	WI	·	× .000	·
MI	·	× .000	·	WV	·	× .000	·
MN	·	× .000	·	WY	·	× .000	·
MO	·	× .000	·	PR	·	× .000	·
MS	·	× .000	·	VI	·	× .012	·
MT	·	× .000	·				

Total Credit Reduction. Add all amounts shown in the *Credit Reduction* boxes. Enter the total here and on Form 940, line 11 . . . . ·

For Privacy Act and Paperwork Reduction Act Notice, see the Instructions for Form 940. Cat. No. 16997C **Schedule A (Form 940) 2014**

Source: Internal Revenue Service.

5-17B • LO 5, 6 See pages 5-19, 5-20, 5-26, and 5-27

The information listed below refers to the employees of Brennan Company for the year ended December 31, 2016. The wages are separated into the quarters in which they were paid to the individual employees.

Name	Social Security #	1st Qtr.	2nd Qtr.	3rd Qtr.	4th Qtr.	Total
May S. Sun	000-00-0001	$ -0-	$ 6,100	$ 6,300	$ 4,100	$ 16,500
David R. Maro (Foreman)	000-00-0003	4,000	3,800	4,200	4,700	16,700
Randy A. Wade	000-00-1998	2,900	2,700	2,900	3,200	11,700
Hilary B. Cahn	000-00-7413	3,800	4,100	4,900	5,500	18,300
Paul C. Morse (Manager)	000-00-6523	9,000	8,800	9,500	10,000	37,300
Morrie T. Black	000-00-6789	6,500	4,100	-0-	-0-	10,600
Kelly K. Woods	000-00-3334	2,500	2,300	1,900	1,800	8,500
Terry M. Brennan (President)	000-00-1014	15,000	14,700	15,500	16,900	62,100
Art A. Mintz	000-00-7277	-0-	-0-	7,000	9,800	16,800
Megan T. Rudolph	000-00-8111	8,800	8,400	8,900	-0-	26,100
Kurt A. Weiner	000-00-2623	-0-	7,500	7,700	8,400	23,600
Ryan C. Harrow	000-00-3534	5,300	5,700	6,100	2,400	19,500
Totals		$57,800	$68,200	$74,900	$66,800	$267,700

For 2016, State D's contribution rate for Brennan Company, based on the experience-rating system of the state, was 3.6% of the first $7,000 of each employee's earnings. The state tax returns are due one month after the end of each calendar quarter. During 2016, the company paid $3,024.00 of contributions to State D's unemployment fund.

Employer's phone number: (613) 555-0029. Employer's State D reporting number: 00596.

Using the forms supplied on pages 5-54 to 5-56, complete the following for 2016:

a. The last payment of the year is used to pay the FUTA tax for the fourth quarter (the first three-quarter's liability was more than the $500 threshold). State D is not a credit reduction state.

Tax Payment:

Date _____ Amount $_____

b. Employer's Report for Unemployment Compensation, State D—4th quarter only. Item 1 is the number of employees employed in the pay period that includes the 12th of each month in the quarter. For Brennan Company, the number of employees is ten in October, nine in November, and eight in December. All employees earned 13 credit weeks during the last quarter except for Sun (8) and Harrow (9).

c. Employer's Annual Federal Unemployment (FUTA) Tax Return—Form 940

Indicate on each form the date that the form should be submitted and the amount of money that must be paid. The president of the company prepares and signs all tax forms.

5-17B (continued)

b.

State D Form UC-2 REV 02-14, Employer's Report for Unemployment Compensation

QTR./YEAR **4/2017**

Read Instructions – Answer Each Item

DUE DATE **01/31/2017**

1ST MONTH   2ND MONTH   3RD MONTH

INV. ☐   EXAMINED BY: [ ]   1.TOTAL COVERED EMPLOYEES IN PAY PERIOD INCL. 12TH OF MONTH

FOR DEPT. USE

Signature certifies that the information contained herein is true and correct to the best of the signer's knowledge.

2.GROSS WAGES

3.EMPLOYEE CONTRIBUTIONS

10. SIGN HERE-DO NOT PRINT

TITLE _____ DATE _____ PHONE # _____

4.TAXABLE WAGES FOR EMPLOYER CONTRIBUTIONS

11. FILED ☐ PAPER UC-2A ☐ INTERNET UC-2A

12. FEDERAL IDENTIFICATION NUMBER _____

5.EMPLOYER CONTRIBUTIONS DUE (RATE X ITEM 4)

EMPLOYER'S CONTRIBUTION RATE ▷ **3.6%**

EMPLOYER'S ACCT. NO. **00596**   CHECK DIGIT **1**

6.TOTAL CONTRIBUTIONS DUE (ITEMS 3 + 5)

7.INTEREST DUE SEE INSTRUCTIONS

8.PENALTY DUE SEE INSTRUCTIONS

Brennan Company
123 Swamp Road
Pikesville, D State 10777-2017

9.TOTAL REMITTANCE (ITEMS 6 + 7 + 8) $

MAKE CHECKS PAYABLE TO: State D UC FUND

SUBJECTIVITY DATE   REPORT DELINQUENT DATE

Employer name and address
Make any corrections on Form UC-2B

DETACH HERE ▲

State D Form UC-2A, Employer's Quarterly Report of Wages Paid to Each Employee

See instructions on separate sheet. Information MUST be typewritten or printed in BLACK ink. Do NOT use commas (,) or dollar signs ($). If typed, disregard vertical bars and type a consecutive string of characters. If hand printed, print in CAPS and within the boxes as below:

SAMPLE Typed: `1 2 3 4 5 6 . 0 0`   SAMPLE Handwritten: `1 2 3 4 5 6 . 0 0`   SAMPLE Filled-in: ➡ ●

Employer name (make corrections on Form UC-2B)	Employer State D UC account no.	Check digit	Quarter and year Q / YYYY	Quarter ending date MM / DD / YYYY
Brennan Company	00596	1	4/2017	12/31/2017

1. Name and telephone number of preparer

2. Total number of pages in this report

3. Total number of employees listed in item 8 on all pages of Form UC-2A

4. Plant number (if approved)

5. Gross wages, MUST agree with item 2 on UC-2 and the sum of item 11 on all pages of Form UC-2A ▲

6. Fill in this circle if you would like the Department to preprint your employee's names & SSNs on Form UC-2A next quarter ➡ ◉

7. Employee's Social Security Number	8. Employee's name FI MI LAST	9. Gross wages paid this qtr Example: 123456.00	10. Credit Weeks

List any additional employees on continuation sheets in the required format (see instructions).

11. Total gross wages for this page: ➡

12. Total number of employees for this page _____

UC-2A REV 07-12

13. Page ____ of ____

5-17B (continued)

c.

Form **940** for 20--: **Employer's Annual Federal Unemployment (FUTA) Tax Return**
Department of the Treasury — Internal Revenue Service

OMB No. 1545-0028

Employer identification number (EIN): 0 0 – 0 0 0 6 4 2 1

Name (not your trade name): BRENNAN COMPANY

Trade name (if any):

Address: 123 SWAMP ROAD
Number   Street   Suite or room number

PIKESVILLE   D   10777-2017
City   State   ZIP code

Foreign country name   Foreign province/county   Foreign postal code

Type of Return
(Check all that apply.)

☐ **a.** Amended
☐ **b.** Successor employer
☐ **c.** No payments to employees in 20--
☐ **d.** Final: Business closed or stopped paying wages

Instructions and prior-year forms are available at *www.irs.gov/form940.*

Read the separate instructions before you complete this form. Please type or print within the boxes.

Part 1: Tell us about your return. If any line does NOT apply, leave it blank.

1a If you had to pay state unemployment tax in one state only, enter the state abbreviation . **1a** ☐ ☐

1b If you had to pay state unemployment tax in more than one state, you are a multi-state employer . . . . **1b** ☐ Check here. Complete Schedule A (Form 940).

2 If you paid wages in a state that is subject to **CREDIT REDUCTION** . . . . **2** ☐ Check here. Complete Schedule A (Form 940).

Part 2: Determine your FUTA tax before adjustments for 20--. If any line does NOT apply, leave it blank.

3 Total payments to all employees . . . . **3** |___.__|

4 Payments exempt from FUTA tax . . . . . . **4** |___.__|

Check all that apply: **4a** ☐ Fringe benefits **4c** ☐ Retirement/Pension **4e** ☐ Other
4b ☐ Group-term life insurance **4d** ☐ Dependent care

5 Total of payments made to each employee in excess of $7,000 . . . . **5** |___.__|

6 Subtotal (line 4 + line 5 = line 6) . . . . . . **6** |___.__|

7 Total taxable FUTA wages (line 3 – line 6 = line 7) (see instructions) . . . . . **7** |___.__|

8 FUTA tax before adjustments (line 7 x .006 = line 8) . . . . . . **8** |___.__|

Part 3: Determine your adjustments. If any line does NOT apply, leave it blank.

9 If ALL of the taxable FUTA wages you paid were excluded from state unemployment tax, multiply line 7 by .054 (line 7 × .054 = line 9). Go to line 12 . . . . . . **9** |___.__|

10 If SOME of the taxable FUTA wages you paid were excluded from state unemployment tax, OR you paid ANY state unemployment tax late (after the due date for filing Form 940), complete the worksheet in the instructions. Enter the amount from line 7 of the worksheet . . **10** |___.__|

11 If credit reduction applies, enter the total from Schedule A (Form 940) . . . . . . **11** |___.__|

Part 4: Determine your FUTA tax and balance due or overpayment for 20--. If any line does NOT apply, leave it blank.

12 Total FUTA tax after adjustments (lines 8 + 9 + 10 + 11 = line 12) . . . . **12** |___.__|

13 FUTA tax deposited for the year, including any overpayment applied from a prior year . **13** |___.__|

14 Balance due (If line 12 is more than line 13, enter the excess on line 14.)
• If line 14 is more than $500, you must deposit your tax.
• If line 14 is $500 or less, you may pay with this return. (see instructions) . . . . **14** |___.__|

15 Overpayment (If line 13 is more than line 12, enter the excess on line 15 and check a box below.) . . . . **15** |___.__|

▶ You **MUST** complete both pages of this form and **SIGN** it.

Check one: ☐ Apply to next return. ☐ Send a refund.

Next ▶

For Privacy Act and Paperwork Reduction Act Notice, see the back of Form 940-V, Payment Voucher.   Cat. No. 11234O   Form **940** (2014)

5-17B (concluded)

c.

Name *(not your trade name)*	Employer identification number (EIN)
BRENNAN COMPANY	00-0006421

Part 5: Report your FUTA tax liability by quarter only if line 12 is more than $500. If not, go to Part 6.

16 Report the amount of your FUTA tax liability for each quarter; do NOT enter the amount you deposited. If you had no liability for a quarter, leave the line blank.

16a **1st quarter** (January 1 – March 31) . . . . **16a** [.   ]

16b **2nd quarter** (April 1 – June 30) . . . . **16b** [.   ]

16c **3rd quarter** (July 1 – September 30) . . . . . **16c** [.   ]

16d **4th quarter** (October 1 – December 31) . . . . . . **16d** [.   ]

17 **Total tax liability for the year** (lines 16a + 16b + 16c + 16d = line 17) **17** [.   ] **Total must equal line 12.**

Part 6: May we speak with your third-party designee?

Do you want to allow an employee, a paid tax preparer, or another person to discuss this return with the IRS? See the instructions for details.

☐ **Yes.** Designee's name and phone number [   ] [   ]

Select a 5-digit Personal Identification Number (PIN) to use when talking to IRS [ ] [ ] [ ] [ ] [ ]

☐ **No.**

Part 7: Sign here. You MUST complete both pages of this form and SIGN it.

Under penalties of perjury, I declare that I have examined this return, including accompanying schedules and statements, and to the best of my knowledge and belief, it is true, correct, and complete, and that no part of any payment made to a state unemployment fund claimed as a credit was, or is to be, deducted from the payments made to employees. Declaration of preparer (other than taxpayer) is based on all information of which preparer has any knowledge.

X **Sign your name here** [   ]

Print your name here [   ]

Print your title here [   ]

Date [/   /   ]

Best daytime phone [   ]

Paid Preparer Use Only

Check if you are self-employed . ☐

Preparer's name	[ ]	PTIN	[ ]
Preparer's signature	[ ]	Date	[/ /]
Firm's name (or yours if self-employed)	[ ]	EIN	[ ]
Address	[ ]	Phone	[ ]
City	[ ] State [ ]	ZIP code	[ ]

Page **2**

Form **940** (2014)

Source: Internal Revenue Service.

CONTINUING PAYROLL PROBLEM • A

Refer to the partially completed payroll register that you worked on at the end of Chapter 4. You will now compute the employer's liability for unemployment taxes (FUTA and SUTA) for the pay of January 14. These computations will be used at the end of Chapter 6 in recording the payroll tax entries.

To compute the employer's liability for unemployment taxes, proceed as follows:

1. Enter each employee's gross earnings in the Taxable Earnings—FUTA and SUTA columns.
2. Total the Taxable Earnings—FUTA and SUTA columns.
3. At the bottom of your payroll register, compute the following:

a. Net FUTA tax. Since this is the first pay period of the year, none of the employees are near the $7,000 ceiling; therefore, each employee's gross earnings is subject to the FUTA tax.
b. SUTA tax. Since Kipley Company is a new employer, Pennsylvania has assigned the company a contribution rate of 3.6785% on the first $9,000 of each employee's earnings. Employees pay 0.07% on total gross pay.

Note: Retain your partially completed payroll register for use at the end of Chapter 6.

CONTINUING PAYROLL PROBLEM • B

Refer to the partially completed payroll register that you worked on at the end of Chapter 4. You will now compute the employer's liability for unemployment taxes (FUTA and SUTA) for the pay of January 14. These computations will be used at the end of Chapter 6 in recording the payroll tax entries.

To compute the employer's liability for unemployment taxes, proceed as follows:

1. Enter each employee's gross earnings in the Taxable Earnings—FUTA and SUTA columns.
2. Total the Taxable Earnings—FUTA and SUTA columns.
3. At the bottom of your payroll register, compute the following:

a. Net FUTA tax. Since this is the first pay period of the year, none of the employees are near the $7,000 ceiling; therefore, each employee's gross earnings is subject to the FUTA tax.
b. SUTA tax. Since Olney Company is a new employer, Pennsylvania has assigned the company a contribution rate of 3.6785% on the first $9,000 of each employee's earnings. Employees pay 0.07% on total gross pay.

Note: Retain your partially completed payroll register for use at the end of Chapter 6.

CASE PROBLEM

C1. Reducing a High Unemployment Tax Rate.

Over the past two years, Kermit Stone, the controller of Hilton Company, has been concerned that the company has been paying a large amount of money for state unemployment taxes. On reviewing the "unemployment file" with the head accountant, Deborah Murtha, he learns that the company's tax rate is near the top of the range of the state's experience-rating system.

After calling the local unemployment office, Stone realizes that the turnover of employees at Hilton Company has had an adverse effect on the company's tax rates. In addition, after consulting with Murtha, he discovers that the eligibility reports that come from the state unemployment office are just signed and sent back to the state without any review.

The eligibility reports are notices that an ex-employee has filed a claim for unemployment benefits. By signing these reports "blindly," the company, in effect, tells the state that the employee is eligible for the benefits. Any benefits paid are charged by the state against Hilton Company's account.

Stone is convinced that the rates the company is paying are too high, and he feels that part of the reason is the "blind" signing of the eligibility reports. Besides this, he wonders what other steps the company can take to lower its contributions rate and taxes.

Submit recommendations that might help Stone reduce the "unfair" burden that the unemployment compensation taxes are leveling on Hilton Company.

CHAPTER 6

Analyzing and Journalizing Payroll

A s you know, the title of this book is *Payroll Accounting*. In the first five chapters, we focused on payroll discussions. Now is the time to look at the accounting part. You remember—the debits and the credits, the journal and the ledger, the payroll registers, and the employees' earnings records.

Payroll transactions must be journalized—recording the payroll, the employer's payroll taxes, the payment of the payroll-related liabilities, and the adjustment required at the end of the accounting period. These entries must then be posted to the appropriate general ledger accounts.

LEARNING OBJECTIVES

After studying this chapter, you should be able to:

1 Record payrolls in payroll registers and post to employees' earnings records.

2 Understand the various deductions—both voluntary and involuntary (taxes and garnishments)—that are taken out of employees' gross pay.

3 Journalize the entries to record the payroll and payroll taxes.

4 Post to the various general ledger accounts that are used to accumulate information from the payroll entries.

5 Explain the recording of the payroll tax deposits.

6 Understand the need for end-of-period adjustments.

This chapter presents the procedures for recording the payroll in a payroll register, transferring information from the payroll register to the employees' earnings records, recording these transactions in the company's book of original entry, and posting them to the proper ledger accounts. Today, many of these functions are done by sophisticated computer programs. However, the payroll professional must understand the steps that the computer is performing.

We will also look at the various withholdings that can come out of an employee's pay and some issues that the employer must be aware of in making these deductions. In addition, the methods of paying employees are detailed in this chapter.

The Payroll Register

As you have seen in Figure 1.9, on page 1-21, and in completing the Continuing Payroll Problem, the payroll register, which in most cases will be computer-generated, gives detailed information about the payroll for each pay period.

To summarize, the payroll register may provide the following types of information:

1. The title of the form.
2. The period covered by the payroll and the pay date.
3. Department or branch. Some large businesses with many departments or branches prepare a separate sheet in the payroll register for each department or branch on each payday. Other firms provide "distribution"

LO 1

Record payrolls in payroll registers and post to employees' earnings records.

columns such as "Sales Salaries," "Office Salaries," and "Plant Wages" for classifying the gross wages and salaries according to the nature of the wage and salary expense. The total of each distribution column shows the total amount of that department's wage expense.

4. A column to record the name of each employee. Many businesses provide a column to record an identifying number such as the time clock number for each employee.

5. Marital status and number of withholding allowances. This information determines the income tax deductions. In some cases, this information is presented only in the employees' earnings records.

6. A record of time worked. Many companies show detailed information in the payroll register as to hours worked each day by each employee. Separate columns can be used to show a total of regular hours worked and a total of overtime hours worked during the pay period. This information helps a business that schedules much overtime work.

7. The regular rate of pay and the amount earned at the regular rate.

8. A space to record the overtime rate and the total earnings at the overtime rate. Some companies prefer to show an Overtime Premium Earnings column in place of the Overtime Earnings column. With this approach, as discussed in Chapter 2, the regular earnings is equal to the regular hourly rate of pay multiplied by the total hours worked, and the overtime premium is equal to the extra one-half rate of pay multiplied by the overtime hours.

$$\text{e.g., } \text{Collins}[(\$15.20 \times 44 \text{ hours}) + (\$7.60 \times 4 \text{ hours})]$$

9. A column to record the total earnings.

10. Information about deductions from total earnings. A separate column may be provided for each type of deduction. The various deductions will be discussed later in this chapter.

11. A column to show the net amount paid (total earnings less deductions). When paying by check, a company usually provides a column for the number of each employee's paycheck.

12. Some firms provide special columns in the payroll register to indicate that portion of the employee's wages taxable under the Federal Insurance Contributions Act (OASDI and HI) and other laws that require payment of taxes only on wages up to the taxable limits.

FIGURE 6.1
Payroll Register (left side)

NO.	NAME	MARITAL STATUS	NO. W/H ALLOW.	TIME RECORD						REGULAR EARNINGS			OVERTIME EARNINGS		
				M	T	W	T	F	S	HOURS	RATE PER HOUR	AMOUNT	HOURS	RATE PER HOUR	AMOUNT
10	Collins, Chris R.	M	2	8	8	8	8	8	4	40	15 20	6 0 8 00	4	22 80	9 1 20
12	Banks, Carolyn B.	M	4	8	8	8	8	10		40	17 10	6 8 4 00	2	25 65	5 1 30
13	Carson, Henry S.	S	1	8	8	8	8	8		40	16 30	6 5 2 00			
23	O'Brien, LuAnn T.	M	2	8	8	8	8	8	8	40	15 90	6 3 6 00	8	23 85	1 9 0 80
24	Rudolph, Beth M.	S	1	8	8	8	0	8		32	16 10	5 1 5 20			
36	**Totals**											224 9 7 20			22 6 5 50

FOR WEEK ENDING *January 17, 20--*   Payday January 17, 20--

The only information needed to be keystroked will be the employee's number or name and the time worked. In some cases this information would be automatically transferred from the time-keeping device. The program will then calculate and print the other information based on the data stored for each employee and the particular computer program. Only a small number of firms prepare the registers manually. The partial payroll register shown in Figure 6.1 contains most of the information outlined above. This register is used to compute the pay for hourly workers for a weekly pay period. The layout of the section devoted to time or hours worked will vary, depending on the payroll period and the work schedules of each individual business.

Proving the Totals of the Payroll Register

As shown later in this chapter, the payroll register provides the information needed in preparing the journal entries to record (1) the wages earned, deductions from wages, and net amount paid each payday and (2) the employer's payroll taxes. Prior to making the journal entry to record the payroll, check the accuracy of the amounts entered in the payroll register by proving the totals of the money columns. Prove the partial payroll register shown in Figure 6.1 as follows:

Proof:

Regular earnings	$22,497.20	
Overtime earnings	2,265.50	
Total earnings		$24,762.70
FICA tax withheld—OASDI	$ 1,535.29	
FICA tax withheld—HI	359.06	
Federal income taxes withheld	3,714.00	
State income taxes withheld	55.25	
Group insurance withheld	54.70	
Total deductions		$ 5,718.30
Total net pay		19,044.40
Total earnings		$24,762.70

In preparing the journal entry to record a payroll, you make an entry each payday to record the aggregate amount of wages earned, deductions made, and net payments to all employees, as determined from the Totals line of the payroll register. After making the journal entry, you must transfer, or post, the information from the journal to the appropriate general ledger accounts.

FIGURE 6.1 (concluded)
Payroll Register (right side)

DEPT. ACCOUNTING—10

TOTAL EARNINGS	FICA OASDI	HI	FED. INCOME TAX	STATE INCOME TAX	GROUP INS.	CHECK NO.	NET PAID AMOUNT	FICA OASDI	HI	FUTA & SUTA	
6 9 9 20	4 3 35	10 14	39 00	4 78	9 00	898	5 9 2 93	6 9 9 20	6 9 9 20	6 9 9 20	1
7 3 5 30	4 5 59	10 66	26 00	6 11	9 00	899	6 3 7 94	7 3 5 30	7 3 5 30	7 3 5 30	2
6 5 2 00	4 0 42	9 45	71 00	5 04	3 90	900	5 2 2 19	6 5 2 00	6 5 2 00	6 5 2 00	3
8 2 6 80	5 1 26	11 99	58 00	6 14	9 00	901	6 9 0 41	8 2 6 80	8 2 6 80	8 2 6 80	4
5 1 5 20	3 1 94	7 47	50 00	3 90	3 90	902	4 1 7 99	5 1 5 20	5 1 5 20	5 1 5 20	5
247 6 2 70	15 35 29	3 59 06	37 14 00	5 5 25	5 4 70		190 4 4 40	247 6 2 70	247 6 2 70	247 6 2 70	36

In most companies having computer-driven payroll systems, the payroll programs are interfaced with the general ledger programs. In these systems, computers generate the payroll entries into a printed journal-entry format and post to the various general ledger accounts automatically from these entries.

Using the Information in the Payroll Register

In addition to serving as the source for preparing journal entries to record the payroll and the employer's payroll taxes, the payroll register provides information that meets some of the recordkeeping requirements of the various payroll acts. Also, the register provides data used in preparing periodic reports required by various laws (e.g., hours worked each day as required by the Fair Labor Standards Act).

Besides the information contained in the payroll register, businesses must provide information about the accumulated earnings of each employee. Therefore, companies keep a separate payroll record on each employee— the employee's earnings record. This record, introduced in Figure 1.10, on page 1-22, is discussed in the following section.

The Employee's Earnings Record

The employee's earnings record, a supplementary record, provides information for:

1. *Preparing the payroll register* from the earnings records, which contain the information needed to compute gross earnings and to determine the amount to withhold for income tax purposes.
2. *Preparing reports* required by state unemployment compensation or disability laws.
3. *Determining when the accumulated wages of an employee reach the cutoff level* for purposes of FICA (OASDI), FUTA, or SUTA. As shown in Figure 6.2, a special "Cumulative Earnings" column is provided so that the total amount of accumulated wages can be recorded each pay period. Thus, when the FICA (OASDI), FUTA, or SUTA cutoff has been reached, the record shows that the employee or the employer no longer has a liability for that particular tax during the rest of the calendar year. [In Figure 6.1, the FUTA and SUTA taxable wage cutoffs are the same ($7,000). However, another separate column would be needed in the payroll register if there were a different cutoff for the SUTA tax.]
4. *Preparing payroll analyses* for governmental agencies and for internal management control. Information such as the department in which the employee works and the job title serves as the basis for such analyses.
5. *Settling employee grievances* regarding regular pay and overtime pay calculations and the withholding of amounts for income taxes and other purposes.
6. *Completing Forms W-2*, which show for each employee the annual gross earnings, income taxes withheld, wages subject to FICA taxes, and FICA taxes withheld.

A business keeps an employee's earnings record for each employee whose wages are recorded in the payroll register. Each payday, after the information has been recorded in the payroll register, the information for each employee is posted to the employee's earnings record. The columns are arranged so that the information can be transferred easily. The earnings record shown in Figure 6.2 is arranged for weekly pay periods. You will note that totals are provided for each quarter so that you can enter information easily on the quarterly tax returns. The bottom of page 1 of the earnings record shows a line for semiannual totals. The bottom of page 2 of the form, which is not illustrated, shows a line for annual totals, which you will need in preparing Form 940, W-2s, and other annual reports.

FIGURE 6.2
Employee's Earnings Record (page 1)

WEEK	20- WEEK ENDING	TOTAL WORKED DAYS	TOTAL WORKED HRS.	REGULAR EARNINGS HRS.	RATE	AMOUNT	OVERTIME EARNINGS HRS.	RATE	AMOUNT	FICA OASDI	HI	FEDERAL INCOME TAX	STATE INCOME TAX	GROUP INSURANCE	CK. NO.	NET PAID AMOUNT	CUMULATIVE EARNINGS	TIME LOST
1	1/3	5	44	40	15 20	6 0 8 00	4	22 80	9 1 20	4 3 35	1 0 14	3 9 00	4 78	9 00	510	5 9 2 93	6 9 9 20	
2	1/10	5	42	40	15 20	6 0 8 00	2	22 80	4 5 60	4 0 52	9 48	3 4 00	4 47	9 00	706	5 5 6	1 3 5 2 80	
3	1/17	6	44	40	15 20	6 0 8 00	4	22 80	9 1 20	4 3 35	1 0 14	3 9 00	4 78	9 00	898	5 9 2 93	2 0 5 2 00	
4																		
5																		
6																		
7																		
8																		
9																		
10																		
11																		
12																		
13																		
QUARTER TOTAL																		
1																		
2																		
13																		
QUARTER TOTAL																		
SEMIANNUAL TOTAL																		

DEPARTMENT	OCCUPATION	WORKS IN (STATE)	S.S. ACCOUNT NO.	NAME-LAST	FIRST	MIDDLE	NO. W/H ALLOW.
A-10	Adm. Ass't	XXX	000-00-1186	Collins	Chris	Ruth	2

SEX: F [X] / M
MARITAL STATUS M

Recording the Gross Payroll and Withholdings

After you have recorded the payroll in the payroll register and posted to the employees' earnings records, you must enter the information in the employer's accounting system. An entry for the totals of each payroll period should be made in the general journal and posted to the general ledger. You can obtain the amounts needed for this entry from the Totals line at the bottom of the last payroll register sheet.

The following journal entry to record the payroll includes a debit to the appropriate expense account(s) for the gross payroll and credits to the various liability accounts for the withholdings from the pay and for the net amount to be paid employees:

	Debit	Credit
Salary Expense	XXX	
Liabilities (Withholdings)		XXX
Cash or Salaries Payable (Net Pay)		XXX
To record the payment of salaries and the liabilities for the employees' taxes withheld.		

Gross Payroll

You should record the total gross payroll (regular earnings and overtime earnings) as the debit portion of the payroll entry. The account has a title such as *Wages Expense* or *Salaries Expense*. In the case of a company with many departments or cost centers, the accounts would have titles such as *Wages Expense—Department A*, *Wages Expense—Maintenance*, and *Wages Expense—Residential Services*. These accounts show the total gross earnings that the employer incurs as an *expen*se each payday.

FICA Taxes—Employee

LO 2

Understand the various deductions—both voluntary and involuntary (taxes and garnishments)—that are taken out of employees' gross pay.

The employer must withhold FICA taxes for each employee. Since the employer has withheld these taxes from the pay of the employees and now owes this amount to the IRS, the taxes withheld represent a *liability* of the employer. When recording the payroll, you should credit accounts entitled *FICA Taxes Payable—OASDI* and *FICA Taxes Payable—HI* for the amounts withheld.

Federal Income Taxes

Employers must withhold a percentage of their employees' wages for income tax purposes. Chapter 4 presented the methods of determining the amounts to be withheld from wages for income tax purposes. As with FICA taxes withheld, the employer also owes to the IRS the federal income taxes withheld from the employees' pay. You should keep a separate account in the general ledger for recording the employer's *liability* for the amount of federal income taxes withheld.

A suitable title for this account, *Employees Federal Income Taxes Payable*, may be abbreviated to read *Employees FIT Payable*. The account is credited for the total amount of federal income taxes withheld each payday and is subsequently debited for the amounts paid to a depositary or to the IRS.

State and City Income Taxes

Employers may be required to withhold state and city income taxes in addition to the federal income taxes. You should keep a separate account in the general ledger for recording the employer's *liability* for the amount of each kind of income tax withheld. Account titles that may be used include *Employees State Income Taxes (SIT) Payable* and *Employees City Income Taxes (CIT) Payable*.

Employees' Contributions to State Funds

A few states require employees to contribute to state unemployment compensation or disability funds. In states requiring employee contributions, the employer deducts the amount of the contributions from the employees' wages at the time the wages are paid. The *liability* for employees' contributions may be recorded in the same account as the employer's SUTA contributions; namely, *SUTA Taxes Payable*. If employees make contributions to a disability benefit fund, this amount is usually reported separately to the state and should be recorded in a separate liability account such as *Employees Disability Contributions Payable*.

Other Payroll Deductions

Besides FICA taxes, state unemployment contributions, and income taxes, most companies have other deductions that must be taken into consideration when preparing the payroll. Regardless of the number or the types of deductions made from employees' wages, we must provide a systematic means of keeping a record of the total wages for each employee, the deductions for each purpose, and the net amount paid.

Although you should have a separate column in the payroll register for each deduction, the payroll register may become too cumbersome if there are too many columns for deductions. Many businesses, therefore, use a payroll register with a separate column for each of the major deductions and lump all other deductions together in one column headed "Other Deductions." Some companies use only one column for deductions and place the entire total in that column. If this practice is followed, it is necessary to have a supplementary record of deductions showing a detailed breakdown of the total for each employee. This supplementary record serves as the basis for obtaining the figure for total deductions shown in the payroll register.

Many payroll deductions result from company policies, collective bargaining agreements, court orders, or employee authorizations. Some of the purposes for making deductions include:

1. Group insurance.
2. Health insurance.
3. Purchase of government savings bonds.
4. Union dues.
5. Garnishment of wages.
   a. Child support.
   b. Federal tax levy.
6. Pension and retirement contributions.

Group Insurance

Many companies have a group insurance program for employees. Such programs usually permit employees to obtain life insurance at a much lower rate than would be possible if the employee purchased the insurance as an individual. Under some group insurance plans, the employer and the employee share the cost of the insurance premium. The employees' share may be deducted from their wages every payday, every month, or every quarter.

When recording a payroll that makes deductions from employees' wages for group insurance, the amount withheld from their wages is applied toward the payment of their share of the premium. The total amount withheld is credited to a *liability* account with a title such as *Group Insurance Premiums Collected* or *Group Insurance Payments Withheld*. This general ledger account serves the same purpose as the accounts used to record payroll taxes withheld from employees' wages. When the premiums are paid to the insurance company, the liability account will be debited.

Health Insurance

Many companies have developed their own health insurance plans for employees or are members of private insurance groups that provide coverage for employees of companies that are members of the group. If employees bear the cost or a portion of the cost of such insurance, the portion paid by the employees is usually deducted every payday from the wages of the employees. The amounts withheld from the employees' wages for health insurance are credited to a *liability* account such as *Health Insurance Premiums Collected*. If these withholdings are made by means of a salary reduction for a qualified benefit under an Internal Revenue Department approved cafeteria plan, the premiums are paid with pretax dollars (not included in taxable income for FIT withholding).

Employers often pay the premium for health insurance in advance to the insurance carrier. At the time of paying the premium, a prepaid expense account such as *Prepaid Health Insurance* is debited for the amount paid the carrier. This account is adjusted periodically through the health insurance or fringe benefit expense account and, if applicable, the employees' withholding account.

Purchase of Government Savings Bonds

Employees are encouraged to invest a certain amount of their wages in government savings bonds. Such plans or similar savings plans encourage employees to save a certain amount of each salary payment. The theory behind such deductions is that most employees will not miss a small amount that is set aside each payday, and over a period of time the deductions accumulate into a sizable amount.

Employees authorize their employer to make payroll deductions for the purchase of savings bonds by completing authorization forms that indicate the amount to be withheld and the frequency. The amounts withheld from the paychecks are sent to the employers' Treasury Direct accounts which are set up by the employees with the United States Treasury. In their Direct accounts, employees decide what type and dollar value of savings bond they want to purchase.

Union Dues

In companies in which employees are members of unions that require employees to pay dues to the union, many employees pay their dues, assessments, and initiation fees through deductions from wages, known as a check-off system. Amounts withheld from union members' wages are credited to a *liability* account such as *Union Dues Payable*. Monthly, or as agreed upon by the union and the employer, the amounts withheld are turned over to the treasurer of the union. At this time, a journal entry is made in which the payment of union dues is recorded by debiting the liability account and crediting the cash account.

Garnishment of Wages

Garnishment refers to the legal or equitable procedure by which a portion of the wages of any person must be withheld for payment of a debt. Through the garnishment process, a creditor, with the aid of the courts, may require the employer to hold back a portion of the debtor's wages and pay that amount to the court or to the creditor. In some companies, the amounts to be held back are deducted each payday from the employee's wages. Ignoring a garnishment order means the employee's debt becomes the company's debt by default judgment.

Generally, the following priority withholding order applies to these wage attachments: (1) bankruptcy; (2) federal tax levy or child support order, whichever is delivered first; and (3) creditor, student loan, or federal administrative wage garnishments. Bankruptcy orders under Chapter 13 of the Bankruptcy Act have the highest priority over all other claims. All other garnishment withholdings must stop with the exception of child support or repaying an employee's loan from his or her retirement plan account.

The Consumer Credit Protection Act (CCPA) restrictions on the amount of an employee's pay that can be garnished are based on an employee's disposable earnings. **Disposable earnings** are the earnings remaining after withholding for federal and state income taxes, FICA taxes, state unemployment and disability taxes, and deductions required for state employees' retirement systems. Since they do not pass to the employer (cash or additions to debit or credit card receipts), tips are not included in disposable earnings. However, service charges that are passed on to the employee by the employer are considered part of the disposable earnings equation.

The maximum amount of disposable earnings that can be garnished to repay a debt is the lesser of:

25% of disposable earnings for the week; or the amount by which the disposable earnings for the week exceed 30 times the federal minimum wage rate (does not apply to garnishments for bankruptcy, child support or federal or state tax levies).

In general, the Act limits the amount of wages subject to garnishment to

- Child support: 50%–65% of disposable earnings
- Creditor garnishment: 25% of disposable earnings
- Administrative wage garnishment: 15% of disposable earnings
- Student loan garnishment: 15% of disposable earnings

These maximum deductions apply regardless of the number of garnishments received on an employee.

For federal tax levies, the IRS instructs employers to withhold the difference between the employee's take-home pay and the exempt amount. This allows the employee's voluntary deductions to continue. In the case of state tax levies, it is possible that an employee's entire net pay can be used to satisfy a state tax levy (leaving the employee with no paycheck). Garnishments for child or spousal support, bankruptcy repayment agreements, and state tax levies are not affected by the new minimum wage.

The Social Security Administration (SSA) has started to use the administrative wage garnishment to collect delinquent overpayments owed by former beneficiaries of the social security program. Unlike other credits, the SSA does not need a court order to initiate this garnishment process.

The provisions of the Consumer Credit Protection Act prohibit an employer from discharging an employee simply because the employee's wages are subject to garnishment for one indebtedness. If another garnishment for a second indebtedness should arise, the worker could be discharged, provided a considerable amount of time had not elapsed between the two occasions of indebtedness.

The payroll manager should also be aware that state garnishment laws that are more favorable to employees have priority over the federal law.

Child Support

The Family Support Act requires the immediate withholding for child support payments for all cases supported by a court order. The amount withheld is equal to the amount of the delinquency, subject to the limits prescribed in the federal garnishment law. Employers may withhold a fee, set by each state, for administrative costs. (In cases of support orders, the limits on the amounts that can be taken from an employee's pay are 50 percent of disposable income if the employee supports a second family and 60 percent if not. These limits increase to 55 percent and 65 percent if the employee is in arrears for 12 weeks or more.) Tips are part of the disposable earnings for child support purposes—whether in the form of cash, debit or credit card receipts, or a set service charge.

Child support takes precedence over most voluntary and involuntary deductions. In the case of multiple support orders, the employer is to allocate monies to each order from the employee's available disposable income.

In the case of competing orders, the process begins with the deduction of the child support order. Then, the other garnishment is satisfied according to the rules stated above for repayment of a creditor debt.

ON THE **JOB**

State garnishment laws either set a flat weekly exempt amount (e.g., Oregon) or use the state minimum wage to determine an exempt amount (e.g., Illinois).

EXAMPLE 6-1

Huffman Company has a child support order outstanding on one of its employees (Charles Suffert—$170 per week). Charles Suffert's disposable income is $950 per week. A new garnishment is received for a $5,000 debt to a credit card company. The company would take an additional $237.50 out of Suffert's pay.

Lesser of:

25% × $950	=	$237.50 or
$950 − (30 × $7.25)	=	$732.50

All states' child support agencies offer electronic payment options and close to twenty states require employers, who meet certain conditions, to remit the payments electronically. For example, employers in Florida with ten or more employees or that pay $30,000 or more in annual state taxes must remit these support payments electronically.

Federal Tax Levy

Federal tax levies take second priority after wages withheld for child support (if received prior to the tax levy). If a tax levy is in place prior to the child support order, the employer must call the issuing agency so that an alternate payment plan can be worked out with the IRS. The only portions of wages that are exempt from a federal tax levy are the taxpayer's standard deduction (single—$6,300; head of household—$9,250; married—$12,600) and the personal exemptions ($4,000) allowed for the tax year divided by the number of pay periods in the year. These tax levies are also suspended if a debtor declares bankruptcy.

The IRS uses Form 668-W—**Notice of Levy on Wages, Salary and Other Income** (not illustrated)—to notify an employer of a tax levy. Copies of the form must then be forwarded to the employee for completion of a statement of filing status and exemptions. This information will then allow the employer to compute the actual levy. If the employee fails to return the signed statement within three working days to the employer, the exempt amount is based on married-filing-separately status with one personal exemption. The employer must begin the withholding in accordance with the levy within 10 days.

Although the gross pay less the amounts exempted can be seized, the IRS wants employers to withhold the difference between the take-home pay and the exempt amount. The take-home pay is the gross pay less taxes and the deductions in effect before the levy was received.

The tax levy takes effect with the first wage payment made three days from the receipt of the tax levy notice. The employer then returns Part 3 of Form 668-W to the Internal Revenue Service along with the initial payment. Further payments are to be sent on the same day that the employee is paid.

Each year, the IRS supplies tables that can be used to figure the amount exempt from tax levies (see Figure 6.3).

The employer must continue to withhold until Form 668-D—**Release of Levy/Release of Property from Levy** (not illustrated)—is received.

EXAMPLE 6-2

Booz Company received a federal tax levy on John Parlini. Parlini is single, claims two personal exemptions, and had a take-home pay of $535.00 this week. The amount of the tax levy (in 2015) would be:

Take-home pay		$535.00
Standard deduction	$ 6,300	
Personal exemptions ($4,000 × 2)	8,000	
	$14,300 ÷ 52 weeks =	275.00
Federal tax levy		$260.00

FIGURE 6.3

2015 Table for Amount Exempt for Tax Levy (Single Person)

Pay Period	Number of Exemptions Claimed on Statement						
	1	2	3	4	5	6	More Than 6
Daily	39.62	55.00	70.38	85.77	101.15	116.54	24.23 plus 15.38 for each exemption
Weekly	198.08	275.00	351.92	428.85	505.77	582.69	121.15 plus 76.93 for each exemption
Biweekly	396.15	550.00	703.85	857.69	1011.54	1165.38	242.31 plus 153.84 for each exemption
Semimonthly	429.17	595.83	762.50	929.17	1095.83	1262.50	262.50 plus 166.67 for each exemption
Monthly	858.33	1191.67	1525.00	1858.33	2191.67	2525.00	525 plus 333.33 for each exemption

Filing Status: **Single**

Source: Internal Revenue Service.

Pension and Retirement Contributions

Since in many instances social security benefits are inadequate for retired employees and their dependents, many firms provide pension and retirement plans that will supplement the government benefits. Although the benefit formulas and eligibility rules vary, the coverage is about the same for production workers, office employees, and managers. Some pension plans are financed solely by employer contributions, but other plans involve employee contributions. With the passage of the Pension Protection Act of 2006, companies can automatically enroll employees in the company's retirement plan and start deducting contributions from their pays. Once these contributions are deducted from the employees' pay, they become a liability for the employer and are recorded as such in the payroll entry. This would also apply to employee contributions into 401(k) plans.

Some employers also provide their employees with the opportunity to set up their own Individual Retirement Accounts (IRA) through a payroll deduction plan (see page 4-9). These voluntary contributions are deducted from the paychecks of the employees who set up their own retirement accounts. These deductions are recorded as a liability in the payroll entry. This liability account will be cleared as the employer pays the contributions to the financial institution that is in charge of each employee's retirement account.

Net Pay

The total of the net amount paid to the employees each payday is credited to either the *cash* account or the *salaries payable* account.

The journal entry to record the payroll from Figure 6.1, on page 6-2, would be:

	Debit	Credit
Wage Expense	24,762.70	
FICA Taxes Payable—OASDI		1,535.29
FICA Taxes Payable—HI		359.06
FIT Payable		3,714.00
SIT Payable		55.25
Group Insurance Payments W/H		54.70
Cash		19,044.40

LO 3

Journalize the entries to record the payroll and payroll taxes.

SELF-STUDY QUIZ 6-1

The totals from the payroll register of Olt Company for the week of January 25 show:

Gross earnings...	$ 95,190.00
Withholdings:	
FICA taxes—OASDI...	(5,901.78)
FICA taxes—HI	(1,380.26)
Federal income tax	(14,270.00)
State income tax...	(1,427.85)
State unemployment tax—employee portion....................	(951.90)
Net pay..	$ 71,258.21

Journalize the entry to record the payroll of January 25.

Note: Answers are on page 6-31.

Methods of Paying Wages and Salaries

The four main methods used in paying wages and salaries include (1) cash, (2) check, (3) electronic transfer, and (4) pay cards.

Paying in Cash

When a company pays wages and salaries in cash, a common procedure is used, as follows:

1. Compute the total wages earned, the deductions, and the net amount to be paid and record this information in the payroll register, as shown in Figure 1.9, on page 1-21.
2. Prepare a supplementary payroll sheet showing the various denominations of bills and coins needed to pay the salary of each employee. The form in Figure 6.4 provides columns to list the names of the employees, the net amount to be paid, the denominations needed to pay each employee, the total amount needed to pay all employees, and the total number of each denomination needed to pay all employees.

FIGURE 6.4
Supplementary Payroll Sheet

HENDRIX, INC.

SUPPLEMENTARY PAYROLL SHEET   June 30, 20--

Name of Employee	Net Amount to Be Paid	Bills					Coins				
		$50	$20	$10	$5	$1	50¢	25¢	10¢	5¢	1¢
Brandon, Paul C.	$ 268.62	5		1	1	3	1		1		2
Connor, Rose T.	271.40	5	1			1		1	1	1	
Day, Joseph R.	297.28	5	2		1	2		1			3
Gee, Margaret F.	704.92	14				4	1	1	1	1	2
Hawke, Sidney O.	271.64	5	1			1	1		1		4
Kirk, Evelyn A.	788.24	15	1	1	1	3			2		4
Lerro, Doris B.	268.12	5		1	1	3			1		2
Pesiri, Armand G.	878.80	17	1		1	3	1	1		1	
Topkis, Christine W.	284.65	5	1	1		4	1		1	1	
Vogel, John C.	724.10	14	1			4			1		
Total	$4,757.77	90	8	4	5	28	5	4	9	4	17

3. Prepare a payroll slip by using the total amount of each denomination needed for the payroll.
4. Write a check for the total amount of the payroll and present it to the bank with the payroll slip to obtain the proper denominations.
5. Place the amount due to each employee in an envelope with a receipt showing the total earnings, the deductions, and the net amount paid. Distribute the prepared envelopes to the employees.

Paying by Check

When paying wages and salaries by check, the employer prepares and signs the checks in the usual way. The check preparer should ensure the accuracy of the names of the payees and the net amounts of the checks. Employers must give employees a periodic statement showing the deductions that have been made from their wages for tax purposes. The employer may distribute these statements each payday or give them out monthly, quarterly, or annually. Also, employees receive a statement at the time they leave the employ of the company. Most employers who pay wages and salaries by check indicate on each check issued or on the check stub or earnings statement the various deductions made (see Figure 6.5).

Many businesses maintain a payroll account at their bank in addition to their regular checking account. In such a case, all checks to pay wages and salaries are issued against the payroll account rather than against the regular checking account. When the company maintains a separate payroll account, the usual procedure is as follows:

1. Sets up a payroll account with a certain balance to be maintained at all times. A transfer from the regular checking account is made to the payroll account. A small balance is desirable in the payroll account because it may be necessary to issue payroll checks before the regular payday. For example, if mistakes were made in an employee's paycheck, an additional check must be issued. These types of corrections will be shown in the next payday's payroll register.
2. Makes a transfer to payroll, drawn on the regular checking account, equal to the total net pay, and deposited in the special payroll account at the bank.
3. Prepares individual checks, drawn against the special payroll account, and records the numbers of the payroll checks in the payroll register. Many companies having a large number of employees may use automatic means of signing the checks.

By maintaining a separate payroll account at the bank, a listing of the canceled payroll checks, accompanied by a statement of the payroll account balance, are returned separately from the canceled checks lists drawn upon the regular checking account, making it easier to reconcile both accounts. The payroll account balance as shown on the bank statement should always be equal to the sum of the total of the outstanding payroll checks and any maintained balance, less any service charge.

> **ON THE JOB**
>
> In a survey conducted by KPMG Consulting, more than 72 percent of employers were found to have paid their employees on a biweekly basis.

> **ON THE JOB**
>
> The National Automated Clearing House Association estimated that employees spend an average of 8 to 24 hours per year depositing or cashing paychecks. In many cases, these transactions are made on company time.

FIGURE 6.5
Earnings Statement (Check Stub) Showing Payroll Deductions

EMPLOYEE'S NAME	ARTHUR T. COCO							PENLAND EQUIPMENT COMPANY, SAN MATEO, FL 32088-2279		
PAY PERIOD ENDING	HOURS	RATE	GROSS EARNINGS	OASDI TAX	HI TAX	FED. WITH. TAX	STATE WITH. TAX	UNION DUES		NET EARNINGS PAID
5/16/ --	REG. T. 40 O.T. 12	8.25 12.88	484.56	30.04	7.03	46.00		3.00		398.49

EMPLOYEE: THIS IS A STATEMENT OF YOUR EARNINGS AND DEDUCTIONS FOR PERIOD INDICATED. KEEP THIS FOR YOUR PERMANENT RECORD.

Paying by Electronic Transfer

Under an electronic funds transfer system (EFTS), employers do not have to issue a paycheck to each worker, although the worker is given a stub showing the amounts deducted. Instead, the employer creates a computerized record for each employee. This record indicates:

1. The employee's bank.
2. The account number at the bank.
3. The net amount to be paid.

A day or two before payday, the employer sends the information to the company's bank where the amounts due to any employees who also keep their accounts at that bank are removed and deposited to the appropriate accounts. That bank sends the remaining names to an automated clearinghouse which sorts out the other bank names and prepares a computer tape for each bank to receive funds electronically. For banks unable to receive entries in electronic form, the clearinghouse creates a printed statement showing the customers' names and the amounts for which their accounts are to be credited. The actual crediting of accounts and the settlement occur on payday.

Under a "paperless" deposit and bill-paying system, employers may deposit wages in bank accounts designated by the employees if the deposits are voluntarily authorized by the employees. Millions of written checks may be eliminated each month. After their net pay has been electronically transferred directly into their accounts, the employees can pay bills by authorizing the bank to automatically transfer funds from that account to the accounts of creditors such as the utility company and department stores.

Pay Cards

The major problem of direct deposit is to obtain up-to-date and timely banking information—employees changing accounts without notifying their employers, gathering information in time to make payroll for new employees, and paying into closed accounts.

Over 15 million American households do not have bank accounts; however, by using debit card-based accounts, the "unbanked" employees can opt for direct deposit of their paychecks. All transactions are completed electronically by using a pay card to make purchases at any point-of-sale terminal or to access cash at automated teller machines (ATMs) or through a bank teller.

National and regional banks issue these prepaid pay cards. Each pay period, funds are transferred from the employer's payroll account to the financial institution issuing the pay card. The card is then used like any debit or credit card and can also be used to access cash at certain automated teller machines (ATMs). Employees will then receive a monthly statement detailing their transactions.[1] These cards are reloadable, and each payday the cards will be "loaded up" with the pays without the employees needing to be anywhere near their employers.

A debit card can also be opened through a point-of-sale purchase at a retail store. The owner can then use the card like a bank account. ATM withdrawals and retail point-of-service transactions can be initiated using a personal identification number (PIN).

In almost half of the states, employers can eliminate paper paychecks by giving employees the choice between receiving their wages by direct deposit or on a pay card.[2] A few states allow employers to make these e-payment options a condition of employment. For instance, in Iowa it can be mandatory for new hires as long as the employees incur no bank charges. Some states require that the employee be allowed a certain number of free withdrawals from the ATMs. A recent

---

ON THE JOB

Cost per transaction to reload a debit card is about 0.25¢ (0.20¢ for direct deposit) versus $2.00 to issue a paper check.

ON THE JOB

Projections by research firms set the number of payroll card users at 10.8 million, and the gross volume to reach $6.9 billion by 2017.

---

1 "Card-Based Payroll Solutions," *PAYTECH*, April 2002, p. 22.

2 "Pay Cards Are a Win-Win Solution," *PAYTECH*, June 2010, p. 24.

bulletin from the Consumer Finance Protection Bureau (CFPB) cautioned employers to have available to the employees at least one other payment option in addition to payroll cards.

Electronic Paystub

Cost savings can also be realized by offering employees **electronic paystubs**. In these cases, the company will make the information that is usually found on a paper paystub available through a secured Web site, kiosk, or interactive voice response system. As with electronic payments, one can eliminate paper, postage, and distribution costs.

Final Pay

Even though few states have no laws governing the timing of the disbursement of the final pay, most states set a time limit after notice of termination for the payment of an employee's final wage. The deadline depends on whether or not the worker is leaving voluntarily. Most states allow a lag time in which to process the final check. However, if fired, California and Michigan require immediate payment. If the employee quits, California requires payment within 72 hours, while Michigan requires payment as soon as the final wages can be calculated.

In California, employees can sue for an equal amount in penalty wages for failure to timely pay final wages (up to 30 days' pay).[3]

Over the Line

Upon losing a government contract, employees of Catapult Technology, Ltd., accepted employment with a new contractor without giving notice to Catapult. Since the employees did not provide two weeks' notice (as specified in Catapult's employee handbook), Catapult refused to pay for the accrued unpaid universal leave time. The employees sued, and a Maryland appeals court ruled that universal leave is given "in remuneration" for employees' work and constitutes a wage. A company's personnel policy cannot contravene an employee's right to be compensated for his or her work.[4]

Unclaimed Wages

Occasionally, a worker may terminate employment or be terminated and not claim the final wage payment. The payroll manager is then faced with the question of what to do with the worker's unclaimed wages, which then become a form of abandoned property, subject to the state laws of escheat. This unclaimed property could also be in the form of unused payroll cards, expense reimbursements, and other employee benefits, such as flexible spending accounts.

The first step in exercising due diligence would be to send a certified letter to the employee's last known address. If contact is not established during the period specified under state law, the paycheck can be voided and the funds transferred to an escrow account. Even though a uniform law (the Uniform Unclaimed Property Act) exists on the subject of unclaimed property, varying practices occur in those states that provide for the disposition of unclaimed property. The uniform law, followed by most states, provides that the holder of any unclaimed property must file a report after a specified statutory period (one year in most states) and then surrender the money to the state as abandoned property. In other states, the holder of unclaimed property files a report with the state, and the state then

---

3 *Payroll Legal Alert*, March 2012, p. 1.

4 "Employers Cannot Put Strings on Final Wage Payments," *Payroll Manager's Letter*, Volume 24, No. 8, April 21, 2008, p. 3.

files suit for possession of the property. Generally, these reports must be filed annually and must state the employee's name, last known address, description of the abandoned wages, the amount, and the date of the last transaction with the employee.

The state would then hold the funds until the employee or heirs claim the funds. Each state has a website that allows people to search the database for unclaimed funds.[5] All of these issues surrounding uncashed payroll checks can be eliminated if employees are paid by direct deposit.

Audits conducted by a state agency are used to determine the adequacy of a firm's compliance program and, if found to be unsatisfactory, can result in interest, penalties, and even criminal prosecution. State statutory provisions for interest rates vary with the most common rate being 12 percent, and with the penalties for failure to report, ranging from $100–$1,000 per day.

Because of the different practices among states, payroll managers must be well acquainted with the laws of their own states in the event they are faced with the difficult problem of disposing of unclaimed wages. They should periodically review their procedures to test the adequacy of their unclaimed property compliance program. Some of the procedures for the unclaimed paychecks should include an identification process, an aging record, a reporting and remitting plan, and a consistent recordkeeping system.[6]

Recording Payroll Taxes

In this section, we will analyze the journal entries that record the *employer's* payroll taxes, each of which has been discussed in preceding chapters:

1. *FICA:* Taxes imposed under the Federal Insurance Contributions Act for old-age, survivors, and disability insurance (OASDI) and hospital insurance (HI) benefits.
2. *FUTA:* Taxes imposed under the Federal Unemployment Tax Act.
3. *SUTA:* Contributions to the unemployment compensation funds of one or more states.

The following accounts will be needed in the general ledger if the employer is subject to FICA taxes, FUTA taxes, and SUTA taxes:

1. *Payroll Taxes:* An expense account for the FICA, FUTA, and SUTA taxes on the employer.
2. *FICA Taxes Payable—OASDI:* A liability account for the tax withheld from employees' wages plus the employer's portion of the tax.
3. *FICA Taxes Payable—HI:* A liability account for the tax withheld from employees' wages plus the employer's portion of the tax.
4. *FUTA Taxes Payable:* A liability account for the accumulation of the employer's federal unemployment taxes payable to the federal government.
5. *SUTA Taxes Payable:* A liability account for the amount payable to state unemployment compensation fund(s).

The following journal entry to record the payroll taxes includes a debit to the tax expense account for the total of the employer's payroll taxes and a credit to the various tax liability accounts:

	Debit	Credit
Payroll Taxes	XXX	
Liabilities (various taxes)		XXX
To record the payroll taxes and liabilities of the employer.		

5 "How to Handle Uncashed Paychecks," *Payroll Manager's Letter*, Volume 31, No. 8, April 21, 2015, p. 5.

6 "Be Prepared for Unclaimed Property Audits," PAYTECH, April 2014, pp. 34–36.

FICA Taxes—Employer

The law states specifically that deductions made from the wages of employees under FICA should be recorded immediately as liabilities on the books of the company. The law does not require that employers record their part of the FICA taxes at the time the *wages are paid*. However, in order to place the tax expense in the proper accounting period, the common practice is to also record the employer's FICA tax liabilities each payday.

The taxes on the employer represent both business expenses and liabilities of the employer. The employer may deduct the employer's FICA contributions as a business expense in the calculation of the company's net income for federal income tax purposes (and the costs of all other payroll taxes).

SUTA Taxes

Under the state unemployment compensation laws, employers must pay contributions into one or more state unemployment compensation funds. When an employer must make contributions to the state unemployment compensation funds of more than one state, it may be advisable to keep a separate liability account for the contributions payable to each state.

FUTA Tax

An employer subject to the gross FUTA tax of 6.0 percent may be able to claim credit in paying the federal tax because of contributions made to state unemployment compensation funds. As discussed in Chapter 5, the maximum credit is 5.4 percent, even though the amount of state contributions is more or less than 5.4 percent. Thus, the net FUTA tax (6.0% − 5.4%) is 0.6 percent. Although you do not actually claim the credit against the FUTA tax until Form 940 is filed with the Internal Revenue Service, you may record the FUTA tax at the net amount (0.6%) at the time you make the entry to record the employer's payroll taxes for each payroll period.

EXAMPLE 6-3

The employees of Richardson Company earn wages during the year amounting to $26,400, all of which is subject to the gross FUTA tax of 6.0 percent. The company must make contributions to the unemployment compensation fund of the state in which the business is located at the rate of 2.8 percent of the wages paid each employee. Richardson computes the federal and state unemployment taxes as follows:

SUTA tax, 2.8% of $26,400		$739.20
Gross FUTA tax, 6.0% of $26,400	$1,584.00	
Less: Credit for SUTA tax, 5.4% of $26,400	−1,425.60	158.40 (net FUTA tax)
Total unemployment taxes		$897.60

More simply, the net FUTA tax is computed by multiplying the taxable wages, $26,400, by the net FUTA tax rate, 0.6 percent, yielding $158.40.

The FUTA tax, like the FICA taxes and the contributions to the state for unemployment compensation purposes, is a social security tax. Thus, the FUTA tax can be charged to the same expense account as the other payroll taxes on the employer, the payroll taxes account. However, since employers may be required to pay the net FUTA tax quarterly and to pay the FICA taxes more frequently, an employer should keep separate liability accounts for recording these two taxes.

SELF-STUDY QUIZ 6-2

Olt Company's gross payroll for the week of January 25 was $95,190.00. This total pay was taxable for federal (0.6%) and state (3.15%) unemployment taxes.

Journalize the entry to record Olt Company's payroll taxes for this pay.

Entries to Record Wages and Payroll Taxes

In the following illustrations of recording (or journalizing) wages and the payroll taxes imposed under both the federal and state laws, the employer is responsible for the following taxes:

1. FICA tax—OASDI on employees: 6.2%.
2. FICA tax—HI on employees: 1.45% + 0.9% on wages in excess of $200,000.
3. FIT withheld from employees.
4. FICA tax—OASDI on employers: 6.2%.
5. FICA tax—HI on employers: 1.45%.
6. Net FUTA tax: 0.6%.
7. SUTA tax: 2.4%.

LO 4

Post to the various general ledger accounts that are used to accumulate information from the payroll entries.

The weekly payroll amounts to $3,200, and the entire amount is subject to all social security and unemployment taxes. You record this information in two separate journal entries. In the first entry, you record the wages expense of the employer and the liabilities for the FICA taxes and FIT withheld in a two-column general journal as follows:

	Debit	Credit
Wages Expense	3,200.00	
FICA Taxes Payable—OASDI		198.40[7]
FICA Taxes Payable—HI		46.40[8]
Employees FIT Payable		230.00[9]
Cash		2,725.20[10]
To record the payment of wages and the liability for the employees' FICA.		

We can analyze this entry in T-accounts as follows:

WAGES EXPENSE		FICA TAXES PAYABLE—OASDI	
3,200.00			198.40
This debit represents the employees' gross earnings for the pay period. This results in an increase in the operating expenses of the employer.			This credit results in an increase in a liability of the employer.

FICA TAXES PAYABLE—HI		EMPLOYEES FIT PAYABLE	
	46.40		230.00
	This credit results in an increase in a liability of the employer.		This credit results in an increase in a liability of the employer.

CASH	
	2,725.20
	This credit results in a decrease in an asset.

---

7 The amount credited to FICA Taxes Payable—OASDI is computed as follows: 6.2% of $3,200 = $198.40, amount deducted from employees' wages.

8 The amount credited to FICA Taxes Payable—HI is computed as follows: 1.45% of $3,200 = $46.40, amount deducted from employees' wages.

9 The amount credited to Employees FIT Payable is obtained by using one of the withholding methods explained in Chapter 4.

10 The amount credited to Cash is computed as follows:

$3,200.00	gross wages earned
−474.80	employees' taxes withheld
$2,725.20	net amount paid employees

In the second entry, you record the employer's payroll taxes as follows:

	Debit	Credit
Payroll Taxes	340.80[11]	
FICA Taxes Payable—OASDI		198.40
FICA Taxes Payable—HI		46.40
FUTA Taxes Payable		19.20
SUTA Taxes Payable		76.80

    To record the payroll taxes and the employer's for the taxes.

Let's analyze this entry by means of T-accounts as shown below.

PAYROLL TAXES

340.80

This debit results in an increase in the operating expenses.

FICA TAXES PAYABLE—OASDI

198.40
198.40

The second credit amount, representing the employer's OASDI tax, also increases the employer's liability. The amount is determined as shown in the computation of the payroll taxes.

FICA TAXES PAYABLE—HI

46.40
46.40

The second credit amount, representing the employer's HI tax, also increases the employer's liability. The amount is determined as shown in the computation of the payroll taxes.

FUTA TAXES PAYABLE

19.20

This credit results in an increase in a liability of the employer. The amount is determined as shown in the computation of the payroll taxes.

SUTA TAXES PAYABLE

76.80

This credit results in an increase in a liability of the employer. The amount is determined as shown in the computation of the payroll taxes.

In the preceding illustration, no contributions were required of employees for state unemployment compensation purposes. Assume that the employees had been required to make contributions of 1 percent to state unemployment compensation funds. The payroll entry would then appear as shown below.

	Debit	Credit
Wages Expense	3,200.00	
FICA Taxes Payable—OASDI		198.40
FICA Taxes Payable—HI		46.40
Employees FIT Payable		230.00
SUTA Taxes Payable		32.00
Cash		2,693.20

    To record the payment of wages and the liability for the employees' FICA.

In a small company with few employees, you can compute the hours worked, determine net pay, and prepare the paychecks or pay envelopes in a relatively short period of time. For such companies, a journal entry crediting the cash account for the total net pay is a logical, efficient procedure.

---

11 The amount debited to Payroll Taxes is computed as follows:

6.2% of $3,200 =	$198.40	employer's OASDI tax
1.45% of $3,200 =	46.40	employer's HI tax
0.6% of $3,200 =	19.20	employer's net FUTA tax
2.4% of $3,200 =	76.80	employer's SUTA tax
Total payroll taxes	$340.80	

In larger companies, however, the calculation of hours worked, the determination of net pay, and the preparation of paychecks may extend over the greater part of a workday, or even longer. In such companies, because of the workload involved in meeting each payroll and especially when the paychecks must be mailed to far-flung branch offices, the paychecks may be prepared several days in advance of their actual distribution to the workers. Further, the preparation of the workers' paychecks may occur in one accounting period, although the actual payment is made in the following accounting period. Thus, to show an accurate picture of the firm's liability for the payroll, at the time of recording the payroll, the net pay is accrued and credited to a liability account such as Salaries Payable or Accrued Salaries Payable, instead of to the cash account. Later, when the paychecks are given to the workers, an entry is made to record the payment of the payroll.

	Debit	Credit
Salaries Payable	XXX	
Cash		XXX
To record the payment of wages for the pay period ended July 20, 20--.		

Recording Workers' Compensation Insurance Expense

As indicated in Chapter 1, most states have passed laws that require employers to provide workers' compensation insurance to protect their employees against losses due to injury or death incurred during employment. The expense account, *Workers' Compensation Insurance Expense*, can be used to record the premiums paid by the company to provide this coverage. Usually, the employer estimates and pays the premium in advance. The insurance premium, often based upon the total gross payroll of the business, may be stated in terms of an amount for each $100 of weekly wages paid to employees. At the end of the year, all the payrolls are audited, and the company pays an additional premium or receives credit for an overpayment. Since the premium rate varies with the hazard involved in the work performed, your personnel and payroll records should provide for a careful classification of employees by kind or grade of work and a summary of labor costs according to the insurance premium classifications.

EXAMPLE 6-4

McMahon Company has only two different grades of work—office clerical and machine shop. The premium rates for the year are $0.18 per $100 of payroll for the office clerical workers and $2.90 per $100 of payroll for the machine-shop workers. Based upon past experience and budgetary projections for the year, the company estimates its annual premium to be $8,900 and sends a check for that amount to the insurance carrier at the beginning of the year. The entry to record this transaction is as follows:

Workers' Compensation Insurance Expense	8,900.00	
Cash		8,900.00

The effect of this entry, when posted to the ledger accounts, increases the operating expenses of the company and decreases the assets.

At the end of the year, the payrolls for the year are audited and analyzed and the current rates are applied to determine the actual premium as follows:

Work Grade	Total Payroll	Rate per $100	Premium
Office clerical	$ 81,000	$0.18	$ 145.80
Machine shop	312,000	2.90	9,048.00
Total	$393,000		$9,193.80
Less: Estimated premium paid in January			8,900.00
Balance due			$ 293.80

A check is written for the balance due the insurance company, and the following entry is made in the journal:

Workers' Compensation Insurance Expense	293.80	
Cash		293.80

Recording the Deposit or Payment of Payroll Taxes

The journal entries required to record the deposit or payment of FICA taxes and income taxes withheld and the payment of FUTA and SUTA taxes are explained below.

Depositing FICA Taxes and Federal Income Taxes Withheld

As explained in Chapter 3, the requirements for depositing FICA taxes and federal income taxes withheld from employees' wages and the employer's FICA match vary.

LO 5

Explain the recording of the payroll tax deposits.

EXAMPLE 6–5

On April 15, the ledger accounts FICA Taxes Payable—OASDI, FICA Taxes Payable—HI, and Employees FIT Payable of Goosen Company appear as follows:

FICA TAXES PAYABLE—OASDI

4/15	697.07
4/15	697.07
	1,394.14

FICA TAXES PAYABLE—HI

4/15	163.02
4/15	163.02
	326.04

EMPLOYEES FIT PAYABLE

4/15	1,601.19

The company must electronically transfer the FICA and the federal income taxes. The following journal entry records this transaction:

FICA Taxes Payable—OASDI	1,394.14	
FICA Taxes Payable—HI	326.04	
Employees FIT Payable	1,601.19	
Cash		3,321.37

When posted, the debits of $1,394.14 and $326.04 to FICA Taxes Payable—OASDI and FICA Taxes Payable—HI remove the liabilities for the employer's share, as well as the employees' share, of the FICA taxes imposed. The debit to Employees FIT Payable removes the liability for the total amount of federal income taxes withheld from the employees' wages during the period. The credit to Cash reduces the assets of the company.

ON THE JOB

More than 55 percent of companies outsource their payroll tax matters, and the majority of others handle it in-house using tax compliance software.

Paying State or City Income Taxes

When the employer turns over to the state or city the amount of income taxes withheld from employees' wages, the appropriate journal entry would be recorded as follows:

	Debit	Credit
Employees SIT Payable...	XXX	
or		
Employees CIT Payable...	XXX	
Cash		XXX

Paying FUTA and SUTA Taxes

At the time of depositing the FUTA taxes that have accumulated during the preceding calendar quarter, an entry is made as follows:

	Debit	Credit
FUTA Taxes Payable..	XXX	
Cash		XXX

The quarterly payment of state unemployment contributions is recorded as follows:

	Debit	Credit
SUTA Taxes Payable..	XXX	
Cash		XXX

Recording End-of-Period Adjustments

LO 6

Understand the need for end-of-period adjustments.

In most cases, the end of the fiscal (accounting) period does not coincide with the end of the payroll period. Therefore, adjustments are commonly made to record the end-of-period wages and accrued vacation pay.

Wages

To record the adjustment for end-of-period wages, the wages for this last payroll period must be split between the fiscal period just ending (accrued wages) and the fiscal period just beginning. For instance, if the fiscal period ends on Wednesday (e.g., December 31) and payday takes place every Friday, the wages earned by the employees on Monday, Tuesday, and Wednesday are an expense of the fiscal period just ended. However, the wages earned on Thursday and Friday (payday) apply to the new fiscal period.

In order to record the wage expense properly for the fiscal period ended, an adjusting entry must be made on the last day of the fiscal period. However, since there is no actual wage payment and, therefore, no withholding, there is no need to credit any withholding accounts. The debit part of the entry would be based on the gross pay for the workdays to be accrued. The credit part of the entry involves a single liability account for the total wage expense. In the case above, the wage expenses of Monday, Tuesday, and Wednesday would be recorded in the following *adjusting entry*:

	Debit	Credit
Wages Expense	XXX	
Wages Payable..		XXX
To record wages incurred but unpaid as of the end of the fiscal period.		

With a sophisticated timekeeping system, hours worked and earnings for the accrued wages can be easily generated. In other cases, since the accumulation of payroll data (timesheets, registers, etc.) is such a time-consuming process, the amount of the adjustment could be based on a percentage of the previous period's payroll. For instance, if the accrual is for three workdays out of a five-workday week, 60 percent of the prior week's gross pay could be used as the amount of the adjustment.

In a situation where the employer holds back one week's pay (e.g., earnings for the current week are not paid until the following Friday), the adjusting entry for the example shown above would accrue eight days of expense (one full workweek plus Monday, Tuesday, and Wednesday).

Since the employer is not liable for the payroll taxes (FICA, FUTA, and SUTA) until the actual payday, payroll taxes are not accrued.

Vacation Pay

Another adjustment required at the end of the accounting period concerns vacation pay. If a company has a vacation policy, the employees earn the right for paid future absences during the current period. Therefore, an expense account should be created for the amount of the vacation time earned by the employees and a liability should be accrued at the end of the current period. Whether making the adjustment each payday, each month, or each year, the expense must be recorded when the liability is created, which is in the period when the employees earn it.

EXAMPLE 6-6

The employees of Carr Company are entitled to one day's vacation for each month worked. The average daily pay for each of the 50 employees is $130. The adjusting entry to record the vacation expense of $6,500 ($130 × 50) at the end of each month is:

Vacation Benefits Expense	6,500.00	
Vacation Benefits Payable		6,500.00

When employees eventually use their vacation time, the payment entry debits Vacation Benefits Payable, not Wages Expense, since the expense was previously recorded in the adjusting entry, as shown above. Another method that is used by most companies ignores the split between regular pay and vacation pay in the payroll entry. Instead, an adjusting entry is made at the end of each month for the expense and the liability to bring the balance in the liability account (Vacation Benefits Payable) either up to or down to the current total of unused vacation for the company, with the offsetting debit or credit made to a vacation expense account.

Postretirement benefits such as health care and pensions also require adjusting entries of this type. These benefits must be reported as expenses during the employees' working years when they earn the entitlements.

Summary of Accounts Used in Recording Payroll Transactions

The following listing summarizes some of the general ledger accounts that may be used to record payroll transactions:

1. *Wages and Salaries:* An operating expense account in which the gross payroll is recorded.
2. *Payroll Taxes:* An operating expense account in which are recorded all payroll taxes on the employer under FICA, FUTA, and the various state unemployment compensation laws.

3. *Workers' Compensation Insurance Expense:* An operating expense account in which are recorded the premiums paid by the company to provide coverage for employees against employment-related injury or death.

4. *Vacation Benefits Expense:* An operating expense account in which are recorded the costs of the vacation time that has been earned by employees.

5. *FICA Taxes Payable—OASDI:* A current liability account in which are recorded deductions made from employees' wages and the employer's portion of the OASDI tax.

6. *FICA Taxes Payable—HI:* A current liability account in which are recorded deductions made from employees' wages and the employer's portion of the HI tax.

7. *FUTA Taxes Payable:* A current liability account in which are recorded the employer's federal unemployment taxes.

8. *SUTA Taxes Payable:* A current liability account in which are recorded the amounts due the states for the employer's unemployment compensation contributions. This account may also be credited for amounts deducted from employees' wages, if employees must contribute to state unemployment compensation funds.

9. *Employees FIT Payable:* A current liability account in which are recorded deductions made from employees' wages for federal income taxes.

10. *Employees SIT Payable:* A current liability account in which are recorded deductions made from employees' wages for state income taxes.

11. *Health Insurance Premiums Collected:* A current liability account in which are recorded deductions made from employees' wages for their share of the premiums paid for health insurance coverage.

12. *Union Dues Payable:* A current liability account in which are recorded the deductions made from union members' wages for their union dues, assessments, or initiation fees.

13. *Wages Payable:* A current liability account in which are recorded the net wages that have been earned by employees but not yet paid to them.

14. *Vacation Benefits Payable:* A current liability account in which are recorded the costs of the vacation time that has been earned by employees but not yet used.

Illustrative Case

The following illustrative case shows the accounting procedures used by Brookins Company in recording payroll transactions during the third quarter of its fiscal year. The fiscal year of the company ends on June 30, 20--. Brookins pays employees semimonthly on the 15th and the last day of the month. When the 15th or the last day of the month falls on Saturday or Sunday, employees are paid on the preceding Friday.

On January 1, 20--, the balances of the accounts used in recording payroll transactions follow. These account balances are shown in the general ledger on pages 6-29 and 6-30.

Acct. No.	Account Title	Account Balance
11	Cash	$85,000.00
20	FICA Taxes Payable—OASDI	961.00
21	FICA Taxes Payable—HI	224.75
22	FUTA Taxes Payable	91.50
23	SUTA Taxes Payable	350.75
25	Employees FIT Payable	1,472.00
26	Employees SIT Payable	474.42
28	Union Dues Payable	80.00
51	Wages and Salaries	46,500.00
55	Payroll Taxes	4,224.00

The first $118,500 in wages and salaries paid is subject to the OASDI tax on both the employer (6.2%) and the employees (6.2%). The total wages and salaries paid are subject to the HI tax on both the employer (1.45%) and the employees (1.45% + 0.9% on wages in excess of $200,000). The employer is also subject to a net FUTA tax of 0.6 percent, based on the first $7,000 in earnings paid each employee during a calendar year, and a SUTA tax of 2.3 percent, based on the first $7,000 in earnings paid during a calendar year. The state does not require contributions of employees for unemployment compensation or disability insurance.

The wage-bracket method is used to determine the amount of federal income taxes to be withheld from the employees' earnings. The state income tax law requires that a graduated percentage of the gross earnings of each employee be withheld each payday. Under the check-off system, union dues are withheld each payday from the union workers who are employed in the plant. On or before the fourth of each month, the dues collected during the preceding month are turned over to the treasurer of the union.

In the following narrative of transactions, the January 14 (Friday) payroll transaction is explained in detail below. All other transactions are stated briefly. Adjacent to the narrative are the journal entries to record the transactions. The ledger accounts showing the transactions posted are on pages 6-29 and 6-30.

Narrative of Transactions	Journal	P.R.	Debit	Page 15 Credit
	20 --			
Jan. 4. Paid the treasurer of the union $80, representing the union dues withheld from the workers' earnings during the month of December.	Jan. 4 Union Dues Payable	28	80.00	
	Cash	11		80.00
	To record payment of union dues withheld during December.			
Jan. 14. Paid total wages and salaries of all employees, $3,890. All the earnings are taxable under FICA. In addition to the social security taxes, the company withheld $455 from the employees' earnings for federal income taxes, $85.58 for state income taxes, and $45 for union dues. (See the explanation of the January 14 payroll transaction given below.)	14 Wages and Salaries	51	3,890.00	
	FICA Taxes Payable—OASDI	20		241.18
	FICA Taxes Payable—HI	21		56.41
	Employees FIT Payable	25		455.00
	Employees SIT Payable	26		85.58
	Union Dues Payable	28		45.00
	Cash	11		3,006.83
	To record the payment of wages and the liabilities for the employees' taxes withheld.			
Jan. 14. Recorded the employer's payroll taxes for the first pay in January. All the earnings are taxable under FICA, FUTA, and SUTA.	14 Payroll Taxes	55	410.40	
	FICA Taxes Payable—OASDI	20		241.18
	FICA Taxes Payable—HI	21		56.41
	FUTA Taxes Payable	22		23.34
	SUTA Taxes Payable	23		89.47
	To record the payroll taxes and liabilities of the employer.			
Jan. 18. Electronically transferred to the IRS the FICA taxes and employees' federal income taxes withheld on the two December payrolls. At the end of December, the total liability for FICA taxes and federal income taxes withheld was $2,657.75 (January 17—Monday—Martin Luther King, Jr.'s birthday, which is a bank holiday.)	18 FICA Taxes Payable—OASDI	20	961.00	
	FICA Taxes Payable—HI	21	224.75	
	Employees FIT Payable	25	1,472.00	
	Cash	11		2,657.75
	To record deposit of FICA taxes and federal income taxes withheld for the 12/15 and 12/31 payrolls.			

Analysis of the January 14 payroll transaction follows:

1. Wages and Salaries is debited for $3,890, the total of the employees' gross earnings.
2. FICA Taxes Payable—OASDI is credited for $241.18, the amount withheld from the employees' earnings for OASDI taxes.
3. FICA Taxes Payable—HI is credited for $56.41, the amount withheld from the employees' earnings for HI taxes.
4. Employees FIT Payable is credited for $455, the amount withheld from employees' earnings for federal income tax purposes.
5. Employees SIT Payable is credited for $85.58, the amount withheld from employees' earnings for state income taxes.
6. Union Dues Payable is credited for $45, the amount withheld from union members' earnings.
7. Cash is credited for $3,006.83, the net amount paid the employees ($3,890 gross earnings − $241.18 OASDI − $56.41 HI − $455 FIT − $85.58 SIT − $45 union dues).

8. Payroll Taxes is debited for $410.40, the amount of taxes imposed on the employer under FICA, FUTA, and SUTA. The computation of the total payroll taxes is:

FICA—OASDI:	6.2% of $3,890 =	$241.18
FICA—HI:	1.45% of $3,890 =	56.41
FUTA:	0.6% of $3,890 =	23.34
SUTA:	2.3% of $3,890 =	89.47
Total payroll taxes		$410.40

9. FICA Taxes Payable—OASDI is credited for the amount of tax on the employer.
10. FICA Taxes Payable—HI is credited for the amount of tax on the employer.
11. FUTA Taxes Payable is credited for $23.34, the liability incurred because of the taxes imposed on the employer under FUTA.
12. SUTA Taxes Payable is credited for $89.47, the amount of the contributions payable to the state.

Narrative of Transactions		Journal	P.R.	Debit	Page 16 Credit
Jan. 18. Paid to the state the amount of state income taxes withheld from employees' pays for the quarter just ended.	Jan. 18	Employees SIT Payable	26	474.42	
		Cash	11		474.42
		To record payment of state income taxes withheld during 4th quarter.			
Jan. 31. Paid total wages and salaries, $4,100. All of this amount constitutes taxable earnings under FICA. Withheld $483 for federal income taxes, $90.20 for state income taxes, and $45 for union dues.	31	Wages and Salaries	51	4,100.00	
		FICA Taxes Payable—OASDI	20		254.20
		FICA Taxes Payable—HI	21		59.45
		Employees FIT Payable	25		483.00
		Employees SIT Payable	26		90.20
		Union Dues Payable	28		45.00
		Cash	11		3,168.15
		To record the payment of wages and the liabilities for the employees' taxes withheld.			
Jan. 31. Recorded the employer's payroll taxes for this payroll. All the earnings are taxable under FICA, FUTA, and SUTA.	31	Payroll Taxes	55	432.55	
		FICA Taxes Payable—OASDI	20		254.20
		FICA Taxes Payable—HI	21		59.45
		FUTA Taxes Payable	22		24.60
		SUTA Taxes Payable	23		94.30
		To record the payroll taxes and liabilities of the employer.			
Jan. 31. Filed the Employer's Annual Federal Unemployment (FUTA) Tax Return, Form 940, for the preceding calendar year. Electronically transferred $91.50 to remove the liability for FUTA taxes for the fourth quarter of the previous year.	31	FUTA Taxes Payable	22	91.50	
		Cash	11		91.50
		To record the deposit of FUTA taxes for the 4th quarter.			
Jan. 31. Filed the state unemployment contributions return for the quarter ending December 31, and paid $350.75 to the state unemployment compensation fund.	31	SUTA Taxes Payable	23	350.75	
		Cash	11		350.75
		To record payment of contributions to state unemployment compensation fund for the 4th quarter.			

Narrative of Transactions	Journal	P.R.	Debit	Page 16 Credit

Jan. 31. Filed the quarterly return (Form 941) with the IRS Center for the period ended December 31. No journal entry is required since the liability for FICA taxes and employees' federal income taxes withheld was removed by the timely transfer on January 18, 20--. No taxes were paid or deposited at the time of filing Form 941.

Narrative of Transactions	Journal		P.R.	Debit	Credit
Feb. 4. Paid the treasurer of the union $90, representing the union dues withheld from the workers' earnings during the month of January.	Feb. 4	Union Dues Payable...	28	90.00	
		Cash	11		90.00
		To record the payment of the union dues withheld during January.			

Narrative of Transactions	Journal		P.R.	Debit	Page 17 Credit
Feb. 15. Paid total wages and salaries, $4,000. All of this amount is taxable under FICA. Withheld $470 for federal income taxes, $88 for state income taxes, and $45 for union dues.	Feb. 15	Wages and Salaries	51	4,000.00	
		FICA Taxes Payable—OASDI	20		248.00
		FICA Taxes Payable—HI	21		58.00
		Employees FIT Payable	25		470.00
		Employees SIT Payable	26		88.00
		Union Dues Payable..	28		45.00
		Cash	11		3,091.00
		To record the payment of wages and the liabilities for the employees' taxes withheld.			
Feb. 15. Recorded the employer's payroll taxes. All the earnings are taxable under FICA, FUTA, and SUTA.	15	Payroll Taxes	55	422.00	
		FICA Taxes Payable—OASDI	20		248.00
		FICA Taxes Payable—HI	21		58.00
		FUTA Taxes Payable	22		24.00
		SUTA Taxes Payable	23		92.00
		To record the payroll taxes and liabilities of the employer.			
Feb. 15. Electronically transferred $2,160.48 to remove the liability for the FICA taxes and the employees' federal income taxes withheld on the January 14 and January 31 payrolls.	15	FICA Taxes Payable—OASDI......................................	20	990.76	
		FICA Taxes Payable—HI	21	231.72	
		Employees FIT Payable..	25	938.00	
		Cash	11		2,160.48
		To record the deposit of FICA taxes and federal income taxes withheld for the January 14 and January 31 payrolls.			
Feb. 28. Paid total wages and salaries, $4,250. All of this amount is taxable under FICA. Withheld $502 for federal income taxes, $93.50 for state income taxes, and $50 for union dues.	28	Wages and Salaries	51	4,250.00	
		FICA Taxes Payable—OASDI	20		263.50
		FICA Taxes Payable—HI	21		61.63
		Employees FIT Payable	25		502.00
		Employees SIT Payable	26		93.50
		Union Dues Payable..	28		50.00
		Cash	11		3,279.37
		To record the payment of wages and the liabilities for the employees' taxes withheld.			
Feb. 28. Recorded the employer's payroll taxes. All the earnings are taxable under FICA, FUTA, and SUTA.	28	Payroll Taxes	55	448.38	
		FICA Taxes Payable—OASDI	20		263.50
		FICA Taxes Payable—HI	21		61.63
		FUTA Taxes Payable	22		25.50
		SUTA Taxes Payable	23		97.75
		To record the payroll taxes and liabilities of the employer.			

Narrative of Transactions		Journal	P.R.	Debit	Page 17 Credit
Mar. 4. Paid the treasurer of the union $95, representing the union dues withheld from the workers' earnings during the month of February.	Mar. 4	Union Dues Payable..	28	95.00	
		Cash	11		95.00
		To record the payment of the union dues withheld during February.			

Narrative of Transactions		Journal	P.R.	Debit	Page 18 Credit
Mar. 15. Paid total wages and salaries, $4,300. All of this amount is taxable under FICA. Withheld $554 for federal income taxes, $94.60 for state income taxes, and $50 for union dues.	Mar. 15	Wages and Salaries	51	4,300.00	
		FICA Taxes Payable—OASDI	20		266.60
		FICA Taxes Payable—HI	21		62.35
		Employees FIT Payable	25		554.00
		Employees SIT Payable	26		94.60
		Union Dues Payable	28		50.00
		Cash	11		3,272.45
		To record the payment of wages and the liabilities for the employees' taxes withheld.			
Mar. 15. Recorded the employer's payroll taxes. All the earnings are taxable under FICA, FUTA, and SUTA.	15	Payroll Taxes...	55	453.65	
		FICA Taxes Payable—OASDI	20		266.60
		FICA Taxes Payable—HI	21		62.35
		FUTA Taxes Payable	22		25.80
		SUTA Taxes Payable	23		98.90
		To record the payroll taxes and liabilities of the employer.			
Mar. 15. Electronically transferred $2,234.26 to remove the liability for FICA taxes and the employees' federal income taxes withheld on the February 15 and February 28 payrolls.	15	FICA Taxes Payable—OASDI...............................	20	1,023.00	
		FICA Taxes Payable—HI....................................	21	239.26	
		Employees FIT Payable.....................................	25	972.00	
		Cash	11		2,234.26
		To record the deposit of FICA taxes and federal income taxes withheld for the February 15 and February 28 payrolls.			
Mar. 31. Paid total wages and salaries, $4,320. All of this amount is taxable under FICA. Withheld $570 for federal income taxes, $95.04 for state income taxes, and $50 for union dues.	31	Wages and Salaries	51	4,320.00	
		FICA Taxes Payable—OASDI	20		267.84
		FICA Taxes Payable—HI	21		62.64
		Employees FIT Payable	25		570.00
		Employees SIT Payable	26		95.04
		Union Dues Payable	28		50.00
		Cash	11		3,274.48
		To record the payment of wages and the liabilities for the employees' taxes withheld.			
Mar. 31. Recorded the employer's payroll taxes. All of the earnings are taxable under FICA, FUTA, and SUTA.	31	Payroll Taxes...	55	455.76	
		FICA Taxes Payable—OASDI	20		267.84
		FICA Taxes Payable—HI	21		62.64
		FUTA Taxes Payable	22		25.92
		SUTA Taxes Payable	23		99.36
		To record the payroll taxes and liabilities of the employer.			

After journalizing and posting the transactions for January through March, the general ledger payroll accounts as shown on the next two pages carry the following balances:

1. *FICA Taxes Payable—OASDI:* $1,068.88, the amount of the liability for the taxes imposed on both the employer and the employees with respect to wages and salaries paid on March 15 and March 31. The FICA taxes, along with the employees' federal income taxes withheld, must be deposited by April 15.

2. *FICA Taxes Payable—HI:* $249.98, the amount of the liability for the taxes imposed on both the employer and the employees with respect to wages and salaries paid on March 15 and March 31. The FICA taxes, along with the employees' federal income taxes withheld, must be paid by April 15.

3. *FUTA Taxes Payable:* $149.16, the accumulation of the amounts credited to this account each payday during the first three months of the calendar year. The balance of the account on March 31 need not

be deposited since it is $500 or less. The $149.16 will be added to the second quarter's liability and deposited if the $500 threshold is passed.

4. *SUTA Taxes Payable:* $571.78, the amount due to the state unemployment compensation fund. This liability must be paid on or before May 2.

5. *Employees FIT Payable:* $1,124, the amount due for federal income taxes withheld from employees' earnings on March 15 and March 31. This amount, along with the balances of the FICA taxes payable accounts, represents a liability that must be paid by April 15.

6. *Employees SIT Payable:* $546.92, the amount due for state income taxes withheld from employees'

earnings during the first three months of the calendar year. This amount must be paid to the treasurer of the state on the date specified in the state's income tax law.

7. *Union Dues Payable:* $100, amount due the treasurer of the union on or before April 4.

8. *Wages and Salaries:* $71,360, the total gross earnings for the three quarters of the company's fiscal year. The entire amount is an operating expense of the business.

9. *Payroll Taxes:* $6,846.74, the total payroll taxes for the three quarters imposed on the employer under FICA, FUTA, and SUTA. The entire amount is an operating expense of the business.

GENERAL LEDGER

CASH — 11

Date		Item	P.R.	Dr.	Cr.	Balance Dr.	Balance Cr.
20--							
Jan.	1	Bal.	✓				85,000.00
	4		J15		80.00		84,920.00
	14		J15		3,006.83		81,913.17
	18		J15		2,657.75		79,255.42
	18		J16		474.42		78,781.00
	31		J16		3,168.15		75,612.85
	31		J16		91.50		75,521.35
	31		J16		350.75		75,170.60
Feb.	4		J16		90.00		75,080.60
	15		J17		3,091.00		71,989.60
	15		J17		2,160.48		69,829.12
	28		J17		3,279.37		66,549.75
Mar.	4		J17		95.00		66,454.75
	15		J18		3,272.45		63,182.30
	15		J18		2,234.26		60,948.04
	31		J18		3,274.48		57,673.56

FICA TAXES PAYABLE—OASDI — 20

Date		Item	P.R.	Dr.	Cr.	Balance Dr.	Balance Cr.
20--							
Jan.	1	Bal.	✓				961.00
	14		J15		241.18		1,202.18
	14		J15		241.18		1,443.36
	18		J15	961.00			482.36
	31		J16		254.20		736.56
	31		J16		254.20		990.76
Feb.	15		J17		248.00		1,238.76
	15		J17		248.00		1,486.76
	15		J17	990.76			496.00
	28		J17		263.50		759.50
	28		J17		263.50		1,023.00
Mar.	15		J18		266.60		1,289.60
	15		J18		266.60		1,556.20
	15		J18	1,023.00			533.20
	31		J18		267.84		801.04
	31		J18		267.84		1,068.88

FICA TAXES PAYABLE—HI — 21

Date		Item	P.R.	Dr.	Cr.	Balance Dr.	Balance Cr.
20--							
Jan.	1	Bal.	✓				224.75
	14		J15		56.41		281.16
	14		J15		56.41		337.57
	18		J15	224.75			112.82
	31		J16		59.45		172.27
	31		J16		59.45		231.72
Feb.	15		J17		58.00		289.72
	15		J17		58.00		347.72
	15		J17	231.72			116.00
	28		J17		61.63		177.63
	28		J17		61.63		239.26
Mar.	15		J18		62.35		301.61
	15		J18		62.35		363.96
	15		J18	239.26			124.70
	31		J18		62.64		187.34
	31		J18		62.64		249.98

FUTA TAXES PAYABLE — 22

Date		Item	P.R.	Dr.	Cr.	Balance Dr.	Balance Cr.
20--							
Jan.	1	Bal.	✓				91.50
	14		J15		23.34		114.84
	31		J16		24.60		139.44
	31		J16	91.50			47.94
Feb.	15		J17		24.00		71.94
	28		J17		25.50		97.44
Mar.	15		J18		25.80		123.24
	31		J18		25.92		149.16

SUTA TAXES PAYABLE   23

Date		Item	P.R.	Dr.	Cr.	Balance Dr.	Balance Cr.
20 --							
Jan.	1	Bal.	✓				350.75
	14		J15		89.47		440.22
	31		J16		94.30		534.52
	31		J16	350.75			183.77
Feb.	15		J17		92.00		275.77
	28		J17		97.75		373.52
Mar.	15		J18		98.90		472.42
	31		J18		99.36		571.78

EMPLOYEES FIT PAYABLE   25

Date		Item	P.R.	Dr.	Cr.	Balance Dr.	Balance Cr.
20 --							
Jan.	1	Bal.	✓				1,472.00
	14		J15		455.00		1,927.00
	18		J15	1,472.00			455.00
	31		J16		483.00		938.00
Feb.	15		J17		470.00		1,408.00
	15		J17	938.00			470.00
	28		J17		502.00		972.00
Mar.	15		J18		554.00		1,526.00
	15		J18	972.00			554.00
	31		J18		570.00		1,124.00

EMPLOYEES SIT PAYABLE   26

Date		Item	P.R.	Dr.	Cr.	Balance Dr.	Balance Cr.
20 --							
Jan.	1	Bal.	✓				474.42
	14		J15		85.58		560.00
	18		J16	474.42			85.58
	31		J16		90.20		175.78
Feb.	15		J17		88.00		263.78
	28		J17		93.50		357.28
Mar.	15		J18		94.60		451.88
	31		J18		95.04		546.92

UNION DUES PAYABLE   28

Date		Item	P.R.	Dr.	Cr.	Balance Dr.	Balance Cr.
20 --							
Jan.	1	Bal.	✓				80.00
	4		J15	80.00		—	
	14		J15		45.00		45.00
	31		J16		45.00		90.00
Feb.	4		J16	90.00		—	
	15		J17		45.00		45.00
	28		J17		50.00		95.00
Mar.	4		J17	95.00		—	
	15		J18		50.00		50.00
	31		J18		50.00		100.00

WAGES AND SALARIES   51

Date		Item	P.R.	Dr.	Cr.	Balance Dr.	Balance Cr.
20 --							
Jan.	1	Bal.	✓			46,500.00	
	14		J15	3,890.00		50,390.00	
	31		J16	4,100.00		54,490.00	
Feb.	15		J17	4,000.00		58,490.00	
	28		J17	4,250.00		62,740.00	
Mar.	15		J18	4,300.00		67,040.00	
	31		J18	4,320.00		71,360.00	

PAYROLL TAXES   55

Date		Item	P.R.	Dr.	Cr.	Balance Dr.	Balance Cr.
20 --							
Jan.	1	Bal.	✓			4,224.00	
	14		J15	410.40		4,634.40	
	31		J16	432.55		5,066.95	
Feb.	15		J17	422.00		5,488.95	
	28		J17	448.38		5,937.33	
Mar.	15		J18	453.65		6,390.98	
	31		J18	455.76		6,846.74	

KEY TERMS

business expense (p. 6-17)

check-off system (p. 6-8)

disposable earnings (p. 6-9)

electronic funds transfer system (EFTS) (p. 6-14)

electronic paystubs (p. 6-15)

garnishment (p. 6-8)

group insurance (p. 6-7)

journal entries (p. 6-3)

ANSWERS TO SELF-STUDY QUIZZES

Self-Study Quiz 6-1

January 25	Salary Expense	95,190.00	
	FICA Taxes Payable—OASDI		5,901.78
	FICA Taxes Payable—HI		1,380.26
	Employees FIT Payable		14,270.00
	Employees SIT Payable		1,427.85
	SUTA Taxes Payable		951.90
	Salaries Payable (Cash)		71,258.21

Self-Study Quiz 6-2

January 25	Payroll Taxes	10,851.67	
	FICA Taxes Payable—OASDI		5,901.78
	FICA Taxes Payable—HI		1,380.26
	FUTA Taxes Payable		571.14
	SUTA Taxes Payable		2,998.49

KEY POINTS SUMMARY

	Learning Objectives	Key Points	Problem Sets A & B
LO1	Record payrolls in payroll registers and post to employees' earnings records.	• Separate P/R register for each payday.	6-15
		• Separate line for each employee.	
		• Totals of each column are used to record payroll journal entry.	
		• Information on each employee is transferred from the P/R register to the employee's earnings record.	
LO2	Understand the various deductions—both voluntary and involuntary (taxes and garnishments)—that are taken out of employees' gross pay.	• Amounts withheld for taxes (FICA, FIT, SIT, and CIT) are set up as liabilities in the P/R entry.	6-1, 6-2, 6-7, 6-13
		• All other deductions from employees' paychecks are set up as liabilities.	
		• Consumer Credit Protection Act limits the amount of wages subject to garnishment.	
		• With garnishments, child support is first, federal tax levies are second.	

Learning Objectives	Key Points	Problem Sets A & B

L03 Journalize the entries to record the payroll and payroll taxes.	• Wages Expense (gross payroll) XXX
	     Liabilities (all withholdings) XXX
	     Cash/Salary Payroll (net pay) XXX
	
	• Paying in cash, check, electronic transfer, pay cards.
	
	• P/R Tax Expense (total) XXX
	     FICA Payable OASDI (employer's) XXX
	     FICA Payable HI (employer's) XXX
	     FUTA Payable XXX
	     SUTA Payable XXX
		6-3, 6-4, 6-5, 6-6, 6-8, 6-9, 6-16

L04 Post to the various general ledger accounts that are used to accumulate information from the payroll entries.	• Copy the debits and credits from the journal entries into the individual ledger accounts in the general ledger.	

L05 Explain the recording of the payroll tax deposits.	• When tax payments are due:
	     Specify Tax Liability Account XXX
	     Cash XXX
		6-10

L06 Understand the need for end-of-period adjustments.	• End of accounting period and end of payroll period— different endings.
	
	• Adjusting entries needed for end-of-period wages and accrued vacation pay:
	     Wages Expense XXX
	        Wages Payable XXX
	     Vacation Benefits Expense XXX
	        Vacation Benefits Payable XXX
		6-11, 6-12, 6-14

MATCHING QUIZ

_____ 1. Employee's earnings record
_____ 2. Pay cards
_____ 3. Disposable earnings
_____ 4. Regular earnings plus overtime earnings
_____ 5. Payroll Taxes
_____ 6. Overtime premium earnings
_____ 7. Wages Payable
_____ 8. Payroll register
_____ 9. Form 668-W
_____ 10. Garnishment

A. Expense account for FICA, FUTA, and SUTA taxes on the employer
B. Legal procedure by which a portion of the wages of any person is withheld for payment of a debt
C. Debit card-based accounts
D. Notifies employer of a tax levy
E. Used to complete Form W-2
F. Provides information needed in preparing the journal entries for payroll
G. Debit portion of payroll entry
H. Earnings remaining after withholding for income taxes and for other amounts required by law
I. One-half regular pay rate multiplied by overtime hours
J. Liability account for wages that have been earned by employees but not yet paid

QUESTIONS FOR REVIEW

1. What are the main kinds of information contained in a payroll register?
2. For what reason are "distribution" columns sometimes provided in the payroll register?
3. Explain the use of the "Cumulative" column in the employee's earnings record.
4. In Philadelphia, Pennsylvania, most workers are subject to three income taxes upon their earnings—federal, state, and city. Should an employer in Philadelphia record the liability for the withholding of all three income taxes in one liability account such as Income Taxes Payable?
5. What is meant by the garnishment of wages?
6. What is general priority order concerning wage attachments?
7. Under the Consumer Credit Protection Act, what is the maximum percentage that can be deducted from an employee's pay to satisfy a student loan garnishment?
8. What portions of an employee's wages are exempt from a federal tax levy?
9. How will payroll deductions from employees' wages for their portion of 401(k) plans be recorded?
10. How are employees who do not have bank accounts paid by an employer who uses an electronic funds transfer system for payroll?
11. How is the information that is usually on a paper paystub given to an employee if the employer is using electronic paystubs?
12. What must the employer do with unclaimed paychecks?
13. What special accounts must usually be opened in the general ledger to record payroll tax entries?
14. Is it necessary for an employer who is subject to FICA and FUTA taxes to keep a separate expense account for the taxes under each act?
15. What is the effect of each of the following postings upon the assets, liabilities, and owner's equity of a company?
    a. A debit to Wages.
    b. A credit to FICA Taxes Payable—HI.
    c. A debit to SUTA Taxes Payable.
    d. A credit to Cash.
16. Why is it necessary to classify employees by kind of work performed when computing the cost of workers' compensation insurance?
17. What accounts are debited and credited when an employer records the electronic transfer of FICA taxes and federal income taxes that have been withheld?
18. How is the amount of accrual entry for the portion of a weekly payroll that is accrued at the end of an accounting period determined?
19. When are expenses of benefits such as vacation pay and retirement pay recorded? Explain.
20. What payroll-related expenses does an employer incur because of its employees?

QUESTIONS FOR DISCUSSION

1. Would it be a violation of the Consumer Credit Protection Act to suspend, demote, or transfer an employee who is subject to a garnishment?
2. Freisleven Corporation has undertaken a cost study of its operations. One area of concern to the company is the total cost of labor, particularly the cost of employee benefits. Prepare a list of the different kinds of costs that a company might incur as part of its "total package" salary cost.
3. If a salaried exempt employee was paid twice (direct deposit) for one pay period and the company was unable to recover the funds, what options are available to the company to correct this overpayment?

PROBLEM SET • A

Omit the writing of explanations for the journal entries. For rounding rules refer to page 2-33.

6-1A • LO 2 Similar to Example 6-2 on page 6-10

Carson Holiday has a federal tax levy of $4,119.90 against him. If Holiday is married with three personal exemptions and had a take-home pay of $1,020.00 this week, how much would his employer take from his pay to satisfy part of the tax levy?

6-2A • LO 2 Similar to Example 6-1 on page 6-10

Kalen O'Brien earned $730 this week. The deductions from her pay were as follows:

FIT	$72.00
FICA—OASDI	45.26
FICA—HI	10.59
State income tax	36.50
State disability insurance	8.61
Health insurance premium	19.50
Credit union contribution	35.00
United Fund contribution	5.00

O'Brien's employer just received a garnishment order (credit card debt of $3,500) against her pay. Compute the following:

a. O'Brien's disposable earnings... $ _____

b. The amount of her pay subject to the garnishment .... $ _____

6-3A • LO 3 See pages 6-18, 6-19, and 6-21

a. Cal Ruther, an employer, is subject to FICA taxes but exempt from FUTA and SUTA taxes. During the last quarter of the year, his employees earned monthly wages of $8,500, all of which is taxable. The amount of federal income taxes withheld each month is $1,040. Journalize the payment of wages, and record the payroll tax on November 25.

JOURNAL

	DATE		DESCRIPTION	POST. REF.	DEBIT	CREDIT	
1							1
2							2
3							3
4							4
5							5
6							6
7							7
8							8
9							9
10							10

6-3A (concluded)

b. Prior to posting the November 25 payroll transaction, FICA Taxes Payable—OASDI, FICA Taxes Payable—HI, and Employees FIT Payable had zero balances. Ruther must pay the FICA taxes and income taxes withheld on the November 25 payroll. Journalize the electronic transfer of the payroll taxes on December 15.

JOURNAL

	DATE	DESCRIPTION	POST. REF.	DEBIT	CREDIT	
1						1
2						2
3						3
4						4
5						5
6						6

6-4A • LO 3 **See pages 6-18 and 6-19**

The employees of Donnelly Music Company earn total wages of $4,690 during January. The total amount is taxable under FICA, FUTA, and SUTA. The state contribution rate for the company is 3.6%. The amount withheld for federal income taxes is $685. Journalize the payment of the monthly wages, and record the payroll taxes.

JOURNAL

	DATE	DESCRIPTION	POST. REF.	DEBIT	CREDIT	
1						1
2						2
3						3
4						4
5						5
6						6
7						7
8						8
9						9
10						10
11						11
12						12
13						13
14						14

6-5A • LO 3   See pages 6-18 and 6-19

Vulcra, Inc., has a semimonthly payroll of $67,000 on September 15. The total payroll is taxable under FICA Taxes—HI; $63,850 is taxable under FICA Taxes—OASDI; and $10,300 is taxable under FUTA and SUTA. The state contribution rate for the company is 4.1%. The amount withheld for federal income taxes is $9,911. The amount withheld for state income taxes is $1,410.

a. Journalize the payment of the wages, and record the payroll taxes on September 15.

b. Assume that the employees of Vulcra, Inc., must also pay state contributions (disability insurance) of 1% on the taxable payroll of $62,100 and that the employees' contributions are to be deducted by the employer. Journalize the September 15 payment of wages, assuming that the state contributions of the employees are kept in a separate account.

JOURNAL

	DATE	DESCRIPTION	POST. REF.	DEBIT	CREDIT	
1						1
2						2
3						3
4						4
5						5
6						6
7						7
8						8
9						9
10						10
11						11
12						12
13						13
14						14
15						15
16						16
17						17
18						18
19						19
20						20
21						21
22						22
23						23
24						24
25						25
26						26
27						27

6-6A • LO 3   See page 6-12

Pauley, Inc., pays its employees' weekly wages in cash. A supplementary payroll sheet that lists the employees' names and their earnings for a certain week is shown below. Complete the payroll sheet by calculating the total amount of payroll and indicating the least possible number of denominations that can be used in paying each employee. However, no employees are to be given bills in denominations greater than $20.

PAULEY, INC.

Supplementary Payroll Sheet

For Period Ending August 15, 20--

Name of Employee	Net Amount Paid	Bills					Coins				
		$20	$10	$5	$1	50¢	25¢	10¢	5¢	1¢	
Chad T. Biskis	$251.75										
Nicole A. Cibik	256.52										
Domingo M. Diaz	384.94										
Laura B. Elias	202.59										
Ari M. Fleischer	253.64										
Diane Y. Germano	296.50										
Arnold B. Herst	594.26										
Edward C. Kenner	399.89										
Kathleen J. Marfia	234.01										
Kimberly A. Picket	595.80										
Total											

6-7A • LO 2, 3   See pages 6-11 and 6-19

Kip Bowman is owner and sole employee of KB Corporation. He pays himself a salary of $1,500 each week.

Additional tax information includes:

FICA tax—OASDI...	6.2% on first $118,500
FICA tax—HI	1.45% on total pay
Federal income tax...	$232.00 per pay
State income tax...	22% of the federal income tax withholding
Federal unemployment tax..	0.6% on first $7,000
State unemployment tax..	0.05% on first $14,000

Additional payroll deductions include:

401(k) plan	3% per pay
Child support garnishment	$100 per pay
Health insurance premium..	$95 per pay

Record the payroll entry and payroll tax entry for the pay of the week ended June 3 (his year-to-date pay is $31,500).

JOURNAL

	DATE		DESCRIPTION	POST. REF.	DEBIT	CREDIT	
1							1
2							2
3							3
4							4
5							5
6							6
7							7
8							8
9							9
10							10
11							11
12							12
13							13
14							14
15							15
16							16
17							17
18							18
19							19
20							20

6-8A • LO 3   **See pages 6-18 and 6-19**

The employees of Pelter Company earn wages of $12,000 for the two weeks ending April 15. FIT taxes of $260 were withheld. The entire amount of wages is subject to the FICA taxes, but only $9,800 is taxable under the federal and state unemployment compensation laws. The state contribution rate of the employer is 2.9%. All employees are subject to state unemployment contributions of 0.5% on the April 15 taxable wages of $9,800, and the employees' contributions are to be deducted by the employer. Journalize the payment of the wages, and record the payroll taxes, assuming that the contributions of the employer and the employees are recorded in one account, SUTA Taxes Payable.

JOURNAL

	DATE	DESCRIPTION	POST. REF.	DEBIT	CREDIT	
1						1
2						2
3						3
4						4
5						5
6						6
7						7
8						8
9						9
10						10
11						11
12						12
13						13
14						14
15						15

6-9A • LO 3   **See pages 6-18 and 6-19**

The following information pertains to the payroll of Texera Tile Company on June 3:

- **a.** The total wages earned by employees are $17,210.

- **b.** The state unemployment insurance contribution rate is 3.5%.

- **c.** The entire amount of wages is taxable under FICA, FUTA, and SUTA.

- **d.** The amount withheld from the employees' wages for federal income taxes is $1,890; for state income taxes, $369.40; and for group insurance, $193.00.

Journalize the payment of wages, and record the payroll taxes on June 3.

JOURNAL

	DATE	DESCRIPTION	POST. REF.	DEBIT	CREDIT	
1						1
2						2
3						3
4						4
5						5
6						6
7						7
8						8
9						9
10						10
11						11
12						12
13						13
14						14
15						15
16						16
17						17

6-10A • LO 5 See page 6-22

On December 31, 2016, Reuter Company has a balance of $98.75 in the FUTA taxes payable account. This represents the employer's liability for the fourth quarter taxes. Journalize the entry Reuter Company should make in January 2017 to record the last transfer (payment) of FUTA taxes for 2016.

JOURNAL

	DATE	DESCRIPTION	POST. REF.	DEBIT	CREDIT	
1						1
2						2
3						3
4						4
5						5
6						6

6-11A • LO 6 See page 6-22

On December 31, 20--, Karmansky Company needed to record its accrued wages for year-end. If December 31 is a Tuesday, then Karmansky Company must account for two days of wages.

The company operates on a five-day workweek, the prior week's gross pay was $32,650, and the net pay was $21,330.

Journalize the adjusting entry to be made on December 31 for the accrued wages.

JOURNAL

	DATE	DESCRIPTION	POST. REF.	DEBIT	CREDIT	
1						1
2						2
3						3
4						4
5						5
6						6

6-12A • LO 6   See pages 6-2 and 6-22

Kelsey Gunn is the only employee of Arsenault Company. His pay rate is $23.00 per hour with an overtime rate of $1\frac{1}{2}$ times for hours over 40 in a workweek.

For the week ending March 31, 20--, he worked 48 hours. Calculate his gross pay for the week using the overtime premium approach to calculate the overtime pay.

Since the company holds back one week of pay, Gunn will not be paid until April 7, 20--. What adjusting entry would the company make in order to record Gunn's salary in the first quarter of this year?

a. Regular pay .... $ _____

b. Overtime premium pay .... $ _____

c. Gross pay .... $ _____

d. Adjusting entry

JOURNAL

	DATE	DESCRIPTION	POST. REF.	DEBIT	CREDIT	
1						1
2						2
3						3

6-13A • LO 2   Similar to Example 6-4 on page 6-20

In Oregon, employers who are covered by the state workers' compensation law withhold employee contributions from the wages of covered employees for the workers' benefit fund at the rate of 1.65¢ for each hour or part of an hour that the worker is employed. Every covered employer is also assessed 1.65¢ per hour for each worker employed for each hour or part of an hour. The employer-employee contributions for workers' compensation are collected monthly, quarterly, or annually by the employer's insurance carrier, according to a schedule agreed upon by the employer and the carrier. The insurance carrier remits the contributions to the state's Workers' Compensation Department.

Cortez Company, a covered employer in Oregon, turns over the employer-employee workers' compensation contributions to its insurance carrier by the 15th of each month for the preceding month. During the month of July, the number of full-time employee-hours worked by the company's employees was 8,270; the number of part-time employee-hours was 1,950.

a. The amount the company should have withheld from its full- and part-time employees during the month of July for workers' compensation insurance is $ _____

b. The title you would give to the general ledger liability account to which the amount withheld from the employees' earnings would be credited is:

_____

c. Journalize the entry on July 29 to record the employer's liability for workers' compensation insurance for the month.

JOURNAL

	DATE	DESCRIPTION	POST. REF.	DEBIT	CREDIT	
1						1
2						2
3						3
4						4
5						5

6-13A (concluded)

d. Journalize the entry on August 15 to record payment to the insurance carrier of the amount withheld from the employees' earnings for workers' compensation insurance and the amount of the employer's liability.

JOURNAL

	DATE	DESCRIPTION	POST. REF.	DEBIT	CREDIT	
1						1
2						2
3						3
4						4
5						5

6-14A • LO 6   Similar to Example 6-6 on page 6-23

At the end of April, Hernandez Company had a balance of $37,910 in the vacation benefits payable account. During May, employees earned an additional $2,790 in vacation benefits, but some employees used vacation days that amounted to $2,050 of the vacation benefits. The $2,050 was charged to Wage Expense when it was paid in May. What adjusting entry would Hernandez Company make at the end of May to bring the vacation benefits payable account up to date?

JOURNAL

	DATE	DESCRIPTION	POST. REF.	DEBIT	CREDIT	
1						1
2						2
3						3

6-15A • LO 1   See pages 6-3 and 6-17

The form on page 6-45 shows the amounts that appear in the Earnings to Date column of the employees' earnings records for 10 full-time and part-time workers in Unger Company. These amounts represent the cumulative earnings for each worker as of October 7, the company's last payday. The form also gives the gross amount of earnings to be paid each worker on the next payday, October 14.

In the state where Unger Company is located, the tax rates and bases are as follows:

Tax on Employees:

FICA—OASDI	6.2% on first $118,500
FICA—HI	1.45% on *total earnings*
SUTA	0.5% on first $8,000

Tax on Employer:

FICA—OASDI	6.2% on first $118,500
FICA—HI	1.45% on *total earnings*
FUTA	0.6% on first $7,000
SUTA	1.8% on first $8,000

In the appropriate columns of the form on page 6-45, do the following:

1. Compute the amount to be withheld from each employee's earnings on October 14 for (a) FICA—OASDI, (b) FICA—HI, and (c) SUTA, and determine the total employee taxes.

2. Record the portion of each employee's earnings that is taxable under FICA, FUTA, and SUTA, and calculate the total employer's payroll taxes on the October 14 payroll.

6-15A (concluded)

UNGER COMPANY

	Employee	Earnings to Date	Gross Earnings Oct. 14	Taxes to Be Withheld from Employees' Earnings Under			Employer Taxes: Portion of Employees' Earnings Taxable Under			
				FICA		SUTA	FICA		FUTA	SUTA
				OASDI	HI		OASDI	HI		
1.	Weiser, Robert A.	$118,790	$1,790							
2.	Stankard, Laurie C.	14,950	295							
3.	Grow, Joan L.	4,060	240							
4.	Rowe, Paul C.	8,190	235							
5.	McNamara, Joyce M.	7,460	195							
6.	O'Connor, Roger T.	118,210	1,810							
7.	Carson, Ronald B.	8,905	280							
8.	Kenny, Ginni C.	4,325	175							
9.	Devery, Virginia S.	57,010	590							
10.	Wilson, Joe W.	3,615	205							
	Total employee taxes....................			$_____ 1.(a)	$_____ 1.(b)	$_____ 1.(c)	$_____	$_____	$_____	$_____

Total taxable earnings . . . .

× Applicable tax rate . . . .

Totals . . . .

Total payroll taxes . . . . $_____

2.

6-16A • LO 3, 4, 5, 6   See pages 6-24 through 6-30

In the Illustrative Case in this chapter, payroll transactions for Brookins Company were analyzed, journalized, and posted for the third quarter of the fiscal year. In this problem, you are to record the payroll transactions for the last quarter of the firm's fiscal year. The last quarter begins on April 1, 20--.

Refer to the Illustrative Case on pages 6-24 to 6-30 and proceed as follows:

a. Analyze and journalize the transactions described in the following narrative. Use the two-column journal paper provided on pages 6-48 to 6-51. Omit the writing of explanations in the journal entries.

b. Post the journal entries to the general ledger accounts on pages 6-52 to 6-57.

Narrative of Transactions:

Apr.	1.	Paid the treasurer of the union the amount of union dues withheld from workers' earnings during March.
	15.	Payroll: $6,105. All wages and salaries taxable. Withheld $565 for federal income taxes, $107.32 for state income taxes, and $50 for union dues.
	15.	Paid the treasurer of the state the amount of state income taxes withheld from workers' earnings during the first quarter.
	15.	Electronically transferred funds to remove the liability for FICA taxes and employees' federal income taxes withheld on the March payrolls.
	29.	Payroll: $5,850. All wages and salaries taxable. Withheld $509 for federal income taxes, $128.90 for state income taxes, and $55 for union dues.
	29.	Filed the Employer's Quarterly Federal Tax Return (Form 941) for the period ended March 31. No journal entry is required, since the FICA taxes and federal income taxes withheld have been timely paid.
	29.	Filed the state contribution return for the quarter ended March 31 and paid the amount to the state unemployment compensation fund.
May	2.	Paid the treasurer of the union the amount of union dues withheld from workers' earnings during April.
	13.	Payroll: $5,810. All wages and salaries taxable. Withheld $507 for federal income taxes, $125.05 for state income taxes, and $55 for union dues.
	16.	Electronically transferred funds to remove the liability for FICA taxes and federal income taxes withheld on the April payrolls.
	31.	Payroll: $6,060. All wages and salaries taxable. Withheld $533 for federal income taxes, $119.00 for state income taxes, and $50 for union dues.
June	3.	Paid the treasurer of the union the amount of union dues withheld from workers' earnings during May.
	15.	Payroll: $6,380. All wages and salaries taxable, except only $5,000 is taxable under FUTA and SUTA. Withheld $549 for federal income taxes, $128.70 for state income taxes, and $50 for union dues.
	15.	Electronically transferred funds to remove the liability for FICA taxes and federal income taxes withheld on the May payrolls.
	30.	Payroll: $6,250. All wages and salaries taxable, except only $4,770 is taxable under FUTA and SUTA. Withheld $538 for federal income taxes, $127.60 for state income taxes, and $50 for union dues.

6-16A (continued)

c. Answer the following questions:

1. The total amount of the liability for FICA taxes and federal income taxes withheld as of June 30 is .... $ _____

2. The total amount of the liability for state income taxes withheld as of June 30 is.. $ _____

3. The amount of FUTA taxes that must be paid to the federal government on or before August 1 (assume July 31 is a Sunday) is .... $ _____

4. The amount of contributions that must be paid into the state unemployment compensation fund on or before August 1 is... $ _____

5. The total amount due the treasurer of the union is .... $ _____

6. The total amount of wages and salaries expense since the beginning of the fiscal year is .... $ _____

7. The total amount of payroll taxes expense since the beginning of the fiscal year is... $ _____

8. Using the partial journal below, journalize the entry to record the vacation accrual at the end of the company's fiscal year. The amount of Brookins Company's vacation accrual for the fiscal year is $15,000.

JOURNAL

	DATE	DESCRIPTION	POST. REF.	DEBIT	CREDIT	
1						1
2						2
3						3
4						4
5						5
6						6

6-16A (continued)

JOURNAL

	DATE		DESCRIPTION	POST. REF.	DEBIT	CREDIT	
1							1
2							2
3							3
4							4
5							5
6							6
7							7
8							8
9							9
10							10
11							11
12							12
13							13
14							14
15							15
16							16
17							17
18							18
19							19
20							20
21							21
22							22
23							23
24							24
25							25
26							26
27							27
28							28
29							29
30							30
31							31
32							32
33							33
34							34

6-16A (continued)

JOURNAL

Page 20

	DATE		DESCRIPTION	POST. REF.	DEBIT	CREDIT	
1							1
2							2
3							3
4							4
5							5
6							6
7							7
8							8
9							9
10							10
11							11
12							12
13							13
14							14
15							15
16							16
17							17
18							18
19							19
20							20
21							21
22							22
23							23
24							24
25							25
26							26
27							27
28							28
29							29
30							30
31							31
32							32
33							33
34							34

6-16A (continued)

JOURNAL

	DATE	DESCRIPTION	POST. REF.	DEBIT	CREDIT	
1						1
2						2
3						3
4						4
5						5
6						6
7						7
8						8
9						9
10						10
11						11
12						12
13						13
14						14
15						15
16						16
17						17
18						18
19						19
20						20
21						21
22						22
23						23
24						24
25						25
26						26
27						27
28						28
29						29
30						30
31						31
32						32
33						33
34						34

6-16A (continued)

JOURNAL

Page 22

	DATE		DESCRIPTION	POST. REF.	DEBIT	CREDIT	
1							1
2							2
3							3
4							4
5							5
6							6
7							7
8							8
9							9
10							10
11							11
12							12
13							13
14							14
15							15
16							16
17							17
18							18
19							19
20							20
21							21
22							22
23							23
24							24
25							25
26							26
27							27
28							28
29							29
30							30
31							31
32							32
33							33
34							34

6-16A (continued)

ACCOUNT **CASH**   ACCOUNT NO. **11**

DATE		ITEM	POST. REF.	DEBIT	CREDIT	BALANCE	
						DEBIT	CREDIT
20-- Apr.	1	Balance	✓			5 7 6 7 3 56	

6-16A (continued)

ACCOUNT **FICA TAXES PAYABLE—OASDI**   ACCOUNT NO. **20**

DATE		ITEM	POST. REF.	DEBIT	CREDIT	BALANCE	
						DEBIT	CREDIT
20-- Apr.	1	Balance	✓				1 0 6 8 88

6-16A (continued)

ACCOUNT **FICA TAXES PAYABLE—HI**   ACCOUNT NO. 21

DATE		ITEM	POST. REF.	DEBIT	CREDIT	BALANCE	
						DEBIT	CREDIT
20-- Apr.	1	Balance	✓				2 4 9 98

6-16A (continued)

ACCOUNT   **FUTA TAXES PAYABLE**   ACCOUNT NO. 22

DATE		ITEM	POST. REF.	DEBIT	CREDIT	BALANCE	
						DEBIT	CREDIT
20-- Apr.	1	Balance	✓				1 4 9 16

ACCOUNT   **SUTA TAXES PAYABLE**   ACCOUNT NO. 23

DATE		ITEM	POST. REF.	DEBIT	CREDIT	BALANCE	
						DEBIT	CREDIT
20-- Apr.	1	Balance	✓				5 7 1 78

6-16A (continued)

ACCOUNT **EMPLOYEES FIT PAYABLE**   ACCOUNT NO. 25

DATE		ITEM	POST. REF.	DEBIT	CREDIT	BALANCE	
						DEBIT	CREDIT
20-- Apr.	1	Balance	✓				1 1 2 4 00

ACCOUNT **EMPLOYEES SIT PAYABLE**   ACCOUNT NO. 26

DATE		ITEM	POST. REF.	DEBIT	CREDIT	BALANCE	
						DEBIT	CREDIT
20-- Apr.	1	Balance	✓				5 4 6 92

6-16A (concluded)

ACCOUNT **UNION DUES PAYABLE**   ACCOUNT NO. 28

DATE		ITEM	POST. REF.	DEBIT	CREDIT	BALANCE	
						DEBIT	CREDIT
20-- Apr.	1	Balance	✓				1 0 0 00

ACCOUNT **WAGES AND SALARIES**   ACCOUNT NO. 51

DATE		ITEM	POST. REF.	DEBIT	CREDIT	BALANCE	
						DEBIT	CREDIT
20-- Apr.	1	Balance	✓			7 1 3 6 0 00	

ACCOUNT **PAYROLL TAXES**   ACCOUNT NO. 55

DATE		ITEM	POST. REF.	DEBIT	CREDIT	BALANCE	
						DEBIT	CREDIT
20-- Apr.	1	Balance	✓			6 8 4 6 74	

PROBLEM SET • B

Omit the writing of explanations for the journal entries. For rounding rules refer to page 2-33.

6-1B • LO 2 Similar to Example 6-2 on page 6-10

Karen Most has a federal tax levy of $2,100.50 against her. If Most is single with two personal exemptions and had a take-home pay of $499.00 this week, how much would her employer take from her pay to satisfy part of the tax levy?

6-2B • LO 2 Similar to Example 6-1 on page 6-10

Garrett Hudson earned $895 this week. The deductions from his pay were as follows:

FIT	$96.00
FICA—OASDI	55.49
FICA—HI	12.98
State income tax	27.75
State disability insurance	6.71
Health insurance premium	31.00
Credit union contribution	50.00
United Fund contribution	10.00

Hudson's employer just received a garnishment order (credit card debt of $2,140) against his pay. Compute the following:

a. Hudson's disposable earnings .... $ _____

b. The amount of his pay subject to the garnishment .... $ _____

6-3B • LO 3 See pages 6-18, 6-19, and 6-21

a. Harriet Pandel, an employer, is subject to FICA taxes but exempt from FUTA and SUTA taxes. During the last quarter of the year, her employees earned monthly wages of $16,900, all of which is taxable. The amount of federal income taxes withheld each month is $1,698. Journalize the payment of wages, and record the payroll tax on November 25.

JOURNAL

	DATE	DESCRIPTION	POST. REF.	DEBIT	CREDIT	
1						1
2						2
3						3
4						4
5						5
6						6
7						7
8						8
9						9
10						10

6-3B (concluded)

b. Prior to posting the November 25 payroll transaction, FICA Taxes Payable—OASDI, FICA Taxes Payable—HI, and Employees FIT Payable had zero balances. Pandel must pay the FICA taxes and income taxes withheld on the November 25 payroll. Journalize the electronic transfer of the payroll taxes on December 15.

JOURNAL

	DATE	DESCRIPTION	POST. REF.	DEBIT	CREDIT	
1						1
2						2
3						3
4						4
5						5
6						6

6-4B • LO 3   See pages 6-18 and 6-19

The employees of Carson Bakery Company earn total wages of $7,780 during January. The total amount is taxable under FICA, FUTA, and SUTA. The state contribution rate for the company is 4.3%. The amount withheld for federal income taxes is $998. Journalize the payment of the monthly wages, and record the payroll taxes.

JOURNAL

	DATE	DESCRIPTION	POST. REF.	DEBIT	CREDIT	
1						1
2						2
3						3
4						4
5						5
6						6
7						7
8						8
9						9
10						10
11						11
12						12
13						13
14						14

6-5B • LO 3   See pages 6-18 and 6-19

Purnell, Inc., has a semimonthly payroll of $53,900 on September 15. The total payroll is taxable under FICA Taxes—HI; $50,400 is taxable under FICA Taxes—OASDI; and $7,300 is taxable under FUTA and SUTA. The state contribution rate for the company is 3.1%. The amount withheld for federal income taxes is $6,995. The amount withheld for state income taxes is $1,010.

a. Journalize the payment of the wages, and record the payroll taxes on September 15.

b. Assume that the employees of Purnell, Inc., must also pay state contributions (disability insurance) of 1% on the taxable payroll of $24,100 and that the employees' contributions are to be deducted by the employer. Journalize the September 15 payment of wages, assuming that the state contributions of the employees are kept in a separate account.

JOURNAL

	DATE		DESCRIPTION	POST. REF.	DEBIT	CREDIT	
1							1
2							2
3							3
4							4
5							5
6							6
7							7
8							8
9							9
10							10
11							11
12							12
13							13
14							14
15							15
16							16
17							17
18							18
19							19
20							20
21							21
22							22
23							23
24							24
25							25
26							26
27							27

6-6B • LO 3   See page 6-12

Adams, Inc., pays its employees' weekly wages in cash. A supplementary payroll sheet that lists the employees' names and their earnings for a certain week is shown below. Complete the payroll sheet by calculating the total amount of payroll and indicating the least possible number of denominations that can be used in paying each employee. However, no employees are to be given bills in denominations greater than $20.

ADAMS, INC.

Supplementary Payroll Sheet

For Period Ending August 15, 20--

Name of Employee	Net Amount Paid	Bills					Coins			
		$20	$10	$5	$1	50¢	25¢	10¢	5¢	1¢
Ben Dowd	$639.57									
Erin Martin	248.95									
Dot Ruiz	491.95									
Randi Heavner	832.14									
Rex Sundry	710.15									
Hal Roach	709.13									
Mandy Arnold	519.13									
Faye Montgomery	227.24									
Max Held	473.18									
Pedro Rodries	590.90									
Total										

6-7B • LO 2, 3   See pages 6-11 and 6-19

Carmen Santos is owner and sole employee of CS Corporation. He pays himself a salary of $2,400 this week.

Additional tax information includes:

FICA tax—OASDI..	6.2% on first $118,500
FICA tax—HI...	1.45% on total pay
Federal income tax	$532.00 per pay
State income tax	22% of the federal income tax withholding
Federal unemployment tax	0.6% on first $7,000
State unemployment tax	0.05% on first $14,000

Additional payroll deductions include:

401(k) plan	3% per pay
Child support garnishment	$125 per pay
Health insurance premium	$110 per pay

Record the payroll entry and payroll tax entry for the pay of the week ended June 3 (his year-to-date pay is $51,500).

JOURNAL

	DATE	DESCRIPTION	POST. REF.	DEBIT	CREDIT	
1						1
2						2
3						3
4						4
5						5
6						6
7						7
8						8
9						9
10						10
11						11
12						12
13						13
14						14
15						15
16						16
17						17
18						18
19						19
20						20

6-8B • LO 3   See pages 6-18 and 6-19

The employees of Portonegra Company earn wages of $15,600 for the two weeks ending April 15. FIT taxes of $424 were withheld. The entire amount of wages is subject to the FICA taxes, but only $10,800 is taxable under the federal and state unemployment compensation laws. The state contribution rate of the employer is 3.9%. All employees are subject to state unemployment contributions of 0.5% on the April 15 taxable wages of $10,800, and the employees' contributions are to be deducted by the employer. Journalize the payment of the wages, and record the payroll taxes, assuming that the contributions of the employer and the employees are recorded in one account, SUTA Taxes Payable.

JOURNAL

	DATE	DESCRIPTION	POST. REF.	DEBIT	CREDIT	
1						1
2						2
3						3
4						4
5						5
6						6
7						7
8						8
9						9
10						10
11						11
12						12
13						13
14						14
15						15

6-9B • LO 3   See pages 6-18 and 6-19

The following information pertains to the payroll of Fanelli Fashion Company on June 3:

a. The total wages earned by employees are $2,910.

b. The state unemployment insurance contribution rate is 3.75%.

c. The entire amount of wages is taxable under FICA, FUTA, and SUTA.

d. The amount withheld from the employees' wages for federal income taxes is $491; for state income taxes, $49.10; and for group insurance, $87.10.

Journalize the payment of wages, and record the payroll taxes on June 3.

JOURNAL

	DATE	DESCRIPTION	POST. REF.	DEBIT	CREDIT	
1						1
2						2
3						3
4						4
5						5
6						6
7						7
8						8
9						9
10						10
11						11
12						12
13						13
14						14
15						15
16						16
17						17

6-10B • LO 5   See page 6-22

On December 31, 2016, Santucci Company has a balance of $619.24 in the FUTA taxes payable account. This represents the employer's liability for the fourth quarter taxes. Journalize the entry Santucci Company should make in January 2017 to record the last transfer (payment) of FUTA taxes for 2016.

JOURNAL

	DATE	DESCRIPTION	POST. REF.	DEBIT	CREDIT	
1						1
2						2
3						3
4						4
5						5
6						6

6-11B • LO 6   See page 6-22

On December 31, 20--, Sanchez Company needed to record its accrued wages for year-end. If December 31 is a Wednesday, then Sanchez Company must account for three days of wages.

The company operates on a five-day workweek, the prior week's gross pay was $29,870, and the net pay was $19,995.

Journalize the adjusting entry to be made on December 31 for the accrued wages.

JOURNAL

	DATE	DESCRIPTION	POST. REF.	DEBIT	CREDIT	
1						1
2						2
3						3
4						4
5						5
6						6

6-12B • LO 6   See pages 6-2 and 6-22

John Torre is the only employee of Bambert Company. His pay rate is $19.70 per hour with an overtime rate of $1\frac{1}{2}$ times for hours over 40 in a workweek.

For the week ending March 31, 20--, he worked 44 hours. Calculate his gross pay for the week using the overtime premium approach to calculate the overtime pay.

Since the company holds back one week of pay, Torre will not be paid until April 7, 20--. What adjusting entry would the company make in order to record Torre's salary in the first quarter of this year?

a. Regular pay .... $ _____

b. Overtime premium pay .... $ _____

c. Gross pay .... $ _____

d. Adjusting entry

JOURNAL

	DATE	DESCRIPTION	POST. REF.	DEBIT	CREDIT	
1						1
2						2
3						3

6-13B • LO 2   Similar to Example 6-4 on page 6-20

In Oregon, employers who are covered by the state workers' compensation law withhold employee contributions from the wages of covered employees for the workers' benefit fund at the rate of 1.65¢ for each hour or part of an hour that the worker is employed. Every covered employer is also assessed 1.65¢ per hour for each worker employed for each hour or part of an hour. The employer-employee contributions for workers' compensation are collected monthly, quarterly, or annually by the employer's insurance carrier, according to a schedule agreed upon by the employer and the carrier. The insurance carrier remits the contributions to the state's Workers' Compensation Department.

Umber Company, a covered employer in Oregon, turns over the employer-employee workers' compensation contributions to its insurance carrier by the 15th of each month for the preceding month. During the month of July, the number of full-time employee-hours worked by the company's employees was 26,110; the number of part-time employee-hours was 3,490.

a. The amount the company should have withheld from its full- and part-time employees during the month of July for workers' compensation insurance is $ _____

b. The title you would give to the general ledger account to which the amount withheld from the employees' earnings would be credited is:

_____

c. Journalize the entry on July 29 to record the employer's liability for workers' compensation insurance for the month.

JOURNAL

	DATE	DESCRIPTION	POST. REF.	DEBIT	CREDIT	
1						1
2						2
3						3
4						4
5						5

6-13B (concluded)

d. Journalize the entry on August 15 to record payment to the insurance carrier of the amount withheld from the employees' earnings for workers' compensation insurance and the amount of the employer's liability.

JOURNAL

	DATE	DESCRIPTION	POST. REF.	DEBIT	CREDIT	
1						1
2						2
3						3
4						4
5						5

6-14B • LO 6   **Similar to Example 6-6 on page 6-23**

At the end of June, Morton Company had a balance of $49,900 in the vacation benefits payable account. During July, employees earned an additional $3,110 in vacation benefits, but some employees used vacation days that amounted to $2,490 of the vacation benefits. The $2,490 was charged to Wage Expense when it was paid in July. What adjusting entry would Morton Company make at the end of July to bring the vacation benefits payable account up to date?

JOURNAL

	DATE	DESCRIPTION	POST. REF.	DEBIT	CREDIT	
1						1
2						2
3						3

6-15B • LO 1   **See pages 6-3 and 6-17**

The form on page 6-69 shows the amounts that appear in the Earnings to Date column of the employees' earnings records for 10 full-time and part-time workers in Ranger Company. These amounts represent the cumulative earnings for each worker as of November 4, the company's last payday. The form also gives the gross amount of earnings to be paid each worker on the next payday, November 11.

In the state where Ranger Company is located, the tax rates and bases are as follows:

Tax on Employees:
FICA—OASDI	6.2% on first $118,500
FICA—HI	1.45% on *total earnings*
SUTA	0.5% on first $8,000

Tax on Employer:
FICA—OASDI	6.2% on first $118,500
FICA—HI	1.45% on *total earnings*
FUTA	0.6% on first $7,000
SUTA	2.8% on first $8,000

In the appropriate columns of the form on page 6-69, do the following:

1. Compute the amount to be withheld from each employee's earnings on November 11 for (a) FICA—OASDI, (b) FICA—HI, and (c) SUTA, and determine the total employee taxes.

2. Record the portion of each employee's earnings that is taxable under FICA, FUTA, and SUTA, and calculate the total employer's payroll taxes on the November 11 payroll.

6-15B (concluded)

RANGER COMPANY

Employee	Earnings to Date	Gross Earnings Nov. 11	Taxes to Be Withheld from Employees' Earnings Under FICA OASDI	HI	SUTA	Employer Taxes: Portion of Employees' Earnings Taxable Under FICA OSADI	HI	FUTA	SUTA
1. Watson, Ruth T.	$118,900	$1,890							
2. Kinder, Ralph A.	14,950	410							
3. Sanchez, Robert T.	4,060	395							
4. Carey, Mary C.	8,190	295							
5. Cox, Mason M.	6,460	425							
6. Kenni, Jack T.	118,300	1,850							
7. Britmayer, Tim A.	8,905	490							
8. Candi, Mark B.	6,825	325							
9. Boxer, Barbara C.	57,010	1,150							
10. McBride, James W.	3,615	195							
Total employee taxes			$	$	$	$	$	$	$
			1.(a)	1.(b)	1.(c)				

Total taxable earnings ....

× Applicable tax rate ....

Totals .... $ $ $ $

Total payroll taxes .... 2.

6-16B • LO 3, 4, 5, 6   See pages 6-24 through 6-30

In the Illustrative Case in this chapter, payroll transactions for Brookins Company were analyzed, journalized, and posted for the third quarter of the fiscal year. In this problem, you are to record the payroll transactions for the last quarter of the firm's fiscal year. The last quarter begins on April 1, 20--.

Refer to the Illustrative Case on pages 6-24 to 6-30 and proceed as follows:

a. Analyze and journalize the transactions described in the following narrative. Use the two-column journal paper provided on pages 6-72 to 6-75. Omit the writing of explanations in the journal entries.

b. Post the journal entries to the general ledger accounts on pages 6-76 to 6-81.

Narrative of Transactions:

Apr. 1. Paid the treasurer of the union the amount of union dues withheld from workers' earnings during March.

15. Payroll: $8,310. All wages and salaries taxable. Withheld $890 for federal income taxes, $166.20 for state income taxes, and $140 for union dues.

15. Paid the treasurer of the state the amount of state income taxes withheld from workers' earnings during the first quarter.

15. Electronically transferred funds to remove the liability for FICA taxes and employees' federal income taxes withheld on the March payrolls.

29. Payroll: $7,975. All wages and salaries taxable. Withheld $815 for federal income taxes, $151.50 for state income taxes, and $135 for union dues.

29. Filed the Employer's Quarterly Federal Tax Return (Form 941) for the period ended March 31. No journal entry is required, since the FICA taxes and federal income taxes withheld have been timely paid.

29. Filed the state contribution return for the quarter ended March 31 and paid the amount to the state unemployment compensation fund.

May 2. Paid the treasurer of the union the amount of union dues withheld from workers' earnings during April.

13. Payroll: $8,190. All wages and salaries taxable. Withheld $875 for federal income taxes, $160.05 for state income taxes, and $135 for union dues.

16. Electronically transferred funds to remove the liability for FICA taxes and federal income taxes withheld on the April payrolls.

31. Payroll: $8,755. All wages and salaries taxable. Withheld $971 for federal income taxes, $174.05 for state income taxes, and $140 for union dues.

June 3. Paid the treasurer of the union the amount of union dues withheld from workers' earnings during May.

15. Payroll: $9,110. All wages and salaries taxable, except only $4,210 is taxable under FUTA and SUTA. Withheld $1,029 for federal income taxes, $187.15 for state income taxes, and $145 for union dues.

15. Electronically transferred funds to remove the liability for FICA taxes and federal income taxes withheld on the May payrolls.

30. Payroll: $8,960. All wages and salaries taxable, except only $2,280 is taxable under FUTA and SUTA. Withheld $988 for federal income taxes, $183.95 for state income taxes, and $145 for union dues.

6-16B (continued)

c. Answer the following questions:

1. The total amount of the liability for FICA taxes and federal income taxes withheld as of June 30 is .... $ _____

2. The total amount of the liability for state income taxes withheld as of June 30 is... $ _____

3. The amount of FUTA taxes that must be paid to the federal government on or before August 1 (assume July 31 is a Sunday) is .... $ _____

4. The amount of contributions that must be paid into the state unemployment compensation fund on or before August 1 is.. $ _____
$ _____

5. The total amount due the treasurer of the union is .... $ _____

6. The total amount of wages and salaries expense since the beginning of the fiscal year is .... $ _____

7. The total amount of payroll taxes expense since the beginning of the fiscal year is... $ _____

8. Using the partial journal below, journalize the entry to record the vacation accrual at the end of the company's fiscal year. The amount of Brookins Company's vacation accrual for the fiscal year is $15,000.

JOURNAL

	DATE	DESCRIPTION	POST. REF.	DEBIT	CREDIT	
1						1
2						2
3						3
4						4
5						5
6						6

6-16B (continued)

JOURNAL

	DATE		DESCRIPTION	POST. REF.	DEBIT	CREDIT	
1							1
2							2
3							3
4							4
5							5
6							6
7							7
8							8
9							9
10							10
11							11
12							12
13							13
14							14
15							15
16							16
17							17
18							18
19							19
20							20
21							21
22							22
23							23
24							24
25							25
26							26
27							27
28							28
29							29
30							30
31							31
32							32
33							33
34							34

6-16B (continued)

JOURNAL

Page 20

	DATE		DESCRIPTION	POST. REF.	DEBIT	CREDIT	
1							1
2							2
3							3
4							4
5							5
6							6
7							7
8							8
9							9
10							10
11							11
12							12
13							13
14							14
15							15
16							16
17							17
18							18
19							19
20							20
21							21
22							22
23							23
24							24
25							25
26							26
27							27
28							28
29							29
30							30
31							31
32							32
33							33
34							34

6-16B (continued)

JOURNAL

	DATE	DESCRIPTION	POST. REF.	DEBIT	CREDIT	
1						1
2						2
3						3
4						4
5						5
6						6
7						7
8						8
9						9
10						10
11						11
12						12
13						13
14						14
15						15
16						16
17						17
18						18
19						19
20						20
21						21
22						22
23						23
24						24
25						25
26						26
27						27
28						28
29						29
30						30
31						31
32						32
33						33
34						34

6-16B (continued)

JOURNAL   Page 22

	DATE		DESCRIPTION	POST. REF.	DEBIT	CREDIT	
1							1
2							2
3							3
4							4
5							5
6							6
7							7
8							8
9							9
10							10
11							11
12							12
13							13
14							14
15							15
16							16
17							17
18							18
19							19
20							20
21							21
22							22
23							23
24							24
25							25
26							26
27							27
28							28
29							29
30							30
31							31
32							32
33							33
34							34

6-16B (continued)

ACCOUNT **CASH** ACCOUNT NO. **11**

DATE		ITEM	POST. REF.	DEBIT	CREDIT	BALANCE	
						DEBIT	CREDIT
20-- Apr.	1	*Balance*	✓			5 7 6 7 3 56	

6-16B (continued)

ACCOUNT **FICA TAXES PAYABLE—OASDI**   ACCOUNT NO. 20

DATE		ITEM	POST. REF.	DEBIT	CREDIT	BALANCE	
						DEBIT	CREDIT
20-- Apr.	1	Balance	✓				1 0 6 8 88

6-16B (continued)

ACCOUNT **FICA TAXES PAYABLE—HI**   ACCOUNT NO. 21

DATE		ITEM	POST. REF.	DEBIT	CREDIT	BALANCE	
						DEBIT	CREDIT
20-- Apr.	1	Balance	✓				2 4 9 98

6-16B (continued)

ACCOUNT **FUTA TAXES PAYABLE**   ACCOUNT NO. 22

DATE		ITEM	POST. REF.	DEBIT	CREDIT	BALANCE	
						DEBIT	CREDIT
20-- Apr.	1	Balance	✓				1 4 9 16

ACCOUNT **SUTA TAXES PAYABLE**   ACCOUNT NO. 23

DATE		ITEM	POST. REF.	DEBIT	CREDIT	BALANCE	
						DEBIT	CREDIT
20-- Apr.	1	Balance	✓				5 7 1 78

6-16B (continued)

ACCOUNT **EMPLOYEES FIT PAYABLE**   ACCOUNT NO. 25

DATE		ITEM	POST. REF.	DEBIT	CREDIT	BALANCE	
						DEBIT	CREDIT
20-- Apr.	1	Balance	✓				1 1 2 4 00

ACCOUNT **EMPLOYEES SIT PAYABLE**   ACCOUNT NO. 26

DATE		ITEM	POST. REF.	DEBIT	CREDIT	BALANCE	
						DEBIT	CREDIT
20-- Apr.	1	Balance	✓				5 4 6 92

6-16B (concluded)

ACCOUNT   **UNION DUES PAYABLE**   ACCOUNT NO. 28

DATE		ITEM	POST. REF.	DEBIT	CREDIT	BALANCE	
						DEBIT	CREDIT
20-- Apr.	1	Balance	✓				1 0 0 00

ACCOUNT   **WAGES AND SALARIES**   ACCOUNT NO. 51

DATE		ITEM	POST. REF.	DEBIT	CREDIT	BALANCE	
						DEBIT	CREDIT
20-- Apr.	1	Balance	✓			7 1 3 6 0 00	

ACCOUNT   **PAYROLL TAXES**   ACCOUNT NO. 55

DATE		ITEM	POST. REF.	DEBIT	CREDIT	BALANCE	
						DEBIT	CREDIT
20-- Apr.	1	Balance	✓			6 8 4 6 74	

CONTINUING PAYROLL PROBLEM • A

In this last phase of your work on the Continuing Payroll Problem A, you will record the amounts withheld for group and health insurance and calculate the net pay for each employee. Refer to the partially completed payroll registers upon which you were working at the end of Chapter 5, and proceed as follows:

1. In the appropriate column of the payroll register, record the amount to be withheld for group life insurance. Each employee contributes 85¢ each week toward the cost of group insurance coverage, with the exception of Smith and Schork (Kipley Company), who are not yet eligible for coverage under the company plan.
2. Record the amount to be withheld for health insurance. Each employee contributes $1.65 each week toward the cost of health insurance.
3. Record the net pay for each employee. The net pay for each employee is obtained by subtracting the total amount of all deductions from the total earnings.
4. Each worker is to be paid by check. Assign check numbers commencing with No. 313.
5. Foot all money columns of the payroll register, and prove the accuracy of the column totals.

6. On a separate sheet of paper:

   a. Prepare the journal entries as of January 12 to record the payroll and the payroll taxes for the week ending January 8. Credit Salaries Payable for the total net pay.

   Use the following tax rates and bases: employer's FICA—OASDI, 6.2% on the first $118,500; employer's FICA—HI, 1.45% on total earnings; FUTA, 0.6% on the first $7,000; and SUTA, 3.6785% on the first $9,000.

   b. Prepare the journal entry to record the payment of the payroll on January 14 when the paychecks are distributed to all workers.

Your work on the Continuing Payroll Problem A is now completed, and you may be asked to submit your payroll register to your instructor. The experience you have gained in working on each of the succeeding phases of the Continuing Payroll Problem will aid you in undertaking the payroll work involved in Chapter 7. In the Comprehensive Payroll Project, you will be responsible for all aspects of payroll operations for a company for an entire calendar quarter.

CONTINUING PAYROLL PROBLEM • B

In this last phase of your work on the Continuing Payroll Problem B, you will record the amounts withheld for group and health insurance and calculate the net pay for each employee. Refer to the partially completed payroll registers upon which you were working at the end of Chapter 5, and proceed as follows:

1. In the appropriate column of the payroll register, record the amount to be withheld for group life insurance. Each employee contributes 85¢ each week toward the cost of group insurance coverage, with the exception of Palmetto and Wichman (Olney Company) who are not yet eligible for coverage under the company plan.
2. Record the amount to be withheld for health insurance. Each employee contributes $1.65 each week toward the cost of health insurance.
3. Record the net pay for each employee. The net pay for each employee is obtained by subtracting the total amount of all deductions from the total earnings.
4. Each worker is to be paid by check. Assign check numbers commencing with No. 313.
5. Foot all money columns of the payroll register, and prove the accuracy of the column totals.

6. On a separate sheet of paper:

   a. Prepare the journal entries as of January 12 to record the payroll and the payroll taxes for the week ending January 8. Credit Salaries Payable for the total net pay.

   Use the following tax rates and bases: employer's FICA—OASDI, 6.2% on the first $118,500; employer's FICA—HI, 1.45% on total earnings; FUTA, 0.6% on the first $7,000; and SUTA, 3.6785% on the first $9,000.

   b. Prepare the journal entry to record the payment of the payroll on January 14 when the paychecks are distributed to all workers.

Your work on the Continuing Payroll Problem B is now completed, and you may be asked to submit your payroll register to your instructor. The experience you have gained in working on each of the succeeding phases of the Continuing Payroll Problem will aid you in undertaking the payroll work involved in Chapter 7. In the Comprehensive Payroll Project, you will be responsible for all aspects of payroll operations for a company for an entire calendar quarter.

CASE PROBLEM

C1. Budgeting for Additional Payroll Costs.

Frank Flynn is the payroll manager for Powlus Supply Company. During the budgeting process, Sam Kinder, director of finance, asked Flynn to arrive at a set percentage that could be applied to each budgeted salary figure to cover the additional cost that will be incurred by Powlus Supply for each employee. After some discussion, it was determined that the best way to compute this percentage would be to base these additional costs of payroll on the average salary paid by the company.

Kinder wants this additional payroll cost percentage to cover payroll taxes (FICA, FUTA, and SUTA) and other payroll costs covered by the company (workers' compensation expense, health insurance costs, and vacation pay).

Flynn gathers the following information in order to complete the analysis:

Average annual salary	$24,000
FICA rates	6.2% and 1.45%
FUTA	0.6% on 1st $7,000
SUTA	3.3% on 1st $10,400
Workers' compensation costs	$0.97 per $100 of payroll
Health insurance costs	$75.15 per month
Vacation pay earned	2 weeks' pay earned each year to be used in following year

Compute the percentage that can be used in the budget.

Payroll Project

What now? Can we process a payroll? How about the accounting entries and postings? Can we complete the deposit forms and the "dreaded" payroll tax returns? What have we learned in the previous six chapters? Did I waste this semester?

Let's find out. Here's your real-world test.

LEARNING OBJECTIVES

Chapter 7 consists of a simulation, or practice set, for payroll accounting. You will apply the knowledge acquired in this course to practical payroll situations. This simulation is a culmination of the information presented in the textbook.

After completing this chapter, you should be able to:

1 Prepare payroll registers.
2 Maintain employees' earnings records.
3 Journalize and post payroll and payroll tax entries.
4 Complete federal, state, and city tax deposit forms and journalize the transactions.
5 Prepare various quarter-end and year-end payroll tax forms.
6 Make the accrual entries for the payroll at the end of a year.

The Payroll Project will provide you with extended practice in keeping payroll records and accounting for payroll transactions. Your completion of this project involves an application of the information learned in the preceding chapters. The work provided resembles that prevailing in the office of every employer in the United States subject to the provisions of the Federal Wage and Hour Law, income tax withholding laws, social security laws, and unemployment compensation laws. Even though most payroll systems now employ computers, it is important that the practitioner understand the operations performed by the computer.

If your assignment involves the use of Appendix A (computerized option) to complete this project, it is suggested that you do at least one of the payrolls manually so that you gain a thorough understanding of the steps needed to be completed on a typical payday.

In this project, you are employed by Glo-Brite Paint Company. As the payroll clerk in the Accounting Department, you have been in charge of the payroll records since the company first began operations on January 5 of the current year. The company employs about 800 individuals; but for the purpose of this project, payroll records will be kept for only a dozen or so employees. By understanding the principles of payroll accounting for a few employees, you should be able to keep similar records for several hundred employees.

For purposes of this project, you will assume that the payroll records, tax reports, and deposits have been completed and filed for the first three quarters of this year. Your work will involve the processing of the payrolls for the last quarter of the year and the completion of the last quarterly and annual tax reports and forms.

Books of Account and Payroll Records

The books of account and payroll records that you will use in this project are described in this section.

Journal

You will use a two-column general journal to record all transactions affecting the accounts in the general ledger. This book of original entry serves as a posting medium for transactions affecting the payroll accounts.

General Ledger

A general ledger, used in keeping the payroll accounts, is ruled with balance-column ruling, which makes it possible to keep a continuous record of each account balance. Some of the ledger accounts will have beginning balances carried over from the first three quarters of the year.

The chart of accounts in Figure 7.1 has been used in opening the general ledger accounts (pages 7-34 to 7-41). Glo-Brite Paint Company has other accounts in its general ledger, but those listed in the partial chart of accounts are the only accounts required in completing this project.

Payroll Register

The payroll register provides the information needed for journalizing each payroll and for posting to the employees' earnings records.

FIGURE 7.1
Partial Chart of Accounts

Account Title	Account No.
Cash	11
Payroll Cash	12
FICA Taxes Payable—OASDI	20.1
FICA Taxes Payable—HI	20.2
FUTA Taxes Payable	21
SUTA Taxes Payable—Employer	22
Employees FIT Payable	24
Employees SIT Payable	25
Employees SUTA Payable	25.1
Employees CIT Payable	26
Group Insurance Premiums Collected	27
Union Dues Payable	28
Administrative Salaries	51
Office Salaries	52
Sales Salaries	53
Plant Wages	54
Payroll Taxes	56

Employee's Earnings Record

The employee's earnings record provides a summary of each employee's earnings, deductions, and taxable wages. The information recorded in this record is posted from the payroll register.

From the personnel data given in Figure 7.2 an employee's earnings record has been maintained for each employee (pages 7-43 to 7-47). The first line of each of these records shows the employee's cumulative figures for the first three quarters of the year. Note that only one-half page has been used for each employee's earnings record.

General Information

The home office and the manufacturing plant of Glo-Brite Paint Company are located at 2215 Salvador Street, Philadelphia, PA 19175-0682. The company's phone number is (215) 555-9559. The company's federal identification number is 00-0000660; the state account number, 000-0-3300; and the city identifying number, 000-0001855.

Regular Hours of Work

The workweek for all employees is 40 hours, except for the student's 36-hour schedule. The office is open from 8:00 a.m. to 5:00 p.m. each day, except weekends. Glo-Brite allows one hour for lunch, 12:00 p.m. to 1:00 p.m. The plant operates on a five-day workweek of eight hours per day, with normal working hours from 7:00 a.m. to 11:00 a.m. and 12:00 p.m. to 4:00 p.m.

FIGURE 7.2
Glo-Brite Employees

Personnel Data—October 1, 20--

BONNO, Anthony Victor, 694 Bristol Avenue, Philadelphia, PA 19135-0617. Married, claiming 4 withholding allowances. Telephone, 555-9827. Social Security No. 000-00-3481. Position, mixer operator in plant. Wages, $17.65 per hour. Group insurance, $55,000.

FERGUSON, James Claude, 808 Sixth Street, Philadelphia, PA 19106-0995. Married, claiming 5 withholding allowances. Telephone, 555-8065. Social Security No. 000-00-8645. Position, sales manager. Salary, $58,500 per year. Group insurance, $88,000. Department: Sales.

FORD, Catherine Louise, 18 Dundee Avenue, Philadelphia, PA 19151-1919. Divorced, claiming 2 withholding allowances. Telephone, 555-0235. Social Security No. 000-00-4567. Position, executive secretary. Salary, $2,643.33 per month. Group insurance, $48,000. Department: Office.

MANN, Dewey Wilson, 3007 Bisque Drive, Philadelphia, PA 19199-0718. Married, claiming 4 withholding allowances. Telephone, 555-0774. Social Security No. 000-00-9352. Position, sales representative. Salary, $2,925 per month. Group insurance, $53,000. Department: Sales.

O'NEILL, Joseph Tyler, 2100 Broad Street, Philadelphia, PA 19121-7189. Married, claiming 3 withholding allowances. Telephone, 555-2332. Social Security No. 000-00-1534. Position, president. Salary, $60,000 per year. Group insurance, $90,000. Department: Administrative.

RUSSELL, Virginia Aloise, 8004 Dowling Road, Philadelphia, PA 19135-9001. Single, claiming 1 withholding allowance. Telephone, 555-3681. Social Security No. 000-00-6337. Position, time clerk. Salary, $2,600 per month. Group insurance, $47,000. Department: Office.

RYAN, Norman Allen, 7300 Harrison Street, Philadelphia, PA 19124-6699. Married, claiming 4 withholding allowances. Telephone, 555-6660. Social Security No. 000-00-1223. Position, electrician in plant. Wages, $18.00 per hour. Group insurance, $56,000.

SOKOWSKI, Thomas James, 133 Cornwells Street, Philadelphia, PA 19171-5718. Married, claiming 2 withholding allowances. Telephone, 555-5136. Social Security No. 000-00-8832. Position, supervisor in plant. Salary, $1,025 per week. Group insurance, $80,000.

STUDENT, 7018 Erdrick Street, Philadelphia, PA 19135-8517. Single, claiming 1 withholding allowance. Position, accounting trainee. Wages, $14.00 per hour. Group insurance, $39,000. Department: Office.

WILLIAMS, Ruth Virginia, 9433 State Street, Philadelphia, PA 19149-0819. Single, claiming 0 withholding allowances. Telephone, 555-5845. Social Security No. 000-00-6741. Position, programmer. Salary, $2,650 per month. Group insurance, $48,000. Department: Office.

PAY POINTS

For rounding rules refer to instructions on page 2-33.

Overtime

All employees except for the exempt administrative employees—the president (*O'Neill*), the sales manager (*Ferguson*), sales representative (*Mann*), and supervisor (*Sokowski*)—are paid *time and a half* for any overtime exceeding 40 hours a week. Workers in the plant (*Bonno and Ryan*) are paid *time and a half* for any hours worked over eight each workday and for work on Saturdays and *twice* the regular hourly rate of pay for work on Sundays or holidays.

Timekeeping

All office and plant employees, except the president, the sales manager, sales representatives, and supervisors, must ring in and out daily on a time clock. Also, those employees who ring in and out must notify the time clerk of the reason for lost time. (The unemployment compensation laws of some states require this information.) The time clerk prepares a weekly report of the hours worked by each employee.

The calendar for the last quarter of the year is presented below.

October

S	M	T	W	T	F	S
				1	2	3
4	5	6	7	8	9	10
11	12	13	14	15	16	17
18	19	20	21	22	23	24
25	26	27	28	29	30	31

November

S	M	T	W	T	F	S
1	2	3	4	5	6	7
8	9	10	11	12	13	14
15	16	17	18	19	20	21
22	23	24	25	26	27	28
29	30					

December

S	M	T	W	T	F	S
		1	2	3	4	5
6	7	8	9	10	11	12
13	14	15	16	17	18	19
20	21	22	23	24	25	26
27	28	29	30	31		

Payday

Employees are paid biweekly on Friday. The first payday in the fourth quarter is Friday, October 9. Since the weekly time clerk's report is not finished until the Monday following the end of each week, the first pay (October 9) will be for the two weeks September 20–26 and September 27–October 3. The company, in effect, holds back one week's pay. This policy applies to all employees. The next payday (October 23) will cover the days worked in the weeks ending October 10 and October 17.

Payroll Taxes—Contributions and Withholdings

Payroll taxes are levied upon Glo-Brite Paint Company and its employees as shown in Figure 7.3.

Depositing Taxes

The company must deposit federal, state, and city taxes during this quarter. The deposit rules that affect the company appear in Figure 7.4.

FIGURE 7.3
Glo-Brite Payroll Taxes

	Payroll Taxes Levied Upon Glo-Brite Paint Company and Its Employees	
Federal Income Taxes (FIT)	Withheld from each employee's gross earnings in accordance with information given on Form W-4 and employee's earnings record. Wage-bracket method is used to determine FIT withholding.*	
Pennsylvania State Income Taxes (SIT)	3.07 percent withheld from each employee's gross earnings during the fourth quarter.*	
Philadelphia City Income Taxes (CIT)	3.92 percent withheld from gross earnings of each resident employee.*	
Pennsylvania State Unemployment Taxes (SUTA)	*Employee:*	0.07 percent (0.0007) on total gross earnings (No limit for the employee's portion.).*
	Employer:	3.6785 percent on first $9,000 gross earnings paid each employee during the calendar year (PA rate for new employers).
Federal Unemployment Taxes (FUTA)	Net tax rate of 0.6 percent on first $7,000 gross earnings paid each worker in the calendar year.	
Federal Insurance Contributions Act (FICA)	*OASDI—Employee and Employer:*	6.2 percent on first $118,500 of gross earnings paid each worker in the calendar year (maximum OASDI tax of $7,347).
	HI—Employee:	1.45 percent on total gross earnings paid each worker in the calendar year, plus an additional 0.9 percent on wages over $200,000.
	HI—Employer:	1.45 percent on total gross earnings paid each worker in the calendar year.

*Tax withholdings for FIT, FICA, SIT, CIT, and SUTA are based on rates used in 2015. Rates for 2016 were not available at the time of publishing.

Group Insurance

The company carries group-term life insurance on all its employees in an amount equal to one and one-half times the annual salary or wages paid each employee (rounded to the nearest thousand). The group insurance program covers full-time employees. A notation has been made on each employee's earnings record to show that each month *30¢ for each $1,000* of insurance coverage is deducted from the employee's earnings to pay a portion of the premium cost. The amount withheld is credited to a liability account entitled Group Insurance Premiums Collected. The taxable portion of group-term life insurance in excess of $50,000 is disregarded because the employees pay for group-term life insurance.

PAY POINTS

Deduct insurance premiums only on the last payday of each month.

FIGURE 7.4
Deposit Rules

	Deposit Rules for Glo-Brite Paint Company
Federal	The FICA taxes and FIT taxes must be deposited *on or before the 15th of the month following the month* in which the taxes were withheld. Since Glo-Brite is a new employer and has no tax liabilities during the lookback period, the company is subject to the monthly deposit rule.
Pennsylvania	Since the state income taxes withheld total $1,000 or more each quarter, the company must remit the withheld taxes semimonthly. The taxes must be remitted within three banking days after the semimonthly periods ending *on the 15th and the last day of the month.*
Philadelphia	Since the city income taxes withheld are more than $350 but less than $16,000 each month, the company is subject to the monthly rule. The city income taxes withheld during the month must be remitted *by the 15th day of the following month.*

Union Dues

Both workers in the plant *(Bonno and Ryan)* are union members. Under the check-off system, $8 is deducted *each payday* from the plant workers' earnings for union dues, assessments, and initiation fees. A notation to this effect has been made on each plant worker's earnings record. On or before the tenth of each month, the amounts withheld during the preceding month are turned over to the treasurer of the union.

Distribution of Labor Costs

Figure 7.5 shows how the salaries and wages are to be charged to the labor cost accounts.

Start of Payroll Project

October 9, 20--

No. 1   The first payroll in October covered the two workweeks that ended on September 26 and October 3. This payroll transaction has been entered for you in the payroll register, the employees' earnings records, the general journal, and the general ledger. By reviewing the calculations of the wages and deductions in the payroll register and the posting of the information to the employees' earnings records, you can see the procedure to be followed each payday.

Wages and salaries are paid by issuing special payroll checks. When the bank on which they are drawn receives such checks, they will be charged against the payroll cash account.

Observe the following rules in computing earnings each pay period:

1.   Do not make any deduction from an employee's earnings if the employee loses less than 15 minutes of time in any day. Time lost that exceeds 15 minutes is rounded to the nearest quarter-hour and deducted. If the time lost by an employee is not to be deducted, the time clerk will make a notation to that effect on the Time Clerk's Report.

FIGURE 7.5
Glo-Brite Labor Cost Accounts

Personnel	Accounts to Be Charged
President (O'Neill)	Administrative Salaries
Executive Secretary (Ford) Programmer (Williams) Time Clerk (Russell) Accounting Trainee (Student)	Office Salaries
Sales Manager (Ferguson) Sales Representative (Mann)	Sales Salaries
Workers (Bonno and Ryan) Supervisor (Sokowski)	Plant Wages

2. In completing the time record columns of the payroll register for all workers, you should place an 8 in the day column for each full day worked (refer to page PR-1 at the end of the book). If an employee works less than a full day, show the actual hours for which the employee will be paid.

3. In the case of an employee who begins work during a pay period, compute the earnings by paying the employees their weekly rate for *any full week* worked. For any *partial week*, compute the earnings for that week by multiplying the hours worked by the hourly rate of pay.

4. If time lost is to be deducted from a salaried employee's pay, the employee's pay must be determined by multiplying the actual hours worked for that week by the hourly rate. If hours are missed but no pay is deducted, include those hours in the Time Record columns on the payroll register. The following schedule shows the weekly and hourly wage rates of the salaried employees:

Employee	Weekly Rate	Hourly Rate
Ferguson, James C.	$1,125.00	$28.13
Ford, Catherine L.	610.00	15.25
Mann, Dewey W.	675.00	16.88
O'Neill, Joseph T.	1,153.85	28.85
Russell, Virginia A.	600.00	15.00
Sokowski, Thomas J.	1,025.00	25.63
Williams, Ruth V.	611.54	15.29

5. Plant workers (*Bonno and Ryan*), other than supervisors, are employed on an hourly basis. Compute the wages by multiplying the number of hours worked during the pay period by the employee's hourly rate.

6. The information needed and the sequence of steps that are completed for the payroll are presented in the following discussion.

Time Clerk's Report No. 38
For the Week Ending September 26, 20--

Employee	Time Record							Time Worked	Time Lost
	S	M	T	W	T	F	S		
Bonno, A. V.		8	8	8	8	8		40 hrs.	. . .
Ford, C. L.		8	8	8	8	8		40 hrs.	. . .
Russell, V. A.		8	8	8	8	8		40 hrs.	. . .
Ryan, N. A.		8	8	8	8	8		40 hrs.	. . .
Student		8	8	8	8	4		36 hrs.	. . .
Williams, R. V. . . .		8	8	D	8	8		32 hrs.	8 hrs.*

*Time lost because of personal business; charged to personal leave; no deduction for this time lost.
D = lost full day

Time Clerk's Report No. 39 For the Week Ending October 3, 20--									
Employee	**Time Record**							**Time Worked**	**Time Lost**
	S	M	T	W	T	F	S		
Bonno, A. V.. . . .		8	8	8	8	8		40 hrs.	. . .
Ford, C. L.		8	8	8	8	8		40 hrs.	. . .
Russell, V. A. . . .		8	8	8	8	8		40 hrs.	. . .
Ryan, N. A..		8	8	8	8	8		40 hrs.	. . .
Student		8	8	8	8	4		36 hrs.	. . .
Williams, R. V.. . .		8	8	8	8	8		40 hrs.	. . .

The time clerk prepared Time Clerk's Report Nos. 38 and 39 from the time cards used by the employees for these workweeks. *Inasmuch as the president, sales manager, sales representatives, and supervisors do not ring in and out on the time clock, their records are not included in the time clerks report, but their salaries must be included in the payroll.*

① The following schedule shows the hourly wage rates of the three hourly employees used in preparing the payroll register for the payday on October 9.

Employee	Hourly Rate
Bonno, Anthony V.	$17.65
Ryan, Norman A.	18.00
Student...	14.00

PAY POINTS

Tax calculations are to be taken to three decimal places and then rounded to two places.

② The entry required for each employee is recorded in the payroll register. The names of all employees are listed in alphabetical order, including yours as "Student." The fold-out payroll register forms needed to complete this project are bound at the back of the book (pages PR-2, PR-3, and PR-4).

No deduction has been made for the time lost by Williams. Thus, the total number of hours (80) for which payment was made is recorded in the Regular Earnings Hours column of the payroll register. However, a notation of the time lost (D) was made in the Time Record column. When posting to Williams's earnings record, 80 hours is recorded in the Regular Earnings Hours column (no deduction for the time lost).

In computing the federal income taxes to be withheld, the wage-bracket tables in Tax Table B at the back of the book were used (pages T-5 to T-14).

PAY POINTS

Use tax tables for biweekly payroll period.

Each payday, $8 was deducted from the earnings of the two plant workers for union dues *(Bonno and Ryan)*.

Payroll check numbers were assigned beginning with check no. 672.

In the Labor Cost Distribution columns at the extreme right of the payroll register, each employee's gross earnings were recorded in the column that identifies the department in which the employee regularly works. The totals of the Labor Cost Distribution columns provide the amounts to be charged to the appropriate salary and wage expense accounts and aid department managers and supervisors in comparing the actual labor costs with the budgeted amounts.

Once the net pay of each employee was computed, all the amount columns in the payroll register were footed, proved, and ruled.

③ An entry was made in the journal (page 7-25) transferring from the regular cash account to the payroll cash account the amount of the check issued to Payroll to cover the net amount of the payroll; next, the entry was posted.

④ Information from the payroll register was posted to the employees' earnings records (see pages 7-43 to 7-47).

Note that when posting the deductions for each employee, a column has been provided in the earnings record for recording each deduction for FICA (OASDI and HI), FIT, SIT, SUTA, and CIT. All other deductions for each employee are to be totaled and recorded as one amount in the Other Deductions column. Subsidiary ledgers are maintained for Group Insurance Premiums Collected and Union Dues Withheld. Thus, any question about the amounts withheld from an employee's earnings may be answered by referring to the appropriate subsidiary ledger. In this project, your work will not involve any recording in or reference to the subsidiary ledgers.

⑤ The proper journal entry recorded salaries, wages, taxes, and the net amount of cash paid from the totals of the payroll register. The journal entry to record the payroll for the first pay in the fourth quarter appears below and in the general journal (page 7-25).

Administrative Salaries	2,307.69	
Office Salaries	4,651.08	
Sales Salaries	3,600.00	
Plant Wages	4,902.00	
FICA Taxes Payable—OASDI		958.57
FICA Taxes Payable—HI		224.19
Employees FIT Payable		1,125.00
Employees SIT Payable		474.67
Employees SUTA Payable		10.85
Employees CIT Payable		606.05
Union Dues Payable		16.00
Payroll Cash		12,045.44

The amounts charged the salary and wage expense accounts were obtained from the totals of the Labor Cost Distribution columns in the payroll register. As shown in the listing of the labor cost accounts in Figure 7.5 on page 7-6 the salaries and wages were charged as follows:

Administrative Salaries

Joseph T. O'Neill (President)

Office Salaries

Catherine L. Ford (Executive Secretary)
Virginia A. Russell (Time Clerk)
Student (Accounting Trainee)
Ruth V. Williams (Programmer)

Sales Salaries

James C. Ferguson (Sales Manager)
Dewey W. Mann (Sales Representative)

Plant Wages

Anthony V. Bonno (Mixer Operator)
Norman A. Ryan (Electrician)
Thomas J. Sokowski (Supervisor)

FICA Taxes Payable—OASDI and FICA Taxes Payable—HI were credited for $958.57 and $224.19, respectively, the amounts deducted from employees' wages.

Employees FIT Payable, Employees SIT Payable, Employees SUTA Payable, Employees CIT Payable, and Union Dues Payable were credited for the total amount withheld for each kind of deduction from employees' wages. In subsequent payroll transactions, Group Insurance Premiums Collected will be credited for the amounts withheld from employees' wages for this type of deduction. Finally, Payroll Cash was credited for the sum of the net amounts paid all employees.

⑥ The payroll taxes for this pay were then recorded in the general journal (page 7-25) as follows:

Payroll Taxes	1,381.42	
FICA Taxes Payable—OASDI		958.57
FICA Taxes Payable—HI		224.18
FUTA Taxes Payable		22.91
SUTA Taxes Payable—Employer		175.76

Payroll Taxes was debited for the sum of the employer's FICA, FUTA, and SUTA taxes. The taxable earnings used in computing each of these payroll taxes were obtained from the appropriate column totals of the payroll register. Note that only part of *Ford's* wages are taxable ($700 out of $1,220 gross pay) for FUTA ($7,000 limit). The computation of the debit to Payroll Taxes was:

FICA—OASDI:	6.2% of $15,460.77 =	$ 958.57
FICA—HI:	1.45% of $15,460.77 =	224.18
FUTA:	0.6% of $3,818.00 =	22.91
SUTA:	3.6785% of $4,778.00 =	175.76
Total Payroll Taxes		$ 1,381.42

FICA Taxes Payable—OASDI was credited for $958.57, the amount of the liability for the employer's portion of the tax. FICA Taxes Payable—HI was credited for $224.18, the amount of the liability for the employer's share of this tax. FUTA Taxes Payable was credited for the amount of the tax on the employer for federal unemployment purposes ($22.91). SUTA Taxes Payable—Employer was credited for $175.76, which is the amount of the contribution required of *the employer* under the state unemployment compensation law.

⑦ The journal entries were posted to the proper ledger accounts (pages 7-34 to 7-41).

October 15

This is the day on which the deposits of FICA and FIT taxes and the city of Philadelphia income taxes for the September payrolls are due. However, in order to concentrate on the fourth-quarter payrolls, we will assume that the deposits for the third quarter and the appropriate entries were already completed.

October 20

No. 2   On this date, Glo-Brite Paint Company must deposit the Pennsylvania state income taxes withheld from the October 9 payroll.

The deposit rule states that if the employer expects the aggregate amount withheld each quarter to be $1,000 or more, the employer must pay the withheld tax semimonthly.

The tax must be remitted within three banking days after the close of the semimonthly periods ending on the 15th and the last day of the month.

① Prepare the journal entry to record the deposit of the taxes, and post to the appropriate ledger accounts.

② Pennsylvania has eliminated the filing of paper forms (replaced by telefile or online filing). The information needed to telefile is listed on page 7-51—complete the information worksheet needed for the first semimonthly period of October. The company's Pennsylvania employer account number is 000-0-3300, its EIN is 00-0000660, its filing password is GBPCOM, and its telephone number is (215) 555-9559.

October 23

No. 3   Prepare the payroll for the last pay period of October from Time Clerk's Report Nos. 40 and 41.

The proper procedure in recording the payroll follows:

① Complete the payroll register.

In as much as only a portion of the payroll register sheet was used in recording the October 9 payroll, the October 23 payroll should be recorded on the same sheet to save space. On the first blank ruled line after the October 9 payroll, insert "Payday October 23—For Period Ending October 17, 20--." On the following lines, record the payroll information for the last pay date of October. When recording succeeding payrolls, continue to conserve space by recording two payrolls on each separate payroll register sheet.

The workers in the plant (*Bonno and Ryan*) are paid *time and a half* for any hours worked over eight each workday and for work on Saturdays and are paid *twice* the regular hourly rate for work on Sundays or holidays.

With this pay period, the *cumulative earnings* of several employees exceed the taxable income base set up by FUTA and SUTA. This factor must be considered in preparing the payroll register and in computing the employer's payroll taxes. Refer to each employee's earnings record to see the amount of cumulative earnings.

LO 1
Prepare payroll registers.

PAY POINTS

Even though they are not on the time clerk's report, remember to pay the president, sales manager, sales representatives, and supervisors.

LO 2
Maintain employees' earnings records.

Time Clerk's Report No. 40
For the Week Ending October 10, 20--

Employee	Time Record							Time Worked	Time Lost
	S	M	T	W	T	F	S		
Bonno, A. V.		8	8	8	8	8	4	44 hrs.	. . .
Ford, C. L.		4	8	8	8	8		36 hrs.	4 hrs.*
Russell, V. A.		8	8	8	8	8		40 hrs.	. . .
Ryan, N. A.		8	8	8	8	8		40 hrs.	. . .
Student		8	8	8	8	4		36 hrs.	. . .
Williams, R. V. . . .		8	8	8	8	8		40 hrs.	. . .

*Time lost on account of death of relative; charged against annual personal leave; no deduction for time lost.

Time Clerk's Report No. 41
For the Week Ending October 17, 20--

Employee	Time Record							Time Worked	Time Lost
	S	M	T	W	T	F	S		
Bonno, A. V. . . .		8	8	8	8	8		40 hrs.	. . .
Ford, C. L.		8	8	8	8	8		40 hrs.	. . .
Russell, V. A. . . .		8	8	8	8	8		40 hrs.	. . .
Ryan, N. A.		8	8	8	8	8	8	48 hrs.	. . .
Student		8	8	8	8	4		36 hrs.	. . .
Williams, R. V. . .		8	8	8	8	8		40 hrs.	. . .

PAY POINTS

The employees' Pennsylvania State Unemployment Tax (SUTA) is calculated (0.0007) on the total wages of each employee. There is no taxable wage limit on the employees' portion of the tax.

PAY POINTS

Be sure to deduct 30¢ premium for each $1,000 of group insurance carried by each employee (last payday of each month).

② Make the entry transferring from Cash to Payroll Cash the net amount of the total payroll, and post.

③ Post the required information from the payroll register to each employee's earnings record.

④ Record in the journal the salaries, wages, taxes withheld, group insurance premiums collected, union dues withheld, and net amount paid, and post to the proper ledger accounts.

The entry required to record the October 23 payroll is the same as that to record the October 9 payroll, except it is necessary to record the liability for the amount withheld from the employees' wages to pay their part of the group insurance premium. The amount withheld should be recorded as a credit to Group Insurance Premiums Collected.

⑤ Record in the journal the employer's payroll taxes and the liabilities created; post to the appropriate ledger accounts.

November 4

No. 4   Deposit with the state of Pennsylvania the amount of state income taxes withheld from the October 23 payroll and complete information worksheet.

No. 5   *Virginia Russell* completed a new Form W-4, changing the number of withholding allowances to 2. Change Russell's earnings record (her marital status has not changed).

No. 6   *Thomas J. Sokowski* completed a new Form W-4, showing that his marital status changed to single and that the number of withholding allowances remains at 2. Change Sokowski's earnings record accordingly.

No. 7   *Dewey Mann* completed a new Form W-4, leaving his marital status as married but dropping the number of withholding allowances to 0. Change Mann's earnings record accordingly.

November 6

No. 8   Pay the treasurer of the union the amount of union dues withheld during the month of October.

Time Clerk's Report No. 42 For the Week Ending October 24, 20--									
Employee	**Time Record**							**Time Worked**	**Time Lost**
	S	M	T	W	T	F	S		
Bonno, A. V. ...		8	8	8	8	8		40 hrs.	...
Ford, C. L.		8	8	8	8	8		40 hrs.	...
Russell, V. A. ...		8	8	8	8	6		38 hrs.	2 hrs.*
Ryan, N. A.		8	8	8	8	8		40 hrs.	...
Student.........		8	8	8	8	4		36 hrs.	...
Williams, R. V. ...		8	8	8	7	8		39 hrs.	1 hr.**

*Time lost on account of family function; deduct 2 hours' pay.
**Time lost because of tardiness; deduct 1 hour's pay.

Time Clerk's Report No. 43
For the Week Ending October 31, 20--

Employee	Time Record							Time Worked	Time Lost
	S	M	T	W	T	F	S		
Bonno, A. V. ...		8	8	8	8	8		40 hrs.	...
Ford, C. L.		8	8	8	8	8		40 hrs.	...
Russell, V. A. ...		8	8	8	8	8		40 hrs.	...
Ryan, N. A.		8	8	8	8	8		40 hrs.	...
Student........		8	8	8	8	4		36 hrs.	...
Williams, R. V. ...		8	8	8	8	8		40 hrs.	...

No. 9   Prepare the payroll for the first pay period in November from Time Clerk's Report Nos. 42 and 43 and record the paychecks issued to all employees. Record this payroll at the top of the second payroll register sheet.

Note: Virginia Russell worked only 38 hours in the week ending October 24. Therefore, compute her pay for that week by multiplying 38 by $15.00 (her hourly rate). *Ruth Williams* worked only 39 hours in the week ending October 24. Therefore, compute her pay for that week by multiplying 39 by $15.29 (her hourly rate).

Also, record the employer's payroll taxes.

PAY POINTS

Make changes in November 6 pay. Refers to Nos. 5, 6, and 7.

November 13

No. 10   Because of her excessive tardiness and absenteeism during the year, the company discharged *Ruth Williams* today. For the week ending November 7, she was late a total of six hours; and for this week, she missed two full days and was late two hours on another day. In lieu of two weeks' notice, Williams was given two full weeks' pay ($1,223.08). Along with her dismissal pay ($1,223.08), she was paid for the week ending November 7 (34 hours, or $519.86) and the days worked this current week (22 hours, or $336.38). The total pay for the two partial weeks is $856.24.

① Record a separate payroll register (on one line) to show Williams's total earnings, deductions, and net pay. The two weeks' dismissal pay is subject to all payroll taxes. Include dismissal pay with the total earnings but do not show the hours in the Time Record columns. Use the tax table for the biweekly payroll period for the total gross pay ($2,079.32) of Williams.

The deduction for group insurance premiums is $14.40. In the Time Record column, make a note of Williams's discharge as of this date. Indicate the payroll check number used to prepare the final check for Williams. When posting to the earnings record, make a notation of Williams's discharge on this date.

② Prepare the journal entries to transfer the net cash and to record Williams's final pay and the employer's payroll taxes. Post to the ledger accounts.

③ Use the blank Form W-2 on page 7-60. Box "a" should be left blank, since the Glo-Brite Paint Company does not use a control number to identify individual Forms W-2.

PAY POINTS

Prepare a Wage and Tax Statement, Form W-2, to be given to Williams.

LO 4

Complete federal, state, and city tax deposit forms and journalize the transactions.

PAY POINTS

On all tax and deposit forms requiring a signature, use Joseph O'Neill's name.

November 16

No. 11 Electronically deposit the amount of FICA taxes and federal income taxes for the October payrolls and complete the Federal Deposit Information Worksheet (page 7-50). Since the company is subject to the monthly deposit rule, the deposit is due on the 15th of the following month. See the deposit requirements explained on pages 3-16 to 3-19. November 15 is a Sunday; therefore, the deposit is to be made on the next business day.

Prepare the journal entry to record the deposit of the taxes, and post to the appropriate ledger accounts.

No. 12 Since Glo-Brite Paint Company withholds the city of Philadelphia income tax, you must deposit the taxes with the Department of Revenue. The deposit rule that affects Glo-Brite Paint Company states that if the withheld taxes are between $350 and $16,000 per month, the company must deposit the tax monthly by the 15th of the following month. The withheld taxes for the October payrolls were $1,224.72.

① Prepare the journal entry to record the deposit of the taxes, and post to the appropriate ledger accounts.

② Complete the Philadelphia Employer's Return of Tax Withheld coupon (Monthly Wage Tax), which appears on page 7-52.

November 17

No. 13 Prepare an employee's earnings record for *Beth Anne Woods*, a new employee who began work today, Tuesday. Woods is single and claims one withholding allowance. She is employed as a programmer at a monthly salary of $2,600. Address, 8102 Franklin Court, Philadelphia, PA 19105-0915. Telephone, 555-1128. Social Security No. 000-00-1587. She is eligible for group insurance coverage of $47,000 immediately, although her first deduction for group insurance will not be made until December 18.

> Department: Office
> Weekly rate: $600.00
> Hourly rate: $15.00

November 18

No. 14 Deposit with the state of Pennsylvania the amount of state income taxes withheld from the November 6 and 13 (*Ruth Williams*) payrolls and complete the information worksheet.

November 20

No. 15 With this pay, the company has decided to offer employees a Savings Incentive Match Plan (SIMPLE Retirement Plan). Most of the employees opted to wait until the start of the following year to participate. However, the following employees have decided to take part in the plan for the remaining pay periods of the year.

James Ferguson:	$500 contribution per pay period
Dewey Mann:	$250 contribution per pay period
Joseph O'Neill:	$700 contribution per pay period
Norman Ryan:	$200 contribution per pay period

The contributions are to be deducted from the participating employee's pay and are excluded from the employee's income for federal income tax purposes. The other payroll taxes still apply. On the payroll registers and the earnings record, use the blank column under "Deductions" for these contributions. Use the term "SIMPLE" as the new heading for this deduction column (on both the payroll register and employee's earnings record).

Use the account in the general ledger for SIMPLE Contributions Payable—account no. 29.

The company must match these contributions dollar for dollar, up to 3 percent of the employee's compensation. These payments will be processed through the Accounts Payable Department.

Prepare the payroll for the last pay period of November from Time Clerk's Report Nos. 44 and 45, and record the paychecks issued all employees. Also, record the employer's payroll taxes.

PAY POINTS

Remember to deduct the premiums on the group insurance for each employee.

Time Clerk's Report No. 44
For the Week Ending November 7, 20--

Employee	Time Record							Time Worked	Time Lost
	S	M	T	W	T	F	S		
Bonno, A. V. . . .		8	8	8	8	8		40 hrs.	. . .
Ford, C. L.		8	8	8	8	8		40 hrs.	. . .
Russell, V. A. . . .		6	8	8	8	8		38 hrs.	2 hrs.*
Ryan, N. A.		8	8	8	8	8		40 hrs.	. . .
Student		8	8	8	8	4		36 hrs.	. . .
Williams, R. V. . .		6	8	7	7	6		34 hrs.	6 hrs.**

*Time lost for personal business; deduct 2 hours' pay.
**Time lost because of tardiness; deduct 6 hours' pay.

Time Clerk's Report No. 45
For the Week Ending November 14, 20--

Employee	Time Record							Time Worked	Time Lost
	S	M	T	W	T	F	S		
Bonno, A. V. . . .		. . .	. . .	8	8	8		24 hrs.	. . .
Ford, C. L.		8	8	8	8	8		40 hrs.	. . .
Russell, V. A. . . .		8	8	8	8	8		40 hrs.	. . .
Ryan, N. A.		8	8	8	8	8		40 hrs.	. . .
Student		8	8	8	8	4		36 hrs.	. . .
Williams, R. V. . .		D	D	8	6	8		22 hrs.	18 hrs.*

*Time lost because of tardiness; deduct 2 hours' pay. Unexcused absences; deduct 16 hours' pay.

No. 16 Salary increases of $30 per week, *effective for the two weeks covered in the December 4 payroll*, are given to *Catherine L. Ford* and *Virginia A. Russell*. The group insurance coverage for Ford will be increased to $50,000; for Russell, it will be increased to $49,000. Update the employees' earnings records accordingly. The new wage rates are listed below.

PAY POINTS

The new wage rates are effective for the December 4 payroll.

Employee	Weekly Rate	Hourly Rate
Ford, Catherine L.	$640.00	$16.00
Russell, Virginia A.	630.00	15.75

November 30

No. 17 Prepare an employee's earnings record for *Paul Winston Young*, the president's nephew, who began work today. Young is single and claims one withholding allowance. He is training as a field sales representative in the city where the home office is located. His beginning salary is $2,730 per month. Address, 7936 Holmes Drive, Philadelphia, PA 19107-6107. Telephone, 555-2096. Social Security No. 000-00-6057. Young is eligible for group insurance coverage of $49,000.

> Department: Sales
> Weekly rate: $630.00
> Hourly rate: $15.75

 ## Start of Short Version of Payroll Project (Continuation of Payroll Project)

December 3

No. 18 Deposit with the state of Pennsylvania the amount of state income taxes withheld from the November 20 payroll and complete the information worksheet.

December 4

No. 19 Prepare the payroll for the first pay period of December from Time Clerk's Report Nos. 46 and 47, and record the paychecks issued all employees. Record this payroll at the top of the third payroll register sheet.

Note: Thursday, November 26, is a paid holiday for all workers.

Also, record the employer's payroll taxes.

Time Clerk's Report No. 46 For the Week Ending November 21, 20--									
Employee	**Time Record**							**Time Worked**	**Time Lost**
	S	M	T	W	T	F	S		
Bonno, A. V. ...		8	8	8	8	8		40 hrs.	...
Ford, C. L.		8	8	8	8	8		40 hrs.	...
Russell, V. A. ...		8	8	8	8	8		40 hrs.	...
Ryan, N. A.		8	8	8	4	8		36 hrs.	4 hrs.*
Student........		8	8	8	4	8		36 hrs.	...
Woods, B. A. ...		...	8	8	8	8		32 hrs.	...

*Time lost on account of personal business; deduct 4 hours' pay.

Time Clerk's Report No. 47 For the Week Ending November 28, 20--									
Employee	**Time Record**							**Time Worked**	**Time Lost**
	S	M	T	W	T	F	S		
Bonno, A. V.	8*	8	8	8	PAID HOLIDAY	8		48 hrs.	...
Ford, C. L.		8	8	8	PAID HOLIDAY	8		40 hrs.	...
Russell, V. A.		8	8	8	PAID HOLIDAY	8		40 hrs.	...
Ryan, N. A.		9	10	8	PAID HOLIDAY	8		43 hrs.	...
Student.........		8	8	8	PAID HOLIDAY	4		36 hrs.	...
Woods, B. A.		8	8	8	PAID HOLIDAY	8		40 hrs.	...

*Double time.

No. 20 *Anthony V. Bonno* reports the birth of a son and completes an amended Form W-4, showing his total withholding allowances to be five. Change his earnings record accordingly, *effective with the December 18 pay.*

No. 21 Both *Anthony Bonno* and *Norman Ryan* have been notified that their union dues will increase to $9 per pay, starting with the last pay period of the year. *Reflect these increases in the December 18 pay* and show the changes on their earnings records.

December 9

No. 22 Pay the treasurer of the union the amount of union dues withheld during the month of November.

December 11

No. 23 The Payroll Department was informed that *Virginia A. Russell* died in an automobile accident on her way home from work Thursday, December 10.

December 14

No. 24 ① Make a separate entry (on one line) in the payroll register to record the issuance of a check payable to the ***Estate of Virginia A. Russell***. This check covers Russell's work for the weeks ending December 5 and 12 ($1,134.00) plus her accrued vacation pay ($1,260.00). Do not show the vacation hours in the Time Record columns on the payroll register, but include them in the Total Earnings column.

Russell's final biweekly pay for time worked and the vacation pay are subject to FICA, FUTA, and SUTA (employer and employee) taxes. Since Russell's cumulative earnings have surpassed the taxable earnings figures established by FUTA and SUTA, there will not be any unemployment tax on the *employer*. The deduction for group insurance premiums is $14.70.

② Make a notation of Russell's death in the payroll register and on her earnings record.

③ Prepare journal entries to transfer the net pay and to record Russell's final pay and the employer's payroll taxes. Post to the ledger accounts.

④ Include the final gross pay ($2,394.00) in Boxes 3 and 5, but not in Boxes 1, 16, and 18. Use the blank Form W-2 on page 7-60.

In addition, the last wage payment and vacation pay must be reported on Form 1099-MISC. A Form 1096 must also be completed. These forms will be completed in February before their due date. (See Transaction Nos. 41 and 42 on page 7-67.)

> **PAY** POINTS
>
> This final pay is not subject to withholding for FIT, SIT, or CIT purposes.

> **PAY** POINTS
>
> Prepare a Wage and Tax Statement, Form W-2, which will be given to the executor of the estate along with the final paycheck.

December 15

No. 25 Electronically deposit the amount of FICA taxes and federal income taxes for the November payrolls and complete the Federal Deposit Information Worksheet.

No. 26 Deposit with the city of Philadelphia the amount of city income taxes withheld from the November payrolls.

December 18

No. 27 Deposit with the state of Pennsylvania the amount of state income taxes withheld from the December 4 payroll and complete the information worksheet.

No. 28 Glo-Brite has been notified by the insurance company that there will be no premium charge for the month of December on the policy for *Virginia*

Russell. Prepare the entry for the check made payable to the estate of Virginia A. Russell, for the amount that was withheld for insurance from her December 14 pay.

No. 29 Prepare an employee's earnings record for *Richard Lloyd Zimmerman,* who was employed today as time clerk to take the place left vacant by the death of Virginia A. Russell last week. His beginning salary is $2,600 per month. Address, 900 South Clark Street, Philadelphia, PA 19195-6247. Telephone, 555-2104. Social Security No. 000-00-1502. Zimmerman is married and claims one withholding allowance. Zimmerman is eligible for group insurance coverage of $47,000, although no deduction for group insurance premiums will be made until the last payday in January.

> Department: Office
> Weekly rate: $600.00
> Hourly rate: $15.00

No. 30 Prepare the payroll for the latter pay of December from Time Clerk's Report Nos. 48 and 49 and record the paychecks issued all employees. Also, record the employer's payroll taxes.

Effective with this pay, *O'Neill* completed a new Form W-4, changing his total withholding allowances to four. Previously, he had claimed fewer allowances than he had been using on his tax return. Change his earnings record accordingly.

In this pay, the president of the company, *Joseph O'Neill,* is paid his annual bonus. This does not affect O'Neill's insurance coverage, which is based on regular pay. This year, his bonus is *$75,000.* For withholding purposes, the bonus is considered a supplemental payment and is added to his gross pay, and the aggregate amount is taxed. For this pay, O'Neill *has increased his SIMPLE deduction to $4,000.* To determine the federal income tax, use the *Table of Allowance Values* along with *Tax Table A* (pages T-2 to T-4). In calculating the tax, do not round the *aggregate* to the nearest *earnings* dollar. In this pay, O'Neill has reached the OASDI ceiling. **To calculate O'Neill's OASDI tax, multiply the OASDI ceiling of $118,500 by 6.2 percent and then subtract the year-to-date OASDI taxes withheld up to this pay.**

Note: After posting the information for this last pay to the employees' earnings records, calculate and enter the quarterly and yearly totals on each earnings record.

PAY POINTS

Remember to deduct the premiums on the group insurance for each employee.

Time Clerk's Report No. 48 For the Week Ending December 5, 20--										
Employee	**Time Record**								**Time Worked**	**Time Lost**
	S	M	T	W	T	F	S		
Bonno, A. V. . . .	4	8	8	8	8	8		44 hrs.	. . .
Ford, C. L.		8	8	8	8	8		40 hrs.	. . .
Russell, V. A. . . .		8	8	8	8	8		40 hrs.	. . .
Ryan, N. A.		8	9	9	9	9		44 hrs.	. . .
Student		8	8	7	8	4		35 hrs.	1 hr.*
Woods, B. A. . . .		8	8	8	8	8		40 hrs.	. . .
Young, P. W. . . .		8	8	8	8	8		40 hrs.	. . .

*Time lost because of tardiness; deduct 1 hour's pay.

Time Clerk's Report No. 49								
For the Week Ending December 12, 20--								

Employee	Time Record						Time Worked	Time Lost
	S	M	T	W	T	F	S		
Bonno, A. V. . . .	8	8	8	8	8	8		48 hrs.	. . .
Ford, C. L.		4	8	8	8	8		36 hrs.	4 hrs.*
Russell, V. A. . . .		8	8	8	8	D		32 hrs.	8 hrs.
Ryan, N. A.		10	8	8	9	8		43 hrs.	. . .
Student		4	8	8	8	4		32 hrs.	4 hrs.**
Woods, B. A. . . .		8	8	8	8	8		40 hrs.	. . .
Young, P. W. . . .		8	8	8	8	8		40 hrs.	

*Time spent in training session; no deduction in pay.
**Time lost in dentist appointment; no deduction in pay.

Note: This completes the project insofar as recording the payroll transactions for the last quarter is concerned. The following additional transactions are given to illustrate different types of transactions arising in connection with the accounting for payrolls and payroll taxes. Record these transactions in the journal, but do not post to the ledger.

January 6

No. 31 Deposit with the state of Pennsylvania the amount of state income taxes withheld from the December 18 payroll and complete the information worksheet.

January 8

No. 32 Pay the treasurer of the union the amount of union dues withheld during the month of December.

January 15

No. 33 Electronically deposit the amount of FICA taxes and federal income taxes for the December payrolls, and complete the Federal Deposit Information Worksheet.

No. 34 Deposit with the city of Philadelphia the amount of city income taxes withheld from the December payrolls.

February 1

No. 35 Prepare *Form 941, Employer's Quarterly Federal Tax Return*, with respect to wages paid during the last calendar quarter. Pages 7-55 and 7-56 contain a blank Form 941. The information needed in preparing the return should be obtained from the ledger accounts, payroll registers, employees' earnings records, and Federal Tax Deposit forms.

Form 941 and all forms that follow are to be signed by the president of the company, *Joseph T. O'Neill.*

ON THE JOB

January						
Su	Mo	Tu	We	Th	Fr	Sa
					1	2
3	4	5	6	7	8	9
10	11	12	13	14	15	16
17	18	19	20	21	22	23
24	25	26	27	28	29	30
31						

LO 5

Prepare various quarter-end and year-end payroll tax forms.

WASHINGTON UPDATE

EMPLOYERS IN "CREDIT REDUCTION" STATES MUST CALCULATE A CREDIT REDUCTION AS AN ADJUSTMENT TO THEIR FUTA TAX ON THEIR FORM 940 EMPLOYER'S ANNUAL FEDERAL UNEMPLOYMENT (FUTA) TAX RETURN. CREDIT REDUCTION STATES ARE STATES THAT DID NOT REPAY THE MONEY THEY BORROWED FROM THE FEDERAL GOVERNMENT TO PAY UNEMPLOYMENT BENEFITS. EMPLOYERS IN THESE STATES MUST USE SCHEDULE A (FORM 940) TO COMPUTE THE CREDIT REDUCTION. IN 2015 PENNSYLVANIA WAS NOT A CREDIT REDUCTION STATE.

No. 36 ① Complete *Form 940, Employer's Federal Unemployment (FUTA) Tax Return*, using the blank forms reproduced on pages 7-57 and 7-58. Also, complete the Federal Deposit Information Worksheet, using the blank form reproduced on page 7-50.

a. Total wages for the first three quarters was $142,224.57. FUTA taxable wages for the first three quarters was $65,490.00.
b. FUTA tax liability by quarter:

> 1st quarter—$204.53
> 2nd quarter—$105.25
> 3rd quarter—$83.16

The first FUTA deposit is now due.
c. Journalize the entry to record the electronic deposit for the FUTA tax liability.

No. 37 ① Prepare *Form UC-2, Employer's Report for Unemployment Compensation—Fourth Quarter*, using the blank form reproduced on page 7-59. In Pennsylvania, a credit week is any calendar week during the quarter in which the employee earned at least $50 (without regard to when paid). The maximum number of credit weeks in a quarter is 13. The telephone number of the company is (215) 555-9559. All other information needed in preparing the form can be obtained from the ledger accounts, the payroll registers, and the employees' earnings records.

② Journalize the entry to record the payment of the taxes for the fourth quarter.

No. 38 Complete *Form W-2, Wage and Tax Statement*, for each current employee, using the blank statements reproduced on pages 7-61 to 7-65. Use each employee's earnings record to obtain the information needed to complete the forms. The two plant workers (Bonno and Ryan) have had $121.00 in union dues withheld during the year.

No. 39 Complete *Form W-3, Transmittal of Wage and Tax Statements*, using the blank form reproduced on page 7-66. Use the information on all Forms W-2 to complete this form.

No. 40 Complete Pennsylvania *Form REV-1667, W-2 Transmittal*, using the blank form reproduced on page 7-66. Use the information on Forms W-2 to complete this report. The wages paid and the Pennsylvania tax withheld for the first three quarters are:

1st	$34,088.75	$1,046.52
2nd	$45,535.62	$1,397.94
3rd	$62,600.20	$1,921.83

No. 41 Complete *Form 1099-MISC, Miscellaneous Income,* for the payment to *the estate of Virginia A. Russell.* The full amount of the December 14 payment must be reported in Box 3. Page 7-67 contains a blank form.

Note: These wages are to be reported as other income in Box 3 so that the IRS will not seek self-employment tax on such amounts.

No. 42 Complete *Form 1096, Annual Summary and Transmittal of U.S. Information Returns,* using the blank form on page 7-67. Use the information on Form 1099-MISC to complete this form.

No. 43 Pennsylvania's Quarterly Reconciliation of Income Tax Withheld is filed electronically. The information worksheet to be completed is on page 7-53. The telephone number of the company is (215) 555-9559.

No. 44 Prepare the Annual Reconciliation of Employer Wage Tax for Philadelphia, using the blank form on page 7-54. For lines 1, 3, and 4, use gross wages and salaries per general ledger less exempt wages paid to Russell ($2,394.00) on December 14. (This amount should agree with Form W-3 Box 18, local wages.) Tax paid during the first three quarters was $5,575.21. For reporting purposes, there were 10 Philadelphia residents for whom wage tax was remitted for the pay period ending March 12, 20--.

QUESTIONS ON THE PAYROLL PROJECT

1. The total payroll tax expense incurred by the employer on salaries and wages paid during the quarter ended December 31 was ....$_____

2. The total payroll tax expense incurred by the employer on the total earnings of Joseph T. O'Neill during the fourth quarter was ....$_____

3. The amount of the group insurance premiums collected from employees during the quarter ended December 31 was ....$_____

4. O'Neill has decided to give all current employees (excluding himself) a bonus payment during January equal to 5% of their total gross pay for last year. Determine the total of this bonus payment ....$_____

5. On the financial statements prepared at the end of its first year of operations, the company must show an accurate picture of all expenses and all liabilities incurred. The last payday of the year was December 18. However, the payment to the employees on that day did not include the weeks ending December 19 and 26 and the four days (December 28–31) in the following week. These earnings will be reflected in the January payrolls. Two-column journal paper is provided for use in journalizing the following entry on page 7-23.

    Prepare the adjusting entry as of December 31 to record the salaries and wages that have accrued but remain unpaid as of the end of the year. When calculating the amount of the accrual for each hourly worker, assume each employee worked eight hours on each day during the period with no overtime (student works a 36-hour week—student worked 32 hours for the period December 28 through December 31). For each salaried worker, the accrual will amount to 14/10 of the worker's biweekly earnings, except for Zimmerman who worked only 10 days.

    Each of the labor cost accounts should be debited for the appropriate amount of the accrual, and Salaries and Wages Payable should be credited for the total amount of the accrual. There is no liability for payroll taxes on the accrued salaries and wages until the workers are actually paid. Therefore, the company follows the practice of not accruing payroll taxes.

6. Also, prepare the adjusting entry as of December 31 to record the accrued vacation pay as of the end of the year. Record the expense in a vacation benefits expense account, and credit the appropriate liability account. Use the journal paper provided.

    As of December 31, the vacation time earned but not used by each employee is listed here.

Bonno	80 hours
Ferguson	three weeks
Ford	two weeks
Mann....................................	one week
O'Neill.................................	four weeks
Ryan	80 hours
Sokowski	two weeks
Student.................................	72 hours
Woods	none
Young...................................	none
Zimmerman.........................	none

LO 6

Make the accrual entries for the payroll at the end of a year.

JOURNAL   Page _____

DATE	DESCRIPTION	POST. REF.	DEBIT	CREDIT

ACCOUNTING RECORDS AND REPORTS

Contents

Item	To Be Used with	Page
Journal	Payroll Project	7-23
General Ledger	Payroll Project	7-34
Employees' Earnings Records	Payroll Project	7-42
Federal Deposit Information Worksheet	Payroll Project	7-50
State Filing Information Worksheet	Payroll Project	7-51
Employer's Coupons of Tax Withheld—City of Philadelphia	Payroll Project	7-52
PA Employer's Quarterly Reconciliation Worksheet	Payroll Project	7-53
Annual Reconciliation of Employer Wage Tax—Philadelphia	Payroll Project	7-54
Employer's Quarterly Federal Tax Return (Form 941)	Payroll Project	7-55
Employer's Annual Federal Unemployment (FUTA) Tax Return (Form 940)	Payroll Project	7-57
Employer's Report for Unemployment Compensation—Pennsylvania (Form UC-2)	Payroll Project	7-59
Wage and Tax Statements (Form W-2)	Payroll Project	7-60
Transmittal of Wage and Tax Statements (Form W-3)	Payroll Project	7-66
W-2 Transmittal—Pennsylvania (Form REV-1667 AS)	Payroll Project	7-66
Miscellaneous Income (Form 1099-MISC)	Payroll Project	7-67
Annual Summary and Transmittal of U.S. Information Returns (Form 1096)	Payroll Project	7-67
Payroll Register—Kipley Company	Continuing Payroll Problem A	PR-1
Payroll Register—Olney Company	Continuing Payroll Problem B	PR-1
Payroll Register—Glo-Brite Paint Company	Payroll Project	PR-2

	DATE		DESCRIPTION	POST. REF.	DEBIT	CREDIT	
1	20-- Oct.	9	Payroll Cash	12	1 2 0 4 5 44		1
2			Cash	11		1 2 0 4 5 44	2
3							3
4		9	Administrative Salaries	51	2 3 0 7 69		4
5			Office Salaries	52	4 6 5 1 08		5
6			Sales Salaries	53	3 6 0 0 00		6
7			Plant Wages	54	4 9 0 2 00		7
8			FICA Taxes Payable—OASDI	20.1		9 5 8 57	8
9			FICA Taxes Payable—HI	20.2		2 2 4 19	9
10			Employees FIT Payable	24		1 1 2 5 00	10
11			Employees SIT Payable	25		4 7 4 05	11
12			Employees SUTA Payable	25.1		1 0 85	12
13			Employees CIT Payable	26		6 0 6 05	13
14			Union Dues Payable	28		1 6 00	14
15			Payroll Cash	12		1 2 0 4 5 44	15
16							16
17		9	Payroll Taxes	56	1 3 8 1 42		17
18			FICA Taxes Payable—OASDI	20.1		9 5 8 57	18
19			FICA Taxes Payable—HI	20.2		2 2 4 18	19
20			FUTA Taxes Payable	21		2 2 91	20
21			SUTA Taxes Payable—Employer	22		1 7 5 76	21
22							22
23							23
24							24
25							25
26							26
27							27
28							28
29							29
30							30
31							31
32							32
33							33
34							34

	DATE		DESCRIPTION	POST. REF.	DEBIT	CREDIT	
1							1
2							2
3							3
4							4
5							5
6							6
7							7
8							8
9							9
10							10
11							11
12							12
13							13
14							14
15							15
16							16
17							17
18							18
19							19
20							20
21							21
22							22
23							23
24							24
25							25
26							26
27							27
28							28
29							29
30							30
31							31
32							32
33							33
34							34

	DATE		DESCRIPTION	POST. REF.	DEBIT	CREDIT	
1							1
2							2
3							3
4							4
5							5
6							6
7							7
8							8
9							9
10							10
11							11
12							12
13							13
14							14
15							15
16							16
17							17
18							18
19							19
20							20
21							21
22							22
23							23
24							24
25							25
26							26
27							27
28							28
29							29
30							30
31							31
32							32
33							33
34							34

	DATE		DESCRIPTION	POST. REF.	DEBIT	CREDIT	
1							1
2							2
3							3
4							4
5							5
6							6
7							7
8							8
9							9
10							10
11							11
12							12
13							13
14							14
15							15
16							16
17							17
18							18
19							19
20							20
21							21
22							22
23							23
24							24
25							25
26							26
27							27
28							28
29							29
30							30
31							31
32							32
33							33
34							34

	DATE		DESCRIPTION	POST. REF.	DEBIT	CREDIT	
1							1
2							2
3							3
4							4
5							5
6							6
7							7
8							8
9							9
10							10
11							11
12							12
13							13
14							14
15							15
16							16
17							17
18							18
19							19
20							20
21							21
22							22
23							23
24							24
25							25
26							26
27							27
28							28
29							29
30							30
31							31
32							32
33							33
34							34

	DATE		DESCRIPTION	POST. REF.	DEBIT	CREDIT	
1							1
2							2
3							3
4							4
5							5
6							6
7							7
8							8
9							9
10							10
11							11
12							12
13							13
14							14
15							15
16							16
17							17
18							18
19							19
20							20
21							21
22							22
23							23
24							24
25							25
26							26
27							27
28							28
29							29
30							30
31							31
32							32
33							33
34							34

JOURNAL

	DATE	DESCRIPTION	POST. REF.	DEBIT	CREDIT	
1						1
2						2
3						3
4						4
5						5
6						6
7						7
8						8
9						9
10						10
11						11
12						12
13						13
14						14
15						15
16						16
17						17
18						18
19						19
20						20
21						21
22						22
23						23
24						24
25						25
26						26
27						27
28						28
29						29
30						30
31						31
32						32
33						33
34						34

	DATE	DESCRIPTION	POST. REF.	DEBIT	CREDIT	
1						1
2						2
3						3
4						4
5						5
6						6
7						7
8						8
9						9
10						10
11						11
12						12
13						13
14						14
15						15
16						16
17						17
18						18
19						19
20						20
21						21
22						22
23						23
24						24
25						25
26						26
27						27
28						28
29						29
30						30
31						31
32						32
33						33
34						34

	DATE		DESCRIPTION	POST. REF.	DEBIT	CREDIT	
1							1
2							2
3							3
4							4
5							5
6							6
7							7
8							8
9							9
10							10
11							11
12							12
13							13
14							14
15							15
16							16
17							17
18							18
19							19
20							20
21							21
22							22
23							23
24							24
25							25
26							26
27							27
28							28
29							29
30							30
31							31
32							32
33							33
34							34

GENERAL LEDGER

ACCOUNT **CASH**   ACCOUNT NO. **11**

DATE		ITEM	POST. REF.	DEBIT	CREDIT	BALANCE	
						DEBIT	CREDIT
20-- Oct.	1	*Balance*	✓			19 984 633	
	9		J41		1 204 544	18 780 089	

DATE		ITEM	POST. REF.	DEBIT	CREDIT	BALANCE	
						DEBIT	CREDIT
20-- Oct.	9		J41	1 2 0 4 5 44		1 2 0 4 5 44	
	9		J41		1 2 0 4 5 44	– – – –	– – – –

DATE		ITEM	POST. REF.	DEBIT	CREDIT	BALANCE	
						DEBIT	CREDIT
20-- Oct.	9		J41		9 5 8 57		9 5 8 57
	9		J41		9 5 8 57		1 9 1 7 14

ACCOUNT FICA TAXES PAYABLE—HI

ACCOUNT NO. 20.2

DATE		ITEM	POST. REF.	DEBIT	CREDIT	BALANCE DEBIT	BALANCE CREDIT
20-- Oct.	9		J41		2 2 4 19		2 2 4 19
	9		J41		2 2 4 18		4 4 8 37

ACCOUNT FUTA TAXES PAYABLE

ACCOUNT NO. 21

DATE		ITEM	POST. REF.	DEBIT	CREDIT	BALANCE DEBIT	BALANCE CREDIT
20-- Oct.	1	*Balance*	✓				3 9 2 94
	9		J41		2 2 91		4 1 5 85

ACCOUNT SUTA TAXES PAYABLE—EMPLOYER

ACCOUNT NO. 22

DATE		ITEM	POST. REF.	DEBIT	CREDIT	BALANCE DEBIT	BALANCE CREDIT
20-- Oct.	9		J41		1 7 5 76		1 7 5 76

ACCOUNT **EMPLOYEES FIT PAYABLE**   ACCOUNT NO. **24**

DATE		ITEM	POST. REF.	DEBIT	CREDIT	BALANCE	
						DEBIT	CREDIT
20-- Oct.	9		J41		1 1 2 5 00		1 1 2 5 00

ACCOUNT **EMPLOYEES SIT PAYABLE**   ACCOUNT NO. **25**

DATE		ITEM	POST. REF.	DEBIT	CREDIT	BALANCE	
						DEBIT	CREDIT
20-- Oct.	9		J41		4 7 4 67		4 7 4 67

ACCOUNT **EMPLOYEES SUTA PAYABLE**   ACCOUNT NO. **25.1**

DATE		ITEM	POST. REF.	DEBIT	CREDIT	BALANCE	
						DEBIT	CREDIT
20-- Oct.	9		J41		1 0 85		1 0 85

ACCOUNT **EMPLOYEES CIT PAYABLE**   ACCOUNT NO. **26**

DATE		ITEM	POST. REF.	DEBIT	CREDIT	BALANCE	
						DEBIT	CREDIT
20-- Oct.	9		J41		6 0 6 05		6 0 6 05

ACCOUNT **GROUP INSURANCE PREMIUMS COLLECTED**   ACCOUNT NO. **27**

DATE	ITEM	POST. REF.	DEBIT	CREDIT	BALANCE	
					DEBIT	CREDIT

ACCOUNT **UNION DUES PAYABLE**   ACCOUNT NO. **28**

DATE		ITEM	POST. REF.	DEBIT	CREDIT	BALANCE	
						DEBIT	CREDIT
20-- Oct.	9		J41		1 6 00		1 6 00

ACCOUNT **SIMPLE CONTRIBUTIONS PAYABLE**   ACCOUNT NO. **29**

DATE	ITEM	POST. REF.	DEBIT	CREDIT	BALANCE DEBIT	BALANCE CREDIT

ACCOUNT **ADMINISTRATIVE SALARIES**   ACCOUNT NO. **51**

DATE		ITEM	POST. REF.	DEBIT	CREDIT	BALANCE DEBIT	BALANCE CREDIT
20-- Oct.	1	*Balance*	✓			4 2 6 9 2 27	
	9		J41	2 3 0 7 69		4 4 9 9 9 96	

ACCOUNT **OFFICE SALARIES**   ACCOUNT NO. **52**

DATE		ITEM	POST. REF.	DEBIT	CREDIT	BALANCE DEBIT	BALANCE CREDIT
20-- Oct.	1	*Balance*	✓			2 8 3 5 0 00	
	9		J41	4 6 5 1 08		3 3 0 0 1 08	

ACCOUNT **SALES SALARIES**   ACCOUNT NO. **53**

DATE		ITEM	POST. REF.	DEBIT	CREDIT	BALANCE	
						DEBIT	CREDIT
20-- Oct.	1	Balance	✓			2 8 5 2 5 00	
	9		J41	3 6 0 0 00		3 2 1 2 5 00	

ACCOUNT **PLANT WAGES**   ACCOUNT NO. **54**

DATE		ITEM	POST. REF.	DEBIT	CREDIT	BALANCE	
						DEBIT	CREDIT
20-- Oct.	1	Balance	✓			4 2 6 5 7 30	
	9		J41	4 9 0 2 00		4 7 5 5 9 30	

ACCOUNT **PAYROLL TAXES**   ACCOUNT NO. **56**

DATE		ITEM	POST. REF.	DEBIT	CREDIT	BALANCE	
						DEBIT	CREDIT
20-- Oct.	1	Balance	✓			1 4 1 2 3 59	
	9		J41	1 3 8 1 42		1 5 5 0 5 01	

Employees' Earnings Record

Employee Earnings Record — BONNO, Anthony Victor

Field	Value
DEPARTMENT	Plant
OCCUPATION	Mixer Operator
WORKS IN (STATE)	PA
S.S. ACCOUNT NO.	000-00-3481
SEX	M — X
NAME—LAST	BONNO
FIRST	Anthony
MIDDLE	Victor
MARITAL STATUS	M
W/H ALLOW.	4
GROUP INSURANCE	$55,000—30¢/M
OTHER DEDUCTIONS INFORMATION — UNION DUES	$8 each pay
SALARY	$
WEEKLY RATE	$
HOURLY RATE	$ 17.65
OVERTIME RATE	$ 26.48

20__ PAYDAY	REG. HRS	REG. RATE	REG. AMOUNT	OT HRS	OT RATE	OT AMOUNT	CUMULATIVE EARNINGS	FICA OASDI	FICA HI	FIT	SIT	SUTA	CIT	OTHER DEDUCTIONS	CK. NO.	NET PAID AMOUNT
YEAR-TO-DATE TOTAL			10293 40			1028 60	11322 00	701 96	164 17	810 00	347 59	7 93	443 82	216 80		8629 73
1 10/9	80	17 65	1412 00				12734 00	87 54	20 47	46 00	43 35	0 99	55 35	8 00	672	1150 30
2																
3																
4																
5																
6																
QUARTER TOTAL																
YEARLY TOTAL																

Employee Earnings Record — FERGUSON, James Claude

Field	Value
DEPARTMENT	Sales
OCCUPATION	Sales Manager
WORKS IN (STATE)	PA
S.S. ACCOUNT NO.	000-00-8645
SEX	M — X
NAME—LAST	FERGUSON
FIRST	James
MIDDLE	Claude
MARITAL STATUS	M
W/H ALLOW.	5
GROUP INSURANCE	$88,000—30¢/M
SALARY	$ 58,500/yr.
WEEKLY RATE	$ 1,125.00
HOURLY RATE	$
OVERTIME RATE	$ 28.13

20__ PAYDAY	REG. HRS	REG. RATE	REG. AMOUNT	OT HRS	OT RATE	OT AMOUNT	CUMULATIVE EARNINGS	FICA OASDI	FICA HI	FIT	SIT	SUTA	CIT	OTHER DEDUCTIONS	CK. NO.	NET PAID AMOUNT
YEAR-TO-DATE TOTAL			23125 00				23125 00	1433 75	335 31	2291 00	709 94	16 19	906 50	132 30		17300 01
1 10/9	80		2250 00				25375 00	139 50	32 63	137 00	69 08	1 58	88 20		673	1782 01
2																
3																
4																
5																
6																
QUARTER TOTAL																
YEARLY TOTAL																

Employee Earnings Record — FORD, Catherine Louise

Field	Value
DEPARTMENT	Office
OCCUPATION	Executive Secretary
WORKS IN (STATE)	PA
S.S. ACCOUNT NO.	000-00-4567
SEX	F X
NAME—LAST	FORD
FIRST	Catherine
MIDDLE	Louise
MARITAL STATUS	S
W/H ALLOW.	2
SALARY	$2,643.33/mo.
WEEKLY RATE	$610.00
HOURLY RATE	$15.25
OVERTIME RATE	$22.88
GROUP INSURANCE	$48,000—30¢/M

20__ PAYDAY	REG HRS	REG RATE	REG AMOUNT	OT HRS	OT RATE	OT AMOUNT	CUMULATIVE EARNINGS	FICA OASDI	FICA HI	FIT	SIT	SUTA	CIT	OTHER DEDUCTIONS	CK. NO.	NET PAID AMOUNT
YEAR-TO-DATE TOTAL			63 0 0 00				63 0 0 00	39 0 60	9 1 35	6 3 9 00	1 9 3 41	4 41	2 4 6 96			46 9 6 47
1 10/9	80		12 2 0 00				75 2 0 00	7 5 64	1 7 69	1 0 7 00	3 7 45	0 85	4 7 82	3 7 80	674	9 3 3 55
2																
3																
4																
5																
6																
QUARTER TOTAL																
YEARLY TOTAL																

Employee Earnings Record — MANN, Dewey Wilson

Field	Value
DEPARTMENT	Sales
OCCUPATION	Sales Representative
WORKS IN (STATE)	PA
S.S. ACCOUNT NO.	000-00-9352
SEX	M X
NAME—LAST	MANN
FIRST	Dewey
MIDDLE	Wilson
MARITAL STATUS	M
W/H ALLOW.	4
SALARY	$2,925/mo.
WEEKLY RATE	$675.00
HOURLY RATE	$16.88
GROUP INSURANCE	$53,000—30¢/M

20__ PAYDAY	REG HRS	REG RATE	REG AMOUNT	OT HRS	OT RATE	OT AMOUNT	CUMULATIVE EARNINGS	FICA OASDI	FICA HI	FIT	SIT	SUTA	CIT	OTHER DEDUCTIONS	CK. NO.	NET PAID AMOUNT
YEAR-TO-DATE TOTAL			54 0 0 00				54 0 0 00	3 3 4 80	7 8 30	3 3 2 00	16 5 78	3 78	2 1 1 68			42 4 2 16
1 10/9	80		13 5 0 00				67 5 0 00	8 3 70	1 9 58	4 0 00	4 1 45	0 95	5 2 92	3 1 50	675	11 1 1 40
2																
3																
4																
5																
6																
QUARTER TOTAL																
YEARLY TOTAL																

Employee Earnings Record — O'Neill

Field	Value
DEPARTMENT	Admin.
OCCUPATION	President
WORKS IN (STATE)	PA
S.S. ACCOUNT NO.	000-00-1534
SEX	M X F
NAME—LAST	O'NEILL
FIRST	Joseph
MIDDLE	Tyler
MARITAL STATUS	M
W/H ALLOW.	3
SALARY	$60,000/yr.
WEEKLY RATE	$1,153.85
HOURLY RATE	$28.85
OVERTIME RATE	$
GROUP INSURANCE	$90,000—30¢/M

OTHER DEDUCTIONS INFORMATION: UNION DUES / OTHER

PAYDAY 20__	REG. HRS.	REG. RATE	REG. AMOUNT	OT HRS.	OT RATE	OT AMOUNT	CUMULATIVE EARNINGS	FICA OASDI	FICA HI	FIT	SIT	SUTA	CIT	OTHER DEDUCTIONS	CK. NO.	NET PAID AMOUNT
YEAR-TO-DATE TOTAL			426 9 2 27				426 9 2 27	26 4 6 92	6 1 9 04	6 116 00	13 1 0 65	29 88	167 3 54	2 0 2 50		300 9 3 74
1 10/9	80		23 0 7 69				449 9 9 96	1 4 3 08	3 3 46	1 9 2 00	7 0 85	1 62	9 0 46		676	17 7 6 22
2																
3																
4																
5																
6																
QUARTER TOTAL																
YEARLY TOTAL																

Employee Earnings Record — Russell

Field	Value
DEPARTMENT	Office
OCCUPATION	Time Clerk
WORKS IN (STATE)	PA
S.S. ACCOUNT NO.	000-00-6337
SEX	M F X
NAME—LAST	RUSSELL
FIRST	Virginia
MIDDLE	Aloise
MARITAL STATUS	S
W/H ALLOW.	1
SALARY	$2,600/mo.
WEEKLY RATE	$600.00
HOURLY RATE	$15.00
OVERTIME RATE	$22.50
GROUP INSURANCE	$47,000—30¢/M

OTHER DEDUCTIONS INFORMATION: UNION DUES / OTHER

PAYDAY 20__	REG. HRS.	REG. RATE	REG. AMOUNT	OT HRS.	OT RATE	OT AMOUNT	CUMULATIVE EARNINGS	FICA OASDI	FICA HI	FIT	SIT	SUTA	CIT	OTHER DEDUCTIONS	CK. NO.	NET PAID AMOUNT
YEAR-TO-DATE TOTAL			62 4 0 00				62 4 0 00	3 8 6 88	9 0 48	6 4 2 00	1 9 1 56	4 37	2 4 4 61	3 1 50		46 4 8 60
1 10/9	80		12 0 0 00				74 4 0 00	7 4 40	1 7 40	1 2 7 00	3 6 84	0 84	4 7 04		677	8 9 6 48
2																
3																
4																
5																
6																
QUARTER TOTAL																
YEARLY TOTAL																

Employee Earnings Record — RYAN, Norman Allen

DEPARTMENT	OCCUPATION	WORKS IN (STATE)	SEX	S.S. ACCOUNT NO.	NAME—LAST	FIRST	MIDDLE
Plant	Electrician	PA	M X	000-00-1223	RYAN	Norman	Allen

MARITAL STATUS	W/H ALLOW.
M	4

GROUP INSURANCE: $56,000—30¢/M
OTHER DEDUCTIONS INFORMATION — UNION DUES: $8 each pay

SALARY: $ ____
WEEKLY RATE: $ ____
HOURLY RATE: $18.00
OVERTIME RATE: $27.00

20__ PAYDAY	REGULAR EARNINGS HRS.	RATE	AMOUNT	OVERTIME EARNINGS HRS.	RATE	AMOUNT	CUMULATIVE EARNINGS
YEAR-TO-DATE TOTAL			132 8 7 50			13 9 7 80	146 8 5 30
1 10/9	80	18 00	144 0 00				161 2 5 30
2							
3							
4							
5							
6							
QUARTER TOTAL							
YEARLY TOTAL							

DEDUCTIONS

20__ PAYDAY	FICA OASDI	HI	FIT	SIT	SUTA	CIT	OTHER DEDUCTIONS	CK. NO.	NET PAID AMOUNT
YEAR-TO-DATE TOTAL	9 1 0 49	2 1 2 94	10 7 0 00	4 5 0 84	1 0 28	5 7 5 66	2 3 5 70		112 1 9 39
1 10/9	8 9 28	2 0 88	5 0 00	4 4 21	1 01	5 6 45	8 00	678	117 0 17

Employee Earnings Record — SOKOWSKI, Thomas James

DEPARTMENT	OCCUPATION	WORKS IN (STATE)	SEX	S.S. ACCOUNT NO.	NAME—LAST	FIRST	MIDDLE
Plant	Supervisor	PA	M X	000-00-8832	SOKOWSKI	Thomas	James

MARITAL STATUS	W/H ALLOW.
M	2

GROUP INSURANCE: $80,000—30¢/M
OTHER DEDUCTIONS INFORMATION — UNION DUES:

SALARY: $1,025.00
WEEKLY RATE: $1,025.00
HOURLY RATE: $25.63
OVERTIME RATE: $ ____

20__ PAYDAY	REGULAR EARNINGS HRS.	RATE	AMOUNT	OVERTIME EARNINGS HRS.	RATE	AMOUNT	CUMULATIVE EARNINGS
YEAR-TO-DATE TOTAL			166 5 0 00				166 5 0 00
1 10/9	80		20 5 0 00				187 0 0 00
2							
3							
4							
5							
6							
QUARTER TOTAL							
YEARLY TOTAL							

DEDUCTIONS

20__ PAYDAY	FICA OASDI	HI	FIT	SIT	SUTA	CIT	OTHER DEDUCTIONS	CK. NO.	NET PAID AMOUNT
YEAR-TO-DATE TOTAL	10 3 2 30	2 4 1 43	20 0 2 00	5 1 1 16	11 66	6 5 2 68			121 0 4 27
1 10/9	12 7 10	2 9 73	17 6 00	6 2 94	1 44	8 0 36	9 4 50	679	15 7 2 43

Employee Payroll Record — Left

Field	Value
DEPARTMENT	Office
OCCUPATION	Accounting Trainee
WORKS IN (STATE)	PA
NAME—LAST	
FIRST	
MIDDLE	
S.S. ACCOUNT NO.	
SEX	M / F
MARITAL STATUS	S
W/H ALLOW.	1
GROUP INSURANCE	$39,000—30¢/M
SALARY	$
WEEKLY RATE	$
HOURLY RATE	$ 14.00
OVERTIME RATE	$ 21.00

20__ PAYDAY	REG HRS	REG RATE	REG AMOUNT	OT HRS	OT RATE	OT AMOUNT	CUMULATIVE EARNINGS	FICA OASDI	FICA HI	FIT	SIT	SUTA	CIT	OTHER DEDUCTIONS	CK. NO.	NET PAID AMOUNT
YEAR-TO-DATE TOTAL			5550 00				5550 00	344 10	80 48	409 00	170 38	3 89	217 56	32 40		4292 19
1 10/9	72	14 00	1008 00				6558 00	62 50	14 62	97 00	30 95	0 71	39 51		680	762 71
2																
3																
4																
5																
6																
QUARTER TOTAL																
YEARLY TOTAL																

Employee Payroll Record — Right

Field	Value
DEPARTMENT	Office
OCCUPATION	Programmer
WORKS IN (STATE)	PA
NAME—LAST	WILLIAMS
FIRST	Ruth
MIDDLE	Virginia
S.S. ACCOUNT NO.	000-00-6741
SEX	M / F X
MARITAL STATUS	S
W/H ALLOW.	0
GROUP INSURANCE	$48,000—30¢/M
SALARY	$ 2,650/mo.
WEEKLY RATE	$ 611.54
HOURLY RATE	$ 15.29
OVERTIME RATE	$ 22.94

20__ PAYDAY	REG HRS	REG RATE	REG AMOUNT	OT HRS	OT RATE	OT AMOUNT	CUMULATIVE EARNINGS	FICA OASDI	FICA HI	FIT	SIT	SUTA	CIT	OTHER DEDUCTIONS	CK. NO.	NET PAID AMOUNT
YEAR-TO-DATE TOTAL			10260 00				10260 00	636 12	148 77	1606 00	314 98	7 18	402 19	59 40		7085 36
1 10/9	80		1223 08				11483 08	75 83	17 73	153 00	37 55	0 86	47 94		681	890 17
2																
3																
4																
5																
6																
QUARTER TOTAL																
YEARLY TOTAL																

DEPARTMENT   OCCUPATION   WORKS IN (STATE)   S.S. ACCOUNT NO.   NAME—LAST   FIRST   MIDDLE

SEX   M   F   MARITAL STATUS   W/H ALLOW.

OTHER DEDUCTIONS INFORMATION   GROUP INSURANCE   UNION DUES   OTHER

SALARY   WEEKLY RATE $ HOURLY RATE $ OVERTIME RATE $

NET PAID   CK. NO.   AMOUNT

DEDUCTIONS   OTHER DEDUCTIONS   CIT   SUTA   SIT   FIT   FICA   HI   OASDI

CUMULATIVE EARNINGS

OVERTIME EARNINGS   HRS.   RATE   AMOUNT

REGULAR EARNINGS   HRS.   RATE   AMOUNT

20 __ PAYDAY   YEAR-TO-DATE TOTAL   1   2   3   4   5   6   QUARTER TOTAL   YEARLY TOTAL

DEPARTMENT   OCCUPATION   WORKS IN (STATE)   S.S. ACCOUNT NO.   NAME—LAST   FIRST   MIDDLE

SEX   M   F   MARITAL STATUS   W/H ALLOW.

OTHER DEDUCTIONS INFORMATION   GROUP INSURANCE   UNION DUES   OTHER

SALARY   WEEKLY RATE $ HOURLY RATE $ OVERTIME RATE $

NET PAID   CK. NO.   AMOUNT

DEDUCTIONS   OTHER DEDUCTIONS   CIT   SUTA   SIT   FIT   FICA   HI   OASDI

CUMULATIVE EARNINGS

OVERTIME EARNINGS   HRS.   RATE   AMOUNT

REGULAR EARNINGS   HRS.   RATE   AMOUNT

20 __ PAYDAY   YEAR-TO-DATE TOTAL   1   2   3   4   5   6   QUARTER TOTAL   YEARLY TOTAL

Payroll Register Form

DEPARTMENT

OCCUPATION

WORKS IN (STATE)

SEX   M   F

S.S. ACCOUNT NO.

NAME—LAST   FIRST   MIDDLE

GROUP INSURANCE

OTHER DEDUCTIONS INFORMATION

UNION DUES

OTHER

SALARY $
WEEKLY RATE $
HOURLY RATE $
OVERTIME RATE $

W/H ALLOW.

MARITAL STATUS

NET PAID

	REGULAR EARNINGS			OVERTIME EARNINGS			CUMULATIVE EARNINGS	DEDUCTIONS								
20___ PAYDAY	HRS.	RATE	AMOUNT	HRS.	RATE	AMOUNT		FICA OASDI	FICA HI	FIT	SIT	SUTA	CIT	OTHER DEDUCTIONS	CK. NO.	AMOUNT
YEAR-TO-DATE TOTAL																
1																
2																
3																
4																
5																
6																
QUARTER TOTAL																
YEARLY TOTAL																

DEPARTMENT

OCCUPATION

WORKS IN (STATE)

SEX   M   F

S.S. ACCOUNT NO.

NAME—LAST   FIRST   MIDDLE

GROUP INSURANCE

OTHER DEDUCTIONS INFORMATION

UNION DUES

OTHER

SALARY $
WEEKLY RATE $
HOURLY RATE $
OVERTIME RATE $

W/H ALLOW.

MARITAL STATUS

NET PAID

	REGULAR EARNINGS			OVERTIME EARNINGS			CUMULATIVE EARNINGS	DEDUCTIONS								
20___ PAYDAY	HRS.	RATE	AMOUNT	HRS.	RATE	AMOUNT		FICA OASDI	FICA HI	FIT	SIT	SUTA	CIT	OTHER DEDUCTIONS	CK. NO.	AMOUNT
YEAR-TO-DATE TOTAL																
1																
2																
3																
4																
5																
6																
QUARTER TOTAL																
YEARLY TOTAL																

Transaction No. 11

FEDERAL DEPOSIT INFORMATION WORKSHEET

Employer
Identification Number _____   Name _____

Month Tax Year Ends _____   Amount of Deposit _____

Type of Tax (Form) _____   Tax Period _____

Address _____   Phone Number _____

City, State, Zip _____

Transaction No. 25

FEDERAL DEPOSIT INFORMATION WORKSHEET

Employer
Identification Number _____   Name _____

Month Tax Year Ends _____   Amount of Deposit _____

Type of Tax (Form) _____   Tax Period _____

Address _____   Phone Number _____

City, State, Zip _____

Transaction No. 33

FEDERAL DEPOSIT INFORMATION WORKSHEET

Employer
Identification Number _____   Name _____

Month Tax Year Ends _____   Amount of Deposit _____

Type of Tax (Form) _____   Tax Period _____

Address _____   Phone Number _____

City, State, Zip _____

Transaction No. 36

FEDERAL DEPOSIT INFORMATION WORKSHEET

Employer
Identification Number _____   Name _____

Month Tax Year Ends _____   Amount of Deposit _____

Type of Tax (Form) _____   Tax Period _____

Address _____   Phone Number _____

City, State, Zip _____

Transaction No. 2

STATE FILING INFORMATION WORKSHEET

Company Name	_____	Payment Frequency	_____
Employer Account #	_____	Gross Compensation	_____
Employer ID #	_____	PA Withholding Tax	_____
Employer Password	_____	Credits	_____
Quarter Ending Date	_____	Interest	_____
Telephone Number	_____	Payment	_____

Transaction No. 4

STATE FILING INFORMATION WORKSHEET

Company Name	_____	Payment Frequency	_____
Employer Account #	_____	Gross Compensation	_____
Employer ID #	_____	PA Withholding Tax	_____
Employer Password	_____	Credits	_____
Quarter Ending Date	_____	Interest	_____
Telephone Number	_____	Payment	_____

Transaction No. 14

STATE FILING INFORMATION WORKSHEET

Company Name	_____	Payment Frequency	_____
Employer Account #	_____	Gross Compensation	_____
Employer ID #	_____	PA Withholding Tax	_____
Employer Password	_____	Credits	_____
Quarter Ending Date	_____	Interest	_____
Telephone Number	_____	Payment	_____

Transaction No. 18

STATE FILING INFORMATION WORKSHEET

Company Name	_____	Payment Frequency	_____
Employer Account #	_____	Gross Compensation	_____
Employer ID #	_____	PA Withholding Tax	_____
Employer Password	_____	Credits	_____
Quarter Ending Date	_____	Interest	_____
Telephone Number	_____	Payment	_____

Transaction No. 27

STATE FILING INFORMATION WORKSHEET

Company Name	_____	Payment Frequency	_____
Employer Account #	_____	Gross Compensation	_____
Employer ID #	_____	PA Withholding Tax	_____
Employer Password	_____	Credits	_____
Quarter Ending Date	_____	Interest	_____
Telephone Number	_____	Payment	_____

Transaction No. 31

STATE FILING INFORMATION WORKSHEET

Company Name	_____	Payment Frequency	_____
Employer Account #	_____	Gross Compensation	_____
Employer ID #	_____	PA Withholding Tax	_____
Employer Password	_____	Credits	_____
Quarter Ending Date	_____	Interest	_____
Telephone Number	_____	Payment	_____

Transaction No. 12

Monthly Wage Tax

GLO-BRITE PAINT COMPANY
2215 SALVADOR STREET
PHILADELPHIA, PA 19175-0682

Signature: _____
I hereby certify that I have examined this return and that it is correct to the best of my knowledge.

Phone #: _____

Account #: **0001855**

Tax Type: **01**

Period/Yr: **10/—**

From: **10/01**

To: **10/31**

Due Date: **11/15**

Philadelphia Revenue Department
P.O. Box 8040
Philadelphia, PA 19101-8040

1. TAX DUE PER WORKSHEET, *Line 8*

2. INTEREST AND PENALTY

3. TOTAL DUE (LINE 1 & 2)

Make checks payable to:
CITY OF PHILADELPHIA

Source: Philadelphia Revenue Department.

Transaction No. 26

Monthly Wage Tax

GLO-BRITE PAINT COMPANY
2215 SALVADOR STREET
PHILADELPHIA, PA 19175-0682

Account #: **0001855**   From: **11/01**

Tax Type: **01**   To: **11/30**

Period/Yr: **11/—**   Due Date: **12/15**

Signature: _____
I hereby certify that I have examined this return
and that it is correct to the best of my knowledge.

Phone #: _____

Philadelphia Revenue Department
P.O. Box 8040
Philadelphia, PA 19101-8040

1. TAX DUE PER WORKSHEET, *Line 8*

2. INTEREST AND PENALTY

3. TOTAL DUE (LINE 1 & 2)

Make checks payable to:
CITY OF PHILADELPHIA

Source: Philadelphia Revenue Department.

Transaction No. 34

Monthly Wage Tax

GLO-BRITE PAINT COMPANY
2215 SALVADOR STREET
PHILADELPHIA, PA 19175-0682

Account #: **0001855**   From: **12/01**

Tax Type: **01**   To: **12/31**

Period/Yr: **12/—**   Due Date: **1/17**

Signature: _____
I hereby certify that I have examined this return
and that it is correct to the best of my knowledge.

Phone #: _____

Philadelphia Revenue Department
P.O. Box 8040
Philadelphia, PA 19101-8040

1. TAX DUE PER WORKSHEET, *Line 8*

2. INTEREST AND PENALTY

3. TOTAL DUE (LINE 1 & 2)

Make checks payable to:
CITY OF PHILADELPHIA

Source: Philadelphia Revenue Department.

Transaction No. 43

PA Employer's Quarterly Reconciliation Worksheet

Company Name _____

Account Number _____

ID # _____

Telephone # _____

Quarter Ending Date _____

Record of PA Withholding Tax:

1st half of month _____

2nd half of month _____

1st half of month _____

2nd half of month _____

1st half of month _____

2nd half of month _____

TOTAL _____

1. Total Compensation _____

2. Total PA W/H Tax _____

3. Total Deposits/Quarter _____

4. Tax Due _____

CITY OF PHILADELPHIA
ANNUAL RECONCILIATION OF
20-- EMPLOYER WAGE TAX

5013

DUE DATE: FEBRUARY 28, 20--

City Account Number
| 0 | 0 | 0 | 1 | 8 | 5 | 5 |

Federal Identification Number
| 0 | 0 | – | 0 | 0 | 0 | 0 | 6 | 6 | 0 |

Taxpayer Name and Address

GLO-BRITE PAINT COMPANY

2215 Salvador Street
Philadelphia, PA 19175-0682

If your business terminated in 20--, enter the termination date **AND** file a CHANGE FORM.

| m | m | – | d | d | – | y | y | y | y |

<u>YOU MUST USE THE CHANGE FORM TO REPORT A
CHANGE OF ADDRESS OR TO CANCEL THIS ACCOUNT.</u>

If this is an amended return place an "X" here:

A. Enter the number of Philadelphia Residents for whom wage tax was remitted for the pay period including March 12, 20--..A.

B. Enter the number of **nonresidents** (employees living outside Philadelphia city limits) for whom wage tax was remitted for the pay period including March 12, 20--.........................B.

C. Total number of employees **for all company locations** reported on the Employer's Federal Quarterly Tax Return for the first quarter of 20-- (for the pay period including March 12, 20--)..............C.

D. Number of employees working **at company locations within Philadelphia city limits**, for the pay period including March 12, 20--...D.

1. Gross Compensation per W-2 forms for all employees.............................1. .00

2. Non-Taxable Gross Compensation included in Line 1.
   (Paid to nonresidents working outside of Philadelphia)............................2. .00

3. Gross Compensation per W-2 forms on which Philadelphia Wage Tax was
   withheld or due (Line 1 minus Line 2)..3. .00

4. **Taxable Gross Compensation paid to <u>residents</u> of Philadelphia
   in 20- -**...4. .00

5. Tax Due (Line 4 times .0392)...5. .00

6. **Taxable Gross Compensation paid to <u>nonresidents</u> of Philadelphia
   in 20- -**...6. .00

7. Tax Due (Line 6 times .034915)...7. .00

8. **Total Tax Due** (Add Lines 5 and 7)..8. .00

9. **Tax previously paid for 20--**..9. .00

10. **ADDITIONAL TAX DUE** If Line 8 is greater than Line 9, enter the amount here...................10. .00

11. **TAX OVERPAID** If Line 9 is greater than Line 8, enter the amount here.
    See instructions for filing a Refund Petition...11. .00

Under penalties of perjury, as set forth in 18 PA C.S. §§ 4902-4903 as amended, I swear that I have reviewed this return and accompanying statements and schedules, and to the best of my knowledge and belief, they are true and complete.

Taxpayer Signature_____ Date_____ Phone #_____

Preparer Signature_____ Date_____ Phone #_____

5013 Internet 11-7-2013

Source: Philadelphia Revenue Department.

Form **941 for 20--:** Employer's QUARTERLY Federal Tax Return
(Rev. January 2015)   Department of the Treasury — Internal Revenue Service

OMB No. 1545-0029

Employer identification number (EIN)   0 0 – 0 0 0 0 6 6 0

Name *(not your trade name)*   GLO-BRITE PAINT COMPANY

Trade name *(if any)*

Address   2215 SALVADOR STREET
Number   Street   Suite or room number

PHILADELPHIA   PA   19175-0682
City   State   ZIP code

Foreign country name   Foreign province/county   Foreign postal code

Report for this Quarter of 20--
(Check one.)

- [ ] **1:** January, February, March
- [ ] **2:** April, May, June
- [ ] **3:** July, August, September
- [ ] **4:** October, November, December

Instructions and prior year forms are available at *www.irs.gov/form941.*

Read the separate instructions before you complete Form 941. Type or print within the boxes.

Part 1:   **Answer these questions for this quarter.**

1   Number of employees who received wages, tips, or other compensation for the pay period including: *Mar. 12* (Quarter 1), *June 12* (Quarter 2), *Sept. 12* (Quarter 3), or *Dec. 12* (Quarter 4)   **1**

2   Wages, tips, and other compensation   **2**

3   Federal income tax withheld from wages, tips, and other compensation   **3**

4   If no wages, tips, and other compensation are subject to social security or Medicare tax   [ ] Check and go to line 6.

	Column 1		Column 2
5a Taxable social security wages . .		× .124 =	
5b Taxable social security tips . . .		× .124 =	
5c Taxable Medicare wages & tips. .		× .029 =	
5d Taxable wages & tips subject to Additional Medicare Tax withholding		× .009 =	

5e   Add Column 2 from lines 5a, 5b, 5c, and 5d   **5e**

5f   Section 3121(q) Notice and Demand—Tax due on unreported tips (see instructions)   **5f**

6   Total taxes before adjustments. Add lines 3, 5e, and 5f   **6**

7   Current quarter's adjustment for fractions of cents   **7**

8   Current quarter's adjustment for sick pay   **8**

9   Current quarter's adjustments for tips and group-term life insurance   **9**

10   Total taxes after adjustments. Combine lines 6 through 9   **10**

11   Total deposits for this quarter, including overpayment applied from a prior quarter and overpayments applied from Form 941-X, 941-X (PR), 944-X, 944-X (PR), or 944-X (SP) filed in the current quarter   **11**

12   Balance due. If line 10 is more than line 11, enter the difference and see instructions   **12**

13   Overpayment. If line 11 is more than line 10, enter the difference   Check one: [ ] Apply to next return.   [ ] Send a refund.

▶ **You MUST complete both pages of Form 941 and SIGN it.**

Next ▶

For Privacy Act and Paperwork Reduction Act Notice, see the back of the Payment Voucher.   Cat. No. 17001Z   Form **941** (Rev. 1-2015)

Transaction No. 35

Name *(not your trade name)*

GLO-BRITE PAINT COMPANY

Employer identification number (EIN)

00-0000660

Part 2:	Tell us about your deposit schedule and tax liability for this quarter.

If you are unsure about whether you are a monthly schedule depositor or a semiweekly schedule depositor, see Pub. 15 (Circular E), section 11.

14 Check one: ☐ Line 10 on this return is less than $2,500 or line 10 on the return for the prior quarter was less than $2,500, and you did not incur a **$100,000 next-day deposit obligation during the current quarter.** If line 10 for the prior quarter was less than $2,500 but line 10 on this return is $100,000 or more, you must provide a record of your federal tax liability. If you are a monthly schedule depositor, complete the deposit schedule below; if you are a semiweekly schedule depositor, attach Schedule B (Form 941). Go to Part 3.

☐ **You were a monthly schedule depositor for the entire quarter.** Enter your tax liability for each month and total liability for the quarter, then go to Part 3.

Tax liability: Month 1 ☐.

Month 2 ☐.

Month 3 ☐.

Total liability for quarter ☐. **Total must equal line 10.**

☐ **You were a semiweekly schedule depositor for any part of this quarter.** Complete Schedule B (Form 941), Report of Tax Liability for Semiweekly Schedule Depositors, and attach it to Form 941.

Part 3:	Tell us about your business. If a question does NOT apply to your business, leave it blank.

15 If your business has closed or you stopped paying wages . . . . ☐ Check here, and

enter the final date you paid wages ☐ / / .

16 If you are a seasonal employer and you do not have to file a return for every quarter of the year . . ☐ Check here.

Part 4:	May we speak with your third-party designee?

Do you want to allow an employee, a paid tax preparer, or another person to discuss this return with the IRS? See the instructions for details.

☐ Yes. Designee's name and phone number

Select a 5-digit Personal Identification Number (PIN) to use when talking to the IRS. ☐ ☐ ☐ ☐ ☐

☐ No.

Part 5:	Sign here. You MUST complete both pages of Form 941 and SIGN it.

Under penalties of perjury, I declare that I have examined this return, including accompanying schedules and statements, and to the best of my knowledge and belief, it is true, correct, and complete. Declaration of preparer (other than taxpayer) is based on all information of which preparer has any knowledge.

X Sign your name here

Print your name here

Print your title here

Date ☐ / /

Best daytime phone

Paid Preparer Use Only

Check if you are self-employed . . . ☐

Preparer's name

PTIN

Preparer's signature

Date / /

Firm's name (or yours if self-employed)

EIN

Address

Phone

City

State

ZIP code

Source: Internal Revenue Service.

Form **940** for 20--: **Employer's Annual Federal Unemployment (FUTA) Tax Return**

Department of the Treasury — Internal Revenue Service

OMB No. 1545-0028

Employer identification number (EIN) 0 0 – 0 0 0 0 6 6 0

Name (not your trade name) GLO-BRITE PAINT COMPANY

Trade name (if any)

Address 2215 SALVADOR STREET

Number   Street   Suite or room number

PHILADELPHIA   PA   19175-0682

City   State   ZIP code

Foreign country name   Foreign province/county   Foreign postal code

Type of Return
(Check all that apply.)

- ☐ **a.** Amended
- ☐ **b.** Successor employer
- ☐ **c.** No payments to employees in 20--
- ☐ **d.** Final: Business closed or stopped paying wages

Instructions and prior-year forms are available at *www.irs.gov/form940*.

Read the separate instructions before you complete this form. Please type or print within the boxes.

Part 1:   Tell us about your return. If any line does NOT apply, leave it blank.

1a If you had to pay state unemployment tax in one state only, enter the state abbreviation .   **1a** ☐☐

1b If you had to pay state unemployment tax in more than one state, you are a multi-state employer . . . .   **1b** ☐ Check here. Complete Schedule A (Form 940).

2 If you paid wages in a state that is subject to CREDIT REDUCTION . . . .   **2** ☐ Check here. Complete Schedule A (Form 940).

Part 2:   Determine your FUTA tax before adjustments for 20--. If any line does NOT apply, leave it blank.

3 Total payments to all employees . . . .   **3** _____ .

4 Payments exempt from FUTA tax . . . . . .   **4** _____ .

Check all that apply: **4a** ☐ Fringe benefits   **4c** ☐ Retirement/Pension   **4e** ☐ Other
4b ☐ Group-term life insurance   **4d** ☐ Dependent care

5 Total of payments made to each employee in excess of $7,000 . . . .   **5** _____ .

6 Subtotal (line 4 + line 5 = line 6) . . . .   **6** _____ .

7 Total taxable FUTA wages (line 3 – line 6 = line 7) (see instructions) . . . . . .   **7** _____ .

8 FUTA tax before adjustments (line 7 x .006 = line 8) . . . .   **8** _____ .

Part 3:   Determine your adjustments. If any line does NOT apply, leave it blank.

9 If ALL of the taxable FUTA wages you paid were excluded from state unemployment tax, multiply line 7 by .054 (line 7 × .054 = line 9). Go to line 12 . . . .   **9** _____ .

10 If SOME of the taxable FUTA wages you paid were excluded from state unemployment tax, OR you paid ANY state unemployment tax late (after the due date for filing Form 940), complete the worksheet in the instructions. Enter the amount from line 7 of the worksheet . .   **10** _____ .

11 If credit reduction applies, enter the total from Schedule A (Form 940) . . . . . .   **11** _____ .

Part 4:   Determine your FUTA tax and balance due or overpayment for 20--. If any line does NOT apply, leave it blank.

12 Total FUTA tax after adjustments (lines 8 + 9 + 10 + 11 = line 12) . . . .   **12** _____ .

13 FUTA tax deposited for the year, including any overpayment applied from a prior year .   **13** _____ .

14 Balance due (If line 12 is more than line 13, enter the excess on line 14.)
- If line 14 is more than $500, you must deposit your tax.
- If line 14 is $500 or less, you may pay with this return. (see instructions) . . . . . .   **14** _____ .

15 Overpayment (If line 13 is more than line 12, enter the excess on line 15 and check a box below.) . . . .   **15** _____ .

▶ You **MUST** complete both pages of this form and **SIGN** it.   Check one: ☐ Apply to next return. ☐ Send a refund.

Next ▶

For Privacy Act and Paperwork Reduction Act Notice, see the back of Form 940-V, Payment Voucher.   Cat. No. 11234O   Form **940** (2014)

Transaction No. 36 (concluded)

Name (not your trade name)	Employer identification number (EIN)
GLO-BRITE PAINT COMPANY	00-0000660

Part 5: Report your FUTA tax liability by quarter only if line 12 is more than $500. If not, go to Part 6.

16 Report the amount of your FUTA tax liability for each quarter; do NOT enter the amount you deposited. If you had no liability for a quarter, leave the line blank.

16a **1st quarter** (January 1 – March 31) . . . . 16a [.   ]

16b **2nd quarter** (April 1 – June 30) . . . . 16b [.   ]

16c **3rd quarter** (July 1 – September 30) . . . . 16c [.   ]

16d **4th quarter** (October 1 – December 31) . . . . . . 16d [.   ]

17 **Total tax liability for the year** (lines 16a + 16b + 16c + 16d = line 17) **17** [.   ] **Total must equal line 12.**

Part 6: May we speak with your third-party designee?

Do you want to allow an employee, a paid tax preparer, or another person to discuss this return with the IRS? See the instructions for details.

☐ **Yes.** Designee's name and phone number [   ] [   ]

Select a 5-digit Personal Identification Number (PIN) to use when talking to IRS [ ][ ][ ][ ][ ]

☐ **No.**

Part 7: Sign here. You MUST complete both pages of this form and SIGN it.

Under penalties of perjury, I declare that I have examined this return, including accompanying schedules and statements, and to the best of my knowledge and belief, it is true, correct, and complete, and that no part of any payment made to a state unemployment fund claimed as a credit was, or is to be, deducted from the payments made to employees. Declaration of preparer (other than taxpayer) is based on all information of which preparer has any knowledge.

✗ **Sign your name here** [   ]   Print your name here [   ]

Print your title here [   ]

Date [/   /   ]   Best daytime phone [   ]

Paid Preparer Use Only   Check if you are self-employed . ☐

Preparer's name	[ ]	PTIN	[ ]
Preparer's signature	[ ]	Date	[/ /]
Firm's name (or yours if self-employed)	[ ]	EIN	[ ]
Address	[ ]	Phone	[ ]
City	[ ]	State [ ]	ZIP code	[ ]

Form **940** (2014)

Source: Internal Revenue Service.

Transaction No. 37

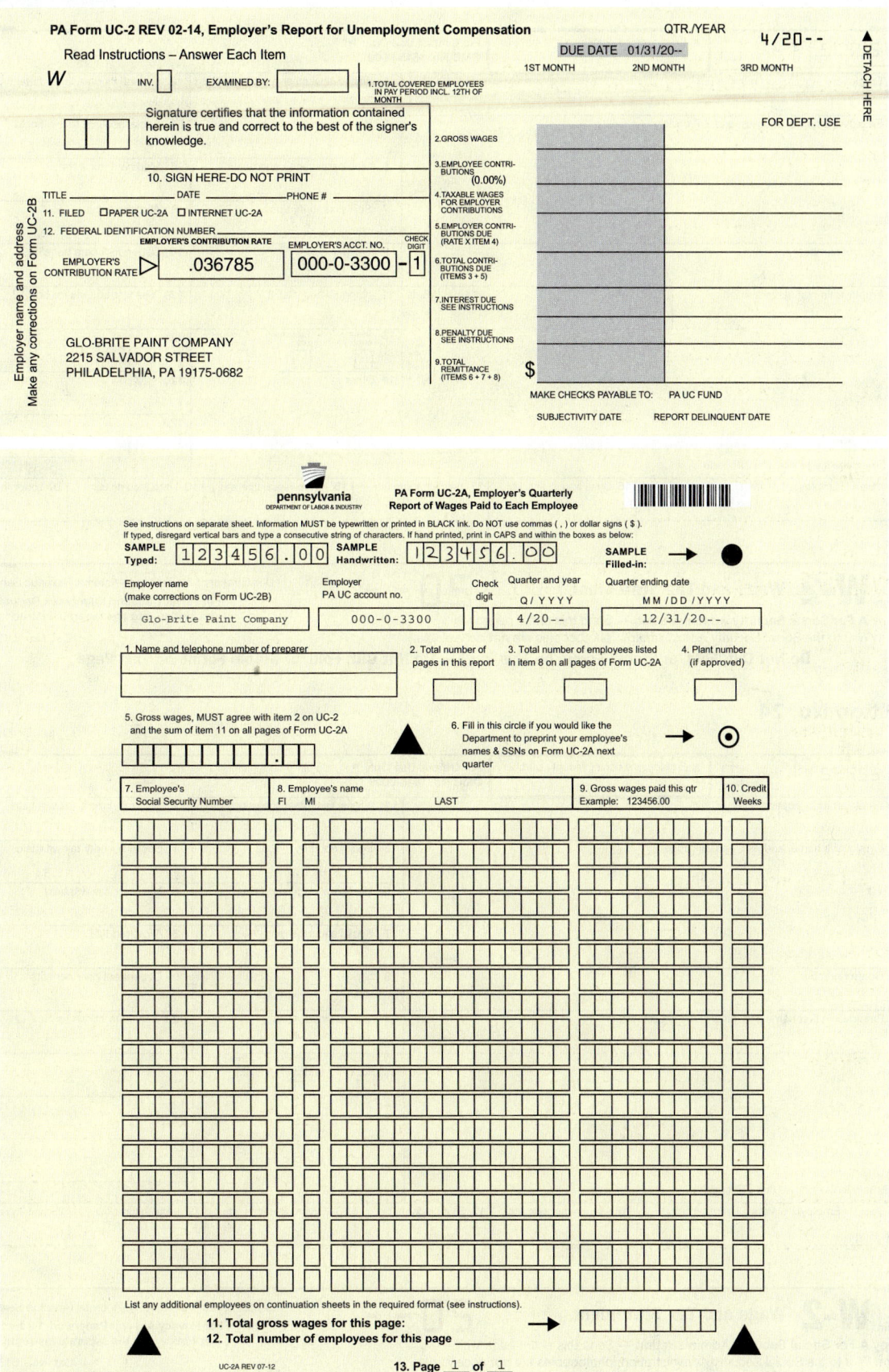

Transaction No. 10

22222	Void ☐	**a** Employee's social security number	For Official Use Only ▶ OMB No. 1545-0008	

b Employer identification number (EIN)	**1** Wages, tips, other compensation	**2** Federal income tax withheld
c Employer's name, address, and ZIP code	**3** Social security wages	**4** Social security tax withheld
	5 Medicare wages and tips	**6** Medicare tax withheld
	7 Social security tips	**8** Allocated tips
d Control number	**9**	**10** Dependent care benefits
e Employee's first name and initial Last name Suff.	**11** Nonqualified plans	**12a** See instructions for box 12
	13 Statutory employee ☐ Retirement plan ☐ Third-party sick pay ☐	**12b**
	14 Other	**12c**
		12d
f Employee's address and ZIP code		

15 State Employer's state ID number	**16** State wages, tips, etc.	**17** State income tax	**18** Local wages, tips, etc.	**19** Local income tax	**20** Locality name

Form W-2 Wage and Tax Statement   **20 - -**   Department of the Treasury—Internal Revenue Service

Copy A For Social Security Administration — Send this entire page with Form W-3 to the Social Security Administration; photocopies are **not** acceptable.

For Privacy Act and Paperwork Reduction Act Notice, see the separate instructions.

Cat. No. 10134D

Do Not Cut, Fold, or Staple Forms on This Page— Do Not Cut, Fold, or Staple Forms on This Page

---

Transaction No. 24

22222	Void ☐	**a** Employee's social security number	For Official Use Only ▶ OMB No. 1545-0008	

b Employer identification number (EIN)	**1** Wages, tips, other compensation	**2** Federal income tax withheld
c Employer's name, address, and ZIP code	**3** Social security wages	**4** Social security tax withheld
	5 Medicare wages and tips	**6** Medicare tax withheld
	7 Social security tips	**8** Allocated tips
d Control number	**9**	**10** Dependent care benefits
e Employee's first name and initial Last name Suff.	**11** Nonqualified plans	**12a** See instructions for box 12
	13 Statutory employee ☐ Retirement plan ☐ Third-party sick pay ☐	**12b**
	14 Other	**12c**
		12d
f Employee's address and ZIP code		

15 State Employer's state ID number	**16** State wages, tips, etc.	**17** State income tax	**18** Local wages, tips, etc.	**19** Local income tax	**20** Locality name

Form W-2 Wage and Tax Statement   **20 - -**   Department of the Treasury—Internal Revenue Service

Copy A For Social Security Administration — Send this entire page with Form W-3 to the Social Security Administration; photocopies are **not** acceptable.

For Privacy Act and Paperwork Reduction Act Notice, see the separate instructions.

Cat. No. 10134D

Do Not Cut, Fold, or Staple Forms on This Page— Do Not Cut, Fold, or Staple Forms on This Page

22222	Void ☐	a Employee's social security number	For Official Use Only ▶ OMB No. 1545-0008		

b Employer identification number (EIN)	1 Wages, tips, other compensation	2 Federal income tax withheld
c Employer's name, address, and ZIP code	3 Social security wages	4 Social security tax withheld
	5 Medicare wages and tips	6 Medicare tax withheld
	7 Social security tips	8 Allocated tips
d Control number	9	10 Dependent care benefits
e Employee's first name and initial Last name Suff.	11 Nonqualified plans	12a See instructions for box 12
	13 Statutory employee Retirement plan Third-party sick pay	12b
	14 Other	12c
		12d
f Employee's address and ZIP code		

15 State Employer's state ID number	16 State wages, tips, etc.	17 State income tax	18 Local wages, tips, etc.	19 Local income tax	20 Locality name

Form **W-2** **Wage and Tax Statement**   **20 - -**

Department of the Treasury—Internal Revenue Service

Copy A For Social Security Administration — Send this entire page with Form W-3 to the Social Security Administration; photocopies are **not** acceptable.

For Privacy Act and Paperwork Reduction Act Notice, see the separate instructions.

Cat. No. 10134D

Do Not Cut, Fold, or Staple Forms on This Page— Do Not Cut, Fold, or Staple Forms on This Page

22222	Void ☐	a Employee's social security number	For Official Use Only ▶ OMB No. 1545-0008		

b Employer identification number (EIN)	1 Wages, tips, other compensation	2 Federal income tax withheld
c Employer's name, address, and ZIP code	3 Social security wages	4 Social security tax withheld
	5 Medicare wages and tips	6 Medicare tax withheld
	7 Social security tips	8 Allocated tips
d Control number	9	10 Dependent care benefits
e Employee's first name and initial Last name Suff.	11 Nonqualified plans	12a See instructions for box 12
	13 Statutory employee Retirement plan Third-party sick pay	12b
	14 Other	12c
		12d
f Employee's address and ZIP code		

15 State Employer's state ID number	16 State wages, tips, etc.	17 State income tax	18 Local wages, tips, etc.	19 Local income tax	20 Locality name

Form **W-2** **Wage and Tax Statement**   **20 - -**

Department of the Treasury—Internal Revenue Service

Copy A For Social Security Administration — Send this entire page with Form W-3 to the Social Security Administration; photocopies are **not** acceptable.

For Privacy Act and Paperwork Reduction Act Notice, see the separate instructions.

Cat. No. 10134D

Do Not Cut, Fold, or Staple Forms on This Page— Do Not Cut, Fold, or Staple Forms on This Page

Source: Internal Revenue Service.

22222	Void ☐	a Employee's social security number	For Official Use Only ▶ OMB No. 1545-0008		

b Employer identification number (EIN)		1 Wages, tips, other compensation	2 Federal income tax withheld

c Employer's name, address, and ZIP code	3 Social security wages	4 Social security tax withheld

5 Medicare wages and tips	6 Medicare tax withheld

7 Social security tips	8 Allocated tips

d Control number	9	10 Dependent care benefits

e Employee's first name and initial	Last name	Suff.	11 Nonqualified plans	12a See instructions for box 12

13 Statutory employee ☐ Retirement plan ☐ Third-party sick pay ☐	12b

14 Other	12c

	12d

f Employee's address and ZIP code

15 State	Employer's state ID number	16 State wages, tips, etc.	17 State income tax	18 Local wages, tips, etc.	19 Local income tax	20 Locality name

Form W-2 Wage and Tax Statement 20 - -

Department of the Treasury—Internal Revenue Service

Copy A For Social Security Administration — Send this entire page with Form W-3 to the Social Security Administration; photocopies are **not** acceptable.

For Privacy Act and Paperwork Reduction Act Notice, see the separate instructions.

Cat. No. 10134D

Do Not Cut, Fold, or Staple Forms on This Page— Do Not Cut, Fold, or Staple Forms on This Page

---

22222	Void ☐	a Employee's social security number	For Official Use Only ▶ OMB No. 1545-0008		

b Employer identification number (EIN)		1 Wages, tips, other compensation	2 Federal income tax withheld

c Employer's name, address, and ZIP code	3 Social security wages	4 Social security tax withheld

5 Medicare wages and tips	6 Medicare tax withheld

7 Social security tips	8 Allocated tips

d Control number	9	10 Dependent care benefits

e Employee's first name and initial	Last name	Suff.	11 Nonqualified plans	12a See instructions for box 12

13 Statutory employee ☐ Retirement plan ☐ Third-party sick pay ☐	12b

14 Other	12c

	12d

f Employee's address and ZIP code

15 State	Employer's state ID number	16 State wages, tips, etc.	17 State income tax	18 Local wages, tips, etc.	19 Local income tax	20 Locality name

Form W-2 Wage and Tax Statement 20 - -

Department of the Treasury—Internal Revenue Service

Copy A For Social Security Administration — Send this entire page with Form W-3 to the Social Security Administration; photocopies are **not** acceptable.

For Privacy Act and Paperwork Reduction Act Notice, see the separate instructions.

Cat. No. 10134D

Do Not Cut, Fold, or Staple Forms on This Page— Do Not Cut, Fold, or Staple Forms on This Page

Source: Internal Revenue Service.

Form W-2 (First)

22222	Void ☐	a Employee's social security number	For Official Use Only ▶ OMB No. 1545-0008

b Employer identification number (EIN)	1 Wages, tips, other compensation	2 Federal income tax withheld

c Employer's name, address, and ZIP code	3 Social security wages	4 Social security tax withheld
	5 Medicare wages and tips	6 Medicare tax withheld
	7 Social security tips	8 Allocated tips

d Control number	9	10 Dependent care benefits

e Employee's first name and initial	Last name	Suff.	11 Nonqualified plans	12a See instructions for box 12
			13 Statutory employee ☐ Retirement plan ☐ Third-party sick pay ☐	12b
			14 Other	12c
				12d

f Employee's address and ZIP code				

15 State	Employer's state ID number	16 State wages, tips, etc.	17 State income tax	18 Local wages, tips, etc.	19 Local income tax	20 Locality name

Form **W-2** **Wage and Tax Statement** 20- -

Department of the Treasury—Internal Revenue Service

Copy A For Social Security Administration — Send this entire page with Form W-3 to the Social Security Administration; photocopies are **not** acceptable.

For Privacy Act and Paperwork Reduction Act Notice, see the separate instructions.

Cat. No. 10134D

Do Not Cut, Fold, or Staple Forms on This Page— Do Not Cut, Fold, or Staple Forms on This Page

Form W-2 (Second)

22222	Void ☐	a Employee's social security number	For Official Use Only ▶ OMB No. 1545-0008

b Employer identification number (EIN)	1 Wages, tips, other compensation	2 Federal income tax withheld

c Employer's name, address, and ZIP code	3 Social security wages	4 Social security tax withheld
	5 Medicare wages and tips	6 Medicare tax withheld
	7 Social security tips	8 Allocated tips

d Control number	9	10 Dependent care benefits

e Employee's first name and initial	Last name	Suff.	11 Nonqualified plans	12a See instructions for box 12
			13 Statutory employee ☐ Retirement plan ☐ Third-party sick pay ☐	12b
			14 Other	12c
				12d

f Employee's address and ZIP code				

15 State	Employer's state ID number	16 State wages, tips, etc.	17 State income tax	18 Local wages, tips, etc.	19 Local income tax	20 Locality name

Form **W-2** **Wage and Tax Statement** 20- -

Department of the Treasury—Internal Revenue Service

Copy A For Social Security Administration — Send this entire page with Form W-3 to the Social Security Administration; photocopies are **not** acceptable.

For Privacy Act and Paperwork Reduction Act Notice, see the separate instructions.

Cat. No. 10134D

Do Not Cut, Fold, or Staple Forms on This Page— Do Not Cut, Fold, or Staple Forms on This Page

22222	Void ☐	a Employee's social security number	For Official Use Only ▶ OMB No. 1545-0008	

b Employer identification number (EIN)	1 Wages, tips, other compensation	2 Federal income tax withheld
c Employer's name, address, and ZIP code	3 Social security wages	4 Social security tax withheld
	5 Medicare wages and tips	6 Medicare tax withheld
	7 Social security tips	8 Allocated tips
d Control number	9	10 Dependent care benefits
e Employee's first name and initial Last name Suff.	11 Nonqualified plans	12a See instructions for box 12
	13 Statutory employee ☐ Retirement plan ☐ Third-party sick pay ☐	12b
	14 Other	12c
		12d
f Employee's address and ZIP code		

15 State Employer's state ID number	16 State wages, tips, etc.	17 State income tax	18 Local wages, tips, etc.	19 Local income tax	20 Locality name

Form **W-2** **Wage and Tax Statement**   **20 - -**

Department of the Treasury—Internal Revenue Service

For Privacy Act and Paperwork Reduction Act Notice, see the separate instructions.

Cat. No. 10134D

Copy A For Social Security Administration — Send this entire page with Form W-3 to the Social Security Administration; photocopies are **not** acceptable.

Do Not Cut, Fold, or Staple Forms on This Page— Do Not Cut, Fold, or Staple Forms on This Page

---

22222	Void ☐	a Employee's social security number	For Official Use Only ▶ OMB No. 1545-0008	

b Employer identification number (EIN)	1 Wages, tips, other compensation	2 Federal income tax withheld
c Employer's name, address, and ZIP code	3 Social security wages	4 Social security tax withheld
	5 Medicare wages and tips	6 Medicare tax withheld
	7 Social security tips	8 Allocated tips
d Control number	9	10 Dependent care benefits
e Employee's first name and initial Last name Suff.	11 Nonqualified plans	12a See instructions for box 12
	13 Statutory employee ☐ Retirement plan ☐ Third-party sick pay ☐	12b
	14 Other	12c
		12d
f Employee's address and ZIP code		

15 State Employer's state ID number	16 State wages, tips, etc.	17 State income tax	18 Local wages, tips, etc.	19 Local income tax	20 Locality name

Form **W-2** **Wage and Tax Statement**   **20 - -**

Department of the Treasury—Internal Revenue Service

For Privacy Act and Paperwork Reduction Act Notice, see the separate instructions.

Cat. No. 10134D

Copy A For Social Security Administration — Send this entire page with Form W-3 to the Social Security Administration; photocopies are **not** acceptable.

Do Not Cut, Fold, or Staple Forms on This Page— Do Not Cut, Fold, or Staple Forms on This Page

Source: Internal Revenue Service.

Transaction No. 38 (concluded)

22222	Void ☐	**a** Employee's social security number	**For Official Use Only ▶** OMB No. 1545-0008		

b Employer identification number (EIN)	**1** Wages, tips, other compensation	**2** Federal income tax withheld
c Employer's name, address, and ZIP code	**3** Social security wages	**4** Social security tax withheld
	5 Medicare wages and tips	**6** Medicare tax withheld
	7 Social security tips	**8** Allocated tips
d Control number	**9**	**10** Dependent care benefits

e Employee's first name and initial	Last name	Suff.	**11** Nonqualified plans	**12a** See instructions for box 12 C o d e

13 Statutory employee ☐ Retirement plan ☐ Third-party sick pay ☐   **12b** C o d e

14 Other   **12c** C o d e

12d C o d e

f Employee's address and ZIP code

15 State	Employer's state ID number	**16** State wages, tips, etc.	**17** State income tax	**18** Local wages, tips, etc.	**19** Local income tax	**20** Locality name

Form **W-2** Wage and Tax Statement   **20- -**   Department of the Treasury—Internal Revenue Service

For Privacy Act and Paperwork Reduction Act Notice, see the separate instructions.

Copy A For Social Security Administration — Send this entire page with Form W-3 to the Social Security Administration; photocopies are **not** acceptable.

Cat. No. 10134D

Do Not Cut, Fold, or Staple Forms on This Page— Do Not Cut, Fold, or Staple Forms on This Page

---

22222	Void ☐	**a** Employee's social security number	**For Official Use Only ▶** OMB No. 1545-0008		

b Employer identification number (EIN)	**1** Wages, tips, other compensation	**2** Federal income tax withheld
c Employer's name, address, and ZIP code	**3** Social security wages	**4** Social security tax withheld
	5 Medicare wages and tips	**6** Medicare tax withheld
	7 Social security tips	**8** Allocated tips
d Control number	**9**	**10** Dependent care benefits

e Employee's first name and initial	Last name	Suff.	**11** Nonqualified plans	**12a** See instructions for box 12 C o d e

13 Statutory employee ☐ Retirement plan ☐ Third-party sick pay ☐   **12b** C o d e

14 Other   **12c** C o d e

12d C o d e

f Employee's address and ZIP code

15 State	Employer's state ID number	**16** State wages, tips, etc.	**17** State income tax	**18** Local wages, tips, etc.	**19** Local income tax	**20** Locality name

Form **W-2** Wage and Tax Statement   **20- -**   Department of the Treasury—Internal Revenue Service

For Privacy Act and Paperwork Reduction Act Notice, see the separate instructions.

Copy A For Social Security Administration — Send this entire page with Form W-3 to the Social Security Administration; photocopies are **not** acceptable.

Cat. No. 10134D

Do Not Cut, Fold, or Staple Forms on This Page— Do Not Cut, Fold, or Staple Forms on This Page

Source: Internal Revenue Service.

Transaction No. 39

DO NOT STAPLE

33333	**a** Control number	**For Official Use Only ▶** OMB No. 1545-0008

b **Kind of Payer** (Check one) ▶	941 ☐ Military ☐ 943 ☐ 944 ☐ CT-1 ☐ Hshld. emp. ☐ Medicare govt. emp. ☐	**Kind of Employer** (Check one) ▶	None apply ☐ 501c non-govt. ☐ State/local non-501c ☐ State/local 501c ☐ Federal govt. ☐	Third-party sick pay ☐ (Check if applicable)

c Total number of Forms W-2	**d** Establishment number	**1** Wages, tips, other compensation	**2** Federal income tax withheld
e Employer identification number (EIN)		**3** Social security wages	**4** Social security tax withheld
f Employer's name		**5** Medicare wages and tips	**6** Medicare tax withheld
		7 Social security tips	**8** Allocated tips
		9	**10** Dependent care benefits
		11 Nonqualified plans	**12a** Deferred compensation
g Employer's address and ZIP code			
h Other EIN used this year		**13** For third-party sick pay use only	**12b**
15 State Employer's state ID number		**14** Income tax withheld by payer of third-party sick pay	
16 State wages, tips, etc.	**17** State income tax	**18** Local wages, tips, etc.	**19** Local income tax
Employer's contact person		Employer's telephone number	For Official Use Only
Employer's fax number		Employer's email address	

Under penalties of perjury, I declare that I have examined this return and accompanying documents and, to the best of my knowledge and belief, they are true, correct, and complete.

Signature ▶ _____   Title ▶ _____   Date ▶ _____

Form **W-3** **Transmittal of Wage and Tax Statements**   20 - -   Department of the Treasury
Internal Revenue Service

Source: Internal Revenue Service.

Transaction No. 40

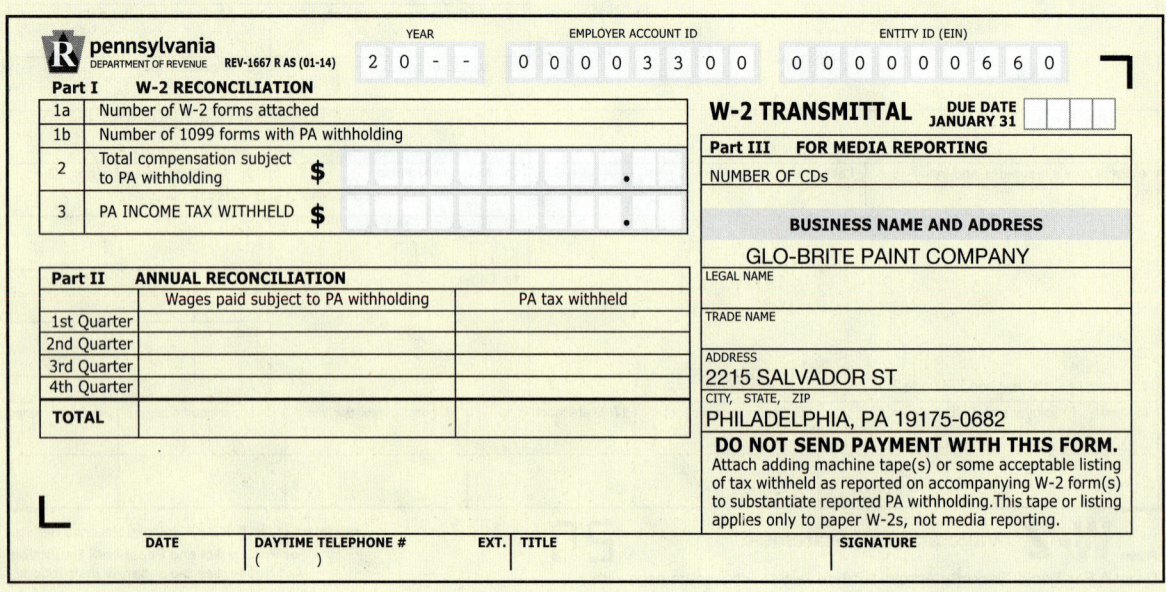

Source: PA Department of Revenue.

Transaction No. 41

9595 ☐ VOID ☐ CORRECTED

PAYER'S name, street address, city or town, state or province, country, ZIP or foreign postal code, and telephone no.		1 Rents $	OMB No. 1545-0115 20-- Form **1099-MISC**	**Miscellaneous Income**
		2 Royalties $		
		3 Other income $	4 Federal income tax withheld $	**Copy A** **For** **Internal Revenue Service Center**
PAYER'S federal identification number	RECIPIENT'S identification number	5 Fishing boat proceeds $	6 Medical and health care payments $	**File with Form 1096.**
RECIPIENT'S name		7 Nonemployee compensation $	8 Substitute payments in lieu of dividends or interest $	For Privacy Act and Paperwork Reduction Act
Street address (including apt. no.)		9 Payer made direct sales of $5,000 or more of consumer products to a buyer (recipient) for resale ► ☐	10 Crop insurance proceeds $	Notice, see the **20-- General Instructions for Certain**
City or town, state or province, country, and ZIP or foreign postal code		11	12	**Information Returns.**
Account number (see instructions)	FATCA filing requirement ☐	2nd TIN not. ☐	13 Excess golden parachute payments $	14 Gross proceeds paid to an attorney $	
15a Section 409A deferrals $	15b Section 409A income $	16 State tax withheld $	17 State/Payer's state no.	18 State income $

Form **1099-MISC**   Cat. No. 14425J   www.irs.gov/form1099misc   Department of the Treasury - Internal Revenue Service

Do Not Cut or Separate Forms on This Page — Do Not Cut or Separate Forms on This Page

Source: Internal Revenue Service.

Transaction No. 42

Do Not Staple   6969

Form **1096** Department of the Treasury Internal Revenue Service	**Annual Summary and Transmittal of U.S. Information Returns**	OMB No. 1545-0108 20--

FILER'S name

Street address (including room or suite number)

City or town, state or province, country, and ZIP or foreign postal code

Name of person to contact	Telephone number	**For Official Use Only**
Email address	Fax number	

1 Employer identification number	2 Social security number	3 Total number of forms	4 Federal income tax withheld $	5 Total amount reported with this Form 1096 $

6 Enter an "X" in only one box below to indicate the type of form being filed.   7 If this is your **final return**, enter an "X" here . . . . ► ☐

W-2G 32	1097-BTC 50	1098 81	1098-C 78	1098-E 84	1098-Q 74	1098-T 83	1099-A 80	1099-B 79	1099-C 85	1099-CAP 73	1099-DIV 91	1099-G 86	1099-INT 92
☐	☐	☐	☐	☐	☐	☐	☐	☐	☐	☐	☐	☐	☐

1099-K 10	1099-LTC 93	1099-MISC 95	1099-OID 96	1099-PATR 97	1099-Q 31	1099-R 98	1099-S 75	1099-SA 94	3921 25	3922 26	5498 28	5498-ESA 72	5498-SA 27
☐	☐	☐	☐	☐	☐	☐	☐	☐	☐	☐	☐	☐	☐

Return this entire page to the Internal Revenue Service. Photocopies are not acceptable.

Under penalties of perjury, I declare that I have examined this return and accompanying documents, and, to the best of my knowledge and belief, they are true, correct, and complete.

Signature ►   Title ►   Date ►

Source: Internal Revenue Service.

Payroll Project Using Online General Ledger (CLGL)

A P P

This edition of *Payroll Accounting* contains two different options for student solution: the complete, full version of the payroll project (which follows), and a short version. Both versions are identical except the short version requires only the completion of the December payrolls (as well as the last quarter and annual tax reports and forms). The short version's step-by-step instructions begin on page A-20 of this appendix. Be sure to ask your instructor which of the two versions you are to complete.

Payroll Project

The payroll project that follows is the computerized version of the same project you completed manually in Chapter 7 beginning on page 7-6 of this text. In this project, you are employed by Glo-Brite Paint Company as the person in the accounting department responsible for the company's payroll processing using the computerized payroll system described in the preceding material. Like the manual project in Chapter 7, you will assume that the payroll records, tax reports, and deposits have been completed and filed for the first three quarters of this year. Your work will involve the computer processing of the payrolls for the last quarter of the year and the completion of the last quarter and annual tax reports and forms. You may complete the required deposit, quarterly, yearly, etc., forms described in Chapter 7. If you have already completed these forms for the manual student project, check them as you progress through this project and note any differences.

To help you get started, the first pay period is provided as a tutorial problem that illustrates the principles and procedures required to process payroll transactions using the *Cengage Learning General Ledger* software. In subsequent pay period processing, whenever a new operational procedure is used for the first time, additional instruction will be provided. Each of the following step-by-step instructions lists a task to be completed at the computer.

This project has been broken down into several assignments comprising all or part of the project in your text. The assignments are delivered online using the CengageNOWv2 learning management system, with each assignment being graded automatically and submitted to your instructor. Your instructor may choose to have you complete only part of this project, so watch the dates and follow the instructions carefully.

Note: Throughout this project, some of the computer-calculated withholding amounts (e.g., federal income tax) will differ slightly from the amounts (from the tax tables) in the manual payroll project in Chapter 7. This occurs because the software uses the annualized percentage method from *IRS Publication 15* rather than the table look-up to compute withholding taxes (see IRS Table 7 on the next page). The differences here should be less than two dollars per pay period, and usually are much less. Also, one- to two-cent differences will occur throughout the solutions because of rounding differences. Finally, some of the account numbers differ slightly from those in your text, but there is a pop-up "Chart of Accounts" available in the software to help you quickly find the accounts you need, or refer to the partial Chart of Accounts below.

TABLE 7—ANNUAL Payroll Period

(a) SINGLE person (including head of household)—

If the amount of wages (after subtracting withholding allowances) is:		The amount of income tax to withhold is:	of excess over—
Not over $2,300		$0	
Over—	**But not over—**		
$2,300	—$11,525 . .	$0.00 plus 10%	—$2,300
$11,525	—$39,750 . .	$922.50 plus 15%	—$11,525
$39,750	—$93,050 . .	$5,156.25 plus 25%	—$39,750
$93,050	—$191,600 . .	$18,481.25 plus 28%	—$93,050
$191,600	—$413,800 . .	$46,075.25 plus 33%	—$191,600
$413,800	—$415,500 . .	$119,401.25 plus 35%	—$413,800
$415,500	. . . .	$119,996.25 plus 39.6%	—$415,500

(b) MARRIED person—

If the amount of wages (after subtracting withholding allowances) is:		The amount of income tax to withhold is:	of excess over—
Not over $8,600		$0	
Over—	**But not over—**		
$8,600	—$27,050 . .	$0.00 plus 10%	—$8,600
$27,050	—$83,500 . .	$1,845.00 plus 15%	—$27,050
$83,500	—$159,800 . .	$10,312.50 plus 25%	—$83,500
$159,800	—$239,050 . .	$29,387.50 plus 28%	—$159,800
$239,050	—$420,100 . .	$51,577.50 plus 33%	—$239,050
$420,100	—$473,450 . .	$111,324.00 plus 35%	—$420,100
$473,450	. . . .	$129,996.50 plus 39.6%	—$473,450

Glo-Brite Paint Company			
Partial Chart of Accounts			
9/30/2016			
Classification	Account Number	Text Account Number	Account Title
Assets	11	11	Cash
	12	12	Payroll Cash
	13	n/a	Accounts Receivable
Liabilities	15	n/a	Accounts Payable
	19	20.1	FICA Taxes Payable--OASDI
	20	20.2	FICA Taxes Payable--HI
	21	21	FUTA Taxes Payable
	22	22	SUTA Taxes Payable
	24	24	Employees FIT Payable
	25	25	Employees SIT Payable
	n/a	25.1	SUTA Taxes Payable-Employer (combined with account 22)
	26	26	Employees CIT Payable
	27	27	Grp. Ins. Prem. Collected
	28	28	Union Dues Payable
	29	29	Simple Contrib. Payable
Capital	30	n/a	Capital
	31	n/a	Drawing
	39	n/a	Income Summary
Expenses	51	51	Administrative Salaries
	52	52	Office Salaries
	53	53	Sales Salaries
	54	54	Plant Wages
	56	56	Payroll Taxes

October 9 Payroll

Some of the accounting forms in this project can be wider than your computer screen, depending on its resolution. If a form scrolls off the screen to the right, you can maximize screen space by clicking on the << icon on the left menu bar to shrink that menu. You can then grab the top of any form window and drag it to the left of your screen, and use the horizontal scroll bars at the bottom of the form window, or the bottom of your screen, to move the form more comfortably into view.

To get the left menu bar back, just click on the >> icon.

Follow the steps below to complete the **October 9** payroll transactions using **Cengage Learning General Ledger**. To access additional Help for any function, click on the **Help** button that appears at the bottom of the screen. There is a **Help** screen with additional information and sample screens for every menu option in the program. Click on the **Save** button at the upper right of your screen at any point to save your work if you need to stop working to continue later. Your work will automatically be restored when you return.

STUDENT PROJECT AUDIT TEST

At the start of each assignment, remove the Student Project Audit Test beginning on page A-35. Answer the questions for each pay period as you complete processing for each pay period.

1. Set the **System Date** at the bottom of the screen to **October 9, 2016**. Note that the year needs to be **2016** in order for the problem to grade correctly.
2. Click on the **General Ledger** tab and select the **Chart of Accounts** from the **Account Lists** section. Review this list to understand how the software designates the Payroll accounts.
3. Enter the employee maintenance data. Click on the top bar **Payroll** tab and the **Maintain Employees** task from the left menu bar. Scroll down to select employee number **180** (Student), enter your own name in the **Employee Name** field (enter your last name in all capital letters similar to the other employees), then **Tab** out of the field. Click on the **Close** button, and answer "Yes" to accept your changes. *Note:* Do not change any of the other fields. If you do, your solutions will not be correct.
4. Enter the Payroll transactions for the period using the detailed instructions in steps (a) through (j) below. Refer to the following pay list for this period:

Employees to Be Paid This Pay Period							
Check Number	Employee Number	Employee Name	Salary / Reg.Hrs.	Overtime @ Time 1½	Overtime @ Double	Group Ins.	Union Dues
672	100	Bonno, Anthony Victor	80				$8.00
673	110	Ferguson, James Claude	reg. salary				
674	120	Ford, Catherine Louise	reg. salary				
675	130	Mann, Dewey Wilson	reg. salary				
676	140	O'Neill, Joseph Tyler	reg. salary				
677	150	Russell, Virginia Aloise	reg. salary				
678	160	Ryan, Norman Allen	80				$8.00
679	170	Sokowski, Thomas James	reg. salary				
680	180	Student (your name)	72				
681	190	Williams, Ruth Virginia	reg. salary				

To enter the payroll records, click on the **Pay Employees** task from the left menu bar. As noted above, you will probably have to shrink the left menu bar (using the << icon) and grab the top of the Payroll form with your mouse to reposition it to better fit on your screen. You should also scroll over to grab the lower-right corner of the form to drag it down to fill the screen.

a. The prior quarter payroll information is already entered, and will show up in the reports, but NOT in the payroll entry screens. Click on the **Deductions** button to display the **Voluntary Deductions** check boxes. Uncheck the **Group Insurance** and **Simple Plan** (which is the same as Simple Contributions Payable) boxes, and click **OK**, as they will not be withheld this pay period.

b. For each pay period, you will need to add a new record to this payroll register for each employee to be paid. Click on the **Add** button to add a new pay record for each of the above employees, and then enter the corresponding fields. You may need to scroll down to the bottom of the payroll form to see the newly added line.

c. **Date:** Make sure the date is set to **10/09/16** for each new record, or use the pop-up calendar to change it. Payroll recording is <u>very</u> dependent on having the correct dates, so **verify this date**, especially for the first employee in any payroll set.

d. **Employee Name:** Select the name from the drop-down list or key the first letter of the employee's last name until the correct name appears.

e. **Check No.:** Start with check number **672** to continue from where the previous quarter left off. This number will automatically increase by 1 for each subsequent employee. It is critical to get this check number correct for each employee, along with the date, as this is how the software matches up your entries for grading.

f. **Salary or Hours worked:** For salaried employees, the salary should display automatically. For hourly employees, click on the **Reg. Hours** field and enter the number of regular work hours shown above.

g. For the two union employees noted above, change the **Union Dues** field to $8.00, which is this period's dues amount.

h. Click on the **Calculate Taxes** button for each employee to fill the remaining fields. **Net Pay** will calculate automatically, and **Gross Pay** will display at the bottom of the form.

i. Review the amounts calculated for reasonableness.

j. Click **Add** to start a new employee or **Close** when done. You may need to confirm the data you entered or the changes you made. If you make a mistake, just go to the appropriate line and field, and change the value. Click on the **Calculate Taxes** button to recalculate these amounts. **Net Pay** will re-compute automatically.

5. Display the Employee List report. Click on the **Employee List** from the **Payroll** left menu bar. The report is shown in Figure A-1. Verify the accuracy of the maintenance input from step 4 above and make any corrections via the **Maintain Employees** menu option.

Employee List	Figure A-1	? – □ ×

Glo-Brite Paint Company
Employee List
10/09/16

Emp. No.	Employee Name/Address	Social Security/Marital Status	# Pay Periods	G.L. Account	Salary/Rate
100	BONNO, Anthony Victor 694 Bristol Avenue Philadelphia, PA 19135-0617	000-00-3481 Married W/H 4	26	54	0.00 17.65
110	FERGUSON, James Claude 808 Sixth Street Philadelphia, PA 19106-0995	000-00-8645 Married W/H 5	26	53	2,250.00 0.00
120	FORD, Catherine Louise 18 Dundee Avenue Philadelphia, PA 19151-1919	000-00-4567 Single W/H 2	26	52	1,220.00 0.00
130	MANN, Dewey Wilson 3007 Bisque Drive Philadelphia, PA 19199-0718	000-00-9352 Married W/H 4	26	53	1,350.00 0.00
140	O'NEILL, Joseph Tyler 2100 Broad Street Philadelphia, PA 19121-7189	000-00-1534 Married W/H 3	26	51	2,307.69 0.00
150	RUSSELL, Virginia Aloise 8004 Dowling Road Philadelphia, PA 19135-9001	000-00-6337 Single W/H 1	26	52	1,200.00 0.00
160	RYAN, Norman Allen 7300 Harrison Street Philadelphia, PA 19124-6699	000-00-1233 Married W/H 4	26	54	0.00 18.00
170	SOKOWSKI, Thomas James 133 Cornwells Street Philadelphia, PA 19171-5718	000-00-8832 Married W/H 2	26	54	2,050.00 0.00
180	STUDENT 7018 Erdrick Street Philadelphia, PA 19135-8517	000-00-5555 Single W/H 1	26	52	0.00 14.00
190	WILLIAMS, Ruth Virginia 9433 State Street Philadelphia, PA 19149-0819	000-00-6741 Single W/H 0	26	52	1,223.08 0.00

6. Display the Payroll report. Click on the **Payroll Report** item from the left menu bar. The payroll report for Employee 100; Bonno, Anthony Victor, followed by the payroll summary, is shown in Figure A-2 on the next page. Due to its length, only the first employee and the summary are shown. If the summary is incorrect, review the list of employees to be paid from step 5 above. Check your numbers, and make any changes using the **Pay Employees** task.

7. Generate and post the journal entry for the current payroll. Click on the **Current Payroll Journal Entry** task on the left menu bar. Click **Yes** when asked if you want to generate the journal entry. If your journal entries do not match those shown in Figure A-3 on the next page, check your employee list and payroll report for keying errors, and go back to make the necessary corrections. If they are correct, click on **Post**. The journal entry will reappear, posted, in the General Journal. *Note:* The software combines both the entries for Employee's SUTA Tax Payable and Employer's SUTA Tax Payable into one account.

8. Generate and post the employer's payroll taxes journal entry. Click on the **Employer's Payroll Taxes Journal Entry** task on the left menu bar. Compare your entries as they appear in the **Payroll Taxes Journal Entries** dialog box, to Figure A-4 on page A-7. Click **Yes** when asked if you want to generate the journal entry. If they are correct, click on **Post**, otherwise go back and re-check your inputs. After you accept the entries, they will reappear, posted, in the General Journal. Note that there is only one SUTA Taxes Payable account in CLGL, rather than separate payable accounts for employers and employees.

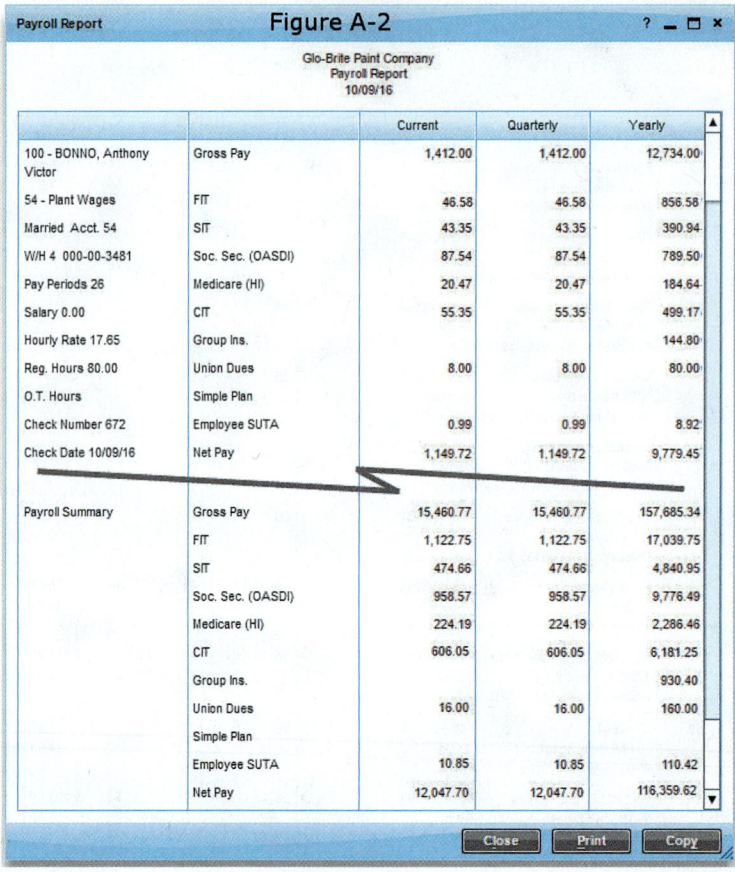

Figure A-2

Glo-Brite Paint Company
Payroll Report
10/09/16

		Current	Quarterly	Yearly
100 - BONNO, Anthony Victor	Gross Pay	1,412.00	1,412.00	12,734.00
54 - Plant Wages	FIT	46.58	46.58	856.58
Married Acct. 54	SIT	43.35	43.35	390.94
W/H 4 000-00-3481	Soc. Sec. (OASDI)	87.54	87.54	789.50
Pay Periods 26	Medicare (HI)	20.47	20.47	184.64
Salary 0.00	CIT	55.35	55.35	499.17
Hourly Rate 17.65	Group Ins.			144.80
Reg. Hours 80.00	Union Dues	8.00	8.00	80.00
O.T. Hours	Simple Plan			
Check Number 672	Employee SUTA	0.99	0.99	8.92
Check Date 10/09/16	Net Pay	1,149.72	1,149.72	9,779.45
Payroll Summary	Gross Pay	15,460.77	15,460.77	157,685.34
	FIT	1,122.75	1,122.75	17,039.75
	SIT	474.66	474.66	4,840.95
	Soc. Sec. (OASDI)	958.57	958.57	9,776.49
	Medicare (HI)	224.19	224.19	2,286.46
	CIT	606.05	606.05	6,181.25
	Group Ins.			930.40
	Union Dues	16.00	16.00	160.00
	Simple Plan			
	Employee SUTA	10.85	10.85	110.42
	Net Pay	12,047.70	12,047.70	116,359.62

Close Print Copy

Figure A-3

Current Payroll Journal Entries

Account #	Account Title	Debit	Credit
54	Plant Wages	4,902.00	
52	Office Salaries	4,651.08	
53	Sales Salaries	3,600.00	
51	Administrative Salaries	2,307.69	
28	Union Dues Payable		16.00
25	Employees SIT Payable		474.66
24	Employees FIT Payable		1,122.75
26	Employees CIT Payable		606.05
12	Payroll Cash		12,047.70
22	SUTA Taxes Payable		10.85
19	FICA Taxes Payable--OASDI		958.57
20	FICA Taxes Payable--HI		224.19

Post Close

Payroll Taxes Journal Entries Figure A-4   ? — □ ×

Account #	Account Title	Debit	Credit
56	Payroll Taxes	1,381.43	
19	FICA Taxes Payable--OASDI		958.57
20	FICA Taxes Payable--HI		224.19
21	FUTA Taxes Payable		22.91
22	SUTA Taxes Payable		175.76

Post   Close

9. Enter and post the October 9 General Journal entry to record the deposit
    of cash for the total net amount owed to employees in the payroll cash
    account. This is also found as the current period **Net Pay** value on the Pay-
    roll Report. Click on the **General Ledger** top tab and the **General Journal**
    task. Enter the journal transaction shown in Figure A-5 below by first
    clicking on the **Add New Entry** button. Verify the date and enter **General**
    as the reference. Next, click on the **Insert Debit/Credit** button, enter the
    first account number (**12**) or click on the pop-up **Chart of Accounts** icon
    to display a list for selection. Enter the debit amount to clear the existing
    credit to **Payroll Cash** from the first journal entry above. Then **Tab** to the
    next row, or click on **Insert Debit/Credit** again to enter the credit to the
    Cash account (**11**). Finally, click on the **Post** button to post this entry to
    the General Ledger.

Figure A-5

10. Display the General Journal report. With the **General Ledger** tab still
    displayed, click on the **General Journal** report from the **Journal Reports**
    section of the left menu bar. The General Journal report is shown in
    Figure A-6 on the next page. Note that you can change the dates of the
    report to match the dates of the assignment, which you will need to do for
    subsequent assignments. You can also customize the report to display only
    certain **Reference** values or account numbers.

11. Display the General Ledger report. With the **General Ledger** top tab
    selected, click on **General Ledger** from the **Ledger Reports** section of the
    left menu bar. The General Ledger report is shown in Figure A-7 on page
    A-9. Note that accounts not relevant to this simulation, and accounts with
    a zero balance have been removed from the figure. You can also customize
    this report to list only a selected range of accounts.

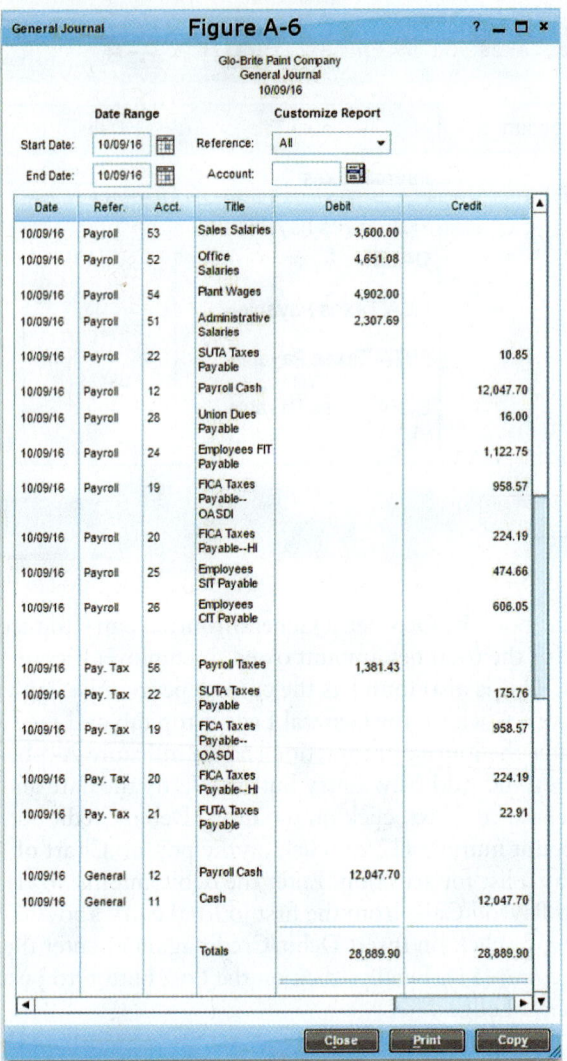

Figure A-6

12. Generate a labor distribution graph. Click on the **Company** top tab and the **Labor Distribution** item from the left menu bar to generate the graph shown in Figure A-8 on page A-10. Note that the CLGL software creates the graph from the year-to-date values.

13. If there is a **Check My Work** link on upper right of your screen, click on that link to review your work. Any errors you have will be noted with a red X, so try to locate the source of the errors and correct them. If the account values are incorrect, you will likely find an individual employee listed in the error detail report that is also incorrect. After fixing individual employees using the **Pay Employees** task, you can delete any of the journal entries, using the **General Journal** task under the **General Ledger** top tab, and retry any or all of the steps above.

14. When you are comfortable that you have completed all steps of the problem correctly click on the **Submit Assignment for Grading** button on the upper right of your screen. You will be graded primarily on three criteria for the payroll problems:

   • Are the pay settings for each employee correct (rate, deductions, etc.)?
   • Are all period's payroll entries correct for each employee?
   • Are the ending balances in each General Ledger account correct?

Note that the journal entries themselves are not graded. If the journal entries are correct, the final General Ledger balances will then also be correct. This allows you to create, edit, delete, and re-enter journal entries in any order.

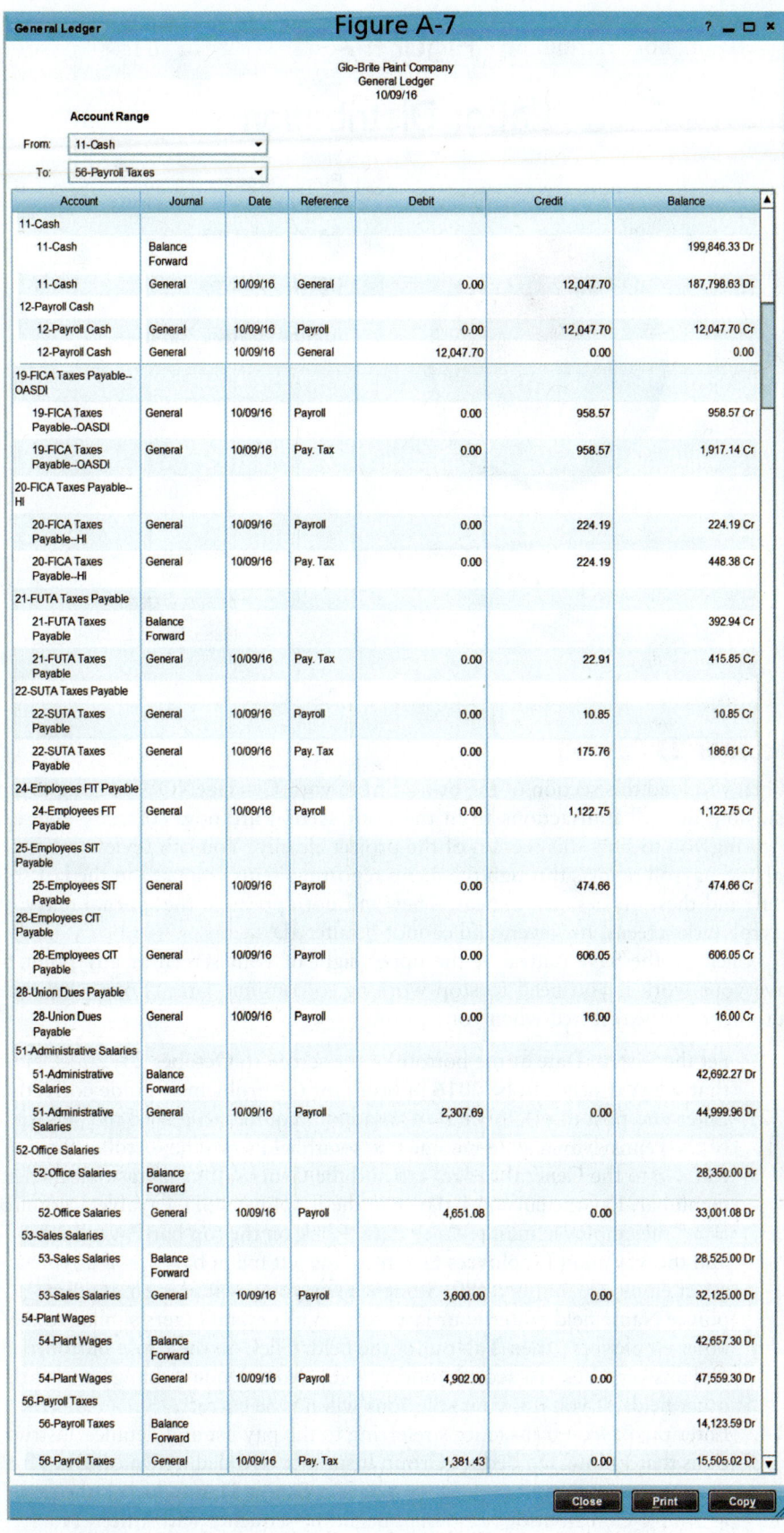

Figure A-7

| General Ledger | | | | | | | ? _ □ ✕ |

Glo-Brite Paint Company
General Ledger
10/09/16

Account Range

From: 11-Cash ▾
To: 56-Payroll Taxes ▾

Account	Journal	Date	Reference	Debit	Credit	Balance
11-Cash						
11-Cash	Balance Forward					199,846.33 Dr
11-Cash	General	10/09/16	General	0.00	12,047.70	187,798.63 Dr
12-Payroll Cash						
12-Payroll Cash	General	10/09/16	Payroll	0.00	12,047.70	12,047.70 Cr
12-Payroll Cash	General	10/09/16	General	12,047.70	0.00	0.00
19-FICA Taxes Payable--OASDI						
19-FICA Taxes Payable--OASDI	General	10/09/16	Payroll	0.00	958.57	958.57 Cr
19-FICA Taxes Payable--OASDI	General	10/09/16	Pay. Tax	0.00	958.57	1,917.14 Cr
20-FICA Taxes Payable--HI						
20-FICA Taxes Payable--HI	General	10/09/16	Payroll	0.00	224.19	224.19 Cr
20-FICA Taxes Payable--HI	General	10/09/16	Pay. Tax	0.00	224.19	448.38 Cr
21-FUTA Taxes Payable						
21-FUTA Taxes Payable	Balance Forward					392.94 Cr
21-FUTA Taxes Payable	General	10/09/16	Pay. Tax	0.00	22.91	415.85 Cr
22-SUTA Taxes Payable						
22-SUTA Taxes Payable	General	10/09/16	Payroll	0.00	10.85	10.85 Cr
22-SUTA Taxes Payable	General	10/09/16	Pay. Tax	0.00	175.76	186.61 Cr
24-Employees FIT Payable						
24-Employees FIT Payable	General	10/09/16	Payroll	0.00	1,122.75	1,122.75 Cr
25-Employees SIT Payable						
25-Employees SIT Payable	General	10/09/16	Payroll	0.00	474.66	474.66 Cr
26-Employees CIT Payable						
26-Employees CIT Payable	General	10/09/16	Payroll	0.00	606.05	606.05 Cr
28-Union Dues Payable						
28-Union Dues Payable	General	10/09/16	Payroll	0.00	16.00	16.00 Cr
51-Administrative Salaries						
51-Administrative Salaries	Balance Forward					42,692.27 Dr
51-Administrative Salaries	General	10/09/16	Payroll	2,307.69	0.00	44,999.96 Dr
52-Office Salaries						
52-Office Salaries	Balance Forward					28,350.00 Dr
52-Office Salaries	General	10/09/16	Payroll	4,651.08	0.00	33,001.08 Dr
53-Sales Salaries						
53-Sales Salaries	Balance Forward					28,525.00 Dr
53-Sales Salaries	General	10/09/16	Payroll	3,600.00	0.00	32,125.00 Dr
54-Plant Wages						
54-Plant Wages	Balance Forward					42,657.30 Dr
54-Plant Wages	General	10/09/16	Payroll	4,902.00	0.00	47,559.30 Dr
56-Payroll Taxes						
56-Payroll Taxes	Balance Forward					14,123.59 Dr
56-Payroll Taxes	General	10/09/16	Pay. Tax	1,381.43	0.00	15,505.02 Dr

Close   Print   Copy

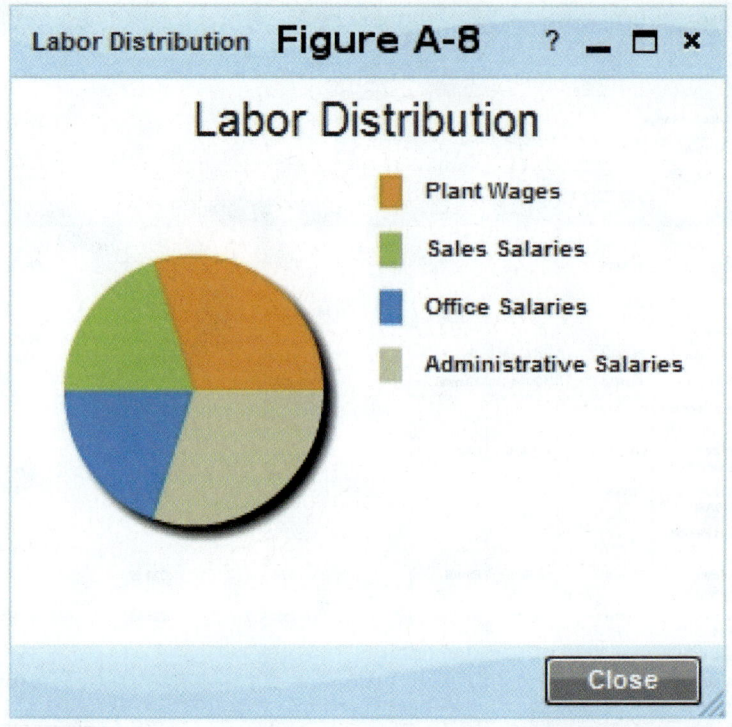

Figure A-8

October 23 Payroll

When you load this section of the project from your **CengageNOWv2** assignment list, note that all transactions from the prior section are now correctly entered, allowing you to start this section of the project cleanly. You can review the journal and payroll reports through the menu reporting items you used in the last session, and these entries will appear. They will not appear in the journal entry or payroll task screens, however, and cannot be altered.

Click on the **Save** button at the upper right of your screen at any point to save your work if you need to stop working to continue later. Your work will automatically be restored when you return.

1. Set the **System Date** at the bottom of the screen to **October 23, 2016**. Note that the year needs to be **2016** in order for the problem to grade correctly.
2. Enter and post the October 20 transaction required to record the deposit of the Pennsylvania state income taxes withheld from the October 9 payroll. Go to the **General Ledger** tab and the **General Journal** task on the left menu bar. Pay the current balance in the Employees SIT Payable account.
3. Enter the employee maintenance data. Click on the top bar **Payroll** tab and the **Maintain Employees** task from the left menu bar. Scroll down to select employee number **180** (Student), key your own name in the **Employee Name** field (enter your last name in all capital letters similar to the other employees), then **Tab** out of the field. Click on the **Close** button, and answer "Yes" to accept your changes. *Note:* Do not change any of the other fields. If you do, your solutions will not be correct.
4. Enter the Payroll transactions referring to the pay list and detailed instructions that follow. <u>Do</u> deduct Group Insurance. <u>Do</u> deduct Union Dues for the appropriate employees. <u>Do not</u> deduct Simple Plan (which is the same as Simple Contributions Payable). Begin the sequence with **Check No. 682**. Note that the group insurance amounts are monthly, and will not be the same as past quarterly payments. In addition, note that two employees

have earned overtime pay, with the hours to be recorded in the "**OT 1 1/2**" column of the payroll record.

Check Number	Employee Number	Employee Name	Salary / Reg.Hrs.	Overtime @ Time 1½	Overtime @ Double	Group Ins.	Union Dues
682	100	Bonno, Anthony Victor	80	4		$ 16.50	$8.00
683	110	Ferguson, James Claude	reg. salary			$ 26.40	
684	120	Ford, Catherine Louise	reg. salary			$ 14.40	
685	130	Mann, Dewey Wilson	reg. salary			$ 15.90	
686	140	O'Neill, Joseph Tyler	reg. salary			$ 27.00	
687	150	Russell, Virginia Aloise	reg. salary			$ 14.10	
688	160	Ryan, Norman Allen	80	8		$ 16.80	$8.00
689	170	Sokowski, Thomas James	reg. salary			$ 24.00	
690	180	Student (your name)	72			$ 11.70	
691	190	Williams, Ruth Virginia	reg. salary			$ 14.40	

Employees to Be Paid This Pay Period

To enter the payroll records, click on the **Pay Employees** task from the left menu bar. As noted above, you will probably have to shrink the left menu bar (using the << icon) and grab the top of the Payroll form with your mouse to reposition it to better fit on your screen. You should also scroll over to grab the lower-right corner of the form to drag it down to fill the screen. Enter the information for each employee as you did for the previous payroll period, and click on the **Calculate Taxes** button after entering all deductions for each employee to fill the remaining fields.

5. Display the Payroll report. Click on the **Payroll Report** item from the left menu bar and verify the results compared with input data.

6. Generate and post the journal entry for the current payroll by selecting **Current Payroll Journal Entry** on the left menu bar. Click **Yes** when asked if you want to generate the journal entry. When the entry appears in the Current Payroll Journal Entries dialog box, click on **Post**. The journal entry will reappear, posted, in the General Journal.

7. Generate and post the employer's payroll taxes journal entry. With the **Payroll** top tab still selected, click on the **Employer's Payroll Taxes Journal Entry** task from the left menu bar. Click **Yes** when asked if you want to generate the journal entry. Verify the result and click **Post** to post the entry to the General Journal. After you accept the entries, they will reappear, posted, in the General Journal.

8. Enter and post the October 23 General Journal entry to record the deposit of cash for the total net amount owed to employees in the payroll cash account. Click on the **General Ledger** top tab and the **General Journal** task. Based on the current period Net Pay summary information in the payroll report, enter the journal transaction.

9. Display the General Journal report. With the **General Ledger** tab still displayed, click on the **General Journal** report from the **Journal Reports** section of the left menu bar. Note that you can change the dates of the report to match the dates of the assignment (10/20/16 through 10/23/16) to view only the entries for this part of the assignment.

10. Display the General Ledger report. With the **General Ledger** top tab selected, click on **General Ledger** from the **Ledger Reports** section of the left menu bar. Review the entries for the period.

11. If there is a **Check your Work** link on upper right of your screen, click on that link to review your work. Any errors you have will be noted with a red X, so try to locate the source of the errors and correct them. If the

account values are incorrect, you will likely find an individual employee listed in the error detail report that is also incorrect. After fixing individual employees using the **Pay Employees** task, you can delete any of the journal entries, using the **General Journal** task under the **General Ledger** top tab, and retry any or all of the steps above.

12. When you are comfortable that you have completed all steps of the problem correctly click on the **Submit Assignment for Grading** button on the upper right of your screen.

November 6 Payroll

Follow the steps below to complete the **November 6** payroll transactions, for the period ending October 31, using **Cengage Learning General Ledger**.

1. Set the **System Date** at the bottom of the screen to **November 6, 2016.** Note that the year needs to be **2016** in order for the problem to grade correctly.
2. Enter and post the following transactions, using the **General Journal** task under the **General Ledger** tab. You can determine current account balances from the **General Ledger** Report item in the left menu bar.

    - November 4: Deposited the Pennsylvania state income taxes withheld from the October 23 payroll. Pay the balance in the Employees SIT Payable account (25).
    - November 6: Paid the treasurer of the union the amount of union dues withheld during the month of October. Pay the balance in the Union Dues Payable account (28).

3. Enter the following information, using the **Maintain Employees** task under the **Payroll** tab.

    - Change employee 180 from "Student" to your name.
    - Change Virginia Russell's number of withholding allowances to 2.
    - Change Thomas J. Sokowski's marital status to Single (his number of withholding allowances remains at 2).
    - Change Dewey Mann's number of withholding allowances to 0.

4. Enter the Payroll transactions referring to the pay list and detailed instructions that follow. <u>Do not</u> deduct Group Insurance. <u>Do</u> deduct Union Dues for the appropriate employees. <u>Do not</u> deduct Simple Plan (which is the same as Simple Contributions Payable). Begin the sequence with **Check No. 692.** Note that you need to enter the salary amounts shown for Virginia Russell and Ruth Williams to override their regular salary amounts.

Employees to Be Paid This Pay Period							
Check Number	Employee Number	Employee Name	Salary / Reg.Hrs.	Overtime @ Time 1½	Overtime @ Double	Group Ins.	Union Dues
692	100	Bonno, Anthony Victor	80				$8.00
693	110	Ferguson, James Claude	reg. salary				
694	120	Ford, Catherine Louise	reg. salary				
695	130	Mann, Dewey Wilson	reg. salary				
696	140	O'Neill, Joseph Tyler	reg. salary				
697	150	Russell, Virginia Aloise	$1,170.00 (loss of 2 hours)				
698	160	Ryan, Norman Allen	80				$8.00
699	170	Sokowski, Thomas James	reg. salary				
700	180	Student (your name)	72				
701	190	Williams, Ruth Virginia	$1,207.85 (loss of 1 hour)				

5. Display an **Employee List** report and verify the changes you made in step 4 on the previous page.

6. Display and review the Payroll report.

7. Generate and post the journal entry for the current payroll by selecting **Current Payroll Journal Entry** on the left menu bar. Click **Yes** when asked if you want to generate the journal entry. When the entry appears in the Current Payroll Journal Entries dialog box, click on **Post**. The journal entry will reappear, posted, in the General Journal.

8. Generate and post the employer's payroll taxes journal entry. With the **Payroll** top tab still selected, click on the **Employer's Payroll Taxes Journal Entry** task from the left menu bar. Click **Yes** on when asked if you want to generate the journal entry. Verify the result and click **Post** to post the entry to the General Journal. After you accept the entries, they will reappear, posted, in the General Journal.

9. Enter and post the November 6 General Journal entry to record the deposit of cash for the total net amount owed to employees in the payroll cash account. Click on the **General Ledger** top tab and the **General Journal** task. Based on the current period Net Pay summary information in the payroll report, enter the journal transaction.

10. Display and review the General Journal report. With the **General Ledger** tab still displayed, click on the **General Journal** report from the **Journal Reports** section of the left menu bar. Note that you should change the dates of the report to match the dates of the assignment (11/4/16 through 11/6/16) to view only the entries for this part of the assignment.

11. Display the General Ledger report. With the **General Ledger** top tab selected, click on **General Ledger** from the **Ledger Reports** section of the left menu bar.

12. If there is a **Check your Work** link on upper right of your screen, click on that link to review your work. Any errors you have will be noted with a red X, so try to locate the source of the errors and correct them.

13. When you are comfortable that you have completed all steps of the problem correctly click on the **Submit Assignment for Grading** button on the upper right of your screen.

November 13 Payroll

A special payroll needs to be run to process a discharged employee (Ruth Williams has been discharged because of her excessive tardiness and absenteeism). The step-by-step instructions for completing the November 13 special payroll are listed below.

1. Set the **System Date** at the bottom of the screen to **November 13, 2016**.

2. Enter Ruth V. Williams' payroll transaction (<u>do</u> deduct Group Ins of $14.40). Enter **Check No. 702** with $2,079.32 in her salary—two partial weeks of work ($856.24), plus two full weeks' pay ($1,223.08) in lieu of two weeks' notice for her final pay. To enter the payroll record, click on the **Pay Employees** task from the left menu bar under the **Payroll** tab. Click on the **Calculate Taxes** button after entering all information to fill the remaining fields.

3. Display and review the Payroll report. Click on the **Payroll Report** item from the left menu bar.

4. Generate and post the journal entry for the current payroll by selecting **Current Payroll Journal Entry** on the left menu bar. Click **Yes** when asked if you want to generate the journal entry. When the entry appears in the Current Payroll Journal Entries dialog box, click on **Post**. The journal entry will reappear, posted, in the General Journal.

5. Generate and post the employer's payroll taxes journal entry. With the **Payroll** top tab still selected, click on the **Employer's Payroll Taxes Journal Entry** task from the left menu bar. Click **Yes** when asked if you want to generate the journal entry. Verify the result and click **Post** to post the entry to the General Journal. After you accept the entries, they will reappear, posted, in the General Journal.

6. Enter and post the November 13 general journal entry to record the deposit of cash for the total net amount of Ruth Williams' pay in the payroll cash account. Click on the **General Ledger** top tab and the **General Journal** task. Based on the current period Net Pay summary information in the Payroll Report, enter the journal transaction.

7. Display and review the **General Journal** report for 11/7/2016 through 11/13/2016.

8. Display and review the **General Ledger** report.

9. If there is a **Check your Work** link on upper right of your screen, click on that link to review your work. Any errors you have will be noted with a red X, so try to locate the source of the errors and correct them.

10. When you are comfortable that you have completed all steps of the problem correctly click on the **Submit Assignment for Grading** button on the upper right of your screen.

November 20 Payroll

Follow the steps below to complete the **November 20** payroll transactions, for the period ending November 14, using **Cengage Learning General Ledger**.

1. Set the **System Date** at the bottom of the screen to **November 20, 2016**.

2. Enter and post the following transactions, using the **General Journal** task under the **General Ledger** tab. You can determine current account balances from the **General Ledger** Report item in the left menu bar.

   • November 16: Deposited with City Bank the amount of FICA taxes and federal income taxes for the October payrolls. Pay the balance in the two FICA Taxes Payable accounts (19 and 20) and Employees FIT Payable (24) as of the end of October.
   • November 16: Deposited the city of Philadelphia employees withheld income tax ($1,224.72) with the Department of Revenue for the October payrolls (see the Employees CIT Payable account balance in the general ledger report as of the end of October).
   • November 18: Deposited the Pennsylvania state income taxes withheld from the November 6 regular payroll and November 13 special payroll (pay the balance in the Employees SIT Payable account.)

3. Enter the following information, using the **Maintain Employees** task under the **Payroll** tab.

   • Change employee 180 from "Student" to your name.
   • Add new employee: Employee number 200; WOODS, Beth Anne; 8102 Franklin Court, Philadelphia, PA 19105-0915; social security number, 000-00-1587; single, salaried, $1,200.00; number of pay periods per year, 26; withholding allowances, 1; Account No. 52 (Office Salaries).

4. Make sure the **System Date** at the bottom of the screen is set to 11/20/16, and enter the Payroll transactions, using the **Pay Employees** task and referring to the pay list and detailed instructions that follow. Do deduct Group Insurance. Do deduct Union Dues for the appropriate employees. Do deduct Simple Plan savings deduction as shown. Begin the sequence with **Check No. 703**. In addition, note that you need to enter the salary amount shown for Virginia Russell to override her regular salary amount.

NOTE: This is the first pay in which the company offers a savings incentive match plan. The computer software has been designed to use the key terms 'Simple Plan' to instruct it to exclude this deduction from the employee's income for FIT purposes. The general ledger account **Simple Contributions Payable** is associated with this deduction for updating during payroll transaction processing.

NOTE: You need to press the **Calculate Taxes** button AFTER you enter the Simple Plan amount for each employee in order for taxes to calculate correctly, as this value affects the FIT calculation.

Employees to Be Paid This Pay Period								
Check Number	Employee Number	Employee Name	Salary / Reg.Hrs.	Overtime @ Time 1½	Overtime @ Double	Group Ins.	Union Dues	Simple Plan
703	100	Bonno, Anthony Victor	64			$ 16.50	$8.00	
704	110	Ferguson, James Claude	reg. salary			$ 26.40		$500.00
705	120	Ford, Catherine Louise	reg. salary			$ 14.40		
706	130	Mann, Dewey Wilson	reg. salary			$ 15.90		$250.00
707	140	O'Neill, Joseph Tyler	reg. salary			$ 27.00		$700.00
708	150	Russell, Virginia Aloise	$1,170.00 (loss of 2 hours)			$ 14.10		
709	160	Ryan, Norman Allen	80			$ 16.80	$8.00	$200.00
710	170	Sokowski, Thomas James	reg. salary			$ 24.00		
711	180	Student (your name)	72			$ 11.70		

5. Display an **Employee List** report and verify information on the new employee.
6. Display and review the **Payroll Report**.
7. Generate and post the journal entry for the current payroll by selecting **Current Payroll Journal Entry** on the left menu bar. Click **Yes** when asked if you want to generate the journal entry. When the entry appears in the Current Payroll Journal Entries dialog box, click on **Post**. The journal entry will reappear, posted, in the General Journal.
8. Generate and post the employer's payroll taxes journal entry. With the **Payroll** top tab still selected, click on the **Employer's Payroll Taxes Journal Entry** task from the left menu bar. Click **Yes** when asked if you want to generate the journal entry. Verify the result and click **Post** to post the entry to the General Journal. After you accept the entries, they will reappear, posted, in the General Journal.
9. Enter and post the November 20 General Journal entry to record the deposit of cash for the total net amount owed to employees in the payroll cash account. Click on the **General Ledger** top tab and the **General Journal** task. Based on the current period Net Pay summary information in the Payroll Report, enter the journal transaction.
10. Display and review the **General Journal** report for 11/14/2016 through 11/20/2016.
11. Display and review the **General Ledger** report.
12. If there is a **Check your Work** link on upper right of your screen, click on that link to review your work. Any errors you have will be noted with a red X, so try to locate the source of the errors and correct them.
13. When you are comfortable that you have completed all steps of the problem correctly, click on the **Submit Assignment for Grading** button on the upper right of your screen.

December 4 Payroll

Follow the steps below to complete the **December 4** payroll transactions, for the period ending November 30, using **Cengage Learning General Ledger**.

1. Set the **System Date** at the bottom of the screen to **December 4, 2016**.
2. Enter and post the following transaction, using the **General Journal** task under the **General Ledger** tab. You can determine current account balances from the **General Ledger** Report item in the left menu bar.

   • December 3: Deposited the Pennsylvania state income taxes withheld from the November 20 payroll (Employees SIT Payable).

3. Enter the following information, using the **Maintain Employees** task under the **Payroll** tab.

   • Change employee 180 from "Student" to your name.
   • Change Catherine L. Ford's salary amount to $1,280.00 because of a salary increase.
   • Change Virginia Russell's salary amount to $1,260.00 because of a salary increase.
   • Add new employee: Employee number 210; YOUNG, Paul Winston; 7936 Holmes Drive, Philadelphia, PA 19107-6107; social security number, 000-00-6057; single, salaried, $1,260.00; number of pay periods per year, 26; withholding allowances, 1; Account No. 53 (Sales Salaries).

4. Make sure the **System Date** at the bottom of the screen is set to 12/04/16, and enter the Payroll transactions, using the **Pay Employees** task and referring to the pay list and detailed instructions that follow. Do not deduct Group Insurance. Do deduct Union Dues for the appropriate employees. Do deduct Simple Plan savings deduction for the appropriate employees. Begin the sequence with **Check No. 712**. Finally, note that one employee has earned hours of double time pay, so put those hours in the **OT Double** column. Enter the information for each employee as you did for the previous payroll period, and click on the **Calculate Taxes** button after entering all deductions for each employee to fill the remaining fields.

		Employees to Be Paid This Pay Period						
Check Number	Employee Number	Employee Name	Salary / Reg.Hrs.	Overtime @ Time 1½	Overtime @ Double	Group Ins.	Union Dues	Simple Plan
712	100	Bonno, Anthony Victor	80		8		$8.00	
713	110	Ferguson, James Claude	reg. salary					$500.00
714	120	Ford, Catherine Louise	reg. salary					
715	130	Mann, Dewey Wilson	reg. salary					$250.00
716	140	O'Neill, Joseph Tyler	reg. salary					$700.00
717	150	Russell, Virginia Aloise	reg. salary					
718	160	Ryan, Norman Allen	76	3			$8.00	$200.00
719	170	Sokowski, Thomas James	reg. salary					
720	180	Student (your name)	72					
721	200	Woods, Beth Ann	$1,080.00 (first payroll)					

5. Display an **Employee List** report under the **Payroll** tab, and verify information you changed and added.
6. Display and review the **Payroll Report**.
7. Generate and post the journal entry for the current payroll by selecting **Current Payroll Journal Entry** on the left menu bar. Click **Yes** when asked

if you want to generate the journal entry. When the entry appears in the Current Payroll Journal Entries dialog box, click on **Post**. The journal entry will reappear, posted, in the General Journal.

8. Generate and post the employer's payroll taxes journal entry. With the **Payroll** top tab still selected, click on the **Employer's Payroll Taxes Journal Entry** task from the left menu bar. Click **Yes** when asked if you want to generate the journal entry. Verify the result and click **Post** to post the entry to the General Journal. After you accept the entries, they will reappear, posted, in the General Journal.

9. Enter and post the December 4 General Journal entry to record the deposit of cash for the total net amount owed to employees in the payroll cash account. Click on the **General Ledger** top tab and the **General Journal** task. Based on the current period Net Pay summary information in the Payroll Report, enter the journal transaction.

10. Display and review the **General Journal** report for 11/21/2016 through 12/04/2016.

11. Display and review the **General Ledger** report.

12. If there is a **Check your Work** link on upper right of your screen, click on that link to review your work. Any errors you have will be noted with a red X, so try to locate the source of the errors and correct them.

13. When you are comfortable that you have completed all steps of the problem correctly click on the **Submit Assignment for Grading** button on the upper right of your screen.

December 14 Payroll

A special payroll needs to be run to process the death of an employee (Virginia A. Russell). The step-by-step instructions for completing the December 14 special payroll follow.

1. Set the **System Date** at the bottom of the screen to **December 9, 2016**.
2. Enter and post the following transaction, using the **General Journal** task under the **General Ledger** tab. You can determine current account balances from the **General Ledger** Report item in the left menu bar.

   • December 9: Paid the treasurer of the union the amount of union dues withheld during the month of November (the balance in Union Dues Payable as of Nov. 30).

3. Enter the following information, using the **Maintain Employees** task under the **Payroll** tab.

   • Change Anthony V. Bonno's number of withholding allowances to 5.

4. Change the **System Date** to **December 14, 2016**. Pay Virginia A. Russell (pay will go to her estate). Enter $2,394.00 in her salary amount, using **Check No. 722**, which is two partial weeks of work ($1,134.00) plus her accrued vacation pay ($1,260.00) for her final check. *Note:* After clicking on the **Calculate Taxes** button, remove the calculated withholding amounts for FIT, SIT, and CIT by keying zeros in these grid cells (final pay is not subject to these withholdings). Do deduct $14.70 for her Group Insurance.

5. Display the **Employee List** report and verify information you changed and added.

6. Display and review the **Payroll Report**.

7. Generate and post the journal entry for the current payroll by selecting **Current Payroll Journal Entry** on the left menu bar. Click **Yes** when asked if you want to generate the journal entry. When the entry appears in the Current Payroll Journal Entries dialog box, click on **Post**. The journal entry will reappear, posted, in the General Journal.

8. Generate and post the employer's payroll taxes journal entry. With the **Payroll** top tab still selected, click on the **Employer's Payroll Taxes Journal Entry** task from the left menu bar. Click **Yes** when asked if you want to generate the journal entry. Verify the result and click **Post** to post the entry to the General Journal. After you accept the entries, they will reappear, posted, in the General Journal.

9. Enter and post the December 14 general journal entry to record the deposit of cash for Virginia A. Russell's net amount in the payroll cash account. Click on the **General Ledger** top tab and the **General Journal** task. Based on the current period Net Pay summary information in the Payroll Report, enter the journal transaction.

10. Display and review the **General Journal** report for 12/5/2016 through 12/14/2016.

11. Display and review the **General Ledger** report.

12. If there is a **Check your Work** link on upper right of your screen, click on that link to review your work. Any errors you have will be noted with a red X, so try to locate the source of the errors and correct them.

13. When you are comfortable that you have completed all steps of the problem correctly click on the **Submit Assignment for Grading** button on the upper right of your screen.

December 18 Payroll

Follow the steps below to complete the **December 18** payroll transactions, for the period ending December 15, using **Cengage Learning General Ledger**.

1. Set the **System Date** at the bottom of the screen to **December 15, 2016**.

2. Enter and post the following transactions, using the **General Journal** task under the **General Ledger** tab. You can determine current account balances from the **General Ledger** Report item in the left menu bar.

   • December 15: Deposited with City Bank the amount of FICA taxes and federal income taxes for the November payrolls. Pay the balance in the two FICA Taxes Payable accounts (19 and 20) and Employees FIT Payable (24) as of the end of November.

   • December 15: Deposited the city of Philadelphia employees withheld income tax with the Department of Revenue for the November payrolls (see the Employees CIT Payable account balance in the general ledger report as of the end of November).

   • December 18: Deposited the Pennsylvania state income taxes withheld from the December 4 payroll (Employees SIT Payable).

   • December 18: Wrote check to Virginia Russell's estate from the regular cash account to reimburse the amount withheld from her December 14 pay for insurance (review the December 14 credit to Group Insurance Premiums Payable to determine this amount).

3. Enter the following information, using the **Maintain Employees** task under the **Payroll** tab.

   • Change employee 180 from "Student" to your name.

   • Change: Employee number 140; O'Neill, Joseph Tyler withholding allowances to 4.

   • Add new employee: Employee number 220; ZIMMERMAN, Richard Lewis; 900 South Clark Street, Philadelphia, PA 19195-6247; social security number, 000-00-1502; married, salaried, $1,300.00; number of pay periods per year, 26; withholding allowances, 1; Account No. 52 (Office Salaries).

4. Enter the Payroll transactions, using the **Pay Employees** task and referring to the pay list and detailed instructions that follow. Do deduct Group

Insurance. <u>Do</u> deduct Union Dues for the appropriate employees. <u>Do</u> deduct Simple Plan savings deduction for the appropriate employees. Begin the sequence with **Check No. 723.** Note: Be sure to enter the changes and amounts of Group Insurance deductions for the new employees and the $9.00 Union Dues, as noted below. Also, add Joseph O'Neill's bonus to his regular pay, and be sure to enter the change to his Simple Plan deduction. Click on the **Calculate Taxes** button after entering all deductions for each employee to fill the remaining fields.

		Employees to Be Paid This Pay Period						
Check Number	Employee Number	Employee Name	Salary / Reg.Hrs.	Overtime @ Time 1½	Overtime @ Double	Group Ins.	Union Dues	Simple Plan
723	100	Bonno, Anthony Victor	80		12	$ 16.50	$9.00	
724	110	Ferguson, James Claude	reg. salary			$ 26.40		$500.00
725	120	Ford, Catherine Louise	reg. salary			$ 15.00		
726	130	Mann, Dewey Wilson	reg. salary			$ 15.90		$250.00
727	140	O'Neill, Joseph Tyler	$77,307.69 (reg. salary + $75,000 bonus)			$ 27.00		$4,000.00
728	160	Ryan, Norman Allen	80	7		$ 16.80	$9.00	$200.00
729	170	Sokowski, Thomas James	reg. salary			$ 24.00		
730	180	Student (your name)	71			$ 11.70		
731	200	Woods, Beth Ann	reg. salary			$ 14.10		
732	210	Young, Paul Winston	reg. salary			$ 14.70		

5. Display an **Employee List** report and verify information you changed and added.

6. Display and review the **Payroll Report**.

7. Generate and post the journal entry for the current payroll by selecting **Current Payroll Journal Entry** on the left menu bar. Click **Yes** when asked if you want to generate the journal entry. When the entry appears in the Current Payroll Journal Entries dialog box, click on **Post**. The journal entry will reappear, posted, in the General Journal.

8. Generate and post the employer's payroll taxes journal entry. With the **Payroll** top tab still selected, click on the **Employer's Payroll Taxes Journal Entry** task from the left menu bar. Click **Yes** when asked if you want to generate the journal entry. Verify the result and click **Post** to post the entry to the General Journal. After you accept the entries, they will reappear, posted, in the General Journal.

9. Enter and post the December 18 General Journal entry to record the deposit of cash for the total net amount owed to employees in the payroll cash account using the **General Journal** task under the **General Ledger** top tab. Based on the current period Net Pay summary information in the Payroll Report, enter the journal transaction.

10. Display and review the **General Journal** report for 12/15/2016 through 12/18/2016.

11. Display and review the **General Ledger** report.

12. If there is a **Check your Work** link on upper right of your screen, click on that link to review your work. Any errors you have will be noted with a red X, so try to locate the source of the errors and correct them.

13. When you are comfortable that you have completed all steps of the problem correctly click on the **Submit Assignment for Grading** button on the upper right of your screen.

If assigned by your instructor, continue to the "Optional Activities" section on page A-32.

Payroll Project (Short Version)

The payroll project that follows is the online version of the same project you completed manually in Chapter 7 of your text. For this project, you will use the **Cengage Learning General Ledger** to simulate how a real company would use general ledger software to maintain payroll records and payroll journal transactions. In this project, you are employed by Glo-Brite Paint Company as the person in the accounting department responsible for the company's payroll processing using the computerized payroll system.

However, unlike the payroll project in Chapter 7, you will only complete the payrolls for the month of December and the optional last quarter and year-end activities. The opening balance file you will use will already contain all the processing for the first two months of the quarter.

Your work will involve the computer processing of the payrolls for the last month of the year and the completion of the last quarter and annual tax reports and forms. You may complete the required deposit, quarterly, yearly, etc., forms described in Chapter 7. If you have already completed these forms for the manual student project, you can use these as a reference as you progress through this project.

To help you get started, the first pay period of December is provided as a tutorial problem that illustrates the principles and procedures required to process payroll transactions using the **Cengage Learning General Ledger** software. In subsequent pay period processing, whenever a new operational procedure is used for the first time, additional instruction will be provided.

This project has been broken down into several assignments comprising all or part of the project in your text. The assignments are delivered online using the **CengageNOWv2** learning management system, with each assignment being graded automatically and submitted to your instructor. Your instructor may choose to have you complete only part of this project, so watch the dates and follow the instructions carefully.

Note: Throughout this project, some of the computer-calculated withholding amounts (e.g., federal income tax) will differ slightly from the amounts (from the tax tables) in the manual payroll project in Chapter 7. This occurs because the software uses the annualized percentage method from *IRS Publication 15* rather than the table look-up to compute withholding taxes (see IRS Table 7 below). The differences here should be less than two dollars per pay period, and usually are much less. Also, one- to two-cent differences will occur throughout the solutions because of rounding differences. Finally, some of the account numbers differ slightly from those in your text, but there is a pop-up "Chart of Accounts" available in the software to help you quickly find the accounts you need, or refer to the partial Chart of Accounts on the following page.

TABLE 7—ANNUAL Payroll Period

(a) SINGLE person (including head of household)—				(b) MARRIED person—			
If the amount of wages (after subtracting withholding allowances) is:		The amount of income tax to withhold is:		If the amount of wages (after subtracting withholding allowances) is:		The amount of income tax to withhold is:	
Not over $2,300		$0		Not over $8,600		$0	
Over—	But not over—		of excess over—	Over—	But not over—		of excess over—
$2,300	—$11,525 . .	$0.00 plus 10%	—$2,300	$8,600	—$27,050 . .	$0.00 plus 10%	—$8,600
$11,525	—$39,750 . .	$922.50 plus 15%	—$11,525	$27,050	—$83,500 . .	$1,845.00 plus 15%	—$27,050
$39,750	—$93,050 . .	$5,156.25 plus 25%	—$39,750	$83,500	—$159,800 . .	$10,312.50 plus 25%	—$83,500
$93,050	—$191,600 . .	$18,481.25 plus 28%	—$93,050	$159,800	—$239,050 . .	$29,387.50 plus 28%	—$159,800
$191,600	—$413,800 . .	$46,075.25 plus 33%	—$191,600	$239,050	—$420,100 . .	$51,577.50 plus 33%	—$239,050
$413,800	—$415,500 . .	$119,401.25 plus 35%	—$413,800	$420,100	—$473,450 . .	$111,324.00 plus 35%	—$420,100
$415,500	. . . .	$119,996.25 plus 39.6%	—$415,500	$473,450	. . . .	$129,996.50 plus 39.6%	—$473,450

		Text	
	Glo-Brite Paint Company		
	Partial Chart of Accounts		
	9/30/2016		
Classification	Account Number	Text Account Number	Account Title
Assets	11	11	Cash
	12	12	Payroll Cash
	13	n/a	Accounts Receivable
Liabilities	15	n/a	Accounts Payable
	19	20.1	FICA Taxes Payable--OASDI
	20	20.2	FICA Taxes Payable--HI
	21	21	FUTA Taxes Payable
	22	22	SUTA Taxes Payable
	24	24	Employees FIT Payable
	25	25	Employees SIT Payable
	n/a	25.1	SUTA Taxes Payable-Employer (combined with account 22)
	26	26	Employees CIT Payable
	27	27	Grp. Ins. Prem. Collected
	28	28	Union Dues Payable
	29	29	Simple Contrib. Payable
Capital	30	n/a	Capital
	31	n/a	Drawing
	39	n/a	Income Summary
Expenses	51	51	Administrative Salaries
	52	52	Office Salaries
	53	53	Sales Salaries
	54	54	Plant Wages
	56	56	Payroll Taxes

December 4 Payroll

Follow the steps below to complete the December 4 payroll transactions using **Cengage Learning General Ledger**. To access additional Help for any function, click on the **Help** button that appears at the bottom of the screen. There is a Help screen with additional information and sample screens for every menu option in the program. Click on the **Save** button at the upper right of your screen at any point to save your work if you need to stop working to continue later. Your work will automatically be restored when you return.

1. Set the **System Date** at the bottom of the screen to **December 4, 2016**. Note that the year needs to be **2016** in order for the problem to grade correctly.
2. Click on the **General Ledger** tab and select the **Chart of Accounts** from the **Account Lists** section. Review this list to understand how the software designates the Payroll accounts.
3. Enter the employee maintenance data. Click on the top bar **Payroll** tab and the **Maintain Employees** task from the left menu bar.

   - Change Catherine L. Ford's salary amount to $1,280.00 because of a salary increase.
   - Change Virginia Russell's salary amount to $1,260.00 because of a salary increase.
   - Scroll down to select employee number **180** (Student), key your own name in the **Employee Name** field (enter your last name in all capital

letters similar to the other employees), then **Tab** out of the field. Note: Do not change any of the other fields. If you do, your solutions will not be correct.

- Add new employee: Employee number 210; YOUNG, Paul Winston; 7936 Holmes Drive, Philadelphia, PA 19107-6107; social security number, 000-00-6057; single, salaried, $1,260.00; number of pay periods per year, 26; withholding allowances, 1; Account No. 53 (Sales Salaries).
- Click on the **Close** button, and click "Yes" to accept your changes.

4. Enter and post the following transaction, which is shown in Figure A-9 below.

- December 3: Deposited the Pennsylvania state income taxes withheld from the November 20 payroll (Employees SIT Payable). First determine current account balances using the **General Ledger Report** in the left menu bar under the **General Ledger** tab. Look for the outstanding balance in account #25. Next, select the **General Journal** task and click on the **Add New Entry button**. Enter the first account number (**25**) or click on the pop-up **Chart of Accounts** icon to display a list for selection. Enter the debit amount to clear the existing credit to **Employees SIT Payable**. Then **Tab** to the next row, or click on **Insert Debit/Credit** again to enter the credit (the same amount) to the **Cash** account (**11**). Finally, click on the **Post** button to post this entry to the General Ledger.

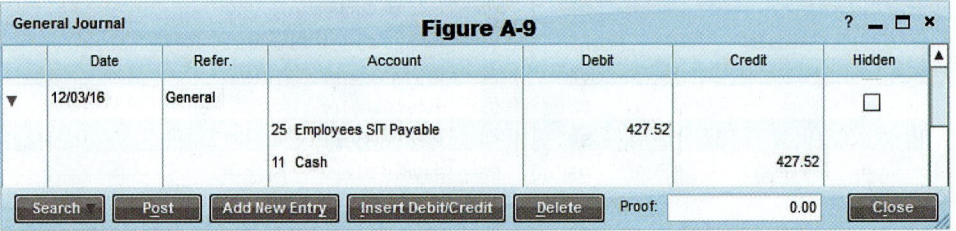

5. Enter the Payroll transactions for the period using the detailed instructions in steps (a) through (j) on the next page. Refer to the following pay list for this period.

Employees to Be Paid This Pay Period								
Check Number	Employee Number	Employee Name	Salary / Reg.Hrs.	Overtime @ Time 1½	Overtime @ Double	Group Ins.	Union Dues	Simple Plan
712	100	Bonno, Anthony Victor	80		8		$8.00	
713	110	Ferguson, James Claude	reg. salary					$500.00
714	120	Ford, Catherine Louise	reg. salary					
715	130	Mann, Dewey Wilson	reg. salary					$250.00
716	140	O'Neill, Joseph Tyler	reg. salary					$700.00
717	150	Russell, Virginia Aloise	reg. salary					
718	160	Ryan, Norman Allen	76	3			$8.00	$200.00
719	170	Sokowski, Thomas James	reg. salary					
720	180	Student (your name)	72					
721	200	Woods, Beth Ann	$1,080.00 (first payroll)					

To enter the payroll records, click on the **Pay Employees** task from the left menu bar. As noted above, you will probably have to shrink the left menu bar (using the << icon) and grab the top of the Payroll form with your mouse to reposition it to better fit on your screen. You should also scroll over to grab the lower-right corner of the form to drag it down to fill the screen.

a. The prior months' payroll information is already entered, and will show up in the reports, but NOT in the payroll entry screens. Click on the **Deductions** button to display the **Voluntary Deductions** check boxes. Uncheck the **Group Insurance**, but check **Union Dues** and **Simple Plan** (which is the same as Simple Contributions Payable) boxes, and click **OK**.

b. For each pay period, you will need to add a new record to this payroll register for each employee to be paid. Click on the **Add** button to add a new pay record for each of the above employees, and then enter the corresponding fields. You may need to scroll down to the bottom of the payroll form to see the newly added line.

c. **Date:** Make sure the date is set to **12/04/16**, or use the pop-up calendar to change it. Payroll recording is very dependent on having the correct dates, so **verify this date**, especially for the first employee in any payroll set.

d. **Employee Name:** Select the name from the drop-down list or key the first letter of the employee's last name until the correct name appears.

e. **Check No.:** Start with check number **712** to continue from where the previous month left off. This number will automatically increase by 1 for each subsequent employee. It is critical to get this check number correct for each employee, along with the date, as this is how the software matches up your entries for grading.

f. **Salary or Hours worked:** For salaried employees, the salary should display automatically. For hourly employees, click on the **Reg. Hours** field and enter the number of regular work hours shown above. When shown, enter the number of hours in the "**OT 1 1/2**" and "**OT Double**" boxes to record the appropriate overtime hours. Note that you need to enter the salary amount shown for Beth Anne Woods to override the regular salary amount.

g. For the two union employees noted above, change the **Union Dues** field to $8, which is this period's dues amount.

h. Click on the **Calculate Taxes** button for each employee to fill the remaining fields. **Net Pay** will calculate automatically, and **Gross Pay** will display at the bottom of the form. Review the amounts calculated for reasonableness.

    i. Click **Add** to start a new employee or **Close** when done. You may need to confirm the data you entered or the changes you made. If you make a mistake, just go to the appropriate line and field, and change the value. Click on the **Calculate Taxes** button again to recalculate those amounts. **Net Pay** will re-compute automatically.

6. Display the Employee List report. Click on the **Employee List** from the **Payroll** left menu bar. The report is shown in Figure A-10 below. Verify the accuracy of the maintenance input from step 4 on page A-22 and make any corrections via the **Maintain Employees** menu option.

Employee List			**Figure A-10**			? _ □ ✕

Glo-Brite Paint Company
Employee List
12/04/16

Emp. No.	Employee Name/Address	Social Security/Marital Status	# Pay Periods	G.L. Account	Salary/Rate
100	BONNO, Anthony Victor 694 Bristol Avenue Philadelphia, PA 19135-0617	000-00-3481 Married W/H 4	26	54	0.00 17.65
110	FERGUSON, James Claude 808 Sixth Street Philadelphia, PA 19106-0995	000-00-8645 Married W/H 5	26	53	2,250.00 0.00
120	FORD, Catherine Louise 18 Dundee Avenue Philadelphia, PA 19151-1919	000-00-4567 Single W/H 2	26	52	1,280.00 0.00
130	MANN, Dewey Wilson 3007 Bisque Drive Philadelphia, PA 19199-0718	000-00-9352 Married W/H 0	26	53	1,350.00 0.00
140	O'NEILL, Joseph Tyler 2100 Broad Street Philadelphia, PA 19121-7189	000-00-1534 Married W/H 3	26	51	2,307.69 0.00
150	RUSSELL, Virginia Aloise 8004 Dowling Road Philadelphia, PA 19135-9001	000-00-6337 Single W/H 2	26	52	1,260.00 0.00
160	RYAN, Norman Allen 7300 Harrison Street Philadelphia, PA 19124-6699	000-00-1233 Married W/H 4	26	54	0.00 18.00
170	SOKOWSKI, Thomas James 133 Cornwells Street Philadelphia, PA 19171-5718	000-00-8832 Single W/H 2	26	54	2,050.00 0.00
180	STUDENT 7018 Erdrick Street Philadelphia, PA 19135-8517	000-00-5555 Single W/H 1	26	52	0.00 14.00
190	WILLIAMS, Ruth Virginia 9433 State Street Philadelphia, PA 19149-0819	000-00-6741 Single W/H 0	26	52	1,223.08 0.00
200	WOODS, Beth Anne 8102 Franklin Court Philadelphia, PA 19105-0915	000-00-1587 Single W/H 1	26	52	1,200.00 0.00
210	YOUNG, Paul Winston 7936 Holmes Drive Philadelphia, PA 19107-6107	000-00-6057 Single W/H 1	26	53	1,260.00 0.00

		Close	Print	Copy

7. Display the Payroll report. Click on the **Payroll Report** item from the left menu bar. The payroll report for Employee 100; Bonno, Anthony Victor, followed by the payroll summary, is shown in Figure A-11. Due to its length, only the first employee and the summary are shown. If the summary is incorrect, review the list of employees to be paid from step 5 on page A-22. Check your numbers, and make any changes using the **Pay Employees** task.

8. Generate and post the journal entry for the current payroll. Click on the **Current Payroll Journal Entry** task on the left menu bar. Click **Yes** when asked if you want to generate the journal entry. If your journal entries do not match those shown in Figure A-12 on page A-26, check your

Payroll Report   **Figure A-11**   ? _ □ ✕

Glo-Brite Paint Company
Payroll Report
12/04/16

		Current	Quarterly	Yearly
100 - BONNO, Anthony Victor	Gross Pay	1,694.40	7,165.90	18,487.90
54 - Plant Wages	FIT	76.76	245.43	1,055.43
Married Acct. 54	SIT	52.02	220.00	567.59
W/H 4 000-00-3481	Soc. Sec. (OASDI)	105.05	444.28	1,146.24
Pay Periods 26	Medicare (HI)	24.57	103.90	268.07
Salary 0.00	CIT	66.42	280.90	724.72
Hourly Rate 17.65	Group Ins.		33.00	177.80
Reg. Hours 80.00	Union Dues	8.00	40.00	112.00
O.T. Hours 8.00	Simple Plan			
Check Number 712	Employee SUTA	1.19	5.02	12.95
Check Date 12/04/16	Net Pay	1,360.39	5,793.37	14,423.10
Payroll Summary	Gross Pay	15,729.09	78,392.68	220,617.25
	FIT	1,022.15	5,713.57	21,630.57
	SIT	482.90	2,406.73	6,773.02
	Soc. Sec. (OASDI)	975.21	4,860.38	13,678.30
	Medicare (HI)	228.09	1,136.77	3,199.04
	CIT	616.58	3,072.95	8,648.15
	Group Ins.		362.40	1,292.80
	Union Dues	16.00	80.00	224.00
	Simple Plan	1,650.00	3,300.00	3,300.00
	Employee SUTA	11.04	55.01	154.58
	Net Pay	10,727.12	57,404.87	161,716.79

[Close]   [Print]   [Copy]

employee list and payroll report for keying errors, and go back to make
the necessary corrections. If they are correct, click on **Post**. The journal
entry will reappear, posted, in the General Journal. *Note:* The software
combines both the entries for Employee's SUTA Tax Payable and Employer's SUTA Tax Payable into one account.

9. Generate and post the employer's payroll taxes journal entry. Click on the
    Employer's Payroll Taxes Journal Entry task on the left menu bar.
    Compare your entries as they appear in the Payroll Taxes Journal Entries
    dialog box, to Figure A-13 on page A-26. Click **Yes** when asked if you
    want to generate the journal entry. If they are correct, click on **Post**, other-
    wise go back and re-check your inputs. After you accept the entries, they
    will reappear, posted, in the General Journal.

10. Enter and post the December 4 General Journal entry to record the deposit
    of cash for the total net amount owed to employees in the payroll cash
    account. This is also found as the current period **Net Pay** value on the Pay-
    roll Report. Click on the **General Ledger** top tab and the **General Journal**
    task. Enter the transaction shown in Figure A-14 on page A-27 by first
    clicking on the **Add New Entry** button. Verify the date and enter **General**
    as the reference. Next, click on the **Insert Debit/Credit** button, enter the

Current Payroll Journal Entries   **Figure A-12**

Account #	Account Title	Debit	Credit
54	Plant Wages	5,193.40	
52	Office Salaries	4,628.00	
53	Sales Salaries	3,600.00	
51	Administrative Salaries	2,307.69	
12	Payroll Cash		10,727.12
19	FICA Taxes Payable-- OASDI		975.21
22	SUTA Taxes Payable		11.04
28	Union Dues Payable		16.00
26	Employees CIT Payable		616.58
25	Employees SIT Payable		482.90
29	Simple Contrib. Payable		1,650.00
24	Employees FIT Payable		1,022.15
20	FICA Taxes Payable--HI		228.09

Post   Close

Payroll Taxes Journal Entries   **Figure A-13**

Account #	Account Title	Debit	Credit
56	Payroll Taxes	1,249.51	
19	FICA Taxes Payable-- OASDI		975.21
20	FICA Taxes Payable--HI		228.09
22	SUTA Taxes Payable		6.48
21	FUTA Taxes Payable		39.73

Post   Close

first account number (**12**) or click on the pop-up **Chart of Accounts** icon to display a list for selection. Enter the debit amount to clear the existing credit to **Payroll Cash** from the first journal entry above. Then **Tab** to the next row, or click on **Insert Debit/Credit** again to enter the credit to the **Cash** account. Finally, click on the **Post** button to post this entry to the General Ledger.

11. Display the General Journal report. With the General Ledger tab still displayed, click on the **General Journal** report from the **Journal Reports** section of the left menu bar. The General Journal report is shown in Figure A-15. Note that you need to change the dates of the report to match the dates of the assignment, 11/21/2016 through 12/04/2016. You can also customize the report to display only certain **Reference** values or account numbers.

12. Display the General Ledger report. With the **General Ledger** top tab selected, click on **General Ledger** from the **Ledger Reports** section of the left menu bar. A partial General Ledger report is shown in Figure A-16. You can also customize this report to list only a selected range of accounts.

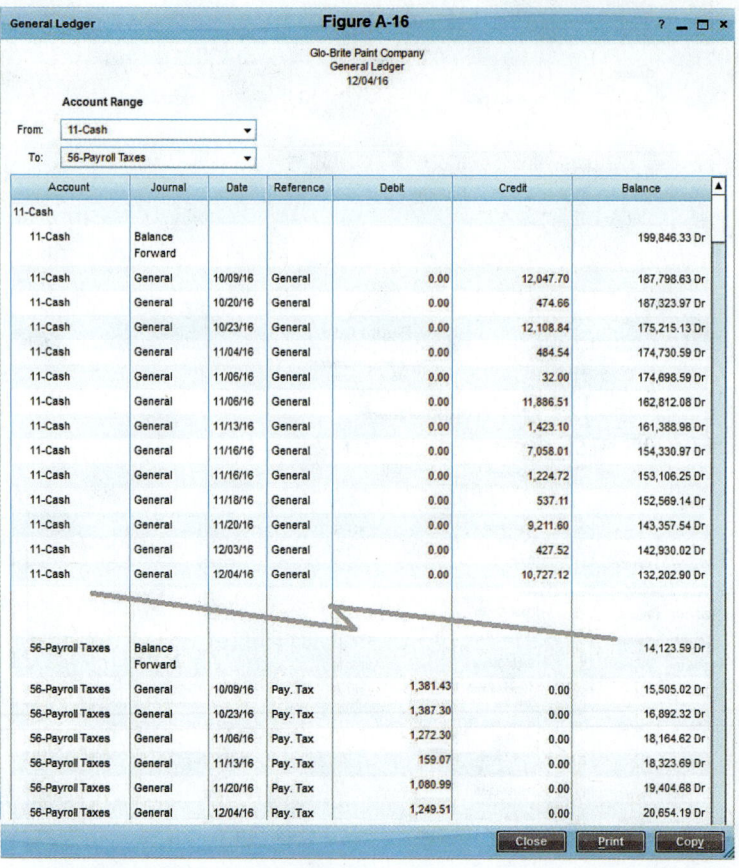

Figure A-16

13. Generate a labor distribution graph. Click on the **Company** top tab and the **Labor Distribution** item from the left menu bar to generate the graph shown in Figure A-17. Note that the software creates the graph from the year-to-date values, rather than the month-to-date values in the key.

14. If there is a **Check My Work** link on upper right of your screen, click on that link to review your work. Any errors you have will be noted with a red X, so try to locate the source of the errors and correct them. If the account values are incorrect, you will likely find an individual employee listed in the error detail report that is also incorrect. After fixing individual employees using the **Pay Employees** task, you can delete any of the journal entries, using the **General Journal** task under the **General Ledger** top tab, and retry any or all of the steps above.

15. When you are comfortable that you have completed all steps of the problem correctly click on the **Submit Assignment for Grading** button on the upper right of your screen. You will be graded primarily on three criteria for the payroll problems:

- Are the pay settings for each employee correct (rate, deductions, etc.)?
- Are all period's payroll entries correct for each employee?
- Are the ending balances in each General Ledger account correct?

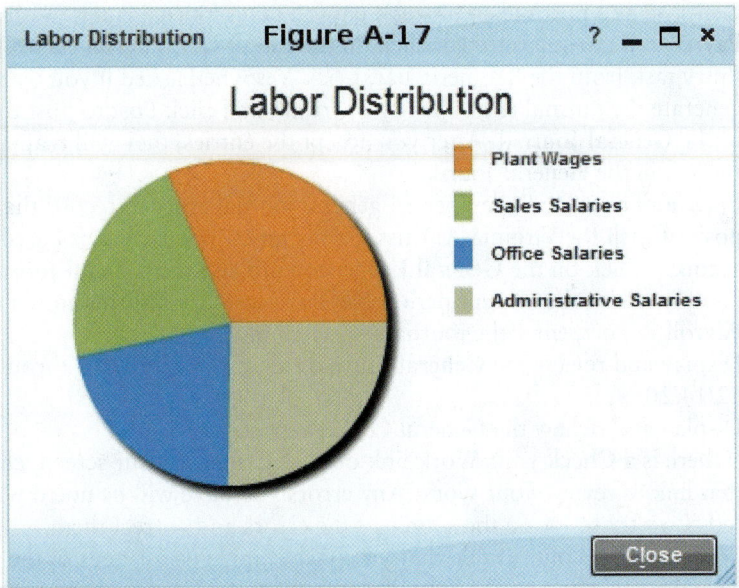

Figure A-17

Note that the journal entries themselves are not graded. If the journal entries are correct, the final General Ledger balances will then also be correct.

December 14 Payroll

A special payroll needs to be run to process the death of an employee (Virginia A. Russell). The step-by-step instructions for completing the December 14 special payroll follow.

1. Set the **System Date** at the bottom of the screen to **December 9, 2016**.
2. Enter and post the following transaction, using the **General Journal** task under the **General Ledger** tab. You can determine current account balances from the **General Ledger** Report item in the left menu bar.

   - December 9: Paid the treasurer of the union the amount of union dues withheld during the month of November (the balance in Union Dues Payable as of Nov. 30).

3. Enter the following information, using the **Maintain Employees** task under the **Payroll** tab.

   - Change Anthony V. Bonno's number of withholding allowances to 5.

4. Change the **System Date** to **December 14, 2016**. Pay Virginia A. Russell (pay will go to her estate). Enter $2,394.00 in her salary amount, using **Check No. 722**, which is two partial weeks of work ($1,134.00) plus her accrued vacation pay ($1,260.00) for her final check. *Note:* After clicking on the **Calculate Taxes** button, remove the calculated withholding amounts for FIT, SIT, and CIT by keying zeros in these grid cells (final pay is not subject to these withholdings). <u>Do</u> deduct $14.70 for her Group Insurance.
5. Display the **Employee List** report and verify information you changed and added.
6. Display and review the **Payroll Report**.
7. Generate and post the journal entry for the current payroll by selecting **Current Payroll Journal Entry** on the left menu bar. Click **Yes** when asked if you want to generate the journal entry. When the entry appears in the Current Payroll Journal Entries dialog box, click on **Post**. The journal entry will reappear, posted, in the General Journal.

8. Generate and post the employer's payroll taxes journal entry. With the **Payroll** top tab still selected, click on the **Employer's Payroll Taxes Journal Entry** task from the left menu bar. Click **Yes** when asked if you want to generate the journal entry. Verify the result and click **Post** to post the entry to the General Journal. After you accept the entries, they will reappear, posted, in the General Journal.

9. Enter and post the December 14 general journal entry to record the deposit of cash for Virginia A. Russell's net amount in the payroll cash account. Click on the **General Ledger** top tab and the **General Journal** task. Based on the current period Net Pay summary information in the Payroll Report, enter the journal transaction.

10. Display and review the **General Journal** report for 12/5/2016 through 12/14/2016.

11. Display and review the **General Ledger** report.

12. If there is a **Check your Work** link on upper right of your screen, click on that link to review your work. Any errors you have will be noted with a red **X**, so try to locate the source of the errors and correct them.

13. When you are comfortable that you have completed all steps of the problem correctly click on the **Submit Assignment for Grading** button on the upper right of your screen.

December 18 Payroll

Follow the steps below to complete the **December 18** payroll transactions, for the period ending December 15, using **Cengage Learning General Ledger**.

1. Set the **System Date** at the bottom of the screen to **December 15, 2016**.

2. Enter and post the following transactions, using the **General Journal** task under the **General Ledger** tab. You can determine current account balances from the **General Ledger** Report item in the left menu bar.

   - December 15: Deposited with City Bank the amount of FICA taxes and federal income taxes for the November payrolls. Pay the balance in the two FICA Taxes Payable accounts (19 and 20) and Employees FIT Payable (24) as of the end of November.

   - December 15: Deposited the city of Philadelphia employees withheld income tax with the Department of Revenue for the November payrolls (see the Employees CIT Payable account balance in the general ledger report as of the end of November).

   - December 18: Deposited the Pennsylvania state income taxes withheld from the December 4 payroll (Employees SIT Payable).

   - December 18: Wrote check to Virginia Russell's estate from the regular cash account to reimburse the amount withheld from her December 14 pay for insurance (review the December 14 credit to Group Insurance Premiums Payable to determine this amount).

3. Enter the following information, using the **Maintain Employees** task under the **Payroll** tab.

   - Change employee 180 from "Student" to your name.
   - Change: Employee number 140; O'Neill, Joseph Tyler withholding allowances to 4.
   - Add new employee: Employee number 220; ZIMMERMAN, Richard Lewis; 900 South Clark Street, Philadelphia, PA 19195-6247; social security number, 000-00-1502; married, salaried, $1,300.00; number of pay periods per year, 26; withholding allowances, 1; Account No. 52 (Office Salaries).

4. Enter the Payroll transactions, using the **Pay Employees** task and referring to the pay list and detailed instructions that follow. D̲o̲ deduct Group

Insurance. <u>Do</u> deduct Union Dues for the appropriate employees. <u>Do</u> deduct Simple Plan savings deduction for the appropriate employees. Begin the sequence with **Check No. 723**. *Note:* Be sure to enter the changes and amounts of Group Insurance deductions for the new employees and the $9.00 Union Dues, as noted below. Also, add Joseph O'Neill's bonus to his regular pay, and be sure to enter the change to his Simple Plan deduction. Click on the **Calculate Taxes** button after entering all deductions for each employee to fill the remaining fields.

Check Number	Employee Number	Employee Name	Salary / Reg.Hrs.	Overtime @ Time 1½	Overtime @ Double	Group Ins.	Union Dues	Simple Plan
723	100	Bonno, Anthony Victor	80		12	$ 16.50	$9.00	
724	110	Ferguson, James Claude	reg. salary			$ 26.40		$500.00
725	120	Ford, Catherine Louise	reg. salary			$ 15.00		
726	130	Mann, Dewey Wilson	reg. salary			$ 15.90		$250.00
727	140	O'Neill, Joseph Tyler	$77,307.69 (reg. salary + $75,000 bonus)			$ 27.00		$4,000.00
728	160	Ryan, Norman Allen	80	7		$ 16.80	$9.00	$200.00
729	170	Sokowski, Thomas James	reg. salary			$ 24.00		
730	180	Student (your name)	71			$ 11.70		
731	200	Woods, Beth Ann	reg. salary			$ 14.10		
732	210	Young, Paul Winston	reg. salary			$ 14.70		

Employees to Be Paid This Pay Period

5. Display an **Employee List** report and verify information you changed and added.
6. Display and review the **Payroll Report**.
7. Generate and post the journal entry for the current payroll by selecting **Current Payroll Journal Entry** on the left menu bar. Click **Yes** when asked if you want to generate the journal entry. When the entry appears in the Current Payroll Journal Entries dialog box, click on **Post**. The journal entry will reappear, posted, in the General Journal.
8. Generate and post the employer's payroll taxes journal entry. With the **Payroll** top tab still selected, click on the **Employer's Payroll Taxes Journal Entry** task from the left menu bar. Click **Yes** when asked if you want to generate the journal entry. Verify the result and click **Post** to post the entry to the General Journal. After you accept the entries, they will reappear, posted, in the General Journal.
9. Enter and post the December 18 General Journal entry to record the deposit of cash for the total net amount owed to employees in the payroll cash account using the **General Journal** task under the **General Ledger** top tab. Based on the current period Net Pay summary information in the Payroll Report, enter the journal transaction.
10. Display and review the **General Journal** report for 12/15/2016 through 12/18/2016.
11. Display and review the **General Ledger** report.
12. If there is a **Check your Work** link on upper right of your screen, click on that link to review your work. Any errors you have will be noted with a red X, so try to locate the source of the errors and correct them.
13. When you are comfortable that you have completed all steps of the problem correctly click on the **Submit Assignment for Grading** button on the upper right of your screen.
14. If assigned by your instructor, continue to the "Optional Activities" section.

Optional Activities

The following optional additional transactions are given to illustrate different types of transactions arising in the subsequent year in connection with the accounting for payrolls and payroll taxes. These correspond with the activities beginning in the Chapter 7 Payroll Project beginning with the date of January 6.

Note: before you begin this activity, you should have a printed copy of the December 18 Payroll Report. If you do not have this report, you need to print one BEFORE you change the date in Step 1 below. It is found under the **Payroll** tab in the **Reports** section of the left menu. In addition, if requested by your instructor, print out the **W2 Statements**, also found in the **Reports** section.

1. Set the **System Date** at the bottom of the screen to **January 6, 2017**. Make sure the year has advanced to **2017**.

2. Enter and post the following transactions, using the **General Journal** task under the **General Ledger** tab. You can determine current account balances from the **General Ledger Report** item in the left menu bar.

   • January 6: Deposited the Pennsylvania state income taxes withheld from the December 18 payroll. Use the current balance of account 25, Employees SIT Payable.

   • January 8: Paid the treasurer of the union the amount of union dues withheld during the month of December. Use the current balance of account 28, Union Dues Payable.

   • January 15: Deposited with City Bank the amount of FICA taxes and federal income taxes for the December payrolls. Pay the balance in the two FICA Taxes Payable accounts (19 and 20) and Employees FIT Payable (24) as of the end of December.

   • January 15: Deposited the city of Philadelphia employees' income tax withheld with the Department of Revenue from the December payrolls. Use the current balance of account 26, Employees CIT Payable.

   • February 1: Deposited FUTA Taxes Payable for the quarter. Use the current balance of account 21.

   • February 1: Paid the SUTA Taxes Payable and Employees SUTA Payable for the fourth quarter. Note that in the computerized simulation you have just completed, Employees SUTA Payable has been combined into one account with the employer's assessment. Use the current balance of account 22.

3. Display and review the **General Journal** report for 1/1/2017 through 2/1/2017. Make any corrections necessary to the General Journal.

4. If there is a **Check your Work** link on upper right of your screen, click on that link to review your work. Any errors you have will be noted with a red **X**, so try to locate the source of the errors and correct them. Do not submit your assignment for grading until you have completed the forms requested by your instructor in step 5 below, as you will need to review some of the reports in the software to extract key numbers.

5. Use the information contained in the payroll accounting reports to complete the following forms, if not completed in the Student Project in Chapter 7. If completed in Chapter 7, check the forms and note any differences. Because of calculation rounding and the use of the percentage method for Federal Income Tax calculation, some amounts may differ. Refer to the February 1 narrative regarding the forms to be completed (on pages 7-54 through 7-67) in the manual student project in Chapter 7, if necessary. Complete those forms assigned by your instructor.

a. Form 941, Employer's Quarterly Federal Tax Return. Use the total Quarterly numbers in the December 18 **Payroll Report**. The final wages paid to Virginia Russell ($2,394.00) and the Simple Plan quarterly need to be deducted from the Line 2 total quarterly wages. Line 3 is the total quarterly FIT amount withheld. Line 5a wages are total quarterly wages paid less the amount paid to Joseph O'Neill in excess of the $118,500 cap on Social Security wages, while Line 5c is total quarterly wages. To calculate the Line 1 amounts, review the **General Journal** report for the total amount paid to the federal government in the transactions of 11/16/2016, 12/15/2016, and 1/15/2017 (also shown in the General Ledger report for accounts 19).

b. Form 940, Employer's Annual Federal Unemployment (FUTA) Tax Return. Line 3 is the annual gross pay from the December 18 Payroll Report. For Line 7, subtract $7,000 each for ten employees ($70,000) and the under $7,000 total wages for Beth Anne Woods and Paul Winston Young. Lines 5 and 6 are the difference between these two amounts. The Line 8 total tax paid should equal the February 1 payment.

c. Form UC-2, Employer's Report for Unemployment Compensation—Fourth Quarter. Total fourth quarter wages come from the December 18 Payroll Report quarterly column. Employee SUTA contributions were $120.52 for the quarter. Taxable SUTA wages were $16,050.00.

d. Form W-2. Review the Wage and Tax Statement for each employee if you printed them in preparation for this activity. Note that you will need to manually calculate the taxable federal wages for employees with Simple deductions. You will also need to issue a manually corrected W-2 for Virginia Russell to show that Line 1 Wages do not include her last pay of $2,394.00.

e. Form W-3, Transmittal of Wage and Tax Statements. The final wages paid to Virginia Russell and the Simple Plan total need to be deducted from the total annual wages on the December 18 Payroll Report for computing Box 1. Box 3 wages are total annual wages paid less the amount paid to Joseph O'Neill in excess of the $118,500 cap on Social Security wages. Box 16 and 18 wages are total annual wages less the final wages paid to Virginia Russell. The other values can be derived from the December 18 Payroll Report.

f. Pennsylvania Form REV-1667, W-2 Transmittal. Use the amounts below for the wages paid and the Pennsylvania tax withheld for the first three quarters. The Line 2 annual and Part II fourth quarter gross pay amounts are the total gross pay minus Virginia Russell's final wages. Find SIT taxes withheld for the quarter from the last Payroll Report.

Quarter	Wages Paid	Tax Withheld
1st	$34,088.75	$1,046.52
2nd	$45,535.62	$1,397.94
3rd	$62,600.20	$1,921.83

g. Form 1099-MISC, Miscellaneous Income (for Virginia A. Russell). This is the gross amount of her last (December 14) pay. Because that check was written to her estate, this amount is reported as "Other income" and should not appear on her W-2, as noted in step (d) above.

    h. Form 1096, Annual Summary and Transmittal of U.S. Information
       Returns (same amount as 1099-MISC). This form must also be com-
       pleted for Virginia A. Russell's last pay.

    i. City of Philadelphia Annual Reconciliation of Employer Wage Tax. For
      Line 1, deduct Virginia Russell's final wages from the annual gross
      wages paid (rounded to the nearest dollar). Note that ten employees
      were residents of Philadelphia in March.

    When you are comfortable that you have completed all steps of the Optional
Activities problem correctly, click on the **Submit Assignment for Grading** button
on the upper right of your screen. This concludes the Payroll Project.

Name_____

Student Project Audit Test

OCTOBER 9 PAYROLL: (As you complete your work, answer the following questions for the October 9 payroll.)

Payroll Report
1. What is the number of withholding allowances for James C. Ferguson?...................... _____
2. What is the current gross pay for Norman A. Ryan? .... _____
3. What is the amount of HI withheld for the current pay period for Ruth V. Williams? . _____
4. What is the total current net pay for all employees?.. _____
5. What is the total yearly SIT withheld for all employees?.. _____

Journal Entries Report
6. What is the amount of the debit to Office Salaries?.. _____
7. What is the amount of the debit to Payroll Taxes?.. _____
8. What is the amount of the credit to Cash? .... _____

General Ledger
9. What is the Cash (account number 11) account balance? .... _____
10. What is the total Administrative Salaries paid to date? .... _____

Name_____

Student Project Audit Test

OCTOBER 23 PAYROLL: (As you complete your work, answer the following questions for the October 23 payroll.)

Payroll Report
1. What is the current gross pay for Anthony V. Bonno?.. _____
2. What is the current amount of OASDI withheld for Catherine L. Ford?...................... _____
3. What is the total current net pay for all employees?.. _____
4. What is the total quarterly gross pay for all employees? .... _____
5. What is the total current amount of group insurance withheld for all employees?........ _____

Journal Entries Report
6. What is the amount of the credit to Employees SIT Payable?....................................... _____
7. What is the amount of the debit to Payroll Taxes?.. _____

General Ledger
8. What is the amount of FICA Taxes Payable—OASDI for the month of October?........ _____
9. What is the amount of Union Dues withheld for the employees for the month of
   October?.. _____

Name_____

Student Project Audit Test

NOVEMBER 6 PAYROLL: (As you complete your work, answer the following questions for the November 6 payroll.)

Payroll Report
  1. What is the current amount of FIT withheld for Joseph T. O'Neill? .... _____
  2. What is the total current gross pay for all employees? .... _____
  3. What is the total current amount of CIT withheld for all employees? .... _____
  4. What is the total current net pay for all employees? .... _____

Journal Entries Report
  5. What is the amount of the credit to FICA Taxes Payable—OASDI for employees? ...... _____
  6. What is the amount of the credit to FICA Taxes Payable—HI for employees? .... _____
  7. What is the amount of the debit to Payroll Taxes? .... _____

General Ledger
  8. What is the balance in the Cash (account number 11) account? .... _____
  9. What is the amount of Sales Salaries paid to date? .... _____

Name_____

Student Project Audit Test

NOVEMBER 13 PAYROLL: (As you complete your work, answer the following questions for the special November 13 payroll.)

Payroll Report
  1. What is the amount of FIT withheld for the year for Ruth V. Williams? .... _____
  2. What is Ruth V. Williams' current net pay? .... _____
  3. In what department did Ruth V. Williams work? .... _____

Journal Entries Report
  4. What is the amount of Ruth V. Williams' Group Insurance withheld? .... _____

General Ledger
  5. What is the total amount of Payroll Taxes (account number 56) to date? .... _____

Name_____

Student Project Audit Test

NOVEMBER 20 PAYROLL: (As you complete your work, answer the following questions for the November 20 payroll.)

Payroll Report

1. What is the amount of FIT withheld for the current pay period for Dewey W. Mann?   _____
2. What is the total current net pay for all employees?..   _____
3. What is the total current gross pay for all employees? ....   _____

Journal Entries Report

4. What is the November 16 credit to Cash for the deposit of FICA & FIT taxes?...........   _____
5. What is the amount of the debit to Payroll Taxes?..   _____
6. What is the amount of the debit to Plant Wages?..   _____

General Ledger

7. What is the balance of Employees SIT Payable?..   _____
8. What is the amount of Office Salaries paid to date?...   _____
9. What is the balance of Simple Contributions Payable? ....   _____

Name_____

Student Project Audit Test

DECEMBER 4 PAYROLL: (As you complete your work, answer the following questions for the December 4 payroll.)

Payroll Report

1. What is the current net pay for Joseph T. O'Neill? ....   _____
2. What is the current amount of OASDI withheld for Norman A. Ryan? ....   _____
3. What is the total current net pay for all employees?..   _____
4. What is the total current CIT withheld for all employees? ....   _____

Journal Entries Report

5. What is the amount of the debit to Administrative Salaries?..................................   _____
6. What is the amount of the credit to Employees SIT Payable?.................................   _____
7. What is the amount of the debit to Payroll Taxes?...   _____

General Ledger

8. What is the balance of SUTA Taxes Payable? ....   _____
9. What is the balance of Sales Salaries?..   _____

Name_____

Student Project Audit Test

DECEMBER 14 PAYROLL: (As you complete your work, answer the following questions for the December 14 payroll.)

Payroll Report
  1. What was Virginia A. Russell's social security number? .... _____
  2. What was the amount of net pay received by Virginia A. Russell's estate? .... _____

Journal Entries Report
  3. What is the amount of the debit to Office Salaries? .... _____

General Ledger
  4. What is the amount that was credited to Group Insurance Premiums Collected
     (account number 27) during this period? .... _____
  5. What is the amount paid for office salaries to date? .... _____

Name_____

Student Project Audit Test

DECEMBER 18 PAYROLL: (As you complete your work, answer the following questions for the December 18 payroll.)

Payroll Report
  1. What is the current amount of SIT withheld for Thomas J. Sokowski? .... _____
  2. What is the total current net pay for all employees? .... _____
  3. What is the total yearly gross pay for all employees? .... _____

Journal Entries Report
  4. What is the amount of the debit to Administrative Salaries? .... _____
  5. What is the amount of the debit to Payroll Taxes? .... _____

General Ledger
  6. What is the balance in the Cash account? .... _____
  7. What is the total amount of Plant Wages to date? .... _____
  8. What is the total amount of Payroll Taxes to date? .... _____

Name_____

Student Project Audit Test

OPTIONAL ACTIVITIES: (Use the General Journal Report dated 2/01/2017 to answer the following questions.)

Journal Entries Report

1. What is the amount of the deposit for Pennsylvania state income taxes withheld from the December 18 payroll?.. _____

2. What is the amount of Union Dues withheld during the month of December? .... _____

3. What is the amount of FICA Taxes Payable—OASDI deposited from the December payrolls?.. _____

4. What is the amount of the city of Philadelphia employees income tax deposited from the December payrolls? .... _____

5. What is the amount of FUTA Taxes Payable deposited for the quarter?....................... _____

6. What is the amount of SUTA Taxes Payable for the fourth quarter? .... _____

7. What is the amount of Employees FIT Taxes Payable deposited from the December payrolls?.. _____

The following tables were in effect during 2015.

TABLE OF ALLOWANCE VALUES

Payroll Period	One Withholding Allowance
Weekly	$ 76.90
Biweekly	153.80
Semimonthly	166.70
Monthly	333.30
Quarterly	1,000.00
Semiannually	2,000.00
Annually	4,000.00
Daily or miscellaneous (each day of the payroll period)	15.40

Percentage Method Tables for Income Tax Withholding

(For Wages Paid in 2015)

TABLE 1—WEEKLY Payroll Period

(a) SINGLE person (including head of household)—

If the amount of wages (after subtracting withholding allowances) is:		The amount of income tax to withhold is:	
Not over $44		$0	
Over—	But not over—		of excess over—
$44	—$222 . .	$0.00 plus 10%	—$44
$222	—$764 . .	$17.80 plus 15%	—$222
$764	—$1,789 . .	$99.10 plus 25%	—$764
$1,789	—$3,685 . .	$355.35 plus 28%	—$1,789
$3,685	—$7,958 . .	$886.23 plus 33%	—$3,685
$7,958	—$7,990 . .	$2,296.32 plus 35%	—$7,958
$7,990		$2,307.52 plus 39.6%	—$7,990

(b) MARRIED person—

If the amount of wages (after subtracting withholding allowances) is:		The amount of income tax to withhold is:	
Not over $165		$0	
Over—	But not over—		of excess over—
$165	—$520 . .	$0.00 plus 10%	—$165
$520	—$1,606 . .	$35.50 plus 15%	—$520
$1,606	—$3,073 . .	$198.40 plus 25%	—$1,606
$3,073	—$4,597 . .	$565.15 plus 28%	—$3,073
$4,597	—$8,079 . .	$991.87 plus 33%	—$4,597
$8,079	—$9,105 . .	$2,140.93 plus 35%	—$8,079
$9,105		$2,500.03 plus 39.6%	—$9,105

TABLE 2—BIWEEKLY Payroll Period

(a) SINGLE person (including head of household)—

If the amount of wages (after subtracting withholding allowances) is:		The amount of income tax to withhold is:	
Not over $88		$0	
Over—	But not over—		of excess over—
$88	—$443 . .	$0.00 plus 10%	—$88
$443	—$1,529 . .	$35.50 plus 15%	—$443
$1,529	—$3,579 . .	$198.40 plus 25%	—$1,529
$3,579	—$7,369 . .	$710.90 plus 28%	—$3,579
$7,369	—$15,915 . .	$1,772.10 plus 33%	—$7,369
$15,915	—$15,981 . .	$4,592.28 plus 35%	—$15,915
$15,981		$4,615.38 plus 39.6%	—$15,981

(b) MARRIED person—

If the amount of wages (after subtracting withholding allowances) is:		The amount of income tax to withhold is:	
Not over $331		$0	
Over—	But not over—		of excess over—
$331	—$1,040 . .	$0.00 plus 10%	—$331
$1,040	—$3,212 . .	$70.90 plus 15%	—$1,040
$3,212	—$6,146 . .	$396.70 plus 25%	—$3,212
$6,146	—$9,194 . .	$1,130.20 plus 28%	—$6,146
$9,194	—$16,158 . .	$1,983.64 plus 33%	—$9,194
$16,158	—$18,210 . .	$4,281.76 plus 35%	—$16,158
$18,210		$4,999.96 plus 39.6%	—$18,210

TABLE 3—SEMIMONTHLY Payroll Period

(a) SINGLE person (including head of household)—

If the amount of wages (after subtracting withholding allowances) is:		The amount of income tax to withhold is:	
Not over $96		$0	
Over—	But not over—		of excess over—
$96	—$480 . .	$0.00 plus 10%	—$96
$480	—$1,656 . .	$38.40 plus 15%	—$480
$1,656	—$3,877 . .	$214.80 plus 25%	—$1,656
$3,877	—$7,983 . .	$770.05 plus 28%	—$3,877
$7,983	—$17,242 . .	$1,919.73 plus 33%	—$7,983
$17,242	—$17,313 . .	$4,975.20 plus 35%	—$17,242
$17,313		$5,000.05 plus 39.6%	—$17,313

(b) MARRIED person—

If the amount of wages (after subtracting withholding allowances) is:		The amount of income tax to withhold is:	
Not over $358		$0	
Over—	But not over—		of excess over—
$358	—$1,127 . .	$0.00 plus 10%	—$358
$1,127	—$3,479 . .	$76.90 plus 15%	—$1,127
$3,479	—$6,658 . .	$429.70 plus 25%	—$3,479
$6,658	—$9,960 . .	$1,224.45 plus 28%	—$6,658
$9,960	—$17,504 . .	$2,149.01 plus 33%	—$9,960
$17,504	—$19,727 . .	$4,638.53 plus 35%	—$17,504
$19,727		$5,416.58 plus 39.6%	—$19,727

TABLE 4—MONTHLY Payroll Period

(a) SINGLE person (including head of household)—

If the amount of wages (after subtracting withholding allowances) is:		The amount of income tax to withhold is:	
Not over $192		$0	
Over—	But not over—		of excess over—
$192	—$960 . .	$0.00 plus 10%	—$192
$960	—$3,313 . .	$76.80 plus 15%	—$960
$3,313	—$7,754 . .	$429.75 plus 25%	—$3,313
$7,754	—$15,967 . .	$1,540.00 plus 28%	—$7,754
$15,967	—$34,483 . .	$3,839.64 plus 33%	—$15,967
$34,483	—$34,625 . .	$9,949.92 plus 35%	—$34,483
$34,625		$9,999.62 plus 39.6%	—$34,625

(b) MARRIED person—

If the amount of wages (after subtracting withholding allowances) is:		The amount of income tax to withhold is:	
Not over $717		$0	
Over—	But not over—		of excess over—
$717	—$2,254 . .	$0.00 plus 10%	—$717
$2,254	—$6,958 . .	$153.70 plus 15%	—$2,254
$6,958	—$13,317 . .	$859.30 plus 25%	—$6,958
$13,317	—$19,921 . .	$2,449.05 plus 28%	—$13,317
$19,921	—$35,008 . .	$4,298.17 plus 33%	—$19,921
$35,008	—$39,454 . .	$9,276.88 plus 35%	—$35,008
$39,454		$10,832.98 plus 39.6%	—$39,454

Percentage Method Tables for Income Tax Withholding (continued)

(For Wages Paid in 2015)

TABLE 5—QUARTERLY Payroll Period

(a) SINGLE person (including head of household)—

If the amount of wages (after subtracting withholding allowances) is: / The amount of income tax to withhold is:

Not over $575 . . . . $0

Over—	But not over—		of excess over—
$575	—$2,881	$0.00 plus 10%	—$575
$2,881	—$9,938	$230.60 plus 15%	—$2,881
$9,938	—$23,263	$1,289.15 plus 25%	—$9,938
$23,263	—$47,900	$4,620.40 plus 28%	—$23,263
$47,900	—$103,450	$11,518.76 plus 33%	—$47,900
$103,450	—$103,875	$29,850.26 plus 35%	—$103,450
$103,875		$29,999.01 plus 39.6%	—$103,875

(b) MARRIED person—

If the amount of wages (after subtracting withholding allowances) is: / The amount of income tax to withhold is:

Not over $2,150 . . . . $0

Over—	But not over—		of excess over—
$2,150	—$6,763	$0.00 plus 10%	—$2,150
$6,763	—$20,875	$461.30 plus 15%	—$6,763
$20,875	—$39,950	$2,578.10 plus 25%	—$20,875
$39,950	—$59,763	$7,346.85 plus 28%	—$39,950
$59,763	—$105,025	$12,894.49 plus 33%	—$59,763
$105,025	—$118,363	$27,830.95 plus 35%	—$105,025
$118,363		$32,499.25 plus 39.6%	—$118,363

TABLE 6—SEMIANNUAL Payroll Period

(a) SINGLE person (including head of household)—

If the amount of wages (after subtracting withholding allowances) is: / The amount of income tax to withhold is:

Not over $1,150 . . . . $0

Over—	But not over—		of excess over—
$1,150	—$5,763	$0.00 plus 10%	—$1,150
$5,763	—$19,875	$461.30 plus 15%	—$5,763
$19,875	—$46,525	$2,578.10 plus 25%	—$19,875
$46,525	—$95,800	$9,240.60 plus 28%	—$46,525
$95,800	—$206,900	$23,037.60 plus 33%	—$95,800
$206,900	—$207,750	$59,700.60 plus 35%	—$206,900
$207,750		$59,998.10 plus 39.6%	—$207,750

(b) MARRIED person—

If the amount of wages (after subtracting withholding allowances) is: / The amount of income tax to withhold is:

Not over $4,300 . . . . $0

Over—	But not over—		of excess over—
$4,300	—$13,525	$0.00 plus 10%	—$4,300
$13,525	—$41,750	$922.50 plus 15%	—$13,525
$41,750	—$79,900	$5,156.25 plus 25%	—$41,750
$79,900	—$119,525	$14,693.75 plus 28%	—$79,900
$119,525	—$210,050	$25,788.75 plus 33%	—$119,525
$210,050	—$236,725	$55,662.00 plus 35%	—$210,050
$236,725		$64,998.25 plus 39.6%	—$236,725

TABLE 7—ANNUAL Payroll Period

(a) SINGLE person (including head of household)—

If the amount of wages (after subtracting withholding allowances) is: / The amount of income tax to withhold is:

Not over $2,300 . . . . $0

Over—	But not over—		of excess over—
$2,300	—$11,525	$0.00 plus 10%	—$2,300
$11,525	—$39,750	$922.50 plus 15%	—$11,525
$39,750	—$93,050	$5,156.25 plus 25%	—$39,750
$93,050	—$191,600	$18,481.25 plus 28%	—$93,050
$191,600	—$413,800	$46,075.25 plus 33%	—$191,600
$413,800	—$415,500	$119,401.25 plus 35%	—$413,800
$415,500		$119,996.25 plus 39.6%	—$415,500

(b) MARRIED person—

If the amount of wages (after subtracting withholding allowances) is: / The amount of income tax to withhold is:

Not over $8,600 . . . . $0

Over—	But not over—		of excess over—
$8,600	—$27,050	$0.00 plus 10%	—$8,600
$27,050	—$83,500	$1,845.00 plus 15%	—$27,050
$83,500	—$159,800	$10,312.50 plus 25%	—$83,500
$159,800	—$239,050	$29,387.50 plus 28%	—$159,800
$239,050	—$420,100	$51,577.50 plus 33%	—$239,050
$420,100	—$473,450	$111,324.00 plus 35%	—$420,100
$473,450		$129,996.50 plus 39.6%	—$473,450

TABLE 8—DAILY or MISCELLANEOUS Payroll Period

(a) SINGLE person (including head of household)—

If the amount of wages (after subtracting withholding allowances) divided by the number of days in the payroll period is: / The amount of income tax to withhold per day is:

Not over $8.80 . . . . $0

Over—	But not over—		of excess over—
$8.80	—$44.30	$0.00 plus 10%	—$8.80
$44.30	—$152.90	$3.55 plus 15%	—$44.30
$152.90	—$357.90	$19.84 plus 25%	—$152.90
$357.90	—$736.90	$71.09 plus 28%	—$357.90
$736.90	—$1,591.50	$177.21 plus 33%	—$736.90
$1,591.50	—$1,598.10	$459.23 plus 35%	—$1,591.50
$1,598.10		$461.54 plus 39.6%	—$1,598.10

(b) MARRIED person—

If the amount of wages (after subtracting withholding allowances) divided by the number of days in the payroll period is: / The amount of income tax to withhold per day is:

Not over $33.10 . . . . $0

Over—	But not over—		of excess over—
$33.10	—$104.00	$0.00 plus 10%	—$33.10
$104.00	—$321.20	$7.09 plus 15%	—$104.00
$321.20	—$614.60	$39.67 plus 25%	—$321.20
$614.60	—$919.40	$113.02 plus 28%	—$614.60
$919.40	—$1,615.80	$198.36 plus 33%	—$919.40
$1,615.80	—$1,821.00	$428.17 plus 35%	—$1,615.80
$1,821.00		$499.99 plus 39.6%	—$1,821.00

WAGE BRACKET METHOD TABLES FOR INCOME TAX WITHHOLDING

SINGLE Persons—WEEKLY Payroll Period
(For Wages Paid through December 31, 2015)

| And the wages are— | | And the number of withholding allowances claimed is— | | | | | | | | | | |
At least	But less than	0	1	2	3	4	5	6	7	8	9	10
		The amount of income tax to be withheld is—										
$0	$55	$0	$0	$0	$0	$0	$0	$0	$0	$0	$0	$0
55	60	1	0	0	0	0	0	0	0	0	0	0
60	65	2	0	0	0	0	0	0	0	0	0	0
65	70	2	0	0	0	0	0	0	0	0	0	0
70	75	3	0	0	0	0	0	0	0	0	0	0
75	80	3	0	0	0	0	0	0	0	0	0	0
80	85	4	0	0	0	0	0	0	0	0	0	0
85	90	4	0	0	0	0	0	0	0	0	0	0
90	95	5	0	0	0	0	0	0	0	0	0	0
95	100	5	0	0	0	0	0	0	0	0	0	0
100	105	6	0	0	0	0	0	0	0	0	0	0
105	110	6	0	0	0	0	0	0	0	0	0	0
110	115	7	0	0	0	0	0	0	0	0	0	0
115	120	7	0	0	0	0	0	0	0	0	0	0
120	125	8	0	0	0	0	0	0	0	0	0	0
125	130	8	1	0	0	0	0	0	0	0	0	0
130	135	9	1	0	0	0	0	0	0	0	0	0
135	140	9	2	0	0	0	0	0	0	0	0	0
140	145	10	2	0	0	0	0	0	0	0	0	0
145	150	10	3	0	0	0	0	0	0	0	0	0
150	155	11	3	0	0	0	0	0	0	0	0	0
155	160	11	4	0	0	0	0	0	0	0	0	0
160	165	12	4	0	0	0	0	0	0	0	0	0
165	170	12	5	0	0	0	0	0	0	0	0	0
170	175	13	5	0	0	0	0	0	0	0	0	0
175	180	13	6	0	0	0	0	0	0	0	0	0
180	185	14	6	0	0	0	0	0	0	0	0	0
185	190	14	7	0	0	0	0	0	0	0	0	0
190	195	15	7	0	0	0	0	0	0	0	0	0
195	200	15	8	0	0	0	0	0	0	0	0	0
200	210	16	8	1	0	0	0	0	0	0	0	0
210	220	17	9	2	0	0	0	0	0	0	0	0
220	230	18	10	3	0	0	0	0	0	0	0	0
230	240	20	11	4	0	0	0	0	0	0	0	0
240	250	21	12	5	0	0	0	0	0	0	0	0
250	260	23	13	6	0	0	0	0	0	0	0	0
260	270	24	14	7	0	0	0	0	0	0	0	0
270	280	26	15	8	0	0	0	0	0	0	0	0
280	290	27	16	9	1	0	0	0	0	0	0	0
290	300	29	17	10	2	0	0	0	0	0	0	0
300	310	30	19	11	3	0	0	0	0	0	0	0
310	320	32	20	12	4	0	0	0	0	0	0	0
320	330	33	22	13	5	0	0	0	0	0	0	0
330	340	35	23	14	6	0	0	0	0	0	0	0
340	350	36	25	15	7	0	0	0	0	0	0	0
350	360	38	26	16	8	0	0	0	0	0	0	0
360	370	39	28	17	9	1	0	0	0	0	0	0
370	380	41	29	18	10	2	0	0	0	0	0	0
380	390	42	31	19	11	3	0	0	0	0	0	0
390	400	44	32	20	12	4	0	0	0	0	0	0
400	410	45	34	22	13	5	0	0	0	0	0	0
410	420	47	35	23	14	6	0	0	0	0	0	0
420	430	48	37	25	15	7	0	0	0	0	0	0
430	440	50	38	26	16	8	0	0	0	0	0	0
440	450	51	40	28	17	9	1	0	0	0	0	0
450	460	53	41	29	17	10	2	0	0	0	0	0
460	470	54	43	31	19	11	3	0	0	0	0	0
470	480	56	44	32	21	12	4	0	0	0	0	0
480	490	57	46	34	22	13	5	0	0	0	0	0
490	500	59	47	35	24	14	6	0	0	0	0	0
500	510	60	49	37	25	15	7	0	0	0	0	0
510	520	62	50	38	27	16	8	0	0	0	0	0
520	530	63	52	40	28	17	9	1	0	0	0	0
530	540	65	53	41	30	18	10	2	0	0	0	0
540	550	66	55	43	31	20	11	3	0	0	0	0
550	560	68	56	44	33	21	12	4	0	0	0	0
560	570	69	58	46	34	23	13	5	0	0	0	0
570	580	71	59	47	36	24	14	6	0	0	0	0
580	590	72	61	49	37	26	15	7	0	0	0	0
590	600	74	62	50	39	27	16	8	1	0	0	0
600	610	75	64	52	40	29	17	9	2	0	0	0
610	620	77	65	53	42	30	18	10	3	0	0	0
620	630	78	67	55	43	32	20	11	4	0	0	0
630	640	80	68	56	45	33	21	12	5	0	0	0
640	650	81	70	58	46	35	23	13	6	0	0	0
650	660	83	71	59	48	36	24	14	7	0	0	0
660	670	84	73	61	49	38	26	15	8	0	0	0
670	680	86	74	62	51	39	27	16	9	1	0	0
680	690	87	76	64	52	41	29	17	10	2	0	0
690	700	89	77	65	54	42	30	19	11	3	0	0
700	710	90	79	67	55	44	32	20	12	4	0	0
710	720	92	80	68	57	45	33	22	13	5	0	0
720	730	93	82	70	58	47	35	23	14	6	0	0
730	740	95	83	71	60	48	36	25	15	7	0	0
740	750	96	85	73	61	50	38	26	16	8	0	0
750	760	98	86	74	63	51	39	28	17	9	1	0
760	770	99	88	76	64	53	41	29	18	10	2	0
770	780	102	89	77	66	54	42	31	19	11	3	0
780	790	104	91	79	67	56	44	32	20	12	4	0
790	800	107	92	80	69	57	45	34	22	13	5	0
800	810	109	94	82	70	59	47	35	23	14	6	0
810	820	112	95	83	72	60	48	37	25	15	7	0
820	830	114	97	85	73	62	50	38	26	16	8	0
830	840	117	98	86	75	63	51	40	28	17	9	1
840	850	119	100	88	76	65	53	41	29	18	10	2
850	860	122	102	89	78	66	54	43	31	19	11	3
860	870	124	105	91	79	68	56	44	32	21	12	4
870	880	127	107	92	81	69	57	46	34	22	13	5
880	890	129	110	94	82	71	59	47	35	24	14	6
890	900	132	112	95	84	72	60	49	37	25	15	7
900	910	134	115	97	85	74	62	50	38	27	16	8
910	920	137	117	98	87	75	63	52	40	28	17	9
920	930	139	120	100	88	77	65	53	41	30	18	10
930	940	142	122	103	90	78	66	55	43	31	20	11
940	950	144	125	105	91	80	68	56	44	33	21	12
950	960	147	127	108	93	81	69	58	46	34	23	13
960	970	149	130	110	94	83	71	59	47	36	24	14
970	980	152	132	113	96	84	72	61	49	37	26	15
980	990	154	135	115	97	86	74	62	50	39	27	16
990	1,000	157	137	118	99	87	75	64	52	40	29	17
1,000	1,010	159	140	120	101	89	77	65	53	42	30	18
1,010	1,020	162	142	123	103	90	78	67	55	43	32	20
1,020	1,030	164	145	125	106	92	80	68	56	45	33	21
1,030	1,040	167	147	128	108	93	81	70	58	46	35	23
1,040	1,050	169	150	130	111	95	83	71	59	48	36	24
1,050	1,060	172	152	133	113	96	84	73	61	49	38	26
1,060	1,070	174	155	135	116	98	86	74	62	51	39	27
1,070	1,080	177	157	138	118	99	87	76	64	52	41	29
1,080	1,090	179	160	140	121	101	89	77	65	54	42	30
1,090	1,100	182	162	143	123	104	90	79	67	55	44	32
1,100	1,110	184	165	145	126	106	92	80	68	57	45	33
1,110	1,120	187	167	148	128	109	93	82	70	58	47	35
1,120	1,130	189	170	150	131	111	95	83	71	60	48	36
1,130	1,140	192	172	153	133	114	96	85	73	61	50	38
1,140	1,150	194	175	155	136	116	98	86	74	63	51	39
1,150	1,160	197	177	158	138	119	99	88	76	64	53	41
1,160	1,170	199	180	160	141	121	102	89	77	66	54	42
1,170	1,180	202	182	163	143	124	104	91	79	67	56	44
1,180	1,190	204	185	165	146	126	107	92	80	69	57	45
1,190	1,200	207	187	168	148	129	109	94	82	70	59	47
1,200	1,210	209	190	170	151	131	112	95	83	72	60	48
1,210	1,220	212	192	173	153	134	114	97	85	73	62	50
1,220	1,230	214	195	175	156	136	117	98	86	75	63	51
1,230	1,240	217	197	178	158	139	119	100	88	76	65	53
1,240	1,250	219	200	180	161	141	122	103	89	78	66	54

$1,250 and over   Use Table 1(a) for a **SINGLE person** on page 45. Also see the instructions on page 43.

WEEKLY SINGLE PERSON

WAGE BRACKET METHOD TABLES FOR INCOME TAX WITHHOLDING

MARRIED Persons—WEEKLY Payroll Period
(For Wages Paid through December 31, 2015)

And the wages are—		And the number of withholding allowances claimed is—										
At least	But less than	0	1	2	3	4	5	6	7	8	9	10
		The amount of income tax to be withheld is—										
$0	$170	$0	$0	$0	$0	$0	$0	$0	$0	$0	$0	$0
170	175	1	0	0	0	0	0	0	0	0	0	0
175	180	1	0	0	0	0	0	0	0	0	0	0
180	185	2	0	0	0	0	0	0	0	0	0	0
185	190	2	0	0	0	0	0	0	0	0	0	0
190	195	3	0	0	0	0	0	0	0	0	0	0
195	200	3	0	0	0	0	0	0	0	0	0	0
200	210	4	0	0	0	0	0	0	0	0	0	0
210	220	5	0	0	0	0	0	0	0	0	0	0
220	230	6	0	0	0	0	0	0	0	0	0	0
230	240	7	0	0	0	0	0	0	0	0	0	0
240	250	8	0	0	0	0	0	0	0	0	0	0
250	260	9	1	0	0	0	0	0	0	0	0	0
260	270	10	2	0	0	0	0	0	0	0	0	0
270	280	11	3	0	0	0	0	0	0	0	0	0
280	290	12	4	0	0	0	0	0	0	0	0	0
290	300	13	5	0	0	0	0	0	0	0	0	0
300	310	14	6	0	0	0	0	0	0	0	0	0
310	320	15	7	0	0	0	0	0	0	0	0	0
320	330	16	8	1	0	0	0	0	0	0	0	0
330	340	17	9	1	0	0	0	0	0	0	0	0
340	350	18	10	2	0	0	0	0	0	0	0	0
350	360	19	11	3	0	0	0	0	0	0	0	0
360	370	20	12	4	0	0	0	0	0	0	0	0
370	380	21	13	5	0	0	0	0	0	0	0	0
380	390	22	14	6	0	0	0	0	0	0	0	0
390	400	23	15	7	0	0	0	0	0	0	0	0
400	410	24	16	8	1	0	0	0	0	0	0	0
410	420	25	17	9	1	0	0	0	0	0	0	0
420	430	26	18	10	2	0	0	0	0	0	0	0
430	440	27	19	11	3	0	0	0	0	0	0	0
440	450	28	20	12	4	0	0	0	0	0	0	0
450	460	29	21	13	5	0	0	0	0	0	0	0
460	470	30	22	14	6	0	0	0	0	0	0	0
470	480	31	23	15	7	0	0	0	0	0	0	0
480	490	32	24	16	8	1	0	0	0	0	0	0
490	500	33	25	17	9	1	0	0	0	0	0	0
500	510	34	26	18	10	2	0	0	0	0	0	0
510	520	35	27	19	11	3	0	0	0	0	0	0
520	530	36	28	20	12	4	0	0	0	0	0	0
530	540	38	29	21	13	5	0	0	0	0	0	0
540	550	39	30	22	14	6	0	0	0	0	0	0
550	560	41	31	23	15	7	0	0	0	0	0	0
560	570	42	32	24	16	8	1	0	0	0	0	0
570	580	44	33	25	17	9	1	0	0	0	0	0
580	590	45	34	26	18	10	2	0	0	0	0	0
590	600	47	35	27	19	11	3	0	0	0	0	0
600	610	48	37	28	20	12	4	0	0	0	0	0
610	620	50	38	29	21	13	5	0	0	0	0	0
620	630	51	40	30	22	14	6	0	0	0	0	0
630	640	53	41	31	23	15	7	0	0	0	0	0
640	650	54	43	32	24	16	8	1	0	0	0	0
650	660	56	44	33	25	17	9	1	0	0	0	0
660	670	57	46	34	26	18	10	2	0	0	0	0
670	680	59	47	35	27	19	11	3	0	0	0	0
680	690	60	49	36	28	20	12	4	0	0	0	0
690	700	62	50	38	29	21	13	5	0	0	0	0
700	710	63	52	39	30	22	14	6	0	0	0	0
710	720	65	53	41	31	23	15	7	0	0	0	0
720	730	66	55	42	32	24	16	8	1	0	0	0
730	740	68	56	44	33	25	17	9	1	0	0	0
740	750	69	58	45	34	26	18	10	2	0	0	0
750	760	71	59	47	35	27	19	11	3	0	0	0
760	770	72	61	48	36	28	20	12	4	0	0	0
770	780	74	62	50	37	29	21	13	5	0	0	0
780	790	75	64	51	39	30	22	14	6	0	0	0
790	800	77	65	53	41	32	23	15	7	1	0	0

(WEEKLY MARRIED PERSONS)

MARRIED Persons—WEEKLY Payroll Period
(For Wages Paid through December 31, 2015)

And the wages are—		And the number of withholding allowances claimed is—										
At least	But less than	0	1	2	3	4	5	6	7	8	9	10
		The amount of income tax to be withheld is—										
$800	$810	$78	$67	$55	$44	$33	$26	$18	$10	$2	$0	$0
810	820	80	68	57	45	34	27	19	11	3	0	0
820	830	81	70	58	47	35	28	20	12	4	0	0
830	840	83	71	60	48	37	29	21	13	5	0	0
840	850	84	73	61	50	38	30	22	14	6	0	0
850	860	86	74	63	51	40	31	23	15	7	0	0
860	870	87	76	64	53	41	32	24	16	8	0	0
870	880	89	77	66	54	43	33	25	17	9	1	0
880	890	90	79	67	56	44	34	26	18	10	2	0
890	900	92	80	69	57	46	35	27	19	11	3	0
900	910	93	82	70	59	47	36	28	20	12	4	0
910	920	95	83	72	60	49	37	29	21	13	5	0
920	930	96	85	73	62	50	39	30	22	14	6	0
930	940	98	86	75	63	52	40	31	23	15	7	0
940	950	99	88	76	65	53	42	32	24	16	8	0
950	960	101	89	78	66	55	43	33	25	17	9	1
960	970	102	91	79	68	56	45	34	26	18	10	2
970	980	104	92	81	69	58	46	35	27	19	11	3
980	990	105	94	82	71	59	48	37	28	20	12	4
990	1,000	107	95	84	72	61	49	38	29	21	13	5
1,000	1,010	108	97	85	74	62	51	39	30	22	14	6
1,010	1,020	110	98	87	75	64	52	41	31	23	15	7
1,020	1,030	111	100	88	77	65	54	42	32	24	16	8
1,030	1,040	113	101	90	78	67	55	44	33	25	17	9
1,040	1,050	114	103	91	80	68	57	45	34	26	18	10
1,050	1,060	116	104	93	81	70	58	47	35	27	19	11
1,060	1,070	117	106	94	83	71	60	48	36	28	20	12
1,070	1,080	119	107	96	84	73	61	50	38	29	21	13
1,080	1,090	120	109	97	86	74	63	51	39	30	22	14
1,090	1,100	122	110	99	87	76	64	53	41	31	23	15
1,100	1,110	123	112	100	89	77	66	54	42	32	24	16
1,110	1,120	125	113	102	90	79	67	56	44	33	25	17
1,120	1,130	126	115	103	92	80	69	57	45	34	26	18
1,130	1,140	128	116	105	93	82	70	59	47	35	27	19
1,140	1,150	129	118	106	95	83	72	60	48	37	28	20
1,150	1,160	131	119	108	96	85	73	62	50	38	29	21
1,160	1,170	132	121	109	98	86	75	63	51	40	30	22
1,170	1,180	134	122	111	99	88	76	65	53	41	31	23
1,180	1,190	135	124	112	101	89	78	66	54	43	32	24
1,190	1,200	137	125	114	102	91	79	68	56	44	33	25
1,200	1,210	138	127	115	104	92	81	69	57	46	35	27
1,210	1,220	140	128	117	105	94	82	71	59	47	36	28
1,220	1,230	141	130	118	107	95	84	72	60	49	37	29
1,230	1,240	143	131	120	108	97	85	74	62	50	39	30
1,240	1,250	144	133	121	110	98	87	75	63	52	40	31
1,250	1,260	146	134	123	111	100	88	77	65	53	42	32
1,260	1,270	147	136	124	113	101	90	78	66	55	43	33
1,270	1,280	149	137	126	114	103	91	80	68	56	45	34
1,280	1,290	150	139	127	116	104	93	81	69	58	46	35
1,290	1,300	152	140	129	117	106	94	83	71	59	48	36
1,300	1,310	153	142	130	119	107	96	84	72	61	49	38
1,310	1,320	155	143	132	120	109	97	86	74	62	51	39
1,320	1,330	156	145	133	122	110	99	87	75	64	52	41
1,330	1,340	158	146	135	123	112	100	89	77	65	54	42
1,340	1,350	159	148	136	125	113	102	90	78	67	55	44
1,350	1,360	161	149	138	126	115	103	92	80	68	57	45
1,360	1,370	162	151	139	128	116	105	93	81	70	58	47
1,370	1,380	164	152	141	129	118	106	95	83	71	60	48
1,380	1,390	165	154	142	131	119	108	96	84	73	61	50
1,390	1,400	167	155	144	132	121	109	98	86	74	63	51
1,400	1,410	168	157	145	134	122	111	99	87	76	64	53
1,410	1,420	170	158	147	135	124	112	101	89	77	66	54
1,420	1,430	171	160	148	137	125	114	102	90	79	67	56
1,430	1,440	173	161	150	138	127	115	104	92	80	69	57
1,440	1,450	174	163	151	140	128	117	105	93	82	70	59
1,450	1,460	176	164	153	141	130	118	106	95	83	72	60
1,460	1,470	177	166	154	143	131	120	108	96	85	73	61
1,470	1,480	179	167	156	144	133	121	109	98	86	75	63
1,480	1,490	180	169	157	146	134	123	111	99	88	76	65

$1,490 and over   Use Table 1(b) for a **MARRIED person** on page 45. Also see the instructions on page 43.

WAGE BRACKET METHOD TABLES FOR INCOME TAX WITHHOLDING

SINGLE Persons—BIWEEKLY Payroll Period
(For Wages Paid through December 31, 2015)

| And the wages are— | | And the number of withholding allowances claimed is— | | | | | | | | | | |
At least	But less than	0	1	2	3	4	5	6	7	8	9	10
		The amount of income tax to be withheld is—										
$0	$105	$0	$0	$0	$0	$0	$0	$0	$0	$0	$0	$0
105	110	2	0	0	0	0	0	0	0	0	0	0
110	115	2	0	0	0	0	0	0	0	0	0	0
115	120	3	0	0	0	0	0	0	0	0	0	0
120	125	3	0	0	0	0	0	0	0	0	0	0
125	130	4	0	0	0	0	0	0	0	0	0	0
130	135	4	0	0	0	0	0	0	0	0	0	0
135	140	5	0	0	0	0	0	0	0	0	0	0
140	145	5	0	0	0	0	0	0	0	0	0	0
145	150	6	0	0	0	0	0	0	0	0	0	0
150	155	6	0	0	0	0	0	0	0	0	0	0
155	160	7	0	0	0	0	0	0	0	0	0	0
160	165	7	0	0	0	0	0	0	0	0	0	0
165	170	8	0	0	0	0	0	0	0	0	0	0
170	175	8	0	0	0	0	0	0	0	0	0	0
175	180	9	0	0	0	0	0	0	0	0	0	0
180	185	9	0	0	0	0	0	0	0	0	0	0
185	190	10	0	0	0	0	0	0	0	0	0	0
190	195	10	0	0	0	0	0	0	0	0	0	0
195	200	11	0	0	0	0	0	0	0	0	0	0
200	205	11	0	0	0	0	0	0	0	0	0	0
205	210	12	0	0	0	0	0	0	0	0	0	0
210	215	12	0	0	0	0	0	0	0	0	0	0
215	220	13	0	0	0	0	0	0	0	0	0	0
220	225	13	0	0	0	0	0	0	0	0	0	0
225	230	14	0	0	0	0	0	0	0	0	0	0
230	235	14	0	0	0	0	0	0	0	0	0	0
235	240	15	0	0	0	0	0	0	0	0	0	0
240	245	15	0	0	0	0	0	0	0	0	0	0
245	250	16	1	0	0	0	0	0	0	0	0	0
250	260	17	1	0	0	0	0	0	0	0	0	0
260	270	18	2	0	0	0	0	0	0	0	0	0
270	280	19	3	0	0	0	0	0	0	0	0	0
280	290	20	4	0	0	0	0	0	0	0	0	0
290	300	21	5	0	0	0	0	0	0	0	0	0
300	310	22	6	0	0	0	0	0	0	0	0	0
310	320	23	7	0	0	0	0	0	0	0	0	0
320	330	24	8	0	0	0	0	0	0	0	0	0
330	340	25	9	0	0	0	0	0	0	0	0	0
340	350	26	10	0	0	0	0	0	0	0	0	0
350	360	27	11	0	0	0	0	0	0	0	0	0
360	370	28	12	0	0	0	0	0	0	0	0	0
370	380	29	13	0	0	0	0	0	0	0	0	0
380	390	30	14	0	0	0	0	0	0	0	0	0
390	400	31	15	0	0	0	0	0	0	0	0	0
400	410	32	16	1	0	0	0	0	0	0	0	0
410	420	33	17	2	0	0	0	0	0	0	0	0
420	430	34	18	3	0	0	0	0	0	0	0	0
430	440	35	19	4	0	0	0	0	0	0	0	0
440	450	36	20	5	0	0	0	0	0	0	0	0
450	460	37	21	6	0	0	0	0	0	0	0	0
460	470	39	22	7	0	0	0	0	0	0	0	0
470	480	40	23	8	0	0	0	0	0	0	0	0
480	490	42	24	9	0	0	0	0	0	0	0	0
490	500	43	25	10	0	0	0	0	0	0	0	0
500	520	45	27	11	0	0	0	0	0	0	0	0
520	540	48	29	13	0	0	0	0	0	0	0	0
540	560	51	31	15	0	0	0	0	0	0	0	0
560	580	54	33	17	2	0	0	0	0	0	0	0
580	600	57	35	19	4	0	0	0	0	0	0	0
600	620	60	37	21	6	0	0	0	0	0	0	0
620	640	63	40	23	8	0	0	0	0	0	0	0
640	660	66	43	25	10	0	0	0	0	0	0	0
660	680	69	46	27	12	0	0	0	0	0	0	0
680	700	72	49	29	14	0	0	0	0	0	0	0
700	720	75	52	31	16	1	0	0	0	0	0	0
720	740	78	55	33	18	3	0	0	0	0	0	0
740	760	81	58	35	20	5	0	0	0	0	0	0
760	780	84	61	38	22	7	0	0	0	0	0	0
780	800	87	64	41	24	9	0	0	0	0	0	0

SINGLE Persons—BIWEEKLY Payroll Period
(For Wages Paid through December 31, 2015)

| And the wages are— | | And the number of withholding allowances claimed is— | | | | | | | | | | |
At least	But less than	0	1	2	3	4	5	6	7	8	9	10
		The amount of income tax to be withheld is—										
$800	$820	$90	$67	$44	$26	$11	$0	$0	$0	$0	$0	$0
820	840	93	70	47	28	13	0	0	0	0	0	0
840	860	96	73	50	30	15	0	0	0	0	0	0
860	880	99	76	53	32	17	1	0	0	0	0	0
880	900	102	79	56	34	19	3	0	0	0	0	0
900	920	105	82	59	36	21	5	0	0	0	0	0
920	940	108	85	62	39	23	7	0	0	0	0	0
940	960	111	88	65	42	25	9	0	0	0	0	0
960	980	114	91	68	45	27	11	0	0	0	0	0
980	1,000	117	94	71	48	29	13	0	0	0	0	0
1,000	1,020	120	97	74	51	31	15	0	0	0	0	0
1,020	1,040	123	100	77	54	33	17	2	0	0	0	0
1,040	1,060	126	103	80	57	35	19	4	0	0	0	0
1,060	1,080	129	106	83	60	37	21	6	0	0	0	0
1,080	1,100	132	109	86	63	40	23	8	0	0	0	0
1,100	1,120	135	112	89	66	43	25	10	0	0	0	0
1,120	1,140	138	115	92	69	46	27	12	0	0	0	0
1,140	1,160	141	118	95	72	49	29	14	0	0	0	0
1,160	1,180	144	121	98	75	52	31	16	1	0	0	0
1,180	1,200	147	124	101	78	55	33	18	3	0	0	0
1,200	1,220	150	127	104	81	58	35	20	5	0	0	0
1,220	1,240	153	130	107	84	61	38	22	7	0	0	0
1,240	1,260	156	133	110	87	64	41	24	9	0	0	0
1,260	1,280	159	136	113	90	67	44	26	11	0	0	0
1,280	1,300	162	139	116	93	70	47	28	13	0	0	0
1,300	1,320	165	142	119	96	73	50	30	15	0	0	0
1,320	1,340	168	145	122	99	76	53	32	17	1	0	0
1,340	1,360	171	148	125	102	79	56	34	19	3	0	0
1,360	1,380	174	151	128	105	82	59	36	21	5	0	0
1,380	1,400	177	154	131	108	85	62	39	23	7	0	0
1,400	1,420	180	157	134	111	88	65	42	25	9	0	0
1,420	1,440	183	160	137	114	91	68	45	27	11	0	0
1,440	1,460	186	163	140	117	94	71	48	29	13	0	0
1,460	1,480	189	166	143	120	97	74	51	31	15	0	0
1,480	1,500	192	169	146	123	100	77	54	33	17	2	0
1,500	1,520	195	172	149	126	103	80	57	35	19	4	0
1,520	1,540	199	175	152	129	106	83	60	37	21	6	0
1,540	1,560	204	178	155	132	109	86	63	40	23	8	0
1,560	1,580	209	181	158	135	112	89	66	43	25	10	0
1,580	1,600	214	184	161	138	115	92	69	46	27	12	0
1,600	1,620	219	187	164	141	118	95	72	49	29	14	0
1,620	1,640	224	190	167	144	121	98	75	52	31	16	0
1,640	1,660	229	193	170	147	124	101	78	55	33	18	2
1,660	1,680	234	196	173	150	127	104	81	58	35	20	4
1,680	1,700	239	200	176	153	130	107	84	61	38	22	6
1,700	1,720	244	205	179	156	133	110	87	64	41	24	8
1,720	1,740	249	210	182	159	136	113	90	67	44	26	10
1,740	1,760	254	215	185	162	139	116	93	70	47	28	12
1,760	1,780	259	220	188	165	142	119	96	73	50	30	14
1,780	1,800	264	225	191	168	145	122	99	76	53	32	16
1,800	1,820	269	230	194	171	148	125	102	79	56	34	18
1,820	1,840	274	235	197	174	151	128	105	82	59	36	20
1,840	1,860	279	240	202	177	154	131	108	85	62	39	22
1,860	1,880	284	245	207	180	157	134	111	88	65	42	24
1,880	1,900	289	250	212	183	160	137	114	91	68	45	26
1,900	1,920	294	255	217	186	163	140	117	94	71	48	28
1,920	1,940	299	260	222	189	166	143	120	97	74	51	30
1,940	1,960	304	265	227	192	169	146	123	100	77	54	32
1,960	1,980	309	270	232	195	172	149	126	103	80	57	34
1,980	2,000	314	275	237	198	175	152	129	106	83	60	37
2,000	2,020	319	280	242	203	178	155	132	109	86	63	40
2,020	2,040	324	285	247	208	181	158	135	112	89	66	43
2,040	2,060	329	290	252	213	184	161	138	115	92	69	46
2,060	2,080	334	295	257	218	187	164	141	118	95	72	49
2,080	2,100	339	300	262	223	190	167	144	121	98	75	52

$2,100 and over — Use Table 2(a) for a **SINGLE person** on page 45. Also see the instructions on page 43.

BIWEEKLY
SINGLE PERSONS

WAGE BRACKET METHOD TABLES FOR INCOME TAX WITHHOLDING

MARRIED Persons—BIWEEKLY Payroll Period
(For Wages Paid through December 31, 2015)

And the wages are—		And the number of withholding allowances claimed is—										
At least	But less than	0	1	2	3	4	5	6	7	8	9	10
		The amount of income tax to be withheld is—										
$0	340	$0	$0	$0	$0	$0	$0	$0	$0	$0	$0	$0
340	350	1	0	0	0	0	0	0	0	0	0	0
350	360	2	0	0	0	0	0	0	0	0	0	0
360	370	3	0	0	0	0	0	0	0	0	0	0
370	380	4	0	0	0	0	0	0	0	0	0	0
380	390	5	0	0	0	0	0	0	0	0	0	0
390	400	6	0	0	0	0	0	0	0	0	0	0
400	410	7	0	0	0	0	0	0	0	0	0	0
410	420	8	0	0	0	0	0	0	0	0	0	0
420	430	9	0	0	0	0	0	0	0	0	0	0
430	440	10	0	0	0	0	0	0	0	0	0	0
440	450	11	0	0	0	0	0	0	0	0	0	0
450	460	12	0	0	0	0	0	0	0	0	0	0
460	470	13	0	0	0	0	0	0	0	0	0	0
470	480	14	0	0	0	0	0	0	0	0	0	0
480	490	15	0	0	0	0	0	0	0	0	0	0
490	500	16	1	0	0	0	0	0	0	0	0	0
500	520	18	3	0	0	0	0	0	0	0	0	0
520	540	20	5	0	0	0	0	0	0	0	0	0
540	560	22	7	0	0	0	0	0	0	0	0	0
560	580	24	9	0	0	0	0	0	0	0	0	0
580	600	26	11	0	0	0	0	0	0	0	0	0
600	620	28	13	0	0	0	0	0	0	0	0	0
620	640	30	15	0	0	0	0	0	0	0	0	0
640	660	32	17	1	0	0	0	0	0	0	0	0
660	680	34	19	3	0	0	0	0	0	0	0	0
680	700	36	21	5	0	0	0	0	0	0	0	0
700	720	38	23	7	0	0	0	0	0	0	0	0
720	740	40	25	9	0	0	0	0	0	0	0	0
740	760	42	27	11	0	0	0	0	0	0	0	0
760	780	44	29	13	0	0	0	0	0	0	0	0
780	800	46	31	15	0	0	0	0	0	0	0	0
800	820	48	33	17	2	0	0	0	0	0	0	0
820	840	50	35	19	4	0	0	0	0	0	0	0
840	860	52	37	21	6	0	0	0	0	0	0	0
860	880	54	39	23	8	0	0	0	0	0	0	0
880	900	56	41	25	10	0	0	0	0	0	0	0
900	920	58	43	27	12	0	0	0	0	0	0	0
920	940	60	45	29	14	0	0	0	0	0	0	0
940	960	62	47	31	16	0	0	0	0	0	0	0
960	980	64	49	33	18	2	0	0	0	0	0	0
980	1,000	66	51	35	20	4	0	0	0	0	0	0
1,000	1,020	68	53	37	22	6	0	0	0	0	0	0
1,020	1,040	70	55	39	24	8	0	0	0	0	0	0
1,040	1,060	72	57	41	26	10	0	0	0	0	0	0
1,060	1,080	75	59	43	28	12	0	0	0	0	0	0
1,080	1,100	78	61	45	30	14	0	0	0	0	0	0
1,100	1,120	81	63	47	32	16	1	0	0	0	0	0
1,120	1,140	84	65	49	34	18	3	0	0	0	0	0
1,140	1,160	87	67	51	36	20	5	0	0	0	0	0
1,160	1,180	90	69	53	38	22	7	0	0	0	0	0
1,180	1,200	93	71	55	40	24	9	0	0	0	0	0
1,200	1,220	96	73	57	42	26	11	0	0	0	0	0
1,220	1,240	99	76	59	44	28	13	0	0	0	0	0
1,240	1,260	102	79	61	46	30	15	0	0	0	0	0
1,260	1,280	105	82	63	48	32	17	2	0	0	0	0
1,280	1,300	108	85	65	50	34	19	4	0	0	0	0
1,300	1,320	111	88	67	52	36	21	6	0	0	0	0
1,320	1,340	114	91	69	54	38	23	8	0	0	0	0
1,340	1,360	117	94	71	56	40	25	10	0	0	0	0
1,360	1,380	120	97	74	58	42	27	12	0	0	0	0
1,380	1,400	123	100	77	60	44	29	14	0	0	0	0
1,400	1,420	126	103	80	62	46	31	16	0	0	0	0
1,420	1,440	129	106	83	64	48	33	18	2	0	0	0
1,440	1,460	132	109	86	66	50	35	20	4	0	0	0
1,460	1,480	135	112	89	68	52	37	22	6	0	0	0
1,480	1,500	138	115	92	70	54	39	24	8	0	0	0

BIWEEKLY MARRIED PERSONS

MARRIED Persons—BIWEEKLY Payroll Period
(For Wages Paid through December 31, 2015)

And the wages are—		And the number of withholding allowances claimed is—										
At least	But less than	0	1	2	3	4	5	6	7	8	9	10
		The amount of income tax to be withheld is—										
$1,500	$1,520	$141	$118	$95	$72	$56	$41	$26	$10	$0	$0	$0
1,520	1,540	144	121	98	75	58	43	28	12	0	0	0
1,540	1,560	147	124	101	78	60	45	30	14	0	0	0
1,560	1,580	150	127	104	81	62	47	32	16	1	0	0
1,580	1,600	153	130	107	84	64	49	34	18	3	0	0
1,600	1,620	156	133	110	87	66	51	36	20	5	0	0
1,620	1,640	159	136	113	90	68	53	38	22	7	1	0
1,640	1,660	162	139	116	93	70	55	40	24	9	3	0
1,660	1,680	165	142	119	96	73	57	42	26	11	5	0
1,680	1,700	168	145	122	99	76	59	44	28	13	7	0
1,700	1,720	171	148	125	102	79	61	46	30	15	9	0
1,720	1,740	174	151	128	105	82	63	48	32	17	11	1
1,740	1,760	177	154	131	108	85	65	50	34	19	13	3
1,760	1,780	180	157	134	111	88	67	52	36	21	15	5
1,780	1,800	183	160	137	114	91	69	54	38	23	17	7
1,800	1,820	186	163	140	117	94	71	56	40	25	19	9
1,820	1,840	189	166	143	120	97	74	58	42	27	21	11
1,840	1,860	192	169	146	123	100	77	60	44	29	23	13
1,860	1,880	195	172	149	126	103	80	62	46	31	25	15
1,880	1,900	198	175	152	129	106	83	64	48	33	27	17
1,900	1,920	201	178	155	132	109	86	66	50	35	29	19
1,920	1,940	204	181	158	135	112	89	68	52	37	31	21
1,940	1,960	207	184	161	138	115	92	70	54	39	33	23
1,960	1,980	210	187	164	141	118	95	72	56	41	35	25
1,980	2,000	213	190	167	144	121	98	75	58	43	37	27
2,000	2,020	216	193	170	147	124	101	78	60	45	39	29
2,020	2,040	219	196	173	150	127	104	81	62	47	41	31
2,040	2,060	222	199	176	153	130	107	84	64	49	43	33
2,060	2,080	225	202	179	156	133	110	87	66	51	45	35
2,080	2,100	228	205	182	159	136	113	90	68	53	47	37
2,100	2,120	231	208	185	162	139	116	93	70	55	49	39
2,120	2,140	234	211	188	165	142	119	96	73	57	51	41
2,140	2,160	237	214	191	168	145	122	99	76	59	53	43
2,160	2,180	240	217	194	171	148	125	102	79	61	55	45
2,180	2,200	243	220	197	174	151	128	105	82	63	57	47
2,200	2,220	246	223	200	177	154	131	108	85	65	59	49
2,220	2,240	249	226	203	180	157	134	111	88	67	61	51
2,240	2,260	252	229	206	183	160	137	114	91	69	63	53
2,260	2,280	255	232	209	186	163	140	117	94	71	65	55
2,280	2,300	258	235	212	189	166	143	120	97	74	67	57
2,300	2,320	261	238	215	192	169	146	123	100	77	69	59
2,320	2,340	264	241	218	195	172	149	126	103	80	71	61
2,340	2,360	267	244	221	198	175	152	129	106	83	73	63
2,360	2,380	270	247	224	201	178	155	132	109	86	75	65
2,380	2,400	273	250	227	204	181	158	135	112	89	77	67
2,400	2,420	276	253	230	207	184	161	138	115	92	79	69
2,420	2,440	279	256	233	210	187	164	141	118	95	81	71
2,440	2,460	282	259	236	213	190	167	144	121	98	83	73
2,460	2,480	285	262	239	216	193	170	147	124	101	85	75
2,480	2,500	288	265	242	219	196	173	150	127	104	87	77
2,500	2,520	291	268	245	222	199	176	153	130	107	89	79
2,520	2,540	294	271	248	225	202	179	156	133	110	91	81
2,540	2,560	297	274	251	228	205	182	159	136	113	93	83
2,560	2,580	300	277	254	231	208	185	162	139	116	95	85
2,580	2,600	303	280	257	234	211	188	165	142	119	97	87
2,600	2,620	306	283	260	237	214	191	168	145	122	99	89
2,620	2,640	309	286	263	240	217	194	171	148	125	102	91
2,640	2,660	312	289	266	243	220	197	174	151	128	105	93
2,660	2,680	315	292	269	246	223	200	177	154	131	108	95
2,680	2,700	318	295	272	249	226	203	180	157	134	111	97
2,700	2,720	321	298	275	252	229	206	183	160	137	114	99
2,720	2,740	324	301	278	255	232	209	186	163	140	117	102
2,740	2,760	327	304	281	258	235	212	189	166	143	120	103
2,760	2,780	330	307	284	261	238	215	192	169	146	123	106
2,780	2,800	333	310	287	264	241	218	195	172	149	126	109
2,800	2,820	336	313	290	267	244	221	198	175	152	129	112
2,820	2,840	339	316	293	270	247	224	201	178	155	132	115
2,840	2,860	342	319	296	273	250	227	204	181	158	135	118
2,860	2,880	345	322	299	276	253	230	207	184	161	138	121

$2,880 and over

Use Table 2(b) for a **MARRIED person** on page 45. Also see the instructions on page 43.

WAGE BRACKET METHOD TABLES FOR INCOME TAX WITHHOLDING

SINGLE Persons—SEMIMONTHLY Payroll Period
(For Wages Paid through December 31, 2015)

SEMIMONTHLY SINGLE PERSONS

| And the wages are— | | And the number of withholding allowances claimed is— | | | | | | | | | | |
At least	But less than	0	1	2	3	4	5	6	7	8	9	10
					The amount of income tax to be withheld is—							
$0	$115	$0	$0	$0	$0	$0	$0	$0	$0	$0	$0	$0
115	120	2	0	0	0	0	0	0	0	0	0	0
120	125	3	0	0	0	0	0	0	0	0	0	0
125	130	3	0	0	0	0	0	0	0	0	0	0
130	135	4	0	0	0	0	0	0	0	0	0	0
135	140	4	0	0	0	0	0	0	0	0	0	0
140	145	5	0	0	0	0	0	0	0	0	0	0
145	150	5	0	0	0	0	0	0	0	0	0	0
150	155	6	0	0	0	0	0	0	0	0	0	0
155	160	6	0	0	0	0	0	0	0	0	0	0
160	165	7	0	0	0	0	0	0	0	0	0	0
165	170	7	0	0	0	0	0	0	0	0	0	0
170	175	8	0	0	0	0	0	0	0	0	0	0
175	180	8	0	0	0	0	0	0	0	0	0	0
180	185	9	0	0	0	0	0	0	0	0	0	0
185	190	9	0	0	0	0	0	0	0	0	0	0
190	195	10	0	0	0	0	0	0	0	0	0	0
195	200	10	0	0	0	0	0	0	0	0	0	0
200	205	11	0	0	0	0	0	0	0	0	0	0
205	210	11	0	0	0	0	0	0	0	0	0	0
210	215	12	0	0	0	0	0	0	0	0	0	0
215	220	12	0	0	0	0	0	0	0	0	0	0
220	225	13	0	0	0	0	0	0	0	0	0	0
225	230	13	0	0	0	0	0	0	0	0	0	0
230	235	14	0	0	0	0	0	0	0	0	0	0
235	240	14	0	0	0	0	0	0	0	0	0	0
240	245	15	0	0	0	0	0	0	0	0	0	0
245	250	15	0	0	0	0	0	0	0	0	0	0
250	260	16	0	0	0	0	0	0	0	0	0	0
260	270	17	0	0	0	0	0	0	0	0	0	0
270	280	18	1	0	0	0	0	0	0	0	0	0
280	290	19	2	0	0	0	0	0	0	0	0	0
290	300	20	3	0	0	0	0	0	0	0	0	0
300	310	21	4	0	0	0	0	0	0	0	0	0
310	320	22	5	0	0	0	0	0	0	0	0	0
320	330	23	6	0	0	0	0	0	0	0	0	0
330	340	24	7	0	0	0	0	0	0	0	0	0
340	350	25	8	0	0	0	0	0	0	0	0	0
350	360	26	9	0	0	0	0	0	0	0	0	0
360	370	27	10	0	0	0	0	0	0	0	0	0
370	380	28	11	0	0	0	0	0	0	0	0	0
380	390	29	12	0	0	0	0	0	0	0	0	0
390	400	30	13	0	0	0	0	0	0	0	0	0
400	410	31	14	0	0	0	0	0	0	0	0	0
410	420	32	15	0	0	0	0	0	0	0	0	0
420	430	33	16	0	0	0	0	0	0	0	0	0
430	440	34	17	1	0	0	0	0	0	0	0	0
440	450	35	18	2	0	0	0	0	0	0	0	0
450	460	36	19	3	0	0	0	0	0	0	0	0
460	470	37	20	4	0	0	0	0	0	0	0	0
470	480	38	21	5	0	0	0	0	0	0	0	0
480	490	39	22	6	0	0	0	0	0	0	0	0
490	500	41	23	7	0	0	0	0	0	0	0	0
500	520	43	25	8	0	0	0	0	0	0	0	0
520	540	46	27	10	0	0	0	0	0	0	0	0
540	560	49	29	12	0	0	0	0	0	0	0	0
560	580	52	31	14	0	0	0	0	0	0	0	0
580	600	55	33	16	0	0	0	0	0	0	0	0
600	620	58	35	18	1	0	0	0	0	0	0	0
620	640	61	37	20	3	0	0	0	0	0	0	0
640	660	64	39	22	5	0	0	0	0	0	0	0
660	680	67	42	24	7	0	0	0	0	0	0	0
680	700	70	45	26	9	0	0	0	0	0	0	0
700	720	73	48	28	11	0	0	0	0	0	0	0
720	740	76	51	30	13	0	0	0	0	0	0	0
740	760	79	54	32	15	0	0	0	0	0	0	0
760	780	82	57	34	17	1	0	0	0	0	0	0
780	800	85	60	36	19	3	0	0	0	0	0	0

SINGLE Persons—SEMIMONTHLY Payroll Period
(For Wages Paid through December 31, 2015)

| And the wages are— | | And the number of withholding allowances claimed is— | | | | | | | | | | |
At least	But less than	0	1	2	3	4	5	6	7	8	9	10
					The amount of income tax to be withheld is—							
$800	$820	$88	$63	$38	$21	$5	$0	$0	$0	$0	$0	$0
820	840	91	66	41	23	7	0	0	0	0	0	0
840	860	94	69	44	25	9	0	0	0	0	0	0
860	880	97	72	47	27	11	0	0	0	0	0	0
880	900	100	75	50	29	13	0	0	0	0	0	0
900	920	103	78	53	31	15	0	0	0	0	0	0
920	940	106	81	56	33	17	0	0	0	0	0	0
940	960	109	84	59	35	19	2	0	0	0	0	0
960	980	112	87	62	37	21	4	0	0	0	0	0
980	1,000	115	90	65	40	23	6	0	0	0	0	0
1,000	1,020	118	93	68	43	25	8	0	0	0	0	0
1,020	1,040	121	96	71	46	27	10	0	0	0	0	0
1,040	1,060	124	99	74	49	29	12	0	0	0	0	0
1,060	1,080	127	102	77	52	31	14	0	0	0	0	0
1,080	1,100	130	105	80	55	33	16	0	0	0	0	0
1,100	1,120	133	108	83	58	35	18	1	0	0	0	0
1,120	1,140	136	111	86	61	37	20	3	0	0	0	0
1,140	1,160	139	114	89	64	39	22	5	0	0	0	0
1,160	1,180	142	117	92	67	42	24	7	0	0	0	0
1,180	1,200	145	120	95	70	45	26	9	0	0	0	0
1,200	1,220	148	123	98	73	48	28	11	0	0	0	0
1,220	1,240	151	126	101	76	51	30	13	0	0	0	0
1,240	1,260	154	129	104	79	54	32	15	0	0	0	0
1,260	1,280	157	132	107	82	57	34	17	1	0	0	0
1,280	1,300	160	135	110	85	60	36	19	3	0	0	0
1,300	1,320	163	138	113	88	63	38	21	5	0	0	0
1,320	1,340	166	141	116	91	66	41	23	7	0	0	0
1,340	1,360	169	144	119	94	69	44	25	9	0	0	0
1,360	1,380	172	147	122	97	72	47	27	11	0	0	0
1,380	1,400	175	150	125	100	75	50	29	13	0	0	0
1,400	1,420	178	153	128	103	78	53	31	15	0	0	0
1,420	1,440	181	156	131	106	81	56	33	17	0	0	0
1,440	1,460	184	159	134	109	84	59	35	19	2	0	0
1,460	1,480	187	162	137	112	87	62	37	21	4	0	0
1,480	1,500	190	165	140	115	90	65	40	23	6	0	0
1,500	1,520	193	168	143	118	93	68	43	25	8	0	0
1,520	1,540	196	171	146	121	96	71	46	27	10	0	0
1,540	1,560	199	174	149	124	99	74	49	29	12	0	0
1,560	1,580	202	177	152	127	102	77	52	31	14	0	0
1,580	1,600	205	180	155	130	105	80	55	33	16	0	0
1,600	1,620	208	183	158	133	108	83	58	35	18	1	0
1,620	1,640	211	186	161	136	111	86	61	37	20	3	0
1,640	1,660	214	189	164	139	114	89	64	39	22	5	0
1,660	1,680	218	192	167	142	117	92	67	42	24	7	0
1,680	1,700	223	195	170	145	120	95	70	45	26	9	0
1,700	1,720	228	198	173	148	123	98	73	48	28	11	0
1,720	1,740	233	201	176	151	126	101	76	51	30	13	0
1,740	1,760	238	204	179	154	129	104	79	54	32	15	0
1,760	1,780	243	207	182	157	132	107	82	57	34	17	1
1,780	1,800	248	210	185	160	135	110	85	60	36	19	3
1,800	1,820	253	213	188	163	138	113	88	63	38	21	5
1,820	1,840	258	217	191	166	141	116	91	66	41	23	7
1,840	1,860	263	222	194	169	144	119	94	69	44	25	9
1,860	1,880	268	227	197	172	147	122	97	72	47	27	11
1,880	1,900	273	232	200	175	150	125	100	75	50	29	13
1,900	1,920	278	237	203	178	153	128	103	78	53	31	15
1,920	1,940	283	242	206	181	156	131	106	81	56	33	17
1,940	1,960	288	247	209	184	159	134	109	84	59	35	19
1,960	1,980	293	252	212	187	162	137	112	87	62	37	21
1,980	2,000	298	257	215	190	165	140	115	90	65	40	23
2,000	2,020	303	262	220	193	168	143	118	93	68	43	25
2,020	2,040	308	267	225	196	171	146	121	96	71	46	27
2,040	2,060	313	272	230	199	174	149	124	99	74	49	29
2,060	2,080	318	277	235	202	177	152	127	102	77	52	31
2,080	2,100	323	282	240	205	180	155	130	105	80	55	33
2,100	2,120	328	287	245	208	183	158	133	108	83	58	35
2,120	2,140	333	292	250	211	186	161	136	111	86	61	37

$2,140 and over   Use Table 3(a) for a **SINGLE person** on page 43. Also see the instructions on page 45.

WAGE BRACKET METHOD TABLES FOR INCOME TAX WITHHOLDING

MARRIED Persons—SEMIMONTHLY Payroll Period
(For Wages Paid through December 31, 2015)

And the wages are—		And the number of withholding allowances claimed is—										
At least	But less than	0	1	2	3	4	5	6	7	8	9	10
		The amount of income tax to be withheld is—										
$0	360	$0	$0	$0	$0	$0	$0	$0	$0	$0	$0	$0
360	370	1	0	0	0	0	0	0	0	0	0	0
370	380	2	0	0	0	0	0	0	0	0	0	0
380	390	3	0	0	0	0	0	0	0	0	0	0
390	400	4	0	0	0	0	0	0	0	0	0	0
400	410	5	0	0	0	0	0	0	0	0	0	0
410	420	6	0	0	0	0	0	0	0	0	0	0
420	430	7	0	0	0	0	0	0	0	0	0	0
430	440	8	0	0	0	0	0	0	0	0	0	0
440	450	9	0	0	0	0	0	0	0	0	0	0
450	460	10	0	0	0	0	0	0	0	0	0	0
460	470	11	0	0	0	0	0	0	0	0	0	0
470	480	12	0	0	0	0	0	0	0	0	0	0
480	490	13	0	0	0	0	0	0	0	0	0	0
490	500	14	0	0	0	0	0	0	0	0	0	0
500	520	15	0	0	0	0	0	0	0	0	0	0
520	540	17	1	0	0	0	0	0	0	0	0	0
540	560	19	3	0	0	0	0	0	0	0	0	0
560	580	21	5	0	0	0	0	0	0	0	0	0
580	600	23	7	0	0	0	0	0	0	0	0	0
600	620	25	9	0	0	0	0	0	0	0	0	0
620	640	27	11	0	0	0	0	0	0	0	0	0
640	660	29	13	0	0	0	0	0	0	0	0	0
660	680	31	15	0	0	0	0	0	0	0	0	0
680	700	33	17	0	0	0	0	0	0	0	0	0
700	720	35	19	2	0	0	0	0	0	0	0	0
720	740	37	21	4	0	0	0	0	0	0	0	0
740	760	39	23	6	0	0	0	0	0	0	0	0
760	780	41	25	8	0	0	0	0	0	0	0	0
780	800	43	27	10	0	0	0	0	0	0	0	0
800	820	45	29	12	0	0	0	0	0	0	0	0
820	840	47	31	14	0	0	0	0	0	0	0	0
840	860	49	33	16	0	0	0	0	0	0	0	0
860	880	51	35	18	1	0	0	0	0	0	0	0
880	900	53	37	20	3	0	0	0	0	0	0	0
900	920	55	39	22	5	0	0	0	0	0	0	0
920	940	57	41	24	7	0	0	0	0	0	0	0
940	960	59	43	26	9	0	0	0	0	0	0	0
960	980	61	45	28	11	0	0	0	0	0	0	0
980	1,000	63	47	30	13	0	0	0	0	0	0	0
1,000	1,020	65	49	32	15	0	0	0	0	0	0	0
1,020	1,040	67	51	34	17	1	0	0	0	0	0	0
1,040	1,060	69	53	36	19	3	0	0	0	0	0	0
1,060	1,080	71	55	38	21	5	0	0	0	0	0	0
1,080	1,100	73	57	40	23	7	0	0	0	0	0	0
1,100	1,120	75	59	42	25	9	0	0	0	0	0	0
1,120	1,140	77	61	44	27	11	0	0	0	0	0	0
1,140	1,160	80	63	46	29	13	0	0	0	0	0	0
1,160	1,180	83	65	48	31	15	0	0	0	0	0	0
1,180	1,200	86	67	50	33	17	0	0	0	0	0	0
1,200	1,220	89	69	52	35	19	2	0	0	0	0	0
1,220	1,240	92	71	54	37	21	4	0	0	0	0	0
1,240	1,260	95	73	56	39	23	6	0	0	0	0	0
1,260	1,280	98	75	58	41	25	8	0	0	0	0	0
1,280	1,300	101	77	60	43	27	10	0	0	0	0	0
1,300	1,320	104	79	62	45	29	12	0	0	0	0	0
1,320	1,340	107	82	64	47	31	14	0	0	0	0	0
1,340	1,360	110	85	66	49	33	16	0	0	0	0	0
1,360	1,380	113	88	68	51	35	18	1	0	0	0	0
1,380	1,400	116	91	70	53	37	20	3	0	0	0	0
1,400	1,420	119	94	72	55	39	22	5	0	0	0	0
1,420	1,440	122	97	74	57	41	24	7	0	0	0	0
1,440	1,460	125	100	76	59	43	26	9	0	0	0	0
1,460	1,480	128	103	78	61	45	28	11	0	0	0	0
1,480	1,500	131	106	81	63	47	30	13	0	0	0	0
1,500	1,520	134	109	84	65	49	32	15	0	0	0	0
1,520	1,540	137	112	87	67	51	34	17	1	0	0	0
1,540	1,560	140	115	90	69	53	36	19	3	0	0	0
1,560	1,580	143	118	93	71	55	38	21	5	0	0	0
1,580	1,600	146	121	96	73	57	40	23	7	0	0	0

SEMIMONTHLY MARRIED PERSONS

MARRIED Persons—SEMIMONTHLY Payroll Period
(For Wages Paid through December 31, 2015)

And the wages are—		And the number of withholding allowances claimed is—										
At least	But less than	0	1	2	3	4	5	6	7	8	9	10
		The amount of income tax to be withheld is—										
$1,600	1,620	$149	$124	$99	$75	$59	$42	$25	$9	$0	$0	$0
1,620	1,640	152	127	102	77	61	44	27	11	0	0	0
1,640	1,660	155	130	105	80	63	46	29	13	0	0	0
1,660	1,680	158	133	108	83	65	48	31	15	0	0	0
1,680	1,700	161	136	111	86	67	50	33	17	0	0	0
1,700	1,720	164	139	114	89	69	52	35	19	2	0	0
1,720	1,740	167	142	117	92	71	54	37	21	4	0	0
1,740	1,760	170	145	120	95	73	56	39	23	6	0	0
1,760	1,780	173	148	123	98	75	58	41	25	8	0	0
1,780	1,800	176	151	126	101	77	60	43	27	10	0	0
1,800	1,820	179	154	129	104	79	62	45	29	12	0	0
1,820	1,840	182	157	132	107	82	64	47	31	14	0	0
1,840	1,860	185	160	135	110	85	66	49	33	16	0	0
1,860	1,880	188	163	138	113	88	68	51	35	18	1	0
1,880	1,900	191	166	141	116	91	70	53	37	20	3	0
1,900	1,920	194	169	144	119	94	72	55	39	22	5	0
1,920	1,940	197	172	147	122	97	74	57	41	24	7	0
1,940	1,960	200	175	150	125	100	76	59	43	26	9	0
1,960	1,980	203	178	153	128	103	78	61	45	28	11	0
1,980	2,000	206	181	156	131	106	81	63	47	30	13	0
2,000	2,020	209	184	159	134	109	84	65	49	32	15	1
2,020	2,040	212	187	162	137	112	87	67	51	34	17	3
2,040	2,060	215	190	165	140	115	90	69	53	36	19	5
2,060	2,080	218	193	168	143	118	93	71	55	38	21	7
2,080	2,100	221	196	171	146	121	96	73	57	40	23	9
2,100	2,120	224	199	174	149	124	99	75	59	42	25	11
2,120	2,140	227	202	177	152	127	102	77	61	44	27	13
2,140	2,160	230	205	180	155	130	105	80	63	46	29	15
2,160	2,180	233	208	183	158	133	108	83	65	48	31	17
2,180	2,200	236	211	186	161	136	111	86	67	50	33	19
2,200	2,220	239	214	189	164	139	114	89	69	52	35	21
2,220	2,240	242	217	192	167	142	117	92	71	54	37	23
2,240	2,260	245	220	195	170	145	120	95	73	56	39	25
2,260	2,280	248	223	198	173	148	123	98	75	58	41	27
2,280	2,300	251	226	201	176	151	126	101	77	60	43	29
2,300	2,320	254	229	204	179	154	129	104	79	62	45	31
2,320	2,340	257	232	207	182	157	132	107	82	64	47	33
2,340	2,360	260	235	210	185	160	135	110	85	66	49	35
2,360	2,380	263	238	213	188	163	138	113	88	68	51	37
2,380	2,400	266	241	216	191	166	141	116	91	70	53	39
2,400	2,420	269	244	219	194	169	144	119	94	72	55	41
2,420	2,440	272	247	222	197	172	147	122	97	74	57	43
2,440	2,460	275	250	225	200	175	150	125	100	76	59	45
2,460	2,480	278	253	228	203	178	153	128	103	78	61	47
2,480	2,500	281	256	231	206	181	156	131	106	81	63	49
2,500	2,520	284	259	234	209	184	159	134	109	84	65	51
2,520	2,540	287	262	237	212	187	162	137	112	87	67	53
2,540	2,560	290	265	240	215	190	165	140	115	90	69	55
2,560	2,580	293	268	243	218	193	168	143	118	93	71	57
2,580	2,600	296	271	246	221	196	171	146	121	96	73	59
2,600	2,620	299	274	249	224	199	174	149	124	99	75	61
2,620	2,640	302	277	252	227	202	177	152	127	102	77	63
2,640	2,660	305	280	255	230	205	180	155	130	105	80	65
2,660	2,680	308	283	258	233	208	183	158	133	108	83	67
2,680	2,700	311	286	261	236	211	186	161	136	111	86	69
2,700	2,720	314	289	264	239	214	189	164	139	114	89	71
2,720	2,740	317	292	267	242	217	192	167	142	117	92	73
2,740	2,760	320	295	270	245	220	195	170	145	120	95	75
2,760	2,780	323	298	273	248	223	198	173	148	123	98	77
2,780	2,800	326	301	276	251	226	201	176	151	126	101	79
2,800	2,820	329	304	279	254	229	204	179	154	129	104	82
2,820	2,840	332	307	282	257	232	207	182	157	132	107	85
2,840	2,860	335	310	285	260	235	210	185	160	135	110	88
2,860	2,880	338	313	288	263	238	213	188	163	138	113	91
2,880	2,900	341	316	291	266	241	216	191	166	141	116	94
2,900	2,920	344	319	294	269	244	219	194	169	144	119	94

$2,920 and over   Use Table 3(b) for a MARRIED person on page 45. Also see the instructions on page 43.

WAGE BRACKET METHOD TABLES FOR INCOME TAX WITHHOLDING

SINGLE Persons—MONTHLY Payroll Period
(For Wages Paid through December 31, 2015)

MONTHLY SINGLE PERSONS

And the wages are—		And the number of withholding allowances claimed is—										
At least	But less than	0	1	2	3	4	5	6	7	8	9	10
		The amount of income tax to be withheld is—										
$0	$220	$0	$0	$0	$0	$0	$0	$0	$0	$0	$0	$0
220	230	3	0	0	0	0	0	0	0	0	0	0
230	240	4	0	0	0	0	0	0	0	0	0	0
240	250	5	0	0	0	0	0	0	0	0	0	0
250	260	6	0	0	0	0	0	0	0	0	0	0
260	270	7	0	0	0	0	0	0	0	0	0	0
270	280	8	0	0	0	0	0	0	0	0	0	0
280	290	9	0	0	0	0	0	0	0	0	0	0
290	300	10	0	0	0	0	0	0	0	0	0	0
300	320	12	0	0	0	0	0	0	0	0	0	0
320	340	14	0	0	0	0	0	0	0	0	0	0
340	360	16	0	0	0	0	0	0	0	0	0	0
360	380	18	0	0	0	0	0	0	0	0	0	0
380	400	20	0	0	0	0	0	0	0	0	0	0
400	420	22	0	0	0	0	0	0	0	0	0	0
420	440	24	0	0	0	0	0	0	0	0	0	0
440	460	26	0	0	0	0	0	0	0	0	0	0
460	480	28	0	0	0	0	0	0	0	0	0	0
480	500	30	0	0	0	0	0	0	0	0	0	0
500	520	32	0	0	0	0	0	0	0	0	0	0
520	540	34	1	0	0	0	0	0	0	0	0	0
540	560	36	3	0	0	0	0	0	0	0	0	0
560	580	38	5	0	0	0	0	0	0	0	0	0
580	600	40	7	0	0	0	0	0	0	0	0	0
600	640	43	10	0	0	0	0	0	0	0	0	0
640	680	47	14	0	0	0	0	0	0	0	0	0
680	720	51	18	0	0	0	0	0	0	0	0	0
720	760	55	22	0	0	0	0	0	0	0	0	0
760	800	59	26	0	0	0	0	0	0	0	0	0
800	840	63	30	0	0	0	0	0	0	0	0	0
840	880	67	34	0	0	0	0	0	0	0	0	0
880	920	71	38	4	0	0	0	0	0	0	0	0
920	960	75	42	8	0	0	0	0	0	0	0	0
960	1,000	80	46	12	0	0	0	0	0	0	0	0
1,000	1,040	86	50	16	0	0	0	0	0	0	0	0
1,040	1,080	92	54	20	0	0	0	0	0	0	0	0
1,080	1,120	98	58	24	0	0	0	0	0	0	0	0
1,120	1,160	104	62	28	0	0	0	0	0	0	0	0
1,160	1,200	110	66	32	0	0	0	0	0	0	0	0
1,200	1,240	116	70	36	3	0	0	0	0	0	0	0
1,240	1,280	122	74	40	7	0	0	0	0	0	0	0
1,280	1,320	128	78	44	11	0	0	0	0	0	0	0
1,320	1,360	134	84	48	15	0	0	0	0	0	0	0
1,360	1,400	140	90	52	19	0	0	0	0	0	0	0
1,400	1,440	146	96	56	23	0	0	0	0	0	0	0
1,440	1,480	152	102	60	27	0	0	0	0	0	0	0
1,480	1,520	158	108	64	31	0	0	0	0	0	0	0
1,520	1,560	164	114	68	35	4	0	0	0	0	0	0
1,560	1,600	170	120	72	39	8	0	0	0	0	0	0
1,600	1,640	176	126	76	43	12	0	0	0	0	0	0
1,640	1,680	182	132	82	47	16	0	0	0	0	0	0
1,680	1,720	188	138	88	51	20	0	0	0	0	0	0
1,720	1,760	194	144	94	55	24	0	0	0	0	0	0
1,760	1,800	200	150	100	59	28	0	0	0	0	0	0
1,800	1,840	206	156	106	63	32	0	0	0	0	0	0
1,840	1,880	212	162	112	67	36	0	0	0	0	0	0
1,880	1,920	218	168	118	71	40	4	0	0	0	0	0
1,920	1,960	224	174	124	75	44	8	0	0	0	0	0
1,960	2,000	230	180	130	80	48	12	0	0	0	0	0
2,000	2,040	236	186	136	86	52	16	0	0	0	0	0
2,040	2,080	242	192	142	92	56	20	0	0	0	0	0
2,080	2,120	248	198	148	98	60	24	0	0	0	0	0
2,120	2,160	254	204	154	104	64	28	0	0	0	0	0
2,160	2,200	260	210	160	110	68	32	0	0	0	0	0
2,200	2,240	266	216	166	116	72	36	3	0	0	0	0
2,240	2,280	272	222	172	122	76	40	7	0	0	0	0
2,280	2,320	278	228	178	128	80	44	11	0	0	0	0
2,320	2,360	284	234	184	134	84	48	15	0	0	0	0
2,360	2,400	290	240	190	140	90	52	19	0	0	0	0

SINGLE Persons—MONTHLY Payroll Period
(For Wages Paid through December 31, 2015)

And the wages are—		And the number of withholding allowances claimed is—										
At least	But less than	0	1	2	3	4	5	6	7	8	9	10
		The amount of income tax to be withheld is—										
$2,400	$2,440	$296	$246	$196	$146	$96	$56	$23	$0	$0	$0	$0
2,440	2,480	302	252	202	152	102	60	27	0	0	0	0
2,480	2,520	308	258	208	158	108	64	31	0	0	0	0
2,520	2,560	314	264	214	164	114	68	35	2	0	0	0
2,560	2,600	320	270	220	170	120	72	39	6	0	0	0
2,600	2,640	326	276	226	176	126	76	43	10	0	0	0
2,640	2,680	332	282	232	182	132	82	47	14	0	0	0
2,680	2,720	338	288	238	188	138	88	51	18	0	0	0
2,720	2,760	344	294	244	194	144	94	55	22	0	0	0
2,760	2,800	350	300	250	200	150	100	59	26	0	0	0
2,800	2,840	356	306	256	206	156	106	63	30	0	0	0
2,840	2,880	362	312	262	212	162	112	67	34	0	0	0
2,880	2,920	368	318	268	218	168	118	71	38	4	0	0
2,920	2,960	374	324	274	224	174	124	75	42	8	0	0
2,960	3,000	380	330	280	230	180	130	80	46	12	0	0
3,000	3,040	386	336	286	236	186	136	86	50	16	0	0
3,040	3,080	392	342	292	242	192	142	92	54	20	0	0
3,080	3,120	398	348	298	248	198	148	98	58	24	0	0
3,120	3,160	404	354	304	254	204	154	104	62	28	0	0
3,160	3,200	410	360	310	260	210	160	110	66	32	0	0
3,200	3,240	416	366	316	266	216	166	116	70	36	3	0
3,240	3,280	422	372	322	272	222	172	122	74	40	7	0
3,280	3,320	428	378	328	278	228	178	128	78	44	11	0
3,320	3,360	437	384	334	284	234	184	134	84	48	15	0
3,360	3,400	447	390	340	290	240	190	140	90	52	19	0
3,400	3,440	457	396	346	296	246	196	146	96	56	23	0
3,440	3,480	467	402	352	302	252	202	152	102	60	27	0
3,480	3,520	477	408	358	308	258	208	158	108	64	31	0
3,520	3,560	487	414	364	314	264	214	164	114	68	35	2
3,560	3,600	497	420	370	320	270	220	170	120	72	39	6
3,600	3,640	507	426	376	326	276	226	176	126	76	43	10
3,640	3,680	517	433	382	332	282	232	182	132	82	47	14
3,680	3,720	527	443	388	338	288	238	188	138	88	51	18
3,720	3,760	537	453	394	344	294	244	194	144	94	55	22
3,760	3,800	547	463	400	350	300	250	200	150	100	59	26
3,800	3,840	557	473	406	356	306	256	206	156	106	63	30
3,840	3,880	567	483	412	362	312	262	212	162	112	67	34
3,880	3,920	577	493	418	368	318	268	218	168	118	71	38
3,920	3,960	587	503	424	374	324	274	224	174	124	75	42
3,960	4,000	597	513	430	380	330	280	230	180	130	80	46
4,000	4,040	607	523	440	386	336	286	236	186	136	86	50
4,040	4,080	617	533	450	392	342	292	242	192	142	92	54
4,080	4,120	627	543	460	398	348	298	248	198	148	98	58
4,120	4,160	637	553	470	404	354	304	254	204	154	104	62
4,160	4,200	647	563	480	410	360	310	260	210	160	110	66
4,200	4,240	657	573	490	416	366	316	266	216	166	116	70
4,240	4,280	667	583	500	422	372	322	272	222	172	122	74
4,280	4,320	677	593	510	428	378	328	278	228	178	128	78
4,320	4,360	687	603	520	437	384	334	284	234	184	134	84
4,360	4,400	697	613	530	447	390	340	290	240	190	140	90
4,400	4,440	707	623	540	457	396	346	296	246	196	146	96
4,440	4,480	717	633	550	467	402	352	302	252	202	152	102
4,480	4,520	727	643	560	477	408	358	308	258	208	158	108
4,520	4,560	737	653	570	487	414	364	314	264	214	164	114
4,560	4,600	747	663	580	497	420	370	320	270	220	170	120
4,600	4,640	757	673	590	507	426	376	326	276	226	176	126
4,640	4,680	767	683	600	517	433	382	332	282	232	182	132
4,680	4,720	777	693	610	527	443	388	338	288	238	188	138
4,720	4,760	787	703	620	537	453	394	344	294	244	194	144
4,760	4,800	797	713	630	547	463	400	350	300	250	200	150
4,800	4,840	807	723	640	557	473	406	356	306	256	206	156
4,840	4,880	817	733	650	567	483	412	362	312	262	212	162
4,880	4,920	827	743	660	577	493	418	368	318	268	218	168
4,920	4,960	837	753	670	587	503	424	374	324	274	224	174
4,960	5,000	847	763	680	597	513	430	380	330	280	230	180
5,000	5,040	857	773	690	607	523	440	386	336	286	236	186
5,040	5,080	867	783	700	617	533	450	392	342	292	242	192
$5,080 and over		Use Table 4(a) for a **SINGLE person** on page 45. Also see the instructions on page 43.										

WAGE BRACKET METHOD TABLES FOR INCOME TAX WITHHOLDING

MARRIED Persons—MONTHLY Payroll Period
(For Wages Paid through December 31, 2015)

And the wages are—		And the number of withholding allowances claimed is—										
At least	But less than	0	1	2	3	4	5	6	7	8	9	10
		The amount of income tax to be withheld is—										
$0	$720	$0	$0	$0	$0	$0	$0	$0	$0	$0	$0	$0
720	760	2	0	0	0	0	0	0	0	0	0	0
760	800	6	0	0	0	0	0	0	0	0	0	0
800	840	10	0	0	0	0	0	0	0	0	0	0
840	880	14	0	0	0	0	0	0	0	0	0	0
880	920	18	0	0	0	0	0	0	0	0	0	0
920	960	22	0	0	0	0	0	0	0	0	0	0
960	1,000	26	0	0	0	0	0	0	0	0	0	0
1,000	1,040	30	0	0	0	0	0	0	0	0	0	0
1,040	1,080	34	1	0	0	0	0	0	0	0	0	0
1,080	1,120	38	5	0	0	0	0	0	0	0	0	0
1,120	1,160	42	9	0	0	0	0	0	0	0	0	0
1,160	1,200	46	13	0	0	0	0	0	0	0	0	0
1,200	1,240	50	17	0	0	0	0	0	0	0	0	0
1,240	1,280	54	21	0	0	0	0	0	0	0	0	0
1,280	1,320	58	25	0	0	0	0	0	0	0	0	0
1,320	1,360	62	29	0	0	0	0	0	0	0	0	0
1,360	1,400	66	33	0	0	0	0	0	0	0	0	0
1,400	1,440	70	37	4	0	0	0	0	0	0	0	0
1,440	1,480	74	41	8	0	0	0	0	0	0	0	0
1,480	1,520	78	45	12	0	0	0	0	0	0	0	0
1,520	1,560	82	49	16	0	0	0	0	0	0	0	0
1,560	1,600	86	53	20	0	0	0	0	0	0	0	0
1,600	1,640	90	57	24	0	0	0	0	0	0	0	0
1,640	1,680	94	61	28	0	0	0	0	0	0	0	0
1,680	1,720	98	65	32	0	0	0	0	0	0	0	0
1,720	1,760	102	69	36	2	0	0	0	0	0	0	0
1,760	1,800	106	73	40	6	0	0	0	0	0	0	0
1,800	1,840	110	77	44	10	0	0	0	0	0	0	0
1,840	1,880	114	81	48	14	0	0	0	0	0	0	0
1,880	1,920	118	85	52	18	0	0	0	0	0	0	0
1,920	1,960	122	89	56	22	0	0	0	0	0	0	0
1,960	2,000	126	93	60	26	0	0	0	0	0	0	0
2,000	2,040	130	97	64	30	0	0	0	0	0	0	0
2,040	2,080	134	101	68	34	1	0	0	0	0	0	0
2,080	2,120	138	105	72	38	5	0	0	0	0	0	0
2,120	2,160	142	109	76	42	9	0	0	0	0	0	0
2,160	2,200	146	113	80	46	13	0	0	0	0	0	0
2,200	2,240	150	117	84	50	17	0	0	0	0	0	0
2,240	2,280	155	121	88	54	21	0	0	0	0	0	0
2,280	2,320	161	125	92	58	25	0	0	0	0	0	0
2,320	2,360	167	129	96	62	29	0	0	0	0	0	0
2,360	2,400	173	133	100	66	33	0	0	0	0	0	0
2,400	2,440	179	137	104	70	37	4	0	0	0	0	0
2,440	2,480	185	141	108	74	41	8	0	0	0	0	0
2,480	2,520	191	145	112	78	45	12	0	0	0	0	0
2,520	2,560	197	149	116	82	49	16	0	0	0	0	0
2,560	2,600	203	153	120	86	53	20	0	0	0	0	0
2,600	2,640	209	159	124	90	57	24	0	0	0	0	0
2,640	2,680	215	165	128	94	61	28	0	0	0	0	0
2,680	2,720	221	171	132	98	65	32	0	0	0	0	0
2,720	2,760	227	177	136	102	69	36	2	0	0	0	0
2,760	2,800	233	183	140	106	73	40	6	0	0	0	0
2,800	2,840	239	189	144	110	77	44	10	0	0	0	0
2,840	2,880	245	195	148	114	81	48	14	0	0	0	0
2,880	2,920	251	201	152	118	85	52	18	0	0	0	0
2,920	2,960	257	207	157	122	89	56	22	0	0	0	0
2,960	3,000	263	213	163	126	93	60	26	0	0	0	0
3,000	3,040	269	219	169	130	97	64	30	0	0	0	0
3,040	3,080	275	225	175	134	101	68	34	1	0	0	0
3,080	3,120	281	231	181	138	105	72	38	5	0	0	0
3,120	3,160	287	237	187	142	109	76	42	9	0	0	0
3,160	3,200	293	243	193	146	113	80	46	13	0	0	0
3,200	3,240	299	249	199	150	117	84	50	17	0	0	0
3,240	3,280	305	255	205	155	121	88	54	21	0	0	0
3,280	3,320	311	261	211	161	125	92	58	25	0	0	0
3,320	3,360	317	267	217	167	129	96	62	29	0	0	0
3,360	3,400	323	273	223	173	133	100	66	33	0	0	0

MONTHLY MARRIED PERSONS

MARRIED Persons—MONTHLY Payroll Period
(For Wages Paid through December 31, 2015)

And the wages are—		And the number of withholding allowances claimed is—										
At least	But less than	0	1	2	3	4	5	6	7	8	9	10
		The amount of income tax to be withheld is—										
$3,400	$3,440	$329	$279	$229	$179	$137	$104	$70	$37	$4	$0	$0
3,440	3,480	335	285	235	185	141	108	74	41	8	0	0
3,480	3,520	341	291	241	191	145	112	78	45	12	0	0
3,520	3,560	347	297	247	197	149	116	82	49	16	0	0
3,560	3,600	353	303	253	203	153	120	86	53	20	0	0
3,600	3,640	359	309	259	209	159	124	90	57	24	0	0
3,640	3,680	365	315	265	215	165	128	94	61	28	0	0
3,680	3,720	371	321	271	221	171	132	98	65	32	0	0
3,720	3,760	377	327	277	227	177	136	102	69	36	2	0
3,760	3,800	383	333	283	233	183	140	106	73	40	6	0
3,800	3,840	389	339	289	239	189	144	110	77	44	10	0
3,840	3,880	395	345	295	245	195	148	114	81	48	14	0
3,880	3,920	401	351	301	251	201	152	118	85	52	18	0
3,920	3,960	407	357	307	257	207	157	122	89	56	22	0
3,960	4,000	413	363	313	263	213	163	126	93	60	26	0
4,000	4,040	419	369	319	269	219	169	130	97	64	30	0
4,040	4,080	425	375	325	275	225	175	134	101	68	34	1
4,080	4,120	431	381	331	281	231	181	138	105	72	38	5
4,120	4,160	437	387	337	287	237	187	142	109	76	42	9
4,160	4,200	443	393	343	293	243	193	146	113	80	46	13
4,200	4,240	449	399	349	299	249	199	150	117	84	50	17
4,240	4,280	455	405	355	305	255	205	155	121	88	54	21
4,280	4,320	461	411	361	311	261	211	161	125	92	58	25
4,320	4,360	467	417	367	317	267	217	167	129	96	62	29
4,360	4,400	473	423	373	323	273	223	173	133	100	66	33
4,400	4,440	479	429	379	329	279	229	179	137	104	70	37
4,440	4,480	485	435	385	335	285	235	185	141	108	74	41
4,480	4,520	491	441	391	341	291	241	191	145	112	78	45
4,520	4,560	497	447	397	347	297	247	197	149	116	82	49
4,560	4,600	503	453	403	353	303	253	203	153	120	86	53
4,600	4,640	509	459	409	359	309	259	209	159	124	90	57
4,640	4,680	515	465	415	365	315	265	215	165	128	94	61
4,680	4,720	521	471	421	371	321	271	221	171	132	98	65
4,720	4,760	527	477	427	377	327	277	227	177	136	102	69
4,760	4,800	533	483	433	383	333	283	233	183	140	106	73
4,800	4,840	539	489	439	389	339	289	239	189	144	110	77
4,840	4,880	545	495	445	395	345	295	245	195	148	114	81
4,880	4,920	551	501	451	401	351	301	251	201	152	118	85
4,920	4,960	557	507	457	407	357	307	257	207	157	122	89
4,960	5,000	563	513	463	413	363	313	263	213	163	126	93
5,000	5,040	569	519	469	419	369	319	269	219	169	130	97
5,040	5,080	575	525	475	425	375	325	275	225	175	134	101
5,080	5,120	581	531	481	431	381	331	281	231	181	138	105
5,120	5,160	587	537	487	437	387	337	287	237	187	142	109
5,160	5,200	593	543	493	443	393	343	293	243	193	146	113
5,200	5,240	599	549	499	449	399	349	299	249	199	150	117
5,240	5,280	605	555	505	455	405	355	305	255	205	155	121
5,280	5,320	611	561	511	461	411	361	311	261	211	161	125
5,320	5,360	617	567	517	467	417	367	317	267	217	167	129
5,360	5,400	623	573	523	473	423	373	323	273	223	173	133
5,400	5,440	629	579	529	479	429	379	329	279	229	179	137
5,440	5,480	635	585	535	485	435	385	335	285	235	185	141
5,480	5,520	641	591	541	491	441	391	341	291	241	191	145
5,520	5,560	647	597	547	497	447	397	347	297	247	197	149
5,560	5,600	653	603	553	503	453	403	353	303	253	203	153
5,600	5,640	659	609	559	509	459	409	359	309	259	209	159
5,640	5,680	665	615	565	515	465	415	365	315	265	215	165
5,680	5,720	671	621	571	521	471	421	371	321	271	221	171
5,720	5,760	677	627	577	527	477	427	377	327	277	227	177
5,760	5,800	683	633	583	533	483	433	383	333	283	233	183
5,800	5,840	689	639	589	539	489	439	389	339	289	239	189
5,840	5,880	695	645	595	545	495	445	395	345	295	245	195
5,880	5,920	701	651	601	551	501	451	401	351	301	251	201
5,920	5,960	707	657	607	557	507	457	407	357	307	257	207
5,960	6,000	713	663	613	563	513	463	413	363	313	263	213
6,000	6,040	719	669	619	569	519	469	419	369	319	269	219
6,040	6,080	725	675	625	575	525	475	425	375	325	275	225
6,080	6,120	731	681	631	581	531	481	431	381	331	281	231

$6,120 and over   Use Table 4(b) for a MARRIED person on page 45. Also see the instructions on page 43.

WAGE BRACKET METHOD TABLES FOR INCOME TAX WITHHOLDING

SINGLE Persons—DAILY Payroll Period
(For Wages Paid through December 31, 2015)

DAILY SINGLE PERSONS

And the wages are—		And the number of withholding allowances claimed is—										
At least	But less than	0	1	2	3	4	5	6	7	8	9	10
		The amount of income tax to be withheld is—										
$0	$15	$0	$0	$0	$0	$0	$0	$0	$0	$0	$0	$0
15	18	1	0	0	0	0	0	0	0	0	0	0
18	21	1	0	0	0	0	0	0	0	0	0	0
21	24	1	0	0	0	0	0	0	0	0	0	0
24	27	2	0	0	0	0	0	0	0	0	0	0
27	30	2	0	0	0	0	0	0	0	0	0	0
30	33	2	1	0	0	0	0	0	0	0	0	0
33	36	3	1	0	0	0	0	0	0	0	0	0
36	39	3	1	0	0	0	0	0	0	0	0	0
39	42	3	2	0	0	0	0	0	0	0	0	0
42	45	4	2	0	0	0	0	0	0	0	0	0
45	48	4	3	1	0	0	0	0	0	0	0	0
48	51	5	3	1	0	0	0	0	0	0	0	0
51	54	5	3	2	0	0	0	0	0	0	0	0
54	57	6	4	2	0	0	0	0	0	0	0	0
57	60	6	4	2	1	0	0	0	0	0	0	0
60	63	7	5	3	1	0	0	0	0	0	0	0
63	66	7	5	3	1	0	0	0	0	0	0	0
66	69	7	6	4	2	0	0	0	0	0	0	0
69	72	8	6	4	2	1	0	0	0	0	0	0
72	75	8	7	5	3	1	0	0	0	0	0	0
75	78	9	7	5	3	1	0	0	0	0	0	0
78	81	9	7	6	4	2	0	0	0	0	0	0
81	84	10	8	6	4	2	1	0	0	0	0	0
84	87	10	8	7	5	3	1	0	0	0	0	0
87	90	10	9	7	5	3	1	0	0	0	0	0
90	93	11	9	8	6	4	2	0	0	0	0	0
93	96	11	10	8	6	4	2	1	0	0	0	0
96	99	12	10	9	7	5	3	1	0	0	0	0
99	102	12	11	9	7	5	3	1	0	0	0	0
102	105	13	11	10	8	6	4	2	0	0	0	0
105	108	13	12	10	8	6	4	2	1	0	0	0
108	111	14	12	11	9	7	5	3	1	0	0	0
111	114	14	13	11	9	7	5	3	1	0	0	0
114	117	14	13	12	10	8	6	4	2	0	0	0
117	120	15	14	12	10	8	6	4	2	1	0	0
120	123	16	14	13	11	9	7	5	3	1	0	0
123	126	17	15	13	11	9	7	5	3	1	0	0
126	129	18	16	14	12	10	8	6	4	2	0	0
129	132	19	16	14	12	10	8	6	4	2	1	0
132	135	20	17	15	13	11	9	7	5	3	1	0
135	138	21	18	15	13	11	9	7	5	3	1	0
138	141	22	19	16	14	12	10	8	6	4	2	0
141	144	23	20	17	14	12	10	8	6	4	2	1
144	147	24	21	18	15	13	11	9	7	5	3	1
147	150	25	22	19	16	14	12	10	8	6	4	2
150	153	26	23	20	17	15	13	11	9	7	5	3
153	156	27	24	21	18	15	13	11	9	7	5	3
156	159	28	25	22	19	16	14	12	10	8	6	4
159	162	29	26	23	20	17	15	13	11	9	7	5
162	165	30	27	24	21	18	15	13	11	9	7	5
165	168	31	28	25	22	19	16	14	12	10	8	6
168	171	31	28	25	22	19	17	15	13	11	9	7
171	174	32	29	26	23	20	17	15	13	11	9	7
174	177	33	30	27	24	21	18	16	14	12	10	8
177	180	34	31	28	25	22	19	17	15	13	11	9
180	183	34	31	28	25	22	19	17	15	13	11	9
183	186	35	32	29	26	23	20	18	16	14	12	10
186	189	36	33	30	27	24	21	18	16	14	12	10
189	192	37	34	31	28	25	22	19	17	15	13	11
192	195	37	34	31	28	25	22	19	17	15	13	11
195	198	38	35	32	29	26	23	20	18	16	14	12
198	201	39	36	33	30	27	24	21	18	16	14	12
201	204	40	37	34	31	28	25	22	19	17	15	13
204	207	41	38	35	32	29	26	23	20	18	16	14
207	210	42	39	36	33	30	27	24	21	18	16	14
210	213	43	40	37	34	31	28	25	22	19	17	15
213	216	44	41	38	35	32	29	26	23	20	18	16
216	219	45	42	39	36	33	30	27	24	21	18	16
219	222	46	43	40	37	34	31	28	25	22	19	17
222	225	47	44	41	38	35	32	29	26	23	20	18

SINGLE Persons—DAILY Payroll Period
(For Wages Paid through December 31, 2015)

And the wages are—		And the number of withholding allowances claimed is—										
At least	But less than	0	1	2	3	4	5	6	7	8	9	10
		The amount of income tax to be withheld is—										
$225	$228	$38	$34	$31	$27	$23	$19	$17	$15	$12	$10	$8
228	231	39	35	31	28	24	20	17	16	13	11	9
231	234	40	36	32	28	25	21	18	16	14	11	9
234	237	40	37	33	29	25	21	19	17	14	12	10
237	240	41	37	34	30	26	22	19	17	15	12	10
240	243	42	38	34	30	27	23	20	18	15	13	10
243	246	43	39	35	31	27	24	20	18	16	13	11
246	249	43	40	36	32	28	24	21	19	16	14	11
249	252	44	40	37	33	29	25	22	19	17	14	12
252	255	45	41	37	33	30	26	22	20	17	15	12
255	258	46	42	38	34	30	27	23	20	18	15	13
258	261	46	43	39	35	31	27	24	21	18	16	13
261	264	47	43	40	36	32	28	24	21	19	16	14
264	267	48	44	40	36	33	29	25	22	19	17	14
267	270	49	45	41	37	33	30	26	23	20	17	15
270	273	49	46	42	38	34	30	26	23	20	18	15
273	276	50	46	43	39	35	31	28	24	21	18	16
276	279	51	47	43	39	36	32	28	25	21	19	16
279	282	52	48	44	40	36	33	29	25	22	19	17
282	285	52	49	45	41	37	33	29	26	22	20	17
285	288	53	49	46	42	38	34	30	27	23	20	18
288	291	54	50	46	43	39	35	31	27	24	21	19
291	294	55	51	47	43	40	36	32	28	24	22	19
294	297	56	52	48	44	40	37	33	29	25	22	20
297	300	56	52	49	45	41	37	33	29	26	23	21
300	303	57	53	49	45	42	38	34	30	26	23	22
303	306	58	54	50	46	42	39	35	31	28	24	23
306	309	58	55	51	47	43	39	35	32	28	25	24
309	312	59	56	52	48	44	40	36	32	29	25	25
312	315	60	56	52	49	45	41	37	33	29	26	26
315	318	61	57	53	49	45	42	38	34	30	26	27
318	321	61	58	54	50	46	42	38	35	31	28	28
321	324	62	58	55	51	47	43	39	35	32	28	28
324	327	63	59	56	52	48	44	40	36	33	29	29
327	330	64	60	56	52	49	45	41	37	33	30	31
330	333	64	61	57	53	49	45	41	38	34	30	32
333	336	65	61	58	54	50	46	42	38	34	31	33
336	339	66	62	58	54	51	47	43	39	35	32	33
339	341	67	63	59	55	51	47	44	40	36	32	34
341	343	68	64	60	56	52	48	44	41	37	33	35
343	345	68	65	61	57	53	49	45	41	38	34	35
345	347	68	65	61	58	54	50	46	42	38	35	36
347	349	69	66	62	58	54	50	46	43	39	35	37
349	351	69	67	63	59	55	51	47	43	40	36	38
351	353	70	67	63	59	56	52	48	44	40	37	38
353	355	70	66	63	59	55	51	47	43	39	35	32
355	357	71	67	63	59	56	52	48	44	40	36	33
357	359	71	68	64	60	56	52	49	45	41	37	33
359	361	72	68	64	61	57	53	49	45	41	37	34
361	363	73	69	65	61	57	53	50	46	42	38	34
363	365	73	69	65	62	58	54	50	46	42	38	35
365	367	74	70	66	62	58	54	51	47	43	39	35
367	369	74	71	67	63	59	55	51	47	44	40	36
369	371	75	71	67	63	60	56	52	48	44	40	37
371	373	76	72	68	64	60	56	52	48	45	41	37
373	375	76	72	68	65	61	57	53	49	45	41	38
375	377	77	73	69	65	61	57	53	50	46	42	38
377	379	77	74	70	66	62	58	54	50	46	43	39
379	381	78	74	70	66	63	59	55	51	47	43	40
381	383	78	75	71	67	63	59	55	51	48	44	40
383	385	78	75	71	67	63	59	55	51	47	43	39
385	387	79	75	72	68	64	60	56	52	48	44	40
387	389	80	76	72	69	65	61	57	53	49	45	41
389	391	80	76	73	69	65	61	57	54	50	46	42
391	393	81	77	73	69	66	62	58	54	50	45	41
$393 and over		Use Table 8(a) for a **SINGLE** person on page 46. Also see the instructions on page 43.										

WAGE BRACKET METHOD TABLES FOR INCOME TAX WITHHOLDING

DAILY MARRIED PERSONS

MARRIED Persons—DAILY Payroll Period
(For Wages Paid through December 31, 2015)

And the wages are—		And the number of withholding allowances claimed is—										
At least	But less than	0	1	2	3	4	5	6	7	8	9	10
		The amount of income tax to be withheld is—										
$0	39	$0	$0	$0	$0	$0	$0	$0	$0	$0	$0	$0
39	42	0	0	0	0	0	0	0	0	0	0	0
42	45	1	0	0	0	0	0	0	0	0	0	0
45	48	1	0	0	0	0	0	0	0	0	0	0
48	51	2	0	0	0	0	0	0	0	0	0	0
51	54	2	0	0	0	0	0	0	0	0	0	0
54	57	2	0	0	0	0	0	0	0	0	0	0
57	60	3	1	0	0	0	0	0	0	0	0	0
60	63	3	1	0	0	0	0	0	0	0	0	0
63	66	3	1	0	0	0	0	0	0	0	0	0
66	69	4	2	0	0	0	0	0	0	0	0	0
69	72	4	2	0	0	0	0	0	0	0	0	0
72	75	5	3	0	0	0	0	0	0	0	0	0
75	78	5	3	0	0	0	0	0	0	0	0	0
78	81	5	3	0	0	0	0	0	0	0	0	0
81	84	6	4	1	0	0	0	0	0	0	0	0
84	87	6	4	1	0	0	0	0	0	0	0	0
87	90	7	5	2	0	0	0	0	0	0	0	0
90	93	7	5	2	0	0	0	0	0	0	0	0
93	96	7	5	2	0	0	0	0	0	0	0	0
96	99	8	6	3	1	0	0	0	0	0	0	0
99	102	8	6	3	1	0	0	0	0	0	0	0
102	105	9	7	4	2	0	0	0	0	0	0	0
105	108	9	7	4	2	0	0	0	0	0	0	0
108	111	10	8	5	3	1	0	0	0	0	0	0
111	114	10	8	5	3	1	0	0	0	0	0	0
114	117	10	8	5	3	1	0	0	0	0	0	0
117	120	11	9	6	4	2	0	0	0	0	0	0
120	123	11	9	6	4	2	0	0	0	0	0	0
123	126	12	10	7	5	3	1	0	0	0	0	0
126	129	12	10	7	5	3	1	0	0	0	0	0
129	132	12	10	7	5	3	1	0	0	0	0	0
132	135	13	11	8	6	4	2	0	0	0	0	0
135	138	13	11	8	6	4	2	0	0	0	0	0
138	141	14	12	9	7	5	3	0	0	0	0	0
141	144	14	12	9	7	5	3	0	0	0	0	0
144	147	14	12	9	7	5	3	0	0	0	0	0
147	150	15	13	10	8	6	4	1	0	0	0	0
150	153	15	13	10	8	6	4	1	0	0	0	0
153	156	16	14	11	9	7	5	2	0	0	0	0
156	159	16	14	11	9	7	5	2	0	0	0	0
159	162	17	15	12	10	8	6	3	1	0	0	0
162	165	17	15	12	10	8	6	3	1	0	0	0
165	168	17	15	12	10	8	6	3	1	0	0	0
168	171	18	16	13	11	9	7	4	2	0	0	0
171	174	18	16	13	11	9	7	4	2	0	0	0
174	177	19	17	14	12	10	8	5	3	1	0	0
177	180	19	17	14	12	10	8	5	3	1	0	0
180	183	19	17	14	12	10	8	5	3	1	0	0
183	186	20	18	15	13	11	9	6	4	2	0	0
186	189	20	18	15	13	11	9	6	4	2	0	0
189	192	21	19	16	14	12	10	7	5	3	0	0
192	195	21	19	16	14	12	10	7	5	3	0	0
195	198	22	20	17	15	13	11	8	6	4	1	0
198	201	22	20	17	15	13	11	8	6	4	1	0
201	204	22	20	17	15	13	11	8	6	4	1	0
204	207	23	21	18	16	14	12	9	7	5	2	0
207	210	23	21	18	16	14	12	9	7	5	2	0
210	213	24	22	19	17	15	13	10	8	6	3	1
213	216	24	22	19	17	15	13	10	8	6	3	1
216	219	24	22	19	17	15	13	10	8	6	3	1
219	222	25	23	20	18	16	14	11	9	7	4	2
222	225	25	23	20	18	16	14	11	9	7	4	2
225	228	26	24	21	19	17	15	12	10	8	5	3
228	231	26	24	21	19	17	15	12	10	8	5	3
231	234	26	24	21	19	17	15	12	10	8	5	3
234	237	27	25	22	20	18	16	13	11	9	6	4
237	240	27	25	22	20	18	16	13	11	9	6	4
240	243	28	26	23	21	19	17	14	12	10	7	5
243	246	28	26	23	21	19	17	14	12	10	7	5
246	249	29	27	24	22	20	18	15	13	11	8	6

MARRIED Persons—DAILY Payroll Period
(For Wages Paid through December 31, 2015)

And the wages are—		And the number of withholding allowances claimed is—										
At least	But less than	0	1	2	3	4	5	6	7	8	9	10
		The amount of income tax to be withheld is—										
$249	$252	$29	$27	$24	$22	$20	$18	$15	$13	$11	$8	$6
252	255	30	28	25	23	21	19	16	14	12	9	7
255	258	30	28	25	23	21	19	16	14	12	9	7
258	261	30	28	25	23	21	19	16	14	12	9	7
261	264	31	29	26	24	22	20	17	15	13	10	8
264	267	31	29	26	24	22	20	17	15	13	10	8
267	270	32	30	27	25	23	21	18	16	14	11	9
270	273	32	30	27	25	23	21	18	16	14	11	9
273	276	33	31	28	26	24	22	19	17	15	12	10
276	279	33	31	28	26	24	22	19	17	15	12	10
279	282	34	32	29	27	25	23	20	18	16	13	11
282	285	34	32	29	27	25	23	20	18	16	13	11
285	288	34	32	29	27	25	23	20	18	16	13	11
288	291	35	33	30	28	26	24	21	19	17	14	12
291	294	35	33	30	28	26	24	21	19	17	14	12
294	297	36	34	31	29	27	25	22	20	18	15	13
297	300	36	34	31	29	27	25	22	20	18	15	13
300	303	37	35	32	30	28	26	23	21	19	16	14
303	306	37	35	32	30	28	26	23	21	19	16	14
306	309	38	36	33	31	29	27	24	22	20	17	15
309	312	38	36	33	31	29	27	24	22	20	17	15
312	315	39	37	34	32	30	28	25	23	21	18	16
315	318	39	37	34	32	30	28	25	23	21	18	16
318	321	39	37	34	32	30	28	25	23	21	18	16
321	324	40	38	35	33	31	29	26	24	22	19	17
324	327	41	38	36	34	32	29	27	25	23	20	18
327	330	42	39	37	34	32	30	28	25	23	21	18
330	333	42	39	37	35	33	30	28	26	24	21	19
333	336	43	40	38	35	33	31	29	26	24	22	19
336	339	44	40	38	36	34	31	29	27	25	22	20
339	341	44	41	39	36	34	32	30	27	25	23	20
341	343	45	41	39	37	35	32	30	28	26	23	21
343	345	45	42	40	37	35	33	31	28	26	24	21
345	347	46	42	40	38	36	33	31	29	27	24	22
347	349	46	43	41	38	36	34	32	29	27	25	22
349	351	47	43	41	39	37	34	32	30	28	25	23
351	353	47	44	42	39	37	35	33	30	28	26	23
353	355	48	44	42	40	38	35	33	31	29	26	24
355	357	48	45	43	40	38	36	34	31	29	27	24
357	359	49	45	43	41	39	36	34	32	30	27	25
359	361	49	46	44	41	39	37	35	32	30	28	25
361	363	50	46	44	42	40	37	35	33	31	28	26
363	365	50	47	45	42	40	38	36	33	31	29	26
365	367	51	47	45	43	41	38	36	34	32	29	27
367	369	51	48	46	43	41	39	37	34	32	30	27
369	371	52	48	46	44	42	39	37	35	33	30	28
371	373	52	49	47	44	42	40	38	35	33	31	28
373	375	53	49	47	45	43	40	38	36	34	31	29
375	377	53	50	48	45	43	41	39	36	34	32	29
377	379	54	50	48	46	44	41	39	37	35	32	30
379	381	54	51	49	46	44	42	40	37	35	33	30
381	383	55	51	49	47	45	42	40	38	36	33	31
383	385	55	52	50	47	45	43	41	38	36	34	31
385	387	56	52	50	48	46	43	41	39	37	34	32
387	389	56	53	51	48	46	44	42	39	37	35	32
389	391	57	53	51	49	47	44	42	40	38	35	33
391	393	57	54	52	49	47	45	43	40	38	36	33
393	395	58	54	52	50	48	45	43	41	39	36	34
395	397	58	55	53	50	48	46	44	41	39	37	34
397	399	59	55	53	51	49	46	44	42	40	37	35
399	401	59	56	54	51	49	47	45	42	40	38	35
401	403	60	56	54	52	50	47	45	43	41	38	36
403	405	60	57	55	52	50	48	46	43	41	39	36
405	407	61	57	55	53	51	48	46	44	42	39	37
407	409	61	58	56	53	51	49	47	44	42	40	37
$409 and over		Use Table 8(b) for a **MARRIED person** on page 46. Also see the instructions on page 43.										

CHECK FIGURES

Chapter 2 Problems

2–1a. (c) $228.29
2–3a. (b) total gross earnings, $2,252.60
2–5a. (b) overtime pay, $11.52
2–7a. (b) total earnings, $747.40
2–9a. (e) total earnings, $850.50
2–11a. (e) total weekly earnings, $476.78
2–13a. (c) total earnings, $825.35
2–15a. (c) total earnings, $1,474.28
2–17a. (b) total earnings, $1,137.52
2–19a. (c) total earnings, $619.75
2–21a. (d) total weekly earnings, $498.96

Chapter 3 Problems

3–1a. total employees' FICA taxes, $457.89; $107.09
3–3a. (a) FICA taxes, $56.73; $13.27
3–5a. November 15 (Hanks), FICA taxes, $31.00; $85.55
3–7a. employees' taxes, $263.50; $61.65
3–9a. total employees' FICA taxes, $2,921.07; $704.91
3–11a. total taxes—line 10, $21,771.83
3–13a. total taxes—line 10, $12,008.76
3–15a. (b) last due date, April 6
3–17a. total OASDI taxes, $6,237.82

Chapter 4 Problems

4–1a. net pay, $167.80
4–3a. Corn tax, $62.68; $63.00
4–5a. total FIT, $543.73

4–7a. net pay, $646.85
4–9a. net pay, $60,957.50
4–11a. (c) take-home pay, $472.03
4–13a. Form W-3, box 2, Federal Income Tax Withheld $23,504.00

Chapter 5 Problems

5–1a. (c) total unemployment taxes, $6,663.60
5–3a. (b) net SUTA tax, $3,104.30
5–5a. (b) Net FUTA, $528.60
5–7a. (b) $235.60
5–9a. (b) SUTA tax, $1,416.00
5–11a. (c) $974.70
5–13a. (a) voluntary = $1,190.00
5–15a. (b) tax rate = 5.5%
5–17a. Form 940, line 8, = $474.60

Chapter 6 Problems

6–1a. federal tax levy, $546.92
6–3a. (a) payroll taxes debit, $650.25
6–5a. (a) cash credit, $50,748.80
6–7a. cash credit, $862.21
6–9a. cash credit, $13,441.03
6–11a. wages debit, $13,060.00
6–13a. (a) July w/h, $168.63
6–15a. (2) total payroll taxes, $258.02

Chapter 7 Problems

Net Paid, October 23, $12,108.81
Net Paid, November 6, $11,885.85

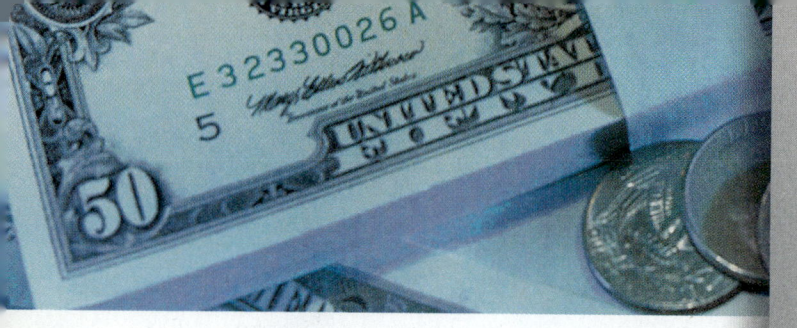

GLOSSARY

This glossary includes terms from Appendices C and D. These appendices are available on the Bieg 2016 product Web site at www.cengagebrain.com.

A

Annualizing wages method of determining amount of income taxes to be withheld by multiplying the wages for one payroll period by the number of periods in the year, determining the annual amount of withholding required on the total wages, and dividing the annual withholding by the number of payroll periods.

Application form personnel record which gives the applicant an opportunity to provide complete information as to personal qualifications, training, and experience.

Average indexed monthly earnings a worker's average monthly earnings, updated to reflect changes in wage levels.

B

Backup withholding amount of income tax withheld by payers of taxable interest, dividends, and certain other payments made to payees who have failed to furnish the payers with correct identification numbers.

Biweekly every two weeks.

Business expense cost of operating a business that is deductible by the employer for federal income tax purposes.

C

Change in payroll rate form document that notifies the proper departments of a change in the employee's rate of remuneration.

Check-off system withholding of union dues from employees' wages by the employer.

Commission stated percentage of revenue paid an employee who transacts a piece of business or performs a service.

Common-law relationship the state existing when the employer has the right to control both what work will be done and how it will be done.

Constructively paid remunerations that are credited to the account of, or set apart for, an employee so that they may be drawn upon at any time, even though they are not actually possessed by the employee.

Continental system method of recording time on time cards in which the day is divided into one 24-hour period, with time running from 12 midnight to 12 midnight.

Contribution report quarterly tax return filed with the state by the employer that provides a summary of the wages paid during the period and shows the computation of the tax or contribution.

Currently insured criterion used to determine eligibility for social security benefits; persons must have at least six quarters of coverage during the 13-quarter period ending with (1) the quarter in which they died or (2) the quarter in which they became entitled to old-age insurance benefits or most recently became entitled to disability benefits.

D

De minimis fringe benefit any property or service the value of which is so small that accounting for it would be unreasonable or impractical.

Defined contribution plan a retirement plan that provides future benefits based solely on the amount paid by each employee and employer into the account, plus investment gains.

Dependency allowance an additional weekly benefit paid to unemployed workers with dependents.

Disability benefits payments to employees who are absent from their jobs because of illness, accident, or disease not arising out of their employment.

Discretionary bonus a bonus not agreed on, announced, or promised before payment.

Dismissal payments amounts paid by employers to workers who have been separated from employment; also known as *payments in lieu of notice, separation pay,* or *terminal leave pay.*

Disposable earnings the earnings remaining after withholding for federal and state income taxes, FICA taxes, state unemployment and disability taxes, and deductions required for state employees' retirement systems.

Domestic service services of a household nature performed in or about a private home of the person who employs the domestic.

E

Educational assistance the expenses that an employer pays for an employee's education, such as tuition, fees, and payments for books, supplies, and equipment.

Electronic funds transfer system (EFTS) system whereby the employer transfers employees' net pays to employees' bank accounts with electronic equipment rather than issuing paychecks.

Electronic paystub paystub information made available through a secured Web site, kiosk, or interactive voice response system.

Employee any individual performing services for an employer in the legal relationship of employer and employee.

Employee history record continuous record of the relationship between the employer and the employee.

Employee's earnings record payroll record for each employee that is used to provide complete information about the accumulated earnings of each employee.

Employer any person or organization who employs one or more individuals for the performance of services, unless such services or employment are specifically excepted by law.

Employment any service performed by employees for their employer, regardless of the citizenship or residence of either.

Enterprise coverage applied to determine if employees of an enterprise are covered under the provisions of the FLSA. The test criteria are at least two employees engaged in interstate commerce and an annual gross sales volume of at least $500,000.

Executive orders regulations issued by the federal government that ban, in employment on government contracts, discrimination based on race, color, religion, sex, or national origin.

Exempt employees workers exempt from some, or all, of the FLSA requirements such as minimum wages, equal pay, and overtime pay.

Experience rating method by which employer contribution payments may be adjusted because of a favorable employment record; also known as *merit rating.*

F

Fair employment practices laws that deal with discrimination on the basis of age, race, color, religion, gender, or national origin as a condition of employment.

Form I-9, Employment Eligibility Verification form that lists the documents an employee must furnish to the employer; they identify the employee and, if an alien, verify authorization to work in the United States.

Form W-2, Wage and Tax Statement form used by the employer to report the amount of wages paid each worker in the course of the trade or business of the employer.

Fully insured criterion used to determine eligibility for most retirement and disability benefits; generally, a worker needs between 6 and 40 quarters of coverage.

G

Garnishment legal or equitable procedure by means of which a portion of the wages of any person must be withheld for payment of a debt.

Gross earnings total regular earnings and total overtime earnings, also known as *gross pay*.

Gross-up supplementals gross-up amount of payment so that after the appropriate payroll taxes are withheld, the net amount left is equal to the original intended payment.

Group insurance life insurance program for employees at a low cost.

H

Hiring notice form that is sent to the Payroll Department so that new employees are properly added to the payroll.

Hospital insurance (HI) plan program of medical care that provides protection against costs of certain hospital and related services; also known as *Basic Medicare* or *Part A Medicare*.

Human resources system those procedures and methods related to recruiting, selecting, orienting, training, and terminating personnel.

I

Income tax levy on the earnings of most employees that is deducted from their gross pay.

Independent contractors persons who follow an independent trade, business, or profession where services are offered to the public.

Indexing updating, or adjusting, a dollar amount over any particular time period (such as a calendar year) to reflect changes in wage levels that have occurred since a predetermined base time period.

Individual employee coverage applied to determine if the FLSA covers an employee. The test is that the employee either engages in interstate commerce or produces goods for such commerce.

Individual-account plan supplemental unemployment benefits plan in which the employers' contributions are paid into a separate trust for each employee.

Information returns forms upon which an employer reports compensation paid to individuals who are not employees.

Interstate employee an individual who works in more than one state.

Investigative consumer report study done by a consumer reporting agency on a job applicant or current employee concerning the individual's character, general reputation, and mode of living.

J

Journal entries transactions recorded in the accounting system of a business.

L

Lookback period the block of time, consisting of four quarters beginning July 1 of the second preceding year and ending June 30 of the prior year, used to determine if an employer is a monthly or a semiweekly depositor.

M

Medicaid program of medical assistance provided to aged and needy persons by means of a joint federal-state program.

Merit rating *see* experience rating.

Monthly depositor one who reported employment taxes of $50,000 or less for the four quarters in the lookback period.

N

Negative-balance employers those whose reserve accounts have been charged for more benefits paid out than contributions paid in to the fund.

Nondiscretionary bonus a bonus normally based on hours worked, units produced, production efficiency, or work quality.

O

Overtime premium method of calculating overtime pay by multiplying the total hours worked (including overtime hours) by the regular rate of pay and then multiplying the overtime hours by one-half the regular hourly rate.

P

Partial unemployment employment by the individual's regular employer on a reduced scale because of lack of work.

Partial unemployment notices forms completed by the employer and given to partially unemployed workers so that supplemental unemployment benefits may be obtained.

Part-year employment another method of calculating the withholding of federal income tax from an employee's pay.

Payroll accounting system those procedures and methods related to the disbursement of pay to employees.

Payroll register multicolumn form used to assemble and summarize the data needed at the end of each payroll period. It lists all employees who earned remuneration, the amount of remuneration, the deductions, and the net amount paid.

Percentage method method of determining amount of income taxes to be withheld using Table of Allowance Values and Percentage Method Withholding Table.

Person an entity defined by law as an individual, a trust or estate, a partnership, or a corporation.

Personal allowance a deduction allowed in computing taxable income; also known as a *personal exemption*.

Piece-rate system compensation plan under which workers are paid according to their output (units or pieces produced).

Pooled-fund laws unemployment insurance system wherein the cost of unemployment benefits is spread among all employers in a particular state.

Pooled-fund plan supplemental unemployment benefits plan financed by employers' contributions into a general fund; also known as the *auto* or *Ford-type plan*.

Positive-balance employers those who have built up a balance in their reserve accounts (contributions paid in less benefits charged).

Pre-hire inquiries questions asked in the employment interview and on application forms, résumés of experience or education required of an applicant, and any kind of written testing.

Primary insurance amount (PIA) a person's monthly retirement or disability benefit, which is the base upon which monthly benefits of the worker's family and survivors are computed.

Principal activities those tasks employees must perform for the employer.

Profit-sharing plans compensation plans in which employer shares with employees a portion of the profits of the business.

Q

Quarter of coverage criterion used to determine if workers are fully insured, currently insured, or insured for disability benefits; the minimum amount of wages or self-employment income with which individuals must be credited in a calendar quarter if they are to receive credit toward being insured for that period.

Quarterly averaging method of determining the amount of income taxes to be withheld by estimating the employee's average wages for the calendar quarter, computing an average payment, and withholding an amount based on the average payment.

R

Reciprocal agreement arrangement entered into by two or more states whereby the resident of one state working in another state will not be subject to the withholding of income taxes by the state in which the person is employed if that state has entered into a similar agreement with the employee's resident state.

Reciprocal arrangements agreements between states to provide unemployment insurance coverage and payment of benefits to interstate workers.

Reference inquiry form document used by the employer to investigate the references given on the application blank by the job applicant.

Requisition for personnel document submitted by a department head to the Human Resources Department asking for additional or replacement employees.

Reserve-ratio formula experience-rating plan used in most states, based on: Contributions − Benefits Paid ÷ Average Payroll.

S

Safe harbor rule rule that determines if an employer has satisfied the deposit obligations by (a) having no shortfall (under deposit) that exceeds the greater of $100 or 2 percent of the amount of employment taxes required to be deposited and (b) having deposited the shortfall on or before the shortfall make-up date.

Salary remuneration paid on a monthly, biweekly, semimonthly, or yearly basis.

Self-employment income the net earnings derived by individuals from a business or profession carried on as a sole proprietorship or as a partnership.

Semimonthly twice a month.

Semiweekly depositor one who reported employment taxes of more than $50,000 for the four quarters in the lookback period.

Separation report report that provides a wage and employment record of the separated employee and the reason for leaving.

Shortfall the excess of the amount of employment taxes required to be deposited over the amount deposited on or before the last date prescribed for the deposit.

Sick pay any payment made to individuals because of their personal injury or sickness that does not constitute wages.

Social security benefits payments made under Title II of the Social Security Act to retired workers, their spouses, children and parents, as well as widows, widowers, and some divorced persons; also known as *OASDI benefits* and *Title II benefits*.

Special withholding allowance allowance claimed by employees so that wages which are below the level subject to the income tax will not be subject to withholding.

Standard deduction an amount of money used to reduce an individual's adjusted gross income in computing taxable income.

Status report initial statement filed by new employers with their state unemployment office, which determines their liability to make contributions into the state unemployment compensation fund.

Supplemental Unemployment Benefits (SUB) private supplementation of state unemployment compensation benefits to employees during periods of layoff.

Supplemental wage payments additional compensation such as vacation pay, bonuses, and commissions paid to employees.

Supplementary medical insurance plan program of voluntary medical care for aged and disabled persons designed to cover costs of doctors' services and other items and services not covered under the basic program; also known as *supplementary* or *voluntary Medicare* or *Part B Medicare*.

T

Taxable wage base the maximum amount of wages during a calendar year that is subject to a particular tax, such as FICA.

Time card form on which employee's time worked is recorded manually by the worker or automatically by a time clock.

Time sheet form that indicates an employee's time of arrival and time of departure.

Tip gift or gratuity given by a customer in recognition of service performed for him or her.

Tipped employee one engaged in an occupation in which tips of more than $30 a month are customarily and regularly received.

Title XII advances funds borrowed from the federal government by states who, due to financial difficulties, cannot pay their unemployment compensation benefits.

U

Unemployment compensation benefits payments made to workers who are temporarily unemployed.

Unemployment insurance a federal-state program that provides economic security for workers during periods of temporary unemployment.

V

Vesting the process of conveying to employees the right to share in a retirement fund in the event they are terminated before the normal retirement age.

Voluntary contributions payments deliberately made by employers to their state funds in order to qualify for a lower unemployment compensation tax rate.

W

Wage remuneration paid on an hourly, weekly, or piece-work basis; total compensation paid to employees for services.

Wage and tax statements statements furnished by employers to their employees informing them of the wages paid during the calendar year and the amount of taxes withheld from those wages.

Wage information reports statements filed by the employer, usually with the quarterly contribution report, which lists employee names, social security numbers, taxable wages, taxable tips, state in which worker was employed during the reported quarter, and employer's federal account number.

Wage-bracket method method of determining amount of income taxes to be withheld by reading amount from tables provided by the IRS, which take into consideration length of payroll period, gross earnings, marital status, and number of withholding allowances claimed.

Workers' compensation insurance protection provided to employees and their dependents against losses due to injury or death incurred during employment.

Workweek fixed and regularly recurring period of 168 hours—7 consecutive 24-hour periods.

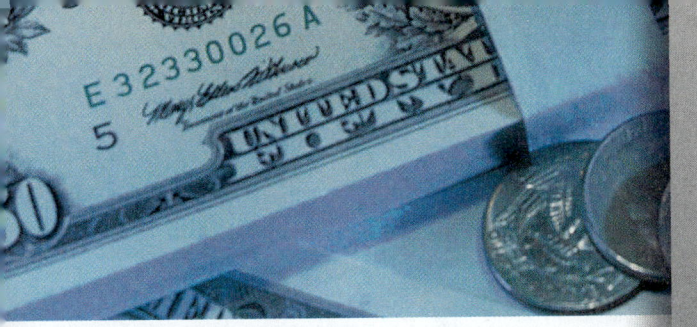

INDEX

A

ABC test, SUTA coverage, 5-4
Absences, 2-17
Account and payroll records, books of, 7-2
Accountable plan for traveling expenses, 4-5
Accounts used in recording payroll transactions, summary of, 6-23
Activities, preliminary and postliminary, 2-16
Additional withholding allowance, 4-10
Adjustments, recording end-of-period, 6-22
ADP (Automatic Data Processing), 1-23
Affordable Care Act of 2010 (ACA), 1-11, 4-21
Age Discrimination in Employment Act of 1967 (ADEA), 1-7
Agent-drivers, 3-3, 5-3
Agricultural employees, 5-2
    Form 943, 3-19, 4-27
Agricultural occupations, 2-12
Agricultural workers, deposit requirements for employers of, 3-19
ALEs, (applicable large employers), 1-11
Allowances
    for dependents, 4-10
    personal, 4-10
American Payroll Association (APA), 1-2
Americans with Disabilities Act of 1990 (ADA), 1-7
Americans working overseas, coverage of, 5-7
Annual FUTA return—Form 940, 5-18
Annual Return of Withheld Federal Income Tax, Form 945, 4-27
Annual statements, 4-33
Annualizing wages, def., 4-17
Annuities, distributions from, Form 1099-R, 4-28
Annuity payments, withholding for, 4-13
APA code of ethics, illus., 1-3
Application for employment, 1-14, illus., 1-15–1-16
Application form, def., 1-14
Archer Medical Savings Accounts, 4-7
ATIP, (Attributed Tip Income Program), 3-7
ATM (automated teller machines), 6-14
Auto plan. *See* Pooled-fund plan

B

Backup withholding, 4-27
    def., 4-29
Bad checks, 3-30
Badge systems, 2-18
Bankruptcy Act, Chapter 13 of, 6-8
Base of operations, location of, 5-5
BELO plan, 2-25
Benefit Cost Ratio (BCR), 5-11
Biometrics, timekeeping, 2-20
Biweekly, def., 2-4

Bonus, discretionary or nondiscretionary, 2-4
Business expense, def., 6-17

C

Cafeteria plans, 4-6
Card-generated systems, 2-18
Cardless and badgeless systems, 2-18
Cash, paying wages and salaries in, 6-12
Certificate of age, 2-12
Change in payroll rate, 1-19
    form, def., 1-19
Change in status form, illus., 1-19
Chart of accounts, partial, illus., 7-2
Check, paying wages and salaries by, 6-13
Check-off system, def., 6-8
Child support, 6-9
Child-labor restrictions, 2-11
Circular E, Employer's Tax Guide, 4-4, 4-27
Civil Rights Act
    of 1964, 1-4
    of 1991, 1-6
Code of ethics, 1-2
Commission, def., 2-28
Commission-drivers, 3-3, 5-3
Common-law relationship, def., 2-3
Common-law test, 3-2, 5-3
Compensation plans, contributions to deferred, 3-8
Compensatory time off, 2-9
Computerized time and attendance recording systems, 2-18
Constructively paid, def., 5-8
Consumer Credit Protection Act (CCPA), 6-9
Consumer Finance protection Bureau (CFPB), 6-15
Consumer Price Index, 3-9
Continental system, def., 2-18
Contribution rate, computing, 5-15
Contribution report, def., 5-26
Contributions
    and withholdings, payroll taxes, 7-4
    pension and retirement, 6-11
    to deferred compensation plans, 3-8
Control of operations, location of, 5-5
Convenience of the employer, 3-7
Corporation, employees of, 2-3
Credit week, 5-26
Credits
    against FUTA tax, 5-9
    unemployment compensation taxes and, 5-8
Cumulative earnings, 7-11

D

Davis-Bacon Act (1931), 1-8
De minimis, 2-17
    fringe benefit, def., 4-4

Deferred arrangements, 4-8
Deferred compensation plans, contributions to, 3-8
Defined contribution plan, def., 4-8
Department of Homeland Security, 1-9
Department of Labor, 2-5, 2-11
Dependents, allowances for, 4-10
Deposit requirements for
    employers of agricultural workers, 3-19
    employers of household employees, 3-19
    nonagricultural workers, 3-16
    state and local government employers, 3-19
Deposit rules, illus., 7-5
Depositing taxes, 7-4
Depositor
    monthly, 3-17, 3-18
    semiweekly, 3-17, 3-18
Deposits
    electronic, 3-20
    failure to make timely, 3-29
    procedures for making, 3-20
Direction of operations, location of, 5-5
Director of corporation, 2-3
Disability benefits, def., 1-12
Disclosure requirements, ERISA, 1-10
Discretionary bonus, def., 2-4
Dismissal payments, def., 5-8
Disposable earnings, def., 6-9
Dividends and Distributions, Form 1099-DIV, 4-28
Doctor's appointments, 2-16
Domestic service, def., 2-3
Domestics, 2-3
Dumping, 5-18

E

Earnings statement (check stub) showing payroll deductions, illus., 6-13
Educational assistance
    def., 3-8
    payments for, 3-8
Electronic deposits, 3-20
Electronic Federal Tax Payment System (EFTPS), 3-20, 5-24
Electronic filing
    Form W-2 and information returns, 4-30
    of Form 941, 3-26
Electronic funds transfer system (EFTS), def., 6-14
Electronic paystub, def., 6-15
Electronic transfer, paying wages and salaries by, 6-14
Employee Retirement Income Security Act of 1974. *See* ERISA
Employee(s), 3-2
    access of personnel files, 1-20
    agricultural, 5-2
    contributions, 5-14, 6-7

Employee(s) (cont.)
def., 2-2
exempt, 2-9, 3-4
FICA (OASDI/HI) taxes and
   withholdings, 3-10, 6-6
*Form 4070, Employee's Report of Tips to
   Employer,* 3-5, illus., 3-7
*Form SS-5, Application for a Social
   Security Card,* 3-14
*Form SS-8, Determination of Employee
   Work Status,* 2-2
*Form W-4, Employee's Withholding
   Allowance Certificate,* 4-10, illus.,
   4-11
FUTA, 5-3
history record, def., 1-19
hospital, 2-8
household, 3-3
in retail, 2-8
in service industries, 2-8
list report, illus., A-5, A-24
of a corporation, 2-3
of the government, 3-3
penalties, 4-13
personnel data, illus., 7-3
receiving remedial education, 2-9
residence, location of, 5-6
salaried nonexempt, 2-24
salaried with fluctuating workweek, 2-24
SUTA, 5-4
taxable payments to, illus., 4-3
terminating, 1-19
tipped, 2-6, 2-8
W-4, Withholding Allowance Certificate,
   1-7
work time, determining, 2-13
Employee's earnings record, 1-21, 6-4, 7-3,
   7-42
def., 1-22
illus., 1-22
page 1, illus., 6-5
Employer identification number (EIN), 3-14
application for, *Form SS-4, illus.,* 3-15
Employer-employee relationship, 4-2
Employer(s), 2-2
contributions, 5-14
convenience of, 3-7
def., 3-2
FICA (OASDI taxes), 3-11, 6-17
*Form 940, Employer's Annual Federal
   Unemployment (FUTA) Tax Return,*
   5-18, 7-20, illus.,5-19, 5-20
*Form 941, Employer's Quarterly Federal
   Tax Return,* 3-16, 3-17, 3-21, 4-21,
   4-27, 7-19, illus., 3-22, 3-23
*Form 941-PR, Employer's Quarterly
   Federal Tax Return,* 3-17
*Form 941-SS, Employer's Quarterly
   Federal Tax Return,* 3-17
*Form 941-X, Adjusted Employer's
   Quarterly Federal Tax Return or Claim
   for Refund,* 3-17, 3-27
*Form 943, Employer's Annual Tax
   Return for Agricultural Employees,*
   3-17, 3-19, 4-27
*Form 944, Employer's Annual Federal
   Tax Return,* 3-16, 3-17, 3-27, 4-27
*Form 945, Annual Return of Withheld
   Federal Income Tax,* 3-16, 3-17
*Form 8027, Employer's Annual
   Information Return of Tip Income and
   Allocated Tips,* 3-6, 4-28
*Form UC-2, Employer's Report for
   Unemployment Compensation—
   Fourth Quarter,* 7-20

FUTA, 5-2
household, 3-19, 5-2, 5-25
major returns filed by, illus., 4-27
negative-balance, 5-15
new, 3-18
positive-balance, 5-15
*Quarterly Contribution Return and
   Report of Wages,* 4-31
returns they must complete, 4-27
seasonal, 3-26
successor, 3-12
SUTA, 5-3
Tax Guide, Circular E, 4-4, 4-27
unemployment compensation reports
   required of, 5-18
Employment
application for, 1-14, illus., 1-15–1-16
def., 3-2
exempt, illus., 3-2
family, 3-3
reciprocal arrangements, 5-6
transfers of, 5-6
Employment Eligibility Verification, Form
   I-9, 1-8
Employment Reference Release, 1-18
Employment tax returns, failure to file,
   3-28
Employment taxes, failure to fully pay, 3-28
End-of-period adjustments, recording, 6-22
Enterprise coverage, def., 2-2
Equal Employment Opportunity, 1-4
   Commission (EEOC), 1-4
Equal Pay Act, 2-11
Equal Pay Law, 2-11
ERISA, 1-10
disclosure requirements, 1-10
Pension Benefit Guaranty Corporation,
   1-10
vesting, 1-10
E-verify, 1-9
Executive orders, def., 1-6
Exempt employees, 3-4
def., 2-9
Exempt employment, illus., 3-2
Exempt payments, 3-7
illus., 4-6
Exempt status
indications of, illus., 2-10
of workers under FLSA, illus., 2-10
Exemptions
blue-collar workers, 2-11
Equal Pay Act, 2-11
from FLSA requirements, 2-9
from income tax withholding, 4-12
salary basis, 2-9
test of, 2-9
white-collar workers, 2-9
Expatriates, 3-3
Experience rating, 5-14
def., 5-10

F

Failure to
file employment tax returns, 3-28
fully pay employment taxes, 3-28
furnish information returns, 3-29
furnish payee statements, 3-29
make timely deposits, 3-29
Failure-to-comply penalties, 3-27
Fair Credit Reporting Act of 1968, 1-18
Fair employment laws, 1-4
Fair employment practices, def., 1-4
Fair Labor Standards Act. *See* FLSA
Fair Minimum Wage Act of 2007, 2-4

Family and Medical Leave Act of 1993
   (FMLA), 1-9
Family employment, 3-3
Family Support Act, 6-9
Federal Disability Insurance Trust Fund, 1-3
Federal income tax (FIT), 1-4, 6-6
depositing of withheld, 6-21
withholding, 4-15
Federal Income Tax Withholding Law, 4-2
coverage under, 4-1
Federal Insurance Contributions Act. *See*
   FICA
Federal laws affecting the need for payroll
   and personnel records
illus., 1-8
other, 1-7
Federal Old-Age and Survivors' Trust Fund,
   1-3
Federal payroll laws, summary of
   information required by, illus., 1-5
Federal Personal Responsibility and Work
   Opportunity Reconciliation Act of
   1996 (PRWORA), 1-7
Federal Reserve Bank
ACH credit method, 3-20
ACH debit method, 3-20
Federal tax levy, 6-10
Federal Unemployment Tax Act. *See* FUTA
Federal Wage and Hour Division, 2-12
Federal Wage and Hour Law, 1-3, 2-1
FICA, 1-3, 3-1
contributions to deferred compensation
   plans, 3-8
coverage under, 3-1
educational assistance, 3-8
exempt employees, 3-4
exempt payments, 3-7
family employment, 3-3
Federal Disability Insurance Trust Fund,
   1-3
Federal Old-Age and Survivors' Trust
   Fund, 1-3
government employees, 3-3
Health Insurance Plan, 1-3
household employee, 3-3
independent contractors, 3-4
international agreements, 3-3
lookback period, 3-16
meals and lodging, 3-7
Medicare, 1-3
occupations specifically covered by, 3-2
returns required for social security
   purposes, 3-16
Self-Employment Contribution Act
   (SECA), 1-3
sick pay, 3-7
statutory employees, 5-3
tax rates, 3-9
tax returns and deposits, major forms for
   preparing, illus., 3-17
taxable wage base, 3-9
taxable wages, 3-5
tips, 3-5
voluntary coverage, 3-4
FICA taxes
depositing of withheld, , 6-21
employee, 3-10, 6-6
employer, 3-11, 6-17
Final pay, 6-15
FIRE (Filing Information Returns
   Electronically), 4-22
Flat 25 percent rate, 4-19
Flat 25 percent supplement wage rate, 4-4
Flexible reporting, 4-4
Flexible-spending accounts, 4-7

FLSA, 1-3, 1-20, 2-1, 2-4
  agricultural occupations, 2-12
  areas not covered by, 2-13
  blue-collar workers, 2-11
  certificate of age, 2-12
  child-labor restrictions, 2-11
  coverage, 2-2
  employee, 2-2
  employer, 2-2
  enterprise coverage, 2-2
  Equal Pay Act, 2-1
  exempt employees, 2-9
  exemption status of workers under, illus.,
    2-10
  individual employee coverage, 2-2
  minimum wage, 2-4
  nonfarm occupations, 2-12
  overtime hours and overtime pay, 2-7
  penalties, 2-13
  records used for timekeeping, 2-17
  requirements, exemptions from, 2-9
  salary basis, 2-9
  test of exemption, 2-9
  tips, 2-6
  wages, 2-4
  white-collar workers, 2-9
  workweek, 2-7
FMLA leave, 2-11
Ford-type plan. *See* Pooled-fund plan
*Form 668-D, Release of Levy/Release of
    Property from Levy,* 6-10
*Form 668-W, Notice of Levy on Wages,
    Salary and Other Income,* 6-10
*Form 940, Employer's Annual Federal
    Unemployment (FUTA) Tax Return,*
    5-18, 5-22, 5-24, 7-20
  illus., 5-19, 5-20, 5-21
  Schedule A, multi-state employers, 5-22,
    illus., 5-23
*Form 941, Employer's Quarterly Federal
    Tax Return,* 3-16, 3-17, 3-21, 3-26,
    3-27, 4-21, 4-27, 7-19
  illus., 3-22, 3-23, 3-24
  *Schedule B, Report of Tax Liability for
    Semiweekly Schedule Depositors,* 3-21,
    illus., 3-25
*Form 941-PR, Employer's Quarterly
    Federal Tax Return,* 3-17
*Form 941-SS, Employer's Quarterly Federal
    Tax Return,* 3-17
Form 941-V, Form 941 Payment Voucher,
    3-17, 3-26
*Form 941-X, Adjusted Employer's
    Quarterly Federal Tax Return or Claim
    for Refund,* 3-17, 3-27
*Form 943, Employer's Annual Tax Return
    for Agricultural Employees,* 3-17, 3-19,
    4-27
*Form 944, Employer's Annual Federal Tax
    Return,* 3-16, 3-17, 3-27, 4-27
*Form 945, Annual Return of Withheld
    Federal Income Tax,* 3-16, 3-17, 3-21,
    4-27, 4-29
Form 1040, Individual Income Tax Return,
    3-11
  Schedule C, Profit or Loss from Business,
    3-13
  *Schedule SE, Self-Employment
    Tax,* 3-13
*Form 1096, Annual Summary and
    Transmittal of U.S. Information
    Returns,* 4-28, 7-21
Form 1099, 3-4
*Form 1099-DIV, Dividends and
    Distributions,* 4-28

*Form 1099-G, Certain Government
    Payments,* 4-28
Form 1099-INT, Interest Income, 4-28
Form 1099-MISC, Miscellaneous Income,
    4-28, 7-21, illus., 4-29
*Form 1099-PATR, Taxable Distributions
    Received From Cooperatives,* 4-28
*Form 1099-R, Distributions From Pensions,
    Annuities, Retirement or Profit-Sharing
    Plans, IRAs, Insurance Contracts, etc.,*
    4-28
*Form 4070, Employee's Report of Tips to
    Employer,* 3-5, illus., 3-7
*Form 4137, Social Security and Medicare
    Tax on Unreported Tip Income,* 3-21
*Form 4419, Application for Filing
    Information Returns Electronically,*
    4-30
Form 5498, IRA Contribution Information,
    4-28
Form 5500, pension plan annual report,
    1-10
*Form 8027, Employer's Annual
    Information Return of Tip Income and
    Allocated Tips,* 3-6, 4-28
*Form 8809, Request for Extension of Time
    to File Information Returns,* 4-22
*Form 8846, Credit for Employer Social
    Security and Medicare Taxes Paid on
    Certain Employee Tips,* 3-6
*Form 9779, EFTPS Business Enrollment
    Form,* 3-20
*Form DE 88ALL, California Payroll Tax
    Deposit,* illus., 4-31
*Form DE 9c, California Quarterly
    Contribution Return and Report of
    Wages,* illus., 4-32
*Form I-9, Employment Eligibility
    Verification,* def., 1-8
*Form SS-4, Application for Employer
    Identification Number,* illus., 3-15
*Form SS-5, Application for a Social Security
    Card,* 3-14
*Form SS-8, Determination of Employee
    Work Status,* 2-2
*Form UC-2, Employer's Report for
    Unemployment Compensation
    Fourth Quarter,* 7-20
  Part I, Pennsylvania Form, illus., 5-26
*Form UC-2A, Employer's Report for
    Unemployment Compensation—Part
    II, Pennsylvania Form,* illus., 5-27
Form W-2 and information returns,
    electronic filing, 4-30
Form W-2, Wage and Tax Statement, 3-5,
    3-19, 4-21, 7-20
  def., 1-22
  illus., 4-22, 4-23, 4-24
*Form W-2c, Corrected Wage and Tax
    Statement,* 4-22, illus., 4-25
*Form W-3, Transmittal of Wage and Tax
    Statements,* 4-24, 7-20
  illus., 4-26
*Form W-3c, Transmittal of Corrected
    Income and Tax Statements,* 4-27
*Form W-4, Employee's Withholding
    Allowance Certificate,* 1-7, 4-10, 4-11,
    4-13
  electronic filing of, 4-12
  illus., 4-11, 4-13
Form W-4P, 4-14
*Form W-4S, Request for Federal Income
    Tax Withholding from Sick
    Pay,* 4-14
Form W-4V, 4-14

*Form W-7, Application for IRS Individual
    Taxpayer Identification Number
    (ITIN),* 3-16
401(k) plans, 4-8, 6-11
Fringe benefits, 4-3
  de minimis, 4-4
  nontaxable, 4-4
  withholding on, 4-3
Fundamental Payroll Certification, 1-2
FUTA, 1-4, 5-1
  coverage under, 5-2
  employees, 5-3
  employers, 5-2
  excluded coverage from, 5-3, 5-4
  nontaxable wages for unemployment
    purposes, 5-8
  penalties, 5-25
  quarterly deposit form, 5-24
  tax rate, 5-9
  taxable wages for unemployment
    purposes, 5-7
  wages, 5-7
FUTA tax, 6-17, 6-22
  credits against, 5-9

G

Garnishment, def., 6-8
General journal entry to record payroll
    cash, illus., A-7, A-22, A-27
General journal report, illus., A-27, A-8
General ledger, 7-2
  report, illus., A-28, A-9
Government employees, 3-3
Government employers, deposit
    requirements for state and local, 3-19
Government payments, withholding on,
    4-14
Government savings bonds, purchase of,
    6-8
Gross amount, 4-2
Gross earnings, def., 2-20
Gross income, 3-12
Gross payroll, 6-6
  and withholdings, recording, 6-6
Gross-up, def., 4-21
Gross-up supplementals, 4-20
Group insurance, 7-5
  def., 6-7

H

Health Care and Education Reconciliation
    Act, 1-11
Health insurance, 6-8
  plan, 1-3
  program (HI), 3-1
Health savings accounts, 4-7
Hiring notice, def., illus., 1-18
Hiring process, human resources
    department procedure, illus., 1-13
Hospital employees, 2-8
Hourly rates
  converting biweekly wage rates to, 2-22
  converting monthly salary rates to, 2-23
  converting semimonthly salary rates to,
    2-23
  converting weekly wage rates to, 2-22
Household employee, 3-3
  deposit requirements for employers of,
    3-19
Household employer, 5-2
  taxes, 5-25
Household Employment Taxes, Schedule H,
    5-25

Human resources and payroll accounting systems, 1-12
Human Resources Department, 1-12
  procedure in the hiring process, illus., 1-13
Human resources system, def., 1-13

I

Idle time, 2-15
Illustrative case, Brookins Company, 6-24–6-30
Immigration Reform and Control Act of 1986 (IRCA), 1-8
Income
  gross, 3-12
  self-employment, 3-12
Income tax
  def., 1-4
  state and city, 6-6
  withholding local, 4-33
Income Tax Code of 1914, 4-2
Income Tax Reform Act of 1986, 4-2
Income tax withholding
  exemption from, 4-12
  percentage method tables for, T-3–T-4
  wage-bracket tables for, T-5–T-14
Income tax withholding laws, 1-4
  coverage under federal, 4-1
Independent contractor
  def., 3-4
  payments, 4-28
  status, test for, illus., 3-5
Individual employee coverage, def., 2-2
Individual Retirement Account Contribution Information, Form 5498, 4-28
Individual retirement accounts (IRAs), 4-9, 6-11
  distributions from, Form 1099-R, 4-28
  Roth, 4-10
Individual's distributive share, 3-12
Information reports—SUTA, 5-25
Information required by major federal payroll laws, summary of, illus., 1-5
Information returns, 4-33
  def., 4-28
  electronic filing Form W-2 and, 4-30
  failure to furnish, 3-29
  major, illus., 4-28
Inpatriates, 3-3
Insurance
  contracts, distributions from, Form 1099-R, 4-28
  group, 6-7, 7-5
  health, 6-8
Interest Income, Form 1099-INT, 4-28
International agreements, 3-3
Internet, timekeeping, 2-20
Interns, 2-4
Interstate employee
  coverage of, 5-4
  def., 5-4
Interstate Reciprocal Coverage Arrangement, 5-6
Investigative consumer report, def., 1-18
IRA. *See* Individual retirement accounts
IVR (Interactive Voice Response), 2-20

J

Job descriptions, 1-14
Journal, 7-2
Journal entries
  current payroll, illus., A-6, A-26

  def., 6-3
  payroll taxes, illus., A-7, A-26

L

Labor cost accounts, illus., 7-6
Labor costs, distribution of, 7-6
Labor distribution graph, illus., A-10, A-29
"Living wage", 2-5
Lookback period
  def., 3-16
  for calendar year 2016, illus., 3-17

M

Makeup pay for military duty, 3-8
Mark-sense time card used in the timekeeper computerized system, illus., 2-19
McNamara-O'Hara Service Contract Act (1965), 1-8
Meal periods, 2-15
Meals and lodging, 3-7
Medicare, 1-3, 3-1
Merit rating, def., 5-10
Military duty, makeup pay for, 3-8
Minimum wage, 2-4
  paying less than, 2-5
  paying more than, 2-5
Monthly depositor, 3-17
  def., 3-18
Multi-state employers, Schedule A of Form 940, 5-22
  illus., 5-23

N

National Call Center, 2-2
National Directory of New Hires, 1-7
Negative-balance employers, def., 5-15
Net pay, 6-11
Ninety-eight percent rule. *See* Safe harbor rule
Nonaccountable plan for traveling expenses, 4-5
Nonagricultural workers (deposit requirements), 3-16
Nondiscretionary bonus, 2-28
  def., 2-4
Nonemployees/statutory employees, 4-2
Nonexempt employees, salaried, 2-24
Nonfarm occupations, 2-12
Nonpayroll reporting, 4-29
Nonprofits, 5-17
Nonresident aliens, withholding on, 4-13
Nontaxable fringe benefits, 4-4
Nontaxable wages for unemployment purposes, 5-8

O

Obamacare. *See* Affordable Care Act
Occupational Safety and Health Act (OSHA) (1970), 1-8
Occupations specifically covered by FICA, 3-2
Office of Child Support Enforcement (OCSE), 1-7
Old-age, survivors, and disability insurance (OASDI), 3-1
One day rule, 3-18
Operations
  location of base of, 5-5
  location of direction or control of, 5-5
Optional activities, A-32
Outsourcing payroll, 1-22

Overtime, 7-4
  different rates for different jobs, 2-22
  paid in advance, 2-22
Overtime earnings for pieceworkers
  method A, 2-26
  method B, 2-27
Overtime hours and overtime pay, 2-7
  exceptions to, 2-8
Overtime pay, calculating, 2-21
Overtime premium, def., 2-21

P

PA Form REV-1667, W-2 Transmittal, 7-20
Paid family leave plans, 1-10
Partial unemployment, def., 5-28
Partial unemployment notices, def., 5-28
Partnerships, 2-3
Part-year employment, def., 4-17
Patient Protection and Affordable Care Act, 1-11
Pay cards, 6-14
Pay, final, 6-15
Paycheck, 1-22
  with stub showing current and year-to-date earnings and deductions, illus., 1-23
Payday, 7-4
Payee statements, failure to furnish, 3-29
Paying a "living wage", 2-5
Payments
  exempt from withholding, 4-5
  for educational assistance, 3-8
Payroll
  current journal entries, illus., A-6, A-26
  general journal entry to record, illus., A-7, A-22, A-27
  outsourcing, 1-22
Payroll accounting system, 1-1
  def., 1-1
  human resources and, 1-12
  procedures, illus., 1-21
Payroll deductions
  earnings statement (check stub), illus., 6-13
  other, 6-7
Payroll Department, 1-12
Payroll Guide, 1-2
Payroll profession, 1-2
Payroll Professional Certification, 1-2
Payroll project, 7-6
  short version, 7-16, A-20
  using online general ledger (CLGL), A-1
Payroll rate, change in, 1-19
  form, change in, 1-19
Payroll records
  and personnel records, federal laws affecting the need for, illus., 1-8
  books of account and, 7-2
  other federal laws affecting the need for, 1-7
  other state laws affecting the need for, 1-11
Payroll register, 6-1, 7-2
  def., 1-20
  illus., 1-21, 6-2, 6-3
  proving the totals of, 6-3
  using the information in, 6-4
Payroll report, illus., A-6, A-25
Payroll Tax Deposit Coupon, 4-31
Payroll taxes
  contributions and withholdings, 7-4
  entries to record wages and, 6-18
  illus., 7-5
  journal entries, illus., A-7, A-26
  recording, 6-16, 6-21

Payroll transactions, summary of accounts used in recording, 6-23
Paystub, electronic, 6-14
Penalties, 2-13, 4-26
  employee, 4-13
  failure-to-comply, 3-27
  FUTA, 5-25
  SUTA, 5-28
Pension Benefit Guaranty Corporation, 1-10
Pension Protection Act of 2006, 6-11
Pensions
  and retirement contributions, 6-11
  distributions from, Form 1099-R, 4-28
  payments, withholding for, 4-13
Percentage method, 4-15
  def., 4-15
Periodic withholding returns, 4-31
Person
  def., 3-2
  self-employed, 3-12
  unemployed, 5-2
Personal allowance, def., 4-10
Personal computer-based systems, 2-18
Personal identification number (PIN), 3-20, 3-26, 6-14
Personnel
  employee access of files, 1-20
  requisition for, 1-14
Personnel records
  federal laws affecting the need for payroll and, illus., 1-8
  other federal laws affecting the need for, 1-7
  other state laws affecting the need for, 1-11
Piece rate, 2-26
Piece-rate system, def., 2-26
Pooled-fund laws, def., 5-11
Portal-to-Portal Act, 2-16
Positive-balance employers, def., 5-15
Postliminary activities, 2-16
Prehire inquiries, def., 1-17
Preliminary activities, 2-16
Premiere Payroll Tax Research Library, 1-4
Pretax salary reductions, 4-5
Principal activities, def., 2-13
Privately printed forms, 4-27
Profit-sharing plans
  def., 2-29
  distributions from, Form 1099-R, 4-28

Q
Quarterly averaging, def., 4-17
Quarterly Contribution Return and Report of Wages, 4-31
Quarterly deposit form, FUTA, 5-24

R
Rate(s)
  computing contribution, 5-15
  converting biweekly wage rates to hourly, 2-22
  converting monthly salary rates to hourly, 2-23
  converting semimonthly salary rates to hourly, 2-23
  converting weekly wage rates to hourly, 2-22
  table of decimal equivalents to convert into weekly, hourly, and hourly overtime salary, illus., 2-24
  tax, 3-9
Reciprocal agreement, 4-30
  def., 4-31

Reciprocal arrangements, def., 5-6
Reconciliation returns, 4-31
Recording systems, computerized time and attendance, 2-18
Recordkeeping requirements, 1-4
Recordkeeping system, 1-20
Reference inquiry, 1-17
  form, def., 1-17
Requisition for personnel, def., 1-14
Reserve-ratio formula, def., 5-15
Retail, employees in, 2-8
Retirement accounts, tax-deferred, 4-8
Retirement contributions, pension and, 6-11
Retirement plans, distributions from, Form 1099-R, 4-28
Returns
  employers must complete, 4-27
  filed by employers, major, illus., 4-27
  major information illus., 4-28
Roth IRA, 4-10
  See also Individual retirement accounts

S
Safe harbor rule, def., 3-19
Salaried employees with fluctuating workweek, 2-24
Salaried nonexempt employees, 2-24
Salaries
  def., 2-4
  methods of computing, 2-20
  methods of paying, 6-12
  paying by check, 6-13
  paying by electronic transfer, 6-14
  paying in cash, 6-12
Salary reductions, pretax, 4-5
Salespersons, 3-3, 5-3
Schedule A of Form 940, multi-state employers, 5-22
  illus., 5-23
Schedule B of Form 941, Report of Tax Liability for Semiweekly Schedule Depositors, 3-21
  illus., 3-25
Schedule C (Form 1040), Profit or Loss from Business, 3-13
Schedule H, *Household Employment Taxes*, 5-25
Schedule SE (Form 1040), Self-Employment Tax, 3-13
Seasonal employers, 3-26
Section 403(b) plan, 4-8
Section 457(b) plan, 4-8
Self-employed person, 3-12
Self-Employment Contributions Act (SECA), 1-3, 3-1, 3-12
Self-employment income
  def., 3-12
  reporting, 3-13
Self-employment OASDI/HI taxes, 3-13
Semimonthly, def., 2-4
Semiweekly depositor, 3-17
  def., 3-18
Separation report, def., 5-26
Service industries, employees in, 2-8
Shortfall, def., 3-19
Sick pay, 3-7
  def., 3-7
  withholding from, 4-14
Simple plans, 4-8
Sleep time, 2-16
Small Business Administration, 3-4
Small Business Job Protection Act, 2-6
Social Security Act, 1-4, 3-9, 5-1

Social Security Administration (SSA), 1-9, 6-9
Social Security numbers, verifying, 3-16
Social Security purposes, returns required for, 3-16
Social Security Tax Law, 4-2
Society for Human Resource Management, 1-18, 2-14
Special incentive plans, 2-27
Special period rule, 4-4
Special withholding allowance, def., 4-10
Standard deduction, def., 4-15
State and city income taxes, 6-6
  paying, 6-22
State and local government employers, deposit requirements for, 3-19
State disability benefit laws, 1-12
State income tax
  returns and reports, 4-31
  withholding, 4-30
State laws affecting the need for payroll and personnel records, 1-11
State laws for minimum wage and overtime rules, 2-5
State unemployment compensation laws (2015), summary of, illus., 5-12, 5-13
State Unemployment Tax Act. *See* SUTA
States' minimum wage and maximum hours laws, 1-3
Status report, def., 5-25
Statutory employees, 2-3, 4-2
Statutory nonemployees, 2-4, 4-2
Successor employer, 3-12
Supplemental wage payments, def., 4-18
Supplemental wages paid separately from regular wages, 4-19
  method A, 4-20
  method B, 4-20
Supplemental wages paid with regular wages, 4-19
Supplementary payroll sheet, illus, 6-12
SUTA, 1-4, 5-1
  Americans working overseas, 5-7
  computing the contribution rate, 5-15
  contribution reports, 5-26
  coverage under, 5-2
  employee contributions, 5-14
  employees, 5-4
  employer contributions, 5-14
  employers, 5-3
  experience rating, 5-14
  information reports, 5-25
  interstate employee, 5-4
  partial unemployment notices, 5-28
  penalties, 5-28
  pooled-fund laws, 5-11
  reciprocal arrangements, 5-6
  separation reports, 5-26
  status reports, 5-25
  tax rates, 5-11
  voluntary contributions, 5-17
  wage information reports, 5-26
  wages, 5-8
SUTA Dumping Prevention Act, 5-18
SUTA taxes, 6-17
  paying FUTA and, 6-22

T
Table, annual payroll period, illus., A-2, A-20
Table for amount exempt for tax levy (single person), 2015, illus., 6-11
Table of allowance values for 2014, illus., 4-16

Table of decimal equivalents to convert into weekly, hourly, and hourly overtime salary rates, illus., 2-24
Taking work home, 2-15
Tardiness, 2-17
Tax levy, (single person) 2015 table for amount exempt for, illus., 6-11
Tax rates, 3-9
    FUTA, 5-9
    SUTA, 5-11
Tax tables, T-2–T-14
Taxable payments to employees, illus., 4-3
Taxable tips, 4-4
Taxable wage base, def., 3-9
Taxable wages, 3-5, 4-2
    for unemployment purposes, 5-7
    other types of, illus., 3-6
Taxable year, 3-13
Tax-deferred retirement accounts, 4-8
Tax-deferred retirement plans, 3-8
Taxes
    and withholdings, employees' FICA (OASDIHI), 3-10
    depositing, 6-21, 7-4
    employee FICA, 6-6
    employer FICA, 6-17
    entries to record payroll, 6-18
    failure to fully pay employment, 3-28
    federal income, 6-6
    FUTA, 6-17, 6-22
    household employers, 5-25
    paying state or city income, 6-22
    payroll, 6-16, 6-21, 7-4, illus., 7-5
    self-employment OASDI/HI, 3-13
    state and city income, 6-6
    SUTA, 6-17, 6-22
    unemployment compensation credits and, 5-8
    withholding local income, 4-33
Taxpayer identification number (TIN), 4-29
Time and a half, 7-4, 7-11
Time card
    def., 2-18
    illus., 2-19
    used in timekeeper computerized system, mark-sense, illus., 2-19
Time rate, 2-20
Time sheet, def., 2-18
Timekeeping, 7-4
    badge systems, 2-18
    biometrics, 2-20
    card-generated systems, 2-18
    cardless and badgeless systems, 2-18
    Internet, 2-20
    IVR, 2-20
    next generation, 2-19
    personal computer-based systems, 2-18
    records used for, 2-17
    touch-screen technology, 2-20
Tipped employee, 2-8
    def., 2-6
Tips, 3-5
    allocated, 4-5
    def., 2-6
    Form 8027, 4-28
    taxable, 4-4
    withholding from, 4-5
Title VII of the Civil rights Act of 1964, 1-4
Title XII advances, def., 5-11
Touch-screen technology, timekeeping, 2-20
Training sessions, 2-16

Transfers of employment, 5-6
Travel time, 2-14
Traveling expenses, 4-5
    accountable plan, 4-5
    nonaccountable plan, 4-5
Traveling salesperson, 3-3, 5-3

U

U.S. Chamber of Commerce, 1-18
U.S. Citizenship and Immigration Services (USCIS), 1-9
U.S. Department of Labor (DOL), 2-1
    Employment Standards Administration homepage, 2-2
U.S. Immigration and Customs Enforcement Agency, 1-8
U.S. Supreme Court, 2-9
Unclaimed wages, 6-15
Unemployed persons, 5-2
Unemployment compensation
    reports required of the employer, 5-18
    taxes and credits, 5-8
Unemployment purposes
    nontaxable wages for, 5-8
    taxable wages for, 5-7
Unemployment tax acts, 1-4
Uniformed Services Employment and Reemployment Rights Act (USERRA) of 1994, 1-10
Uniformed Unclaimed Property Act, 6-15
Union dues, 6-8, 7-6
Unpaid leave, 1-9

V

Vacation pay, 4-19, 6-23
Vesting, def., 1-10
Vietnam Era Veterans' Readjustment Act (1974), 1-8
Vocational Rehabilitation Act (1973), 1-8
Voluntary contributions, def., 5-17
Voluntary coverage, 3-4

W

W-2 Transmittal, PA Form REV-1667, 7-20
W-4 form (Employee's Withholding Allowance Certificate), 1-7
Wage, def., 2-4
Wage and Hour Law, 2-11
Wage and Tax Statement
    def., 4-21
    Form W-2, 1-22, 3-5, 3-19, 4-21, 7-20, illus., 4-22
    Form W-2c, corrected, 4-22, illus., 4-25
    Form W-3, Transmittal of, 4-24, 7-20, illus., 4-26
    Form W-3c, Transmittal of Corrected, 4-27
Wage information reports, def., 5-26
Wage tax coupon, Philadelphia, illus., 4-33
Wage-bracket method, 4-16
    def., 4-15
    married persons—weekly payroll period, illus., 4-17
Wages, 6-22
    and payroll taxes, entries to record, 6-18
    annualizing, 4-17
    def., 2-4, 4-2
    FUTA, 5-7
    garnishment of, 6-8
    methods of computing, 2-20

methods of paying, 6-12
    other types of taxable, illus., 3-6
    paying by check, 6-13
    paying by electronic transfer, 6-14
    paying in cash, 6-12
    supplemental paid separately from regular, 4-19, 4-20
    supplemental paid with regular, 4-19
    supplemental payments, 4-18
    SUTA, 5-8
    taxable, 3-5
    unclaimed, 6-15
Walsh-Healey Public Contracts Act (1936), 1-8
Withholding
    backup, 4-27, 4-29
    employees' FICA (OASDIHI) taxes and, 3-10
    exemption from income tax, 4-12
    federal income tax, 4-15
    for pension or annuity payments, 4-13
    from sick pay, 4-14
    from tips, 4-5
    local income taxes, 4-33
    on fringe benefits, 4-3
    on government payments, 4-14
    on nonresident aliens, 4-13
    other methods of, 4-17
    other, 4-13
    payments exempt from, 4-5
    payroll taxes—contributions and, 7-4
    recording gross payroll and, 6-6
    state income tax, 4-30
Withholding agreements, additional and voluntary, 4-12
Withholding allowances, 4-9, 4-11
    additional, 4-10
    other, 4-10
    special, 4-10
Withholding laws, coverage under federal income tax, 4-1
Withholding rate, 39.6 percent, 4-19
Work
    location of, 5-5
    regular hours of, 7-3
Work time
    absences, 2-17
    clothes-changing time and wash up, 2-14
    doctor's appointments, 2-16
    fractional parts of an hour, 2-17
    idle time, 2-15
    meal periods, 2-15
    preliminary and postliminary activities, 2-16
    principal activities, 2-13
    rest periods and coffee breaks, 2-15
    sleep time, 2-16
    taking work home, 2-15
    tardiness, 2-17
    training sessions, 2-16
    travel time, 2-14
    waiting time, 2-15
Work-at-home individuals, 3-3
Workbooks, B-1
Workers' compensation insurance
    def., 1-12
    recording expense, 6-20
Workers' compensation laws, 1-12
Worksheet
    def., 2-7
    salaried employees with fluctuating, 2-24